BUSINESS ETHICS

BUSINESS ETHICS

A Stakeholder and Issues Management Approach

SEVENTH EDITION

Joseph W. Weiss

BK

Berrett–Koehler Publishers, Inc.

Berrett-Koehler Publishers, Inc.
1333 Broadway, Suite 1000
Oakland, CA 94612-1921
Tel: (510) 817-2277   Fax: (510) 817-2278
www.bkconnection.com

Ordering Information
Quantity sales. Special discounts are available on quantity purchases by corporations, associations, and others. For details, contact the "Special Sales Department" at the Berrett-Koehler address above.

Individual sales. Berrett-Koehler publications are available through most bookstores. They can also be ordered directly from Berrett-Koehler: Tel: (800) 929-2929; Fax: (802) 864-7626; www.bkconnection.com.

Orders for college textbook/course adoption use. Please contact Berrett-Koehler: Tel: (800) 929-2929; Fax: (802) 864-7626.

Distributed to the U.S. trade and internationally by Penguin Random House Publisher Services.

Berrett-Koehler and the BK logo are registered trademarks of Berrett-Koehler Publishers, Inc.

Printed in Canada

Berrett-Koehler books are printed on long-lasting acid-free paper. When it is available, we choose paper that has been manufactured by environmentally responsible processes. These may include using trees grown in sustainable forests, incorporating recycled paper, minimizing chlorine in bleaching, or recycling the energy produced at the paper mill.

Library of Congress Cataloging-in-Publication Data

Names: Weiss, Joseph W., author.
Title: Business ethics : a stakeholder and issues
  management approach / Joseph W. Weiss.
Description: Seventh Edition. | Oakland, CA :
  Berrett-Koehler, 2021. | Revised edition of
  the author's Business ethics, [2014] |
  Includes bibliographical references and index.
Identifiers: LCCN 2021034188 (print) |
  LCCN 2021034189 (ebook) |
  ISBN 9781523091546 (paperback) |
  ISBN 9781523091553 (adobe pdf) |
  ISBN 9781523091560 (epub)
Subjects: LCSH: Business ethics. |
  Social responsibility of business.
Classification: LCC HF5387 .W45 2021
  (print) | LCC HF5387 (ebook) |
  DDC 174/.4—dc23
LC record available at https://lccn.loc
  .gov/2021034188
LC ebook record available at https://lccn.loc
  .gov/2021034189

First Edition
27 26 25 24 23 22 21 10 9 8 7 6 5 4 3 2 1

Book producer: Westchester Publishing
Services
Cover designer: Rob Johnson

Brief Contents

■ Contents

Chapter 6
The Corporation and Internal Stakeholders: Values-Based Moral Leadership, Culture, Strategy, and Self-Regulation   351

The seventh edition of *Business Ethics: A Stakeholder and Issues Management Approach* continues the mission of providing a practical, easy-to-read, engaging, and contemporary text with detailed contemporary and classic cases for students. This text updates the previous edition, adding new cases in addition to other new features.

We continue our quest to assist colleagues and students in understanding the changing environment using combined stakeholder and issues management approaches, based on the theory and practice that firms depend on stakeholders as well as stockholders for their survival and success. Acting morally while doing business is a serious matter. The United States in particular has recently experienced instabilities in its governance, political, global trade, and international alliance relationships. Covid-19 jarred the country's economy, health care systems, and businesses of all sizes, just as the United States was recovering from the subprime-lending crisis. These recent disruptions present even more drastic challenges. Ethical behaviors are required, not optional, for this and future generations. Learning to think and reason ethically is a necessity, not a luxury.

Business ethics dilemmas are matters that involve deciding and doing what is right over what is wrong, while acting in helpful over harmful ways and seeking the common good as well as our own welfare. This text addresses this foundational way of thinking by asking why the modern corporation exists in the first place. What is its raison d'être and purpose? How does it treat its stakeholders? Business ethics engages these essential questions; and it is also about the purpose, values, and transactions of and between individuals, groups, and companies and their global alliances. Stakeholder theory and management, in particular, are what concern nonfinancial as well as the financial aspects of business behavior, policies, and actions. A stakeholder view of the firm complements the stockholder view and includes all parties and participants who have an interest—a stake—in the environment and society in which business operates.

Students and professionals need straightforward frameworks to thoughtfully and objectively analyze and then sort through complex issues in order to make decisions that matter—ethically, economically, socially, legally, and spiritually. The United States and indeed the whole world have been jolted by Covid-19 and the Black Lives Matter movement. Then there are the ongoing corporate scandals, the continuing consequences of the Arab Spring, race relations, the role of police and other public service agencies, security issues worldwide, escalating immigration problems, the increasing inequalities in income distribution and wealth, the decay and now survival of the middle classes, global warming and climate change—all developments that are changing institutions, livelihoods, careers, business practices, and the very survival of human lives internationally. This text attempts to identify and help analyze many of these issues and opportunities for change, using relevant stakeholder, issues management, and ethical frameworks. Ethics always has and, we argue, will continue to matter.

The Revised Seventh Edition: Why and How This Text Is Different

This edition builds on previous success factors to provide:

1. A competent, contemporary text grounded in factual and detailed research, while being easy to read and applying concepts and methods to real-time, business-related situations
2. Interesting and contemporary news stories, exercises, and examples
3. In-depth and customized cases (22 in this edition) specifically designed for this book
4. Ethical dilemmas experienced by real individuals, not hypothetical stories
5. A detailed chapter on both stakeholder and issues management methods, with step-by-step explanations, not summarized or theoretical abstractions
6. A straightforward business and managerial perspective supported by the latest research—not only a philosophical approach
7. One of the most comprehensive texts on the topics of workforce and workplace demographics, generational trends, and issues relating to ethical issues
8. Comprehensive coverage of such foundational laws as the Sarbanes-Oxley Act, federal sentencing guidelines, and codes of conduct
9. Personal, professional, organizational, and global perspectives, with information and strategies for addressing ethical dilemmas
10. A decision-maker role for students in exercises and examples

This edition adds features that enhance your ethical understanding and interest in contemporary issues in the business world. It also aligns even more closely with the international requirements of the Association to Advance Collegiate Schools of Business (AACSB) to help students, managers, and leaders achieve in their respective fields. Among the additions and changes are the following:

- A Point/CounterPoint exercise has been added to several chapters to challenge students' thinking and arguments on contemporary issues. Topics include "too big to fail" (TBTF) institutions, student loan debt, and continuing issues related to file sharing and other forms of online sharing.
- New cases cover issues relating to the Boeing 737 MAX, Wells Fargo, Facebook, artificial intelligence (AI), Covid-19, university admissions, Uber, and the opioid crisis.
- The effects of the Covid-19 crisis are interspersed across the chapters.
- National ethics survey data has been updated.

- New perspectives on generational differences and ethical workplace issues have been added.
- Each chapter has new and updated lead-off cases and scenarios to attract students' attention.
- Data on global and international issues has been updated.
- Updated research and business press findings and stories have been added to each chapter to explain concepts and perspectives.
- The material on stakeholder and issues management (Chapter 3) has a section explaining stakeholder theory in more depth.
- Chapter 4 has updated research throughout, with new Ethical Insight inserts.
- Chapters 5, 6, 7, and 8 are updated, as are the cases.

An Action Approach

The seventh edition puts the students in the decision-maker role when identifying and addressing ethical dilemmas with thought-provoking cases and discussion questions that ask, "What would you do if you had to decide a course of action?" Readers are encouraged to articulate and share their decision-making rationales and strategies. Readers will also learn how to examine changing ethical issues and business problems with a critical eye. We take a close look at the business reporting of the online editions of the *Wall Street Journal*, CBS *60 Minutes*, the *New York Times*, *Businessweek*, *The Economist*, and other sources.

Stakeholder and Issues Management Analysis

The combination of stakeholder and issues management analysis is a comprehensive approach for identifying issues, groups, strategies, and outcomes. These methods are presented in an updated and more integrative Chapter 3. This chapter is a useful starting point for mapping the who, what, when, where, why, and how of ethical problems relating to organizations and their stakeholders. Issues and crisis management frameworks are explained and integrated into approaches that complement the stakeholder analysis. Quick tests and negotiation techniques are presented in Chapters 2 and 8. In addition, this seventh edition includes:

- An updated instructor's manual and PowerPoint slides
- Streamlined case teaching notes
- Suggested videos and websites for each chapter

Objectives and Advantages of This Textbook

- To use an *action-oriented* stakeholder and issues management approach for understanding the ethical dimensions of business, organizational, and professional complex issues, crises, and events that are happening now.
- To introduce and *motivate students* about the relevance of ethical concepts, principles, and examples through actual moral dilemmas that are

occurring in their own lives, as well as with known national and international people, companies, and groups.

- To present a *simple, straightforward* way of using stakeholder and issues management methods with ethical reasoning in the marketplace and in workplace relationships.
- To *engage and expand* readers' awareness of ethical and unethical practices in business at the individual, group, organizational, and multinational levels through *real-time*—not hypothetical—ethical dilemmas, stories, and cases.
- To instill *self-confidence and competence* in the reader's ability to think and act according to moral principles. The classroom becomes a lab for real-life decisions.

Structure of the Book

- Chapter 1 defines business ethics and familiarizes the reader with examples of ethics in business practices, levels of ethical analysis, and what can be expected from a course in business ethics. A Point/ CounterPoint exercise engages students immediately.
- Chapter 2 engages students in a discussion of ethics at the personal, professional, organizational, and international levels. The foundations of ethical principles are presented in context with contemporary ethical decision-making approaches. Individual styles of moral decision making are also discussed. Although the approach here is a micro-level one, these principles can be used to examine and explain corporate strategies and actions as well. (Executives, managers, employees, coalitions, government officials, and other external stakeholder groups are treated as individuals.)
- Chapter 3 introduces action-oriented methods for studying social responsibility relationships at the individual employee, group, and organizational levels. These methods provide and encourage the incorporation of ethical principles and concepts from the entire book.
- Chapter 4 presents ethical issues and problems that firms face with external consumers, government, and environmental groups. How moral can and should corporations be and act in commercial dealings? Do corporations have a conscience? Classic and recent crises resulting from corporate and environmental problems are covered.
- Chapter 5 explains ethical problems that consumers face in the marketplace: product safety and liability, advertising, privacy, and the Internet. The following questions are addressed: How free is "free speech," and what effect is weaponized disinformation having on socie- ties? How much are you willing to pay for safety? Who owns the environment? Who regulates the regulators in an open society?
- Chapter 6 presents the corporation as internal stakeholder and discusses ethical leadership, strategy, structure, alliances, culture, and systems as dominant themes regarding how to lead, manage, and be a responsible follower in organizations today.

- Chapter 7 focuses on the individual employee stakeholder and examines the new and changing workforce/workplace trends, moral issues, and dilemmas employees and managers face and must respond to in order to survive and compete in national and global economies. This chapter has been described as a "must-read" for every human resources professional.
- Chapter 8 begins by asking students if they are ready for professional international assignments as well as a changed Covid-19 environment. Ethical and leadership competencies of new entrants into the global workforce are introduced, before moving the discussion to global and multinational enterprises (MNEs) and ethical issues between MNEs, host countries, and other groups. Issues resulting from globalization are presented along with stakeholders who monitor corporate responsibility internationally. Negotiation techniques for professionals responsibly doing business abroad are presented.

Cases

Chapter 1

1. Education Pushed to the Brink: How Covid-19 Is Redefining Recruitment and Admissions Decisions
2. Classic Ponzi Scheme: Bernard L. Madoff Investment Securities LLC: Wall Street Trading Firm
3. Cyberbullying: Who's to Blame and What Can Be Done?

Chapter 2

4. Ford's Pinto Fires: The Retrospective View of Ford's Field Recall Coordinator
5. Jerome Kerviel: Rogue Trader or Misguided Employee? What Really Happened at the Société Générale?
6. Samuel Waksal at ImClone

Chapter 3

7. The BP *Deepwater Horizon* Explosion and Oil Spill: Crisis and Aftermath
8. Ethics and AI (Artificial Intelligence): Opportunities and Threats
9. Genetic Discrimination

Chapter 4

10. Conscious Capitalism: What Is It? Why Do We Need It? Does It Work?
11. Uber and the Ride-Sharing Economy
12. The Crisis at Wells Fargo Bank: Then and Now

■ Acknowledgments

This book continues the practice that has endured over the last several years that I have been teaching business ethics to undergraduates, MBA students, and executives. My consulting work also informs this edition in numerous ways. I would like to thank all my students for their questions, challenges, and class contributions, which have stimulated the research and presentations in this text. I also thank all the professional staff at Berrett-Koehler, especially Edward Wade and Neal Maillet, who helped make this edition possible; and the faculty and staff at Bentley University, who contributed resources and motivation for this edition. I pay tribute to the late pioneering Michael Hoffman and his staff at Bentley University's Center for Business Ethics, and to his successor Jeff Moriarty, whose shared resources and friendship also helped with this edition. I also recognize Rachel Marvin, Kinberly Saenz de la Cruz, Cindy Wu, Sean MacDogall, and the graduate students listed as coauthors of cases.

Thanks, also, to the main reviewers Jeffrey Kulic, marketing instructor at George Mason University School of Business; and Professor Judith Herzberg of Springfield College in Boston, Massachusetts, whose comments were helpful. The many graduate and undergraduate students at Bentley University also provided invaluable assistance in updating the research and text.

Joseph W. Weiss
Bentley University

▪ Case Authorship

Case 1 Education Pushed to the Brink: How Covid-19 Is Redefining Recruitment and Admissions Decisions

Gordon Berridge

Case 2 Classic Ponzi Scheme: Bernard L. Madoff Investment Securities LLC: Wall Street Trading Firm

Alba Skurti, Bentley University, under the direction of Professor Joseph W. Weiss, Bentley University

Case 3 Cyberbullying: Who's to Blame and What Can Be Done?

Roseleen Dello Russo and Lauren Westling, Bentley University, under the direction of Professor Joseph W. Weiss, Bentley University

Case 4 Ford's Pinto Fires: The Retrospective View of Ford's Field Recall Coordinator

Dennis A. Gioia, professor of Organizational Behavior, Smeal College of Business, Pennsylvania State University, provided the personal reflections in this case. Michael K. McCuddy, Valparaiso University, provided background information and discussion questions.

Case 5 Jerome Kerviel: Rogue Trader or Misguided Employee? What Really Happened at the Société Générale?

Steve D'Aquila, Bentley University, under the direction of Professor Joseph W. Weiss, Bentley University

Case 6 Samuel Waksal at ImClone

Amy Vensku, MBA Bentley student under the direction of Professor Joseph W. Weiss; edited and adapted for this text by Michael K. McCuddy, Valparaiso University, and Matt Zamorski, Bentley University

Case 7 The BP *Deepwater Horizon* Explosion and Oil Spill: Crisis and Aftermath

Jill Stonehouse and Bianlbahen Patel, Bentley University, under the direction of Professor Joseph W. Weiss, Bentley University

Case 8 Ethics and AI (Artificial Intelligence): Opportunities and Threats

Joseph W. Weiss, with Kristina Hagmeier

Case 9 Genetic Discrimination

Jaclyn Publicover, Bentley University, with Joseph W. Weiss, Bentley University

Case 10 Conscious Capitalism: What Is It? Why Do We Need It? Does It Work?

John Warden, Bentley University, edited by Professor Joseph W. Weiss

Case 11 Uber and the Ride-Sharing Economy

Dhara Patel and Jon Malchiodi, with Joseph W. Weiss

Case 12 The Crisis at Wells Fargo Bank: Then and Now

Joseph W. Weiss, with Cindy Wu

Case 13 For-Profit Universities: Opportunities, Issues, and Promises

Alicia Cabrera and Nate Pullen, Bentley University, under the direction of Professor Joseph W. Weiss, Bentley University

Case 14 Fracking: Drilling for Disaster?

Lauren Casas and Ned Coffee, MBA Bentley students, under the direction of Professor Joseph W. Weiss, Bentley University, with editorial revisions made by Laura Gray, Matt Zamorski, and Lu Bai

Case 15 Neuromarketing

Eddy Fitzgerald and Jennifer Johnson, Bentley University, under the direction of Professor Joseph W. Weiss, Bentley University

Case 16 Opioid Crisis in America

Mati Litwin and A. Forestieri, with Joseph W. Weiss

Case 17 Corporate Responsibility in the Age of Big Data: Facebook's Obligations to Protect Consumers

A. Aquino, with Joseph W. Weiss

Case 18 Boeing: The 737 "MAX-imum" Mistake

Amanda Walker, with Joseph W. Weiss

Case 19 Women on Wall Street: Fighting for Equality in a Male-Dominated Industry

Monica Meunier, under the direction of Professor Joseph W. Weiss, and adapted and edited for this text by Michael K. McCuddy, Valparaiso University

Case 20 Plastic in the Ocean: An International Climate Change Problem

Terry DelRossi

Case 21 Sweatshops: Not Only a Global Issue

Michael K. McCuddy, the Louis S. and Mary L. Morgal Chair of Christian Business Ethics and Professor of Management, College of Business Administration, Valparaiso University

Case 22 The U.S. Industrial Food System

Brenda Pasquarello, with Joseph W. Weiss

1

BUSINESS ETHICS, THE CHANGING ENVIRONMENT, AND STAKEHOLDER MANAGEMENT

OPENING CASE

Blogger: "Hi. i download music and movies, limewire, torrent [and other sites]. Is it illegal for me to download or is it just illegal for the person uploading it. Does anyone know someone who was caught and got into trouble for it, what happened to them. Personally I don't see a difference between downloading a song or taping it on a cassette from a radio!"[1]

The Covid-19 crisis has accelerated the use of online technologies, particularly social media, mobile phone apps, entertainment, and communication sites. Illegal file sharing continues to be problematic. "The U.S. Chamber of Commerce's Global Innovation Policy Center estimated in 2019 that online piracy accounts for 26.6 billion views of U.S.-produced movies and 126.7 billion views of U.S.-produced TV episodes every year. The economic impact of digital video piracy extends far beyond the movie and television industries; in total, it is responsible for at least $29.2 billion in lost domestic revenues, 230,000 in lost American jobs, and $47.5 billion in reduced GDP [gross domestic product]."[2] The Recording Industry Association of America (RIAA), on behalf of its member companies and copyright owners, has sued more than 20,000 people and settled 2,500 cases for unlawful downloading. RIAA detectives log on to peer-to-peer networks where they easily identify illegal activity since users' shared folders are visible to all. The majority of these cases have been settled out of court for $1,000 to $3,000, but fines per music track can go up to $150,000 under the Copyright Act.

More recently, a practice known as "torrenting" has contributed to illegal file sharing, particularly with books, movies, and games. A "torrent" or "tracker" breaks up "the big file and chops it up into little pieces, called 'packets' . . . that are shared throughout a network of computers also downloading the same file you are." You are usually downloading it from a network of peers. Copyrighted files are illegal to download without paying, and some of these technologies make downloading easier. The risks for becoming part of a "torrent community" or downloading copyrighted files for "free" can be substantial. Trolls, hackers, and other vipers can track, steal, and corrupt your computer system. "Anti-piracy activists claim that copyright infringement (most of it done through torrenting) is costing the U.S. economy $250 billion per year."[3]

The nation's first file-sharing defendant to challenge an RIAA lawsuit, Jammie Thomas-Rasset, reached the end of the appeals process to overturn a jury-determined $222,000 fine in 2013. She was ordered to pay this amount, which she argued was unconstitutionally excessive, for downloading and sharing 24 copyrighted songs using the now-defunct file-sharing service Kazaa. The Supreme Court has not yet heard a file-sharing case, having also declined without comment to review the only other appeal following Thomas-Rasset's case. (In that case, the court let stand a federal jury–imposed fine of $675,000 against Joel Tenenbaum for downloading and sharing 30 songs.) "As I've said from the beginning, I do not have now, nor do I anticipate in the future, having $220,000 to pay this," Thomas-Rasset said. "If they do decide to try and collect, I will file for bankruptcy as I have no other option."[4]

Once the well-funded RIAA initiates a lawsuit, many defendants are pressured to settle out of court in order to avoid oppressive legal expenses. Others simply can't take the risk of large fines that juries have shown themselves willing to impose.

New technologies and the trend toward digital consumption, as noted above, have made intellectual property both more critical to businesses' bottom lines and more difficult to protect. No company, big or small, is immune to the intellectual property protection challenge. Illegal downloads of music are not the only concern. In 2011, the U.S. Copyright Group initiated what it called "the largest illegal downloading case in U.S. history" at the time, suing over 23,000 file sharers who illegally downloaded Sylvester Stallone's movie *The Expendables.* This case was expanded to include the 25,000 users who also downloaded Voltage Pictures' *The Hurt Locker,* which increased the total number of defendants to approximately 50,000, all of whom used peer-to-peer downloading through BitTorrent. The lawsuits were filed based on the illegal downloads made from an Internet Protocol (IP) address. The use of an IP address as identifier presents ethical issues—for example, should a parent be responsible for a child downloading a movie through the family's IP address? What about a landlord who supplied Internet to a tenant?

Digital books are also now in play. In 2012, a now-classic lawsuit was filed in China against technology giant Apple for sales of illegal book downloads through its App Store. Nine Chinese authors are demanding payment of $1.88 million for unauthorized versions of their books that were submitted to the App Store and sold to consumers for a profit. Again, the individual IP addresses are the primary way of determining who performed the illegal download. Telecom providers and their customers face privacy concerns, as companies are being asked for the names of customers associated with IP addresses identified with certain downloads.

Privacy activists argue that an IP address (which identifies the subscriber but not the person operating the computer) is private, protected information that can be shown during criminal but not civil investigations. Fred von Lohmann, a senior staff attorney with the Electronic Frontier Foundation, has suggested on his organization's blog that "courts are not prepared to simply award default judgments worth tens of thousands of dollars against individuals based on a piece of paper backed by no evidence."[5]

1.1 Business Ethics and the Changing Environment

The Internet, Zoom, and other apps—with enhanced use during Covid-19—are now among the primary ways of communicating, doing business, and managing life—individually, organizationally, nationally, and internationally. Those less fortunate in the United States as well as the last "third billion" of people in undeveloped countries who are not and cannot afford broadband access are particularly disadvantaged.[6] Covid-19 has been a wake-up call to the health and welfare and technological needs of the United States and businesses worldwide. Also, as this chapter's opening case shows, there is more than one side to every complex issue and debate involving businesses, consumers, families, other institutions, and professionals. When stakeholders, governments, and companies cannot agree or negotiate competing claims among themselves, the issues generally go to the courts, as was shown in the 2020 U.S. presidential election.

Stakeholders are individuals, companies, groups, and even governments and their subsystems that cause and respond to external issues, opportunities, and threats. Global crises, natural disasters, corporate scandals, globalization, deregulation, mergers, technology, and global cyberterrorism have accelerated the rate of change and brought about a climate of uncertainty in which stakeholders must make business and moral decisions. Issues concerning questionable ethical and illegal business practices confront everyone, as exemplified in some of the following examples:

- Covid-19 and events surrounding and heightened by it have ushered in a host of contemporary issues that have both legal and ethical urgency. Cybersecurity is a necessity for all. Hackers demanding and getting ransomware extracted $144 million in 2020 from municipality governments, universities, and private businesses.[7]

- Public outrage over institutional racism, triggered by the May 2020 murder of George Floyd, gave rise to the Black Lives Matter movement nationally and internationally and has pressured police and other criminal justice institutions to reimagine their organizations and practices.

- While Covid-19 has in many ways overshadowed other previous crises, the subprime-lending crisis of 2008 is also memorable, as it affected stakeholders as varied as consumers, banks, mortgage companies, real estate firms, and homeowners. Many companies that sold mortgages to unqualified buyers lied about low-risk, high-return products. Wall Street companies, while thriving, are also settling lawsuits stemming from the 2008 crisis. Hundreds of thousands of subprime borrowers struggled from that crisis, and many lost their homes. Subprime securities still pose a significant legal risk to the firms that packaged them, using capital that could be gainfully applied to the current economy."[8] Standing now as a landmark financial crisis, in 2011, Bank of America announced that it would "take a whopping $20 billion hit to put the fallout from the subprime bust behind it and satisfy claims from angry investors."[9] The ethics and decisions precipitating the crisis contributed to tilt the U.S. economy toward recession, with long-lasting effects.

- The corporate scandals in the 1990s through 2001 at Enron, Adelphia, Halliburton, MCI WorldCom, Tyco, Arthur Andersen, Global Crossing, Dynegy, Qwest, and Merrill Lynch are now deemed "classic cases" economically and in business ethics; and similar scandals could reoccur at other firms without responsible diligence, especially with democracies across the globe threatened by domestic terrorism, lax citizen and environmental protection policies, and shared governance by stakeholders and stockholders. We reference these classic cases since they jolted shareholder and public confidence in Wall Street and corporate governance. Enron's bankruptcy with assets of $63.4 billion defies imagination, and WorldCom's bankruptcy set the record for the largest corporate bankruptcy in U.S. history.[10] Only 22 percent of Americans express a great deal or quite a lot of confidence in big business, compared to 65 percent who express confidence in small business.[11] Confidence in big business reached its highest point in 1974 at 34 percent, and even during the dot-com boom in the late 1990s it hovered at 30 percent. The lowest rating of 16 percent was polled in 2009 after the subprime-lending crisis, and although public confidence has since increased slightly, the significant differential in American confidence between big and small business belies a public mistrust of big business that may not be easily repaired.[12]

- According to the *New York Times*, "Even as millions of people have lost their jobs during the [Covid-19] pandemic, the soaring stock market since the spring of 2020 has delivered outsized gains to the wealthiest Americans. And few among the superrich have done as well as corporate executives who received stock awards this year."[13] Moreover, the debate continues over excessive pay to those chief executive officers (CEOs) who continue to post poor corporate performance. Large bonuses paid out during the financial crisis made executive pay a controversial topic, yet investors did little to solve the issue. "Investors had the opportunity to provide advisory votes on executive pay at financial firms that received TARP [Troubled Asset Relief Program] funds in 2009, and they gave thumbs up to pay packages at every single one of those institutions. This proxy season, with advisory votes now widely available (thanks to the Dodd-Frank Act), only five companies' executive compensation packages have received a thumbs down from shareholders."[14] "Realized CEO compensation grew 105.1% from 2009 to 2019, the period capturing the recovery from the Great Recession; in that period granted CEO compensation grew 35.7%. In contrast, typical workers in these large firms saw their average annual compensation grow by just 7.6% over the last 10 years."[15] A recent analysis showed that in 2020, the average multiple of CEO compensation to that of rank-and-file workers is 320."[16]

- During the Covid-19 pandemic, some critics on the right of the political spectrum continue to argue that companies still can become overregulated. Others argue that more sufficient and effective regulation of the largest financial and social media companies is needed to overcome the inequalities in income, pay, wealth, and taxes that have been created. The Sarbanes-Oxley Act of 2002 was one response to the scandals in the early 2000s. This act states that corporate officers will serve prison time and pay large fines if they are found guilty of fraudulent financial reporting and of deceiving shareholders. Implementing this legislation requires companies to create accounting oversight boards, establish ethics codes, show financial reports in greater detail to investors, and have the CEO and chief financial officer (CFO) personally sign off on and take responsibility for all financial statements and internal controls. Implementing these provisions is costly for corporations. Some claim their profits and global competitiveness are negatively affected and the regulations are "unenforceable."[17] More recently, Covid-19 and the ensuing economic crisis has exposed an increasing racial divide along with income inequalities between those at the top of the income and wealth spectrum and the shrinking middle- and lower-income levels.

- U.S. firms before Covid were outsourcing work to other countries to cut costs and improve profits, work that some argue could be accomplished in the United States. Estimates of U.S. jobs outsourced range from 104,000 in 2000 to 400,000 in 2004, and on average, 300,000 annually. "Forrester Research estimated that 3.3 million U.S. jobs and about $136 billion in wages would be moved to overseas countries such as India, China, and Russia by 2015. Deloitte Consulting reported that 2 million jobs would move from the United States and Europe to overseas destinations within the financial services business. Across all industries the emigration of service jobs can be as high as 4 million."[18] Do U.S. employees who are laid off and displaced need protection, or is this practice part of another societal business transformation? Is the United States becoming part of a global supply chain in which outsourcing is "business as usual," or is the working middle class in the United States and elsewhere at risk of predatory industrial practices and ineffective government polices?[19] Still, there are critics in 2020 who argue that outsourcing does lower company costs, increases profits for stockholders, and gives lower prices to consumers—resulting in higher standards of living and an overall increase in employment for larger numbers of the population.

- Will robots, robotics, and artificial intelligence (AI) applications replace humans in the workplace? This interesting but disruptive development poses concerns. "The outsourcing of human jobs as a side effect of globalization has arguably contributed to the current unemployment crisis. However, one rather extreme trend sees humans done away with altogether, even in the low-wage countries where many American jobs have landed."[20] What will be the ethical implications of the next wave of AI development, "where full-blown autonomous self-learning systems take us into the realm of science fiction—delivery systems and self-driving vehicles alone could change day-to-day life as we know it, not to mention the social implications."[21] AI also extends into electronic warfare (drones), education (robot assisted or led), and manufacturing (a Taiwanese company replaced a "human force of 1.2 million people with 1 million robots to make laptops, mobile devices, and other electronics hardware for Apple, Hewlett-Packard, Dell, and Sony").[22] One futurist predicted that as many as 50 million jobs could be lost to machines by 2030, and even 50 percent of all human jobs by 2040. These, again, may be extreme views.

These large macro-level issues taken together underlie many ethical dilemmas that affect business and individual decisions among stakeholders in organizations, professions, as well as individual lives. Before discussing stakeholder theory, the management approach that it is based on, and how these perspectives and methods can help individuals and companies better understand how to make more socially responsible decisions, we take a brief look at the broader environmental forces that affect industries, organizations, and individuals.

Seeing the "Big Picture"

Pulitzer Prize–winning journalist Thomas Friedman continues to track mega changes, including those resulting from Covid, on a global scale. His 2011 book, *That Used to Be Us: How America Fell Behind in the World It Invented and How We Can Come Back,* is particularly prophetic now. In it, he suggests an agenda for change to meet larger challenges. His book *The Lexus and the Olive Tree* vividly illustrates a macroenvironmental perspective that provides helpful insights into stakeholder and issues management mind-sets and approaches.[23] Friedman notes:

> Like everyone else trying to adjust to this new globalization system and bring it into focus, I had to retrain myself and develop new lenses to see it. Today, more than ever, the traditional boundaries between politics, culture, technology, finance, national security, and ecology are disappearing. You often cannot explain one without referring to the others, and you cannot explain the whole without reference to them all. I wish I could say I understood all this when I began my career, but I didn't. I came to this approach entirely by accident, as successive changes in my career kept forcing me to add one more lens on top of another, just to survive.[24]

After quoting Murray Gell-Mann, the Nobel laureate and former professor of theoretical physics at Caltech, Friedman continues:

> We need a corpus of people who consider that it is important to take a serious and professional look at the whole system. It has to be a crude look, because you will never master every part or every interconnection. Unfortunately, in a great many places in our society, including academia and most bureaucracies, prestige accrues principally to those who study carefully some [narrow] aspect of a problem, a trade, a technology, or a culture, while discussion of the big picture is relegated to cocktail party conversation. That is crazy. We have to learn not only to have specialists but also people whose specialty is to spot the strong interactions and entanglements of the different dimensions, and then take a crude look at the whole.[25]

■ POINT/COUNTERPOINT

File Sharing: Still a Problem, but Harmful Theft or Sign of the Times?

Instructions: Each student in this exercise must select *either* Point or CounterPoint arguments (no in-between choices), defend that choice, and state why you believe either one or the other. Be ready to argue your choice as the instructor directs. Afterward, the class is debriefed, and there is further discussion as a class.

POINT: File sharing is theft, illegal, and endangers the entire structure of incentives that allows the creation of digital media. Downloading even one copyrighted song, movie, book, or game illegally has severe costs for the musicians and the owners and employees of the companies that produce songs, and for legitimate online music services, not to mention consumers who purchase music legally. Those responsible, even peripherally, for illegal file sharing should be tracked down by any means possible and held accountable for these costs and damages.

COUNTERPOINT: The generation that grew up with the advent of digital media has a well-cultivated expectation of ease and freedom when it comes to accessing music, television, and books using the Internet. Not only younger individuals but consumers worldwide are prone through torrenting and other enticing sites to download "free" materials and are at risk, because their files and devices can also be hacked. Companies are willing to capitalize on that ease to boost their profits. It is unethical to use technology and the legal system to "make examples" of those (possibly innocent bystanders whose IP addresses were used by others) who are simply showing the flaws and gaps in distribution strategies.

> "I watch some of my favorite shows on Hulu.com for free and I buy others on Amazon or iTunes. I pay a fee to use Pandora for ad-free Internet radio, or Spotify for specific music playlists. But like many of my friends, I don't own a TV, so when there is no other way to access a show, I will download it from a torrent [file-sharing] site since I can, and my friends do as well."
> —*Interview with a Generation Y "Millennial"*

> "The Boston Celtics are my favorite basketball team, but unfortunately, I live in the New York area. This means that the local sports channel only shows New York Knicks games and Brooklyn Nets games. With no other way of watching every Celtics game, I am enticed to go on Reddit and watch the Celtics game streamed illegally. Is this my fault? It's available and my friends do it."
> —*Interview with a Generation Y "Millennial"*

Environmental Forces and Stakeholders

Organizations and individuals are embedded in and interact with multiple changing local, national, and international environments, as contemporary media and news and the above discussions illustrate. Each chapter of this book provides some context for reported events, controversies, and ethical arguments. Chapter 8 in particular illustrates and references an international perspective, as do sections throughout this text. These environments are increasingly moving into a global system of dynamically interrelated interactions among businesses and economies, even though some scholars and pundits argue that globalization has been in retreat in part because of the pandemic and also because of emergent nationalistic, autocratic leaders who claim democracies are failing.[26]

Still, the motto "Think globally before acting locally" is relevant in many situations. The macro-level environmental forces shown in Figure 1.1 affect the performance and operation of industries, organizations, and jobs. This

Figure 1.1

Environmental Dimensions Affecting Industries, Organizations, and Jobs

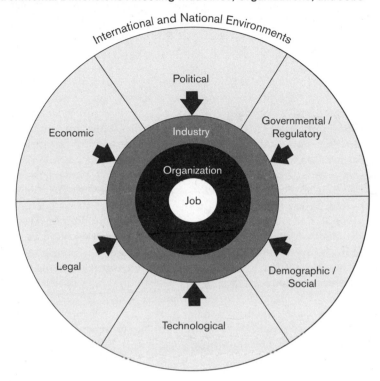

framework can be used as a starting point to identify trends, issues, opportunities, and ethical problems that affect people and stakes in different levels. *A first step toward understanding stakeholder issues is to gain an understanding of environmental forces that influence stakeholders, their issues, and stakes.* As we present an overview of these environmental forces here, think of the effects and pressures each of the forces has on you.

The economic environment is under Covid-19 stress presently but shows potential for rebounding once vaccinations and containment start to work. The global economy, suppressed from 2016 to 2021, will rebound and continue to evolve through renewed global trade, markets, and resource flows, despite previous debates and forced ideologies to the contrary. The rise of China has overshadowed India presently. The United States will have to regain its international presence and credibility post-Covid with new trade opportunities and business practices.

The technological environment has become a necessity, no longer a luxury. Although speed, scope, economy of scale, and efficiency are transforming transactions through information technology, privacy and surveillance issues continue to emerge. The boundary between surveillance and convenience also continues to blur. Has the company or organization for which you work used surveillance to monitor Internet use?

Disinformation and misinformation have plagued and still threaten the United States and some other countries and democracies. International and national "bad actors," domestic terrorist groups, and divides between "red" and "blue" political and ideological mind-sets will have to be mended for real change to occur.

The government and legal environments are also in a state of repair after the brutal January 6, 2021, attack on the U.S. Capitol, with continuing identity and dangerous divisive politics in the U.S. Congress. But regulatory laws such as the Dodd-Frank Act of 2010 that established the Consumer Financial Protection Bureau, whose mission is to protect consumers by carrying out federal consumer financial laws, educating consumers, and hearing complaints from the public, will help citizens with credit card abuses in particular.[27]

The demographic and social environment continues to change as national boundaries experience the effects of globalization and the workforce becomes more diverse. The Black Lives Matter movement has reinvigorated interest in solving institutional racism. Emphasis currently is on addressing concrete national, state, and local (in the United States) policy changes with regard to income inequality, justice of the treatment of Black and minority citizens by law enforcement officers, and inclusiveness policies and practices in and across institutions. Employers and employees are faced with Covid-19 problems of shutdowns, stress, loss, and employment as well as employability. At the same time, employers and employees continue to face tensions with demographic factors related to aging and very young populations; minorities becoming majorities; generational differences; and the effects of downsizing and outsourcing on morale, productivity, and security. Those companies that survive the Covid-19 crisis face economic survival issues, but they also must strive to effectively integrate a workforce that is at once increasingly younger and older, less educated and more educated, technologically sophisticated and technologically unskilled.

In this book these environmental factors are incorporated into a stakeholder and issues management approach that also includes an ethical analysis of actors external and internal to organizations. The larger perspective underlying these analytical approaches is represented by the following question: How can the common good of all stakeholders in controversial situations be realized?

Stakeholder Management Approach

How do companies, the media, political groups, consumers, employees, competitors, and other groups respond in socially ethical and responsible ways when impacted by an issue, dilemma, threat, or opportunity from the environments just described? The stakeholder theory expands a narrow view of corporations from a stockholder-only perspective to include the many stakeholders who are also involved in how corporations envision the future, treat people and the environment, and serve the common good for the many. Implementing this view starts with the ethical imperatives and moral understandings that corporations that use natural resources and the environment must serve, as well as providing for those who buy their products and services. This view and accompanying methods are explained in more detail in Chapters 2 and 3 especially and inform the whole text.

The stakeholder theory begins to address these questions by enabling individuals and groups to articulate collaborative, win-win strategies based on:

1. Identifying and prioritizing issues, threats, or opportunities
2. Mapping who the stakeholders are
3. Identifying their stakes, interests, and power sources
4. Showing who the members of coalitions are or may become
5. Showing what each stakeholder's ethics are (and should be)
6. Developing collaborative strategies and dialogue from a "higher ground" perspective to move plans and interactions to the desired closure for all parties

Chapter 3 lays out specific steps and strategies for analyzing stakeholders. Our aim is to develop awareness of the ethical and social responsibilities of different stakeholders. As Figure 1.2 illustrates, there can be a wide range of stakeholders in any situation. We turn to a general discussion of "business ethics" in

Figure 1.2

Primary versus Secondary Stakeholder Groups

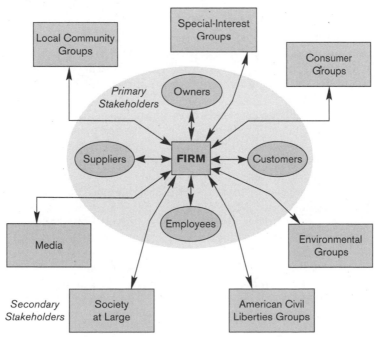

the following section to introduce the subject and motivate you to investigate ethical dimensions of organizational and professional behavior.

1.2 What Is Business Ethics? Why Does It Matter?

Business ethicists ask, "What is right and wrong, good and bad, harmful and beneficial regarding decisions and actions in organizational transactions?" Ethical reasoning and logic is explained in more detail in Chapter 2, but we note here that approaching problems using a moral frame of reference can influence solution paths as well as options and outcomes. Since "solutions" to business and organizational problems may have more than one alternative, and sometimes no right solution may seem available, using principled, ethical thinking provides structured and systematic ways of making decisions based on values, as opposed to relying on perceptions that may be distorted, pressures from others, or the quickest and easiest available options that may prove more harmful.

What Is Ethics, and What Are the Areas of Ethical Theory?

Ethics derives from the Greek word *ethos*—meaning "character"—and is also known as moral philosophy, which is a branch of philosophy that involves "systematizing, defending, and recommending concepts of right and wrong conduct."[28] Ethics involves understanding the differences between right and wrong thinking and actions and using principled decision making to choose actions that do not hurt others. Although intuition and creativity are often involved in having to decide between what seems like two "wrong" or less desirable choices in a dilemma where there are no easy alternatives, using ethical principles to inform our thinking before acting hastily may reduce the negative consequences of our actions. Classic ethical principles are presented in more detail in Chapter 2, but by way of an introduction, three general areas constitute a framework for understanding ethical theories: metaethics, normative ethics, and descriptive ethics.[29]

Metaethics considers where one's ethical principles "come from, and what they mean." Do one's ethical beliefs come from what society has prescribed? Did our parents, family, or religious institutions influence and shape our ethical beliefs? Are our principles part of our emotions and attitudes? Metaethical perspectives address these questions and focus on issues of universal truths, the will of God, the role of reason in ethical judgments, and the meaning of ethical terms themselves.[30] More practically, if we are studying a case or observing an event in the news, we can inquire about what and where a particular CEO's or professional's ethical principles (or lack thereof) are and where in that person's life and work history these beliefs were adopted.

Normative ethics is more practical. It involves prescribing ethical behaviors and evaluating what should be done in the future. We can inquire about specific moral standards that govern and influence right from wrong conduct and behaviors. Normative ethics also deals with what habits we need to develop, what duties and responsibilities we should follow, and the consequences of our behavior and its effects on others. Again, in a business or organizational context, we observe and address ethical problems and issues with individuals, teams, and leaders and address ways of preventing and/or solving ethical dilemmas and problems.

Descriptive ethics involves the examination of other people's beliefs and principles. It also relates to presenting—describing but not interpreting or evaluating—facts, events, and ethical actions in specific situations and places. In any context—organizational, relationship, or business—our aim here is to *understand*, not predict, judge, or solve, an ethical or unethical behavior or action.

Learning to think, reason, and act ethically helps us to become aware of and recognize potential ethical problems. Then we can evaluate values, assumptions, and judgments regarding the problem *before* we act. Ultimately, ethical principles alone cannot answer what the late theologian Paul Tillich called "the courage to be" in serious ethical dilemmas or crises. We can also learn from business case studies, role playing, and discussions on how our actions affect others in different situations. Acting accountably and responsibly is still a choice.

Laura Nash defined business ethics as "the study of how personal moral norms apply to the activities and goals of commercial enterprise. It is not a separate moral standard, but the study of how the business context poses its own unique problems for the moral person who acts as an agent of this system." Nash stated that business ethics deals with three basic areas of managerial decision making: (1) choices about what the laws should be and whether to follow them; (2) choices about economic and social issues outside the domain of law; and (3) choices about the priority of self-interest over the company's interests.[31]

Unethical Business Practices and Employees

The 2020 Global Business Ethics Survey Report from the Ethics and Compliance Initiative (ECI) surveyed responses from 18 countries across global regions, including North America, South America, Europe, Asia Pacific, Africa, and the Middle East.[32]

Some Key Findings from the ECI:

- One in every five employees feels pressure to compromise their organization's ethics standards, policies, or the law.
- Employees who feel pressure are about twice as likely to observe various types of misconduct.
- The incidence of pressure was three times as high for employees with weak leader commitment to organizational values and ethical leadership compared with strong leader commitment.

A 2014 National Business Ethics Survey (NBES)[33] from the reputable Ethics Resource Center identified the types of ethical misconduct that were reported in the United States.

Specific Types of Ethical Misconduct Reported

The most frequently observed types of misconduct were a worker witnessing abusive behavior (18 percent), lying to employees (17 percent), discrimination (12 percent), and sexual harassment (7 percent). Types of misconduct that were viewed less frequently include falsifying company financial data and public reports (3 percent) or bribing officials (2 percent). Many employees still do not report misconduct that they observe, and fear of retaliation is increasingly valid. This retaliation can lead to instability in the workplace by driving away talented employees. Even with increasing investment in ethical programs, the rate of reporting was still within the range of 63 to 65 percent. Detailed data suggests that a potential factor is employees independently attempting to create a solution without the involvement of management.[34]

The Retaliation Trust/Fear/Reality Disconnect

Of the employees who reported witnessing misconduct in the 2014 NBES, approximately 20 percent experienced retaliation. Those companies that practice good business ethics will reap strong results in the future. It provides comfort to employees to speak out on matters, as shown by these statistics: "Reporting rates are higher (72 percent) at companies where the employee thinks retaliation is not tolerated compared to those who think retaliation is tolerated (54 percent)."[35] Even in a scenario where an employee misses an initial opportunity to report misconduct, evidence suggests an improving situation. The willingness for employees who are victims of retaliation to report misconduct *in the future* was 86 percent (compared to the 95 percent of people who did not suffer retaliation but would report it in the future).[36]

An emphasis on and teaching of business ethics is slowly but surely producing positive results and has a strong impact on the company as a whole. The NBES report also made recommendations to help improve the business ethics of the workplaces:

- Maintain commitment to ethics and compliance program and seek industry leadership.
- Focus on efforts to empower employees and deepen their commitment to the company and its long-term success.
- Develop ongoing programs and structures to monitor misconduct within the company.
- Develop initiatives to address the most common forms of misconduct.
- Educate workers about Dodd-Frank and other laws designed to encourage whistle-blowers and protect them from retaliation.[37]

Why Does Ethics Matter in Business?

"Doing the right thing" matters to firms, taxpayers, employees, and other stakeholders, as well as to society. To companies and employers, acting legally and ethically means saving billions of dollars each year in lawsuits, settlements, and theft. One study found that the annual business costs of internal fraud range between the annual gross domestic product (GDP) of Bulgaria ($66 billion) and that of Taiwan ($586 billion). It has also been estimated that theft costs companies $600 billion annually, and that 79 percent of workers admit to or think about stealing from their employers. Other studies have shown that corporations have paid significant financial penalties for acting unethically.[38] The U.S. Department of Commerce noted that as many as one-third of all business failures annually can be attributed to employee theft. "Potential global loss from fraud and employee theft is $2.9 trillion annually. It is also estimated that 33 percent of corporate bankruptcies in the United States are linked to employee theft.[39]

Relationships, Reputation, Morale, and Productivity

Costs to businesses also include deterioration of relationships; damage to reputation; declining employee productivity, creativity, and loyalty; ineffective information flow throughout the organization; and absenteeism. Companies that have a reputation for unethical and uncaring behavior toward employees also have a difficult time recruiting and retaining valued professionals.

Integrity, Culture, Communication, and the Common Good

Strong ethical leadership goes hand in hand with strong integrity. Both ethics and integrity have a significant impact on a company's operations. "History has often shown the importance of ethics in business—even a single lapse in judgment by one employee can significantly affect a company's reputation and its bottom line. Leaders who show a solid moral compass and set a forthright example for their employees foster a work environment where integrity becomes a core value."[40]

Integrity/Ethics

What is the degree to which coworkers, managers, and senior leaders display integrity and ethical conduct? ECI data suggests that companies have been reinforcing the importance of integrity/ethics; namely, 47 percent of U.S. respondents in 2018 reported that they have "personally observed conduct that violated either the law or organization standards." This number dropped from 51 percent reported four years earlier. Of the 47 percent of people, 69 percent of them reported a misbehavior, an all-time high and 23 percent increase since the first study, which was done in 2020. Some reported ethical acts included stealing, sexual harassment, misuse of confidential information, and giving or accepting bribes.[41]

The same study also identifies an important aspect of improving "employee conduct" in culture—which is defined as "the shared understanding of what really matters in an organization and the way things really get done." While a strong culture provides many benefits, unfortunately, only

20 percent of respondents were confident that their company has a strong ethical culture. In an attempt to resolve this issue, suggestions on how to improve workplace ethical culture included the following: "(1) Promote a statement of values throughout the organization and set ethical standards to guide employee actions. (2) Include ethics and compliance in performance goals. (3) Regularly survey employee attitudes about pressures to disregard ethics. (4) Assess the ethical culture in the company and provide support in areas it may be weak. (5) Reinforce cultural norms of the unacceptability of performance without integrity. (6) Make sure company ethics and compliance programs are of high quality."[42]

Working for the Best Companies

Employees care about ethics because they are attracted to ethically and socially responsible companies. *Fortune* magazine regularly publishes a list of the 100 best companies to work for. Although the list continues to change, it is instructive to observe some of the characteristics of good employers that employees repeatedly cite.

Over 252,000 employees at 257 firms doing business in 45 international participated in the 2020 survey. Companies were surveyed by the Great Place to Work Institute, a global research and consulting firm operating in 45 countries around the world. Sixty-six percent of the survey is based on the institute's "Trust Index" survey, which relates to employees attitudes about "management's credibility, job satisfaction, and camaraderie." Thirty-three percent relates to a "Culture Audit" (i.e., pay and benefit programs, hiring practices, communication, training, recognition programs, and diversity efforts).[43]

The public and consumers benefit from organizations acting in an ethically and socially responsible manner. Ethics matters in business because all stakeholders stand to gain when organizations, groups, and individuals seek to do the right thing, as well as to do things the right way. Ethical companies create investor loyalty, customer satisfaction, and business performance and profits.[44] The following section presents different levels on which ethical issues can occur.

1.3 Levels of Business Ethics

Because ethical problems are not only an individual or personal matter, it is helpful to examine where issues originate and how they change. Business leaders and professionals manage a wide range of stakeholders inside and outside their organizations. Understanding these stakeholders and their concerns will facilitate our understanding of the complex relationships between participants involved in solving ethical problems.

Ethical and moral issues in business can be examined on at least five levels. Figure 1.3 illustrates these five levels: individual, organizational, association, societal, and international.[45]

Figure 1.3

Business Ethics Levels

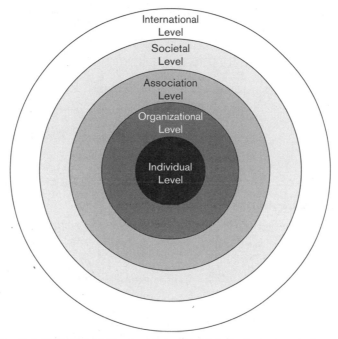

Source: Carroll, A. B. (1978). Linking business ethics to behavior in organizations. *SAM Advanced Management Journal 43(3)*: 7. Reprinted with permission from Society for Advancement of Management, Texas A&M University, College of Business.

■ POINT/COUNTERPOINT

Can Ethics Really Be Taught?

Instructions: Take either one side or the other, Point or CounterPoint, in this exercise. Choose the side you feel the most comfortable with, not how you feel others might think of you or what you wish you could or should do. You'll gain more learning this way. This exercise isn't done to impress; it is designed for you to hear yourself, then others.

POINT: Ethics can't really be taught—it's part intuition, part beliefs, and part choice. Best to think about and study it, but then go with whatever the situation requires you to do and with what you can and are able to.

COUNTERPOINT: If you don't decide by principle(s), then learning ethical ones and practicing with cases, discussion, and reflection will help you. Intuition may not work in a tough or crisis situation. Besides, do you really trust yourself to do "the right thing" under pressure or even in ordinary situations?

Figure 1.4

A Framework for Classifying Ethical Issues and Levels

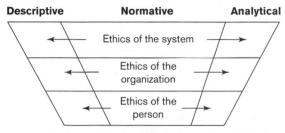

Source: Matthews, J. B., Goodpaster, K. E., and Nash, L. L. (1985). *Policies and persons: A casebook in business ethics.* New York: McGraw-Hill, 509. Reproduced with permission from Kenneth E. Goodpaster.

Asking Key Questions

It is helpful to be aware of the ethical levels of a situation and the possible interaction between these levels when confronting a question that has moral implications. The following questions can be asked when a problematic decision or action is perceived (before it becomes an ethical dilemma):

- What are my core values and beliefs?
- What are the core values and beliefs of my organization?
- Whose values, beliefs, and interests may be at risk in this decision? Why?
- Who will be harmed or helped by my decision or by the decision of my organization?
- How will my own and my organization's core values and beliefs be affected or changed by this decision?
- How will I and my organization be affected by the decision?

Figure 1.4 offers a graphic to help identify the ethics of the system (i.e., a country or region's customs, values, and laws); your organization (i.e., the written formal and informal acceptable norms and ways of doing business); and your own ethics, values, and standards.

In the following section, popular myths about business ethics are presented to challenge misconceptions regarding the nature of ethics and business. You may take the "Quick Test of Your Ethical Beliefs" before reading this section.

Ethical Insight 1.1

Quick Test of Your Ethical Beliefs

Answer each question with your first reaction. Circle the number, from 1 to 4, that best represents your beliefs, where 1 represents "Completely agree," 2 represents "Often agree," 3 represents "Somewhat disagree," and 4 represents "Completely disagree."

1. I consider money to be the most important reason for working at a job or in an organization. 1 2 3 4
2. I would hide truthful information about someone or something at work to save my job. 1 2 3 4
3. Lying is usually necessary to succeed in business. 1 2 3 4
4. Cutthroat competition is part of getting ahead in the business world. 1 2 3 4
5. I would do what is needed to promote my own career in a company, short of committing a serious crime. 1 2 3 4
6. Acting ethically at home and with friends is not the same as acting ethically on the job. 1 2 3 4
7. Rules are for people who don't really want to make it to the top of a company. 1 2 3 4
8. I believe that the "Golden Rule" is that the person who has the gold rules. 1 2 3 4
9. Ethics should be taught at home and in the family, not in professional or higher education. 1 2 3 4
10. I consider myself the type of person who does whatever it takes to get a job done, period. 1 2 3 4

Add up all the points. Your Total Score is: _____

Total your scores by adding up the numbers you circled. The lower your score, the more questionable your ethical principles regarding business activities. The lowest possible score is 10, the highest 40. Be ready to give reasons for your answers in a class discussion.

■ 1.4 Five Myths about Business Ethics

Not everyone agrees that ethics is a relevant subject for business education or dealings. Some have argued that "business ethics" is an oxymoron or a contradiction in terms. Although this book does not advocate a particular ethical position or belief system, it argues that ethics is relevant to business transactions. However, certain myths persist about business ethics. The more popular myths are presented in Figure 1.5.

A myth is "a belief given uncritical acceptance by the members of a group, especially in support of existing or traditional practices and institutions."[46] Myths regarding the relationship between business and ethics do not represent truth but popular and unexamined notions. Which, if any, of the following myths have you accepted as unquestioned truth? Which do you reject? Do you know anyone who holds any of these myths as true?

Myth 1: Ethics Is a Personal, Individual Affair, Not a Public or Debatable Matter

This myth holds that individual ethics is based primarily and often only on personal or religious beliefs and that one decides what is right and wrong in the

Figure 1.5

Five Business Ethics Myths

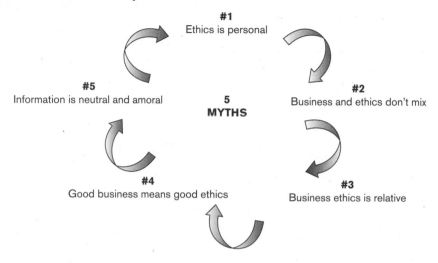

privacy of one's conscience. This myth is supported in part by Milton Friedman, a well-known economist, who views "social responsibility," as an expression of business ethics, to be unsuitable for business professionals to address seriously or professionally because they are not equipped or trained to do so.[47]

Although it is true that individuals must make moral choices in life, including business affairs, it is also true that individuals do not operate in a vacuum. Individual ethical choices are most often influenced by discussions, conversations, and debates and made in group contexts. Individuals often rely on organizations and groups for meaning, direction, and purpose. Moreover, individuals are integral parts of organizational cultures, which have standards to govern what is acceptable. Therefore, to argue that ethics related to business issues is mainly a matter of personal or individual choice is to underestimate the role organizations play in shaping and influencing members' attitudes and behaviors.

Studies indicate that organizations that act in socially irresponsible ways often pay penalties for unethical behavior.[48] In fact, the results of the studies advocate integrating ethics into the strategic management process because it is both the right and the profitable thing to do. Corporate social performance has been found to increase financial performance. One study notes that "analysis of corporate failures and disasters strongly suggests that incorporating ethics in before-profit decision making can improve strategy development and implementation and ultimately maximize corporate profits."[49] Moreover, the popularity of books, training, and articles on learning organizations and the habits of highly effective people among Fortune 500 and 1000 companies suggests that organizational leaders and professionals have a need for purposeful, socially responsible management training and practices.[50]

Myth 2: Business and Ethics Do Not Mix

This myth holds that business practices are basically amoral (not necessarily immoral) because businesses operate in a free market. This myth also asserts that management is based on scientific rather than religious or ethical principles.[51]

Although this myth may have thrived in an earlier industrializing U.S. society and even during the 1960s, it has eroded over the past two decades. The widespread consequences of computer hacking on individual, commercial, and government systems that affect the public's welfare, like identity theft on the Internet (stealing others' Social Security numbers and using their bank accounts and credit cards), and of kickbacks, unsafe products, oil spills, toxic dumping, air and water pollution, and improper use of public funds have contributed to the erosion. The international and national infatuation with a purely scientific understanding of U.S. business practices, in particular, and of a values-free marketing system has been undermined by these events. As one saying goes, "A little experience can inform a lot of theory."

The ethicist Richard DeGeorge has noted that the belief that business is amoral is a myth because it ignores the business involvement of all of us. Business is a human activity, not simply a scientific one, and as such, it can be evaluated from a moral perspective. If everyone in business acted amorally or immorally, as a pseudoscientific notion of business would suggest, businesses would collapse. Employees would openly steal from employers; employers would recklessly fire employees at will; contractors would arrogantly violate obligations; and chaos would prevail. In the United States, business and society often share the same values: rugged individualism in a free-enterprise system, pragmatism over abstraction, freedom, and independence. When business practices violate these American values, society and the public are threatened.

Finally, the belief that businesses operate in totally "free markets" is debatable. Although the value or desirability of the concept of a "free market" is not in question, practices of certain firms in free markets are. At issue are the unjust methods of accumulation and noncompetitive uses of wealth and power in the formation of monopolies and oligopolies (i.e., small numbers of firms dominating the rules and transactions of certain markets). The dominance of AT&T before its breakup is an example of how one powerful conglomerate could control the market. Microsoft and Walmart are other examples. The U.S. market environment can be characterized best as a "mixed economy" that is based on free-market mechanisms but not limited to or explained only by them. Mixed economies rely on some governmental policies and laws for control of deficiencies and inequalities. For example, protective laws are still required, such as those governing minimum wage, antitrust situations, layoffs from plant closings, and instances of labor exploitation. In such mixed economies in which injustices thrive, ethics is a lively topic.

Myth 3: Ethics in Business Is Relative

In this myth, no right or wrong way of believing or acting exists. Right and wrong are in the eyes of the beholder.

The claim that ethics is not based solely on absolutes has some truth to it. However, to argue that all ethics is relative contradicts everyday experience. For example, the view that because a person or society believes something to be right makes it right is problematic when examined. Many societies believed in and practiced slavery; however, in contemporary individuals' experiences, slavery is morally wrong. When individuals and firms do business in societies that promote slavery, does that mean that the individuals and firms must also condone and practice slavery? The simple logic of relativism, which is discussed in Chapter 2, gets complicated when seen in daily experience. The question that can be asked regarding this myth is, Relative to whom or what? And why? The logic of this ethic, which answers that question with "Relative to me, myself, and my interests" as a maxim, does not promote community. Also, if ethical relativism were carried to its logical extreme, no one could disagree with anyone about moral issues because each person's values would be true for that person. Ultimately, this logic would state that no right or wrong exists apart from an individual's or society's principles. How could interactions be completed if ethical relativism were carried to its limit? Moreover, the U.S. government, in its vigorous pursuit of Microsoft, certainly did not practice a relativist style of ethics.

Myth 4: Good Business Means Good Ethics

This myth can translate to "executives and firms that maintain a good corporate image, practice fair and equitable dealings with customers and employees, and earn profits by legitimate, legal means are de facto ethical." Such firms, therefore, would not have to be concerned explicitly with ethics in the workplace. Just do a hard but fair day's work and that has its own moral goodness and rewards.[52]

The faulty reasoning underlying this logic obscures the fact that ethics does not always provide solutions to technical business problems. Moreover, as Rogene Buchholz argued, no correlation exists between "goodness" and material success.[53]

It is also argued that "excellent" companies and corporate cultures have created concern for people in the workplace that exceeds the profit motive. In these cases, excellence seems to be related more to customer service, to maintenance of meaningful public and employee relationships, and to corporate integrity than to profit motive.[54]

The point is that ethics is not something added to business operations; ethics is a necessary part of operations. A more accurate, logical statement from business experience would suggest that "good ethics means good business." This is more in line with observations from successful companies that are ethical first and also profitable.

Finally, the following questions need to be asked: What happens, then, if what should be ethically done is not the best thing for business? What happens when good ethics is not good business? The ethical thing to do may not always be in the best interests of the firm. We should promote business ethics, not because good ethics is good business, but because we are morally required to adopt the moral point of view in all our dealings with other people—and business is no exception. In business, as in all other human endeavors, we must be prepared to pay the costs of ethical behavior. The costs may sometimes seem high, but that is the risk we take in valuing and preserving our integrity.[55]

Myth 5: Information and Computing Are Amoral

This myth holds that information and computing are neither moral nor immoral—they are amoral. They are in a "gray zone," a questionable area regarding ethics. Information and computing have positive dimensions, such as empowerment and enlightenment through the ubiquitous exposure to information, increased efficiency, and quick access to online global communities. It is also true that information and computing have a dark side: information about individuals can be used as "a form of control, power, and manipulation."[56]

The point here is to beware the dark side: the misuse of information—misinformation and disinformation, as well as the "weaponization" of information—especially on social media. Ethical implications are present but veiled. Truth, accuracy, and privacy must be protected and guarded: "Falsehood, inaccuracy, lying, deception, disinformation, misleading information are all vices and enemies of the Information Age, for they undermine it. Fraud, misrepresentation, and falsehood are inimical to all of them."[57]

Logical problems occur in all five of the above myths. In many instances, the myths hold simplistic and even unrealistic notions about ethics in business dealings. In the following sections, the discussion about the nature of business ethics continues by exploring two questions:

- Why use ethical reasoning in business?
- What is the nature of ethical reasoning—and can it be taught?

■ 1.5 Why Use Ethical Reasoning in Business?

Ethical reasoning is required in business for at least three reasons. First, many times laws do not cover all aspects or "gray areas" of a problem.[58] How could tobacco companies have been protected by the law for decades until the settlement in 1997, when the industry agreed to pay $368.5 billion for the first 25 years and then $15 billion a year indefinitely to compensate states for the costs of health care for tobacco-related illnesses? What gray areas in federal and state laws (or the enforcement of those laws) prevailed for decades? What sources of power or help can people turn to in these situations for truthful information, protection, and compensation when laws are not enough?

Second, free-market and regulated-market mechanisms do not effectively inform owners and managers how to respond to complex issues that have far-reaching ethical consequences. Enron's former CEO Jeffrey Skilling believed that his new business model of Enron as an energy trading company was the next big breakthrough in a free-market economy. The idea was innovative and creative; the executive's implementation of the idea was illegal. Perhaps Skilling should have followed Enron's ethics code; it was one of the best available.

A third argument holds that ethical reasoning is necessary because complex moral problems require "an intuitive or learned understanding and concern for fairness, justice, [and] due process to people, groups, and communities."[59] Company policies are limited in scope in covering the human, environmental, and social costs of doing business. Judges have to use intuition and a kind of learn-as-you-go approach in many of their cases. In Microsoft's previous alleged monopoly case, for example, there were no clear precedents in the software industry—or with a company of Microsoft's size and global scope—to offer clear legal direction. Ethics plays a role in business because laws are many times insufficient to guide action.

1.6 Can Business Ethics Be Taught?

Because laws and legal enforcement are not always sufficient to help guide or solve complex human problems relating to business situations, some questions arise: Can ethics help? If so, how? And can business ethics be taught? This ongoing debate has no firm answer, and studies continue to address the issue. One study, for example, that surveyed 125 graduate and undergraduate students in a business ethics course at the beginning of a semester showed that students did not reorder their priorities on the importance of 10 social issues at the end of the semester, but they did change the degree of importance they placed on the majority of the issues surveyed.[60] What, if any, value can be gained from teaching ethical principles and training people to use them in business?

This discussion begins with what business ethics courses cannot or should not, in my judgment, do. Ethics courses should not advocate a set of rules from a single perspective or offer only one best solution to a specific ethical problem. Given the complex circumstances of many situations, more desirable and less desirable courses of action may exist. Decisions depend on facts, inferences, and rigorous ethical reasoning. Neither should ethics courses or training sessions promise superior or absolute ways of thinking and behaving in situations. Informed and conscientious ethical analysis is not the only way to reason through moral problems.

Ethics courses and training can do the following:

- Provide people with rationales, ideas, and a vocabulary to help them participate effectively in ethical decision-making processes.
- Help people "make sense" of their environments by abstracting and selecting ethical priorities.
- Provide intellectual insights to argue with advocates of economic fundamentalism and those who violate ethical standards.
- Enable employees to act as alarm systems for company practices that do not meet society's ethical standards.
- Enhance conscientiousness and sensitivity to moral issues and a commitment to finding moral solutions.
- Enhance moral reflectiveness and strengthen moral courage.

- Increase people's ability to become morally autonomous, ethical dissenters, and the conscience of a group.
- Improve the moral climate of firms by providing ethical concepts and tools for creating ethical codes and social audits.[61]

Other scholars argue that ethical training can add value to the moral environment of a firm and to relationships in the workplace in the following ways:

- Finding a match between an employee's and employer's values
- Managing the pushback point, where an employee's values are tested by peers, employees, and supervisors
- Handling an unethical directive from a boss
- Coping with a performance system that encourages cutting ethical corners[62]

Teaching business ethics and training people to use them does not promise to provide answers to complex moral dilemmas. However, thoughtful and resourceful business ethics educators can facilitate the development of awareness of what is ethical, help individuals and groups realize that their ethical tolerance and decision-making styles decrease unethical blind spots, and enhance the discussion of moral problems openly in the workplace.

■ 1.7 Plan of the Book

This book focuses on applying a stakeholder management approach—based on stakeholder theory—that is integrated with issues management approaches, along with your own critical reasoning to situations that involve groups and individuals who often have competing interpretations of a problem or opportunity. We are all stakeholders in many situations, whether with our friends, network of colleagues, or in organizational and work settings. Because stakeholders are people, they generally act on beliefs, values, and financially motivated strategies. For this reason, ethics- and values-based thinking is an important part of a stakeholder and issues management approach. It is important to understand why stakeholders act and how they make decisions. The stakeholder and issues management approach aims at having all parties reach win-win outcomes through communication and collaborative efforts. Unfortunately, this does not always happen. If we do not have a systematic approach to understanding what happens in complex stakeholder relationships, we cannot learn from past mistakes or plan for more collaborative, socially responsible future outcomes. A schematic of the book's organization is presented in Figure 1.6.

Chapter 2 provides a foundation of ethical principles, quick tests, and scenarios for evaluating motivations for certain decisions and actions. A stakeholder management approach involves knowing and managing stakeholders' ethics, including your own. Chapter 3 provides a systematic approach for structuring and evaluating stakeholder issues, strategies, and options at the outset. Step-by-step methods for collaborating and for forming and evaluating strategies are identified. Chapter 4 then examines an organization's corporate governance and

Figure 1.6

Plan of the Book

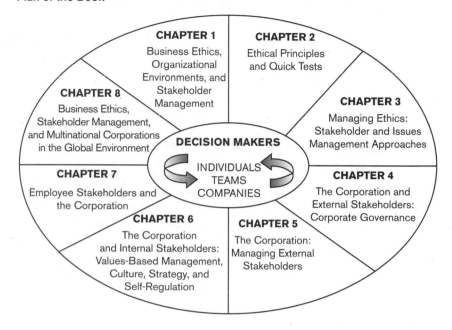

compliance before Chapter 5 looks at how organizations manage external and business issues stakeholders. Chapter 6 looks at internal stakeholders, strategy, culture, and self-regulation in corporations and discusses rights and obligations of employees and employers as stakeholders. Chapter 7 analyzes current trends affecting employees in corporations. Chapter 8, the final chapter, examines globalization and views nations as stakeholders to examine how multinational corporations operate in host countries and different systems of capitalism.

Chapter Summary

Businesses and governments operate in numerous environments, including technological, legal, social, economic, and political dimensions. Presently, the natural environment affected by Covid-19 is overwhelming the other environments. Still, understanding the connections and interactive effects of these environmental forces on industries and organizations—as well as on ourselves, our families, the nation, and other countries—is a first step in identifying stakeholders and the issues that different groups must manage in order to survive and compete. This book explores and illustrates how stakeholders can manage issues and trends in their changing environments in socially responsible, principled ways. Thinking and acting ethically is not a mechanical process; it is also very personal. It is important as a professional in an organization to integrate personal with professional experiences and values.

Business ethics deals with what is "right" and "wrong" in organizational decisions, behavior, and policies. Business ethics provides principles and guidelines that assist people in making informed choices that balance economic interests and social responsibilities. Ethical reasoning also relies on intuition that is reflective and empathetic. Being able to think of other stakeholders' interests can better inform the moral dimension of your own decisions. This is one aim of using a stakeholder management approach.

Seeing the "big picture" of how ethical issues begin and transform requires imagination and some "maps." Because business ethics apply to several levels, this chapter has presented these levels to illustrate the complexity of ethical decision making in business transactions. When you can "connect the dots" among these dimensions, more options for solving problems morally are opened.

The stakeholder management approach also provides a means for mapping complicated relationships between the focal and other stakeholders, a means of identifying the strategies of each stakeholder, and a means for assessing the moral responsibility of all the constituencies.

Five common myths about business ethics have been discussed. Each myth has been illustrated and refuted. You are invited to identify and question your own myths about business ethics. Ethical reasoning in business is explained with steps to guide decision making. Three reasons explain why ethical reasoning is necessary in business: (1) Laws are often insufficient and do not cover all aspects or "gray areas" of a problem; (2) free-market and regulated-market mechanisms do not effectively inform owners and managers on how to respond to complex crises that have far-reaching ethical consequences; and (3) complex moral problems require an understanding and concern for fairness, justice, and due process. Ethical reasoning helps individuals sort through conflicting opinions and information in order to solve moral dilemmas.

Ethical education and training can be useful for developing a broad awareness of the motivations, values, and consequences of our decisions. Business ethics does not, however, provide superior or universally correct solutions to morally complex dilemmas. Principles and guidelines are provided that can enhance—with case analysis, role playing, and group discussion—a person's insight and self-confidence in resolving moral dilemmas that often have two right (or wrong) solutions.

Questions

1. Refer to Figure 1.1 to identify how the Covid-19 virus has affected the other specific environments in which you live, study, and work. Explain how these influences, pressures, and opportunities affect you, and ask yourself how ethically you would like or are striving to be to accomplish your work and goals under pressure.

2. What are the three major ethical issues you face now in your work or student life? What is "ethical" about these issues?

3. Identify some benefits of using a stakeholder approach in ethical decision making. How would using a stakeholder management approach help you plan and/or solve an ethical issue in your working life? Explain.

4. What is a myth? Which, if any, of the five business myths discussed in this chapter do you not accept as a myth (i.e., that you believe is true)? Explain.

5. Identify one myth you had/have about business ethics. Where did it originate? Why is it a "myth"? What led you to abandon this myth, or do you still believe in it? Explain.

6. Identify three reasons presented in this chapter for using ethical reasoning in business situations. Which of these reasons do you find the most valid? The least valid? Explain.

7. Is the law sufficient to help managers and employees solve ethical dilemmas? Explain and offer an example from your own experiences or from a contemporary event.

8. What are some important distinctive characteristics of ethical problems? What distinguishes an ethical from a legal problem?

9. What (if any) specific attitudes, values, beliefs, or behaviors of yours do you think could be changed from an ethics course? Explain.

10. Identify and describe a specific belief or behavior of yours that you feel could be changed through taking a course in ethics.

Exercises

1. Invent and state your own definition of "business ethics." Do you believe that ethics is an important factor in business transactions today? If you were the CEO of a corporation, how would you communicate your perspective on the importance of ethics to your employees, customers, and other stakeholder groups?

2. Conduct your own small survey of two people regarding their opinions on the importance of unethical practices in businesses today. Do your interviewees give more importance to economic performance or socially irresponsible behavior? Or do they think other factors are more important? Summarize your results.

3. You are giving a speech at an important community business association meeting. You are asked to give a presentation called "An Introduction to Business Ethics" for the members. Give an outline of your speech.

4. Explain how a major trend in the environment has affected your profession, job, or skills—as a professional or a student. Be specific. Are any ethical consequences involved, and has this trend affected you?

5. Review Lawrence Kohlberg's levels and stages of moral development. After careful consideration, briefly explain which stage, predominantly or characteristically, defines your ethical level of development. Explain. Has this stage influenced a recent decision you have made or action you have taken? Explain.

6. You are applying to a prestigious organization for an important, highly visible position. The application requires you to describe an ethical dilemma in your history and how you handled it. Describe the dilemma and your ethical position.

Real-Time Ethical Dilemma

You are a staff associate at a major public accounting firm and graduated from college two years ago. You are working on an audit for a small, nonprofit religious publishing firm. After performing tests on the royalty payables system, you discover that for the past five years, the royalty payable system has miscalculated the royalties it owes to authors of their publications. The firm owes almost $100,000 in past-due royalties. All of the contracts with each author are negotiated differently. However, each author's royalty percentage will increase at different milestones in books sold (i.e., 2 percent up to 10,000, and 3 percent thereafter). The software package did not calculate the increases, and none of the authors ever received their increase in royalty payments. At first you can't believe that none of the authors ever realized they were owed their money. You double-check your calculations and then present your findings to the senior auditor on the job. Much to your surprise, his suggestion is to pass over this finding. He suggests that you sample a few additional royalty contracts and document that you expanded your testing and found nothing wrong. The firm's audit approach is well documented in this area and is firmly based on statistical sampling. Because you had found multiple errors in the small number of royalty contracts tested, the firm's approach suggested testing 100 percent of the contracts. This would mean (1) going over the budgeted time/expense estimated to the client; (2) possibly providing a negative audit finding; and (3) confirming that the person who audited the section in the years past may not have performed procedures correctly.

Based on the prior year's work papers, the senior auditor on the job performed the testing phase in all of these years just before his promotion. For some reason, you get the impression that the senior auditor is frustrated with you. The relationship seems strained. He is very intense, constantly checking the staff's progress in the hope of coming in even a half hour under budget for a designated test/audit area. There is a lot of pressure, and you don't know what to do. This person is responsible for writing your review for your personnel file and bonus or promotion review. He is a very popular employee who is "on the fast track" to partnership.

You don't know whether to tell the truth and risk a poor performance review that would jeopardize your future with this company, or to tell the truth, hopefully be exonerated, and be able to live with yourself by "doing the right thing" and facing consequences with a clean conscience.

Questions

1. What would you do as the staff associate in this situation? Why? What are the risks of telling the truth for you? What are the benefits? Explain.
2. What is the "right" thing to do in this situation? What is the "smart" thing to do for your job and career? What is the difference, if there is one, between the "right" and "smart" thing to do in this situation? Explain.
3. Explain what you would say to the senior auditor, your boss, in this situation if you decided to tell the truth as you know it.

Cases

Case 1

Education Pushed to the Brink: How Covid-19 Is Redefining Recruitment and Admissions Decisions

Covid-19 has had a devastating effect on the higher education system. It has had sweeping effects on every aspect of a university, especially on the ability to recruit and admit new students for the fall 2020 term. The purpose of this case is to understand the facts of how the pandemic was and is impacting recruitment within the United State and internationally. The research was conducted through peer-reviewed articles, industry conference sessions, internal reporting, and publicly available government data. The biggest finding was how those universities that were already participating in virtual recruiting pre-pandemic were able to pivot more easily to fully online recruiting compared with those that were not engaged online. The support of key internal stakeholders was also necessary to move to fully online recruiting. Another interesting finding was from the review of an internal survey of 71 new international students. Among these new graduate students, who were expected to start in fall 2020, we found that 74 percent of the international students are still looking for their experience of an American education to be in-person. After reviewing all of the material, it was determined that with the changes in recruitment and admissions brought on by Covid-19, the greatest impact will be felt by the international student applicants.

Facts

Covid-19 by the Numbers

Covid-19 was first discovered in Wuhan, China, by Dr. Li Wenliang in December 2019 (Hauck et al., 2020). Since the novel coronavirus was first discovered, it has raced around the globe infecting millions. As of July 10, 2020, there have been 12,294,117 confirmed cases of the disease, with 555,531 global deaths. The United States has been the worst-hit country with 133,291 deaths, more than double the Covid-19-related deaths of any other country (Johns Hopkins University School of Medicine, 2020). The impact of this disease has added difficulties to all facets of life in the United States. The U.S. economy is currently in a Covid-induced recession that shows little signs of changing anytime soon (Horsley, 2020). The U.S. jobless rate has still not recovered fully since the March unemployment rate skyrocketed to over 14 percent. According to the government's June 2020 report, we are still at a very high unemployment rate of 11.1 percent (U.S. Bureau of Labor Statistics, 2020). All of these facts have driven many local governments, companies, and universities to make difficult decisions, forced by a lack of federal leadership.

Pre-Covid-19 Strategies, Tools, and Resources for Recruiting in Higher Education

There were already challenges facing recruiting and admissions in higher education institutes before the Covid-19 pandemic. According to a 2019 report by

GMAC.org on student mobility, the United States was seeing a decline in international applications because of increased competition from Asia, Europe, and Canada and because of a strong economy and low unemployment rate. Institutions were having to invest large amounts of capital on in-person events both on campus and off campus (Graduate Management Admissions Council, 2019).

On-campus events presented by institutions like the one in which I work were holding events that allowed prospective students to interact with highly skilled professors, current graduate students, and staff in advanced facilities of research and study. These events gave participants the opportunity to get hands-on with the technology in the labs. It gave them the opportunity to picture themselves learning in such an exciting location. Interaction with the support staff was also an important aspect to these on-campus visits, with the staff demonstrating the care and attention that students would receive and how they were truly invested in their success.

Off-campus events allow universities to meet in-person with students who might not be able to travel to the school campus and still give the students an opportunity to put a face and name to the university.

Boston universities like Brandeis, Suffolk, Babson, and Bentley were scheduling events all over the world to interact with potential candidates in face-to-face presentations and information sessions. To share the benefits and resources of their institutions, alumni and admissions directors were engaged. The higher education institutions worked with companies or organizations like EducationUSA, AccessMBA/Masters, The MBA Tour, and QS to set up fairs, college visits, and events in locations around the world, once again, to ensure that face-to-face interaction would occur.

Post-Covid-19 Strategies, Tools, and Resources for Recruiting in Higher Education

In March 2020, universities and colleges around the United States began transitioning to fully online classes (Svrluga and Anderson, 2020). By April 2020, almost every university in the country had transitioned to online learning, shutting down campuses to students, staff, and faculty to protect against the spread of Covid-19. All travel was canceled, as were all in-person recruiting events around the world, forcing universities and their partners to pivot to virtual events and fairs.

Suddenly those in-person connections that admissions departments had depended on to build that relationship was gone. They could no longer meet with alumni for dinner or coffee. Being able to introduce themselves in-person to prospective students at fairs and conferences was also no longer an option. The tools and resources that schools had become accustomed to using no longer could be utilized.

According to the 2020 GMAC annual conference held from June 18 to June 19, 2020, most universities are looking to decrease budgets and shift them to domestic and digital marketing, leaving most budgets in question. Before Covid-19, most schools were predicting that they would maintain their budgets and would be enrolling 50 percent international students in the 2020 class. Most schools are now anticipating a sharp decline in international students for the fall 2020 term, for fear of contracting Covid-19 (Graduate Management Admissions Council, 2020). In addition to the health scare, in July 2020, the U.S. Department of Homeland Security (under the Donald Trump administration) announced that students would be required to attend at least one class on campus or face being deported, which not only sent many current students into a panic (Lee, 2020), but also those students who were expecting to start school in fall 2020. Many students who were accepted are seeing the continued growth in Covid-19 cases and the potential of the school shutting down again and then having to leave the country as worrisome.

Research is showing they are more likely to decide that taking a gap year or deferring until it is safe to start is a better option (Graduate Management Admissions Council, 2020).

How Recruiting and Admissions Were Forced to Adapt

Attending a university is more than just attending class. So much of it is about the experience of the campus and the personal relationships that are developed. According to a recent survey of 71 international students who were accepted to the fall 2020 term for the graduate school of business at my university (see Figure 1), 32 percent prefer on-campus attendance only, 42 percent prefer on-campus

Figure 1

Preferred Attendance for Fall 2020 (New Students)

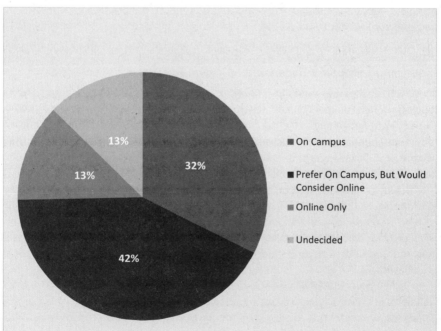

but would consider starting online for the first semester, 13 percent want online only, and 13 percent are undecided. The data shows that 74 percent of students would prefer to be on campus and have that face-to-face experience.

Similar data emerges when students are surveyed about how they want to be contacted to learn about schools. All universities have to create compelling and engaging online information sessions using platforms like Zoom, Facebook, Skype, WeChat, Instagram, TikTok, LinkedIn, and FaceTime. By using the only tool that was left, the name of the game became impact and creativity. More and more schools were looking to create new content marketing that offered more than just information. They are using student-to-prospective student online meetings and engaging with different affinity groups to help drive more engagement to online events (Newton, 2020). Schools like my university are also engaging with corporate partners to offer virtual information sessions that students can use, like "How to Talk with Your Employer about Attending Graduate School" (Bentley University, 2020).

For a lot of U.S.-based schools, strategies have transitioned to focusing on domestic and international students who are already in the United States (Graduate Management Admissions Council, 2020). With so many international students unable to travel or obtain visas to travel, it makes it virtually impossible for those students who are interested to come to the United States to study, forcing universities to look domestically to fill seats left empty by international students. These transitions were coming from internal pressures from university leadership that was already dealing with budget deficits. "At a time when higher education enrollment is already projected to decrease by 15 percent this year as a result of Covid-19, universities are already facing an estimated $23 billion decline in revenues" (Bipartisan Policy Center, 2020). The idea of a further decline in enrollment is leading many universities to make risk-versus-reward decisions.

What Universities Are Doing: Risks versus Rewards

As universities make preparations to welcome students for the fall 2020 term, *the risk versus reward* is how many of them are weighing their options. In looking at plans laid out by several universities like Harvard, MIT, Boston College, Bentley University, Worcester Polytechnic Institute, and the University of Massachusetts-Amherst, there are two decisions that are being instituted: staying 100 percent online and offering a hybrid format.

The risk to be considered for the hybrid format is opening up too much and risking the health and safety of their students and staff. They are also worried about not being able to attract new students, since some want the safety of online courses; others want the robust experience of on-campus, in-person classes; while others want the option to do both.

There are also risks with going 100 percent online. In a recent article, a New York University professor discussed "whether students and parents will be inclined to continue paying top dollar for virtual campus life" (LaRoche, 2020). This is especially true for new students who want the experience of a college, as much as the education. The newest risk to schools that have chosen to go fully online

AO to Stakeholder Flow of Communication

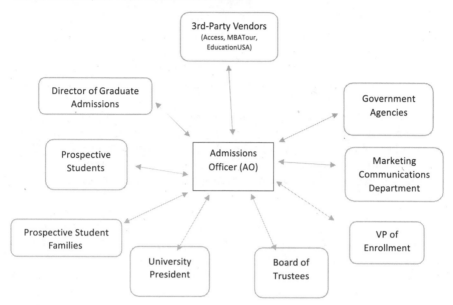

is the new F1 and M1 visa rules that were announced on July 6, 2020. Months after schools like Harvard and MIT announced they would be going fully online, the federal government came out with a statement regarding international students. The new law states that any student on a student visa who is attending classes 100 percent online must leave the country (Lee, 2020). New students will not be able to enter the country as well. All of this leaves universities to balance these risks with the reward of attracting new students and retaining current students.

Stakeholders

Admissions Officer (AO)

At the center of redefining the recruiting and admissions processes for universities during Covid-19 is the admissions officer. AOs are tasked with recruiting and admitting qualified candidates with the best opportunities for success at their schools and within their programs. They must use the tools and services that are given to them to achieve these goals. The success of their task during a worldwide pandemic lies within the strength of the relationship they have formed with the different stakeholders (Figure 2).

Other Stakeholders

Director of Graduate Admissions: AOs report directly to the director of graduate admissions. The AO's economic responsibility is to use financial resources in a way that helps improve outcomes for recruitment and enrollment. Legally, AOs want to make sure that they are using these funds in a way that is not illegal, like buying gifts for prospective students. Ethically they need to make sure that they are using the funds allocated to them in a way that is in line with university standards.

This is why it is important to understand that the director of graduate admissions position has political power to influence decisions about applicants and the application process. The director also has cultural power as well as power over individuals and groups within the admissions and recruitment department. The ethical standards of this position would be based on utilitarianism to fairly weigh the costs and benefits of the department and allocate resources to improve enrollment. It will be important for the AO to instill a supportive strategy, as the potential for cooperation is high. Coalitions: VP of enrollment, university president, board of trustees.

Vice President of Enrollment: The AO has an economic responsibility to recruit and admit enough qualified students to grow the graduate school. The AO needs to recruit and admit students in accordance with federal laws like Title IX, to protect the VP of enrollment and the institution from potential legal or moral issues related to unfair admissions practices. Ethically, AOs need to regularly communicate with the VP regarding what they are doing to ensure a fair and unbiased admissions process. This VP position holds political power in the enrollment decisions of the institution. VPs also hold economic power over budget distribution within the division. As leaders of the enrollment division, they also have power over culture, individuals, and groups. As the head of a large division, their ethical decisions are based on the rights of students enrolling as well as using justice to distribute the tools and burdens to each department within the division. The tactic for the AO will be to involve them as much as possible. They have a shared interest in the goals to recruit and admit strong students. Coalitions: director of graduate admissions, university president, board of trustees, marketing communications department.

Prospective Students: The AO has an economic responsibility to provide accurate information about tuition and associated costs to prospective students about attending the graduate school. This will allow those prospective students who need visas to accurately provide the U.S. government with the correct information, protecting them from illegally filing incorrect documents. Each AO involved with prospective students has an ethical responsibility to submit accurate and truthful costs. The AO should also be volunteering this information in every interaction with prospective students. The type of power prospective students have is voting power. They can influence a university's decision on program offerings, extracurricular activities, and student amenities by their decision to apply or not apply. The type of moral obligation to ethical principles for prospective students is going to be utilitarianism as they weigh the benefits, safety, and price of the institution that they decide to apply to. The best strategy to address prospective students during Covid-19 is to treat them as a mixed blessing. Keep them close and collaborate with them as much as possible to help them in deciding to apply. Coalitions: families of prospective students.

Families of Prospective Students: An AO's economic responsibility to the families is helping them to understand the costs associated with attending school. Legally, the AO does not want to put any false or misleading statements out to the families that could put them in financial jeopardy. The AO has a responsibility to the student and the family to help them make an ethical and informed decision to attend school during the pandemic. By volunteering financial resource information to the families, the AO will be helping families in the long term, even if they decide to wait to enroll. This is important because the largest power that families have is power over the individual student. They can persuade the student on decisions or choices to attend. They also have the power of voting if multiple stakeholder families join together to influence the school. Families can also use economic power if they are paying for school, and that can influence the student or impact the university. Families most likely will imply the ethical behavior of utilitarianism when supporting the decision of a student to attend a school or not. They are going to weigh the cost and benefits of their decision to support the student to enroll in the school. From an admissions and recruiting perspective, you will need to keep these stakeholders collaborating with you to help students and their families on decisions. They are going to be a mixed blessing, for sure. Coalitions: prospective students.

University President: AOs have the same economic responsibility to the university president as they do to the VP of enrollment—namely, to take responsible actions to recruit a full and qualified class of graduate students. Legally, the AO wants to follow all university rules and procedures laid out by the president of the university, again communicating any possible ethical violations through proper channels that might include the president. Voluntarily, each AO should be keeping the president updated on any new laws and regulations regarding university admissions. As the one person hired to run the institution, the university president has the political power to influence and make decisions that affect the institution. Presidents have economic power, as they can influence control over financial resources. They also have legal power with the ability to influence policy and procedure within the university landscape. The strategy to take with presidents of a university is to involve them as much as possible. They will be supportive participants in helping to achieve the goals of enrollment and recruitment. Coalitions: VP of enrollment, board of trustees.

Board of Trustees: The AO has an economic responsibility to all university stakeholders and a fiduciary responsibility to make sure the institution is financially sustainable. Legally, AOs will want to protect the university president and the board of trustees from any issues that might arise that would put the institution at risk. Ethically, the AO wants to represent the university in a way that will not put the school's reputation at risk. The power of the board is in its political power to influence the institutional decision-making processes. Board members can also make major economic decisions that can impact the entire university. They also have the legal power to effect major policy and procedures. Finally, they have voting powers. As a group they can use this power to vote in or out the president or other university-wide policy. The Board of Trustees' moral obligation is to the institution and the students it serves. Board members will use the ethical principal of justice as a way of enacting decisions that are fair and just for everyone at the university. The best strategy to take with the Board of Trustees is to collaborate with them, as they are concerned about the overall well-being of the university, and their actions can move from threat to cooperation depending on the situation. When it comes to recruiting and admissions practices, support is the action the board will most likely take. Coalitions: university president, VP of enrollment, director of graduate admissions.

Government Agencies: In dealing with any government agency, the AO has an economic responsibility to adhere to all laws and regulations. Legally, the AO would not want to put the university at risk of losing accreditation or federal funding. Ethically, the AO would want to keep any government agency informed of any wrongdoings within the institution. AOs can keep updated on any new rules and regulations and volunteer that information to their department or university. Government agencies have a legal power to influence agendas of the university through legislation. They can also use their political power to influence university decisions through accreditation. Rights is how these agencies would use ethics, as they need to follow constitutions and local and federal laws. The type of strategy to best deal with government agencies is to collaborate. They are going to be a mixed blessing to deal with, as they have a high potential for threat and cooperation. Coalitions: other government agencies.

Marketing Communications Department (Marcomm): Admissions officers have an economic responsibility to use marketing funds in a manner that will gain exposure to potential students who are interested in attending the university. Legally, they need to produce accurate and truthful advertising that will not break any false-advertising laws. They also have an ethical responsibility to help promote the safety standards that the university is taking to protect new students from the pandemic. The AO should share any marketing material regarding the safety standards about Covid-19 with all stakeholders. The Marcomm department has the technical power to use new modes of advertising to help influence potential students' decision to attend. Those in marketing communications also have cultural power, as they have the ability to choose which types of social media is used to influence prospective students. Marcomm has to use limited resources in a way that will have maximum impact on making a positive impression. In this way they are using utilitarianism to make the most people "happy" about the university. Marcomm needs to be involved in the process of redeveloping the recruitment plan, as they are going to be very supportive of the efforts. Coalitions: university president, VP of enrollment, director of graduate enrollment.

Third-Party Vendors: An AO has an economic responsibility to third-party vendors to make sure that the university is fulfilling its contractual obligations to pay for and attend their marketed events. Legally, the AO is protecting the university from potential lawsuits for breaking a contract. Ethically, the AO wants to make sure that all communication between the third parties and the school is clear, with no misunderstandings. The AO should be following up periodically with both sides to ensure good communication. These third-party vendors carry influential power of individuals and groups. They can use this power to promote one university over another, depending on contacts. This could greatly assist in recruiting new students. The ethical principles of third-party vendors would be universalism. They treat every institution the same regardless of size, region, or affiliation. As long as there is a contract, they will be very supportive, and involving them in the recruiting process will be helpful. Coalitions: third-party vendors, prospective students.

Issues

In the ongoing pandemic, a review of environmental issues with the resulting impact on the recruitment and admissions process is summarized. There is the very real possibility of the continued spread of Covid-19 for the next year. How will recruitment and admissions handle the continued disruptions of mandated stay-at-home orders, social distancing, and the strain on technological resources? What was the response of the admissions team to third-party vendors who were successful or not successful in being able to pivot from in-person events to online events? Will university leadership mismanage or be unprepared for the long-term effects of a lingering virus? What is the impact of budget cuts on recruiting programs due to fund reallocations?

Being able to quickly pivot to a new method is how an admissions and recruiting team should be able to adapt. Those teams at universities that had already used virtual recruitment techniques as a tool were able to more easily adapt to fully virtual recruitment and admissions.

Having experience with multiple third-party vendors pre-pandemic gave an advantage in terms of knowing which ones were better equipped to go virtual versus those that struggled with online events. Vendors need the right tools to attract quality students and produce successful online events. It was important to evaluate whether a third-party vendor can offer a high-value experience for virtual events that equals the same quality as the pre-pandemic, in-person events, especially if they were charging the same price.

Leadership management during an unforeseen crisis is critical to the success of the entire university. Mismanagement at the top during a pandemic that leads to the removal of the president has an impact on recruiting and enrollment. Potential students looking at applying will have a perception of how stable the university's system is.

Budget cuts to the admissions and recruitment department due to reallocation of funds to support the university will impact the ability to recruit students. Fewer dollars to spend on third-party partners and recruitment tools will leave the admissions officer looking for alternative resources and cheaper partnerships to supplement the loss. An impact on quality and quantity will be felt on recruitment.

How would we rank these issues from most important to least important? The most important issue is how recruitment and admissions will handle the continued disruptions of mandated stay-at-home orders, social distancing, and the strain on technological resources. It is followed by whether university leadership is mismanaged and unprepared for the long-term effects of a lingering virus. Next comes addressing the budget cuts to recruiting programs because of fund real-locations, and finally, the response of the admissions team to third-party vendors who were successful or not successful in being able to pivot from in-person events to online events.

A strategy for resolving the number-one issue of being able to deal with the pandemic and its continued disruption will be to leverage relationships with those stakeholders that have been identified as strong supporters and that can be in-volved in the process. The best strategy for dealing with the mismanagement of senior leadership is to involve lower-level management, like the VP of enrollment and the director of graduate admissions, to help insulate the recruitment process from poor leadership decisions. This strategy can also be used in addressing bud-get cuts. Involving the VP and the director in the recruitment and admissions plan-ning process can help reduce further cuts. Because they have economic power to make budget decisions, they can help to reallocate funds to the AO's recruiting projects.

In dealing with multiple third-party vendors, there should be two strategies. First, there should be monitoring of the vendors' ability to pivot successfully to online events. Once you determine who has the best offering with demonstrable success, then you will move them to a supportive role and involve them in the new recruiting process.

The implementation response should be handled in the order of impor-tance, and the stakeholder analysis should be used where appropriate to maintain the proper strategy and ethical standards. Addressing these con-cerns in order will assist the AO in reducing and resolving each issue in a timely manner.

Monitoring each issue through the established strategy will help you to un-derstand if any change is needed. If, for example, a supportive stakeholder changes to a nonsupportive stakeholder, the AO will want to be able to transition quickly to a defend strategy.

Ethics Involved

After reviewing the stakeholders and issues, the admissions officer has a moral obligation to maintain strong relationships with stakeholders. This means that to be able to transition into a new recruiting strategy, there must be open and fac-tual communication. The AO has to assume that the information that is coming from the VP, director of graduate admissions, and the university president has the institution's safety and best interest in mind. Additionally, the AO is going to want to research as many laws and regulations as possible regarding safe prac-tices. Then the task is applying the information from management and their own research to the new recruitment process. Furthermore, admissions officers would want to make sure that the plans they put into place are applied to all recruitment strategies with any other stakeholders and that they fit in all situations. If a situation was discovered that did not fit within the planned strategy, then it would need to be addressed before it was launched.

Implementing these new strategies to address the ongoing pandemic will be something that admissions officers are going to have to decide. Will the actions that are being put forth keep people safe and free of harm during the pandemic? How will these new strategies keep the stakeholders safe? They will need to review any current facts about the pandemic and make sure that the strategy meets those needs, as well as continue to gather updated information from the university and confirm them against health officials' recommendations. Once this information is gathered, it will need to be determined if these new strategies assure their own safety as well. Once the decision is made to move forward, the AO will need to be consistent in messaging to all stakeholders.

Personal Reflection

Living with these decisions and working to implement them has been both my private and professional life since February 2020. Remaining nimble enough and flexible enough to quickly pivot to any change has been a challenge. Equally challenging was fully understanding the safety concerns of all involved and making decisions that will best serve them and the institution.

The hardest decision that I have had to make since the start of the pandemic is telling students who were expecting to start school with us in the fall that they have to wait to start their career at the university because of government restrictions and safety concerns. This by far has been the biggest challenge, along with the uncertainty of what the fall will be like. Looking at how this pandemic has impacted the different communities at my own institution, I see that those who are most negatively impacted are our international student population. Those international students who are currently on campus have had to already upend their lives just to study in the United States. Unlike our domestic students, these students had the increased stress of dealing with government visa restrictions, forcing them to confront the realization that they may have to make a choice between trying to stay and complete their education or going home.

A lot of prospective graduate students are trying to plan on what to do come September when classes start. Until July 1, 2020, there were no answers, and like a lot of schools, we were waiting for information on what the virus was going to do. I found myself shifting my views, initially taking a pragmatic approach, thinking about the Covid-19 situation and how my decisions would affect what is happening at the institution and then the community at large. Later, I found that I had moved to a more altruistic view by being more concerned with delivering the type of service I felt our prospective students needed. Regardless of my personal safety concerns, I was willing to stay at the university to speak with students and ease their concerns for the benefit of the newly accepted students. I suspect that when we are able to reflect back on this global pandemic when it is over, we will find that the students who were supposed to start school in 2020 were the hardest-hit population, and that there will be a lasting effect on their education far beyond the end of the pandemic.

Questions for Discussion

1. What issues is this author describing as a university recruitment and admissions officer that are different and unusual compared to "normal times"?
2. How did/does Covid-19 affect each of the stakeholders in this case?
3. How are/were you affected as a stakeholder in your university/college/institution during Covid-19?
4. Describe the ethical challenges and for whom (using your own words) in this case.
5. What did you learn in this case that you didn't know regarding higher educational institutions during Covid-19?

Sources

This case was written from the firsthand experience of the case author at Bentley University Graduate School, with some additional material from the following sources:

Bentley University. (2020, May 2). How to talk to employer about grad school. https://www.bentley.edu/graduate/events/previously-recorded.

Bipartisan Policy Center. (2020, July 20). Barring international students could cost universities billions. *Targeted News service*.

Graduate Management Admissions Council. (2019). *Application trends survey report 2019*. Market Intelligence. Reston: GMAC.org. https://www.gmac.com/-/media/files/gmac/research/admissions-and-application-trends/application-trends-survey-report-2019.pdf.

Graduate Management Admissions Council. (2020). Re-imagining marketing and ads expenditure during Covid-19. *GMAC Annual Conference 2020*.

Hauck, G., Gelles, K., Bravo, V., and Thorson, M. (2020, June 23). Five months in: A timeline of how Covid-19 has unfolded in the US. *USA Today News*. https://www.usatoday.com/in-depth/news/nation/2020/04/21/coronavirus-updates-how-covid-19-unfolded-u-s-timeline/2990956001/.

Horsley, S. (2020, June 8). It's official: U.S. economy is in a recession. *NPR.org*. https://www.npr.org/sections/coronavirus-live-updates/2020/06/08/872336272/its-official-scorekeepers-say-u-s-economy-is-in-a-recession

Johns Hopkins University School of Medicine. (2020, July 10). Covid-19 Dashboard by the Center for Systems Science and Engineering (CSSE) at Johns Hopkins University (JHU). Coronavirus Resource Center. https://coronavirus.jhu.edu/map.html

LaRoche, J. (2020, April 20). NYU professor rips colleges for being "drunk on exclusivity," says coronavirus will force change. *Yahoo! Finance*.https://finance.yahoo.com/news/nyu-marketing-pro-expects-tremendous-price-pressure-on-us-colleges-after-coronavirus-201541903.html.

Lee, J. J. (2020, July 8). *International students shouldn't be political pawns. Inside Higher Ed*. https://www.insidehighered.com/views/2020/07/08/government-regulation-about-international-students-strong-arming-colleges-resume.

Newton, D. (2020, June 26). *5 things that Covid-19 will make the new normal in higher ed. Forbes.com*. https://www.forbes.com/sites/dereknewton/2020/06/26/5-things-that-covid-19-will-make-the-new-normal-in-higher-ed/#4015d1236071.

Svrluga, S., and Anderson, N. (2020, March 9). *Amherst College switches to online learning, as universities nationally scramble to respond to Covid-19 outbreak. Washington Post.* https://www.washingtonpost.com/education/2020/03/09 /princeton-requires-lectures-seminars-go-online-only-temporary-move-amid -covid-19-outbreak/.

U.S. Bureau of Labor Statistics. (2020). The employment situation—February 2021 (News Release) https://www.bls.gov/news.release/pdf/empsit.pdf.

Case 2

Classic Ponzi Scheme: Bernard L. Madoff Investment Securities LLC: Wall Street Trading Firm

Bernard L. Madoff, now a commonplace name and memory on Wall Street, to investors, and to business school students studying finance and ethics, was denied a compassionate release from prison. Madoff died in June 2021. This is a retelling of one of the largest, if not the largest, reported Ponzi schemes in recent history. Note: A "Ponzi scheme" is defined as "a form of fraud in which belief in the success of a nonexistent enterprise is fostered by the payment of quick returns to the first investors from money invested by later investors" (Chen, 2021, April 14).

Bernard L. Madoff Investment Securities LLC was founded in the 1960s as a small investment firm on Wall Street. At age 22 and with $5,000 in savings from summer jobs, Madoff launched the firm that in the 1980s would rank with some of the most prestigious and powerful firms on Wall Street. Madoff began as a single stock trader before starting a family-operated business that included his brother, nephew, niece, and his two sons. Each held a position that was quite valuable within the company.

Madoff had also created "an investment-advisory business that managed money for high-net-worth individuals, hedge funds and other institutions." He made profitable and consistent returns by repaying early investors from the money received from new investors. Instead of running an actual hedge fund, Madoff held this investment operation inside his firm on the 17th floor of the building, in a secure area that only two dozen staff members were permitted to enter. Because of the prestige and power that Madoff possessed, no employee dared question the security and confidentiality of the "hedge fund" floor. The $65 billion investment fund was later discovered to be fraudulent, shattering the lives of thousands of individuals, institutions, organizations, and stakeholders worldwide.

The Man with All the Power

Bernard Madoff's charisma and amiable personality were important traits that helped him gain power in the financial community and become one of the largest players on Wall Street. He became a notable authoritative figure by securing important roles on boards and commissions, helping him bypass securities regulations. One of the roles included serving as the chairman of the board of directors of the NASDAQ stock exchange during the early 1990s. Madoff was knowledgeable and smart enough to understand that the more involved he became with regulators, the more "you could shape regulations." He used his reputation as a respected trader and perceived "honest" businessman to take advantage of investors and manipulate them fraudulently. Investors were hoodwinked into believing that it was a privilege to take part in Madoff's elite investments, since Madoff never accepted many clients and used exclusively selective recruiting in order to keep this part of his business a secret.

Madoff was even able to keep his employees quiet, telling them not to speak to the media regarding any of the business activities. While several understood something was not right, they ignored their suspicions because of Madoff's perceived clean record and aura: "He appeared to believe in family, loyalty, and honesty. . . . Never in your wildest imagination would you think he was a fraud-ster" (Creswell and Thomas, 2009, as cited in Perri, 2013, 11).

Madoff has been described as a person who is "typically [like] people with psychopathic personalities [who] don't fear getting caught. . . . They tend to be very narcissistic with a strong sense of entitlement" (Treanor, 2011). This led many analysts of criminal behavior to observe similar traits between Madoff and serial killers like Ted Bundy. Analysts discovered several factors motivating Madoff toward a Ponzi scheme: "A desire to accumulate vast wealth, a need to dominate others, and a need to prove that he was smarter than everyone else" (Creswell and Thomas, 2020). Whatever the motivating factors were, Madoff's behavior was still criminal and affected a large pool of stakeholders.

Early Suspicions Arise

Despite the unrealistic returns and questionable nature of Madoff's business op-erations, investors continued to invest money. In 2000, a whistle-blower from a competing firm—Harry Markopolos, CFE, CFA—discovered Madoff's Ponzi scheme. Markopolos and his small team developed and presented an eight-page document that provided evidence and red flags of the fraud to the Boston re-gional office of the Securities and Exchange Commission (SEC) in May 2000. Markopolos used what he referred to as the "Mosaic Method" to find Madoff's irregularities. The first red flag was when Madoff claimed he was making money when the Standard & Poor's Index was in decline, which is mathematically im-possible. To make matters even worse, Madoff Securities was earning "undis-closed commission" instead of using the standard hedge fund fee (1 percent of the total plus 20 percent of the profits). Markopolos also found out that Madoff "was applying for huge loans from European banks (seemingly unnecessary if Madoff's returns were as high as he said)" (Hayes and Khartit, 2020).

Despite the SEC's lack of response, Markopolos resubmitted the documents again in 2001, 2005, 2007, and 2008. His findings were not taken seriously: "My team and I tried our best to get the Securities and Exchange Commission to in-vestigate and shut down the Madoff Ponzi scheme with repeated and credible warnings." Because Madoff was well respected and powerful on Wall Street, few suspected his fraudulent actions. The status and wealth that Madoff had created gave him the means to manipulate the SEC and regulators alike.

Negligence on All Sides

The negligence and gaps in governmental regulation make it very difficult to point to only one guilty party in the Madoff scandal. The SEC played a crucial role by allowing Madoff's operations to carry on for as long as they did. For over 10 years, the SEC received numerous warnings that Madoff's steady returns were anything but ordinary and nearly impossible. The SEC and the Financial Industry Regulatory Authority, "a nongovernment agency that oversees all securities firms," were known to have investigated Madoff's firm over eight times but brought no charges of criminal activity. Despite the red flags and mathematical proof that Markopolos presented, SEC staff allowed Madoff's operations to continue unchallenged. Spencer Bachus, a politician and a Republican member of the U.S. House of Representatives, stated that "what we may have in the Madoff case is not necessarily a lack of enforcement and oversight tools, but a failure to use them." Unfortunately, there could be another side to the story. David Kotz, currently the SEC's inspector general, planned an ongoing internal investigation to understand the reasoning behind the negligence and to determine if any conflict of interest between SEC staff and the Madoff family could have been part of the problem. Arthur Levitt Jr., who was part of the SEC and a chairman from 1993 to 2001, had close connections with Madoff himself. He would rely on Madoff's advice about the functioning of the market, although Levitt denies all accusations. In September 2009, it was officially stated that no evidence was found relating to any conflict of interest: "The OIG [Office of Inspector General] investigation did not find evidence that any SEC personnel who worked on an SEC examination or investigation of Bernard L. Madoff Investment Securities LLC had any financial or other inappropriate connection with Bernard Madoff or the Madoff family that influenced the conduct of their examination or investigatory work."

Unfortunately, the SEC is not the only party to blame. JPMorgan Chase has also been criticized for its actions regarding the Madoff scandal. Instead of investing clients' money in securities, as Madoff had promised to do, he deposited the funds in a Chase bank account. In 2008, federal court documents show that "the account had mushroomed to $5.5 billion. . . . This translates to $483 million in after-tax profits for the bank holding the Madoff funds." As one of Chase's largest customers, Madoff's account should have been monitored closely. Internal bank compliance systems should have detected such red flags. Unfortunately, Madoff was savvy enough to move millions of dollars between his U.S. and London operations, making it seem like he was actively investing clients' money. The massive account balances of investors should not have been difficult to overlook. Don Jackson, director of SecureWorks Counter Threat Unit Intelligence Services, noted that "the only way to stop this kind of fraud is for the bank to know its clients better and to report things that might be suspicious. It really comes down to human control." This was an area of weakness for JPMorgan Chase at the time.

Where Were the Auditors?

For Madoff to successfully perpetrate such a large scam spanning more than a decade, he needed the help of auditors to certify the financial statements of Bernard L. Madoff Investment Securities. The company's auditing services were provided by a three-person accounting firm, Friehling & Horowitz, formerly run by David Friehling. For over 15 years, Friehling confirmed to the American Institute of Certified Public Accountants (AICPA) that his firm did not conduct any type of audit work. Because of this confirmation, Friehling did not have to "enroll in the AICPA's peer review program, in which experienced auditors assess each firm's audit quality every year...to maintain their licenses to practice." Friehling & Horowitz had in fact been auditing the books of Madoff for over 17 years, providing a clean bill of health each year from 1991 through 2008. Authorities state that if Friehling provided integrity in his findings, the scandal would not have continued for as long as it did: "Mr. Friehling's deception helped foster the illusion that Mr. Madoff legitimately invested his clients' money," stated U.S. Attorney Lev Dassin. In addition to receiving total fees of $186,000 annually from the auditing services provided to Madoff, Friehling also had accounts in Madoff's firm totaling more than $14 million and had withdrawn over $5.5 million since the year 2000. Friehling deceived investors and regulators by providing unauthorized audit work and verifying fraudulent financial statements. Given the size of the accounting firm, a red flag should have been raised. Madoff's operations were too large in size and complexity for the resources of a three-person accounting firm.

Revealing the Fraud

As the U.S. economy entered the 2008 recession period, investors began to panic and withdraw their money from Madoff's accounts, totaling more than $7 billion. Madoff was unable to cover the redemptions and struggled "to obtain the liquidity necessary to meet those obligations." He confessed to his sons that the business he was running was a scam. On December 11, 2008, Bernard Madoff was arrested by federal agents—one day after his sons reported his confession to the authorities.

Global Crisis

The Ponzi scheme that Madoff ran for more than a decade affected the lives of thousands of individuals, institutions, organizations, and stakeholders worldwide. A 162-page list was submitted to the U.S. Bankruptcy Court in Manhattan detailing the affected parties. The lengthy list consisted of some of the wealthiest investors and well-known names around the region: "They reportedly include Philadelphia Eagles owner Norman Braman, New York Mets owner Fred Wilpon, and J. Ezra Merkin, the chairman of GMAC Financial Services." Talk-show host Larry King and actor John Malkovich were on the list, among others. Many investment management firms, such as Tremont Capital Management and Fairfield Greenwich Advisors, had invested large amounts in Madoff's funds and were hit the hardest financially. Major global banks, "including Royal Bank of Scotland, France's largest bank, BNP Paribas, Britain's HSBC Holdings PLC and Spain's Santander" were also known to have lost millions. Charitable foundations, such as the Lautenberg Foundation, and financial institutions, including Bank of America Corp., Citigroup, and JPMorgan Chase, were all stakeholders in the Madoff scandal. Ordinary individuals also invested much of their life savings into what they believed was a "once-in-a-lifetime opportunity." William Woessner, a retiree from the State Department's Foreign Service, agreed that the investors "were made to feel that it was a big favor to be let in if you didn't have a lot of money. It was an exclusive club to belong to." It has been reported that individual losses were between $40,000 to over $1 million in total. There were 3,500 investors from New York and more than 1,700 from Florida.

The repercussions of Madoff's Ponzi scheme have been emotional as well as financial. A French aristocrat and professional investor living within the suburbs of New York, René-Thierry Magon de la Villehuchet, had invested almost $1.4 billion in Madoff's accounts. He had invested both his and his clients' money, only to lose everything. Villehuchet felt personally responsible for the loss of his clients' money: "He had a true concept of capitalism. . . . He felt responsible and he felt guilty," said his brother Bertrand de la Villehuchet. Villehuchet's depression grew to such a point that he committed suicide on December 22, 2008.

Consequences and Aftermath

On June 29, 2009, Judge Denny Chin found Madoff guilty on 11 criminal counts and sentenced him to 150 years in prison, the maximum possible sentence allowed at the time. Chin's severe sentence was influenced by the statements given by Madoff's victims and the 113 letters received and filed with the federal court: "A substantial sentence may in some small measure help the victims in their healing process," stated Judge Chin. Madoff was also forced to pay a $170 billion legal judgment passed by the government, stating that this amount of money "was handled by his firm since its founding in the 1960s." David Friehling, the auditor for Madoff's books, was also arrested on fraud charges. He was initially "released on a $2.5 million bond and had to surrender his passport." Friehling lost his CPA license in 2010, and his sentencing has since been postponed four times. He faces a sentence of more than 100 years in prison.

Lawyer Irving H. Picard is a bankruptcy trustee in the Madoff scandal. As a court-appointed trustee, Picard has filed numerous lawsuits and has collected $1.2 billion in recovered funds from "banks, personal property, and funds around the world." It is estimated that from this $1.2 billion, Picard has earned approximately $15 million. More than $116 million has been given to 237 Madoff victims, each receiving up to $500,000. In order to help the victims of the Madoff scandal, Picard started a program called "Hardship Case." He has also filed a $199 million lawsuit against the Madoff family, including Madoff's brother, his two sons, and niece, all of whom worked alongside Madoff. An additional lawsuit was filed against Madoff's wife for $44.8 million, stating that she had transferred large amounts of money from the firm "over a six-year period." As of now, none of the family members—Madoff's two sons, brother, niece, and wife—have been found guilty on any of the charges. Madoff's oldest son, Mark, committed suicide in December 2010 at age 46. Madoff's other son also died. Madoff's victims took swift action against the negligence of SEC and JPMorgan Chase. U.S. District Court Judge Colleen McMahon threw out most of the $19.9 million charges against JPMorgan in November 2011, however. The then–New York Mets owners paid a settlement of $162 million in March 2012 to avoid going to trial to answer the allegations made by Irving Picard.

Hidden Secrets?

Despite the accusations of negligence that JPMorgan Chase received from the public, it was one of the biggest financial firms to profit in the Madoff scandal. As stated earlier, JPMorgan made a profit of $483 million. During 2006, "the bank had started offering investors a way to leverage their bets on the future performance of two hedge funds that invested with Mr. Madoff" and decided to place $250 million of its own money inside these funds. A few months before Madoff's arrest in 2008, JPMorgan withdrew its $250 million, stating that it had become "concerned about the lack of transparency and its due diligence raised doubts about Madoff's operations." It is surprising that the bank was suspicious and apprehensive toward investments with Madoff yet raised no concerns about the large amount of money being deposited in Madoff's accounts within the bank. JPMorgan also failed to alert investors to move their money, stating that "the issues did not meet the threshold necessary to permit the bank to restructure the notes. . . . We did not have the right to disclose our concerns." Regardless of the public statements made by JPMorgan in support of its actions, many lawyers and investors believe that the bank had knowledge of Madoff's scam but wanted to secure high returns for as long as possible.

Ethical Flaws

In a 2011 *New York Magazine* interview, Madoff stated that he never thought the collapse of his Ponzi scheme would cause the sort of destruction that has befallen his family. He asserted that unidentified banks and hedge funds were somehow "complicit" in his elaborate fraud, an about-face from earlier claims that he was the only person involved. "They had to know," Madoff said. "But the attitude was sort of, 'If you're doing something wrong, we don't want to know.'" To date, none of the major banks or hedge funds that did business with Madoff have been accused by federal prosecutors of knowingly investing in his Ponzi scheme. However, in civil lawsuits Picard has asserted that executives at some banks expressed suspicions for years, yet they continued to do business with Madoff and steer their clients' money into his hands.

In some ways, Madoff has not tried to evade blame. He has made a full confession, saying that nothing justifies what he did. And yet, for Madoff, that doesn't settle the matter. He feels misunderstood. He can't bear the thought that people think he's evil. "I'm not the kind of person I'm being portrayed as," he told *New York Magazine*.

A main issue in this controversy is the continuous fraudulent operations that Madoff was able to maintain for a decade that created a $65 billion Ponzi scheme and shattered the lives of thousands around the world. For most of the world, Bernie Madoff is a monster: He betrayed thousands of investors and bankrupted charities and hedge funds. On paper, his Ponzi scheme lost nearly $65 billion; the effects spread across five continents. And he brought down his own family with him, a more intimate kind of betrayal.

Bernard Madoff was the central stakeholder who manipulated and involved his brother, two sons, and a niece, all of whom worked inside the Bernard L. Madoff

Investment Securities LLC. Other key stakeholders included Madoff's employees, who had invested their money into an operation they believed was legal and ethical. Others from the financial community, including financial institutions, investment management firms, charitable organizations, and global banks, were also major players. The government, specifically the SEC, and the Department of Justice were also heavily involved. The lawyer Irving Picard was a key player, as was the whistle-blower Harry Markopolos and his team who revealed the nature of the scam early on, even though the SEC and other government regulators did not move on the evidence.

As of October 2013, federal authorities were working toward mounting a criminal investigation into JPMorgan Chase, believing that the bank may have intentionally neglected Madoff's Ponzi scheme. Having agreed to a $13 billion settlement with the U.S. government to settle charges that the bank overstated the quality of mortgages it was selling to investors in the run-up to the financial crisis, the threat of criminal charges over the Madoff case represents another major threat to the reputation of the nation's largest bank. In 2013, a "Madoff Victim Fund (MVF)" was created attempting to help compensate those Madoff defrauded. However, the Department of Justice did not begin paying back the approximate $4 billion dollars until late into 2017. Progress has been seemingly made, according to an update that was released in 2018: "We have now paid over 27,300 victims an aggregate recovery of 56.65 percent of their losses, with thousands more set to recover the same amount in the future." And "at least one more significant distribution in 2019" by the fund was anticipated, in the hope of concluding most of these issues (Hayes and Khartit, 2020). A further update on April 14, 2021, shows that the settlement amounts reached over $14.4 billion of settlements, with payouts totaling over $13.5 billion on 2,654 allowed claims. "The Madoff Victim Fund has paid out almost $3.2 billion to more than 36,800 individuals and entities" (Stempel, 2021).

Questions for Discussion

1. What did Madoff do that was illegal and unethical?
2. Identify some of the main reasons that Madoff was able to start and sustain such an enormous Ponzi scheme for as long as he did.
3. Who were/are the major stakeholders involved and affected by Madoff's scheme and scandal?
4. Did Madoff have accomplices in starting and sustaining his scheme, or was he able to do it alone? Explain.
5. How was he caught?
6. What lessons can be learned from the Madoff scandal?

Sources

This case was developed from material contained in the following sources:

Abkowitz, A. (2008, December 19). Madoff's auditor...doesn't audit? *CNNMoney .com.* http://money.cnn.com/2008/12/17/news/companies/madoff.auditor .fortune/.

Berenson, A., and Saltmarsh, M. (2009, January 1). Madoff investor's suicide leaves questions. *NYTimes.com.* http://www.nytimes.com/2009/01/02/business /02madoff.html.

Carozza, D. (2009, May/June). Chasing Madoff: An interview with Harry Markopolos, CFE, CFA. *FraudMagazine.com.* http://www.fraud-magazine.com/article.aspx?id =313.

Creswell, J., and Thomas, L. (2009, January 24). The talented Mr. Madoff. *NYTimes .com.* http://www.nytimes.com/2009/01/25/business/25bernie.html ?pagewanted=1&_r=1 (as cited in Perri (2013, 335).

Creswell, J., and Thomas, L. (2020, updated January 31). The talented Mr. Madoff. *New York Times.* https://www.nytimes.com/2009/01/25/business/25bernie .html.

Dienst, J., and Honan, K. (2010, December 13). Madoff son found dead in suicide. *NBCNewYork.com.* http://www January.nbcnewyork.com/news/local/Mark -111717634.html.

Ellis, D. (5, 2009). Congress looks for answers in Madoff scandal. *CNNMoney.com.* http://money.cnn.com/2009/01/05/news/companies/madoff_hearing/index.htm.

Elstein, A. (2009, August 26). Madoff account netted J.P. Morgan $483M. *Crains NewYork.com.* http://www.crainsnewyork.com/article/20090826/FREE /908269991.

Frank, R., and Efrati, A. (2009, June 30). "Evil" Madoff gets 150 years in epic fraud. *WSJ.com.* http://online.wsj.com/article/SB124604151653862301.html.

Hayes, A., and Khartit, K. (2020, September 24). Bernie Madoff. *Investopedia.* https://www.investopedia.com/terms/b/bernard-madoff.asp.

Hedgpeth, D., and Greenwell, M. (2009, February 6). List brings home impact of Madoff scandal. *WashingtonPost.com.* http://www.washingtonpost.com/wp-dyn/content /article/2009/02/05/AR2009020501865.html?sid=ST2009020501619.

Henriques, D. B. (2009, January 28). JPMorgan exited Madoff-linked funds last fall. *NYTimes.com.* http://www.nytimes.com/2009/01/29/business/29madoff .html?pagewanted=1&_r=1.

Lavan, R. (2008, December 15). Who is Bernard Madoff? *Times Online.* http://www .thetimes.co.uk/tto/business/industries/banking/article2159812.ece.

Luhby, T. (2009, October 2). Madoff relatives sued for $199 million. *CNNMoney.com.* http://money.cnn.com/2009/10/02/news/economy/Madoff_lawsuit_family/.

Madoff victims' lawsuit against JPMorgan Chase tossed. (2011, November 2). *HuffingtonPost.com.* http://www.huffingtonpost.com/2011/11/02/madoff-victims -lawsuit-jp-morgan-chase_n_1071117.html.

Pavlo, W. (2011, September 16). David Friehling, Madoff's accountant, sentencing postponed…again. *Forbes.com.* http://www.forbes.com/sites/walterpavlo /2011/09/16/david-friehling-madoffs-accountant-sentencing-postponed-again/.

Perri, F. (2013). Visionaries or false prophets. *Journal of Contemporary Criminal Justice, 29(3),* 331–350.

Protess, B., and Silver-Greenberg, J. (2013). JPMorgan faces possible penalty in Madoff case. *DealbookNYTimes.com.* http://dealbook.nytimes.com/2013/10/23 /madoff-action-seen-as-possible-for-jpmorgan/?_r=0.

Rashbaum, W. K., and Henriques, D. B. (2009, March 18). Accountant for Madoff is arrested and charged with securities fraud. *NYTimes.com.* http://www.nytimes .com/2009/03/19/business/19madoff.html?_r=1.

Smith, A. (2009, October 14). Madoff victims sue SEC for "negligence." *CNNMoney .com*. http://money.cnn.com/2009/10/14/news/economy/madoff_sec_lawsuit /index.htm.

Stempel, J. (2021, April 14). Key dates in Bernard Madoff's criminal case, recovery efforts for victims. https://www.reuters.com/business/key-dates-bernard-madoffs -criminal-case-recovery-efforts-victims-2021-04-14/

Sundby, A. (2009, November 3). Madoff accountant apologizes to victims. *CBSnews .com*. http://www.cbsnews.com/stories/2009/11/03/cbsnews_investigates /main5510619.shtml.

Case 3

Cyberbullying: Who's to Blame and What Can Be Done?

What Is Cyberbullying?

Cyberbullying is "when a child, preteen, or teen is tormented, threatened, harassed, humiliated, embarrassed, or otherwise targeted by another child, preteen, or teen using the Internet, interactive and digital technologies, or mobile phones" (National Crime Prevention Council, n.d.). Unlike traditional bullying, cyberbullying eliminates the need for physical contact with others in order to make the person feel inferior. Technology as an avenue for intimidation is a hot-button issue for school systems and parents alike. This is uncharted territory, and legislation does not always provide guidance and structure.

The reality is that bullying makes a significantly negative impact on the lives of today's youth. Cyberbullying directly impacts self-esteem and can—and has—led to suicide among its adolescent victims. Schools, parents, and peers must identify and intervene in cases of cyberbullying. Increased awareness and education about cyberbullying and its consequences can help create a safer online community. Individuals should be held morally responsible for the consequences of their actions online.

Why Cyberbullying?

A young adult's behavior is primarily motivated by a desire to meet that individual's basic need for recognition, attention, and approval. In a survey conducted in 1999, students in over 100 schools were asked the following question: "Is it easier for you to get noticed or get attention in this school by doing something positive or something negative?" Almost 100% replied "negative" (Weinhold, 2000). Adolescents turn to cyberbullying to fuel their need for attention and recognition from their peers. It began primarily in chat rooms and instant messaging conversations but has expanded to include social networking (Facebook) and video-sharing websites (YouTube). Text messaging and anonymous web postings are common methods of cyberbullying. Very recently, cyberbullying has established a presence in portable gaming devices through "virtual worlds" and interactive sites.

Cyberbullying is more attractive than traditional bullying for a variety of reasons. First, technology provides the perpetrator with the option of anonymity. Victims often do not know who is targeting them because the bully's identity is hidden through anonymous web posts or fictitious e-mails. Second, bullies are able to expand the scope of their impact because a larger network of individuals may be involved in the cyberattack. With just a few mouse clicks, an entire community may be a participant in the incident, creating the perception that "everyone" knows about it. Many argue that it is psychologically easier to be a cyberbully than a traditional bully. A cyberbully does not have to physically confront the victim and witness the immediate result of a message. Some cyberbullies might not even recognize the severity of their actions, which take place from a different location.

Last, the response to cyberbullying has been slow, suggesting to perpetrators that there are little or no consequences for malicious online actions.

Why Is Cyberbullying a Major Issue?

Today's youth are "wired" and connected to technology 24/7. Statistics suggest that "two-thirds of [American] youth go online every day for schoolwork, to keep in touch with their friends, to play games, to learn about celebrities, to share their digital creations, or for many other reasons." Moreover, "according to a recent nationwide poll, over 40 percent of adults in the United States have been harassed online. People are targeted in a variety of ways—from name-calling to more severe tactics such as being insulted based on their race, gender, or sexual orientation" (Hinduja and Patchin, 2010). Given the accessibility of technology, it should be no surprise that individuals are using the Internet, cell phones, and other electronic instruments to bully each other. A 2010 study revealed that "30% of middle-school students were victims of at least one of nine forms of cyberbullying two or more times in the past 30 days" and "22 percent of middle-school students admitted to engaging in at least one of five forms of cyberbullying two or more times in the past 30 days" (Hinduja and Patchin, 2010). Females are more likely to choose cyberbullying over traditional bullying. The rationale is that females prefer the nonconfrontational nature of technology.

With such a large percentage of today's youth affected by cyberbullying, something has to be done. Cyberbullying is damaging to the self-esteem of the victims. Typically beginning around middle school, self-perception begins to dictate a child's sense of self-worth. Teenagers often feel that they are defined by "their erupting skin and morphing bodies, [and] many seventh-grade students have a hard enough time just walking through the school doors. When dozens of kids vote online, which is not uncommon, about whether a student is fat or stupid or gay, the impact can be devastating" (Weinhold, 2000). Victims of cyberbullying typically report feeling angry, frustrated, sad, embarrassed, and scared.

An adolescent's self-esteem can dramatically decrease during puberty. In one survey, when kids in kindergarten were asked if they like themselves, 95 percent or more said "yes." By fourth grade, the percentage of kids who reported liking themselves was down to 60 percent; by eighth grade, the percentage was down to 40 percent; and by twelfth grade it was down to 5 percent (Weinhold, 2000).

Meet the Victims

Phoebe Prince. On January 14, 2010, Phoebe Prince was found dead in her South Hadley, Massachusetts, home. Phoebe was 15 years old and a recent immigrant from Ireland attending South Hadley High School. As a freshman in high school, she had a romantic fling with a senior football player, upsetting the other girls at her school. They tormented her relentlessly, calling her a "slut." They even followed her home one day, throwing things at her from their moving car. Phoebe took her own life when the intimidation became too much. She was found dead by her 12-year-old sister.

Immediately following the death of Phoebe Prince, the girls who bullied her mocked her death on the Internet. It was confirmed that Phoebe had been a victim of both cyberbullying and daily physical abuse. Many students reported to school officials that Phoebe was the victim of harassment through social networking sites like Facebook and text messages. Two students at South Hadley High School were later suspended as a result. Principal Daniel Smith observed that "the bullying often surrounded arguments about teen dating" (Cullen, 2010). Even the Facebook page created in Phoebe's memory contained cruel messages posted by bullies.

Megan Meier. Another high-profile case was that of Megan Meier, a 13-year-old girl whose suicide was the result of cyberbullying. In October 2006, Tina and Ron Meier found their daughter's body in a bedroom closet. Megan had hanged herself. A few weeks earlier, Megan had established a relationship with a boy using the social networking site MySpace. Megan and the boy, "Josh Evans," quickly formed an online relationship. The catch: Josh Evans was not a real person—it was later discovered to be a fake cover name for Megan's cyberbullies to use. Evans claimed to be a 16-year-old boy who lived in a nearby town but was homeschooled. There were several red flags to suggest that Josh Evans did not exist, but to Megan Meier, an already insecure teenager on medication for depression, the boy seemed very real. "Josh" even told Megan that he did not have a phone, restricting him to virtual communication.

Megan's online relationship with Josh then took a turn for the worse. Megan received a message from Josh on MySpace saying, "I don't know if I want to be friends with you any longer because I hear you're not nice to your friends." A bully was using Josh's account to send cruel messages. Megan called her mother, describing electronic bulletins posted about her saying things like "Megan Meier is a slut. Megan Meier is fat" (Parents: Cyber bullying led to teen's suicide, 2007). Megan had an existing history of depression, and these messages were a crushing blow to her self-esteem. The stress of the situation was too much for Megan, and she took her own life shortly after these messages were posted.

The person orchestrating Josh Evan's fictitious account was actually a neighborhood mother. Lori Drew, age 47 at the time of Megan's death, was the mother of one of Megan's former friends. Lori Drew knew that Megan had been prescribed antidepressants but still used the fraudulent identity to torment Megan. Drew's reasoning was that Megan had been mean to her daughter and needed to be taught a lesson. This highly unusual case went to trial in November 2008, and Drew was found guilty of three misdemeanors. She did not serve any jail time.

The Beverly Vista School. In May 2008, Evan S. Cohen confronted the Beverly Vista School in Beverly Hills, California, for disciplining his eighth-grade daughter J. C. Cohen for cyberbullying. J. C. had videoed friends at a café egging another eighth-grade girl. In the video, J. C. and her friends make mean-spirited comments toward the victim, calling her "ugly," "spoiled," and a "slut." When the video surfaced online, the Beverly Vista School suspended J. C. for two days, along with her accomplices.

Cohen, a lawyer in the music industry, sued the school on behalf of his daughter. "What incensed me," he said, "was that these people were going to suspend my daughter for something that happened outside of school" (Hoffman, 2010). The legal test was whether or not the video had caused the school "substantial" disruption. According to the law, a student can only be suspended when the student's speech interferes "substantially" with the school's educational mission. The judge ruled in favor of Cohen, and the school district was required to pay Cohen's legal expenses amounting to $107,150.80 (Hoffman, 2010). "The judge also threw in an aside that summarizes the conundrum that is adolescent development, acceptable civility, and school authority. The good intentions of the school notwithstanding, he wrote, it cannot discipline a student for speech, simply because young persons are unpredictable or immature, or because, in general, teenagers are emotionally fragile and may often fight over hurtful comments" (Hoffman, 2010).

No case involving student online speech has yet been brought before the Supreme Court. Lower courts have ruled both ways, sometimes siding with schools disciplining their students and other times siding with the individual perpetrator.

Legislation for Cyberbullying

In response to these and other cases, the federal government has taken steps to prevent and to manage cyberbullying, including the drafting of the Megan Meier Cyberbullying Prevention Act (H.R. 1966). This bill proposes that Chapter 41 of Title 18 of the United States Code (related to extortion and threats) be amended to define cyberbullying and related penalties. According to the act, cyberbullying is not limited to social networking sites but also includes e-mail, instant messaging, blogs, websites, telephones, and text messages. "The bill would amend the federal criminal code to impose criminal penalties on anyone who transmits in interstate or foreign commerce a communication intended to coerce, intimidate, harass, or cause substantial emotional distress to another person, using electronic means to support severe, repeated, and hostile behavior" (H.R. 1966: Megan Meier Cyberbullying Prevention Act, 2011).

The Megan Meier bill was introduced to the House of Representatives on April 2, 2009. It was referred to two subcommittees—the House Judiciary Committee and the House Judiciary Subcommittee on Crime, Terrorism, and Homeland Security. The last action was on September 30, 2009, when subcommittee hearings were held. The bill has not become law. It was a part of a previous session of Congress and must be reintroduced in order to be reconsidered for law.

State governments are also considering laws against cyberbullying. On May 3, 2010, Massachusetts Governor Deval Patrick signed new antibullying legislation that places greater responsibility on schools to intervene in bullying situations. "Bullying, as defined by the bill, encompasses crimes such as stalking and harassment. The anti-bullying legislation specifically holds provisions for anti-bully training and mandates that all school employees, including teachers, cafeteria staff, and janitorial staff, must report and investigate incidents involving bullying.

Teachers must also notify all parents of the students involved in the bullying incident. It also includes an anti-bullying curriculum to be taught in both public and private schools" (Clabough, 2010).

Although a step in the right direction, the bill does not assign specific penalties to those who do not intervene in instances of bullying. Following the bill's implementation, bullying continues to be a major issue in Massachusetts schools.

On February 13, 2013, Illinois State Senate representative Ira I. Silverstein introduced the Internet Posting Removal Act–SB 1614. When you read the bill solely through the lens of cyberbullying prevention, it makes sense. But what happens when politicians start using the statute to silence critics? Precise language is a must when it comes to laws; loose lips sink ships, and loose language can annihilate freedoms.

The Impact of Facebook

The growth of social networking sites such as Facebook in the past decade have contributed to the prevalence of cyberbullying. Social networking giants have experience in dealing with cyberbullying. Facebook has accessible help centers that provide postings and suggestions on how users can fight back against cyberbullying.

Facebook gives users the responsibility to manage cyberbullying. On Facebook's Help Menu, advisory information is available for teens and parents regarding how to handle cyberbullying. Facebook provides a mechanism for users to report abusive behavior by another user. After the abuse is reported, Facebook investigates the behavior. Facebook also gives users the ability to block specific individuals and restrict privacy settings. There are comprehensive instructions on Facebook's website to make online safety as user-friendly as possible.

Facebook also encourages users to avoid retaliation, recommending that victims block or report abusers rather than respond via "inbox, wall posting, or Facebook Chat." A section of Facebook's Help Center is dedicated to educating parents about ways to protect their teens from cyberbullying. This page emphasizes the need for communication among parents and teens regarding expectations and the use of common sense. Though Facebook cannot prevent and monitor every issue of online harassment, the company recognizes that cyberbullying is an issue and is doing what it can to empower users.

Although Facebook has taken steps to prevent cyberbullying on its respective websites, WhatsApp and Instagram, these efforts are not enough. Cyberbullying is still a major issue on social networking sites and on other forms of media and communication. To push forward to a solution, questions must be raised about who should be held accountable in instances of cyberbullying.

Conclusion

Cyberbullying is a real issue that deserves recognition. We should be educating adolescents about the potentially damaging effects of their actions, responding to incidents, and holding the appropriate people accountable in instances of cyberbullying. All stakeholders in cyberbullying should take this issue very seriously. Cyberbullying can have an incredibly harmful effect on adolescents if nobody intervenes. Teenagers, parents, schools, and the government especially have a moral responsibility to take action when they come across cyberbullying. From an ethical perspective, we can no longer be bystanders. Take a stand against cyberbullying.

Finally, here are some simple suggestions from Laura Tierney, a member of the Social Institute, to help stop cyberbullying from occurring:

1. **Be on the lookout for anything that makes them feel unsafe**: Teach kids to trust their gut. If something feels wrong to them, they should listen to that.
2. **Take a screenshot**: "With disappearing snaps and with disappearing Instagram stories, it's easy to say, 'Well, I might have seen this, but it's disappeared,'" Tierney says. By taking a screenshot and saving it, your child has solid proof and a record of what they've seen online.
3. **Tell the right people what they've seen**: Don't just tell your child or teenager to "tell somebody" if they see something. Make sure they understand who the right "somebody" is. If they don't know who to turn to and tell, they will likely only tell their peers, and that does nothing to stop cyberbullying.

Another helpful suggestion is for parents to monitor their children's online habits or have easy access to their device. This is for the safety of the child (and potentially the safety of others as well), so be open to them and hopefully they understand the importance of monitoring their online life. A Pew Research Center survey of adults with children 13 to 17 years old, which was published in 2018, found these results about cyberbullying:

- 61 percent of parents checked the websites their teenager visited.
- 60 percent visited their social media accounts.
- 48 percent looked through their phone calls and messages.
- 16 percent track their teenagers' whereabouts through their cell phones.

As soon as you learn about your child's behavior, make sure to address the issue as soon as possible or the situation can spiral out of control. Denying the presence of potential bad behavior does not help either, since this could potentially balloon the negativity of this issue. The best way to solve this matter is to get all the information you can about any incidents and talk to your child about what happened (Idaho Youth Ranch, 2018).

Questions for Discussion

1. Have you or someone you know ever been involved in cyberbullying, as a bully or victim? If so, what are the feelings and effects associated with cyberbullying in the situations with which you are familiar?
2. What are the issues with cyberbullying? Explain.

3. Who are the stakeholders in cyberbullying cases, and what are the stakes for them?
4. Who is ethically responsible for the rise and continuance of cyberbullying?
5. Should social networking sites be censored in an effort to stop cyberbullying? Explain.
6. Is it legal and ethical to censor social networking sites to stop cyberbullying? Explain.
7. What is Congress doing about this situation?

Sources

This case was developed from material contained in the following sources:

Brody, N. (2018, December 11). Commentary: Donald Trump: The diary of a cyberbully. https://www.statesman.com/opinion/20181211/commentary-donald-trump-diary-of-cyberbully.

Chen, J. (2021, April 14). Ponzi scheme. *Investopedia.* https://www.investopedia.com/terms/p/ponzischeme.asp.

Clabough, R. (2010, May 4). Anti-bullying legislation in Massachusetts. *New American.*

Creswell, J., and Thomas, L. (2009, January 24). The talented Mr. Madoff. Retrieved from http://www.nytimes.com/2009/01/25/business/25bernie.html?pagewanted=all, as cited in Perri (2013, 335).

Creswell, J. and L. Thomas (2020, January 31). The talented Mr. Madoff. https://www.bendbulletin.com/business/the-talented-mr-madoff/article_b677edeb-9638-5873-a608-2813064e5ec2.html

Cullen, K. (2010, February 2). No safe haven for bullies. *Boston Globe.*

Cullen, K. (2010, January 24). The untouchable mean girls. *Boston Globe.* http://www.boston.com/news/local/massachusetts/articles/2010/01/24/the_untouchable_mean_girls/.

Hinduja, S., and Patchin, J. W. (2014, October). Cyberbullying identification, prevention, and response. Cyberbullying Research Center. https://cyberbullying.org/Cyberbullying-Identification-Prevention-Response.pdf.

Hinduja, S., and Patchin, J. W. (2010). Fact sheet: Cyberbullying and self-esteem. Cyberbullying Research Center. https://cyberbullying.org/cyberbullying_and_self_esteem_research_fact_sheet.pdf.

Hoffman, J. (2010, June 27). Online bullies pull schools into the fray. *New York Times.* http://www.nytimes.com/2010/06/28/style/28bully.html?_r=1&pagewanted=all.

H.R. 1966: Megan Meier Cyberbullying Prevention Act. (2011, February 2). Govtrack.us. http://www.govtrack.us/congress/bills/111/hr1966.

Idaho Youth Ranch. (2018, September 14). Social media dangers and the effects of cyberbullying. https://www.youthranch.org/blog/social-media-dangers-and-the-effects-of-cyberbullying.

Kowalski, R. M. (2008). *Cyber bullying: Bullying in the digital age.* Malden: Blackwell.

McQuade, S. C. (2009). *Cyber bullying: Protecting kids and adults from online bullies.* Westport: Praeger Publishers.

"Monitoring Internet use." (2011, February 14). Mass.gov.

National Crime Prevention Council. (n.d.). What is cyberbullying, exactly? Stop cyberbullying. *WiredKids.* Accessed June 17, 2020, http://www.stopcyberbullying.org/what_is_cyberbullying_exactly.html.

Parents: Cyber bullying led to teen's suicide." (2007, November 19). *ABC News.* http://abcnews.go.com/GMA/story?id=3882520.

Perri, F. Visionaries or false prophets. (2013). *Journal of Contemporary Criminal Justice, 29(3),* 331–350.

Shariff, S. (2009). *Confronting cyber-bullying.* New York: Cambridge University Press, 2009.

"Social networking sites." (2011, February 14). Mass.gov.

Treanor, T. (2011, August 31). Imagining the Madoff within us. https://dctheatrescene.com/2011/08/31/imagining-the-madoff-within-us/

Weinhold, B. K. (2000, February). Uncovering the hidden causes of bullying and school violence. *Counseling and Human Development* 32(6).

Weir, R. (2010, February 17). Mayor Menino launches anti-cyber bullying hotline. *Boston Herald.* https://www.bostonherald.com/2010/02/17/mayor-menino-launches-anti-bully-hotline/.

Notes

1. Illegal downloading? What's illegal? (n.d.). *Yahoo! Answers.* http://uk.answers. yahoo.com/question/index?qid=20080229100732AAsCQpt.

2. Johnson, A. (2020, February 7). 22 years after the DMCA, online piracy is still a widespread problem. Information Technology and Innovation Foundation. https://itif.org /publications/2020/02/07/22-years-after-dmca-online-piracy-still-widespread-problem.

3. O'Sullivan, F. (2020, July 8). What is torrenting? 4 things you need to know. https:// www.cloudwards.net/what-is-torrenting/.

4. Kravets, D. (2013, March 18). Supreme court OKs $222K verdict for sharing 24 songs. *Wired.com.* http://www.wired.com/threatlevel/2013/03/scotus-jammie-thomas -rasset/.

5. Kirk, J. (2008, February 26). U.S. judge pokes hole in file-sharing lawsuit. *Computerworld.com.* https://www.computerworld.com/article/2814382/u-s--judge-pokes-hole -in-file-sharing-lawsuit.html; Recording Industry Association of America (2004, April). New wave of illegal file sharing lawsuits brought by RIAA. *RIAA.com.* https://tech-insider .org/internet/research/2004/0428.html, accessed, March 7, 2012; McMillan, G. (2011, May 10). Are you one of 23,000 defendants in the US' biggest illegal download lawsuit? *Time.com.* https://techland.time.com/2011/05/10/are-you-one-of-23000-defendants-in -the-us-biggest-illegal-download-lawsuit/; Roth, E. June 11, 2011. 50,000 users of Bit-Torrent sued for illegal movie downloads. https://www.benzinga.com/11/06/1158982/50 -000-users-of-bittorrent-sued-for-illegal-movie-downloads; Brian, M. (2012, January 7). Apple facing $1.88 million lawsuit in China over sales of illegal book downloads. *The Next Web.* https://thenextweb.com/news/apple-facing-1-88-million-lawsuit-in-china -over-sales-of-illegal-book-downloads.

6. Almost half of the world's population has no access to the Internet, according to World Economic Forum data from April 2020 (https://www.weforum.org/agenda /2020/04/coronavirus-covid-19-pandemic-digital-divide-internet-data-broadband -mobbile/). Moreover, "approximately 19 million Americans—6 percent of the population— still lack access to fixed broadband service at threshold speeds. In rural areas, nearly one-fourth of the population—14.5 million people—lack access to this service. In tribal areas, nearly one-third of the population lacks access. Even in areas where broadband is available, approximately 100 million Americans still do not subscribe" (Federal Communications Commission Eighth Broadband Progress Report, https://www.fcc.gov /reports-research/reports/broadband-progress-reports/eighth-broadband-progress -report).

7. Novinson, M. (2020, June 30). The 11 biggest ransomware attacks of 2020 (so far). *CRN.com.*

8. Chatham House (2018, January 12). The lasting effects of the financial crisis have yet to be felt. https://www.chathamhouse.org/2018/01/lasting-effects-financial-crisis-have -yet-be-felt.

9. Schwartz, N. D., and E. Dash (2011, June 29). Bank of America settles claims stemming from mortgage crisis. *NYTimes.com,* http://www.nytimes.com/2011/06/30/business /30mortgage.html?_r=1&pagewanted=all.

10. Hayes, A. (2021). Enron. Investopdia, https://www.investopedia.com/terms/e /enron.asp

11. Confidence in institutions. (n.d.). *Gallup.com.* http://www.gallup.com/poll/1597 /confidence-institutions.aspx#3, accessed August 21, 2013.

12. Ibid.

13. Eavis, P. (2020, October 8). While millions lost jobs, some executives made millions in company stock. *New York Times.* https://www.nytimes.com/2020/10/08/business /executive-stock-awards-coronavirus.html

14. Bloxham, E. (2011, April 13). How can we address excessive CEO pay? *Fortune.* https://fortune.com/2011/04/13/how-can-we-address-excessive-ceo-pay/.

15. Mishel, L., and Jori Kandra. (2020, August 18). CEO compensation surged 14% in 2019 to $21.3 million. *Economic Policy Institute.* https://www.epi.org/publication/ceo -compensation-surged-14-in-2019-to-21-3-million-ceos-now-earn-320-times-as -much-as-a-typical-worker/.

16. Ibid.

17. Smith, P. (2002, July 18). Sarbanes bill is "unenforceable." *AccountancyAge.com.* http:// www.accountancyage.com/News/112993, accessed March 7, 2012.

18. O'Sullivan, K., and Durfree, D. (2004, June 1). Offshoring by the numbers. *CFO Magazine, 20(7)*, 49–54. http://www.cfo.com/article.cfm/3014067.

19. Ricciuti, M., and Yamamoto, M. (2004, May 5). Outsourcing: Where to draw the line? *CNET News.* http://www.zdnet.com/news/outsourcing-where-to-draw-the-line /135880.

20. West, N. (2012, May 6). 5 ways robots are outsourcing humans in the workforce. *Activist Post.* http://www.activistpost.com/2012/05/5-ways-robots-are-outsourcing-humans -in.html.

21. Ibid.

22. Ibid.

23. Friedman, T. (2000). *The Lexus and the olive tree.* New York: Anchor Books, 17, 20, 24.

24. Ibid., 2, 20.

25. Ibid., p. 28.

26. Irwin, D. (2020, December 17). Globalization in retreat. *Wall Street Journal*, R13.

27. The Consumer Financial Protection Bureau's official website is http://www .consumerfinance.gov/. See also the bureau's 2013–2017 strategic plan at http://www .consumerfinance.gov/strategic-plan/.

28. Fieser, J. (2009). Ethics. *Internet Encyclopedia of Philosophy.* http://www.iep.utm.edu /ethics/.

29. Ibid.

30. Ibid.

31. Nash, L. (1990). *Good intentions aside: A manager's guide to resolving ethical problems.* Boston: Harvard Business School Press, 5.

32. Ethics and Compliance Initiative. (2020). *Global business ethics survey.* https://www .ethics.org/global-business-ethics-survey/.

33. Ethics Resource Center. (2014). National business ethics survey: Workplace ethics in transition. *Ethics.org.* http://www.ethics.org/nbes/files/FinalNBES-web.pdf, accessed January 26, 2021.

34. Ibid.

35. Ibid.

36. Ibid.

37. Ibid.

38. Morse, J. R. (2003, October). The economic costs of sin. *American Enterprise 14(7)*, 14–14); Frooman, J. (1997). Socially irresponsible and illegal behavior and shareholder wealth. *Business & Society, 36(3)*, 221–229.

39. Zuckerman, A. (2020, May 29). 39 Employee theft statistics: 2019/2020 impact and costs to business. https://comparecamp.com/employee-theft-statistics/.

40. (2011, June). Integrity seen as top leadership trait. *E-Scan Newsletter, 37(6)*, p. 7; see also Horton, M. (2020, July 2). The importance of business ethics, https://www.investopedia.com/ask/answers/040815/why-are-business-ethics-important.asp.

41. Verschoor, C. C. (2018). Survey of workplace ethics. *Strategic Finance.* https://sfmagazine.com/post-entry/july-2018-survey-of-workplace-ethics/#:~:text=The%20 2018%20percentage%20of%20U.S.,part%20of%20an%20ongoing%20pattern.

42. Ibid.

43. Fortune. (n.d.). 100 best companies to work for. *CNNMoney.com.* https://money .cnn.com/magazines/fortune/best-companies/2014/methodology/index.html?iid=BC14 _sp_method.

44. Graves, S., and Waddock, S. (1993). Institutional owners and corporate social performance: Maybe not so myopic after all. *Proceedings of the International Association for Business and Society*, San Diego; Graves, S., and Waddock, S. (1997). The corporate social performance–financial performance link. *Strategic Management Journal, 18*, 303–319.

45. Carroll, A. (1993). *Business and society: Ethics and stakeholder management*, 3rd ed. Cincinnati: South-Western, 110–112.

46. See also Josephson Institute of Business Ethics. (2014, April 16). Making ethical decisions: things to ask yourself. https://blink.ucsd.edu/finance/accountability/ethics/ask.html.

47. Friedman, M. (1970, September 13). The social responsibility of business is to increase its profits. *New York Times Magazine*, 33.

48. Frooman (1997), op. cit.

49. Key, S., and Popkin, S. (1998). Integrating ethics into the strategic management process: Doing well by doing good. *Management Decision, 36(5)*, 331–338. See also Allinson, R. (1993). *Global disasters: Inquiries into management ethics*. New York: Prentice Hall; and Arthur, H. (1984). Making business ethics useful. *Strategic Management Journal, 5*, 319–333.

50. Senge, P. (1990). *The fifth discipline: The art and practice of the learning organization*. New York: Doubleday. See also In search of the holy performance grail. Rummler, G. (1996, April). *Training and Development, 50(4)*, 26–32; and Covey, S. R. (1989). *The seven habits of highly effective people*. New York: Simon & Schuster.

51. DeGeorge, R. (1999). *Business ethics*, 5th ed. Upper Saddle River, NJ: Prentice Hall.

52. Stone, C. D. (1975). *Where the law ends*. New York: Harper & Row.

53. Buchholz, R. (1989). *Fundamental concepts and problems in business ethics*. Englewood Cliffs, NJ: Prentice Hall. For more information, see Buchholz, R. A. (1995). *Business environment and public policy*, 5th ed. Englewood Cliffs, NJ: Prentice Hall.

54. Newton, L. (1986). The internal morality of the corporation. *Journal of Business Ethics, 5*, 249–258.

55. Hoffman, M., and Moore, J. (1995). *Business ethics: Readings and cases in corporate morality*, 3rd ed. New York: McGraw-Hill.

56. DeGeorge, R. (2000). Business ethics and the challenge of the information age. *Business Ethics Quarterly, 10(1)*, 63–72.

57. Ibid.

58. Stone (1975), op. cit.

59. Carroll (1993), op. cit.

60. Stead, B., and Miller, J. (1988). Can social awareness be decreased through business school curriculum? *Journal of Business Ethics, 7(7)*, 30.

61. Jones, T. (1989). Ethics education in business: Theoretical considerations. *Organizational Behavior Teaching Review, 13(4)*, 1–18.

62. Hanson, K. O. (1987, September). What good are ethics courses? *Across the Board*, 10–11.

2

ETHICAL PRINCIPLES, QUICK TESTS, AND DECISION-MAKING GUIDELINES

OPENING CASE

Louise Simms, an American and newly graduated with a master of business administration (MBA) degree, was hired by a firm based in the United States. With minimal training, she was sent to join a company partner to negotiate with a high-ranking Middle Eastern government official. The partner informed Simms that he would introduce her to the government contact and then leave her to "get the job done." Her assignment was to "do whatever it takes to win the contract: it's worth millions to us." The contract would allow Simms's firm to select and manage technology companies that would install a multimillion-dollar computer system for that government. While in the country, Simms was told by the official that Simms's firm had "an excellent chance of getting the contract" if the official's nephew, who owned and operated a computer company in that country, could be assured "a good piece of the action."

On two different occasions, while discussing details, the official attempted unwelcome advances toward Simms. He backed off both times when he observed her subtle negative responses. Simms was told that "the deal" would remain a confidential matter, and the official closed by saying, "That's how we do business here; take it or leave it." Simms was frustrated about the terms of the deal and about the advances toward her. She called her superior in Chicago and urged him not to accept these conditions because of the questionable arrangements and also because of the disrespect shown toward her, which she said reflected on the company as well. Simms's supervisor responded, "Take the deal! And don't let your emotions get involved; we assigned you there because of your independent maturity as a responsible woman. You're in another culture. Use your charm to our competitive advantage. Go with the flow. Accept the offer and get the contract groundwork started. Use your best judgment on how to handle the details."

Simms couldn't sleep that night. She now had doubts about her supervisor's and the government administrator's "ethics." She felt discrimination as a woman and wondered about the culture of the company and her business unit. This was her first job and a significant opportunity. At the same time, she had to live with herself and prove to her boss that she could handle risk responsibly.

■ 2.1 Ethical Reasoning and Moral Decision Making

An important basis for ethics is clear: Much human behavior has consequences for the welfare of others. We are capable of acting toward others in such a way as to increase or decrease the quality of their lives. We are capable of helping or harming. . . . The proper role of ethical reasoning is to highlight acts of two kinds: those that enhance the well-being of others—that warrant our praise—and those that harm or diminish the well-being of others—and thus warrant our criticism. Developing one's ethical reasoning abilities is crucial because there is in human nature a strong tendency toward egotism, prejudice, self-justification, and self-deception.[1]

Ethical reasoning helps determine and differentiate between *right* thinking, decisions, and actions and those that are *wrong*, hurtful, and/or harmful—to others and to ourselves. Ethics is based on and motivated by values, beliefs, emotions, and feelings as well as facts. Ethical actions also involve conscientious reasoning of facts based on moral standards and principles. *Business ethics* refers to applying ethical reasoning and principles to commercial activities that are often profit-oriented. A relevant and notable quote states that "you are free to choose, but you're not free from the consequence of your choice." Ethical reasoning involves thinking before acting and gaining an understanding of motives before consequences occur.

Three Criteria in Ethical Reasoning

The following criteria can be used in ethical reasoning. They help to systematize and structure our arguments:[2]

1. Moral reasoning must be logical. Assumptions and premises, both factual and inferred, used to make judgments should be known and made explicit.
2. Factual evidence cited to support a person's judgment should be accurate, relevant, and complete.
3. Ethical standards used in reasoning should be consistent. When inconsistencies are discovered in a person's ethical standards in a decision, one or more of the standards must be modified.

Returning to this chapter's opening case, if Louise Simms were to use these three criteria, she would articulate the assumptions underlying her decision. If she chose to accept the official's offer, she might reason that she assumed it was not a bribe, or that if it were a bribe she would not get caught; and that even if she or her company did get caught, she would be willing to incur any penalty individually, including the loss of her job. Moreover, Louise would want to obtain as many facts as she could about U.S. laws and the Middle Eastern country's laws on negotiating practices. She would gather information from her employer and check the accuracy of the information against her decision.

She would have to be consistent in her standards. If she chooses to accept the foreign official's conditions, she must be willing to accept additional contingencies consistent with those conditions. She could not suddenly decide that her actions were "unethical" and then back out midway through helping the official's nephew obtain part of the contract. She must think through these contingencies *before* she makes a decision.

Finally, a simple but powerful question can be used throughout your decision-making process: What is my *motivation* and *motive* for choosing a course of action? Examining individual motives and separating these from the known motivations of others provides clarity and perspective. Louise, for example, might ask, "Why did I agree to negotiate with the official on his terms? Was it for money? To keep my job? To impress my boss? For adventure?" She also might ask whether her stated motivation from the outset would carry her commitments through the entire contracting process.

Moral Responsibility Criteria

A major aim of ethical reasoning is to gain a clear focus on problems to facilitate acting in morally responsible ways. Individuals are morally responsible for the harmful effects of their actions when (1) *they knowingly and freely acted or caused the act to happen and knew that the act was morally wrong or hurtful to others*; and (2) *they knowingly and freely failed to act or prevent a harmful act, and they knew it would be morally wrong for a person to do this*.[3] Although no universal definition of what constitutes a morally wrong act exists, an act and the consequences of an act can be defined as morally wrong if physical or emotional harm is done to another as a result of the act.

Two conditions that eliminate a person's moral responsibility for causing injury or harm are *ignorance* and *inability*.[4] However, persons who intentionally prevent themselves from knowing that a harmful action will occur are still responsible. Persons who negligently fail to inform themselves about a potentially harmful matter may still be responsible for the resultant action. Of course, some mitigating circumstances can excuse or lessen a person's moral responsibility in a situation. These include circumstances that show (1) a low level or lack of seriousness to cause harm, (2) uncertainty about knowledge of wrongdoing, and (3) the degree to which a harmful injury was caused or averted. As we know from court trials, proving intent for an alleged illegal act is not an easy matter. Legally, a case involving a defendant is generally in jeopardy when there is sufficient physical as well as other evidence demonstrating that a person "knowingly and willingly" showed intent to commit an illegal act. However, the extent to which a person is morally irresponsible can be difficult to determine.

2.2 Ethical Principles and Decision Making

This section discusses five fundamental principles used in ethical reasoning that are both classic and timely in solving dilemmas in everyday life as well as in complex business situations. Observe Figure 2.1 as you read this section. Since we are examining stakeholders in this text, and we all are stakeholders in different situations, we illustrate how the following principles apply to stakeholders using classic principles. The principles are (1) utilitarianism, (2) universalism, (3) rights, (4) justice, and (5) virtue ethics. After reviewing these principles, we show some "quick ethical tests" that can also be used to clarify ethical dilemmas.

Figure 2.1

Summary of Five Ethical Decision-Making Principles with Stakeholder Analysis

Belief Systems	Source of Moral Activity	Stakeholder Analysis Issues
Utilitarianism (Calculation of Costs and Benefits)	Moral authority is determined by the consequences of an act: An act is morally right if the net benefits over costs are greatest for the majority. Also, the greatest good for the greatest number must result from this act.	1. Consider collective as well as particular interests.
		2. Formulate alternatives based on the greatest good for all parties involved.
		3. Estimate costs and benefits of alternatives for groups affected.

Figure 2.1 *–continued*

Belief Systems	Source of Moral Activity	Stakeholder Analysis Issues
Universalism (Duty)	Moral authority is determined by the extent to which the intention of an act treats all persons with respect. Includes the requirement that everyone would act this way in the same circumstances.	1. Identify individuals whose needs and welfare are at risk with a given policy ordecision.
		2. Identify the use or misuse of manipulation, force, coercion, or deceit that may be harmful to individuals.
		3. Identify duties to individuals affected by the decision.
		4. Determine if the desired action or policy would be acceptable to individuals if the decision were implemented.
Rights (Individual Entitlement)	Moral authority is determined by individual rights guaranteed to all in their pursuit of freedom of speech, choice, happiness, and self-respect.	1. Identify individuals and their rights that may be violated by a particular action.
		2. Determine the legal and moral basis of these individual rights.
		3. Determine the moral justification from utilitarian principles if individuals' rights are violated.
Justice (Fairness and Equity)	Moral authority is determined by the extent opportunities, wealth, and burdens are fairly distributed among all.	1. If a particular action is chosen, how equally will costs and benefits be distributed to stakeholders?
		2. How clear and fair are the procedures for distributing the costs and benefits of the decision?
		3. How can those who are unfairly affected by the action be compensated?
Virtue Ethics (Character-Based Virtues)	Moral authority is based on individual character virtues such as truthfulness, integrity, and honesty. An act, policy, or strategy is moral if it reflects these types of virtues.	1. What are the "character virtues" of the individual stakeholder(s), the policy, procedure, or strategy in question?
		2. If a particular action, policy, or strategy is chosen, to what extent will these virtues be evident, or missing?
		3. While seeking a mutually desirable outcome in a conflicting situation, how can conflicting character values and characteristics that are embedded and/or reflected in a decision, policy, or strategy be avoided or negotiated?

Take the quick ethics assessment in Ethical Insight 2.1. After you have read and reflected on the five principles, return to the assessment and see which of the principles you may consciously or routinely use in your everyday decision making or when deciding complex dilemmas. Which principle would "work" for you?

Ethical Insight 2.1

Are You Ethical?

Answer each question with your first reaction. Circle the number, from 1 to 4, that best represents your beliefs, where 1 represents "Completely agree," 2 represents "Often agree," 3 represents "Somewhat disagree," and 4 represents "Completely disagree."

1. I consider myself the type of person who does whatever it takes to get the job done, period. 1 2 3 4
2. Ethics should be taught at home and in the family, not in professional or higher education. 1 2 3 4
3. I believe that the "golden rule" is that the person who has the gold rules. 1 2 3 4
4. Rules are for people who don't really want to make it to the top of a company. 1 2 3 4
5. Acting ethically at home and with friends is not the same as acting ethically on the job. 1 2 3 4
6. I would do what is needed to promote my own career in a company, short of committing a serious crime. 1 2 3 4
7. Cutthroat competition is part of getting ahead in the business world. 1 2 3 4
8. Lying is usually necessary to succeed in business. 1 2 3 4
9. I would hide truthful information about someone or something at work to save my job. 1 2 3 4
10. I consider money to be the most important reason for working at a job or in an organization. 1 2 3 4

Add up all the points. Your Total Score is: _____

Total your scores by adding up the numbers you circled. The lower your score, the more questionable your (business-related) ethical principles. The lowest possible score is 10, which indicates you are highly unethical; the highest score is 40, indicating you are highly ethical; 20 signals "questionable ethics"; 30 indicates you are more ethical than unethical, but caution should be taken about consequences of your behaviors.

Source: © Joseph W. Weiss. No part or the whole of this document should be reprinted or duplicated in any form without the express written/typed consent of the author, jweiss@bentley.edu.

Utilitarianism: A Consequentialist (Results-Based) Approach

Jeremy Bentham (1748–1832) and John Stuart Mill (1806–1873) are acknowledged as founders of the concept of *utilitarianism*. Although various interpretations of the concept exist, the basic utilitarian view holds that an action is judged as right or good on the basis of its consequences. The ends of an action justify the means taken to reach those ends. As a *consequentialist principle,* the moral authority that drives utilitarianism is the calculated *consequences*, or results, of an action, regardless of other principles that determine the means or motivations for taking the action. Utilitarianism also includes the following tenets:[5]

1. An action is morally right if it produces the greatest good for the greatest number of people.
2. An action is morally right if the net benefits over costs are greatest for all affected, compared with the net benefits of all other possible choices.
3. An action is morally right if its benefits are greatest for each individual and if these benefits outweigh the costs and benefits of the alternatives.

There are also two types of criteria used in utilitarianism: *rule*-based and *act*-based.[6] Rule-based utilitarianism argues that general principles are used as criteria for deciding the greatest benefit to be achieved from acting a certain way. The act itself is not the basis used for examining whether the greatest good can be gained. For example, "stealing is not acceptable" could be a principle that rule-based utilitarians would follow to gain the greatest utility from acting a certain way. "Stealing is not acceptable" is not an absolute principle that rule-based utilitarians would follow in every situation. Rule-based utilitarians might choose another principle over "stealing is not acceptable" if the other principle provided a greater good.

Act-based utilitarians, on the other hand, analyze a particular action or behavior to determine whether the greatest utility or good can be achieved. Act-based utilitarians might also choose an action over a principle if the greatest utility could be gained. For example, an employee might reason that illegally removing an untested chemical substance from company storage would save the lives of hundreds of infants in a less advantaged country because that chemical is being used in an infant formula manufactured in that country. The employee could lose his job if caught; still he calculates that stealing the chemical in this situation provides the greatest utility.

Utilitarian concepts are widely practiced by government policy makers, economists, and business professionals. Utilitarianism is a useful principle for conducting a stakeholder analysis, because it forces decision makers to (1) consider collective as well as particular interests, (2) formulate alternatives based on the greatest good for all parties involved in a decision, and (3) estimate the costs and benefits of alternatives for the affected groups.[7]

Louise Simms could use utilitarian principles in her decision making by identifying each of the stakeholders who would be affected by her decision. She would then calculate the costs and benefits of her decision as they affect each group. Finally, she would decide on a course of action based on the greatest good for the greatest number. For example, after identifying all the stakeholders in her decision, including her own interests, Simms might believe that her firm's capabilities were not competitive and that rejecting the offer would produce the greatest good for the people of the country where the contract would be negotiated, because obtaining bids from the most technically qualified companies would best serve the interests of those receiving the services.

Problems with utilitarianism include the following:

1. No agreement exists about the definition of "good" for all concerned. Is it truth, health, peace, profits, pleasure, cost reductions, or national security?[8]
2. No agreement exists about who decides. Who decides what is good for whom? Whose interests are primary in the decisions?
3. The actions are not judged, but rather their consequences. What if some actions are simply wrong? Should decision makers proceed to take those actions based only on their consequences?
4. How are the costs and benefits of nonmonetary stakes, such as health, safety, and public welfare, measured? Should a monetary value be assigned to nonmarketed benefits and costs?[9] What if the actual or even potentially harmful effects of an action cannot be measured in the short term, but the action is believed to have potentially long-term effects, say, in 20 or 30 years? Should that action be chosen?
5. Utilitarianism does not consider the individual. It is the collective for whom the greatest good is estimated. Do instances exist when individuals and their interests should be valued in a decision?
6. The principles of justice and rights are ignored in utilitarianism. The principle of justice is concerned with the distribution of good, not the amount of total good in a decision. The principle of rights is concerned with individual entitlements, regardless of the collective calculated benefits.

Even given these problems, the principle of utilitarianism is still valuable under some conditions: when resources are fixed or scarce; when priorities are in conflict; when no clear choice fulfills everyone's needs; and when large or diverse collectives are involved in a zero-sum decision—that is, when a gain for some corresponds to a loss for others.[10]

Utilitarianism and Stakeholder Analysis

Because businesses use utilitarian principles when conducting a stakeholder analysis, you, as a decision maker, should:

1. Define how costs and benefits will be measured in selecting one course of action over another—including social, economic, and monetary costs and benefits as well as long-term and short-term costs and benefits. On what principle, if any, would you base your utilitarian analysis?
2. Define what information you will need to determine the costs and benefits for comparisons.
3. Identify the procedures and policies you will use to explain and justify your cost–benefit analysis.
4. State your assumptions when defining and justifying your analysis and conclusions.
5. Ask yourself what moral obligations you have toward each of your stakeholders after the costs and benefits have been estimated.

Universalism: A Deontological (Duty-Based) Approach

Immanuel Kant (1724–1804) is considered one of the leading founders of the principle of *universalism*. Universalism, which is also called deontological ethics, holds that the ends do not justify the means of an action—the right thing must always be done, even if doing the wrong thing would do the most good for the most people. Universalism, therefore, is also referred to as a *nonconsequentialist* ethic. The term "deontology" is derived from the Greek word *deon*, or duty. Regardless of consequences, this approach is based on universal principles, such as justice, rights, fairness, honesty, and respect.[11]

Kant's principle of the *categorical imperative*, unlike utilitarianism, places the moral authority for taking action on an individual's duty toward other individuals and "humanity." The categorical imperative consists of two parts. The first part states that *a person should choose to act if and only if that person would be willing to have every person on earth, in that same situation, act exactly that way.* This principle is absolute and allows for no qualifications across situations or circumstances. The second part of the categorical imperative states that, in an ethical dilemma, *a person should act in a way that respects and treats all others involved as ends as well as means to an end.*[12]

Kant's categorical imperative forces decision makers to take into account their duty to act responsibly and respectfully toward all individuals in a situation. Individual human welfare is a primary stake in any decision. Decision makers must also consider formulating their justifications as principles to be applied to everyone.

In Louise Simms's situation, if she followed deontological principles of universalism, she might ask, "If I accept the official's offer, could I justify that anyone anywhere would act the same way?" Or, "Since I value my own self-respect and believe my duty is to uphold self-respect for others, I will not accept this assignment because my self-respect has been and may again be violated."

The major weaknesses of universalism and Kant's categorical imperative include these criticisms: First, these principles are imprecise and lack practical utility. It is difficult to think of all humanity each time one must make a decision in an ethical dilemma. Second, it is hard to resolve conflicts of interest when using a criterion that states that all individuals must be treated equally. Degrees of differences in stakeholders' interests and relative power exist. However, Kant would remind us that the human being's humanity must be considered above the stakes, power bases, or consequences of our actions. Still, it is often impractical not to consider other elements in a dilemma. Finally, what if a decision maker's duties conflict in an ethical dilemma? The categorical imperative does not allow for prioritizing. A primary purpose of the stakeholder analysis is to prioritize conflicting duties. It is, again, difficult to take absolute positions when limited resources and time and conflicting values are factors.

Universalism and Stakeholder Analysis

The logic underlying universalism and the categorical imperative can be helpful for applying a stakeholder analysis. Even though we may not be able to employ Kant's principles absolutely, we can consider the following as guide-lines for using his ethics:

1. Take into account the welfare and risks of all parties when considering policy decisions and outcomes.
2. Identify the needs of individuals involved in a decision, the choices they have, and the information they need to protect their welfare.
3. Identify any manipulation, force, coercion, or deceit that might harm individuals involved in a decision.
4. Recognize the duties of respecting and responding to individuals affected by particular decisions before adopting policies and actions that affect them.
5. Ask if the desired action would be acceptable to the individuals involved. Under what conditions would they accept the decision?
6. Ask if individuals in a similar situation would repeat the designated action or policy as a principle. If not, why not? And would they continue to employ the designated action?

Rights: A Moral and Legal (Entitlement-Based) Approach

Rights are based on several sources of authority.[13] *Legal rights* are entitlements that are limited to a particular legal system and jurisdiction. In the United States, the Constitution and Declaration of Independence are the basis for citizens' legal rights—for example, the right to life, liberty, and the pursuit of happiness, and the right to freedom of speech. *Moral* (and *human*) *rights*, on the other hand, are universal and based on norms in every society—for example, the right not to be enslaved and the right to work.

Moral and legal rights are linked to individuals and, in some cases, groups, not to societies, as is the case with a utilitarian ethic. Moral rights are also connected with duties—that is, my moral rights imply that others have a duty toward me to not violate those rights, and vice versa. Moral rights also provide the freedom to pursue one's interests, as long as those interests do not violate others' rights. Moral rights also allow individuals to justify their actions and seek protection from others in doing so.

There are also special rights and duties, or *contractual rights*. Contracts provide individuals with mutually binding duties that are based on a legal system with defined transactions and boundaries. Moral rules can apply to contracts. For instance, (1) the contract should not commit the parties to unethical or immoral conduct; (2) both parties should freely and without force enter the contractual agreement; (3) neither individual should misrepresent or misinterpret facts in the contract; and (4) both individuals should have complete knowledge of the nature of the contract and its terms before they are bound by it.[14]

Finally, the concept of *negative* and *positive rights* defines yet another dimension of ethical principles.[15] A *negative right* refers to the duty others have to not interfere with actions related to a person's rights. For example, if you have the right to freedom of speech, others—including your employer—have the duty not to interfere with that right. Of course, there are circumstances that constrain "free speech," which we will discuss in Chapter 4. A *positive right* imposes a duty on others to provide for your needs to achieve your goals, not just protect your right to pursue them. Some of these rights may be part of national, state, or local legislation. For example, you may have the right to equal educational opportunities for your child if you are a parent. This implies that you have the right to send your child to a public school that has the same standards as any other school in your community.

Positive rights were given attention in the twentieth century. National legislation that promoted different groups' rights and the United Nations' Universal Declaration of Human Rights served as sources for positive rights. Negative rights were emphasized in the seventeenth and eighteenth centuries and were based on the Bill of Rights in the Declaration of Independence. Currently, American political parties and advocates who are either politically to the "left" or to the "right" debate on whether certain moral rights are "negative" or "positive" and to what extent taxpayer dollars and government funds should support these rights. For example, "conservative" writers like Milton Friedman[16] have endorsed government support of negative rights (like protecting property and enforcing law and order) and argued against public spending on positive rights (like medical assistance, job training, and housing). As you can see, the concept of rights has several sources of moral authority. Understanding and applying the concept of rights to stakeholders in business situations adds another dimension of ethical discovery to your analysis.

Louise Simms might ask what her rights are in her situation. If she believes that her constitutional and moral rights would be violated by accepting the offer, she would consider refusing to negotiate on the foreign official's terms.

The principle of rights has these limitations:

1. The justification that individuals are entitled to rights can be used to disguise and manipulate selfish, unjust political claims and interests.
2. Protection of rights can exaggerate certain entitlements in society at the expense of others. Fairness and equity issues may be raised when the rights of an individual or group take precedence over the rights of others. Issues of reverse discrimination, for example, have arisen from this reasoning.
3. The limits of rights come into question. To what extent should practices that may benefit society, but threaten certain rights, be permitted?

Rights and Stakeholder Analysis

The principle of rights is particularly useful in stakeholder analysis when conflicting legal or moral rights of individuals occur or when rights may be violated if certain courses of action are pursued. The following are guidelines for observing this principle:[17]

1. Identify the individuals whose rights may be violated.
2. Determine the legal and moral bases of these individuals' rights. Does the decision violate these rights on such bases?

3. Determine to what extent the action has moral justification from utilitarian or other principles if individual rights may be violated. National crises and emergencies may warrant overriding individual rights for the public good.

Justice: Procedures, Compensation, and Retribution

The principle of *justice* deals with fairness and equality. Here, the moral authority that decides what is right and wrong concerns the fair distribution of opportunities, as well as hardships, to all. The principle of justice also pertains to punishment for wrong done to the undeserving. John Rawls, a contemporary philosopher, offers two principles of fairness that are widely recognized as representative of the principle of justice:[18]

1. Each person has an equal right to the most extensive basic liberties that are compatible with similar liberties for others.
2. Social and economic inequalities are arranged so that they are both (a) reasonably expected to be to everyone's advantage and (b) attached to positions and offices open to all.

The first principle states that all individuals should be treated equally. The second principle states that justice is served when all persons have equal opportunities and advantages (through their positions and offices) to society's opportunities and burdens. Equal opportunity or access to opportunity does not guarantee equal distribution of wealth. Society's disadvantaged may not be justly treated, some critics claim, when only equal opportunity is offered. The principle of justice also addresses the unfair distribution of wealth and the infliction of harm.

Richard DeGeorge identifies four types of justice:[19]

1. *Compensatory justice* concerns compensating someone for a past harm or injustice. For example, affirmative action programs, discussed in Chapter 7, are justified, in part, as compensation for decades of injustice that minorities have suffered.
2. *Retributive justice* means serving punishment to someone who has inflicted harm on another. A criterion for applying this justice principle is: "Does the punishment fit the crime?"
3. *Distributive justice* refers to the fair distribution of benefits and burdens. Have certain stakeholders received an unfair share of costs accompanying a policy or action? Have others unfairly profited from a policy?
4. *Procedural justice* designates fair decision practices, procedures, and agreements among parties. This criterion asks, "Have the rules and processes that govern the distribution of rewards, punishments, benefits, and costs been fair?"

These four types of justice are part of the larger principle of justice. How they are formulated and applied varies with societies and governmental systems.

Following the principle of justice, Louise Simms might ask whether accepting the government official's offer would provide a fair distribution of goods and services to the recipients of the new technological system. Also, are the conditions demanded by the government administrator fair for all parties concerned? If Simms determined that justice would not be served by enabling her company to be awarded the contract without a fair bidding process, she might well recommend that her firm reject the offer.

The obvious practical problems of using the principle of justice include the following: Outside the jurisdiction of the state and its judicial systems, where ethical dilemmas are solved by procedure and law, who decides who is right and who is wrong? Who has the moral authority to punish whom? Can opportunities and burdens be fairly distributed to all when it is not in the interest of those in power to do so?

Even with these shortcomings, the principle of justice adds an essential contribution to the other ethical principles discussed so far. Beyond the utilitarian calculation of moral responsibility based on consequences, and the universalist absolute duty to treat everyone as a means and not an end, and the principle of rights, which values unquestionable claims, the principle of justice forces us to ask how fairly benefits and costs are distributed, regardless of power, position, or wealth.

Rights, Power, and "Transforming Justice"

Justice, rights, and power are really intertwined. Rights plus power equals "transforming justice." T. McMahon states, "While natural rights are the basis for justice, rights cannot be realized nor justice become operative without power."[20] Judges and juries exercise power when two opposing parties, both of whom are "right," seek justice from the courts.

Power generally is defined and exercised through inheritance, authority, contracts, competition, manipulation, and force. Power exercised through manipulation cannot be used to obtain justice legitimately. The steps in exercising "transforming justice" are as follows:

1. Be aware of your rights and power. McMahon states, "It is important to determine what rights and how much legitimate power are necessary to exercise these rights without trampling on other rights. For example, an employer might have the right and the power to fire an insolent employee, but she or he might not have enough to challenge union regulations."[21]

2. Establish legitimate power as a means for obtaining and establishing rights. According to McMahon, "If the legitimacy of transforming justice cannot be established, its exercise may then be reduced to spurious power plays to get what someone wants, rather than a means of fulfilling rights."[22]

3. This interrelationship of rights, justice, and power is particularly helpful in studying stakeholder management relationships. Since stakeholders exercise power to implement their interests, the concept of "rights plus power equals transforming justice" adds value in determining justice (procedural, compensatory, and retributive). The question of justice in complex, competitive situations becomes not only "Whose rights are more right?" but also "By what means and to what end was power exercised?"

Justice and Stakeholder Analysis

In a stakeholder analysis, the principle of justice can be applied by asking the following questions:

1. How equitable will the distribution of benefits and costs, pleasure and pain, and reward and punishment be among stakeholders if you pursue a particular course of action? Would all stakeholders' self-respect be acknowledged?

2. How clearly have the procedures for distributing the costs and benefits of a course of action or policy been defined and communicated? How fair are these procedures to all affected?

3. What provisions can be made to compensate those who will be unfairly affected by the costs of the decision? What provisions can we make to redistribute benefits among those who have been unfairly or overly compensated by the decision?

Virtue Ethics: Character-Based Virtues

Plato and Aristotle are recognized as the founders of virtue ethics, which also has roots in ancient Chinese and Greek philosophy. Virtue ethics emphasizes moral character in contrast to moral rules (deontology) or consequences of actions (consequentialism).[23]

Virtue ethics is grounded in "character traits"—that is:

A disposition which is well entrenched in its possessor, something that, as we say "goes all the way down", unlike a habit such as being a tea-drinker—but the disposition in question, far from being a single track disposition to do honest actions, or even honest actions for certain reasons, is multi-track. It is concerned with many other actions as well, with emotions and emotional reactions, choices, values, desires, perceptions, attitudes, interests, expectations, and sensibilities. To possess a virtue is to be a certain sort of person with a certain complex mindset. (Hence the extreme recklessness of attributing a virtue on the basis of a single action.)[24]

The concepts of virtue ethics derived from ancient Greek philosophy are the following: virtue, practical wisdom, and eudaemonia (or happiness, flourishing, and well-being). Virtue ethics focuses on the type of person we ought to be, not on specific actions that should be taken. It is grounded in good character, motives, and core values. Virtue ethics argue that the possessor of good character is and acts morally, feels good, is happy, and flourishes. Practical wisdom, however, is often required to be virtuous. Adults can be culpable in their intentions and actions by being "thoughtless, insensitive, reckless, impulsive, shortsighted, and by assuming that what suits them will suit everyone instead of taking a more objective viewpoint. They are also, importantly, culpable if their understanding of what is beneficial and harmful is mistaken.

It is part of practical wisdom to know how to secure real benefits effectively; those who have practical wisdom will not make the mistake of concealing the hurtful truth from the person who really needs to know it in the belief that they are benefiting him."[25]

Critiques of virtue ethics include the following major arguments:

First, virtue ethics fails to adequately address dilemmas which arise in applied ethics, such as abortion. For, virtue theory is not designed to offer precise guidelines of obligation. Second, virtue theory cannot correctly assess the occasional tragic actions of virtuous people. . . . Since virtue theory focuses on the general notion of a good person, it has little to say about particular tragic acts. Third, some acts are so intolerable, such as murder, that we must devise a special list of offenses which are prohibited. Virtue theory does not provide such a list. Fourth, character traits change, and unless we stay in practice, we risk losing our proficiency in these areas. This suggests a need for a more character-free way of assessing our conduct. Finally, there is the problem of moral backsliding. Since virtue theory emphasizes long-term characteristics, this runs the risk of overlooking particular lies, or acts of selfishness, on the grounds that such acts are temporary aberrations.[26]

These same criticisms also apply to other ethical principles and schools of thought.

Virtue Ethics and Stakeholder Analysis

Virtue ethics adds an important dimension to rules and consequentialist ethics by contributing a different perspective for understanding and executing stakeholder management. Examining the motives and character of stakeholders can be helpful in discovering underlying motivations of strategies, actions, and outcomes in complex business and corporate transactions. With regard to corporate scandals, virtue ethics can explain some of the motives of several corporate officers' actions that center on greed, extravagant habits, irrational thinking, and egotistical character traits.

Virtue ethics also adds a practical perspective. Beauchamp and Childress state that "a practical consequence of this view is that the education of, for example medical doctors, should include the cultivation of virtues such as compassion, discernment, trustworthiness, integrity, conscientiousness as well as benevolence (desire to help) and nonmalevolence (desire to avoid harm)."[27] These authors also note that "persons of 'good character' can certainly formulate 'bad policy' or make a 'poor choice'—we need to evaluate those policies and choices according to moral principles."

The Common Good

Plato and Aristotle are believed to be the authors of the common good concept. The ethicist John Rawls has developed and redefined the notion of the *common good* as "certain general conditions that are . . . equally to everyone's advantage."[28] The common good has also been defined as "the sum of those conditions of social life which allow social groups and their individual members relatively thorough and ready access to their own fulfillment."[29] The common good includes the broader interdependent institutions, social systems, environments, and services and goods. Examples of the common good include the health care system; legislative and judicial systems; political, economic, and legal systems; and the physical environment. These systems exist at the local, regional, national, and global levels. Individuals, groups, and populations are dependent on these interlocking systems.[30] The common good must be created and maintained in societies. Cooperative and collaborative effort is required. "The common good is a good to which all members of society have access, and from whose enjoyment no one can be easily excluded. All persons, for example, enjoy the benefits of clean air or an unpolluted environment or any of our society's other common goods. In fact, something counts as a common good only to the extent that it is a good to which all have access."[31]

The ethic of the common good suggests that decision makers take into consideration the intent as well as the effects of their actions and decisions on the broader society and the common good of the many. There are four major constraining factors and arguments on the notion of the common good:

1. A unitary notion of the common good is not viable in a pluralistic society. The common good means different things to different people.
2. Relatedly, in an individualistic society, people are rewarded to provide and succeed by themselves. The logic of the common good runs counter in many instances to this individualist cultural orientation.
3. "Free riders" abuse the provision of the common good by taking advantage of the benefits while not contributing to the upkeep of common goods. A critical mass of free riders can and does destroy common goods, such as parts of the environment.
4. Finally, helping create and sustain common goods means unequal sharing of burdens and sacrifices by some groups, since not all groups will exert such efforts. Expecting some groups to support the common good while others will not is unjust and perhaps impractical.

Given these obstacles, the ethic of the common good calls us to share in a common vision of a society that is beneficial for all members while respecting individual differences. Using this ethic in our decision making also calls us to take goals and actions that include others besides ourselves and our own interest into account. Such a logic is not just partly altruistic but, in many circumstances, practical. We thrive when we breathe clean air, drink clean water, and can trust that the food we eat is not contaminated. This logic may also apply to business decisions that involve our customers and employees, as well as our neighbors, family members, and ourselves as members of a society as well as an organization. By using this principle, Louise would consider what good would be gained from actions taken not only for the professionals involved in her company and the client's company, but also for the host society.

She would have to evaluate ethical principles that serve the common good of the people in that country.

Ethical Relativism: A Self-Interest Approach

Ethical relativism holds that no universal standards or rules can be used to guide or evaluate the morality of an act. This view argues that people set their own moral standards for judging their actions. Only the individual's self-interest and values are relevant for judging that person's behavior. This form of relativism is also referred to as *naive relativism*.

Individuals, professionals, and organizations using this approach can consider finding out what the industry and/or professional standard or norm is with regard to an issue. Another suggestion would be to inflict no undue harm with a course of action taken.[32]

If Louise Simms were to adopt the principle of ethical relativism for her decision making, she might choose to accept the government official's offer to promote her own standing in his firm. She might reason that her self-interest would be served best by making any deal that would push her career ahead. But Simms could also use ethical relativism to justify her rejection of the offer. She might say that any possible form of such a questionable negotiation is against her beliefs. The point behind this principle is that individual standards are the basis of moral authority.

The logic of ethical relativism also extends to cultures. *Cultural relativism* argues that "when in Rome, do as the Romans do." What is morally right for one society or culture may be wrong for another. Moral standards vary from one culture to another. Cultural relativists would argue that firms and business professionals doing business in a country are obliged to follow that country's laws and moral codes. A criterion that relativists would use to justify their actions would be: "Are my beliefs, moral standards, and customs satisfied with this action or outcome?"

The benefit of ethical and cultural relativism is that they recognize the distinction between individual and social values and customs. These views take seriously the different belief systems of individuals and societies. Social norms and mores are seen in a cultural context.

However, relativism can lead to several problems. (It can be argued that this perspective is actually not ethical.) First, these views imply an underlying laziness.[33] Individuals who justify their morality only from their personal beliefs, without taking into consideration other ethical principles, may use the logic of relativism as an excuse for not having or developing moral standards. Second, this view contradicts everyday experience. Moral reasoning is developed from conversation, interaction, and argument. What I believe or perceive as "facts" in a situation may or may not be accurate. How can I validate or disprove my ethical reasoning if I do not communicate, share, and remain open to changing my own standards?

Ethical relativism can create absolutists—individuals who claim their moral standards are right regardless of whether others view the standards as right or wrong. For example, what if my beliefs conflict with yours? Whose relativism is right, then? Who decides and on what grounds? In practice, ethical relativism does not effectively or efficiently solve complicated conflicts that involve many parties because these situations require tolerating doubts and permitting our observations and beliefs to be informed.

Cultural relativism embodies the same problems as ethical relativism. Although the values and moral customs of all cultures should be observed and respected, especially because business professionals are increasingly operating across national boundaries, we must not be blindly absolute or divorce ourselves from rigorous moral reasoning or laws aimed at protecting individual rights and justice. For example, R. Edward Freeman and Daniel Gilbert Jr. ask, "Must American managers in Saudi Arabia treat women as the Saudis treat them? Should Saudis in the U.S. treat women as they do in Saudi Arabia? Must American managers in South Africa [during the apartheid years] treat blacks as white South Africans treat them? Must white South Africans treat blacks in the United States as U.S. managers treat them? Must Saudis in the United States treat women as U.S. managers treat them?"[34] They continue, "It makes sense to question whether the norms of the Nazi society were in fact morally correct."[35] Using rigorous ethical reasoning to solve moral dilemmas is important across cultures.

However, this does not suggest that flexibility, sensitivity, and awareness of individual and cultural moral differences are not necessary. It does mean that upholding principles of rights, justice, and freedom in some situations may conflict with the other person's or culture's belief system. Depending on the actions taken and decisions made based on a person's moral standards, a price may be paid for maintaining them. Often, negotiation agreements and understanding can be reached without overt conflict when different ethical principles or cultural standards clash.

Finally, it could be argued that cultural relativism does provide an argument against cultural imperialism. Why should American laws, customs, and values that are embedded in a U.S. firm's policies be enforced in another country that has differing laws and values regarding the activities in question?

Ethical Relativism and Stakeholder Analysis

When considering the perspectives of relativism in a stakeholder analysis, ask the following questions:

1. What are the major moral beliefs and principles at issue for each stakeholder affected by this decision?
2. What are my moral beliefs and principles in this decision?
3. To what extent will my ethical principles clash if a particular course of action is taken? Why?
4. How can conflicting moral beliefs be avoided or resolved in seeking a desirable outcome?
5. What is the industry standard and norm with regard to this issue(s)?

A now-classic case of ethical relativism is Samuel Waksal, who in 2002 resigned as chief executive officer (CEO) of ImClone, a manufacturer of drugs for cancer and other treatment therapies. He was later arrested and indicted for bank fraud, securities fraud, and perjury. He pleaded guilty to all of the counts in the indictment. (He also implicated his daughter and father in his insider-trading schemes.) In addition, he pleaded guilty to tax evasion for not paying New York State sales tax on pieces of art that he had purchased. He was sentenced to 87 months in prison and was ordered to pay a $3 million fine and $1.2 million in restitution to the New York State Sales Tax Commission. He began serving his prison sentence on July 23, 2003. Martha Stewart, an ImClone stockholder, was sentenced to five months in prison and five months of house arrest for using insider-trading knowledge to sell shares of ImClone stock. She was also ordered to pay $30,000 in fines and court fees. Her broker, Peter Bacanovic, was given the same sentence but a lower fine of $4,000. Bacanovic's assistant, Douglas Faneuil, was spared prison time and fined $2,000.[36] When asked in an interview how he got into this "mess," Waksal said, "It certainly wasn't because I thought about it carefully ahead of time. I think I was arrogant enough at the time to believe that I could cut corners, not care about details that were going on, and not think about consequences."[37]

Immoral, Amoral, and Moral Management

In addition to the classic ethical principles, there are three broad, straight moral orientations that can be applied to individuals, groups, and organizations: immorality, amorality, and morality.

Immoral management of employees, stakeholders, and constituencies signifies a minimally ethical or unethical approach, such as laying off employees without fair notice or compensation, offering upper-level management undeserved salary increases and perks, and giving "golden parachutes" (attractive payments or settlement contracts to selected employees) when a change in company control is negotiated. (Such payments are often made at the expense of shareholders' dividends without their knowledge or consent.) Managing immorally means intentionally going against the ethical principles of justice and fair and equitable treatment of other stakeholders.

Amoral management happens when owners, supervisors, and managers treat shareholders, outside stakeholders, and employees without concern or care for the consequences of their actions. No willful wrong may be intended, but neither is thought given to moral behavior or outcomes. Minimal action is taken while setting policies that are solely profit-oriented, production-centered, or short-term. Employees and other stakeholders are viewed as instruments for executing the economic interests of the firm. Strategies, control systems, leadership style, and interactions in such organizations also reflect an amoral, minimalist approach toward stakeholders. Nevertheless, the harmful consequences of amoral actions are real for the persons affected.

Moral management places value on fair treatment of shareholders, employees, customers, and other stakeholders. Ethics codes are established, communicated, and included in training; employee rights are built into visible policies that are enforced; and employees and other stakeholders are treated with respect and trust. The firm's corporate strategy, control and incentive systems, leadership style, and interactions reflect a morally managed organization. Moral management is the preferred mode of acting toward stakeholders since respect and fairness are considered in decisions.

It is helpful to consider these three orientations while observing managers, owners, employees, and coworkers. Have you seen amoral policies, procedures, and decisions in organizations? The next section summarizes four social responsibility roles that business executives view as moral for decision makers. The model presented complements the five ethical principles by providing a broad framework for describing ethical orientations toward business decisions. You can also use the following framework to characterize your own moral and responsible roles, those of your boss and colleagues, and even those of contemporary international figures in government or business.

POINT/COUNTERPOINT

Instructions: Each student must select *either* Point or CounterPoint arguments (no in-between choices), defend that choice, and state why you believe either one or the other. In this particular Point/CounterPoint, select one or more of the ethical principles along with your "ethical reasoning" to defend/explain your choice. Be ready to argue your choice as the instructor directs. Afterward, the class is debriefed, and there is further discussion as a class.

POINT: The "common good" is a nice concept and goal, but in real time, it is mostly idealistic. I would not disagree with it, but truthfully, in my everyday life and in general, I do what I have to do and what I can do to make ends meet. Also, "It's who you know, not just what you know" and luck that really count. "No harm, no foul." You live life the way you want, and so will I.

COUNTERPOINT: Without believing and living the common good, as much as I can, I believe that human life wouldn't be meaningful. Look what happens when narcissism and "dog eat dog" reasoning happens. So I strive to live toward the common good and have it live inside me, otherwise I would be angry and down a lot.

2.3 Four Social Responsibility Roles

What social obligations do businesses and their executives have toward their stockholders and society? The traditional view is that the responsibility of corporate owners and managers is to serve only, or primarily, their stockholders' interests. This view has been challenged and modified—but not abandoned—since the turn of this century. The debate continues about whether the roles of businesses and managers include serving social stakeholders along with economic stockholders. Because of changing demographic and educational characteristics of the workplace and the advent of laws, policies, and procedures

Figure 2.2

Four Social Responsibility Modes and Roles

		Stockholder Model	Stakeholder Model
		ORIENTATIONS	
MOTIVES	Self-Interest	1 Productivism	2 Progressivism
	Moral Duty	3 Philanthropy	4 Ethical Idealism

Source: Buono, Anthony F., and Nicholas, Lawrence. (1990). Stockholder and stakeholder interpretations of business' social role. In Hoffman, Michael, and Moore, Jennifer (eds.), *Business ethics: Readings and cases in corporate morality*, 2nd ed., 172. New York: McGraw-Hill. Reproduced with the permission of Anthony F. Buono.

that recognize greater awareness of employee and other stakeholders' rights, distinctions have been made about the responsibility of the business to its employees and to the larger society.

Four ethical interpretations of the social roles and modes of decision making are discussed and illustrated in Figure 2.2. The four social responsibility modes reflect business roles toward stockholders and a wider audience of stakeholders.[38]

Notice the two distinct social responsibility orientations of businesses and managers toward society: the *stockholder model* (the primary responsibility of the corporation to its economic stockholders) and the *stakeholder model* (the responsibility of the corporation to its social stakeholders outside the corporation). The two sets of motives underlying these two orientations are "self-interest" and "moral duty."

The stockholder self-interest (cell 1 in Figure 2.2) and moral duty (cell 3) orientations are discussed first, followed by the stakeholder self-interest (cell 2) and moral duty (cell 4) orientations. The two stockholder orientations are productivism and philanthropy.

Productivists (who hold a free-market ethic) view the corporation's social responsibility in terms of rational self-interest and the direct fulfillment of stockholder interests. The free market values the basis of rewards and punishments in the organization. This ethic drives internal and external vision, mission, values, policies, and decisions—including salaries, promotion, and demotions. Productivists believe the major—and, some would say, only—mission of business is to obtain profit. The free market is the best guarantee of moral corporate conduct in this view. Supply-side economists as productivists, for example, argue that the private sector is the vehicle for social improvement. Tax reduction and economic incentives that boost private industry are policies that productivists advocate as socially responsible. Former president George W. Bush's initial response to the subprime-lending crisis exemplifies a productivist approach; as the BBC News reported, Bush's efforts included "reform tax laws to help troubled borrowers refinance their loans, but the President added that it was not the government's job to bail out speculators."[39] President Bush eased that position as the U.S. and global economies approached a near collapse. U.S. presidents must make policy decisions that balance all these responsibility modes, while being very concerned about stakeholders, many of whom are the public citizenry.

Although all the ethical principles discussed earlier could be used by organizational leaders within each of these responsibility modes, productivists might find themselves advocating the use of *negative rights* to promote policies that protect shareholders' interests over positive rights that would cost taxpayers and use government resources to assist those more economically dependent on government services—who, productivists would argue, add an economic burden to the free-market system.

A free-market-based ethic is widely used by owners and managers who must make tough workplace decisions: (1) How many and which people are to be laid off because of a market downturn and significantly lower profits? (2) What constitutes fair notice and compensation to employees who are to be terminated from employment? (3) How can employees be disciplined fairly in situations in which people's rights have been violated? A company is entitled to private property rights and responsibilities to shareholders. Robert Nozick, a libertarian philosopher, is an advocate of a market-based ethic. He makes a case for a market-based principle of justice and entitlement in his classic book *Anarchy, State, and Utopia*. Opponents of the market-based ethic argue that the rights of less advantaged people also count; that property rights are not absolute in all situations; that there are times when the state can be justified in protecting the rights of others in disputes against property owners; and that the distribution of justice depends on the conditions of a situation— if war, illegal entry, fraud, or theft occur, some form of redistribution of wealth can be justified.[40]

Philanthropists, who also have a stockholder view of the corporation, hold that social responsibility is justified in terms of a moral duty toward helping less advantaged members of society through organized, tax-deductible charity and *stewardship*. Proponents of this view believe that the primary social role of the corporation is still to obtain profits. However, moral duty drives their motives instead of self-interest (the productivist view). Advocates of this view are stewards and believe that those who have wealth ought to share it with disadvantaged people. As stockholder stewards, philanthropists share profits primarily through their tax-deductible activities. Warren Buffett gave 85 percent of his wealth, estimated over $44 billion, to philanthropic causes, including the Bill and Melinda Gates Foundation. The remainder will be given to foundations operated by his children.[41]

Philanthropists might argue from principles of utilitarianism, duty, and universalism to justify their giving. Corporate philanthropy, generally speaking, is based primarily on the profit motive. Corporate philanthropists' sense of stewardship is contingent on their available and calculated use of wealth to help the less economically advantaged.

Progressivism and *ethical idealism* are the two social responsibility modes in the stakeholder model, the other dominant orientation. *Progressivists* believe corporate behavior is motivated by self-interest, but they also hold that corporations should take a broader view of responsibility toward social change. Pope John Paul II and, some would argue, Pope Francis might be considered as ethical idealists. Enlightened self-interest is a value that also characterizes progressivists. The renowned theologian Reinhold Niebuhr is a modern example of a progressivist who argued for the involvement of the church in politics to bring about reasoned, orderly reform. He also worked with unions and other groups to improve workers' job conditions and wages. Progressivists support policies such as affirmative action, environmental protection, employee stock option programs (ESOPs), and energy conservation. Is the anti-corruption Russian activist Alexei Navalny an example of ethical idealism? He was poisoned with a Novichok nerve agent—allegedly, but not proven, by state officials because of his vocal dissent against the government. He was flown to and hospitalized in Germany, where he almost died. He then returned to Russia and called for more open protests against the government. At the time of this writing, his physical condition has deteriorated in prison, and his fate is uncertain.

Finally, *ethical idealists* believe that social responsibility is justified when corporate behavior directly supports stakeholder interests. Ethical idealists, as exemplified by American activist Ralph Nader earlier in his career, hold that, to be fully responsible, corporate activity should help transform businesses into institutions where workers can realize their full potential. Employee ownership, cooperatives, and community-owned service industries are examples of the type of corporate transformation that ethical idealists advocate. The boundaries between business and society are fluid for ethical idealists. Corporate profits are to be shared for humanitarian purposes—to help bring about a more humane society.

Of course, as noted previously, a spectrum of beliefs exists for each of these four modes. For example, ethical idealists profess different visions regarding the obligations of business to society. Progressivists and ethical idealists generally tend to base their moral authority on legal and moral rights, justice, and universalism. Organizational leaders and professionals are obviously concerned with the operational solvency and even profitability (especially for-profit firms) of their companies. Still, they tend to believe that stakeholder interests and welfare are necessary parts of the economic system's effectiveness and success.

Which orientation best characterizes your current beliefs of business responsibility toward society: productivism, philanthropy, progressivism, or ethical idealism? Keep in mind the ethical decision frameworks presented above and also your ethical assessment scores, as we turn to the different levels of ethical decision making.

POINT/COUNTERPOINT

Black Lives Matter versus All Lives Matter

Instructions: Each student in this exercise must select *either* Point or Counter-Point arguments (no in-between choices), defend that choice, and state why you believe either one or the other. In this particular Point/CounterPoint, select one or more than one of the ethical principles along with your "ethical reasoning" to defend/explain your choice. Be ready to argue your choice as the instructor directs. Afterward, the class is debriefed, and there is a further discussion as a class.

POINT: Yes, Black Lives Matter is distinctive and should be separate from "All Lives Matter" as a slogan.

"Black Lives Matter" doesn't mean no other lives matter. Black Lives Matter (BLM) is an anthem, a slogan, a hashtag, and a straightforward statement of fact. While it is not a new movement, the message is central to the nationwide protests that happened in 2020. BLM speaks out against the police brutality and systemic racism that caused the deaths of George Floyd, Ahmaud Arbery, Tony McDade, and Breonna Taylor, as well as the thousands of violent incidents that happen to Black people that aren't recorded, aren't reported, or aren't afforded the outrage they deserve. At its most basic level, it calls for a shift in the statistics that Black people are twice as likely to be killed by a police officer while unarmed, compared to a white individual. "About 1 in every 1,000 black men can expect to be killed by police. Risk of being killed by police peaks between the ages of 20 y and 35 y for men and women and for all racial and ethnic groups."[42] "All lives won't matter until black lives do." "If you break your arm and go to the doctor, and the doctor says 'all your bones matter, not just your arm.' You're gonna look at them [like they're] stupid because yes, all your bones matter but they are fine, your arm needs attention. . . ."[43]

"BLM is that arm, saying all lives matter is redundant."

COUNTERPOINT: No, it shouldn't be a separate slogan.

To separate out any particular class or group of people is also a form of racism whether or not it is intended that way or not. Why not just say "Black lives matter, too." Of course Black lives matter. You don't have to be a white supremacist, a bigot, or an insensitive person to say "All lives matter" and mean Black lives matter too. Why must I or we be blamed, pay, and be responsible for what white and other colonizers did hundreds of years ago? Also, if I believe Black lives matter too, why must I be identified and grouped with those law enforcement officers who mistreat and brutalize, even kill innocent Black people (or any people)? It isn't fair and sends a message that further enflames the racist, segregationist individuals and national (and international) terrorists among us. No one is really more equal than anybody else. Justice is blind. No one is above the law.

■ 2.4 Levels of Ethical Reasoning and Moral Decision Making

Understanding the nature of an ethical dilemma, the source and who is affected are important steps toward responding. In this section, three dimensions of ethical dilemmas taken from Kohlberg's work are described in order to guard against "short-sightedness" when experiencing or analyzing an ethical dilemma.

Many ethical issues and dilemmas result from *pressures* that are experienced at (1) the personal level; (2) the company or organizational level; (3) the industry level; and (4) the societal, international, and global levels.

Personal Level

As the opening case of this chapter illustrates, a person experiences pressures from conflicting demands or circumstances that require a decision. Ethical dilemmas at this level can occur as a result of workplace pressures or from personal circumstances or motivations not related to work. Pressures on Louise stem from a supervisor's assignment, the consequences of which could affect others in the organization and possibly in the host culture. Is Louise being lied to? Is she being pressured to risk her integrity and even job or career by accepting this assignment? Note that what begins as an individual or personal dilemma can escalate into organizational and other levels, as is possible with Louise if the issues are not resolved.

Ethical dilemmas that do not start at the personal level can and do involve and affect individuals along the way. The personal focus on ethical decision making also involves a broader inquiry into how individual personalities, traits, maturity, and styles affect such decisions. For example, narcissism and cynicism are individual differences that influence self-perceptions and perceptions of others. Researchers have shown that these two traits in particular had a negative effect on aspects of ethical decision making, whereas basic personality characteristics, such as conscientiousness and agreeableness, did not have the same effect.[44] It sounds like common sense, but studies confirm— and sometimes dispute—what we think we already know. Similarly, negative affectivity and agreeableness matter, in that these personality traits moderate the relationship between fairness perceptions and retaliation in the workplace.[45] Others have found that moral personality and the centrality of moral identity were associated with a more principled (versus expedient) ethical ideology. That is, moral personality characteristics affect organizational citizenship behavior and the propensity to morally disengage.[46] Ethical personality traits discussed here—agreeableness, conscientiousness, and a principled approach, as contrasted with negativity, narcissism, and cynicism—are associated with ethical activities in the workplace. These studies confirm that the principle of virtue ethics matters in organizational settings.

Moral maturity also matters. Kohlberg's three levels of moral development (which encompass six stages) provide a guide for observing our own and a person's level of moral maturity in everyday life and organizational settings. Whether, and to what extent, ethical education and training contribute to moral development in later years is not known. Most individuals in Kohlberg's 20–year study (limited to males) reached the fourth and fifth stages by adulthood. Only a few attained the sixth stage. While this study has its critics, it remains a widely used and useful concept for discussing moral development and responsibility.

Level 1: Preconventional Level (Self-Orientation)

- Stage 1: Punishment avoidance: avoiding punishment by not breaking rules. The person has little awareness of others' needs.
- Stage 2: Reward seeking: acting to receive rewards for oneself. The person has awareness of others' needs but not of right and wrong as abstract concepts.

Level 2: Conventional Level (Others Orientation)

- Stage 3: Good person: acting "right" to be a "good person" and to be accepted by family and friends, not to fulfill any moral ideal.
- Stage 4: Law and order: acting "right" to comply with law and order and norms in societal institutions.

Level 3: Postconventional, Autonomous, or Principles Level (Universal, Humankind Orientation)

- Stage 5: Social contract: acting "right" to reach consensus by due process and agreement. The person is aware of relativity of values and tolerates differing views.
- Stage 6: Universal ethical principles: acting "right" according to universal, abstract principles of justice and rights. The person reasons and uses conscience and moral rules to guide actions.

Interestingly, one study of 219 corporate managers working in different companies found that managers typically reason at moral stage 3 or 4, which, the author notes, is "similar to most adults in the Western, urban societies or other business managers."[47] Managers in large to medium-size firms reasoned at lower moral stages than managers who were self-employed or who worked at small firms. Reasons offered for this difference in moral reasoning include that larger firms have more complex bureaucracies and layers of structure, more standard policies and procedures, and exert more rule-based control over employees. Employees tend to get isolated from other parts of the organization and feel less involved in the central decision-making process. On the other hand, self-employed professionals and managers in smaller firms tend to interact with people throughout the firm and with external stakeholders. Involvement with and vulnerability to other stakeholders may cause these managers to adhere to social laws more closely and to reason at stage 4.

The same study also found that managers reasoned at a higher level when responding to a moral dilemma in which the main character was not a corporate employee. It could be that managers reason at a higher level when moral problems are not associated with the corporation. The author suggests that the influence of the corporation tends to restrict the manager to lower moral reasoning stages. Or it could be that the nature of the moral dilemma may affect the way managers reason (i.e., some dilemmas may be appropriately addressed with stage 3 or 4 reasoning while other dilemmas may require stage 5 logic).

Stephen Covey's "Moral Continuum" offers a developmental model for progressing from a basic state of dependence to independence and then interdependence using the "seven habits of highly effective people," which can be learned and practiced. The seven habits are (1) Be Proactive, (2) Begin with the End in Mind, (3) Put First Things First, (4) Think Win–Win, (5) Seek First to Understand, then to Be Understood, (6) Synergize, and (7) Sharpen the Saw.

Breaking Out of Dependency to Become Independent

Breaking out of dependency (less morally mature) to become more interdependent (highest level of moral maturity) is a process that involves the heart, mind, and body. According to Covey's Moral Continuum, once the first three habits are developed, a person builds character, and a "Private Victory" is achieved. Developing and following the three habits signals a "Public Victory" on this moral journey. The first habit, "Be Proactive," embodies the "Principle of Personal Vision," or taking control and being responsible for one's own life while acting with integrity. This means that a person also begins to see how others see them, keeping commitments, and deciding to be oneself by developing a plan.[48] The second habit, "Begin with the End in Mind," embodies the "Principle of Personal Leadership" and involves envisioning where one wishes to go in their life, answering what being successful means, and addressing what is really important. During this process, a person "rescripts" their internalized messages and develops their own vision and goals, which entails them seeing the "big picture" around them and developing a "Personal Mission Statement" grounded in principles that matter most to them. The third habit, "Put First Things First," embodies the principle of "Personal Management," which involves implementing concrete plans only after one believes that they will succeed. This habit helps a person refuse distractions and be able to delegate tasks to others to help the person reach their goals. Once these first three habits are achieved, a "Private Victory" from dependence has been accomplished.

From Independence to Interdependence

"Think Win–Win," the fourth habit, is based on the "Principle of Interpersonal Leadership," which involves building relationships through cooperation. A sense of integrity and maturity and an abundance mentality are developed with this habit. The fifth habit, "Seek First to Understand, then to Be Understood," embodies the principle of "Emphatic Communication, which involves communicating as an emphatic listener. Nonjudgmental listening builds goodwill in relationships. The sixth habit, "Synergize," embodies the "Principle of Creative Cooperation" and builds on the previous habits to form relationships that increase the work of two people beyond each individual's maximum efficiency. Synergy makes $1 + 1 = 3$. That is, the results of two individuals working together is to equal the output of three or more individuals working independently. Flexibility, openness, and goodwill are part of this habit. Finally, the seventh habit, "Sharpen the Saw," which embodies the "Principle of Balanced Renewal," is based on the need for continuous self-renewal that requires physical, mental, and emotional effort to achieve life balance. Moral maturity is an ongoing process, not a destination.

With regard to this chapter's opening case and Louise's dilemma, the logic of the Moral Continuum, briefly summarized here, offers an opportunity of reflection for her to consider her personal values, mission, and character in deciding what course of action to follow or not to follow. Ethical decision making in serious dilemmas, or even those that may at first seem trivial, generally involves one's whole self.

Organizational Level

Firms that engage in questionable practices and activities face possible dilemmas with their stakeholders and/or stockholders. Studies show that when corporate values are dominated by financial profits, employees' ethical standards are diminished in their workplace decisions, as compared to corporations that value and reward integrity and good business practices.[49] Former Wells Fargo executives and sales professionals valued profitability above responsibility and accountability to customers, and they almost destroyed the company in the process (see Case 12 in this book).[50]

Or take the example of *Wal-Mart Stores, Inc. v. Dukes.* "The largest sexual discrimination lawsuit in U.S. history was brought against Wal-Mart when a federal appeals court approved class-action status for seven women who claim the retailer was biased in pay and promotions."[51] Plaintiffs in that case estimated that 1.5 million women who had worked for Wal-Mart in the U.S. stores since 1998 were eligible to join that suit. Wal-Mart's reputation and image will not be easily repaired from this and other lawsuits that have recently been brought against the largest retailer. Going forward, Wal-Mart's officers must decide whether or not this type of possible discrimination is worth the legal, social, and media fallout for the company and its stakeholders.

Industry Level

Company officers, managers, and professionals working within and/or across industries may contribute to, and be influenced and affected by, specific business practices in an industry. A recent example of an unethical, illegal industry-wide business practice was Facebook's regulatory troubles in the United States when the Federal Trade Commission (FTC) fined the company $5 billion for deceiving users because of Facebook's inability to protect users' personal information. In that case, an investigation prompted by the Cambridge Analytica data scandal revealed Facebook's irresponsibility. "It was the largest fine ever handed out for violating consumers' privacy and nearly 20 times more than the largest penalty related to data privacy or security ever imposed worldwide."[52]

In this chapter's opening case, Louise could inquire about the business practice in which she is being pressured to engage (i.e., contract negotiations in a foreign country). She can explore whether or not such practices are legal in her company and industry. Even if she finds that such practices are used but are questionable ethically and legally, she will need to decide whether or not she wishes to assume personal liability and the consequences of taking such actions.

Societal, International, and Global Levels

Industry, organizational, professional, and personal ethics may clash at the societal, global, and international levels. For example, although tipping and paying money to government and other business officials may meet local customary practices in some countries, such offerings may also be illegal bribes in other countries (like the United States and Europe). Chapter 8 addresses these types of issues.

In this chapter's opening case, Louise is walking a tightrope in her decision. She needs to consult the Foreign Corrupt Practices Act (discussed in Chapter 8) to determine whether her superiors are asking her personally and professionally—as a representative of her firm—to act illegally. She might also seek advice from someone in her company or in the country regarding cultural norms and business practices.

■ 2.5 Identifying and Addressing Ethical Dilemmas

An ethical dilemma is a problem or issue that confronts a person, group, or organization and that requires a decision or choice among competing claims and interests, all of which may be unethical (i.e., against all parties' principles). Decision choices presented by an ethical dilemma usually involve solutions that do not satisfy all stakeholders. In some situations, there may be a resolution to an ethical dilemma that is the "right" thing to do, although none of the stakeholders' material interests benefit. Ethical dilemmas that involve many stakeholders require a reasoning process that clearly states the dilemma objectively and then proceeds to articulate the issues and different solution alternatives.

Although ethical reasoning has been defined, in part, by acting on "principled thinking," it is also true that moral creativity, negotiating skills, and knowing your own values also help solve tough "real world" situations. Should Louise Simms move to close the lucrative deal or not? Is the official offering her a bribe? What other personal, as well as professional, obligations would she be committing herself to if she accepted? Is the official's request legal? Is it ethical? Is this a setup? If so, who is setting her up? Would Louise be held individually responsible if something went wrong? Who is going to protect her if legal complications arise? How is she supposed to negotiate such a deal? What message is she sending about herself as well as her company? What if she is asked to return and work with these people if the contract is signed? What does Louise stand to win and lose if she does or does not accept the official's offer?

So, what *should* Louise do to act morally responsible in this situation? Is she acting only on behalf of her company or also from her own integrity and beliefs? These are the kinds of questions and issues this chapter raises. No easy answers may exist, but understanding the ethical principles discussed at the outset, sharing ethical dilemmas and outcomes, discussing ethical experiences in depth, and using role playing to analyze situations can help you identify, think, and feel through the issues that underlie ethical dilemmas.

The Louise Simms scenario may be complicated by the international context. This is a good starting point for a chapter on ethics, because business transactions now increasingly involve international players and different "rules of engagement." Chapter 8, on the global environment and stakeholder issues peculiar to multinational corporations, offers additional guidelines for solving dilemmas in international contexts. Deciding what is right and wrong in an international context also involves understanding laws and customs and the level of economic, social, and technological development of the nation or region involved. For example, do European and U.S. standards of doing business in other countries involve certain biases? Would these biases result in consequences that are beneficial or harmful to those in the local culture? On the other hand, we should not easily accept stereotypical descriptions of how to do business by means of what may be considered "local customs." The remainder of this chapter has additional information and ethical assessments and insights on identifying and resolving the moral dimensions of dilemmas in the workplace and in organizational and personal roles and relationships. Ethical Insight 2.2 illustrates a method to describe an ethical dilemma and analyze it using ethical concepts from this chapter.

Ethical Insight 2.2

Your Ethical Dilemma

Complete the following steps:

Step 1: Describe an ethical dilemma that you recently experienced. Be detailed. What was the situation? Whom did it involve? Why? What happened? What did you do? What did you not do? Describe your reasoning process in taking or not taking action. What did others do to you? What was the result?

Step 2: Read the descriptions of relativism, utilitarianism, universalism, rights, justice, and moral decision making in this chapter. Explain which principle best describes your reasoning and your action(s) in the dilemma you presented in step 1.

Step 3: Were you conscious that you were reasoning and acting on these (or other) ethical principles before, during, and after your ethical dilemma? Explain.

Step 4: After reading this chapter, would you have acted any differently in your dilemma than you did? Explain.

Moral Creativity

Moral creativity or imagination relates to recognizing the complexity of some ethical dilemmas that involve interlocking, conflicting interests, and relationships from the point of view of the person, group, and/or organization facing a decision to be made. Creativity is required to gain perspective among the different stakeholders and their interests to sort out and evaluate harmful effects among different alternative actions.[53] What begins as a business–as–usual decision can evolve into a dilemma or even a "defining moment" in one's life.[54] According to Joseph Badaracco at Harvard University:

> An ethical decision typically involves choosing between two options: one we know to be right and another we know to be wrong. A defining moment, however, challenges us in a deeper way by asking us to choose between two or more ideals in which we deeply believe. Such challenges rarely have a "correct" response. Rather, they are situations created by circumstance that ask us to step forward and, in the words of the American philosopher John Dewey, "form, reveal, and test" ourselves. We form our character when we commit to irreversible courses of action that shape our personal and professional identities. We reveal something new about us to ourselves and others because defining moments uncover something that had been hidden or crystallize something that had been only partially known. And we test ourselves because we discover whether we will live up to our personal ideals or only pay them lip service.[55]

Badaracco offers three key questions with creative probes for individuals, work group managers, and company executives to address before acting in a "defining moment." For individuals, the key question is "Who am I?" This question requires individuals to:

1. Identify their feelings and intuitions that are emphasized in the situation.
2. Identify their deepest values in conflict brought up by the situation.
3. Identify the best course of action to understand the right thing to do.[56]

Work group managers can ask, "Who are we?" They can also address these three dimensions of the team and situation:

1. What strong views and understanding of the situation do others have?
2. Which position or view would most likely win over others?
3. Can I coordinate a process that will reveal the values I care about in this organization?

Company executives can ask, "Who is the company?" Three questions they can consider are:

1. Have I strengthened my position and the organization to the best of my ability?
2. Have I considered my organization's role vis-à-vis society and shareholders boldly and creatively?
3. How can I transform my vision into action, combining creativity, courage, and shrewdness?

CEOs and professionals could ask the three sets of questions to help articulate a morally creative response to ethical dilemmas and "defining moments." What might have happened differently had Bernard Madoff, who executed an unprecedented Ponzi scheme fraud that lasted over decades and defrauded customers of $20 billion, sat down, looked in the mirror, and reflected on these questions? Or what could have happened to Enron's Jeffrey Skilling and Ken Lay, or Tyco's Dennis Kozlowski, or Gary Winnick at Global Crossing?

Ethical Dilemma Problem Solving

A range of decision-making resources can help you evaluate moral possibilities and insights when resolving ethical dilemmas. Change begins with having an awareness that helps build confidence by perceiving dilemmas before they are played out and assists you in negotiating solutions with a moral dimension.

12 Questions to Get Started

A first step in addressing ethical dilemmas is to identify the problem. This is particularly necessary for a stakeholder approach because the problems depend on who the stakeholders are and what their stakes entail. Before specific ethical principles are discussed, let's begin by considering important decision criteria for ethical reasoning. How would you apply the criteria to Louise Simms's situation?

To start, here are 12 questions, developed by Laura Nash,[57] to ask yourself during the decision-making period:

1. Have you defined the problem accurately?
2. How would you define the problem if you stood on the other side of the fence?
3. How did the situation occur?
4. To whom and to what do you give your loyalty as a person and as a member of the corporation?
5. What is your intention in making this decision?
6. How does this intention compare with the probable results?
7. Who could your decision injure?
8. Can you discuss the problem with the affected parties before you make your decision?
9. Are you confident that your decision will be valid over a long period?
10. Could you disclose, without qualms, your decision?
11. What is the symbolic potential of your action if understood? If misunderstood?
12. Under what conditions would you allow exceptions?

The above questions can help individuals openly discuss the responsibilities necessary to solve ethical problems. Sharing these questions can facilitate group discussions, build consensus around shared points, serve as an information source, uncover ethical inconsistencies in a company's values, help a CEO see how senior managers think, and increase the nature and range of choices. The discussion process is cathartic.

To return briefly to the opening case, if Louise Simms considered the first question, she might, for example, define the problem she faces from different perspectives (as discussed in Chapter 1). At the *organizational level*, her firm stands to win a sizable contract if she accepts the government official's conditions. Yet her firm's reputation could be jeopardized in the United States if this deal turned out to be a scandal. At the *societal level*, the issues are complicated. In this Middle Eastern country, this type of bargaining might be acceptable. In the United States, however, Louise could have problems with the Foreign Corrupt Practices Act. At the *individual level*, she must decide if her conscience can tolerate the actions and consequences this deal involves. As a woman, she may be at risk because advances were made toward her. Her self-esteem and integrity have also been damaged. She must consider the costs and benefits that she will incur from her company if she decides to accept or reject this assignment. As you can see, these questions can help Louise clarify her goal of making a decision and determine the price she is willing to pay for that decision.

■ 2.6 Individual Ethical Decision-Making Styles

Stanley Krolick defined four styles of ethical decision making: (1) individualism, (2) altruism, (3) pragmatism, and (4) idealism.[58] These four styles are summarized here to complement the social responsibility modes, ethical principles, and moral maturity stages discussed above. Caution must be used when considering any of these schemes to avoid stereotyping. These categories are guides—not prescriptions—for further reflection, discussion, and study.

Individualists are driven by natural reason, personal survival, and preservation. The self is the source and justification of all actions and decisions. Individualists believe that "if I don't take care of my own needs, I will never be able to address the concerns of others."[59] The moral authority of individualists is their own reasoning process, based on self-interest. Individualism is related to the principle of naive ethical relativism and to productivism.

Altruists are concerned primarily with other people. Altruists relinquish their own personal security for the good of others. They would, as an extreme, like to ensure the future of the human race. The altruist's moral authority and motivation is to produce the greatest good for the largest number of people. Unlike utilitarians, altruists would not diligently calculate and measure costs and benefits. Providing benefits is their major concern. Altruists justify their actions by upholding the integrity of the community. They enter relationships from a desire to contribute to the common good and to humankind. Altruists are akin to universalists and philanthropists.

Pragmatists are concerned primarily with the situation at hand, not with the self or the other. The pragmatist's bases for moral authority and motivation are the perceived needs of the moment and the potential consequences of a decision in a specific context. The needs of the moment dictate the importance of self-interest, concern for others, rules, and values. Facts and situational information are justifications for the pragmatist's actions. Pragmatists may abandon significant principles and values to produce certain results. They are closest philosophically to utilitarians. Although this style may seem the most objective and appealing, the shifting ethics of pragmatism make this orientation (and the person who espouses it) difficult and unpredictable in a business environment.

Idealists are driven by principles and rules. Reason, relationships, or the desired consequences of an action do not substitute for the idealist's adherence to principles. Duties are absolute. Idealists' moral authority and motivation are commitment to principles and consistency. Values and rules of conduct are the justification that idealists use to explain their actions. Seen as people with high moral standards, idealists can also be rigid and inflexible. Krolick states, "This absolute adherence to principles may blind the idealist to the potential consequences of a decision for oneself, others, or the situation."[60] This style is related to the social responsibility mode of ethical idealism and to the principle of universalism.

Which of the four styles best characterizes your ethical orientation? The orientation of your colleagues? Your supervisor or boss?

Communicating and Negotiating across Ethical Styles

When working or communicating with an ethical style, you also must observe *the other person's ethical style.* According to Krolick, the first step is to "concede that the other person's values and priorities have their own validity in their own terms and try to keep those values in mind to facilitate the process of reaching an agreement."[61] The following guidelines can help when communicating, negotiating, or working with one of the four ethical styles:

- *Individualist*: Point out the benefits to the other person's self-interest.
- *Altruist*: Focus on the benefits for the various constituencies involved.
- *Pragmatist*: Emphasize the facts and potential consequences of an action.
- *Idealist*: Concentrate on the principles or duties at stake.

Learning to recognize and communicate with people who have other ethical styles and being flexible in accommodating their ethical styles, without sacrificing your own, are important skills for working effectively with others.

2.7 Quick Ethical Tests

In addition to knowing the ethical principles, social responsibility modes, and ethical styles presented in this chapter, businesspeople can take short "ethical tests" before making decisions. Many of these rules reflect the principles discussed in this chapter. These "checkpoints," if observed, could change the actions you would automatically take in ethical dilemmas.

The Center for Business Ethics at Bentley University has articulated six simple questions for the "practical philosopher." Before making a decision or acting, ask the following:

1. Is it right?
2. Is it fair?
3. Who gets hurt?
4. Would you be comfortable if the details of your decision were reported on the front page of your local newspaper?
5. What would you tell your child to do?
6. How does it smell? (How does it feel?)

Other quick ethical tests, some of which are classic, include:

- *The Golden Rule*: "Do unto others as you would have them do unto you." This includes not knowingly doing harm to others.
- *The Intuition Ethic*: We know apart from reason what is right. We have a moral sense about what is right and wrong. We should follow our "gut feeling" about what is right.
- *The Means-Ends Ethic*: We may choose unscrupulous but efficient means to reach an end if the ends are really worthwhile and significant. Be sure the ends are not the means.
- *The Test of Common Sense*: "Does the action I am getting ready to take really make sense?" Think before acting.
- *The Test of One's Best Self*: "Is this action or decision I'm getting ready to take compatible with my concept of myself at my best?"
- *The Test of Ventilation*: Do not isolate yourself with your dilemma. Get others' feedback before acting or deciding.
- *The Test of the Purified Idea*: "Am I thinking this action or decision is right just because someone with authority or knowledge says it is right?" You may still be held responsible for taking the action.[62]

Use these principles and guidelines for examining the motivations of stakeholders' strategies, policies, and actions. Why do stakeholders act and talk as they do? What principles drive these actions?

■ 2.8 Concluding Comments

A definition of ethics and business ethics has been offered along with four types of ethical reasoning to provide a basis for making ethical decisions. Individual stakeholders have a wide range of ethical principles, orientations, and "quick tests" to draw on before solving an ethical dilemma. Moral maturity also affects an individual's ethical reasoning and actions. Kohlberg's stages of moral development and Covey's Moral Continuum are concepts that provide a diagnostic and suggested developmental insights into ethical decision making.

Using moral reflection and creativity is also important when deciding between two "right" or "wrong" choices. Reflecting on one's core values and having a sense of moral courage and shrewdness are also a recommended part of this decision-making process. When there are multiple stakeholders in a dilemma, the moral dimension of the stakeholder approach can be helpful by identifying the "ground rules" or "implicit morality" of institutional members. As R. Edward Freeman and Daniel Gilbert Jr. state:

> Think of the implicit morality of an institution as the rules that must be followed if the institution is to be a good one. The rules are often implicit, because the explicit rules of an institution may be the reason that the institution functions badly. Another way to think of the implicit morality of an institution is as the internal logic of the institution. Once this internal logic is clearly understood, we can evaluate its required behaviors against external standards.[63]

Back to Louise Simms . . .

Let's return to the opening case in which Louise Simms is trying to decide what to do. Put yourself in Louise's situation. Identify your ethical decision-making style. Are you primarily an idealist, pragmatist, altruist, or individualist? What are some of your blind spots? Consider the three questions regarding a "defining moment" at the beginning of the chapter: Who am I? Who are we? Who is the company? What courses of action are available after reviewing your responses to these questions? Then, describe the ethical principles you usually follow in your life: utilitarianism, rights, justice, universalism, ethical virtue, ethical relativism, and the common good ethic. Which of those principles do you aspire to use to act more ethically and morally mature and responsible? What is your moral responsibility to yourself, your family and friends, your colleagues and work team, and to the company? How will you feel about yourself after you make the decision? Now make Louise's decision and share your decision with your classmates and consider their responses. Do you think you made the right decision?

Chapter Summary

Complex ethical dilemmas in business situations involve making tough choices between conflicting interests. This chapter began with classic ethical principles that are used to guide dilemmas and decisions at the individual, group, and organizational levels. Moral maturity and Covey's Moral Continuum were discussed to consider how to approach personal-level dilemmas. Questions were presented for addressing dilemmas and "defining moments" creatively, boldly, and shrewdly. In addition, 12 questions and three decision criteria were given that can assist individuals in determining the most suitable course of action.

Individuals can gain a clear perspective of their own motivations and actions by distinguishing them from those of others. This perspective can be useful for guiding your own decision-making process. Understanding the criteria in this chapter can help you to reason more critically when examining other stakeholders' ethical reasoning.

A primary goal of ethical reasoning is to help individuals act in morally responsible ways. Ignorance and bias are two conditions that cloud moral awareness. Five principles of ethical reasoning were presented to expose you to methods of ethical decision making. Each principle was discussed in terms of the utility and drawbacks characteristic of it. Guidelines for thinking through and applying each principle in a stakeholder analysis were also provided. These principles are not mechanical recipes for selecting a course of action. They are filters or screens to use for clarifying dilemmas.

Three ethical orientations—immoral, amoral, and moral—can be used to evaluate ethics. Immoral and moral motives are more discernible than amoral ones. Amoral orientations include lack of concern for others' interests and well-being. Although no intentional harm or motive may be observed, harmful consequences from ignorance or neglect reflect amoral styles of operating.

Four social responsibility roles or business modes were discussed: productivism and philanthropy (influenced by stockholder concerns) and progressivism and ethical idealism (driven by stockholder concerns but also influenced by external stakeholders). Individuals also have ethical decision-making styles. Four different (but not exclusive) styles are individualism, altruism, pragmatism, and idealism. Another person's ethical decision-making style must be understood when engaging in communication and negotiation. These styles are a starting point for identifying predominant decision-making characteristics.

The chapter concluded by offering quick "ethical tests" that can be used to provide insight into your decision-making process and actions.

Questions

1. Do you believe ethical dilemmas can be prevented and solved morally without the use of principles? Explain. Offer an example from a dilemma you recently experienced or currently are experiencing. Characterize the logic you used in thinking through or having made a decision. Compare the logic you used to principles and quick tests in this chapter. What similarities and differences did you discover? Can you include any of the principles and ethical reasoning in this chapter in dilemmas you may or expect to face? Explain.

2. Why are creativity and moral imagination oftentimes necessary in preventing and resolving ethical dilemmas and "defining moments" of conflict in one's workplace? Offer an example of an ethically questionable situation in which you had to creatively improvise to "do the right thing."

3. What is a first step for addressing ethical dilemmas? What parts of this chapter would and could you use to complement or change your own decision-making methods?

4. How can the discussion of personal-level ethical decision making, moral maturity, and Covey's Moral Continuum assist you in addressing dilemmas in your life and work?

5. What single question is the most powerful for solving ethical dilemmas?
6. What are two conditions that eliminate a person's moral responsibility?
7. Return to the case you selected in question 4 above. Briefly explain which of the chapter's five fundamental principles of ethical reasoning the leaders and/or major stakeholders you identified used and did not use in the case. Which ethical principle(s) would you recommend that they should have used? Why?
8. What are some of the problems characteristic of cultural relativism? Offer an example in the news of a company that has acted unethically according to the perspective of cultural relativism.
9. Why is utilitarianism useful for conducting a stakeholder analysis? What are some of the problems with using this principle? Give an example of when you used utilitarianism to justify an ethically questionable action.
10. Briefly explain the categorical imperative. What does it force you, as a decision maker, to do when choosing an action in a moral dilemma?
11. Explain the difference between the principles of rights and justice. What are some of the strengths and weaknesses of each principle?
12. Which of the four social responsibility modes most accurately characterizes your college/university and place of work? Explain. Do your ethics and moral values agree with these organizations? Explain.
13. Briefly explain your ethical decision-making style as presented in the chapter.
14. How would you describe your level of moral maturity using Kohlberg's stages?
15. What insights did you gain from Covey's Moral Continuum with regard to your ethical decision-making activities? What are some connections between Covey's and Kohlberg's concepts and ethics?
16. Explain what ethical logic and actions people generally take to persuade you to do something that is ethically questionable. Refer to the ethical decision styles in the chapter.
17. Which of the ethical "quick tests" do you prefer? Why?

Exercises

1. Describe a serious ethical dilemma you have experienced. Use the 12 questions developed by Laura Nash to offer a resolution to the problem, even if your resolution is different from the original experience. Did you initially use any of the questions? Would any of these questions have helped you? How? What would you have done differently? Why?
2. Identify an instance when you thought ignorance absolved a person or group from moral responsibility. Then identify an example of a person or group failing to become fully informed about a moral situation. Under what conditions do you think individuals are morally responsible for their actions? Why?
3. With which of the four social responsibility business modes in the chapter do you most identify? Why? Name a company that reflects this orientation. Would you want to work for this company? Would you want to be part of the management team? Explain.

4. Select a corporate leader in the news who acted legally but immorally and one who acted illegally but morally. Explain the differences of the actions and behaviors in each of the two examples. What lessons do you take from your examples?

5. Select two organizations in the same industry that you are familiar with or that are in the media or online news, such as McDonald's and Burger King, Toyota and General Motors, Alaska Airlines and American Airlines. Research some of the latest news items and activities about each company and its officers over the same time period. Now, using ethical principles and the quick tests from this chapter, compare and contrast each. Evaluate how "ethical" each is compared to the other.

I was employed as a certified public accountant (CPA) for a regional account-ing firm that specialized in audits of financial institutions and had many local clients. My responsibilities included supervising staff, collecting evidence to support financial statement assertions, and compiling work papers for man-agers and partners to review. During the audit of a publicly traded bank, I discovered that senior bank executives were under investigation by the Fed-eral Deposit Insurance Corporation (FDIC) for removing funds from the bank. They were also believed to be using bank funds to pay corporate credit card bills for gas and spouses' expenses. The last allegation noted that the execu-tives were issuing loans to relatives without proper collateral.

After reviewing the work papers, I found two checks, made payable to one executive of the bank, that were selected during a cash count from two tellers. There was no indication based on our sampling that expenses were being paid for spouses. My audit manager and the chief financial officer (CFO) of my firm were aware of these problems.

After the fieldwork for the audit was completed, I was called into the CEO's office. The CEO and the chief operating officer (COO) stated that the FDIC examiners wanted to interview the audit manager, two staff accountants, and me. The CEO then asked the following question: "If you were asked by the FDIC about a check or checks made payable to bank executives, how would you answer?" I told them that I would answer the FDIC examiners by stating that, during our audit, we made copies of two checks made payable to an ex-ecutive of the bank for $8,000 each.

The COO stated that during his review of the audit work papers, he had not found any copies of checks made payable to executives. He also stated that a better response to the question regarding the checks would be, "I was not aware of reviewing any checks specifically made payable to the executive in question." The COO then said that the examiners would be in the following day to speak with the audit staff. I was dismissed from the meeting.

Neither the CEO nor the COO asked me if the suggested "better" re-sponse was the response I would give, and I did not volunteer the informa-tion. During the interview, the FDIC investigators never asked me whether I knew about the checks. Should I have volunteered this information?

Questions

1. What would you have done? Volunteered the information or stayed silent? Explain your decision.
2. Was anything unethical going on in this case? Explain.
3. Describe the "ethics" of the officers of the firm in this case.
4. What, if anything, should the officers have done, and why?
5. What lessons, if any, can you take from this case, as an employee working under company officials who have more power than you do?

Cases

Case 4

Ford's Pinto Fires: The Retrospective View of Ford's Field Recall Coordinator

Brief Overview of the Ford Pinto Fires

Determined to compete with fuel-efficient Volkswagen and Japanese imports, the Ford Motor Company introduced the subcompact Pinto in the 1971 model year. Lee Iacocca, Ford's president at the time, insisted that the Pinto weigh no more than 2,000 pounds and cost no more than $2,000. Even with these restrictions, the Pinto met federal safety standards, although some people have argued that strict adherence to the restrictions led Ford engineers to compromise safety. Some 2 million units were sold during the 10-year life of the Pinto.

The Pinto's major design flaw—a fuel tank prone to rupturing with moderate-speed rear-end collisions—surfaced not too long after the Pinto's entrance to the market. In April 1974, the Center for Auto Safety petitioned the National Highway Traffic Safety Administration (NHTSA) to recall Ford Pintos because of the fuel-tank design defect. The Center for Auto Safety's petition was based on reports from attorneys of three deaths and four serious injuries in moderate-speed, rear-end collisions involving Pintos. The NHTSA did not act on this petition until 1977.

As a result of tests performed for the NHTSA, as well as the extraordinary amount of publicity generated by the problem, Ford agreed, on June 9, 1978, to recall 1.5 million 1971–1976 Ford Pintos and 30,000 1975–1976 Mercury Bobcat sedan and hatchback models for modifications to the fuel tank. Recall notices were mailed to the affected Pinto and Bobcat owners in September 1978. Repair parts were to be delivered to all dealers by September 15, 1978.

Unfortunately, the recall was initiated too late for six people. Between June 9 and September 15, 1978, six people died in Pinto fires after a rear impact. Three of these people were teenage girls killed in Indiana in August 1978 when their 1973 Pinto burst into flames after being rear-ended by a van. The fiery deaths of the Indiana teenagers led to criminal prosecution of the Ford Motor Company on charges of reckless homicide, marking the first time that an American corporation was prosecuted on criminal charges. In the trial, which commenced on January 15, 1980, "Indiana state prosecutors alleged that Ford knew Pinto gasoline tanks were prone to catch fire during rear-end collisions but failed to warn the public or fix the problem out of concern for profits." On March 13, 1980, a jury found Ford innocent of the charges. Production of the Pinto was discontinued in the fall of 1980.

Enter Ford's Field Recall Coordinator

Dennis A. Gioia, currently a professor in the Department of Management and Organization at Pennsylvania State University, was the field recall coordinator at

Ford Motor Company when the Pinto fuel-tank defect began unfolding. Gioia's responsibilities included the operational coordination of all the current recall campaigns, tracking incoming information to identify developing problems, and reviewing field reports of alleged component failures that led to accidents. Gioia left Ford in 1975. Subsequently, "reports of Pinto fires escalated, attracting increasing media attention." The remainder of this case, written in the first-person and in Gioia's own words in the early 1990s, is his personal reflection on lessons learned from his experiences involving the Pinto fuel-tank problem.

Why Revisit Decisions from the Early 1970s?

I take this case very personally, even though my name seldom comes up in its many recountings. I was one of those "faceless bureaucrats" who is often portrayed as making decisions without accountability and then walking away from them—even decisions with life-and-death implications. That characterization is, of course, far too stark and superficial. I certainly don't consider myself faceless, and I have always chafed at the label of bureaucrat as applied to me, even though I have found myself unfairly applying it to others. Furthermore, I have been unable to walk away from my decisions in this case. They have a tendency to haunt—especially when they have had such public airings as those involved in the Pinto fires debacle have had.

But why revisit 20-year-old decisions, and why take them so personally? Here's why: because I was in a position to do something about a serious problem . . . and didn't. That simple observation gives me pause for personal reflection and also makes me think about the many difficulties people face in trying to be ethical decision makers in organizations. It also helps me to keep in mind the features of modern business and organizational life that would influence someone like me (me of all people, who purposely set out to be an ethical decision maker!) to overlook basic moral issues in arriving at decisions that, when viewed retrospectively, look absurdly easy to make. But they are not easy to make, and that is perhaps the most important lesson of all.

The Personal Aspect

I would like to reflect on my own experience mainly to emphasize the personal dimensions involved in ethical decision making. Although I recognize that there are strong organizational influences at work as well, I would like to keep the critical lens focused for a moment on me (and you) as individuals. I believe that there are insights and lessons from my experience that can help you think about your own likely involvement in issues with ethical overtones.

First, however, a little personal background. In the late 1960s and early 1970s, I was an engineering/MBA student; I also was an "activist," engaged in protests of social injustice and the social irresponsibility of business, among other things. I held some pretty strong values, and I thought they would stand up to virtually any challenge and enable me to "do the right thing" when I took a career job. I suspect that most of you feel that you also have developed a strongly held value system that will enable you to resist organizational inducements to do something unethical. Perhaps. Unfortunately, the challenges do not often come in overt forms that shout the need for resistance or ethical righteousness. They are much more subtle than that, and thus doubly difficult to deal with because they do not make it easy to see that a situation you are confronting might actually involve an ethical dilemma.

After school, I got the job of my dreams with Ford and, predictably enough, ended up on the fast track to promotion. That fast track enabled me to progress quickly into positions of some notable responsibility. Within two years I became Ford's field recall coordinator, with first-level responsibility for tracking field safety problems. It was the most intense, information-overloaded job you can imagine, frequently dealing with some of the most serious problems in the company. Disasters were a phone call away, and action was the hallmark of the office where I worked. We all knew we were engaged in serious business, and we all took the job seriously. There were no irresponsible bureaucratic ogres there, contrary to popular portrayal.

In this context, I first encountered the neophyte Pinto fires problem—in the form of infrequent reports of cars erupting into horrendous fireballs in very low-speed crashes and the shuddering personal experience of inspecting a car that had burned, killing its trapped occupants. Over the space of a year, I had two distinct opportunities to initiate recall activities concerning the fuel-tank problems, but on both occasions, I voted not to recall, despite my activist history and advocacy of business social responsibility.

The key question is how, after two short years, could I have engaged in a decision process that appeared to violate my own strong values—a decision process whose subsequent manifestations continue to be cited by many observers as a supposedly definitive study of corporate unethical behavior? I tend to discount the obvious accusations: that my values weren't really strongly held; that I had turned my back on my values in the interest of loyalty to Ford; that I was somehow intimidated into making decisions in the best interest of the company; that despite my principled statements, I had not actually achieved a high stage of moral development; and so on. Instead, I believe a more plausible explanation for my own actions looks to the foibles of normal human information processing.

I would argue that the complexity and intensity of the recall coordinator's job required that I develop cognitive strategies for simplifying the overwhelming amount of information I had to deal with. The best way to do that is to structure the information into cognitive "schemas," or more specifically "script schemas," that guide understanding and action when facing common or repetitive situations. Scripts offer marvelous cognitive shortcuts because they allow you to act virtually unconsciously and automatically, and thus permit you to handle complicated situations without being paralyzed by needing to think consciously about every little thing. Such scripts enabled me to discern the characteristic hallmarks of problem cases likely to result in recall and to execute a complicated series of steps required to initiate a recall.

All of us structure information all of the time; we could hardly get through the workday without doing so. But there is a penalty to be paid for this wonderful cognitive efficiency: we do not give sufficient attention to important information that requires special treatment because the general information pattern has surface appearances that indicate that automatic processing will suffice. That, I think, is what happened to me. The beginning stages of the Pinto case looked for all the world like a normal sort of problem. Lurking beneath the cognitive veneer, however, was a nasty set of circumstances waiting to conspire into a dangerous situation. Despite the awful nature of the accidents, the Pinto problem did not fit an existing script; the accidents were relatively rare by recall standards, and the accidents were not initially traceable to a specific component failure. Even when a failure mode suggesting a design flaw was identified, the cars did not perform significantly worse in crash tests than competitor vehicles. One might easily argue that I should have been jolted out of my script by the unusual nature of the accidents (very low speed, otherwise unharmed passengers trapped in a horrific fire), but those facts did not penetrate a script cued for other features. (It also is difficult to convey to the layperson that bad accidents are not a particularly unusual feature of the recall coordinator's information field. Accident severity is not necessarily a recall cue; frequently repeated patterns and identifiable causes are.)

The Corporate Milieu

In addition to the personalized scripting of information processing, there is another important influence on the decisions that led to the Pinto fires mess: the fact that decisions are made by individuals working within a corporate context. It has escaped almost no one's notice that the decisions made by corporate employees tend to be in the best interest of the corporation, even by people who mean to do better. Why? Because the socialization process and the overriding influence of organizational culture provide a strong, if generally subtle, context for defining appropriate ways of seeing and understanding. Because organizational culture can be viewed as a collection of scripts, scripted information processing relates even to organizational-level considerations. Scripts are context bound; they are not free-floating general cognitive structures that apply universally. They are tailored to specific contexts. And there are few more potent contexts than organizational settings.

There is no question that my perspective changed after joining Ford. In retrospect, I would be very surprised if it hadn't. In my former incarnation as a social activist, I had internalized values for doing what was right—as I understood righteousness in grand terms, but I had not internalized a script for applying my values in a pragmatic business context. Ford and the recall coordinator role provided a powerful context for developing scripts—scripts that were inevitably and undeniably oriented toward ways of making sense that were influenced by the corporate and industry culture.

I wanted to do a good job, and I wanted to do what was right. Those are not mutually exclusive desires, but the corporate context affects their synthesis. I came to accept the idea that it was not feasible to fix everything that someone might construe as a problem. I therefore shifted to a value of wanting to do the greatest good for the greatest number (an ethical value tempered by the practical constraints of an economic enterprise). Doing the greatest good for the greatest number meant working with intensity and responsibility on those problems that would spare the most people from injury. It also meant developing scripts that responded to typical problems, not odd patterns like those presented by the Pinto.

Another way of noting how the organizational context so strongly affects individuals is to recognize that one's personal identity becomes heavily influenced by corporate identity. As a student, my identity is centered on being a "good person" (with a certain dose of moral righteousness associated with it). As recall coordinator, my identity shifted to a more corporate definition. This is an extraordinarily important point, especially for students who have not yet held a permanent job role, and I would like to emphasize it. Before assuming your career role, identity derives mainly from social relationships. Upon putting on the mantle of a profession or a responsible position, identity begins to align with your role. And information processing perspective follows from the identity.

I remember accepting the portrayal of the auto industry and Ford as "under attack" from many quarters (oil crises, burgeoning government regulation, inflation, litigious customers, etc.). As we know, groups under assault develop into more cohesive communities that emphasize commonalities and shared identities. I was by then an insider in the industry and the company, sharing some of their beleaguered perceptions that there were significant forces arrayed against us and that the well-being of the company might be threatened.

What happened to the original perception that Ford was a socially irresponsible giant that needed a comeuppance? Well, it looks different from the inside. Over time, a responsible value for action against corporate dominance became tempered by another reasonable value that corporations serve social needs and are not automatically the villains of society. I saw a need for balance among multiple values, and as a result, my identity shifted in degrees toward a more corporate identity.

The Torch Passes to You

So, given my experiences, what would I recommend to you, as a budding organizational decision maker? I have some strong opinions. First, develop your ethical base now! Too many people do not give serious attention to assessing and articulating their own values. People simply do not know what they stand for because they haven't thought about it seriously. Even the ethical scenarios presented in classes or executive programs are treated as interesting little games without apparent implications for deciding how you intend to think or act. These exercises should be used to develop a principled, personal code that you will try to live by. Consciously decide your values. If you don't decide your values now, you are easy prey for others who will gladly decide them for you or influence you implicitly to accept theirs.

Second, recognize that everyone, including you, is an unwitting victim of their cognitive structuring. Many people are surprised and fascinated to learn that they use schemas and scripts to understand and act in the organizational world. The idea that we automatically process so much information so much of the time intrigues us. Indeed, we would all turn into blithering idiots if we did not structure information and expectations, but that very structuring hides information that might be important—information that could require you to confront your values. We get lulled into thinking that automatic information processing is great stuff that obviates the necessity for trying to resolve so many frustrating decisional dilemmas.

Actually, I think too much ethical training focuses on supplying standards for contemplating dilemmas. The far greater problem, as I see it, is recognizing that a dilemma exists in the first place. The insidious problem of people not being aware that they are dealing with a situation that might have ethical overtones is another consequence of schema usage. I would venture that scripted routines seldom include ethical dimensions. Is a person behaving unethically if the situation is not even construed as having ethical implications? People are not necessarily stupid, ill intentioned, or Machiavellian, but they are often unaware. They do indeed spend much of their time cruising on automatic, but the true hallmark of human information processing is the ability to switch from automatic to controlled information processing. What we really need to do is to encourage people to recognize cues that build a "Now Think!" step into their scripts—waving red flags at yourself, so to speak—even though you are engaged in essentially automatic cognition and action.

Third, because scripts are context bound and organizations are potent contexts, be aware of how strongly, yet how subtly, your job role and your organizational culture affect the ways you interpret and make sense of information (and thus affect the ways you develop the scripts that will guide you in unguarded moments). Organizational culture has a much greater effect on individual cognition than you would ever suspect.

Last, be prepared to face critical responsibility at a relatively young age, as I did. You need to know what your values are and you need to know how you think so that you can know how to make a good decision. Before you can do that, you need to articulate and affirm your values now, before you enter the fray. I wasn't really ready. Are you?

Questions for Discussion

1. The Ford Pinto met federal safety standards, yet it had a design flaw that resulted in serious injuries and deaths. Is simply meeting safety standards a sufficient product design goal of ethical companies?
2. Gioia uses the notion of script schemas to help explain why he voted to not initiate a recall of the Ford Pinto. In your opinion, is this a justifiable explanation?
3. How can organizational context influence the decisions made by organizational members?
4. If you had been in Gioia's position, what would you have done? Why?
5. Describe the four key decision-making lessons that Gioia identifies for neophyte decision makers. Discuss how you expect or intend to use these four lessons in your own career.

Sources

This case was developed from material contained in the following sources:

Ford Pinto fuel-fed fires. (n.d.). *The Center for Auto Safety.* Accessed March 6, 2021, https://www.autosafety.org/ford-pinto-fuel-fed-fires.

Ford Pinto reckless homicide trial. (n.d.). *History.com.* Accessed March 6, 2021, https://www.history.com/speeches/ford-pinto-reckless-homicide-trial.

Gioia, D. A. (1992, May). Pinto fires and personal ethics: A script analysis of missed opportunities. *Journal of Business Ethics, 11(5–6)*, 379–390.

Grimshaw v. Ford Motor Company, 1981. (n.d.) American Museum of Tort Law. Accessed, June 22, 2020, https://www.tortmuseum.org/ford-pinto/#:~:text =The%20Pinto%2C%20a%20subcompact%20car,production%20and%20 onto%20the%20market.

Case 5

Jerome Kerviel: Rogue Trader or Misguided Employee? What Really Happened at the Société Générale?

Société Générale: A French Bank Globally Recognized

The French banking company Société Générale ("SocGen" or "the Company") was founded on May 4, 1864. The bank has grown to serve 19.2 million individual customers in 76 countries. It employs 103,000 workers from 114 different nationalities. SocGen operates in three major businesses: retail banking and financial services, global investment management and services, and corporate and investment banking. The core values at the Company are professionalism, team spirit, and innovation.

In 2006, SocGen ranked 67 on *Fortune's* 2006 Global 500 and had managed to build a $72 billion position in European stock index futures. The year before, the Company ranked 152 on *Fortune's* list. In addition to top-line growth, SocGen also posted a more important improvement in overall profitability, at $5.5 billion, up 42 percent from the prior year. It was the 14th-largest company among the banking institutions on the list.

The Beginning of the Story

Things were about to change for SocGen. In 2006, turmoil revolved around the collapsing housing market and a mortgage industry that witnessed loan defaults in record numbers. Several banks engaged in purchasing high-risk mortgage loans, but the overall economic recession, primarily in the United States but also felt globally, constrained this bank's financial status. SocGen saw its stock price cut almost in half throughout the year, but this was not the only potential pitfall for this once-robust Company. It was the actions of one rogue trader, Jerome Kerviel, that could have brought about the ultimate downfall of SocGen.

Who Is Jerome Kerviel, and What Happened at the Bank?

On January 24, 2008, Jerome Kerviel found himself in the international media spotlight, but not as he would have hoped. On this day, SocGen announced to the world that it had discovered a $7.14 billion trading fraud caused by a single trader, Kerviel. Additionally, a nearly $3 billion loss was posted resulting from the loss in investments in the U.S. subprime mortgage industry. The second-largest bank in France had its shares halted to avoid a complete market collapse on the price of the stock.

From his modest roots to the upscale Paris suburb where he resided, friends and family never expected that this unmarried 31-year-old could be capable of such a scandal. With a relatively modest salary ($145,700), Kerviel did not profit from his trading scheme. He had been an employee at SocGen since 2000. He began in a monitoring support role and oversaw the futures traders for five years. He was then promoted to the futures trading desk. He traded European futures by betting on the future performance of these funds. Kerviel saw his trading profits increase throughout 2007 as he bet that the markets would fall during this time. By the end of the year, he needed to mask his significant gains, so he created fictional losing positions to erode his gains. These included the purchasing of 140,000 DAX futures (the German stock index, a blue chip stock market index that includes the 30 major German companies trading on the Frankfurt Stock Exchange). By mid-January, Kerviel had lost over $3 billion. He was hedging more than $73.3 billion, an amount far in excess of the trading limits created by Soc-Gen for a single trader. This amount even exceeded SocGen's overall market cap of $52.6 billion.

Despite the Company's five levels of increased security to prevent traders from assuming positions greater than a predetermined amount and a group compliance division that was put in charge of monitoring trader activity, Kerviel was able to bypass internal controls for over two years.

Kerviel's motive was not to steal from the bank but to have his significant trading gains catapult his career—and to cash in on a significant bonus given to traders who exhibit the type of profitability he created for the Company. Red flags were triggered, but e-mails to his superiors on his trading activity were ignored because of his overall profitability for the Company. Kerviel admitted his wrongdoing but said that SocGen was partially responsible for not monitoring his activities correctly and for rewarding his behavior with a proposed bonus of $440,000. Kerviel stated that his actions were similar to those of other traders; he was just being labeled as the scapegoat in this investigation.

Company Reaction

Once the fraud was detected in mid-January 2008, SocGen immediately reported it to France's central bank, Bank of France. Over the next three trading days, Soc-Gen employees began to unload all of Kerviel's positions into the marketplace. The Company attempted to complete this significant sale of securities in a manner that would not disrupt the normal market movement. The ripple effect of this action may have created additional pressure on the already falling world markets. Some analysts speculated that this action may even have influenced the U.S. Federal Reserve rate cut. SocGen management denied that action after it discovered that the trading fraud had a meaningful impact on the world marketplace. Co-CEO Daniel Bouton stated that the three-day sell-off was in accordance with guidelines and that the liquidation of a position at any one time could not be more than 10 percent of the given market.

After Kerviel admitted his guilt, his employment was terminated along with that of his supervisors. Bouton submitted a formal resignation, along with second-in-command Phillipe Citerne; however, both resignations were rejected by the board of directors. Employees at the Company staged demonstrations where they showed their support for Bouton.

The bank has stated that since the activity was brought to light, there has been a tightening on the internal controls, so that actions such as Kerviel's are no longer possible for a trader. On January 25, 2008, SocGen took out a full-page newspaper article apologizing to its customers for the scandal. On January 30, the board announced the formation of an independent committee to investigate the current monitoring practices and determine what measures could be put in place to prevent it from happening again. The committee would enlist the services of the auditing company PricewaterhouseCoopers. The Company also announced that it needed an influx of capital to stay afloat and began looking to outside help to raise $8.02 billion in new capital.

Government Reaction

On January 26, 2008, Kerviel was taken into police custody for questioning regarding his trading activity at SocGen. Three complaints were issued to police, one by SocGen and two others by small shareholders.

This event was the focus at the World Economic Forum in Davos, Switzerland, which brought to light questions on how risk is managed within organizations. French finance minister Christine Lagarde was assigned the task of investigating the events and compiling a report on the failure of internal controls at SocGen. The report was then publicized in an effort to prevent similar fraudulent trading events from occurring in the future. A timeline of the events leading up to the trading losses was created in an effort to better understand the events that transpired. In the report, Lagarde stated that there should be an increase in penalties for banks that violate the commission's set rules. The then-president of France, Nicolas Sarkozy, stated that the events at SocGen did not affect the "solidity and reliability of France's financial system." He wanted the board of directors to take action against senior management, including Bouton.

On January 28, 2008, Kerviel was charged with unauthorized computer activity and breach of trust. Plans were also announced to charge Kerviel with fraud and misrepresentation, which could carry a maximum prison time of seven years and fines of $1.1 million. At the time of this writing, the fraud charge had not been accepted by the courts; however, prosecutors were seeking to appeal this to a higher court.

The government sought to prevent a hostile takeover of SocGen during this period. However, the European Union was in disagreement with the French government and stated that all bidders should be treated equally: "The same rules apply as in other takeover situations under free movement of capital rules. Potential bidders are to be treated in an undiscriminatory manner." The current stand-out bidder is the largest bank in France, BNP Paribas. Many competitors are contemplating making an offer for the distressed Company—to purchase a portion or all of the bank's assets.

Why It Happened

Kerviel was able to evade detection because of his experience monitoring the traders in his early years at SocGen. Falsifying bank records and computer fraud were part of the intricate scheme that he created. Kerviel knew when he would be monitored by the bank and avoided any activity during those periods. He created a fictitious company and falsified trading records to keep his activity under wraps. Kerviel also used other employees' computer access codes and falsified trading documents.

Related Companies with Similar Troubles

In 1995, Barings, a British bank that had been in existence for more than 230 years, collapsed as the results of the actions of one futures trader, Nick Leeson. Leeson lost more than $1.38 billion when trading futures in the Asian markets.

In 1991, London-based Bank of Credit and Commerce International (BCCI) went bankrupt as the result of illegal trading activity and insider trading, losing over $10 billion.

During the late 1980s and early 1990s, Yasuo Hamanaka, a Japanese copper futures trader, cost his employer, Sumitomo Copper, $2.6 billion.

Is There More to the Story?

A director of SocGen, Robert Day, sold $126.1 million in shares on January 9, 2008, two weeks before the trading fraud was disclosed. He also sold $14.1 million the next day for two charitable trusts he chaired. Trading also occurred on January 18. The total trading activity amounted to $206 million. It was reported that Day traded during the timeframe where it was acceptable for a board member to trade shares of stock. Accusations of insider trading have been denied.

The *Financial Times* in London has reported that SocGen may have known about the trading activities back in November, when the Eurex derivatives exchange questioned Kerviel's trading positions and alerted the Company. This then calls into question the lack of oversight by the Company and what responsibility Soc-Gen has to its shareholders for this oversight. Kerviel accuses his supervisors of turning a blind eye to his activities because he was earning the Company a significant amount of money. He states that his profits should have raised concerns because they far exceeded the parameters of the transactions he was allowed to engage in.

Corporate Controls at SocGen

It has been stated that there were not enough safeguards in place to protect the bank from Kerviel's activities. The following describes the existing safeguards and focuses on the public ethical programs that SocGen had in place.

At SocGen, the board of directors and three corporate governance committees that were established in 1995 are in charge of creating and policing the Company through its internal rules and regulations. The Company engages in risk management by constantly reviewing its risk exposure in the variety of areas in which it operates. Because of the sensitivity of many banking projects, corporate governance remains at the forefront of the bank's activities. The three committees include the audit committee (in charge of reviewing the Company's draft financial statements prior to submission to the board of directors), the compensation committee (in charge of determining executive compensation packages), and the nomination committee (appoints new board members and executive officers).

The board of directors is responsible for the Company's overall strategy and the adherence to its defined set of internal rules. The risk assessment divisions operate autonomously from the other operating units. Reporting directly to general management, this group consists of 2,000 employees who constantly monitor the activities of the other business units, making sure they are in compliance with the internal rules established by the board of directors. Monthly meetings are held to review strategic initiatives, and all new products must first receive the approval of the risk team before implementation may take place.

Internal audit groups have been put in place with the following assignments:

• Detect, measure, and manage the risks incurred.
• Guarantee the reliability, integrity, and availability of financial and management data.
• Verify the quality of the information and communications systems.

All staff members are under constant day-to-day supervision to ensure their compliance with the regulations in place.

The Compliance Department was established in 1997 and is currently responsible for monitoring all banking activities so that the actions of all employees are in the best interest of the Company. A charter is in place that extends beyond local law and attempts to cover the high ethical standards set by the Company. Three key principles of the group are to work only with well-known customers, always assess the economic legitimacy of the action, and have the ability to justify any stance taken.

The trading room had eight compliance staff members in 2006, with the goal of increasing this number in 2007. Anti-money-laundering practices have also been in the spotlight during the last few years. In all, the group has increased overall training for 2006 to 50,000 hours, up from 24,000 hours in 2005. The total number of employees trained is 18,000 individuals.

The role of information technology (IT) has also increased to support the corporate governance initiative. GILT (Group Insider List Tool) monitors potential conflicts of interest and insider-trading activity within the Company, and MUST (Monitoring of Unusual and Suspicious Transactions) is used to detect insider trading and market manipulation. The Company also has standards in place to prevent corruption on the part of Company employees and government officials.

A code of conduct has been in place since March 2005, with the goal of being a reference tool for employees that highlights the principles that the Company wants its employees to uphold. The code was created as the result of the changes in the current business environment in which employees and society alike are expected to have set a higher standard for an individual company's corporate responsibilities. Like many other companies that have a code of conduct, SocGen felt that establishing this code was an essential part of operating in the current business environment.

The SocGen China Group has established strict controls in an effort to prevent internal private information and confidential customer data from leaking to the outside marketplace. Separation is a key component in this control measure, whereby an effort is made to eliminate the chance of conflicts of interest on sensitive projects. There is restricted access to IT programs, and any potential conflict of interest must first be approved and signed off by the Compliance Department.

Compliance structures were put in place beginning in March 2005 as a result of a change in law by the French Banking and Financial Regulation Committee (Regulation No. 97–02). The secretary-general of SocGen heads the Group Compliance Committee. Through monthly meetings, members of the group identify any potential risks on the part of the Company, develop ways to prevent future risks in new products, and engage in employee training in an effort to strengthen the idea of corporate compliance within the company culture.

Stakeholders and Their Roles

The main stakeholder in this case is Jerome Kerviel. His actions were the primary driver behind the significant losses incurred by SocGen. However, although Kerviel may have been the focal stakeholder, there are several other primary stakeholders. Kerviel's direct supervisors were responsible for managing his actions. Senior management and the board of directors were responsible for implementing and enforcing guidelines. Employees of the Company are stakeholders since other traders' actions may have influenced Kerviel's decisions, and the Kerviel case may have jeopardized their own careers within the Company. The final primary stakeholders were the Company's shareholders, who were negatively impacted by the huge trading losses at SocGen brought about by Kerviel.

Secondary stakeholders include the government, which pushed the board of directors for Bouton's resignation, and the court systems prosecuting Kerviel and other individuals indicted on counts of insider trading. There are competitors, including BNP Paribas, which may try to take advantage of this opportunity to purchase a portion of SocGen's operations at a devalued price. Finally, there is the public at large, whose confidence was yet again shaken by another scandal within a financial institution.

Potential coalitions involved in the events leading up to the trading scandal include traders and their managers who may have ignored rules and regulations enacted by the governing committee at SocGen. Current coalitions may include shareholders who want to be reimbursed for the management oversight. Shareholder suits may also be brought against those identified as potentially engaging in insider trading. Finally, competition may be forming a coalition to section off the different business units of SocGen to complete a proposed buyout offer.

From the CEO's perspective, Kerviel might be seen as directly violating the rules put in place by the governing committee. Kerviel's managers also did not fully adhere to the established policies. The board of directors and the CEO were instrumental in the creation of the guidelines. The board rejected Bouton's letter of resignation and many employees have been very supportive of him, stating that he was the person who could guide the Company through this trying time.

Each stakeholder in this case had varying degrees of power. Kerviel had the power to operate with limited supervision (although this was due to his manipulation of the system) and to have a significant impact on the overall bottom line at SocGen. The supervisors of the traders had a degree of power only over the traders, provided they were not blindsided by the traders' fraudulent activities. The board of directors was responsible for providing strategic guidance for the Company, electing a CEO, and establishing rules and regulations for the Company and its employees. The shareholders of SocGen stock had the power to vote on issues, since they are each individual owners of the Company. The government had the power to influence how companies conducted business. Competitors to SocGen impacted the strategies the Company undertook to stay ahead of its competition.

Three Primary Stakeholders and Their Obligations

Kerviel had a legal obligation not to engage in fraudulent behavior; this is evidenced by the fact that he was indicted in the French court system. His economic incentive was to make the most money possible for SocGen while minimizing risk. He was successful for two years, but as he failed to minimize overall risk, his behavior eventually caught up with him. He had an ethical responsibility to management and his colleagues. He could be viewed as both a threat to the Company and a cooperative influence, depending on how management controlled the situation.

Kerviel's supervisors did not have as significant a legal obligation as Kerviel with regard to his specific responsibilities and actions. However, if they had been aware of his actions and did not act, then they can be seen as enabling him to commit illegal acts. They had an economic incentive to uphold the standards that senior management has put in place, since that is part of their job responsibility. Ethically, they had a responsibility to senior management, their colleagues, and their direct reports. It was the responsibility of senior management to work with the supervisors, and it was up to senior management to work with the supervisors to see that rules and regulations were upheld.

The board of directors has an obligation to make sure that the employees of the Company act in accordance with the laws of the country they reside in. The board has an economic responsibility to the shareholders of stock in the Company. Ethically, the board must create rules of conduct and ethical standards and practice a rule by example. The board is a supportive, low-potential-threat stakeholder that will probably cooperate with the CEO in this case.

Where Is He Now?

"A lower court in France convicted Kerviel in October 2010 of forgery, breach of trust, and unauthorized computer use for covering up bets worth nearly 50 billion euros in 2007 and 2008. By the time his trades were discovered and made public, he had amassed losses of almost 5 billion euros on those bets," reported the Associated Press. He lost the subsequent appeal, with the Paris appeals court upholding Kerviel's sentence in its entirety in 2012. "He was sentenced to three years in prison and ordered to pay restitutions of $ 6.8 billion." However, after serving five months in prison, Kerviel was released in 2014.

Questions for Discussion

1. Is Kerviel the only guilty one in this case with regard to his actions? Also, does the punishment fit the crime in this case? Explain both of your answers.
2. Should other individuals and the bank be held legally responsible and liable for Kerviel's actions? Why or why not? Explain.
3. Describe what you believe to have been Kerviel's personal and professional ethics. Use the terms from this chapter as well as your own reasoning.
4. Compare your personal and professional ethics to Kerviel's.
5. Explain how a stakeholder and issues analysis can help you understand this case.
6. What are the lessons students in accounting, business, and organizational studies fields can take away from this case?

Sources

This case was developed from material contained in the following sources:

Accused billion-dollar rogue trader charged, freed. (2008, January 28). *CNN.com.* https://edition.cnn.com/2008/WORLD/europe/01/28/rogue.trader/.

BNP Paribas weighs bid for Société Générale. (2008, January 31). *News A-Z.* http://newsaz.blogspot.com/2008/01/bnp-paribas-weighs-bid-for-societe.html.

Chen, J. (2019, June 25). Jerome Kerviel. *Investopedia.com.* http://investopedia .com/terms/j/jerome-kerviel.asp.

Clark, N. (2010, October 5). Rogue trader at Société Générale gets 3 years. *New York Times.* https://www.nytimes.com/2010/10/06/business/global /06bank.html.

Fortune Global 500. (2008, February 5). *CNN.com.* http://money.cnn.com/magazines /fortune/global500/2006/snapshots/1235.html.

Gumbel, P. (2008, January 25). Financiers never say "sorry." *CNN.com.* http:// money.cnn.com/2008/01/25/magazines/fortune/gumbel_davossorry.fortune /index.htm.

Gumbel, P. (2008, February 1). 4 things I learned from Société Générale. *CNN.com.* http://money.cnn.com/2008/02/01/news/international/socgen_whatilearned .fortune/index.htm.

Judges charge France's "rogue trader." (2008, January 28). *CNN.com.*

Police raid flat of rogue trader Jerome Kerviel (2008, January). *The Telegraph.* http://www.telegraph.co.uk/finance/newsbysector/banksandfinance/2783273 /Police-raid-flat-of-rogue-trader-Jerome-Kerviel.html.

Prosecutor seeks fraud charge for rogue trader. (2008, January 29). *CNN.com.* http://money.cnn.com/2008/01/29/news/international/rogue_trader/index.htm.

Rogue French trader Jerome Kerviel's 3-year sentence, $7 billion fine upheld. (2012, October 24). *DailyFinance.com.*

Rogue Société Générale trader accused of hacking computer systems. (2008, January 28). *ComputerWeekly.com.* http://www.computerweekly.com/news /2240084755/Rogue-Societe-Generale-trader-accused-of-hacking-computer -systems.

"Rogue trader" faces preliminary charges. (2008, January 28). *CNN.com.* http://
    edition.cnn.com/2008/BUSINESS/01/28/soeciete.generale/index.html#cnn
    STCText.

SocGen board rejects CEO resignation. (2008, January 30). *CNN.com.* http://money
    .cnn.com/2008/01/30/news/international/socgen/index.htm.

Société Générale CEOs keep jobs. (2008, January 30). *CNN.com* http://edition.cnn
    .com/2008/WORLD/europe/01/30/french.bank/.

Société Générale ranks No. 67 on *Fortune*'s 2006 Global 500. (2006, September 26).
    CNN.com. http://money.cnn.com/2006/09/21/news/companies/societe_
    generale.fortune/index.htm.

Vandore, Emma. (2008, May 26). Société Générale cites lax management in $7B
    fraud. *ABCNews.com.* http://abcnews.go.com/Business/story?id=4924887.

Case 6

Samuel Waksal at ImClone

Seeking Approval for Erbitux

For several years, ImClone, a biotechnology company, was a darling of Wall Street. Its stock price rose from less than $1 per share in 1994 to $72 a share in November 2001. "The whole time it was producing nothing for sale. It did generate some revenue through licensing agreements with other drug companies—signs that the pharmaceutical industry did think ImClone was on to something." ImClone focused on developing a cancer treatment drug called Erbitux. Erbitux is intended to make cancer treatment more effective by "targeting a protein called epidermal growth factor receptor (EGFR), which exists on the surface of cancer cells and plays a role in their proliferation."

In its 10-K Annual Report for the fiscal year ending December 31, 2001, ImClone described Erbitux as the company's "lead product candidate" and indicated that Erbitux had been shown in early-stage clinical trials to cause tumor reduction in certain cases. ImClone had planned to market the drug in the United States and Canada with its development partner, Bristol-Myers Squibb. On September 19, 2001, ImClone announced that Bristol-Myers Squibb had paid $2 billion for the marketing rights to Erbitux and would codevelop and copromote Erbitux with ImClone.

ImClone was one of at least five pharmaceutical companies with EGFR drugs in mid- to late-stage testing. The winners at commercialization of a new drug class—such as EGFR—are the "companies that beat their rivals to market, since doctors tend to embrace the initial entries." Under this pressure, ImClone took a testing shortcut, using what is known as a single-armed study—one that is conducted without a control group. ImClone's use of the single-armed study failed to meet U.S. Food and Drug Administration (FDA) rigorous criteria for using the methodology.

Samuel Waksal, ImClone's cofounder and CEO at the time, was directly involved in coordinating and publicizing ImClone's efforts to develop Erbitux and to obtain FDA approval for it. On June 28, 2001, ImClone began the process of submitting a rolling application—called a Biologics License Application (BLA)—seeking FDA approval for Erbitux. On October 31, 2001, ImClone submitted to the FDA the final substantial portion of its BLA. The FDA had a 60-day period within which a decision had to be made concerning whether to accept the BLA for filing. The FDA had three options: (1) accept ImClone's BLA for filing; (2) accept the BLA for filing but simultaneously issue a disciplinary review letter notifying ImClone that the BLA still had serious deficiencies that would need to be corrected before the BLA could be approved; or (3) refuse to approve the drug by issuing a Refusal to File (RTF) letter. When the FDA issues an RTF, the applicant must file a new BLA to start the process over.

Samuel Waksal's Reaction to the Impending Refusal to File

On December 25, 2001, Bristol-Myers Squibb learned from a source at the FDA that the federal agency would issue an RTF letter on December 28, 2001. On the evening of December 26, 2001, Waksal learned of the FDA's decision and attempted to sell 79,797 shares of ImClone stock that were held in his brokerage account with Merrill Lynch. He initially told his agent to transfer the shares to his daughter's account. The following morning he instructed his agent to sell the shares. When Waksal's agent called Merrill Lynch to sell the shares, the agent was told that the shares were restricted and could not be sold without the approval of ImClone's legal counsel. When Merrill Lynch refused to conduct the transaction, Waksal ordered his agent to transfer the shares to Bank of America and then sell them. Bank of America also refused to conduct the transaction, and the shares were never sold.

On December 26, 2001, Waksal contacted his father, Jack Waksal, informing him of the impending RTF. The next morning, Jack Waksal placed an order to sell 110,000 shares of ImClone stock. Jack Waksal also called Prudential Securities and placed an order to sell 1,336 shares of ImClone stock from the account of his daughter, Patti Waksal. On December 28, Jack Waksal sold another 25,000 shares of ImClone stock. When questioned by the staff of the Securities and Exchange Commission (SEC), Jack Waksal provided false and misleading explanations for these trades.

On the morning of December 27, 2001, before the stock market opened, Samuel Waksal had a telephone conversation with his daughter Aliza. At that time, Waksal was Aliza's only means of support, and he had control of her bank and brokerage accounts. During their conversation, he directed her to sell all her ImClone shares. Immediately after talking to her father, Aliza placed an order at 9 a.m. to sell 39,472 shares of ImClone stock. By selling her shares at that moment in time, she avoided $630,295 in trading losses.

On December 28, 2001, Waksal purchased 210 ImClone put option contracts, buying them through an account at Discount Bank and Trust AG in Switzerland. He sold all 210 put option contracts on January 4, 2002, which resulted in a profit of $130,130. Waksal also failed to file a statement disclosing a change of ownership of his ImClone securities as required by Section 16(a) of the Exchange Act and Rule 16a-3.

According to the SEC, Waksal violated several sections of the Securities Act when he attempted to sell his own ImClone stock, when he illegally tipped his father about the FDA decision, when he caused Aliza to sell her shares of ImClone stock, and when he purchased ImClone put option contracts.

The Outcome for Samuel Waksal and ImClone

Waksal resigned as ImClone's CEO on May 21, 2002, and on June 12 he was arrested for securities fraud and perjury. Two months later he was indicted for bank fraud, securities fraud, and perjury. On October 15, 2002, Waksal pleaded guilty to all of the counts in the indictment, except those counts based on allegations that he passed material, nonpublic information to his father. On March 3, 2003, he also pleaded guilty to tax-evasion charges for failing to pay New York State sales tax on pieces of art he had purchased. On June 10, 2003, Waksal was sentenced to 87 months in prison and was ordered to pay a $3 million fine and $1.2 million in restitution to the New York State Sales Tax Commission. Waksal began serving his prison sentence on July 23, 2003.

Despite Waksal's actions, ImClone appears to have survived the scandal. Under the leadership of Daniel Lynch, ImClone's former chief financial officer and its current CEO, the company has staged a remarkable turnaround. Most of Im-Clone's 440 employees stayed with the company and helped Lynch revive it. Lynch says the employees stayed for one overpowering reason—they believed in Erbitux. As for himself, Lynch asserted that "what motivated me to get up in the morning was knowing that if I could get this drug approved, it would improve the lives of patients with cancer." Based on a clinical trial by Merck KGaA, ImClone's European marketing partner, the FDA on February 12, 2004 "approved Erbitux for treating patients with advanced colon cancer that has spread to other parts of the body." Thus, Erbitux became ImClone's first commercial product.

Where Are They Now?

Since the scandal, ImClone has since been sold to Eli Lilly for a price of $6.5 billion in 2008. The next year, Waksal was caught up in the Martha Stewart insider trading scandal as well and has since served jail time for his role. Waksal is currently making a comeback in the biotech industry. Waksal started the bio-pharmaceutical firm Kadmon Corp. and planned to open a sister company in China on the Hong Kong Exchange. While some question why people would invest in Kadmon knowing Waksal's history, investors supported the company's initial public offering (IPO) that valued the company at approximately $800 million as of 2016. The company is focused on developing three different treatments believed to cure cancer, autoimmune diseases, and rare disorders.

Questions for Discussion

1. What might motivate an individual or a company to shortcut drug testing that is crucial for FDA approval?
2. Why did Samuel Waksal react as he did pursuant to learning that the FDA would not approve Erbitux?
3. Why were Samuel Waksal's actions unethical?

Sources

This case was developed from material contained in the following sources:

Ackman, D. (2002, October 11). A child's guide to ImClone. *Forbes.com*. http://www.forbes.com/2002/10/11/1011topnews.html.

FDA approves ImClone's Erbitux: Drug at center of insider-trading scandal involving Waksal, Stewart. (2004, February 12). *MSNBC.com*. https://www.nbcnews.com/id/wbna4251347.

Garde, D. (2016, July 26). An ex-con is taking his debt ridden, cash-burning biotech public. Why are people investing? *Statnews.com*. https://www.statnews.com/2016/07/26/kadmon-sam-waksal-biotech-scandal/.

Herper, M. (2002, May 23). ImClone CEO leaves, problems remain. *Forbes.com*. http://www.forbes.com/2002/05/23/0523imclone.html.

Herper, M. (2003, June 10). Samuel Waksal sentenced. *Forbes.com*. http://www
.forbes.com/2003/06/10/cx_mh_0610waksal.html.

SEC v. Samuel D. Waksal. Wayne M. Carlin (WC-2114), Attorney for the SEC. Case 02
Civ. 4407 (NRB). (2003, March 11). Securities and Exchange Commission.
http://www.sec.gov/litigation/complaints/comp18026.htm.

SEC v. Samuel D. Waksal, Jack Waksal, and Patti Waksal. Barry W. Rashover
(BR-6413), Attorney for the SEC. Case 02 Civ. 4407 (NRB). (2003, October 10).
Securities and Exchange Commission. http://www.sec.gov/litigation/complaints
/comp18408.htm.

Shook, D. (2002, February 14). Lessons from ImClone's trial—and error. *Business
Week Online*. https://www.bloomberg.com/news/articles/2002-02-13/lessons
-from-imclones-trial-and-error.

Tirrell, Meg. (2013, September 3). ImClone's Waksal back in biotech with plans
for spinouts. *Bloomberg.com*. http://www.bloomberg.com/news/2013-09-03
/imclone-s-waksal-back-in-biotech-with-plans-for-spinouts.html.

Tischler, L. (2004, September 1). The trials of ImClone. *Fast Company*. https://www
.fastcompany.com/50740/trials-imclone.

Notes

1. Linda Elder, L., and Paul, R. (2011). Ethical reasoning essential to education. *CriticalThinking.org.* http://www.criticalthinking.org/pages/ethical-reasoning-essential-to -education/1036.

2. Velasquez, M. G. (1998). *Business ethics: Concepts and cases,* 4th ed. Englewood Cliffs, NJ: Prentice Hall.

3. Ibid.

4. Ibid.

5. Mill, J. S. (1957). *Utilitarianism.* Indianapolis: Bobbs-Merrill; Carroll, A. (1993). *Business and society: Ethics and stakeholder management,* 2nd ed. Cincinnati: South-Western; Velasquez, M. G. (1992). *Business ethics: Concepts and cases,* 3rd ed. Englewood Cliffs, NJ: Prentice Hall.

6. Brandt, R. (1959). *Ethical theory.* Englewood Cliffs, NJ: Prentice Hall, 253–254; Smart, J., and Williams, B. (1973). *Utilitarianism: For and against.* Cambridge: Cambridge University Press. https://www.utilitarianism.com/utilitarianism-for-and-against.pdf.

7. Delong, J. V., et al. (1981, March/April). Defending cost–benefit analysis: Replies to Steven Kelman. *AEI Journal on Government and Society,* 39–43.

8. Hoffman, W. M., and Moore, J. (1990). *Business ethics: Readings and cases in corporate morality,* 2nd ed. New York: McGraw-Hill.

9. Kelman, S. (1981, January/February). Cost–benefit analysis: An ethical critique. *AEI Journal on Government and Society,* 33–40.

10. Freeman, R. E., and Gilbert, D., Jr. (1988). *Corporate strategy and the search for ethics.* Upper Saddle River, NJ: Prentice Hall.

11. Kant, I. (1964). *Groundwork of the metaphysics of morals.* Translated by H. Paton. New York: Harper & Row.

12. Feldman, F. (1978). *Introductory ethics.* Englewood Cliffs, NJ: Prentice Hall, 119–128.

13. Tuck, R. (1979). *Natural rights theories: Their origin and development.* New York: Cambridge University Press; Stoljar, S. (1984). *An analysis of rights.* New York: St. Martin's Press; Shue, H. (1981). *Basic rights.* Princeton, NJ: Princeton University Press; McCloskey, H. (1965). Rights. *Philosophical Quarterly, 15,* 115–127; Wasserstrom, R. (1964, October 29). Rights, human rights, and racial discrimination. *Journal of Philosophy, 61,* 628–641; Singer, P. (1978). Rights and the market. In Arthur, J., and Shaw, W. (eds.), *Justice and economic distribution,* 207–221. Englewood Cliffs, NJ: Prentice Hall; Hart, H. (1955, April). Are there any natural rights? *Philosophical Review, 64,* 185; Velasquez, M. G. (2002). *Business ethics,* 5th ed. Upper Saddle River, NJ: Prentice Hall.

14. Garrett, T. (1986). *Business ethics,* 2nd ed., 88–91. Englewood Cliffs, NJ: Prentice Hall.

15. Feinberg, J. (1973). *Social philosophy.* Englewood Cliffs, NJ: Prentice Hall.

16. Friedman, M. (1962). *Capitalism and freedom.* Chicago, IL: University of Chicago Press, 22–36.

17. Ibid.

18. Rawls, J. (1971). *A theory of justice.* Cambridge, MA: Harvard University Press.

19. DeGeorge, R. T. (1990). *Business ethics,* 3rd ed. New York: Macmillan.

20. McMahon, T. (1999). Transforming justice: A conceptualization. *Business Ethics Quarterly, 9(4),* 593–602.

21. Ibid., 600.

22. Ibid.

23. Hursthouse, R., and Zalta, E. N. (eds.). (2003, July 18). Virtue ethics. *Stanford Encyclopedia of Philosophy.* http://plato.stanford.edu/archives/fall2003/entries/ethics-virtue/.

24. Ibid.

25. Ibid.

26. Virtue theory (n.d.). *The Internet Encyclopedia of Philosophy.* http://www.iep.utm.edu/virtue/, accessed March 18, 2012. This quote is taken from the section "Loudon's Critique," based on Louden, R. (1984). On some vices of virtue ethics. *American Philosophical Quarterly, 21,* 227–236.

27. Beauchamp, T. L., and Childress, J. F. (2002). *Principles of biomedical ethics,* 5th ed. Oxford: Oxford University Press.

28. Rawls (1971), op. cit.

29. Velasquez, M. G., Andre, C., Shanks, T., S. J., and Meyer, M. J. (2014, August 2). The common good. Markkula Center, Santa Clara University. http://www.scu.edu/ethics/practicing/decision/commongood.html (originally appeared in *Issues in Ethics, 5(2),* Spring 1992.

30. Ibid.

31. Ibid.

32. Beauchamp, T. L., and Childress, J. F. (1994). *Principles of biomedical ethics,* 4th ed. New York: Oxford University Press.

33. Steiner, G. A., and Steiner, J. F. (2000). *Business, government, and society: A managerial perspective,* 9th ed. Boston: McGraw-Hill.

34. Freeman and Gilbert (1988), op. cit., 36.

35. Ibid.

36. Based on the ImClone research of Amy Venskus, master's student at Bentley College, Waltham, MA, 2004.

37. Leung, R. (2003, October 2). Sam Waksal: I was arrogant. *CBSNews.com.* https://www.cbsnews.com/news/sam-waksal-i-was-arrogant-02-10-2003.

38. Buono, A. F., and Nichols, L. T. (1990). Stockholder and stakeholder interpretations of business' social role. In Hoffman, W. M., and Moore, J. M. (eds.), *Business ethics: Readings and cases in corporate morality,* 2nd ed. New York: McGraw-Hill.

39. Bush moves to ease lending crisis. (2007, August 31). *BBCNews.co.uk.* http://news.bbc.co.uk/2/hi/business/6971746.stm.

40. Davis, L. (1976). Comments on Nozick's entitlement theory. *Journal of Philosophy, 73,* 839–842.

41. Barton, N., et al. (2006, June 25). Warren Buffett gives major share of fortune to Gates Foundation. *The Chronicle of Philanthropy.*

42. Edwards, F., Lee, H., and Esposito, M. (2019, August 20). Risk of being killed by police use of force in the United States by age, race–ethnicity, and sex. *Proceedings of the National Academy of Sciences, 116(34).* https://www.pnas.org/content/116/34/16793.

43. Semaj Mitchell@semajmitchell12. May 28, 2020. #BlacklivesMatter #TMCChequered flag. Tweet

44. Antes, A. L., Brown, R. P., Murphy, S. T., Waples, E. P., Mumford, M. D., Connelly, S., and Devenport, L. D. (2007, December). Personality and ethical decision-making in research: The role of perception of self and others. *Journal of Empirical Research on Human Research Ethics, 2(4),* 15–34.

45. Skarlicki, P., Folger, R., and Tesluk, P. (1999). Personality as a moderator in the relationship between fairness and retaliation. *Academy of Management Journal, 42(1),* 100–108.

46. McFerran, B., Aquino, K., and Duffy, M. (2010, January). How personality and moral identity relate to individuals' ethical ideology. *Business Ethics Quarterly, 20(1),* 35–56.

47. Kohlberg, L. (1969). State and sequence: The cognitive developmental approach to socialization. In Gosline, D. A. (ed.), *Handbook of socialization theory and research.* Chicago:

Rand McNally; Jones, T. (1991). Ethical decision making by individuals in organizations: An issue-contingent model. *Academy of Management Review, 16(2)*, 366–395.

48. Covey, S. (1989). *The 7 habits of highly effective people.* New York: Free Press.

49. Wattles, J., Geier, B., Egan, M., and Wiener-Bronner, D. (2018). Wells Fargo's 20-month nightmare. *CNN Business.* https://money.cnn.com/2018/04/24/news/companies/wells-fargo-timeline-shareholders/index.html?iid=EL

50. Kelton, Erika. (2013, January 25). JPMorgan and Jamie Dimon need an extreme makeover. *Forbes.com.* http://www.forbes.com/sites/erikakelton/2013/01/25/jpmorgan-and-jamie-dimon-need-an-extreme-makeover/; Tayan, B. (2019). The Wells Fargo Cross-Selling Scandal. https://corpgov.law.harvard.edu/2019/02/06/the-wells-fargo-cross-selling-scandal-2/

51. Wal-Mart to appeal discrimination suit status. (2007, February 6). *CNN Money.* http://money.cnn.com/2007/02/06/news/companies/walmart/index.htm; Case profile: Wal-Mart lawsuit (re: gender discrimination in USA). (2008, April 14). Business and Human Rights Resource Centre. Accessed March 15, 2012, http://www.business-human rights.org/Categories/Lawlawsuits/Lawsuitsregulatoryaction/LawsuitsSelectedcases/Wal-MartlawsuitregenderdiscriminationinUSA.

52. Jaeger, J. (2019, December 27). Top ethics and compliance failures of 2019. *Compliance Week.* https://www.complianceweek.com/opinion/top-ethics-and-compliance-failures-of-2019/28237.article.

53. Werhane, P. (1999). *Moral imagination and management decision-making.* New York: Oxford University Press.

54. Badaracco, J., Jr. (1998). A guide to defining moments, the discipline of building character. *Harvard Business Review, 76(2)*, 114.

55. Ibid., 114–115.

56. Ibid., 114–121.

57. Nash, L. (1981, November/December). Ethics without the sermon. *Harvard Business Review, 59(6)*, 88.

58. Krolick, S. (1987). *Ethical decision-making style: Survey and interpretive notes.* Beverly, MA: Addison-Wesley.

59. Ibid.

60. Ibid., 18.

61. Ibid., 20.

62. Steiner and Steiner (2000) op. cit.; Freeman and Gilbert (1988), op. cit.; Mill (1957), op. cit.; Carroll (1993), op. cit.; Velasquez (1992), based on Steiner and Steiner, and Carroll, op. cit.

63. Freeman and Gilbert (1988), op. cit.

3

STAKEHOLDER AND ISSUES MANAGEMENT APPROACHES

OPENING CASE

"Before Deepwater, there was this mentality that had set in in the 1990s and 2000s, that the oil and gas industry, as it was going farther offshore, was capable of self-regulating," says Matt Lee Ashley, a researcher at the Center for American Progress. "Then Deepwater happened and burst that set of assumptions."[1]

The oil company BP (formerly British Petroleum) leased/licensed the *Deepwater Horizon* oil rig, operated by Transocean and contracted by Halliburton, that exploded in flames in the Gulf of Mexico on the night of April 20, 2010.[2] The result was 11 deaths, 17 injured, and hundreds of miles of beaches soiled. A "blowout preventer" (specialized valve) designed to prevent crude oil releases failed to activate.[3]

The factual events leading up to the BP blowout unearth a highly complex network of stakeholders, stakes, and circumstances, which though preventable, together culminated in the worst environmental disaster recorded in U.S. history. In March 2008, the U.S. Occupational Safety and Health Administration (OSHA) recorded on public record that BP had one of the worst safety records in its industry. After the explosion when the *Deepwater Horizon* sank, "a sea-floor oil gusher flowed for 87 days, until it was capped on 15 July 2010."[4] The total oil spill was estimated at 210 million U.S. gallons. By September 2010, with all-out efforts by BP and a host of other organizations and crews, the entire well had been sealed, but the legal and ethical issues and stakeholder disputes had only begun. In 2013, over 2.7 million pounds of "oiled material" had been removed from the Louisiana coast, and tar balls were reported daily on Alabama and Florida beaches.

Different phases of the trials are ongoing.[5] BP has already admitted guilt in 2012 to 14 criminal charges that included manslaughter and "negligence in misreading important tests before the explosion." The company agreed to pay $4.5 billion in fines and penalties. "Four current or former employees also face criminal charges. The company has spent more than $42 billion on cleaning up the environment and compensating victims. People and businesses continue to file claims for damages, and there is no cap to the damages."[6]

The Justice Department and Judge Carl Barbier are overseeing and managing a latter part of the trial between the plaintiffs (Transocean, Halliburton, the states of Louisiana and Alabama, and private plaintiffs) and BP (with its partner, Anadarko Petroleum). The main issue at this point in the case that the plaintiffs must prove is whether a total of 4.2 million barrels of oil was discharged as a result of the oil rig exploding into the sea 87 days after the explosion. That amount of oil is the equivalent of nearly one-quarter of all the oil consumed in the United States in one day. Plaintiffs allege that BP's failure of preparation caused the crisis and aftermath of oil flow. BP is defending whether or not it was prepared for a blowout and if its response was adequate once the oil started leaking.[7]

Stakeholders in this crisis number in the thousands. In the federal government alone, stakeholders included the Departments of Energy, Interior, Justice, members of Congress, and even President Obama—who met with BP executives in June 2010 and persuaded them "to create a $20 billion fund to compensate residents and businesses for losses resulting from the spill."[8] Obama also announced plans to empower the Minerals Management Service to oversee offshore drilling. Other key stakeholders include BP employees and their families, BP's partners, and the plaintiffs.

BP agreed to a settlement involving literally thousands of individuals affected by the spill in 2012 totaling $7.8 billion—the amount that BP would have to pay was not capped, however. Over 200,000 individuals and businesses were paid $6.1 billion through the Gulf Coast Claims Facility. Add to this number the state governments and agencies affected by the spill, the lawyers on both sides of the case, insurance companies, auditors, and competitors, all of whom are also stakeholders. In addition, the response and aftermath cleanup "involved thousands of boats, tens of thousands of workers, and millions of feet of containment boom."[9]

BP's then–chief executive officer (CEO) Tony Hayward defended BP against accusations that the company was not prepared and that it cut corners on the design of the well and then attempted to escape responsibility for the consequences. He was replaced by Robert Dudley, BP's managing director after the blowout, when Hayward was criticized for minimizing the scale of the spill and for making remarks such as, "There's no one who wants this thing over more than I do. I'd like my life back"– which particularly offended members of the workers' families who died in the explosion. His presence at a yacht race in June, only months after the spill, reportedly contributed to accusations of insensitivity.[10]

This crisis will be studied and analyzed for years to come. The human, political, economic, environmental, and social costs were enormous. "Tens of thousands of families have been affected by the spill, whether they work in the fishing industry, tourism, or oil. The area of the spill supplies 40 percent of seafood in the U.S."[11] BP has increased its investment "in exploration and projects annual capital spending over the next several years to be $24 billion to $27 billion–at least 25 percent higher than 2011 levels as the company pours cash into projects in Angola, Azerbaijan, Indonesia, and elsewhere," according to CEO Dudley.[12]

"Scientists state that since that oil spill, they now know more about . . . the Gulf of Mexico, as well as the physics, ecology, and chemistry of oil spills, than they ever would have otherwise. . . . It's that old adage, 'you can't manage what you don't understand'–well, you can't protect what you don't understand. . . ."[13]

3.1 Stakeholder Theory and the Stakeholder Management Approach Defined

The BP *Deepwater Horizon* oil spill is, to date, the largest oil spill in the history of marine oil drilling operations. It was a complex crisis not limited to the financial, economic, and corporate interests involved. Since numerous people, businesses, and the environment were affected, and 11 workers lost their lives, an analysis that also encompasses ethical and moral considerations is required.

Stakeholder theory is best described by R. Edward Freeman—its modern founder. As Freeman wrote:

> My thesis is that I can revitalize the concept of managerial capitalism by replacing the notion that managers have a duty to stockholders with the concept that managers bear a fiduciary relationship to stakeholders. Stakeholders are those

groups who have a stake in or claim on the firm. Specifically I include suppliers, customers, employees, stockholders, and the local community, as well as management in its role as agent for these groups. . . . Each of these stakeholder groups has a right not to be treated as a means to some end, and therefore must participate in determining the future direction of the firm in which they have a stake.[14]

Freeman and his collaborators state that it is "a mistake to see stakeholder theory as a specific theory with a single purpose. Researchers would do well to see stakeholder theory as a set of shared ideas that can serve a range of purposes within different disciplines and address different questions."[15]

The *stakeholder management approach* is based on a related instrumental theory that argues "a subset of ethical principles (trust, trustworthiness, and cooperativeness) can result in significant competitive advantage."[16] This approach, then, allows researchers and practitioners to use analytical concepts and methods for identifying, mapping, and evaluating corporate strategy with stakeholders. We refer to the use of this instrumental approach in stakeholder theory as "stakeholder analysis."

The stakeholder management approach, including frameworks for analyzing and evaluating a corporation's relationships (present and potential) with external groups, aims ideally at reaching "win–win" collaborative outcomes. Here, win–win means making moral decisions that benefit the common good of all constituencies within the constraints of justice, fairness, and economic interests. Unfortunately, this does not always happen. There are usually winners and losers in complex situations where there is a perceived zero-sum game (i.e., a situation in which there are limited resources, and what is gained by one person is necessarily lost by the other).

Scholars and consultants, however, have used the stakeholder management approach as a means for planning and implementing collaborative relationships to achieve win–win outcomes among stakeholders.[17] Structured dialogue facilitated by consultants is a major focus in these collaborative communications. The aim in using the stakeholder approach as a communication strategy is to change perceptions and "rules of engagement" to create win–win outcomes.

A stakeholder management approach does not have to result from a crisis, as so many examples from ethics literature and the news provide. It can also be used as a planning method to anticipate and facilitate business decisions, events, and policy outcomes. A stakeholder analysis is not only limited to publicly traded, for-profit enterprises but also applies to nonprofit organizations: "Stakeholder theorists clearly indicate that their theory is intended to [benefit] more than merely for-profit corporations."[18]

A stakeholder management approach also begins, as indicated in Chapter 1, by asking what external forces in the general environment are affecting an organization. This context can often provide clues to responses by stakeholders to opportunities, crises, and extraordinary events. After Enron, corporate scandals revealed that there were several factors in the general environment that were at play, in addition to certain corporate executives' greed. For example, the dot-com technology bubble leading up to the year 2000 created a financial environment where investment funds followed innovative ideas in exorbitant and exuberant ways. Investment banks loaned large amounts to Enron and other companies without due diligence. Stock analysts lied and encouraged deceptive investing from the public. Boards of directors abandoned their fiscal responsibilities, as did large accounting firms like Arthur Andersen (which is no longer in existence). The general legal and enforcement environment during the 1990s appeared indifferent to monitoring corporate activities and protecting shareholders. A similar general environment with low-to-nonexistent government regulation followed, culminating in the 2008 subprime-lending crisis that sent the global economy reeling. Next we define the term "stakeholder."

Stakeholders

A *stakeholder* is "any individual or group who can affect or is affected by the actions, decisions, policies, practices, or goals of the organization."[19] We begin by identifying the *focal stakeholder*. This is the company or group that is the focus or central constituency of an analysis.

The *primary stakeholders* of a firm include its owners, customers, employees, and suppliers. Also of primary importance to a firm's survival are its stockholders and board of directors. The CEO and other top-level executives can be stakeholders, but in the stakeholder analysis they are generally considered actors and representatives of the firm. In this chapter's opening case, BP's CEO and top-level team are focal stakeholders. Coalitional focal stakeholders that may also be connected to BP primary stakeholders include owners, customers, employees, and in this case, Chinese vendors and suppliers.

Secondary stakeholders include all other interested groups, such as the media, consumers, lobbyists, courts, governments, competitors, the public, and society. Halliburton and Transocean were considered "secondary stakeholders" by BP's then CEO and other officers; after the spill, these collaborators became plaintiffs. Control and quality of products and services can be diminished and/or lost with outsourced and licensing relationships if proper monitoring and management is absent. One final report on this case suggested that the real root of the problem was BP's own laissez-faire approach to safety, even though spokespersons from BP denied this allegation.[20]

Stakes

A *stake* is any interest, share, or claim that a group or individual has in the outcome of a corporation's policies, procedures, or actions toward others. Stakes may be based on any type of interest. The stakes of stakeholders are not always obvious. The economic viability of competing firms can be at stake when one firm threatens entry into a market. The physical environment, employees' lives, and the health and welfare of communities can be at stake when corporations like BP either relax or do not have in place proper equipment, safety standards, and emergency plans for crises.

Stakes also can be present, past, or future oriented. For example, stakeholders may seek compensation for a firm's past actions, as has occurred when lawyers argued that certain airlines owed their clients monetary compensation after having threatened their emotional stability when pilots announced an impending disaster (engine failure) that, subsequently, did not occur. Stakeholders may seek future claims; that is, they may seek injunctions against firms that announce plans to drill for oil or build nuclear plants in designated areas or to market or bundle certain products in noncompetitive ways.

3.2 Why Use a Stakeholder Management Approach for Business Ethics?

The stakeholder management approach is a response to the growth and complexity of contemporary corporations and the need to understand how they operate with their stakeholders and stockholders. Stakeholder theory argues that corporations should treat all their constituencies fairly and that doing so allows the companies to perform better in the marketplace.[21] "If organizations want to be effective, they will pay attention to all and only those relationships that can affect or be affected by the achievement of the organization's purposes."[22] Although stakeholder theory includes a fiduciary dimension by nature of its intent, as Freeman was quoted as saying above, we apply this theory in ways that use ethical principles such as justice, utilitarianism, rights, and universalism to individual stakeholders and their interactions with each other and corporations. A case study that integrates a stakeholder approach with issues management and ethics is found in K. T. Berg and S. B. Feldner, "Analyzing the Intersection of Transparency, Issue Management and Ethics: The Case of Big Soda" (*Journal of Media Ethics*, 32[3] [2017]: 154–167).

This chapter applies the stakeholder management approach not only in its theoretical form, but also as a practical method that combines issues management and ethics concepts to analyze how companies deal with their stakeholders. We therefore use the term "stakeholder analysis" (which is part of stakeholder management) to identify strategies, actions, and policy results of firms in their management of employees, competitors, the media, courts, and stockholders. Later in the chapter, we introduce "issues management" as another set of methods for identifying and managing stakeholders. We present issues management and stakeholder theory as complementary theories that use similar methods. Starting with a major issue or opportunity that a company faces is a helpful way to begin a stakeholder analysis.

A more familiar way of understanding corporations is the *stockholder approach*, which focuses on financial and economic relationships. By contrast, a stakeholder management approach is a normative and instrumental approach that studies actors' interests, stakes, and actions.[23] The stakeholder management approach takes into account nonmarket forces that affect organizations and individuals, such as moral, political, legal, and technological interests, as well as economic factors.

Underlying the stakeholder management approach is the ethical imperative that mandates that businesses in their fiduciary relationships to their stockholders: (1) act in the best interests of and for the benefit of customers, employees, suppliers, and stockholders; and (2) respect and fulfill these stakeholders' rights. One study concluded that "multiple objectives—including both economic and social considerations—can be and, in fact, are simultaneously and successfully pursued within large and complex organizations that collectively account for a major part of all economic activity within our society."[24] The larger literature on cross-disciplinary stakeholder theory and methods, not all of which is included, deals with such topics such as stakeholder identification and engagement, multi-stakeholder networks and eco systems, and stakeholder theory applied to multiple international contexts.

Stakeholder Theory: Criticisms and Responses

The dominant criticism of stakeholder theory by some scholars is that corporations should serve only stockholders since they own the corporation.[25] It is important to observe criticisms of stakeholder theory and responses to them in order to understand the purpose of and benefits provided by stakeholder theory. The following criticisms have been offered by scholars: stakeholder theory (1) negates and weakens fiduciary duties that managers owe to stockholders, (2) weakens the influence and power of stakeholder groups, (3) weakens the firm, and (4) changes the long-term character of the capitalist system.[26] Ethically, these arguments are based on property and implied contract rights and on fiduciary duties and responsibilities of managers to stockholders.

Critics claim that some stakeholder groups' power can be weakened by stakeholder theory by treating all stakeholders equally—as stakeholder theory suggests. For example, labor unions can be avoided, hurt, or even eliminated. Corporations can also be weakened in their pursuit of profit if they attempt to serve all stakeholders' interests. The corporation cannot be all things to all stakeholders and protect stockholders' fiduciary interest. Finally, critics who claim that stakeholder theory changes the long-term character of capitalism argue that (1) corporations have no responsibility by law other than to their stockholders, since the market disciplines corporations anyway, and that (2) stakeholder theory permits some managers to "game" corporations by arguing that they are protecting some stakeholder interests, even if interests of others are harmed. Some more leftist thinkers also criticize advocates of stakeholder theory as being naive and utopian. These critics claim that well-intentioned "do-gooders" ignore or mask the reality of capital labor relationships through simplistic notions in stakeholder theory such as "participation," "empowerment," and "realizing human potential."[27]

Despite these criticisms, stakeholder theory continues to be popular and widely used. As noted earlier in this chapter, societies and economies involve market and nonmarket interests of diverse stakeholders as well as stockholders. To understand and effect responsible corporate strategies, methods that include different players and environmental factors—not just stockholders or financial interests—are required. Stakeholder theory addresses these realities. The following point also responds to some of the above criticisms. Stakeholder theory does offer advantages. For example, Susan Key's 1999 critique of stakeholder theory of the firm[28] has been summarized[29] as follows: "Stakeholder theory must account for power and urgency as well as legitimacy, no matter how distasteful or unsettling the results. Managers must know about groups in their environment that hold power and intend to impose their will upon the firm. Power and urgency must be attended to if managers are to serve the legal and moral interests of legitimate stakeholders."

The ethical dimension of stakeholder theory is based on the view that profit maximization is constrained by justice, that regard for individual rights should be extended to all constituencies that have a stake in a business, and that organizations are not only "economic" in nature but can also act in socially responsible ways. To this end, companies *should* act in socially responsible ways, not only because it's the "right thing to do," but also to ensure their legitimacy.[30]

3.3 How to Execute a Stakeholder Analysis

Stakeholder analysis is a pragmatic way of identifying and understanding multiple (often competing) claims of many constituencies. As part of a general stakeholder approach, stakeholder analysis is a method to help understand the relationships between an organization and the groups with which it must interact. Each situation is different and therefore requires a map to guide strategy for an organization dealing with groups, some of whom may not be supportive of issues, such as outsourcing jobs. The aim here is to familiarize you with the framework so that you can apply it in the classroom and to news events that appear in the press and in other media. Even though you may not be an executive or manager, the framework can help you to see the "big picture" of complex corporate dealings and apply ethical reasoning and principles when analyzing strategies used by managers and different stakeholders.

Taking a Third-Party Objective Observer Perspective

In the following discussion, you are asked to assume the role of a CEO of a company to execute a stakeholder analysis. However, it is recommended that you take the role of "third-party objective observer" when doing a stakeholder analysis. Why? In this role, you will need to suspend your belief and value judgments in order to understand the strategies, motives, and actions of the different stakeholders. You may not agree with the focal organization or CEO you are studying. Therefore, the point is to be able to see all sides of an issue and then objectively evaluate the claims, actions, and outcomes of all the parties. Being more objective helps determine who acted responsibly, who won and who lost, and at what costs.

Part of the learning process in this exercise is to see your own blind spots, values, beliefs, and passions toward certain issues and stakeholders. Doing an in-depth stakeholder analysis with a group allows others to see and comment on your reasoning. For the next section, however, take the role of a CEO so that you can get an idea of what it feels like to be in charge of directing an organization-wide analysis.

Role of the CEO in Stakeholder Analysis

Assume for this exercise that you are the CEO, working with your top managers, in a firm that has just been involved in a major controversy of international proportions. The media, some consumer groups, and several major customers have called you. You want to get a handle on the situation without reverting to unnecessary "firefighting" management methods. A couple of your trusted staff members have advised you to adopt a planning approach quickly while responding to immediate concerns and to understand the "who, what, where, when, and why" of the situation before jumping to "how" questions. Your senior strategic planner suggests you lead and participate in a stakeholder analysis. What is the next step?

The stakeholder analysis is a series of steps aimed at the following tasks:[31]

1. Map stakeholder relationships.
2. Map stakeholder coalitions.
3. Assess the nature of each stakeholder's responsibilities.
4. Assess the nature of each stakeholder's power.
5. Construct a framework of stakeholder moral responsibilities and interests.
6. Develop specific strategies and tactics.
7. Monitor shifting coalitions.

Each step is described in the following sections. Let's explore each one and then apply them in our continuing scenario example.

Step 1: Map Stakeholder Relationships

In 1984, R. Edward Freeman offered questions that help begin the analysis of identifying major stakeholders (Figure 3.1). The first five questions in the figure offer a quick jump-start to the analysis. Questions 6 through 9 may be used in later steps, when you assess the nature of each stakeholder's interest and priorities.

Figure 3.1

Sample Questions for Stakeholder Review

1. Who are our stakeholders currently?
2. Who are our potential stakeholders?
3. How does each stakeholder affect us?
4. How do we affect each stakeholder?
5. For each division and business, who are the stakeholders?
6. What assumptions does our current strategy make about each important stakeholder (at each level)?
7. What are the current "environmental variables" that affect us and our stakeholders (initiation, GNP, prime rate, confidence in business [from polls], corporate identity, media image, and so on)?
8. How do we measure each of these variables and their impact on us and our stakeholders?
9. How do we keep score with our stakeholders?

Source: Freeman, R. E. (1984). *Strategic management: A stakeholder approach.* Boston: Pitman, 242. Reproduced with permission of the author.

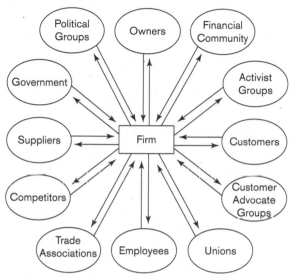

Figure 3.2

Stakeholder Map of a Large Organization

Source: Freeman, R. E. (1984). *Strategic management: A Stakeholder approach.*
Boston: Pitman, 25. Reproduced with permission of the author.

Let's continue our example with you as CEO. While brainstorming about questions 1 through 5 with employees you have selected who are the most knowledgeable, current, and close to the sources of the issues at hand, you may want to draw a stakeholder map and fill in the blanks. Note that your stakeholder analysis is only as valid and reliable as the sources and processes you use to obtain your information. As a CEO in this hypothetical scenario, which is controversial, incomplete, and in which questionable issues arise, you may wish to go outside your immediate planning group to obtain additional information and perspective. You should therefore identify and complete the stakeholder map (Figure 3.2), inserting each relevant stakeholder involved in the particular issue you are studying.

For example, if you were examining the BP spill—and you were not the CEO of that company—you would place BP and then CEO Tony Hayward—later replaced by Robert Dudley—in the center (or focal) stakeholder box in Figure 3.2, then continue identifying the other groups involved: Halliburton, Transocean, employees who were victims and those immediately endangered by the spill, shareholders (members of the lawsuit), affected community victims (families), affected community businesses, the U.S. government (Departments of Justice and the Interior), the U.S. Congress, President Obama, suppliers and distributors, and competitors, among others. In completing a stakeholder map, include real groups, individuals, and organizations—issues are not part of the formal stakeholder map.

Note that in Figure 3.2 the reciprocal arrows represent enacted major strategies and tactics between each stakeholder and the focal stakeholder.

Step 2: Map Stakeholder Coalitions

After you identify and make a map of the stakeholders who are involved with your firm in the incident you are addressing, the next step is to determine and map any coalitions that have formed. Coalitions among stakeholders form around stakes that they have—or seek to have—in common. Interest groups and lobbyists sometimes join forces against a common "enemy." Competitors also may join forces if they see an advantage in numbers. Mapping actual and potential coalitions around issues can help you, as the CEO, anticipate and design strategic responses toward these groups before or after they form.

Step 3: Assess the Nature of Each Stakeholder's Responsibilities

Next you need to identify the nature of each stakeholder's interests and responsibilities in a particular situation. Since each stakeholder has a stake, interest, or claim in the process and outcomes of the situation, opportunity, controversy, or crisis, it is important to assess the nature of the focal organization's responsibilities toward each stakeholder group. As Figure 3.3, which is based on Archie Carroll's work on the Pyramid of Corporate Social Responsibility and the Moral Management of Organizational Stakeholders, illustrates, addressing the legal, economic, ethical, and voluntary nature of a company's responsibility toward owners, customers, employees, community groups, the public, government, and victims brings a moral awareness to the CEO of the focal company. For example, in 2014, the pharmacy chain CVS banned the sale of tobacco

Figure 3.3

Nature of Focal Organization's Ethical Responsibilities

Stakeholders	Economic	Legal	Ethical	Voluntary
Owners				
Leaders and Managers				
Employees				
Customers				
Suppliers				
Communities				
Competitors				
Suppliers				
Media				
Government				
Public				
Victims				
Other?				

Source: Adapted from Carroll, A. (1991, July–August). The pyramid of corporate social responsibility: Toward the moral management of organizational stakeholders. *Business Horizons, 34 (4)*, 44.

products from its 7,600 stores, a decision made with the express intent of help-ing create a smoke-free generation. In 2021, CVS supportively acknowledged a U.S. Food and Drug Administration (FDA) proposed policy to ban menthol cigarettes and flavored cigars that would serve the health interests of the public, including the disproportionate discrimination in selling such products in Black communities. With regard to Figure 3.3, this voluntary decision may affect CVS's short-term profits, but it takes an ethical stand that influences all its stakeholders and stockholders. This step is not limited to the CEO; other stake-holders would benefit from using it. With regard to the BP situation, had the CEO and his core team completed this exercise and acted responsibly, he may not have lost his job.

For example, BP's CEO may see the firm's *economic responsibility* to the owners (as stakeholders) as "preventing as many costly lawsuits as possible." *Legally*, the CEO may want to protect the owners and the executive team from liability and damage; this would entail proactively negotiating disputes out-side the courts, if possible, in a way that is equitable to all. *Ethically*, the CEO may keep the company's stockholders and owners up to date regarding the company's ethical thinking and strategies to show responsibility toward all stakeholders. At stake is the firm's reputation as well as its profitability. In the case of BP and other crises, the CEO's job and future career with the com-pany can be at risk. Missteps in communicating with the media and visible stakeholders, and showing insensitivity to victims or the situation, can cause executives to lose their job during a crisis, as was the case at BP.

Step 4: Assess the Nature of Each Stakeholder's Power

This part of the analysis asks, "What's in it for each stakeholder? Who stands to win, lose, or draw over certain stakes?" Let us examine eight types of power that different stakeholders exert and that you can use in your analysis: (1) *vot-ing power* (the ability of stakeholders to exert control through strength in num-bers); (2) *political power* (the ability to influence decision-making processes and agendas of public and private organizations and institutions); (3) *economic power* (the ability to influence by control over resources—monetary and phys-ical); (4) *technological power* (the ability to influence innovations and decisions through uses of technology); (5) *legal power* (the ability to influence laws, poli-cies, and procedures); (6) *environmental power* (the ability to impact nature); (7) *cultural power* (the ability to influence values, norms, and habits of people and organizations); and (8) *power over individuals and groups* (the ability to in-fluence particular, targeted persons and groups through different forms of persuasion).[32] The BP example suggests that shareholders, members of Con-gress, and individual constituents have voting power over BP's policies and officers' jobs and responsibilities. The president of the United States, govern-ment regulatory agencies, consumers, stock market analysts, and investors all exert economic power over BP in this situation. The U.S. government, reg-ulatory agencies, and interest groups also exert political power over BP's operating and manufacturing policies, processes, and products.

Note that power and influence are exerted in two-way relations: BP toward its stakeholders, and each stakeholder toward BP on a given issue. For exam-ple, owners and stockholders can vote on the firm's decisions regarding a particular issue or opportunity, such as BP's future drilling plans. On the other hand, federal, state, and local governments can exercise their political power by voting on BP's legal obligations toward consumers. New legislation may emerge with regard to the regulation of BP's outsourcing and quality-control methods. In return, consumers can exercise their economic power by boycotting BP's products or buying from other companies. What other sources of stakeholder power exist in this case?

Step 5: Construct a Framework of Stakeholder Moral Responsibilities and Interests

After you map stakeholder relationships and assess the nature of each stakeholder's interest and power, the next step is to identify the moral obligations your company has to each stakeholder.

Chapter 2 explained the ethical principles and guidelines that can assist in this type of decision making. For purposes of completing this matrix, ethical decision making of company representatives can refer to the following ethical principles: *utilitarianism* (weighing costs and benefits—"ends justifying means"); *universalism* (showing respect and concern for human beings—"means count as much as ends"); *rights* (recognizing individual liberties and privileges under laws and constitutions); *justice* (observing the distribution of burdens and benefits of all concerned). *Voluntarily* (i.e., acting freely and from one's own accord), the CEO may advise shareholders to show responsibility by publicly announcing their plans for resolving the issue of the firm's "next steps." This can also be done in more open and conscientious marketing activities as well as in a consciously responsible distribution of products.

This part of the analysis lays the foundation for developing specific strategies toward each stakeholder you have identified. Notice that developing strategies first preempts and may omit putting "first things first." In this case, this means meeting your moral responsibilities to those affected in the situation and not protecting or promoting profit first and at any costs. Although there is a fiduciary responsibility toward your stockholders, you may discover that you can lose your company (bankruptcy) and its assets, including your job, if you do not also attend to powerful noneconomic interests—customers, victims and their families' lives in crisis situations, communities' needs, the media's attacks, and legitimacy with the general public and government.

Step 6: Develop Specific Strategies and Tactics

Using the results from the preceding steps, you can now proceed to outline the specific strategies and tactics you wish to use with each stakeholder. If you are a CEO using this framework, you can use Figure 3.4 along with the previous frameworks in this section to help articulate strategies to employ with different stakeholders.[33]

The typology of organizational stakeholders in Figure 3.4 shows two dimensions: potential for threat and potential for cooperation. Note that stakeholders can move among the quadrants, changing positions as situations and stakes change. Generally, officers of a firm in controversial situations, or situations that offer significant opportunities for an organization, try to influence

Figure 3.4

Diagnostic Typology of Organizational Stakeholders

Stakeholder's Potential for
Threat to Organization

	High	Low
High	Type 4 **MIXED BLESSING** Strategy: **COLLABORATE**	Type 1 **SUPPORTIVE** Strategy: **INVOLVE**
Low	Type 3 **NONSUPPORTIVE** Strategy: **DEFEND**	Type 2 **MARGINAL** Strategy: **MONITOR**

(Row axis label: Stakeholder's Potential for Cooperation with Organization)

Source: Savage, G. T., Nix, T. W., Whitehead, C. J., and Blair, J. D. (1991). Strategies for assessing and managing organizational stakeholders. *Academy of Management Executive, 5,* 65. © 1991 Academy of Management. Reproduced with permission of Academy of Management in the format Textbook via Copyright Clearance Center.

and move stakeholders toward type 1—the *Supportive* stakeholder with a low potential for threat and high potential for cooperation. Here the strategy of the focal company is to *involve* the supportive stakeholder. Think of both internal and external stakeholders who might be supportive and who should be involved in the focal organization's strategy.

In contrast, type 3, the *Nonsupportive* stakeholder, who shows a high potential for threat and a low potential for cooperation, represents an undesirable stance from the perspective of the influencer. The suggested strategy in this situation calls for the focal organization to *defend* its interests and reduce dependence on that stakeholder.

A type 4 stakeholder is a *Mixed Blessing,* with a high potential for both threat and cooperation. This stakeholder calls for a *collaborative* strategy. In this situation, the stakeholder could become a Supportive or Nonsupportive type. A collaborative strategy aims to move the stakeholder to the focal company's interests.

Finally, type 2 is the *Marginal* stakeholder. This stakeholder has a low potential for both threat and cooperation. Such stakeholders may not be interested in the issues of concern. The recommended strategy in this situation is to *monitor* the stakeholder, to "wait and see" and minimize expenditure of resources, until the stakeholder moves to a Mixed Blessing, Supportive, or Nonsupportive position.

With regard to this chapter's opening case, had you been the BP CEO at that time after the explosion, you and your staff would have decided what strategy to pursue with regard to addressing the crisis. The nature of that strategy would have determined who would be the supporters and nonsupporters of BP's decisions. If you had chosen to deny and avoid responsibility for the explosion, or to blame the companies who were outsourced and running those projects, you may have found that your supporters would have been fewer and you may have realized that an avoidance, denial, and/or blame strategy would have pushed more stakeholders to the Nonsupportive space. Nonsupportive stakeholders would be those who sought but did not find support and truthfulness from BP's officers with regard to owning responsibility, offering apologies, and then providing immediate help. Therefore, families of victims of the explosion who appeared in the media, disgruntled and shocked employees from the rig who survived the explosion, community inhabitants in the vicinity of the oil spill, and others would be nonsupportive. Who else would you add to those in opposition to BP at the time of the crisis, shortly afterward, and even a year or two or three down the road? By systematically completing this exercise and brainstorming with others who would be truthful with you, as a CEO in a crisis, you can—before you react—create a broader, more objective, and socially responsible picture of and response to the situation. At stake in such cases as the BP spill is the company's survival and reputation.

Figure 3.5 presents an example of the typology in Figure 3.4, using the BP oil spill case as an example. It is important to insert specific names of groups and individuals when doing an actual analysis. Indicate other stakeholders who might be or were influenced by BP's decision to outsource and recall products. Using your "third-party objective observer" perspective, you can determine the movement among stakeholder positions using the arrows in the figure: Who influenced whom, by what means, and how? As you look at Figure 3.5, ask yourself: Do I agree with this figure as it is completed? Who is likely to move from Supportive to Nonsupportive over time? Or from a Mixed Blessing position to a Nonsupportive or Supportive one? Why? How? Support your logic and defend your position.

From the point of view of the focal stakeholder, if you were CEO, you would develop specific strategies and keep the following points in mind:

1. Your goal is to create a socially responsible, win–win set of outcomes, if possible. However, this may mean economic costs to your firm if, in fact, members of your firm are responsible to certain groups for harm caused as a consequence of your actions.
2. Ask: "What is our business? Who are our customers? What are our responsibilities to the stakeholders, to the public, and to the firm?" Keep your values, mission, and responsibilities in mind as you move forward.
3. Consider probable consequences of your actions. For whom? At what costs? Over what period? Ask: "What does a win–win situation look like for us?"
4. Keep in mind that the means you use can be important as the ends you seek; that is, how you approach and treat each stakeholder can be as important as what you do.

Figure 3.5

Diagnostic Typology of Stakeholders for BP Corporation

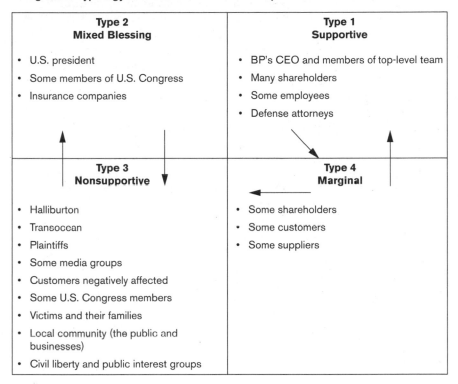

Type 2 Mixed Blessing	Type 1 Supportive
• U.S. president • Some members of U.S. Congress • Insurance companies	• BP's CEO and members of top-level team • Many shareholders • Some employees • Defense attorneys
Type 3 Nonsupportive	Type 4 Marginal
• Halliburton • Transocean • Plaintiffs • Some media groups • Customers negatively affected • Some U.S. Congress members • Victims and their families • Local community (the public and businesses) • Civil liberty and public interest groups	• Some shareholders • Some customers • Some suppliers

Specific strategies now can be articulated and assigned to corporate staff for review and implementation. Remember, social responsibility is a key variable; it is as important as the economic and political factors of a decision because social responsibility is linked to costs and benefits in other areas. At this point, you can ask to what extent your strategies are just and fair and consider the welfare of the stakeholders affected by your decision.

Executives use a range of strategies, especially in long-term crisis situations, to respond to external threats and stakeholders. Their strategies often are short-sighted and begin as a defensive move. When observing and using a stakeholder analysis, question why executives respond to their stakeholders as they do. Following the questions and methods in this chapter systematically will help you understand why key stakeholders respond as they do.

Step 7: Monitor Shifting Coalitions

Because time and events can change the stakes and stakeholders and their strategies, you need to monitor the evolution of the issues and actions of the stakeholders using Figure 3.4. Tracking external trends and events and the resultant stakeholder strategies can help a CEO and the executive's team act and react accordingly. This is a dynamic process that occurs over time and is affected by strategies and actions that you, as CEO, and your team direct with each stakeholder group as events occur. Your decisions are influenced by how effective certain stakeholders respond to (or counteract) you and your team's strategies and actions. As CEO, you would typically follow a utilitarian ethic of weighing costs and benefits of all your strategies and actions toward each major stakeholder group, keeping your company's best interests in mind. However, neglecting the public and common good of all your stakeholders also affects your bottom line. If you followed a universalistic ethic in the BP case, you might attempt to address concerns and make apologies to those who were harmed and extend condolences to the families of those who died in the explosion and aftermath of the disaster. You would have taken immediate action by offering factual information regarding what happened and why and what the company intended to do to resolve the crisis. Ethics is—or should be—an integral part of every corporation's and organization's goals, objectives, strategies, and actions that affect other people. A question in the stakeholder analysis offered here is: What ethical principle(s)—if any—did the CEO of BP follow, and why, given the pressures from different stakeholders?

Summary of Stakeholder Analysis

You have now completed a basic stakeholder analysis and should be able to proceed with strategy implementation in more realistic, thoughtful, interactive, and responsible ways. The stakeholder approach should involve other decision makers inside and outside the focal organization.

Stakeholder analysis provides a rational, systematic basis for understanding issues and the "ethics in action" involved in complex relationships between an organization, its leaders, and constituents. It helps decision makers structure strategic planning sessions and decide how to meet the moral obligations of all stakeholders. The extent to which the resultant strategies and outcomes are moral and effective for a firm and its stakeholders depends on many factors, including the values of the firm's leaders, the stakeholders' power, the legitimacy of the actions, the use of available resources, and the exigencies of the changing environment.

■ 3.4 Negotiation Methods: Resolving Stakeholder Disputes

Disputes are part of stakeholder relationships. Most disputes are handled in the context of mutual trusting relationships between stakeholders; others move into the legal and regulatory system.[34] Disputes occur between different stakeholder levels: for example, between professionals within an organization, consumers and companies, business to business (B2B), governments and businesses, and among coalitions and businesses. It is estimated that Fortune 500 senior human resources (HR) executives are involved in legal disputes 20 percent of their working time. Also, managers generally spend 30 percent of their time handling conflicts. The hidden cost of managing conflicts between and among professionals in organizations can result in absenteeism, turnover, legal costs, and loss of productivity.[35] U.S. retail e-commerce sales in the fourth quarter of 2011 were $51.4 billion, up 15.5 percent from 2010. With that volume, there will be business disputes. A study by the American Arbitration Association surveying 100 senior executives of Fortune 1000 companies found the following:

1. Two out of three executives were concerned about B2B e-commerce disputes with major suppliers, and 50 percent of surveyed executives noted that this type of dispute would significantly impact their business.

2. More than 50 percent noted that the shift to e-commerce will create new and/or different types of stakeholder disputes, with 64 percent of surveyed executives reporting that their companies did not yet have a plan in place to deal with these disputes.

3. Seventy percent agreed that specific guidelines are needed in order to manage e-commerce disputes, and one in four executives noted that their company did nothing to prevent e-commerce disputes.[36]

Stakeholder conflict and dispute resolution methods are clearly necessary.

Stakeholder Dispute Resolution Methods

Dispute resolution is an expertise also known as alternative dispute resolution (ADR). Dispute resolution techniques cover a variety of methods intended to help potential litigants resolve conflicts. The methods can be viewed on a continuum ranging from face-to-face negotiation to litigation, as Figure 3.6 illustrates. Advocates of alternative resolution methods argue that litigation need not be the standard for evaluating other dispute techniques.[37]

Figure 3.6 illustrates the degree to which disputing parties give up control of the process and outcome to a neutral third party. The left side of the continuum is based on consensual, informal dispute resolution methods. Negotiating, facilitation, and some mediation are methods where the parties maintain control over the conflict resolution process. Moving to the right side of the spectrum (adjudicative), disputing parties give up control to third-party arbitrators and then litigators (courts, tribunals, and binding arbitration). For example, with regard to outsourcing issues discussed earlier in the chapter, most companies have the authority to make outsourcing decisions. However, with regard to outsourced government contractors, for example, control over what types of contracts will be used is more complicated. For example, during the effort to start rebuilding Iraq after the invasions were over, Congress debated the use of external contractors for those projects. Halliburton received several exclusive outsourced contracts toward that effort. Using the National Defense Authorization Act for fiscal year 2005, Congress allowed civil service employees in the Departments of Defense and Homeland Security, the Internal Revenue Service, and the Pentagon to control external contractors. It was reported that "between 2003 and 2008, Congress estimated that the

Figure 3.6

The ADR Continuum

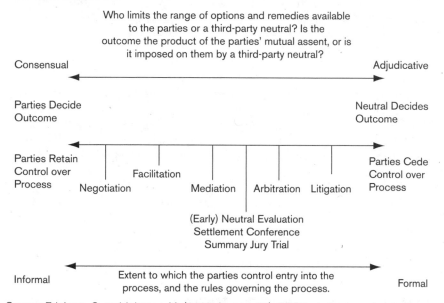

Source: Erickson, S. and Johnson, M. (2012, January 27). ADR techniques and procedures flowing through porous boundaries: Flooding the ADR landscape and confusing the public. Accessed February 11, 2014, http://www.mediate.com/pdf/ADR%20Techniques%20 and%20Procedures%20Flowing%20Through%20Porous%20Boundaries-%20Flooding %20the%20the%20ADR%20Landscape%20and%20Confusing%20the%20Public%20(Revised, %20January%2027,%202012).pdf.

United States had spent $100 billion on contractors in Iraq, or one dollar out of every five spent on the Iraq War at the time. Today, assuming a conservative estimate of $800 billion spent on the war, at least $160 billion has likely ended up in the coffers of private contractors."[38] Lawsuits are still pending in some cases. More recently, the U.S. Congressional appropriations and spending for the war in Afghanistan between 2001 and 2021 is estimated at $2.261 trillion.[39]

The stakeholder management approach involves the full range of dispute resolution techniques, although ideally more *integrative* and *relational* rather than *distributive* or *power-based* methods would be attempted first. (Power-based approaches are based on authoritarian and competition-based methods where the more powerful group or individual "wins" and the opposing group "loses." This approach can cause other disputes to arise.) Integrative approaches are characterized as follows:

- Problems are seen as having more potential solutions than are immediately obvious.
- Resources are seen as expandable; the goal is to "expand the pie" before dividing it.

- Parties attempting to create more potential solutions and processes are thus said to be "value creating."
- Parties attempt to accommodate as many interests of each of the parties as possible.
- It is considered a win–win or "all gain" approach.[40]

Distributive approaches have the following characteristics:

- Problems are seen as zero-sum.
- Resources are imagined as fixed: "Divide the pie."
- They are "value claiming" rather than "value creating."
- They involve haggling or "splitting the difference."[41]

Relational approaches (which consider power, interests, rights, and ethics) include and are based on:

- Relationship building
- Narrative, deliberative, and other "dialogical" (i.e., dialogue-based) approaches to negotiation and mediation
- Restorative justice and reconciliation (i.e., approaches that respect the dignity of every person, build understanding, and provide opportunities for victims to obtain restoration and for offenders to take responsibility for their actions)
- Other transformative approaches to peace building[42]

The process of principled negotiation, from Roger Fisher and William Ury's book *Getting to Yes*, continues to be used for almost any type of dispute. Their four principles are:

1. Separate the people from the problem.
2. Focus on interests rather than positions.
3. Generate a variety of options before settling on an agreement.
4. Insist that the agreement be based on objective criteria.[43]

Adjudicative, legislative, restorative justice, reparation, and rights-based approaches are necessary when rights, property, or other legitimate claims have been violated and harm results. Leaders and professionals practicing a stakeholder management approach incorporate and gain proficiency in using a wide range of conflict and alternative dispute resolution methods.[44]

■ 3.5 Stakeholder Management Approach: Using Ethical Principles and Reasoning

Applying ethical principles and reasoning in a stakeholder approach involves asking: What is equitable, just, fair, and good for those who affect and are affected by business decisions? Who are the weaker stakeholders in terms of power and influence? Who can, who will, and who should help weaker stakeholders make their voices heard and encourage their participation in the decision process? This approach also requires the principal stakeholders to define and fulfill their ethical obligations to the affected constituencies.

Chapter 2 specifically deals with the ethical principles and reasoning used in a stakeholder approach. That chapter presents several ethical frameworks and principles, including the following: (1) the common good principle, (2) rights, (3) justice, (4) utilitarianism, (5) relativism, and (6) universalism, all of which can be applied to individual, group, and organizational belief systems, policies, and motives. You may also refer to Chapters 2 and 3 when using ethical principles (or the lack of such) to describe actual individuals' and groups' observed moral policies, motives, and outcomes in cases that you are studying or creating from your experience or research.

3.6 Moral Responsibilities of Cross-Functional Area Professionals

One goal of a stakeholder analysis is to encourage and prepare organizational managers to articulate their own moral responsibilities, as well as the responsibilities of their company and their profession, toward their different constituencies. Stakeholder analysis focuses the enterprise's attention and moral decision-making process on external events. The stakeholder management approach also applies internally, especially to individual managers in traditional functional areas. These managers can be seen as conduits through which other external stakeholders are influenced.

Because our concern is managing moral responsibility in organizational stakeholder relationships, this section briefly outlines some of the responsibilities of selected functional area managers. While organizational structures and professions have and are undergoing radical shifts, especially with Covid-19 and its variants, cross-functional dimensions and dynamics still are at play. With the Internet, the transparency of all organizational actors and internal stakeholders increases the risk and stakes of unethical practices. Chat rooms, message boards, and breaking-news sites provide instant platforms for exposing both rumor and accurate news about companies. (In the tobacco controversy, it was an anti-smoking researcher and advocate who first posted inside information from a whistle-blower on the Internet. This action was the first step toward opening the tobacco companies' internal documents to public scrutiny and the resulting lawsuits.)

Figure 3.7 illustrates a classical manager's stakeholders. The particular functional area you are interested in can be kept in mind while you read the descriptions discussed next. Note that steps 1 through 7 presented in the stakeholder analysis can also be used for this level of analysis.

Functional and expert areas include marketing, research and development (R&D), manufacturing, public relations (PR), HR management, and accounting and finance. The basic moral dimensions of each of these are discussed below. Even though functional areas are often blurred in some emerging network organizational structures and self-designed teams, many of the respon-

Figure 3.7

A Manager's Stakeholders

Note: The letters K, L, M, and N are hypothetical designations in place of real department names. Dotted lines refer to hypothetical linkages.

Source: Freeman, R. E. (1984). *Strategic management: A stakeholder approach.* Boston: Pitman, 218. Reproduced with permission of the author.

sibilities of these managerial areas remain intact. Understanding these managerial roles from a stakeholder perspective helps to clarify the pressures and moral responsibilities of these job positions. Refer to the section on ethical principles and quick ethical tests for professionals in Chapter 2.

Marketing and Sales Professionals and Managers as Stakeholders

Sales professionals and managers are continuously engaged—electronically and/or face-to-face—with customers, suppliers, and vendors. Sales professionals are also evaluated by quotas and quantitative expectations on a weekly, monthly, and quarterly basis. The stress and pressure to meet expectations is always present. Sales professionals must continually balance their personal ethics and their professional pressures. The dilemma often becomes, "Who do I represent? What weight do my beliefs and ethics have when measured against my department's and company's performance measures for me?" Another key question for sales professionals particularly is, "Where is the line between unethical and ethical practices for me?" Also, because customers are an integral part of business, these professionals must create and maintain customer interest and loyalty. They must be concerned with consumer safety and welfare, while increasing revenue and obtaining new accounts. Many marketing and sales professionals also are responsible for determining and managing the firm's advertising and the truthfulness (and legality) of the data and information they issue to the public about products and services. They must interact with many of the other functional and expertise areas and with advertising agencies, customers, and consumer groups. Moral dilemmas can arise for marketing managers who may be asked to promote unsafe products or to implement advertising campaigns that are untrue or not in the consumer's best interests.

Several equity traders, most notably at Enron during and after the corporate scandals, were involved in lying to customers about "dogs"—stocks they knew were underperforming. Part of their motive was to keep certain stocks popular and in a "buy" mode so that their own sales performance would be valued higher, giving them better bonuses.

A major moral dilemma for marketing managers is having to choose between a profitable decision and a socially responsible one. Stakeholder analysis helps marketing managers in these morally questionable situations by identifying stakeholders and understanding the effects and consequences of profits and services on them. Balancing company profitability with human rights and interests is a moral responsibility of marketers. Companies that have no ethics code or socially responsible policies—as well as those that do have such policies but do not enforce them—increase the personal pressure, pain, and liability of individual professionals. Such tensions can lead to unethical and illegal activities.

R&D, Engineering Professionals, and Managers as Stakeholders

R&D managers and engineers are responsible for the safety and reliability of product design. Faulty products can mean public outcry, which can result in unwanted media exposure and possibly (perhaps justifiably) lawsuits. R&D managers must work and communicate effectively and conscientiously with professionals in manufacturing, marketing, and information systems, and with senior managers, contractors, and government representatives, to name a few of their stakeholders. This chapter's opening case illustrates that a company's operating parts, design, and quality control can involve more care and concern for safety and monitoring to ensure proper functioning of operations than BP's company officers probably envisioned before the now classical *Deepwater Horizon* crisis erupted. Technical issues can quickly escalate to political, cultural, legislative, and judicial levels; ethical issues that may begin as professional ethical codes of engineers can, if a product crisis occurs, transform into legal concerns about international human and consumer rights and justice.

As studies and reports on the tragically memorable Space Shuttle *Challenger* disaster further illustrate, care and attention to the safe functioning of technical parts and processes of any system can mean the difference between life and death. *Challenger* tore apart 73 seconds after liftoff from Cape Canaveral, Florida, on January 28, 1986. Engineers and managers at the National Aeronautics and Space Administration (NASA) and the cooperating company, Morton Thiokol, had different priorities, perceptions, and technical judgments regarding the "go, no-go" decision of that space launch. A follow-up study found that "the commission not only found fault with a failed sealant ring but also with the officials at NASA who allowed the shuttle launch to take place despite concerns voiced by NASA engineers regarding the safety of the launch."[45] The lack of individual responsibility and the poor critical judgment of NASA administrators contributed to the miscommunication and resulting disaster.

Moral dilemmas can arise for R&D engineers whose technical judgments and risk assessments conflict with administrative managers seeking profit and time-to-market deadlines. R&D managers also can benefit from doing a stakeholder analysis before disasters occur. The discussion of the levels of business ethics in Chapter 1 also provides professionals with a way of examining their individual ethics and moral responsibilities.

Accounting and Finance Professionals and Managers as Stakeholders

Accounting and finance professionals are responsible for the welfare of clients and safeguard their financial interests. Financial planners, brokers, accountants, mutual fund managers, bankers, valuation specialists, and insurance agents have the responsibility of ensuring reliable and accurate transactions and reporting of other people's money and assets.[46] Many of these professions are part of regulated industries; however, corporate scandals such as those at Wells Fargo, Boeing, and earlier at Enron, Tyco, Arthur Andersen, and other large firms showed that company culture, individual and team judgment, greed, and lack of integrity contributed to executives' "cooking the books." Financial fraud, stealing, and gambling away employees' pensions and shareholders' investments were part of the illegal activities officers of these firms directed and led. Although the Sarbanes-Oxley Act, the Revised Sentencing Guidelines, and stricter company ethics and reporting codes (see Chapter 4) have helped prevent illegal activity in these professions, problems remain.

Factors in these professions that trigger unethical activities include (1) pressures from senior officers and supervisors to "maximize profits," sometimes at any cost; (2) a lack of integrity (truthfulness, conscience) of leaders, supervisors, and employees; (3) corporate cultures that devalue clients, investors, and employees; (4) requests from clients to change financial statements and tax returns and commit tax fraud; (5) conflict of interest and lack of auditor independence between client and auditing firm; and (6) blurring professional and personal roles and responsibilities between client and professional. These issues are in part related to societal, structural problems. For example, the U.S. financial system emphasizes and rewards short-term, quarterly earnings that help create many of the pressures and poor practices listed above. Chapters 4 and 5 deal with these topics in more detail.

Public Relations Managers as Stakeholders

PR managers must constantly interact with outside groups and corporate executives, especially in an age when communications media, external relations, and public scrutiny play such vital roles. PR managers are responsible for transmitting, receiving, and interpreting information about employees, products, services, and the company. A firm's public credibility, image, and reputation depend on how PR professionals manage stakeholders because PR personnel must often negotiate the boundaries between corporate loyalty and credibility with external groups. These groups often use different criteria than corporate executives do for measuring success and responsibility, especially during crises. Moral dilemmas can arise when PR managers must defend company actions that have possible or known harmful effects on the public or stakeholders. A stakeholder analysis can prepare PR managers and inform them about the situation, the stakes, and the strategies they must address.

Human Resources Managers as Stakeholders

Human resources managers (HRMs) are on the front line of helping other managers recruit, hire, fire, promote, evaluate, reward, discipline, transfer, and counsel employees. They negotiate union settlements and assist the government with enforcing Equal Employment Opportunity Commission (EEOC) standards. HRMs must translate employee rights and laws into practice. They also research, write, and maintain company policies on employee affairs. They face constant ethical pressures and uncertainties over issues about invasion of privacy and violations of employees' rights. With renewed emphasis on diversity, equity, and inclusion, HR professionals' work has taken on even more urgency. Stakeholders of HRMs include employees, other managers and bosses, unions, community groups, government officials, lobbyists, and competitors.

Moral dilemmas can arise for these managers when affirmative action policies are threatened in favor of corporate decisions to hide biases or protect profits. HRMs also straddle the fine line between the individual rights of employees and corporate self-interests, especially when reductions in force and other hiring or firing decisions are involved. As industries restructure, merge, downsize, outsource, and expand internationally, the work of HRMs becomes even more complicated.

Summary of Managerial Moral Responsibilities

Expert and functional area managers are confronted with balancing operational profit goals with corporate moral obligations toward stakeholders. These pressures are considered "part of the job." Unfortunately, clear corporate directions for resolving dilemmas that involve conflicts between individuals' rights and corporate economic interests generally are not available. Using a stakeholder analysis is "like walking in the shoes of another professional"— you get a sense of that person's pressures. Using a stakeholder analysis is a step toward clarifying the issues involved in resolving ethical dilemmas. Chapter 2 presented moral decision-making principles that can help individuals think through these issues and take responsible action.

■ 3.7 Issues Management: Integrating a Stakeholder Framework

Issues management methods complement the stakeholder management approach. It may be helpful to begin by identifying and analyzing major issues before doing a stakeholder analysis. Many reputable large companies use issues managers and methods for identifying, tracking, and responding to trends that offer potential opportunities as well as threats to companies.[47] Before discussing ways of integrating stakeholder management (and analysis) with issues management, issues management is defined.

What Is an Issue?

An issue is a problem, contention, or argument that concerns both an organization and one or more of its stakeholders and/or stockholders. Teresa Yancey Crane, founder of the Issue Management Council, explained the relationship between an issue and issue management the following way: "Think of an issue as a gap between your actions and stakeholder expectations. Second, think of issue management as the process used to close that gap."[48] The gap can be closed in a number of ways, using several strategies. A primary method is using an accommodating policy. Providing public education, community dialogue, and changing expectations through communication are some accommodating strategies used in issues management. Solving complicated issues may sometimes require radical actions, like replacing members from the board of directors and the senior management team.[49]

Issues management is also a formal process used to anticipate and take appropriate action to respond to emerging trends, concerns, or issues that can affect an organization and its stakeholders. "Issues management is a . . . genuine and ethical long-term commitment by the organization to a two-way, inclusive standard of corporate responsibility toward stakeholders. Issues management involves connectivity with, rather than control of, others. Issues managers help identify and close gaps between expectation, performance, communication, and accountability. Issues management blends 'many faces' within the entity into 'one voice.' Like the issues themselves, the process is multi-faceted and is enhanced by the strategic facilitation and integration of diverse viewpoints and skills."[50]

Many national and international business-related controversies develop around the exposure of a single issue that evolves into more serious and costly issues. The so-called attack on the U.S. Capitol resulted in numerous other issues; classically, Enron's now historical problems in the beginning surfaced as an issue of overstated revenue. After months of investigation, members of the highest executive team were found to have been involved in deception, fraud, and theft. The Ford Bridgestone/Firestone Explorer crisis in 2001 resulted from what appeared to have been faulty tires (see Ethical Insight 3.1). The issue escalated to questions about the design of the Ford vehicle itself, then to questions about many international deaths and accidents over a number of years. The CEO of Ford eventually lost his job. You may have noticed that some of these classical ethical failures in companies continue to occur.

Ethical Insight 3.1

Classic Crisis Management Case

- Crisis management experts criticized Bridgestone/Firestone for minimizing their tires' problems during the week of August 11, 2000. The experts gave the company mixed reviews on its handling of the recall of 6.5 million tires that were responsible for 174 deaths and more than 300 incidents involving tires that allegedly shredded on the highway in 1999. The tire maker's spokespersons claimed the poor tread on the tires was caused by underinflation, improper maintenance, and poor road conditions.

- Mark Braverman, principal of CMG Associates, a crisis management firm in Newton, Massachusetts, noted that the company blamed the victim and that Bridgestone/Firestone lacked a visible leader for its crisis management effort. "The CEO should be out there, not executive vice presidents."
- Steven Fink, another crisis management expert, noted that "after they [Bridgestone/Firestone] announced the recall, they were not prepared to deal with it. They were telling consumers they will have to wait up to a year to get tires. And things like busy telephone call lines and overloaded web sites—these are things that can be anticipated. That's basic crisis management."
- Stephen Greyser, professor of marketing and communications at Harvard Business School, stated, "It's about what they didn't do up to now. The fact that [Bridgestone/Firestone] is just stepping up to bat tells me they've never really had the consumer as the principal focus of their thinking."
- Defending the way Bridgestone/Firestone handled the crisis was Dennis Gioia, professor of organizational behavior at Smeal College of Business Administration at Pennsylvania State University: "With hindsight, you can always accuse a company of being too slow, given the history of automotive recalls. Sometimes you can't take hasty action or you would be acting on every hint there's a problem. It can create hysteria."

Question for Discussion

Who do you agree or disagree with these crisis management consultants? Explain.

Source: Consultants split on Bridgestone's crisis management. (2000, August 11). Wall Street Journal, A6.

Other Types of Issues

There are other types of issues arising from the external environment that involve different companies and industries. For example, the issue of obesity has become prominent in the United States. Once considered a personal life-style problem, obesity is now seen as a public health disease, and its treatment can be paid for by one's health insurance. This issue involves insurance companies, the corporations that employ individuals facing this problem, employment attorneys, families of those individuals affected, and taxpayers, to name a few. Another issue that affects numerous stakeholders is drivers who drink. U.S. mothers who have lost their children to this growing phenomenon have discovered that this issue is not a set of isolated events, but widespread. Mothers Against Drunk Driving (MADD) was founded in the 1980s by Candy Lightner, whose 13-year-old daughter, Cari, was killed by a drunken hit-and-run driver as she walked down a suburban street in California. The impact broke almost every bone in her body and fractured her skull, and she died at the scene of the accident. "I promised myself on the day of Cari's death that I would fight to make this needless homicide count for something positive in the years ahead," her mother later wrote.[51]

Programs like *60 Minutes, Dateline,* and *Frontline*, along with other news-oriented blogs and online podcast sources, introduce breaking news that focuses on events, crises, and innovative practices that are being faced and addressed. Stakeholder and issues management frameworks can be used to understand the evolution of these issues in order to responsibly manage or change their effects.

Stakeholder and Issues Management: "Connecting the Dots"

Issues and stakeholder management are used interchangeably by scholars and corporate practitioners, as the two following quotes illustrate:

> For many societal predicaments, stakeholders and issues represent two complementary sides of the same coin.[52]
>
> Stakeholders tend to organize around "hot" issues, and issues are typically associated with certain vocal stakeholder groups. Issues management scholars can therefore explore how issues management requires stakeholder prioritization, and how stakeholder management gets facilitated when managers have deep knowledge of stakeholders' issue agendas. Earlier research also suggests that whether or not stakeholders decide to get involved with certain issues has a profound influence on issue evolution, as does the timing and extent of their involvement.[53]

Applying stakeholder and issues management approaches should not be mechanical. Moral creativity and objectivity help, as discussed in Chapter 1. A general first step is to ask, "What is the issue, opportunity, or precipitating event that an organization is facing or has experienced? How did the issue emerge?" Generally there are several issues that are discovered. The process begins by analyzing and then framing which issues are the most urgent and have (or may have) the greatest impact on the organization. At this point, you can begin to ask who was involved in starting or addressing the issue. This triggers the beginning of a stakeholder analysis and the steps discussed earlier in the chapter. Depending on how the issue evolved into other issues—or whether there was a crisis at the beginning, middle, or end of the issue evolution— you will know which issues management framework from the following section is most relevant for the analysis of the situation.

Actually, stakeholder analysis questions help "connect the dots" in understanding and closing the gaps of issues management. Stakeholder questions help discover "who did what to whom to influence which results, and at what costs and outcomes." A major purpose in analyzing and effectively managing issues and stakeholders is to create environments that allow high-performing people to achieve productive and ethical results.

Moral Dimensions of Stakeholder and Issues Management

Some studies argue that moral reasoning is "issue-dependent" and that "people generally behave better when the moral issue is important."[54] Questions regarding issue recognition include: To what extent do people actually recognize moral issues? Is it by the magnitude of the potential consequences or the actual consequences of the issue? Is it by the social consensus regarding how important the issue is? Is it by how likely it is that the effects of the issue will be felt or how quickly the issue will occur?[55] Ethical reasoning and behavior are an important part of managing stakeholders and issues because ethics is the energy that motivates people to respond to issues. When ethical motives are absent from leaders' and professionals' thinking and feelings, activities can occur that cost all stakeholders. Teaching you methods for detecting and preventing unethical and illegal actions is an aim of this section.

Companies face issues every day. Some issues lead to serious consequences—defective products, financial fraud, fatal side effects of drugs, oil spills, the loss of millions of lives to the effects of tobacco, violence from use of firearms, or the theft of pensions from ordinary employees who worked a lifetime to accrue them. Other issues evolve in a way that leads to spectacular outcomes: the invention and commercialization of the Internet; information technology that provides wireless access to anyone at any time in any place; and the capability to network customers, businesses, suppliers, and vendors. Privately funded space explorations by pioneers such as Jeff Bezos and Richard Branson trigger entrepreneurial inventions. Learning to identify and change issues for the good of the organization and for the common and public good is another goal of the stakeholder management approach.

Types of Issues Management Frameworks

This section presents two general issues frameworks for mapping and managing issues before and after they evolve or erupt into crises. These frameworks can be used with the stakeholder management approach. Using a stakeholder analysis (which is part of the general stakeholder management approach) explains the "who, what, where, why, and what happened" that affects an issue. After you have read the first two issues management approaches, shown in Figures 3.8 and 3.9, you will see that either or both can be used to identify and analyze a major issue (crisis or potential opportunity) for an organization, as is explained below.

Figure 3.8 illustrates a straightforward framework that organizations can use for anticipating and thinking through issues to prevent a crisis. This is a somewhat generic model that has evolved within the issues management field. Identifying, tracking, and developing responses to issues are the thrusts of the process. More recently, companies like General Electric, Patagonia, Costco, and others use issues frameworks with the intent of acting in socially responsible ways, not only to protect their own companies and businesses from environmental and economic "threats," but also to

Figure 3.8

Six-Step Issues Management Process

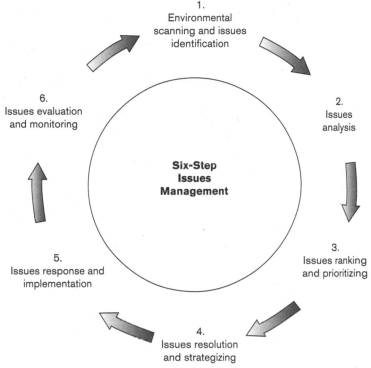

Source: Based on Coates, J., Jarratt, V., and Heinz, L. (1986). *Issues management*. Mt. Airy, MI: Lomond Publications, 19–20.

protect the environment and extend their reputations for "doing the right thing."

The steps in Figure 3.8, then, can also be used to plan and manage issues that may have already affected an organization. Senior officers and staff would probably use this framework in their strategizing and "what if" scenarios. If you are analyzing a case such as the BP rig explosion and oil spill, you can use this framework to show what steps the organization *could* have taken to prevent such disasters and the steps actually taken to manage the issues under investigation. You can also use a stakeholder analysis at any point in this model.

Figure 3.9 is more specific and focuses on the evolution of an issue from inception to resolution. This framework, which is not organization–specific like Figure 3.8, is more likely to be used by analysts, managers, and scholars studying issues with warning signs that, if attention is given to them, can prevent escalating problems. In many cases, a stakeholder analysis can show why strategies and actions of particular stakeholders short-circuited the issue's evolution through all the stages in this figure.

Figure 3.9

Seven-Phase Issue Development Process

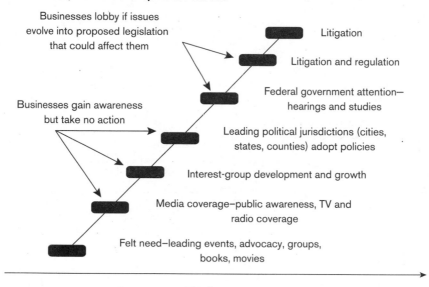

Businesses lobby if issues evolve into proposed legislation that could affect them

Litigation

Litigation and regulation

Federal government attention—hearings and studies

Businesses gain awareness but take no action

Leading political jurisdictions (cities, states, counties) adopt policies

Interest-group development and growth

Media coverage–public awareness, TV and radio coverage

Felt need–leading events, advocacy, groups, books, movies

Timeline

Source: Adapted from Marx, T. (1986). Integrating public affairs and strategic planning. *California Management Review, Fall, 29(1),* 145.

First Approach: Six-Step Issues Management Process

The first method, as noted, is the most straightforward and most appropriate for companies or groups scanning the environment for issues that can impact their businesses and internal environments. A third-party observer could also use this approach to describe how a company acted in retrospect or could act in the future.

However, this model would not be suitable for examining how an issue evolved over time, or for analyzing precrisis signs or symptoms of an event.

The process involves the following steps, illustrated in Figure 3.8.[56]

1. Environmental scanning and issues identification
2. Issues analysis
3. Issues ranking and prioritizing
4. Issues resolution and strategizing
5. Issues response and implementation
6. Issues evaluation and monitoring

These steps are part of a firm's corporate planning process. In the strategic issues management process, a firm uses a selected team to work on emerging trends as they relate to the industry and company. As Robert Heath noted, "The objective of issues management is to make a smart, proactive, and even more respected organization. This sort of organization is one that understands and responds to its stakeseekers and stakeholders."[57]

This framework is a basic approach for proactively mapping, strategizing, and responding to issues that affect an organization. With regard to this chapter's opening case, if you, as an objective third-party observer, were analyzing BP's situation, what issues can you identify that might affect the company? As you identify each issue (step 1), you might begin to analyze any organizational and/or environmental issue that offered clues about the condition of the rig. Then you could examine the issues and their impact on the organization and other stakeholders before and after the explosion (step 2). The remaining steps would involve analyzing how BP handled the crisis (steps 3–6).

This six-step process also allows you to advise upper-level managers and directors in the company regarding precautions to take to avoid the illegal and unethical consequences of an issue. This model sharpens your ability to see the effects of issues on organizations from conception to response and monitoring.

Second Approach: Seven-Phase Issue Development Process

Issues are believed and have been observed to follow a developmental life cycle. Views differ on the stages, phases, and time involved in such a life cycle. Thomas Marx's reasoning fits with the seven-phase evolution of the public's "felt need" or outcry for that need or demand becoming a law. The entire cycle has been estimated to take eight years, as illustrated in Figure 3.9. With the use of the Internet, social media, and mobile devices, this time span will likely be shortened.[58]

1. A felt need arises (from emerging events, advocacy groups, books, movies).
2. Media coverage is developed (television segments, such as on *60 Minutes, 20/20, FOX News, CNN,* and breaking news on the Internet from the *Wall Street Journal, New York Times,* and other news and blogging sources).
3. Interest groups develop and gain momentum and grow.
4. Policies are adopted by leading political jurisdictions (cities, states, counties).
5. The federal government gives attention to the issue (hearings and studies).
6. Issues and policies evolve into legislation and regulation.
7. Issues and policies enter litigation.

How many companies could have averted being hacked and having to pay ransom had they had one of these issue frameworks operating? BP's CEO and top-level team could have used this framework to anticipate and perhaps prevent the explosion—and if not prevent the explosion, they could have responded to the public in a more timely and concerned way. With the Internet, it no longer takes eight years for this model to move from phase one to the last (litigation) phase. Once local and federal legislators learn about a volatile news-breaking public issue, especially if the media has exposed it, company representatives may respond sooner.

"While the accident could have been prevented, BP might have avoided its intense and deserved public flogging if only it had respected the best practices for managing a crisis,"[59] wrote Murray Bryant and Trevor Hunter. They explored who was to blame for the spill:

> BP has for many years publicly claimed to be laser focused on safety. But inside the company, it was clearly focused on cost cutting, at the expense of safety. Furthermore, regulators and environmental groups have not been fooled by BP's public statements, though they have allowed the company to continue to operate as usual. Who then is to blame for the spill? Is it BP, which has been driving cost cutting hard and succeeding? Or its contractors, who have had to operate to meet BP's specifications and who, in order to meet budget, changed operating procedures? Is it government regulators, who have been well aware of BP's violations, but have allowed it not to pay its fines and to continue to operate? Is it the public, users of oil, whose insatiable demands for petrochemical products has led to the overuse of a limited natural resource that, it could be claimed, forced firms like BP to take on ever more risky operations to meet demand (note that figures suggest that the operations in the Gulf account for nearly 20 percent of the United States' domestic oil production)? Or, is it investors, demanding ever higher returns on their investment over shorter periods of time, driving BP executives to squeeze efficiencies from operations that were designed to be effective—not efficient, in order to maximize earnings per share?[60]

Stakeholder management methods can be used with this issue management approach in order to identify those groups and individuals who moved an issue from one phase to another and who helped change the nature of an issue. Usually different stakeholder groups redefine issues as these constituencies compete with one another, using different sources of power, as discussed earlier.

This seven-phase framework is also useful in identifying and following public issues that do not necessarily originate with corporations and could be applied to such issues as drunk driving, obesity, global warming, and even to natural disasters like Covid-19. Some scientists and technology innovators had warned earlier that a devastating global virus like Covid-19 could develop. Issues frameworks and stakeholder analysis can help identify the effectiveness of public and private organizations in detecting and responding to events that result in crises. Sometimes the aftermath of a catastrophic event can result in a larger crisis than the precipitating event itself.

Marx illustrated his model with the origins of the automobile safety-belt issue.[61] The four stages of this case, according to Marx, were reflected by the following events:

1. Social awareness: Ralph Nader's now-classic book *Unsafe at Any Speed,* published in 1965, created a social expectation regarding the safe manufacturing of automobiles. The Chevrolet Corvair, later pulled off the market, was the focus of Nader's astute legal and public advocacy work in exposing manufacturing defects.
2. Political awareness: The National Traffic and Motor Vehicle Safety Act and the resulting safety hearings in 1966 moved this expectation into the political arena.

3. Legislative engagement: In 1966, the Motor Vehicle Safety Act was passed, and four states began requiring the use of seat belts in 1984.
4. Litigation: Social control was established in 1967, when all cars were required to have seat belts. Driver fines and penalties, recalls of products, and litigation concerning defective equipment further reinforced the control stage.

Nader's pioneering consumer advocacy and legal work with regard to U.S. automobile manufacturing set an enduring precedent for watchdog congressional and voluntary advocacy groups that initiated laws that are still in effect.

Many other books have served as catalysts to mobilize the U.S. public and ultimately influence Congress to pass legislation. A brief list includes, for example, Thomas Paine's *Common Sense* (1776), which rallied the public against the British monarchy and is believed to have been the single most powerful influence that mobilized widespread support for the Revolutionary War—over 100,000 copies were sold in the first few months of its publication. Mary Wollstonecraft's *A Vindication of the Rights of Women* (1792) was the first literary statement promoting women's rights and led to the movement that gave women the right to vote in America. Upton Sinclair's novel *The Jungle* (1906) shocked the nation by exposing the wretched conditions of Chicago's meatpacking industry and the impoverished lives of immigrants who worked there. The book influenced legislation on employment laws and safety standards related to meatpacking and the food industry in general. *Silent Spring* (1962) by Rachel Carson brought to the attention of millions the loss of endangered species and the environment and pressured some of the first legislation in these areas.[62] Refer to Chapter 5 to see later books on food and diets that also have made an impact on national policy.

Take any industry or scan the news, then select an issue and see if you can predict and/or observe the possible path the issue may take through these different stages. This issue evolution process provides a window into the emergence and evolution of public policies and laws in U.S. society. Issues are not static or predetermined commodities. Stakeholder interests and actions move or impede an issue's development. To understand how an issue develops (or is unable to develop) is to understand how power works in a political system in which market and nonmarket forces pressure the ethics and values of stockholders and stakeholders.

■ 3.8 Managing Crises

On January 15, 2009, US Airways Flight 1549 took off from LaGuardia Airport in New York City bound for Charlotte/Douglas International Airport, North Carolina, with the ultimate destination of Seattle-Tacoma International Airport in Washington State. During its initial climb, the plane hit a flock of Canadian geese. Despite losing engine power, Captain Chesley Burnett "Sully" Sullenberger III and his crew safely landed the plane on the Hudson River off midtown Manhattan. That landing is now known as the "Miracle on the Hudson." The crew was later awarded the Master's Medal of the Guild of Air Pilots and Air Navigators, which stated, "This emergency ditching and evacuation, with the loss of no lives, is a heroic and unique aviation achievement." It was later described as "the most successful ditching in aviation history."[63]

Captain Sullenberger's crisis leadership style was focused; technically and intuitively accurate; and creative, calm, sympathetic, positive, and transparent. Consequently, his leadership during a time of intense crisis is celebrated as heroic, although he personally does not feel comfortable with that term. Captain Sullenberger's actions that day now serve as an exemplary role model of crisis leadership.

Crisis management methods evolved from the study of how corporations and leaders responded (and should have responded) to crises. Using crisis management methods with stakeholder management methods is essential for understanding and possibly preventing future fiascos because crises continue to occur in a number of areas: product/service crises (e.g., JetBlue's 2007 weather-related mishap); consumer products (the classic crisis with Ford's use of faulty Bridgestone/Firestone tires); financial systems (Enron and the recent subprime-lending crisis); and government/private contractor projects (Boston's 2006 Big Dig tunnel partial ceiling collapse and the 1986 *Challenger* disaster). Captain Sullenberger's response to the crisis he faced in the scenario discussed above is a success story. Unfortunately, most corporate leaders have not responded so courageously.

Crisis management expert Steven Fink states that a crisis is a "turning point for better or worse," a "decisive moment" or "crucial time," or "a situation that has reached a critical phase." He goes on to say that crisis management "is the art of removing much of the risk and uncertainty to allow you to achieve more control over your destiny."[64] Crises, from a corporation's point of view, can deteriorate if the situation escalates in intensity, comes under closer governmental scrutiny, interferes with normal operations, jeopardizes the positive image of the company or its officers, or damages a firm's bottom line. A turn for the worse also could occur if any of the firm's stakeholders were seriously harmed or if the environment was damaged. The following two approaches describe ways that organizations can respond to crises. In addition to the contemporary BP rig explosion and oil spill already discussed, you may turn to Chapter 4 to review some of the classic corporate crises that have occurred over the past few decades. Having such examples as the *Exxon Valdez*, the Ford Pinto disaster, and other crises in mind would be informative as you read how to examine and respond to a crisis from a stakeholder management perspective.

The model in Figure 3.10 shows a crisis consisting of four stages: (1) prodromal (precrisis), (2) acute, (3) chronic, and (4) conflict resolution. Judgment and observation are required to manage these stages. This approach differs from the second one in that a precrisis stage is included.[65]

The *prodromal* stage is the warning stage. If this stage is not recognized or does not actually occur, the second stage (acute crisis) can rush in, requiring damage control. Clues in the prodromal stage must be carefully observed. For

Figure 3.10

Four Crisis-Management Stages

Stage 1	Stage 2	Stage 3	Stage 4
Precrisis	**Crisis Occurs**	**Lingering**	**Health Restored**
PRODROMAL STAGE	ACUTE STAGE	CHRONIC STAGE	CONFLICT RESOLUTION STAGE
Warning, symptoms	Point of no return	Self-doubt, self-analysis	Return to normalcy

Source: Fink, S. (1986). *Crisis management: Planning for the inevitable.* New York: American Management Association, 26.

example, Covid-19 and its variants are also warning signs of what might follow without more vigilance. What happens in the prodromal stage when these types of attitudes and values clash within and between companies and work groups? Was there a warning sign or symptom that employees and managers at BP and/or the licensed companies saw that a crisis was possible? If so, why do you think these warning signs were not taken more seriously? Ethical Insight 3.2 provides an opportunity to show which methods from chapter 3 could apply to this investigation.

Ethical Insight 3.2

The Covid-19 virus apparently originated in Wuhan, China. But did it originate in a biosafety lab, or did it enter a human through an intermediate animal? And what difference does it make anyway?

"World Health Organization investigators said Tuesday, February 9, 2021 that they would no longer pursue research into whether the coronavirus leaked from a lab in Wuhan, China." The team of experts stopped the inquiry because of "lack of evidence." The virus was first identified in December 2019. "In Washington, the State Department's chief spokesman Ned Price said the U.S. would wait to see the WHO [World Health Organization] . . . full report before reaching its own conclusions about the origin of the coronavirus."[66]

The quest to discover whether the virus was released or spread to humans is of interest to a number of stakeholders and their interests: scientists want to know in order to prevent another such disaster; politicians wish to know to discern whether or not this may have been a weaponized activity; people across the globe who lost relatives and loved ones wish to have answers as well.

Exercise: Which method(s) in this chapter would you suggest as an attempt to investigate and explain not only the origin of Covid-19, but how this virus mutated from wherever its origin was to where it is now, and how and why it wasn't contained earlier in a particular national, or locally? What role did politics, economics, strategy—ethics!—play in the evolving events and timeline of what became a disastrous crisis.

In the second stage, *acute crisis,* damage has been done. The point here is to control as much of the damage as possible. This is often the shortest of the stages. In the BP crisis, the explosion took the crew on the rig by surprise. Should they have been more suspecting that a crisis or problem like this could occur?

The third stage, *chronic crisis,* is the cleanup phase. This is a period of recovery, self-analysis, self-doubt, and healing. Congressional investigations, audits, and interviews occur during this stage, which can linger indefinitely, according to Fink. A survey of Fortune 500 CEOs reported that companies that did not have a crisis management plan stayed in this stage two and a half times longer than those that did.

The final stage, *crisis resolution,* is the crisis management goal. The key questions here are: What can and should an organization's leaders do to speed up this phase and resolve a crisis once and for all? Crisis signs of climate change and Covid-19 continue to threaten all countries: governments, businesses, and citizens. Large numbers of leaders in these sectors still deny the reality of these crises.

How Executives Have Responded to Crises

Not all CEOs and organizational leaders respond the same to crises. JetBlue's founder and CEO David Neeleman resigned as CEO and issued a customer "Bill of Rights" after one of the worst crisis in the airline's history during the winter of 2007, when "nine airplanes full of angry passengers sat for six hours or more on the tarmac at John F. Kennedy International Airport in New York,"[67] costing the airline $30 million. A classic crisis management model developed by Archie Carroll suggests a different type of CEO response mode in its five phases of corporate social response to crises related to product crises.[68] This model illustrates how corporations have, and many continue to, actually responded to serious crises. The phases, illustrated in Figure 3.11, are (1) Reaction, (2) Defense, (3) Insight, (4) Accommodation, and (5) Agency. For a full description of the BP crisis, a more thorough case appears at the end

Figure 3.11

Corporate Social Responses

Source: Adapted from Carroll, A. (1977). A three-dimensional conceptual model of corporate performance. *Academy of Management Review, 4(4),* 502.

of this chapter and can be used to apply the crisis management methods presented here. Did BP's then–CEO react first and then respond? If so, why do you think many CEOs go into a "reaction" mode at the first realization of a crisis?

It is interesting to observe how some executives continue to deny and/or avoid responsibility in crises that become disastrous. Knowledge of these stages certainly would be a first step toward corporate awareness. Let's look more closely at each stage.

According to this model, the *Reaction* stage is the first phase when a crisis has occurred. Management lacks complete information and time to analyze the event thoroughly. A reaction made publicly that responds to allegations is required. This stage is important to corporations, because the public, the media, and the stakeholders involved see for the first time who the firm selects as its spokesperson, how the firm responds, and what the message is. A classic case in which the leadership and management of a company responded positively to a crisis—and did not react either negatively or with denial—was the Tylenol case. In 1982, seven people died after taking Tylenol capsules that had been tampered with and laced with cyanide. Tylenol's market share sank from 37 percent to 7 percent. James Burke, Johnson & Johnson's chairman, and a seven-member team focused first on protecting people and customers, then saving the product. Thirty-one million bottles of Tylenol nationally were recalled and all advertising was stopped until the problem was solved. An 800 number was set up and corporate headquarters held several press conferences with a live satellite feed. Two months later, "Tylenol was reintroduced into the market with triple-seal tamper-resistant packaging, [and the company] offered coupons for the products, created a new discounted pricing program, new advertising campaign and gave more than 2,250 presentations to the medical community."[69] Two management crises experts said that Johnson & Johnson actually increased their credibility after the crisis, and that their response became the "gold standard" for responding to crises.[70]

The second stage of the model, *Defense*, signals that the company is overwhelmed by public attention. The firm's image is at stake. This stage usually involves the company's recoiling under media pressure. But this does not always have to be a negative or reactive situation.

The third stage, *Insight*, is the most agonizing time for the firm in the controversy. The stakes are substantial. The firm's existence may be questioned. The company must come to grips with the situation under circumstances that have been generated externally. During this stage, the executives realize and confirm from evidence whether their company is at fault in the safety issues of the product in question.

In the fourth stage, *Accommodation*, the company either acts to remove the product from the market or refutes the charges against product safety. Addressing public pressure and anxiety is the task in this stage.

During the last stage, *Agency*, the company attempts to understand the causes of the safety issue and develop an education program for the public.

How could the CEO in the BP case have performed differently according to this model of crisis management? Research news and media reports on the Internet on this case and other crises. Take special note of how companies respond morally to their stakeholders. Observe the relative amount of attention companies sometimes give to consumers, the media, and government stakeholders. Use the frameworks presented in this chapter to help inform your observations and judgments. Develop a timeline as the crisis unfolds. Notice who the company chooses as its spokesperson. Determine how and why the company is assuming or avoiding responsibility.

Crisis Management Recommendations

A number of suggestions that corporations can follow to respond more effectively to crises are briefly summarized here. More in-depth strategies and tactics can be found in other sources.[71]

- Face the problem: Don't avoid or minimize it. Tell the truth.
- Take your "lumps" in one big news story rather than in bits and pieces. "No comment" implies guilt.
- Recognize that, in the age of instant news, there is no such thing as a private crisis.
- Stage "war games" to observe how your crisis plan holds up under pressure. Train executives to practice press conferences, and train teams to respond to crises that may affect other functional areas or divisions.
- Use the firm's philosophy, motto, or mission statement to respond to a crisis. For example, "We believe in our customer. Service is our business."
- Use the firm's closeness to customers and end users for early feedback on the crisis and to evaluate your effectiveness in responding to the events.

The following tactical recommendations are also helpful crisis prevention and management techniques:

- Understand your entire business and dependencies.
- Understanding your business is the basis on which all subsequent policies and processes are built and, therefore, should not be rushed.
- Carry out a business impact assessment.
- Having identified the mission-critical processes, it is important to determine what the impact would be if a crisis happened. This process should assess the quantitative (e.g., financial and service levels) and the qualitative (e.g., operational, reputational, legal, and regulatory) impacts that might result from a crisis and the minimum level of resource for recovery.
- Complete a 360-degree risk assessment, where managers, their peers and direct reports evaluate each other's style and performance. This is used to determine the internal and external threats that could cause disruption and their likelihood of occurrence. Using recognized risk techniques, a scoring system can be achieved, such as high-medium-low, 1 to 10, or unacceptable/acceptable risk.
- Develop a feasible, relevant, and attractive response in two parts: develop the detailed response to an incident and then formulate the business crisis plan that supports that response.

- Exercise, maintain, and audit the plan. A business crisis plan cannot be considered reliable until it has been tested. Exercising the plan is of considerable importance, as a plan untested becomes a plan untrusted.[72]

Finally, issues and crisis management methods and preventive techniques are only effective in corporations if:

- Top management is supportive and participates.
- Involvement is cross-departmental.
- The issues management unit fits with the firm's culture.
- Output, instead of process, is the focus.[73]

Chapter Summary

Organizations and businesses in this new century are more complex and networked than in any previous historical period. Because of the numerous transactions of corporations, methods are required to understand an organization's moral obligations and relationships to its constituencies.

The stakeholder management approach provides an analytical method for determining how various constituencies affect and are affected by business activities. It also provides a means for assessing the power, legitimacy, and moral responsibility of managers' strategies in terms of how they meet the needs and obligations of stakeholders.

Critics of stakeholder theory argue that corporations should serve only stockholders since they own the corporation. They hold that stakeholder theory (1) negates and weakens fiduciary duties that managers owe to stockholders, (2) weakens the influence and power of stakeholder groups, (3) weakens the firm, and (4) changes the long-term character of the capitalist system. A major response to the critics of stakeholder theory states that societies and economies involve market and nonmarket interests of diverse stakeholders as well as stockholders. To understand and effect responsible corporate strategies, methods that include different players and environmental factors—not just stockholders or financial interests—are required.

A stakeholder analysis is a strategic management tool that allows firms to manage relationships with constituents in any situation. An individual or group is said to have a "stake" in a corporation if it possesses an interest in the outcome of that corporation. A "stakeholder" is defined as an individual or group who can affect or be affected by the actions or policies of the organization.

Recent studies have indicated that profits and stockholder approval may not be the most important driving forces behind management objectives.[74] Job enrichment, concern for employees, and personal well-being are also important objectives. These studies reinforce the importance of the stakeholder management approach as a motivating part of an organization's social responsibility system.

The implementation of a stakeholder analysis involves a series of steps designed to help a corporation understand the complex factors involved in its obligations toward constituencies.

The moral dimensions of managerial roles also have a stakeholder perspective. The stakeholder approach can assist managers in resolving conflicts over individual rights and corporate objectives. This approach can help managers think through and chart morally responsible decisions in their work.

The use of stakeholder analysis by a third party is a means for understanding social responsibility issues between a firm and its constituencies. Ethical reasoning can also be analyzed relative to the stakeholder management approach.

Preventing and effectively negotiating disputes is a vital part of the work of professionals and leaders. We discussed several alternative dispute resolution methods in the chapter, emphasizing consensual, relational, and integrative methods that seek win–win approaches. The full range of dispute resolution methods is important to learn because conflict is part of ongoing organizational change.

Issues and crisis management frameworks complement stakeholder analysis as social responsibility methods. Understanding what the central issues are for a company and how the issues evolved over time can help effectively and responsibly manage changes in a company's direction and operations. Crisis management frameworks help to predict, prevent, and respond to emergencies. Issues and stakeholder management methods used together provide an overall approach to leading and managing organizational change responsibly and ethically.

Questions

1. With regard to this chapter's opening case, what, if anything, could BP's CEO have done differently to have prevented and/or avoided the resulting fallout from the crisis? Explain.
2. Briefly describe a dispute in which you were an important stakeholder. How was the situation resolved (or not resolved)? What methods were used to resolve the situation? Looking back on the situation now, what methods could or should have been used to resolve that situation? For example, what would you now recommend happen to effectively resolve it fairly?
3. Which of the types of power (described in this chapter) that stakeholders can use have you effectively used in a conflict or disagreement over a complex issue? Briefly explain the outcome and evaluate your use(s) of power.
4. Which roles and responsibilities in this chapter have you assumed in an organization? What pressures did you experience in that role that presented ethical dilemmas or issues for you? Explain.
5. What reasons would you offer for encouraging leaders and/or managers to use the stakeholder approach? Would these reasons apply to teams?
6. Give a recent example of a corporation that had to publicly manage a crisis. Did the company spokesperson respond effectively to stakeholders regarding the crisis? What should the company have done differently in its handling of the crisis?
7. Describe how you would feel and what actions you would take if you worked in a company and saw a potential crisis emerging at the prodromal or precrisis stage. What would you say, to whom, and why?

8. Using Figure 3.4, identify a complex issue-related controversy or situation in which you, as a stakeholder, were persuaded to move from one position to another and why—for example, from a Nonsupportive to Supportive position, or from Mixed Blessing to Marginal. Explain why you moved and what the outcome was.

9. Argue both the pros and cons of stakeholder theory, using some of the arguments in the chapter as well as your own. What is your evaluation of the usefulness of the stakeholder management approach in understanding and analyzing complex issues?

Exercises

1. Describe a situation in which you were a stakeholder. What was the issue? What were the stakes? Who were the other stakeholders? What was the outcome? Did you have a win–win resolution? If not, who won, who lost, and why?

2. Recall your personal work history. Who were your manager's most important stakeholders? What, in general, were your manager's major stakes in that particular position?

3. In your company or organization, or one in which you have worked, what is the industry? The major external environments? Your product or service? Describe the major influences of each environment on your company (for example, on its competitiveness and ability to survive). Evaluate how well your company is managing its environments strategically, operationally, and technologically, as well as in relation to products and public reputation.

4. Choose one type of functional area manager described in the chapter. Describe a dilemma involving this manager, taken from a recent media report. Discuss how a stakeholder analysis could have helped or would help that manager work effectively with stakeholders.

5. Describe a complex issue that is evolving in the news or media. Explain how the issue has evolved into other issues. Which issues management framework would help track the evolution of this issue? Explain.

6. Describe a recent crisis that involved a product. Which phase of the crisis management model do you believe is the most important for all involved stakeholders? Explain.

I worked as a marketing manager in Belgium for a midsize engineering company. Total revenues for the company were $120 million. The company had recently gone public and, in two public offerings, had raised more than $60 million. The firm was organized into four distinct strategic business units, based on products. The group that I worked in was responsible for more than $40 million in sales. We had manufacturing plants in four countries.

Our plant in Belgium manufactured a component that was used in several products and brought in $15 million in revenue. However, these products were old technology and were slowly being replaced in the industry. The overhead associated with the plant in Belgium was hurting the company financially, so they decided to sell the facility. The unions in Belgium are very strong and had not approved the final sale agreement. After this sale, the workforce was going to be reduced by half. Those who were laid off were not going to receive full severance pay, which, in Belgium, could take several years, and then workers would receive only 80 percent of total payment—a drastic change from what is offered in the United States. I was surprised that our executives in the United States had stated that the sale agreement was more than fair—contrary to the union's position. A strike was imminent; the materials manager was told to stock 10 weeks of product.

My ethical dilemma started after the strike began. Originally, the company thought the strike would not last longer than a couple days. Instead of causing a panic among our customers, management decided to withhold information on the strike from our customers and sales force. I could understand the delay in telling our customers, but to withhold information from our sales force was, I believed, unconscionable. Inevitably, our inside sales representatives became suspicious when they called the Belgium plant to get the status of an order, and nobody answered. They called me, and I ignored the corporate request and informed them of the strike. When it became obvious that the strike was going to be longer than anticipated, I asked the vice presidents of marketing and sales about our strategy for informing the affected customers. They looked at me quizzically and told me to keep things quiet ("Don't open a can of worms") because the strike should be over soon. In addition, they dictated that customer service should not inform customers of the strike, and excuses should be developed for late shipments.

The strike lasted longer than 12 weeks. In this time, we managed to shut down a production line at Lucent Technologies (a $5 million customer) with only a couple of days' notice and alienated countless other valuable and loyal customers. I did not adhere to the company policy: I informed customers about the strike when they inquired about their order status. I also told customer service to direct any customer calls to me when we were going to miss shipments. This absolved them of the responsibility to tell the customer.

We did not take a proactive stance until 11 weeks into the strike, when the vice president of sales sent a letter informing our customers about the strike—too little and much too late to be of any help. The materials manager was fired because he only stocked 10 weeks of product, even though management thought he should have been conservative with his estimates. Half-way through this ordeal, I updated my résumé and started a search for a new job. It was clear that management was more concerned about their year-end bonus than doing the right thing for the long-term prospects of the company and its customers.

Questions

1. Do you agree with the writer's decision to inform customers about the strike? Explain.
2. Did management have the right to withhold this information from customers? Explain.
3. Explain what you would have done, and why, if you had been in the writer's situation.
4. What should management have done in this case? When? Why?

Cases

Case 7

The BP *Deepwater Horizon* Explosion and Oil Spill: Crisis and Aftermath

The BP *Deepwater Horizon* spill is a multifaceted disaster that, despite popular opinion, cannot be explained by any one root cause. The April 20, 2010, oil spill was a point of crisis for oil giant BP, and CEO Tony Hayward faced a significant challenge in responding to this crisis.

The events leading up to the BP blowout unearth a highly complex network of circumstances, which though preventable, together culminated in the worst environmental disaster in American history. Repercussions of the incident are still felt today, and all stakeholders involved have an opportunity to learn about the significance of crisis management.

Events Leading Up to the BP Spill

In March 2008, the Occupational Safety and Health Administration (OSHA) stated on public record that BP had one of the worst safety records in its industry. This same month, the Minerals Management Service (MMS) gave BP an exclusive right to drill a parcel of Gulf of Mexico floor called Block 252, for a fixed fee of $34 million. Over the coming months, BP boarded a rig to supervise contractors who set out to drill the Macondo well using Transocean rigs.

On October 2009, Hurricane Ida hit the drilling site, damaging BP's oil rig and requiring BP to rent a more technologically sophisticated rig, called *Deepwater Horizon.*

The Point of Crisis

On April 9, 2010, BP exerted unreasonable pressure during drilling and fractured the rock in its well. According to the National Commission on the BP *Deepwater Horizon* Oil Spill and Offshore Drilling (2011, 94), "BP informed its lease partners Anadarko and MOEX that 'well integrity and safety' issues required the rig to stop drilling further." BP management compared safety to profit maximization and made the decision to plug the fractures rather than cease drilling in an effort to maximize profit. The plug worked, but BP knew it was precarious and that it needed to mitigate this risk by balancing pressure carefully. After the incident, the BP wells leader admitted that losing returns "was the No. 1 risk."

The Warning Signs

When BP and Halliburton tested float valves, BP used a decision tree to evaluate the job based on whether there were lost returns on the cement factor, rather than on engineering or risk principles, and decided the test went well enough to excuse Schlumberger technicians, who were also scheduled to perform cement evaluation tests. That decision, which was based on an effort to save the company time and money, was another example of a decision that could have prevented the oil well blowout that is ironically costing over $20 billion in remediation to date.

BP is documented to have sought Halliburton's counsel on how it could use cement centralizers to mitigate some of this drilling risk. However, because of low inventory, BP again allegedly compromised on quality and safety by changing Halliburton's design and using the wrong kind of cement centralizers.

Halliburton conducted a routine cement slurry test revealing that the foam was unstable, but the company did not adequately report or address it. This event was sadly not uncommon among the various subcontractors on the *Deepwater Horizon* project. There appeared to be a team culture of poor communication driven by an effort to save time, money, and reputation, which ironically resulted in catastrophic loss of the same, at the expense of stakeholders of this project.

The company finished its cement job and began to lock down the Macondo well so it could move a smaller rig into place, but BP had amended the *Deepwater*'s procedures to omit a pressure test (which would have checked the bottomhole cement job), among other things. (Incidentally, on April 12, BP had sent its amendments to the procedure to the MMS, but there is no evidence that the new procedures were reviewed.) This combination of events, caused by several actors, was highly uncanny and improbable, and given the circumstances of the weak cement job, their occurrence proved to be deadly. The more that the details of the story were unraveled, the more it became evident that multiple parties and stakeholders participated in the negligence, insufficient funding, and insufficient communication in the lead-up to the *Deepwater Horizon* explosion.

BP was also discovered to have used a broken pressure gauge during this same time. This too became a critical issue that, if it had been prevented, could have possibly averted the disaster. Still, the root cause of these errors is unclear, as the disaster could have been prevented with tighter risk management protocol, more sufficient inspection, as well as closer attention to fluctuation in gauge readings. Nonetheless, incompetence and risk mitigation planning negligence again appeared to be rife on the job.

Other important precrisis warnings included the fact that the well was leaking and was in danger of exploding. The site workers were also found to have not adequately read or responded to the confounding results of the pressure test that showed they needed to use a different gauge to detect a leak that was later found in the well. This also indicated negligence (and incompetence) on behalf of site workers. Drill-pipe pressure increased 250 pounds per square inch (psi) as shown on the monitor, but no one appeared to be checking the monitor. As could be expected from these warnings, the pressure relief valve soon blew. In response, the pumps were shut off; but pressure increased and no one seemed trained to know the significance of this issue and appropriate action was not taken. The warning signs were ignored.

Next, mud emerged on the rig floor, indicating that there was a problem in the well. Six-eight minutes passed before this issue was addressed, and the spill was not diverted overboard. The lack of response indicated negligence in emergency response training and a disregard for the warning signs that a crisis was coming.

After countless emergency indications, a high enough concentration of natural gas leaked into the air to cause an ignition. This explosion forced 5 million barrels of oil into the Gulf of Mexico over 87 days—the worst environmental disaster in American history.

The Aftermath—Response to the Crisis

During the emergency response, scientists, including Ian MacDonald of Florida State University, alleged that BP withheld the facts around the spill, likely to protect its reputation. Possibly because of this obfuscation, it took 87 days until the well was finally capped on July 15, 2010.

Aside from some controlled burning and microbial digestion, only upon the capping of the well did the remediation of the oil's damage truly begin. BP set up a $20 billion claims fund, which was still being administered as of March 2012. It is estimated that BP will pay $585 million in pollution violations. The company "has claimed about $40 billion in charges to cover the costs of litigation and cleanup" and set aside $3.5 billion to cover expected Clean Water Act fines on the estimated 3.2 million barrels spilled. However, the ripple effect of the spill has had no small impact on the Gulf Area tourism and fishing, which has somehow gone unaccounted for in BP's legal restoration.

More recently, a scientific study of the ongoing after effects of the spill on mice and dolphins in that area, found that "the effects on the mouse immune system . . . were strikingly similar to what we saw in the dolphins," says De Guise (an investigating scientist). "We want to show the likelihood of a cause and effect relationship and add to the weight of (evidence that oil impacts the immune system in a way that is very reproducible across species. The changes that we found in the Barataria Bay dolphins are specific to oil and not related to something else" (Hancock, 2021). Importantly, it was reported from the same scientist that, "I think it is the first time we find such evidence across generations in a wild animal population, and that is scary. It raises concern for the long-term recovery of these dolphins. These are long-lived mammals and, in many ways, not unlike humans who live in the area and depend on natural resources. It is interesting science, but it is very scary"(Ibid.).

The legal aftermath of the spill is also very consequential, as hundreds with legal claims charging harm from the disaster are still pending. For example, a Florida man, Christopher F. Causey, whose case represents "the 504 lawsuits still outstanding from ordeal, Florida District Judge Casey Rodgers said in her order filed Jan. 11" (White, 2021). The U.S. Department of Justice (DOJ) earlier in the aftermath filed a civil suit against BP and its business partners. This civil suit is expected to be followed by criminal charges—so much so that BP has already divested some assets. Other legal updates on the spill can be found in White (2021).

Legislatively, oil companies are likely to face much more strict safety, environmental, risk management, and reporting standards in the future. From the federal government level, Barack Obama, who was president at the time of the crisis, began pushing for the cut of oil subsidies, which could lead to higher oil prices for consumers.

This type of large environmental crisis required swift corrective action and strategic public relations. There are many lessons to be learned from the way BP continues to handle the consequences of the accident and the way it employed crisis management.

Fatal Ethical Flaws

The root fatal flaws in this drilling project were not scientific in nature, but rather the tears in the fundamental ethical fabric of the team and its strategic business partners—negligence, poor risk management, and possible willful obfuscation of information for the apparent purpose of salvaging reputation while risking the safety and well-being of BP's stakeholders.

The first ethical flaw is negligence. While some degree of mistakes is unavoidable because of human error, BP and its constituent contractors displayed a systematic failure to prevent error, which could be classified as negligence. Several claims had been filed against BP to this extent, but courts have not rendered a decision, and BP executives expect the case to last until at least 2014. What made the events surrounding the explosion tragic is that there were many opportunities for BP to make choices that could have prevented the disaster, but team members systematically compromised the safety and stakeholder consideration when they cut corners to save time and to maximize profits, flying in the face of justice and utilitarianism (as discussed in the next section). This distinction is both ethically significant and economically consequential for businesses, as it is embedded in our criminal law system, which penalizes on the basis of negligence.

A subset of this negligence was the failure to report safety risks, which was endemic to the broader BP contracting team, including Halliburton, Transocean, and the BP staff. To this point, ironically, BP was celebrating *Deepwater Horizon*'s seven years of safety at the exact moment of the explosion. As the problem was so pervasive, and as the moral burden of a team's culture lies with its leadership, BP is implicated in this failure.

A third classification of ethical failure recognized by the U.S. legal system is willful misconduct, which implies a conscious and willful choice to endanger others when other options are available. Whether or not this charge will be found sufficiently compelling in court, it could be seen in several of BP's decisions, including its decision to drill after fracturing the well and its decision to dismiss Schlumberger before testing the well. At this point in BP's work, BP made both an ethical and financial miscalculation by actively choosing to compromise the safety, economic livelihood, environment, and personal property of many of its stakeholders to maximize its own profits. This decision was systematic and was not made in isolation, suggesting abuse and grounds for liability on the part of BP and its team members.

Whether or not BP will be indicted for criminal charges, BP and nine of its business associates have faced civil charges from the DOJ in pursuit of remediation of the damages under the Oil Pollution Act and the Clean Water Act. In this is an important lesson: companies like BP should consider not just the letter of the law but the spirit of the law, such as the anti-pollution provisions of both the Oil Pollution Act and Clean Water Act when guiding ethical decisions. A big part of BP's damaging ethical tapestry is its failure to consider its stakeholders in driving its corporate strategy. BP's costly mistakes could also have been averted by balancing its focus on short-term profits and considering others in the business, as well as governments, consumers, and the environment. This *stakeholder management approach* identifies corporate strategy by mapping and evaluating the implications of strategy through the lens of stakeholder impact as shown in the following analysis. This approach is built upon "win–win" collaborative outcomes rather than short-term profits by identifying the issue at hand, assessing the nature of stakeholder interest, assessing each stakeholder's power, identifying stakeholder moral responsibilities, and developing the appropriate strategies and tactics. Incidentally, these same outcomes will likely save companies like BP up to billions of dollars in the long run.

Questions for Discussion

1. Who and what factors were responsible for the *Deepwater Horizon* oil spill?
2. Evaluate BP's corporate culture from an ethical standpoint. What role did top management have in shaping that culture?
3. What actions could/should BP management have taken in response to the many early-warning signs? Did the "inaction" of BP demonstrate the company's ethics? Explain.
4. What responsibility did BP's partners and oversight agencies like OSHA have in the crisis?
5. How did BP's corporate strategy affect its ethical decision making?
6. Do companies like BP have an ethical responsibility to protect the environment? Why or why not?

Sources

This case was developed from material contained in the following sources:

Gillis, J. (2010, May 19). Scientists fault lack of studies over gulf oil spill. *New York Times*.

Hancock, E. (2021). Gulf Oil Spill's long-lasting legacy for dolphins. https://www.sciencedaily.com/releases/2021/03/210302150112.htm.

Mauer, R., and Tinsley, A. M. (2010, May 8). Gulf oil spill: BP has a long record of legal, ethical violations. *McClatchy Newspapers*.

National Commission on the BP *Deepwater Horizon* Oil Spill and Offshore Drilling. (2011, January). *Deep Water: The Gulf oil disaster and the future of offshore drilling*. Washington, DC: U.S. Independent Agencies and Commissions.

Passwaters, M. (2010, December 15). DOJ files *Deepwater Horizon* civil suit. http://www
.snl.com/interactivex/article.aspx?id=12278731&KPLT=2. Note: This is a proprietary
research site not accessible to public.

Passwaters, M. (2011, January 6). National commission on BP spill blames cost
cutting, mismanagement. http://www.snl.com/interactivex/article.aspx?id=12178
252&KLPT=6&Printable=1. Note: This is a proprietary research site not accessible
to public.

Swint, B. (2010, June 22). The legal aspects of the BP deep oil spill. *Law and Medicine*.

Swint, B. (2012, February 20). BP could reach settlement for Gulf oil spill this week.
Washington Post. http://www.washingtonpost.com/business/economy/bp-could
-reach-settlement-for-gulf-oil-spill-this-week/2012/02/20/gIQALU52PR_story
.html.

Thomas, P., Johes, L. A., Cloherty, J., and Ryan, J. (2010, May 27). BP's dismal safety
record. *ABC News*. http://abcnews.go.com/WN/bps-dismal-safety-record
/story?id=10763042.

White, B. (2021, January 22). BP Deepwater Horizon Oil Spill claims move forward
with test case. https://topclassactions.com/lawsuit-settlements/lawsuit-news
/bp-deepwater-horizon-oil-spill-test-case/

White House, Office of the Press Secretary. (2010, June 15). Remarks by the
president to the nation on the BP oil spill. https://obamawhitehouse.archives
.gov/the-press-office/remarks-president-nation-bp-oil-spill.

Yanke, G. (2010, June 2). BP's Gulf oil spill: Where ethics and legal advice collide.
Investment Rethink Blog.

Zimmerman, A. (2011, February 12). State officials step up criticism of BP oil-spill fund.
Wall Street Journal. http://online.wsj.com/article/SB10001424052748704329104
576138342199677406.html?KEYWORDS=BP+oil+department+of+justice.

Case 8

Ethics and AI (Artificial Intelligence): Opportunities and Threats

"Success in creating AI would be the biggest event in human history. Unfortunately, it might also be the last, unless we learn how to avoid the risks."
—Stephen Hawking

Introduction

"Artificial intelligence is the simulation of human intelligence processes by machines, especially computer systems. Specific applications of AI include expert systems, natural language processing (NLP), speech recognition and machine vision" (Tech Accelerator, 2020).

The following three features characterize artificial intelligence:

• Learning—the ability to acquire relevant information
• Reasoning—the ability to apply the rules acquired and use them to reach conclusions
• Iterative—the ability to change the process based on newly acquired information

The power of AI has been widely used to aid in Covid-19 efforts by aiding "in detecting, understanding and predicting the spread of disease . . . supporting physicians by automating aspects of diagnosis, prioritizing healthcare resources, and improving vaccine and drug development . . . combating online misinformation about COVID-19" (Tzachor and Whittlestone et al., 2020).

Emergence of Artificial Intelligence

AI as a field was formally founded in 1956 at a conference at Dartmouth College in Hanover, New Hampshire, where the term "artificial intelligence" was coined" (Lewis, 2014). Over the next two decades, artificial intelligence as a field has flourished and is becoming more ubiquitously applied across industries. Government agencies such as the Defense Advanced Research Projects Agency (DARPA) funded special projects to research AI and its ability to translate and transcribe spoken language. "In the 1980's, AI was reignited by two sources: an expansion of the algorithmic toolkit, and a boost of funds" (Anyoha, 2017). Researchers John Hopfield and David Rumelhart popularized "deep learning" techniques and computer-enabled programming for teaching computers to learn from experience. At the same time, researcher Edward Feignenbaum introduced expert systems that could mimic the decision-making process of a human expert in a particular field. Programs were designed to ask experts to respond to a given situation, and once this information was learned, nonexperts could receive advice from that program. During the 1990s and 2000s, AI thrived; many of the landmark goals of artificial intelligence had been achieved. In 1997, IBM's Deep Blue, a chess-playing computer program, defeated reigning world chess champion and grand master Gary Kasparov. This was the first time a world chess champion lost to a computer and served as a huge step toward an artificially intelligent decision-making program. Also in 1997, voice recognition software developed by Dragon Systems was implemented in Windows. AI breakthroughs have already surpassed human ability in certain activities, such as online search functions for photographs, videos, and audio; translation, transcription, lip reading, emotions recognition (including lying); and signature and handwriting recognition and documents forgery (Hancock, Naaman, and Levy, 2020).

Social Issues

"Many forms of bias underlie data sets and can interfere with data quality and how data is analyzed. These problems predate the advent of AI, but they could become more widely encoded into the fabric of the health care system if they are not corrected before AI becomes widespread" (Howard and Borenstein, 2020). Artificial intelligence was created by humans and as such is subject to the same biases prevalent in society. Although the interweaving of said biases was not intentional, it does not make their threat any more real, especially in times of crisis. The data these machines rely on are filled with biases. Data may exist in poor quality or not at all for some groups, which will only further these inequalities. "Infection and mortality data released by the CDC [Centers for Disease Control], while still infrequent and incomplete, paints a bleak picture around how COVID-19 disproportionately kills certain racial and ethnic groups. Alarming rates among black Americans are rooted in longstanding economic and health care inequalities, and the ambiguous racial/ethnic categorization of existing data further obscures disparities" (Smith and Rustagi, 2020). The data is also incomplete for immigrants, the LGBTQ+ community, and other marginalized groups because of their fear of deportation or their lack of resources as they have "economic and social vulnerabilities" (Smith and Rustagi, 2020). On top of that, the data is skewed toward affluent, white communities, as they are most often able to access the limited amount of tests and expensive medical procedures. In order to avoid more drastic and deadly effects of these biases "developers should employ values-based design methods in order to create systems that can be evaluated in terms of providing benefits for all impacted populations, and not only economic value for organizations." As well as ensure the systems are "inclusive, fully taking into account human gender diversity (e.g., research on the impact of the virus across the nonbinary gender spectrum) and economic condition along with environmental sustainability" (IEEE Global Initiative on Ethics of AIS, 2020).

Legal Issues

The legal system is the institution tasked with defending civil rights and liberties. To better understand the legal aspects of AI and applications using this technology, a central question concerns how the law will evolve in response to this technology. Will it be through the imposition of new laws and regulation or through the time-honored tradition of having courts settle disputes, grievances, and harm done from the consequences of AI technology? Courts have already been involved in a number of U.S. decisions. "In Washington v. Emanuel Fair, the defense in a criminal proceeding sought to exclude the results of a genotyping software program that analyzed complex DNA mixtures based on AI while at the same time asking that its source code be disclosed" (Lexology, 2019). "The Court accepted the use of the software and concluded that a number of other states had validated the use of the program without having access to its source code" (Lexology, 2019). "In State v. Loomis, the Wisconsin Supreme Court held that a trial judge's use of an algorithmic risk assessment software in sentencing did not violate the accused's due process rights, even though the methodology used to produce the assessment was neither disclosed to the accused nor to the court" (State v. Loomis, 2017). Another legal consideration revolves around robots. Current legal frameworks do not have rules under which robots shall be held liable for their acts or omissions that cause damage to third parties. Robots can be so sophisticated that it can be questioned if ordinary rules on liability are sufficient. This is an important consideration in cases where cause cannot be traced back to a specific human and where the acts or omissions of robots, which have caused harm, could have been avoided.

Ethical Considerations

Beyond these larger social and economic considerations, data scientists have concerns about bias, ethical implementations of the technology, and the nature of interactions between AI systems and humans. According to Satya Nadella of Microsoft, "The most critical next step in our pursuit of AI is to agree on an ethical and empathetic framework for its design" (Gordon-Murnane, 2018, 40).

Babic and colleagues (2021) frame moral risks of AI as "challenges as problems of responsible algorithm design," since "products and services that make decisions autonomously will also need to resolve ethical dilemmas—a requirement that raises additional risks and regulatory and product development challenges"; namely, "how to automate moral reasoning?" Scholars, they note, give the problem of how Tesla, for example, can and should "program its cars to think in utilitarian cost–benefit terms or Kantian ones, where certain values cannot be traded off regardless of benefits? Even if the answer is utilitarian, quantification is extremely difficult: How should we program a car to value the lives of three elderly people against, say, the life of one middle-aged person? How should businesses balance trade-offs among, say, privacy, fairness, accuracy, and security? Can all those kinds of risks be avoided?"

Companies such as Facebook, Amazon, and Apple have been making tremendous progress in developing AI systems; however, it is imperative that organizations implementing new AI technologies know the risks and impacts these technologies will have. Today, AI designers and developers are creating systems that will affect and influence millions of people. According to Deloitte, "Organizations should consider questions such as whether their applications of technology decrease or increase discriminatory bias; what procedures they have to protect the privacy of worker data; whether technology-made decisions are transparent and explainable; and what policies they have in place to hold humans responsible for those decisions' outputs" (Volini and Denny, 2020). Ethical, human-centric AI must be developed with consideration for the societal or for the community it affects.

Reasonable Solutions Paths to Moral Puzzles

Babic and colleagues (2021) suggest that "executives need to think of machine learning as a living entity, not an inanimate technology." Toward that end, these authors offer the following guidelines: "Think like a regulator and certify first. Businesses should develop plans for certifying machine-learning offerings before they go to market." They also recommend that executives and regulators "monitor continuously; ask the right questions" regarding accuracy and fairness, biases, and agency. For instance, "On which third-party components, including data sources, does the behavior of our machine-learning algorithms depend? How much does it vary when they're used by different types of people—for example, less-skilled ones?" They also encourage those designing and using AI to "develop principles that address your business risks." They also pose a most important question that has ethical as well practical implications: "Are there conditions under which machine learning should not be allowed to make decisions, and if so, what are they?"

Concluding Comments

It seems likely that AI is and will continue to permeate most products and processes in companies and businesses, as well as our individual lives. An enduring ethical and moral question will be: Whose values, principles, and unplanned or anticipated consequences will be used to design, guide, and explain any resulting harm that ensues? It is helpful to note that Europe has a head start on addressing these questions.

The Organisation for Economic Cooperation and Development (OECD) is an international body "that works to build better policies for better lives." It promotes AI that is "innovative and trustworthy" and responsibly transparent. AI "that respects human rights, the rule of law, diversity, and democratic values, and that drives inclusive growth, sustainable development, and well-being" will be acceptable and responsible for its users. OECD also emphasizes the "robustness, safety, security, and continuous risk management of AI systems throughout their life cycles" (OECD, 2019).

Questions for Discussion

1. What are outstanding ethical concerns and issues with AI technology and applications?
2. Who are the stakeholders and stockholders in developing, designing, distributing, and selling these applications?
3. What are some practical solution suggestions for keeping AI technologies ethical and accountable?
4. Do you believe AI technologies and applications will take over most jobs done by humans today or complement the work people do now?

5. How do you think education should and needs to change as AI penetrates all areas of life as we know it today?

Sources

This case was developed from material contained in the following sources:

Anyoha, R. (2017). Can machines think? *The history of artificial intelligence (blog).* http://sitn.hms.harvard.edu/flash/2017/history-artificial-intelligence/.

Babic, B., Cohen, G., Evgeniou, T., and Gerke, S. (2021, January–February). When machine learning goes off the rails: A guide to managing the risks. *Harvard Business Review.* https://hbr.org/2021/01/when-machine-learning-goes-off-the-rails.

Bryson, J. (2015). Artificial intelligence and pro-social behavior. In Misselhorn, C. (ed.), *Collective Agency and Cooperation in Natural and Artificial Systems: Explanation, Implementation and Simulation*, 281–306. Vol. 122 of Philosophical Studies. Berlin: Springer.

Bryson, J. (2018). The past decade and future of AI's impact on society. *OpenMind.* https://www.bbvaopenmind.com/en/articles/the-past-decade-and-future-of-ais-impact-on-society/.

Campolo, A., Sanfilippo, M., Whittaker, M., and Crawford, K. (2017). *AI Now 2017 Report.* https://ainowinstitute.org/AI_Now_2017_Report.pdf.

Dignan, L. (2016). Google's big bet: Machine learning, artificial intelligence will be its secret sauce, winning formula. *ZDNet.* https://www.zdnet.com/article/googles-big-bet-machine-learning-artificial-intelligence-will-be-its-secret-sauce-winning-formula/.

Furst, K., and Wagner, D. (2018). Ethics and the pursuit of artificial intelligence. *International Policy Digest*, https://intpolicydigest.org/2018/08/06/ethics-and-the-pursuit-of-artificial-intelligence/.

Gordon-Murnane, L. (2018, March–April). Ethical, explainable artificial intelligence: Bias and principles. *Online Searcher, 42(2).* https://www.questia.com/read/1G1-532528739/ethical-explainable-artificial-intelligence-bias.

Hancock, J. T., Naaman, M., and Levy, K. (2020, January). AI-mediated communication: Definition, research agenda, and ethical considerations. *Journal of Computer-Mediated Communication, 25(1).* https://doi.org/10.1093/jcmc/zmz022.

Howard, H., and Borenstein, J. (2020). AI, robots, and ethics in the age of COVID-19. https://sloanreview.mit.edu/article/ai-robots-and-ethics-in-the-age-of-covid-19/.

IEEE Global Initiative on Ethics of AIS. (2020). Statement regarding the ethical implementation of artificial intelligence systems (AIS) for addressing the COVID-19 pandemic. https://standards.ieee.org/content/dam/ieee-standards/standards/web/documents/other/gieais-covid.pdf?utm_medium=undefined&utm_source=undefined&utm_campaign=undefined&utm_content=undefined&utm_term=undefined.

Lewis, T. (2014). A brief history of artificial intelligence. *LiveScience.com.* https://www.livescience.com/49007-history-of-artificial-intelligence.html.

Lexology. (2019, July 17). Emerging legal issues in an AI-driven world. https://www.lexology.com/library/detail.aspx?g=4284727f-3bec-43e5-b230-fad2742dd4fb.

OECD. (2019). *What are the OECD principles on AI?* https://www.oecd.org/going-digital/ai/principles/

Smith, G., and Rustagi, I. (2020). The problem with COVID-19 artificial intelligence solutions and how to fix them. https://ssir.org/articles/entry/the_problem_with_covid_19_artificial_intelligence_solutions_and_how_to_fix_them.

State v. Loomis. (2017, March 10). *Harvard Law Review*. https://harvardlawreview
.org/2017/03/state-v-loomis/.

Tech Accelerator. (2020). Artificial intelligence. *SearchEnterpriseAI.com*. https://
searchenterpriseai.techtarget.com/definition/AI-Artificial-Intelligence.

Tzachor, A., Whittlestone, J., Sundaram, L., and Ó hÉigeartaigh, S. (2020). Artificial
intelligence in a crisis needs ethics with urgency. https://www.nature.com/articles
/s42256-020-0195-0.

Volini, E., and Denny, D. (2020). Ethics and the future of work. https://www2.deloitte
.com/xe/en/insights/focus/human-capital-trends/2020/ethical-implications
-of-ai.html.

Case 9

Genetic Discrimination

Genetic discrimination is defined by the Centers for Disease Control and Prevention as "prejudice against those who have or are likely to develop an inherited disorder." With advances in science, it is possible to determine whether specific gene mutations exist and to discover the likelihood of an individual developing a disorder based on the existence of these mutations. These developments have created situations that concern the public: their privacy and possible employment livelihood. One of the major issues noted by the National Human Genome Research Institute (NHGRI) is the possibility that individuals who have taken this testing, and received positive results, will be turned down for health insurance or employment. This possibility will most probably be at issue depending on the political party and dominant political persuasion in power at both the national and state levels, as well as in the Supreme Court.

Many people with family histories or other factors that determine their susceptibility to certain diseases or disorders will have to make a decision about whether to be tested for the existence of certain genetic sequences or mutations. A major factor in this decision will be how this information will be used and who will be able to access the results. Patients may choose to refuse testing that could save their lives or improve their quality of life because they fear future discrimination. Employers with group insurance plans may want to know whether any of their employees are predisposed to a specific disorder. Insurance providers would also like to have the results of genetic testing to assist in underwriting policies. Both of these scenarios are likely to lead to discrimination against or exclusion of certain individuals for either employment or insurance coverage.

Human Genome Project

One of the major catalysts of the advancement of genetic testing and the interpretability of genetic information was the Human Genome Project. It began in 1990 as a joint effort between the National Institutes of Health and the United States Department of Energy. The project had six goals: (1) to identify all of the approximately 20,000 to 25,000 genes in human DNA; (2) to determine the sequence of the 3 billion chemical base pairs that make up human DNA; (3) to store this information in databases; (4) to improve tools for data analysis; (5) to transfer related technologies to the private sector; and (6) to address the ethical, legal, and social issues (ELSI) that may arise from the project. Accomplishments leading to the project's completion in 2003 have contributed to major advances in scientific research and health care, primarily in the areas of medicine and genetic testing. Understanding the genes and sequences associated with common diseases has future implications for the entire human population and will help to detect and possibly remedy disorders with more precise and targeted treatments.

Business Response

Even before the entire human genome had been sequenced and published, and the implications of the discovery had been reviewed to establish guidelines and boundaries, biotechnology companies and others conducting scientific research had begun to develop uses for this new way of looking at human conditions and diseases. One question from this new branch of medical technology is: Who, if anyone, should own gene sequences, and who has the rights to one's genetic information? The issue of patenting gene sequences began long before the map of the human genome was completed and prior to consequences of granting these patents were able to be seriously examined. Companies had already begun to submit applications and receive approval for gene sequences that had some still unknown future use and potential profitability. According to Modern Drug Discovery contributor, Charles W. Schmidt, "Those who seek patents usually want to protect research investments in one of two markets: gene- and protein-based drug development or diagnostic testing that searches for gene sequences linked to a given illness" (Schmidt, 2001). Even without strong federal regulations to guide the use and ownership of test data and eliminate the reluctance of people to agree to testing, companies developing genetic tests believed that patenting is necessary to protect an industry that is someday likely to generate millions in profits. Those in opposition to this view have trouble allowing ownership of something that is so personal. The major caveat to granting these patents is that it limits and slows the competition in the industry to find uses for and make advances in an already-patented gene sequence. However, if there is no guarantee of exclusive ownership with the outcome of research, companies may choose not to move forward in research. The main issue of a significant business response to scientific advancements in genetic testing and gene sequencing is ensuring that laws and regulations keep up with technology and medical advances to prevent major abuse, ownership, and privacy issues.

The two cases that follow illustrate the evolution between 2001 and 2013 of enforcement with regard to the genetic nondiscrimination Title II law.

The Case of Burlington Northern Santa Fe Railway

In February 2001, the Equal Employment Opportunity Commission (EEOC) filed a suit against the Burlington Northern Santa Fe Railway Company for secretly testing some of its employees. The genetic tests conducted had been developed by Athena Diagnostics in Worcester, Massachusetts, to detect a rare neuromuscular disorder, but Burlington Northern had been using them to validate and predict claims of carpal tunnel syndrome made by railroad workers. This incident, and others like it across the United States and Europe over the following years, raised concerns about the access and rights that employers have to their employees' medical and genetic information. In this case, if Burlington Northern had discovered that employees with carpal tunnel syndrome had a genetic predisposition to the injury, the company could have claimed that the ailment was not job related and therefore denied payment of any medical bills. The EEOC filed its suit referencing the Americans with Disabilities Act, which states that "it is unlawful to conduct genetic testing with the intent to discriminate in the workplace." Cases like this alerted lawmakers and activists to the growing concerns of discrimination in the workplace based on genetic information, and on closer examination of the issue, revealed significant inconsistencies and gaps in the laws currently protecting the rights of employees.

Rhonda Jones

The first lawsuit initiated by the EEOC to effectively enforce the Genetic Information Nondiscrimination Act of 2008 (GINA) came in 2013. This case and the previous one summarized above (Burlington Northern Santa Fe Railway Company in Fort Worth, Texas, also for carpal tunnel syndrome in April 2001) emphasize the integral relationship between conduct prohibited under GINA and conduct prohibited under the Americans with Disabilities Act of 1990 as amended (42 U.S.C. §12101 et seq., Pub. L. 101-336). "GINA Title II prohibits both the acquisition and the use of genetic information in employment contexts."

Rhonda Jones was a temporary memo clerk for Fabricut, Inc. Her temporary employment was running out when she applied for a permanent position with Fabricut. The company at first offered her the position before violating the GINA Title II law when, as part of its pre-employment medical examination, it allegedly requested Rhonda Jones's family history with regard to several specific conditions. "GINA defines 'genetic information' broadly to include family medical history." Based on the pre-employment medical examination, Fabricut allegedly "required Jones to obtain additional testing to rule out carpal tunnel syndrome (CTS)." Even though later testing did rule out CTS, because of information she gave the company, Fabricut allegedly withdrew their job offer "on the basis of the pre-employment medical examination and its view that she had CTS."

"As part of the consent decree settling the case, Fabricut agreed to pay $50,000 in damages. The company also agreed to undertake corrective actions that include posting a nondiscrimination notice to employees. GINA requires that employers post a nondiscrimination notice, and 'Equal Employment Opportunity is the Law' posters are readily available on the EEOC website. Fabricut also agreed to have its employees responsible for hiring decisions undergo nondiscrimination training and further agreed to distribute nondiscrimination policies to its employees"(Wagner, 2013).

Government Response to Advances in Genetic Testing and Discrimination

As with most human resources issues, companies cannot always be trusted to act in the best interests of their individual employees, especially where privacy rights are concerned. Throughout the past two decades, the United States has drafted and passed several laws addressing the issue of discrimination by employers and private businesses and protecting employees who speak out against discriminatory behavior. One of the most well-known regulations in this category is the Americans with Disabilities Act of 1990 (ADA), which prohibits discrimination in hiring on the basis of a disability. Similarly, Title VII of the Civil Rights Act of 1974 prohibits employment discrimination on the basis of race, color, religion, sex, and national origin. According to National Institutes of Health Consultant Robert B. Lanman, JD, who was commissioned in May 2005 by the Secretary's Advisory Committee on Genetics, Health, and Society to examine the adequacy of current laws protecting against genetic discrimination, these laws have not been updated to specifically relate to genetic discrimination. They offer protection to the extent that a genetic predisposition is common in a specific race or other group protected under the ADA or Civil Rights Act. In his executive summary, Lanman offered the example of Tay-Sachs disease, which is prevalent in persons of Eastern European Jewish ethnicity. Discrimination based on the genetic information of an individual that is unrelated to an individual's race or ethnicity would not currently fall under the protection of the ADA or Civil Rights Act.

A major section of the pieced-together legislation that is currently protecting citizens from genetic discrimination is the Health Insurance Portability and Accountability Act of 1996 (HIPAA). This act prohibits insurance companies from (1) excluding members because of a preexisting condition that is based solely on the results of genetic testing or family history, (2) imposing eligibility requirements, or (3) restricting coverage based on genetic information. HIPAA does not restrict insurance companies from "requesting, purchasing, or otherwise obtaining genetic information about an individual," and it does not restrict insurance companies from charging higher premiums or including this genetic information in the underwriting process.

The major problem with the state and federal regulations enacted to date is that genetic information is either not mentioned as a basis for discrimination, or it is not defined consistently throughout existing laws. The United States has two primary concerns: protecting the privacy of genetic information, and preventing discrimination based on genetic information—especially by employers and insurance companies. To address this issue, new federal regulation must cover gaps left in existing directives and account for future developments in the industry. The hodgepodge of existing laws combined with the inconsistency of state laws leaves too many loopholes to provide comprehensive protection for the general public.

The History of the Genetic Information Nondiscrimination Act

On February 17, 2005, the Senate passed S.306, the "Genetic Information Nondiscrimination Act of 2005" with a vote of 98–0. The law was then passed on to the House of Representatives on March 10, 2005, where it was referred to the Subcommittee on Health. The proposed bill specifically prohibited "discrimination on the basis of genetic information with respect to health insurance and employment." In addition, it amended the Employee Retirement Income Security Act of 1974 (ERISA) and the Public Health Service Act (PHSA) to include in their definitions of genetic information any results of genetic testing and information pertaining to whether or not testing was performed. It also disallowed insurance companies from adjusting premiums based on the results of genetic testing, and prevented them from requiring genetic tests for subscribers or their dependents.

The law concluded by covering fines and penalties and called for a commission to review advances in science and technology and developments in genetic testing six years after the enactment of the law to make recommendations and amendments. This bill in 2005 was considered dead in the House of Representatives but was resubmitted for consideration in 2007.

Initially, these first attempts to pass the law were met with resistance from the Health Insurance Association of America (HIAA), and the claim that additional federal regulation is not needed. Opponents of the bill see sufficient restrictions in the current existing laws and do not see the necessity of new legislation. However, Lanman's report, "An Analysis of the Adequacy of Current Law in Protecting against Genetic Discrimination in Health Insurance and Employment," points out several shortcomings in the combined efforts to protect individuals from this type of discrimination. More important, future advances in bio- and medical technology need to be accounted for—and somewhat are—by this new proposed bill.

The bill's consequences for employers and health insurance providers are focused around the idea of being informed. Since health insurance costs are rising, and they are likely to continue to rise with advances in medicine, testing, and the ability to prolong life, employers must be more aware of the costs of hiring additional employees. Health insurance providers also must remain competitive in balancing the cost of providing health care coverage and mitigating the financial risk to themselves. If employers and health insurance providers are not privy to all of the information available concerning the insured parties, premiums will not be fair or balanced.

While the health insurance companies will probably not come out ahead in this battle, some of their concerns should be taken into consideration if the bill is to be amended before it is passed. For example, one of the members of the Human Genome Project's Committee for Ethical, Legal, and Social Implications, Nancy L. Fisher, MD, asks if genetic testing and health insurance can coexist. Fisher's main concern is the definition of terms like "preexisting condition" and "genetic information," and how new laws will affect not only the health insurance industry and its ability to survive, but also the financial cost for taxpayers if "society decides that everyone is entitled to comprehensive health care."

May 21, 2008: The Genetic Information Nondiscrimination Act

The Genetic Information Nondiscrimination Act, referred to as "the first civil rights legislation of the 21st century" was reintroduced to Congress and became a law on May 21, 2008. The law prevents employers and insurers from using genetic data against individuals and employees. The law states that (1) employers cannot deny a person a job because the individual is genetically predisposed to develop a particular disease or condition; (2) insurers cannot use an individual's genetic profile to deny coverage or raise his/her premiums; and (3) now protected, an individual benefits from medical genetic testing without concern with regard to results being used against him/her. However, the law does not protect third parties from using an individual's genetic results, including the military. It is also plausible that an individual may still be at risk of being discriminated against with regard to health insurance.

Title II GINA Law Today

The two cases presented earlier, illustrate the difference in EEOC's effectiveness in enforcing the Title II GINA law. Given the history of disputes over genetic testing, ownership and commercialization of genetic tests and research results, and employees at risk and who may or may not have a preexisting genetic condition, this federal law appears at present to be serving its intended purpose. Interesting to note, Utah recently signed into law SB 227, "creating the Genetic Information Privacy Act (GIPA). The law is aimed at protecting genetic data collected from direct-to-consumer (DTC) genetic testing companies. Companies distributing DTC tests should evaluate their current data privacy policies and practices against the obligations the new Utah law imposes on data use and protection, including user consent, data security, and access and deletion rights, to ensure they are in a position to comply with the new law" (Fulton et al., 2021).

Questions for Discussion

1. What is genetic discrimination, and why is it an issue?
2. Who would benefit and who would be at risk if genetic testing and the results of such tests were legal and could be required of employees? Explain.
3. Explain the ethical principle(s) that could be used to (a) argue against genetic testing of employees and (b) argue for genetic testing.
4. Explain your position on the issue of genetic testing by employers.
5. How does the outcome of Rhonda Jones's case affect employers? Is there now a fair balance between the Title II GINA law and employers? Explain.

Sources

This case was developed from material contained in the following sources:

About the Human Genome Project. (n.d.). Human Genome Project Information Archive 1990–2003. Accessed March 16, 2021, https://web.ornl.gov/sci/techresources/Human_Genome/project/index.shtml.

Askari, E. (2003, October 3). Genetic revolution opens door to discrimination by insurance companies. *Knight Ridder Tribune Business News.*

Bates, S. (2001, July 1). Science friction. *HR Magazine,* 34–44.

Fisher, N. L., MD. (2004, January). Genetic testing and health insurance: Can they coexist? *Cleveland Clinic Journal of Medicine, (71)1.*

Fulton, A., Kadish, J., Mullin Richter, S., and Hampton LLP. (2021, April 2). New State Genetic Privacy Law Directed at Consumer Genetic Tests. https://www.jdsupra.com/legalnews/new-state-genetic-privacy-law-directed-1958441/

Genetic discrimination. (n.d.). National Human Genome Research Institute. http://www.genome.gov/10002328.

Genetic testing glossary. (n.d.). Centers for Disease Control National Office of Public Health Genomics. Accessed August 5, 2006, http://www.cdc.gov/genomics/gtesting/ACCE/FBR/CF /CFGlossary2.htm.

H.R. 1227: Genetic Information Nondiscrimination Act of 2005, 109th U.S. Congress (2005–2006). *GovTrack.us.* https://www.congress.gov/bill/109th-congress /house-bill/1227.

H.R. 1227: Genetic Information Nondiscrimination Act of 2005 (Introduced in House). Sec. 208. Disparate Impact. (2005). The Library of Congress. Accessed August 6, 2006, http://thomas.loc.gov/cgi-bin/query/F?c109:3:./temp/~c109cK3bQY: e89590.

H.R. 1227: Genetic Information Nondiscrimination Act of 2005 (Introduced in House). Text of Legislation. (2005). The Library of Congress. Accessed August 6, 2006, http://thomas.loc.gov/cgi-bin/query/z?c109:H.R.1227.

Keim, B. (2008, May 21). Genetic discrimination by insurers, employers becomes a crime. *Wired Science.* http://blog.wired.com/wiredscience/2008/05/the-genetic -inf.html.

Kipper, S. (2003, July 23). The Proposed Genetic Discrimination Model Act (letter). Health Insurance Association of America. Accessed July 29, 2006, http://www .ncoil.org/hearings /HIAATestimony.doc.

Lanman, R. B. (2005, May). An analysis of the adequacy of current law in protecting against genetic discrimination in health insurance and employment. https://osp.od .nih.gov/wp-content/uploads/2014/01/legal_analysis_May2005_0.pdf.

S. 306: Genetic Information Nondiscrimination Act of 2005, 109th U.S. Congress. (2005–2006). *GovTrack.us.* https://www.congress.gov/bill/109th-congress /senate-bill/306.

Schmidt, C. W. (2001, May). Cashing in on gene sequences. *Modern Drug Discovery, (4)5,* 73–74. http://pubs.acs.org/subscribe/journals/mdd/v04/i05/html /05money.html.

Wagner, J. (2013). EEOC files and settles its first GINA-based employment discrimi- nation lawsuit on May 7, 2013. https://theprivacyreport.com/2013/05/13/eeoc -files-and-settles-its-first-gina-based-employment-discrimination-lawsuit-on-may-7 -2013/

Wilner, F. N. (2001, February 19). Test tube ethics. *Traffic World,* 13–14.

Notes

1. Borunda, A. (2020, April 20). We still don't know the full impacts of the BP oil spill, 10 years later. *National Geographic*. https://www.nationalgeographic.com/science /2020/04/bp-oil-spill-still-dont-know-effects-decade-later/.

2. Chen, J. (2020, February 12). BP oil spill. *Investopedia*. https://www.investopedia .com/terms/b/bp-oil-spill.asp; Thomas, P., Johes, L. A., Cloherty, J., and Ryan, J. (2010, May 27). BP's dismal safety record. *ABC News*. http://abcnews.go.com/WN/bps-dismal -safety-record/story?id=10763042; Martin, A. (2011, September 14). BP mostly, but not entirely, to blame for gulf spill—national. *The Atlantic*. https://www.theatlantic.com /national/archive/2011/09/bp-mostly-not-entirely-blame-gulf-spill/337965/.

3. BP oil spill timeline. (2010). *The Guardian*. http://www.theguardian.com/environ- ment/2010/jun/29/bp-oil-spill-timeline-deepwater-horizon; *Deepwater Horizon* oil spill. (2013, October 22). *Wikipedia*. http://en.wikipedia.org/wiki/Deepwater_Horizon_oil _spill#Health_consequences.

4. BP oil spill timeline. (2010), op. cit.

5. Krauss, C. (2013). In BP trial, the amount of oil lost is at issue. *New York Times*. http://www.nytimes.com/2013/09/30/business/energy-environment/bp-trial-in-2nd -phase-to-set-amount-of-oil-spilled.html?pagewanted=1&_r=0.

6. Ibid.

7. Hammer, D. (2013). Oil spill trial: Plaintiffs say BP lied about size of oil spill; BP says response "extraordinary." *Eyewitness News*.

8. Ibid.

9. Ibid.

10. Ibid.

11. Borunda (2020), op. cit.

12. Ibid.

13. Ibid.

14. Freeman, R. E., Harrison, J. S., Wicks, A. C., Parmar, B. L., and De Colle, S. (2010). *Stakeholder theory: The state of the art*, 39. Cambridge: Cambridge University Press.

15. Jones, T. (April 1995). Instrumental stakeholder theory: A synthesis of ethics and economics. *Academy of Management Review, 20(2)*, 404. Also see Freeman et al. (2010), op. cit., 63; and Hasnas, J. (2013). Whither stakeholder theory? A guide for the perplexed revisited. *Journal of Business Ethics, 112(1)*, 47–57.

16. Jones (1995, April), op. cit.

17. Clarkson, M. (ed.) (1998). *The corporation and its stakeholders: Classic and contemporary readings*. Toronto: University of Toronto Press.

18. Hasnas (2013), op. cit.

19. Freeman, R. E. (1984). *Strategic management: A stakeholder approach*, 25. Boston: Pitman.

20. Koenig, T., and Rustad, M. (2012, April 25). Reconceptualizing the BP oil spill as *parens patriae* products liability. *Houston Law Review, 49*, 291–391.

21. Berman, S., Wicks, A., Otha, S., and Jones, T. (1999). Does stakeholder orienta- tion matter? The relationship between stakeholder management models and firm finan- cial performance. *Academy of Management Journal, 42*, 488–506; Ogden, S., and Watson, R. (1999). Corporate performance and stakeholder management: Balancing shareholder and customer interests in the U.K. privatized water industry. *Academy of Management Journal, 42*, 526–538.

22. Freeman, R. E. (1999). Divergent stakeholder theory. *Academy of Management Review, 24*, 233–236.

23. Preston, L., and Sapienza, H. (1990). Stakeholder management and corporate performance. *Journal of Behavioral Economics, 19(4)*, 373. See also Jawahar, M., and Mclaughlin, G. (2001, July). Toward a descriptive stakeholder theory: An organizational life cycle approach. *Academy of Management Review, 26(3)*, 397–414.

24. For a critique of the stakeholder theory, see Reed, D. (1999). Stakeholder management theory: A critical theory perspective. *Business Ethics Quarterly, 9(3)*, 453–483.

25. This section used as a resource, Friedman, A., and Miles, S. (2006). *Stakeholders, theory, and practice.* Oxford: Oxford University Press, 119–148.

26. Marcoux, A. (2000). Business ethics gone wrong. *Cato Policy Report, 22(3)*. Washington, DC: The Cato Institute; Argenti, J. (1993). *Your organization: What is it for?* New York: McGraw-Hill; Sternberg, E. (1994). *Just business: Business ethics in action.* Boston: Little, Brown.

27. Froud, J., Haslam, C., Suckdev, J., and Williams, K. (1996). Stakeholder economy? From utility privatisation to new labour. *Capital and Class, 60*, 119–134; Friedman and Miles (2006), op. cit.

28. Key, S. (1999). Toward a new theory of the firm: A critique of stakeholder "theory." *Management Decision, 37(4)*, 319.

29. Mitchell, R. B., Agle, B. R., and Wood, D. (1997). Toward a theory of stakeholder identification and salience: Defining the principle of who and what really counts. *Academy of Management Review, 22(4)*, 853–886. See also Key (1999), 319.

30. Bowie, N., and Duska, R. (1991). *Business ethics*, 2nd ed. Englewood Cliffs, NJ: Prentice Hall; Frederick, W. (1994). From CSR1 to CSR2: The maturing of business and society thought. *Business & Society, 3(2)*, 150–166; Bowen, H. (1953). *Social responsibilities of businessmen.* New York: Harper.

31. Frederick, W. (1988). *Business and society: Corporate strategy, public policy, ethics*, 6th ed. New York: McGraw-Hill.

32. Freeman (1984), op. cit., 25.

33. Savage, G. T., Nix, T. W., Whitehead, C. J., and Blair, J. D. (1991). Strategies for assessing and managing organizational stakeholders. *Academy of Management Executive, 5(2)*, 61–75.

34. Andriof, J., Waddock, S., Husted, B., and Rahman, S. (eds.) (2002). *Unfolding stakeholder thinking: Theory, responsibility, and engagement.* Sheffield, U.K.: Greenleaf Publishing.

35. Barnes-Slater, C., and Ford, J. (2002, August). Measuring conflict: Both the hidden costs and the benefits of conflict management interventions. *Mediate.com.* https://www.mediate.com/articles/fordSlater.cfm; Lynch, D. (1997, May). Unresolved conflicts affect the bottom line—effects of conflicts on productivity. *HR Magazine.*

36. U.S. Department of Commerce. (2012, February 16). Quarterly retail e-commerce sales 4th quarter 2011. *U.S. Census Bureau News.* http://www.census.gov/retail/mrts/www /data/pdf/ec_current.pdf; B2B e-commerce poised for explosion according to American Arbitration Association study; survey of Fortune 1000 uncovers need for e-commerce rules. (2001, May 17). *Business Wire.*

37. Alternate dispute resolution. (n.d.) *NYCourts.gov.* http://www.courts.state.ny.us /ip/adr/What_Is_ADR.shtml, accessed March 13, 2012.

38. Wilkie, C. (2013). Iraq war contractors fight on against lawsuits, investigations, fines. *Huffington Post.* http://www.huffingtonpost.com/2013/03/20/iraq-war-contractors_n _2901100.html.

39. Crawford, N., and C. Lutz. (2021). U.S. costs to date for the War in Afghanistan, 2001–2021. https://watson.brown.edu/costsofwar/files/cow/imce/figures/2021/Human %20and%20Budgetary%20Costs%20of%20Afghan%20War%2C%202001-2021.pdf.

40. Morris, C. (2002, May). Definitions in the field of dispute resolution and conflict transformation. *Peacemakers Trust.* http://www.peacemakers.ca/publications/ADRdefini tions.html.

41. Ibid.

42. Ibid.

43. Fisher, R., Ury, W., and Patton, B. (1991). *Getting to yes: Negotiating agreement without giving in,* 2nd ed., 11. New York: Penguin Books.

44. It is beyond the scope of this chapter to go into further detail on these methods. The following readings are suggested: Bush, R., and Folger, J. (1994). *The promise of mediation: Responding to conflict through empowerment and recognition.* San Francisco, CA: Jossey-Bass; Cobb, S. (1994). A narrative perspective on mediation: Towards the materialization of the "storytelling" metaphor. In Folger, J., and Jones, T. (eds.), *New directions in mediation: Communication research and perspectives,* 48–66. Thousand Oaks, CA: Sage; Cormick, G., et al. (1997). *Building consensus for a sustainable future: Putting principles into practice.* Ottawa: National Round Table on the Environment and Economy; Fisher et al. (1991), op. cit.; Folger, J., and Bush, R. (2001). *Designing mediation: Approaches to training and practice within a transformative framework.* New York: Institute for the Study of Conflict Transformation.

45. Chinn, G. M. (2008). Ethical issues of the Space Shuttle *Challenger* Disaster Team 2. *WikiSpaces.* https://wikispaces.psu.edu/display/STS245/Ethical+Issues+of+the+Space+Shuttle +Challenger+Disaster+Team+2, accessed March 10, 2021.

46. Duska, R. (2005). Ethics in financial services. Adapted from an article by James Clarke in Hartman, L. (ed.). (2005). *Perspectives in business ethics,* 3rd ed. Boston: McGraw-Hill, 631.

47. Wartick, S., and Heugens, P. (2003, Spring). Guest editorial, future directions of issues management. *Corporate Reputation Review, 6(1),* 7–18.

48. Issue Management Council. (n.d.). Issue management defined (excerpted from a speech by Teresa Yancey Crane). http://issuemanagement.org/learnmore/clarification-of -terms/, accessed March 13, 2012.

49. Wartick and Heugens (2003), op. cit., 15.

50. Ibid.

51. Mothers Against Drunk Driving. (n.d.) History of MADD. http://www.madd.org /about-us/history/cari-lightner-and-laura-lamb-story.pdf, accessed March 13, 2012; MADD successfully realized its goal by reducing alcohol-related deaths by 20 percent in 1997; see Mothers Against Drunk Driving (n.d.). Organization overview. *Activist Facts.* https://www .activistfacts.com/organizations/17-mothers-against-drunk-driving/#:~:text=For%20 the%20first%2015%20years,by%2020%25)%20in%201997.

52. Mahon, J. F., and Heugens, P. (2002). Who's on first–Issues or stakeholder management? In Windsor, D., and Welcomer, S. (eds.), *Proceedings of the Thirteenth Annual Meeting of the International Association for Business and Society.* Oronto, ME: International Association for Business and Society.

53. Bigelow, B., Fahey, L., and Mahon, J. (1991). Political strategy and issues evolution: A framework for analysis and action. In Paul, K. (ed.), *Contemporary issues in business ethics and politics,* 1–26. Lewiston, NY: Edwin Mellen.

54. Jones, T. (1991). Ethical decision making by individuals in organizations: An issue-contingent model. *Academy of Management Review, 16(2),* 366–395.

55. Ibid.

56. King, W. (1987). Strategic issue management. In King, W., and Cleland, D. (eds.), *Strategic planning and management handbook*, 256. New York: Van Nostrand Reinhold; Buchholz, R. (1982). Education for public issues management: Key insights from a survey of top practitioners. *Public Affairs Review, 3*, 65–76; Brown, J. (1979). *This business of issues: Coping with the company's environment.* New York: Conference Board. Also see Carroll, A. B., and Bulchholtz, A. (2003). *Business and society: Ethics and stakeholder management,* 5th ed. Cincinnati: South-Western.

57. Heath, R. (2002, November). Issues management: Its past, present and future. *Journal of Public Affairs, 2(4),* 209.

58. Marx, T. (1986). Integrating public affairs and strategic planning. *California Management Review, 29(1),* 141–147; and Power, P. (2004, August 16). Calm in a crisis. *Lawyer.* http://www.thelawyer.com/calm-in-a-crisis/111565.article, accessed November 4, 2013.

59. Bryant, M., and Hunter, T. (2010, September/October). BP and public issues (mis) management. *Ivey Business Journal.* https://iveybusinessjournal.com/publication/bp-and-public-issues-mismanagement/.

60. Ibid.

61. Ibid. Also see Marx (1986) and Power (2004), op. cit.

62. 10 books that changed America. (2008, March 20). *Listverse.* http://listverse.com/2008/03/20/10-books-that-changed-america/.

63. Wald, M., and Baker, A. (2009, January 18). 1549 to Tower: We're gonna end up in the Hudson. *New York Times,* A29; Gittens, H., Dienst, J., and Hogarty, D. (2009, January 15). Plane crashes into Hudson: Hero pilot saves everyone. *NBC New York.* http://www.nbcnewyork.com/news/archive/Plane-Crashes-in-Hudson-River.html; Olshan, J., and Livingston, I. (2009, January 17). Quiet air hero is Captain America. *New York Post*; US Airways Flight 1549 (n.d.). *Wikipedia.* http://en.wikipedia.org/wiki/US_Airways_Flight_1549.

64. See Marx (1986), op. cit.

65. Ibid.

66. Hjelmgaard, K. (2021, February 9). WHO will end research into "extremely unlikely" theory that COVID-19 originated in Wuhan lab. *USA Today.* https://www.usatoday.com/story/news/world/2021/02/09/covid-origin-world-health-organization-end-research-wuhan-lab-theory/4446839001/.

67. Bailey, J. (2007, February 19). JetBlue's C.E.O. is "mortified" after fliers are stranded. *New York Times.* http://www.nytimes.com/2007/02/19/business/19jetblue.html?pagewanted=1&_r=2&ref=todayspaper.

68. Matthews, J. B., Goodpaster, K., and Nash, L. (1985). *Policies and persons: A casebook in business ethics.* New York: McGraw-Hill.

69. Prbookgroup. (2009, April 13). Case study: Tylenol poisonings. *Crisis communications.* http://crisiscomm.wordpress.com/2009/04/13/case-study-tylenol-poisonings/.

70. Ibid.

71. Mitroff, I., Shrivastava, P., and Firdaus, U. (1987). Effective crisis management. *Academy of Management Executive, 1(7),* 283–292.

72. Power (2004), op. cit.

73. Wartick, S., and Rude, R. (1986). Issues management: Fad or function? *California Management Review, 29(1),* 124–140.

74. Key (1999), op. cit.

4

THE CORPORATION AND EXTERNAL STAKEHOLDERS

Corporate Governance: From the Boardroom to the Marketplace

OPENING CASE

Recently, 205,280 organizations reported they had been hacked in a ransomware attack. Organizations paid on average $84,116 in the last quarter of 2019 to release files, twice as much than the previous quarter. Coveware, a security firm, reported that $190,946 was paid to hackers in the last month of 2019—with many organizations experiencing ransom demands in the millions of dollars.[1]

TJX Companies, Inc., a leading off-price retailer of apparel and home fashions in the United States and worldwide, was lucky. When its systems were hacked some years ago, no ransomware was demanded. The company's security-breach story is a classic but still relevant lesson to all organizations, especially with regard to their corporate social responsibility to customer stakeholders.

When you read the company's "V.A.L.U.E. Corporate Social Responsibility Report 2013" and then chief executive officer (CEO) Carol Meyrowitz's letter, you would never believe the crisis that rocked the company in 2008 ever happened. This case illustrates one difference between companies that learn, change, and grow, and those that do not.

TJX seems to practice its V.A.L.U.E. proposition, "Vendor Social Compliance, Attention to Governance, Leveraging Differences, United with Our Communities, and Environmental Initiatives." Forbes reported in 2013 that the TJX Companies (NYSE: TJX) had taken over the No. 95 spot from Capital One Financial Corp (NYSE: COF). Although the company, as with several other retailers, could improve its customer satisfaction index score, it has recovered from the 2008 crisis recounted here.[2]

On January 17, 2008, TJX announced that the organization had experienced an unauthorized intrusion of its computer systems.[3] Customer information, including credit card, debit card, and driver's license numbers, had been compromised. This intrusion had been discovered in December 2006, and it was thought that data and information as far back as 2003 had been accessed and/or stolen. At the time, approximately 45.6 million credit card numbers had been stolen. In October 2007, the number rose to 94 million accounts,[4] making it one of the largest credit card thefts or unauthorized intrusions in recent history.

Because of the lax security systems at TJX, the hackers had an open doorway to the company's entire computer system. Hackers used a laptop outside of one of TJX's stores in Minnesota and easily cracked the code to enter into the Wi-Fi network. Once in, the hackers were able to access customer databases at the corporate headquarters in Framingham, Massachusetts. The hackers gained access to millions of credit card and debit card numbers, information on refund transactions, and customer addresses and phone numbers. The hackers reportedly used the stolen information to purchase over $8 million in merchandise.[5]

TJX used an outdated WEP (wired equivalent privacy) to secure its networks. The industry standard at the time required TJX to use WPA (Wi-Fi Protected Access) protocols.[6] Even earlier, in 2001, hackers were able to break the code of WEP, which made TJX highly vulnerable to an intrusion. (Similar data breaches have occurred within the past few years at the firms ChoicePoint and CardSystems Solutions.) In August 2007, a Ukrainian man, Maksym Yastremskiy, was arrested in Turkey as a potential suspect in the TJX case. According to police officials, Yastremskiy is "one of the world's important and well-known computer pirates."[7] He led two other men in the scheme.[8]

Even though the intrusion was discovered in December 2006, the company did not publicize it until a month later. Consumers felt that they should have been notified of the breach once it was discovered. However, TJX complied with law enforcement and kept the information confidential until it was told it could notify the public. Retail companies such as TJX that use credit card processing are required to comply with the Payment Card Industry Data Security Standard (PCI DSS). The PCI DSS is a set of requirements for maximizing the security of credit and debit card transactions. A majority of firms have not complied with this standard, as was the case with TJX. Additionally, TJX did not have regular internal or external security or network audits occurring. In fact, 18 months had passed before TJX noticed the data breach, for which the regular audits could have potentially detected. Furthermore, a risk mitigation and management strategy were nonexistent.[9]

A number of stakeholders were involved in this break-in: consumers, who were put at great risk; banks; TJX (its shareholders, management, employees, and other internal parties who did business with and were invested in the firm); the credit card companies; the law enforcement and justice systems; the public; other retail firms; and the media, to name a few. Then CEO Carol Meyrowitz took an active role in informing the public in statements on the company's websites and through the media about the company's responsibility and obligations to its stakeholders during and after the investigation. TJX also contacted various agencies to help with the investigation. A website and hotline were established to answer customer questions and concerns.

The intrusion cost TJX approximately $118 million in after-tax cash charges and $21 million in future charges. Although TJX incurred substantial legal, reimbursement, and improvement costs, the company's pretax sales were not negatively affected. Sales during the second quarter of fiscal year 2008 increased compared to second-quarter sales from fiscal year 2007.[10] During Meyrowitz's tenure, she was able to successfully navigate this crisis and lead TJX to "grow from about $13 billion to $48.3 billion." She retired in June 2015.[11]

At the end of 2007, TJX reached a settlement agreement with six banks and bankers' associations in response to a class-action lawsuit against the company.[12] In the spring of 2008, TJX settled in separate agreements with Visa ($40.9 million with 80 percent acceptance) and Mastercard International (a maximum of $24 million with 90 percent minimum acceptance). There was almost full acceptance of the alternative recovery offers by eligible Mastercard accounts.[13] Note that those issuers who accept the agreements and terms "release and indemnify TJX and its acquiring banks on their claims, the claims of their affiliated issuers, and those of their sponsored issuers as Mastercard issuers related to the intrusion. That includes claims in putative class actions in federal and Massachusetts state courts."[14]

Affected customers were reimbursed for costs such as replacing their driver's licenses and other forms of identification and were offered vouchers at TJX stores and free monitoring of their credit cards for three years. Customer discontent was reportedly expressed after the intrusion; however, customer loyalty returned,[15] as was evidenced in sales numbers.

4.1 Managing Corporate Social Responsibility in the Marketplace

Consumers are as engaged as ever with expectations of social justice and fairness—in society and the marketplace. "Nearly 60% of Americans want the companies they buy products from to have a position about issues such as racial discrimination and social justice, a survey carried out in June [2020] among 1,004 respondents found. Roughly 50% of the survey's respondents said they often do online research to see how a brand reacted to the social issues." Corporate social responsibility (CSR) involves an organization's duty and obligation to respond to its stakeholders' and the stockholders' economic, legal, ethical, and philanthropic concerns and issues. This definition encompasses both the social concerns of stakeholders and the economic and corporate interests of corporations and their stockholders. Generally, society cannot function without the economic, social, and philanthropic benefits that corporations provide. Leaders in corporations who use a stakeholder approach commit to serving broader goals, in addition to economic and financial interests, of those whom they serve, including the public. Typically, corporations will incorporate one of four broad categories of CSR in the workplace: environmental efforts, philanthropy, ethical labor practices, and volunteering.[16]

Managing CSR in the marketplace with multiple stakeholder interests is not easy. Ethics at the personal and professional levels requires reasoned and principled thinking, as well as creativity and courage. When ethics and social responsibility escalate to the corporate level, where companies must make decisions that affect governments, competitors, communities, stockholders, suppliers, distributors, the public, and customers (who are also consumers), moral issues increase in complexity, as this chapter's opening case illustrates. For organizational leaders and professionals, the moral locus of authority involves not only individual conscience but also corporate governance and laws, collective values, and consequences that affect millions of people locally, regionally, and globally. Patagonia, for example, is a company that conducts its outdoor apparel business with a 360-degree focus of responsibility. The company takes responsibility for the actions of all members of its supply chain and for impacts on the environment. This attitude is integrated into the culture of the company, its organizational structure (with a new director of Social/Environmental Responsibility position created in 2010), and its relationship with suppliers. It has developed a "contractor relationship assessment," a scorecard system that is used to rate the performance of each factory. Patagonia, along with many other companies, now recognizes a broader scope of accountability and the interests of multiple stakeholders.[17]

In the opening case, the TJX executives had to deal not only with their own customers, but with banks (in a class-action suit), credit card companies, the media, competitors, and a network of suppliers and distributors—as well as their own reputation. What may have seemed like a routine technical security problem turned into one of the largest-known credit card theft/unauthorized intrusions in history. Had the CEO not stepped in and become a responsible spokesperson and decision maker for the company, customers may not have responded in kind. This involvement from Meyrowitz shortly after the crisis also proved to be beneficial toward TJX's profits, as discussed in the opening case.

The basis of CSR in the marketplace begins with a question: What is the philosophical and ethical context in which CSR and ethical decisions are made? For example, not everyone is convinced that businesses should be as concerned about ethics and social responsibility as they are about profits. Many believe that ethics and social responsibility are important, but not as important as a corporation's performance. This classical debate—and seeming dichotomy—between performance, profitability, and "doing the right thing" continues to surface not only with regard to CSR, but also in political parties and debates over personal and professional ethics. The roots of CSR extend to the topic of what a "free market" is and how corporations should operate in free markets. Stated another way, does the market sufficiently discipline and weed out inefficient "bad apples" and wrongdoers, thereby saving corporations the costs of having to support "soft" ethics programs? Ethical Insight 4.1 asks you to assume a decision-making role, in hindsight, regarding the TJX opening case.

Ethical Insight 4.1

Ethical Issues in the TJX Case

After reading the opening case, answer and be prepared to discuss in class these questions:

1. If you had been assigned to investigate, report, and offer recommendations from this case, how would you respond to this question: Who was to blame for the security breach and why?
2. Which factor, in your judgment, was the most important contributor to TJX's security breach: the lack of a comprehensive security policy and legal procedures, or issues with the company's corporate leadership and culture? Explain.
3. What will work best for TJX in this case: discipline from the legal and judicial system or required changes in the company's leadership and culture regarding security? Explain.
4. Do you believe there should be stricter oversight of private and public companies from regulatory agencies to ensure network and other IT safety procedures are being met? Explain.

The type of information security breach experienced by TJX has become almost commonplace for large organizations, particularly with business trends toward electronic data collection and storage and the increasing complexity of technology. Corporations now have an ethical responsibility for preventive, detective, and corrective actions regarding the protection of stakeholder information. The following is a list of the top-10 "massive security breaches" of recent years:[18]

1. *Court Ventures (now owned by Experian) 2011*: 200 million accounts were breached. A 25-year-old Vietnamese man admitted hacking into Court Ventures databases by posing as a private investigator in the United States. He acquired the money by cash wire transfers between the United States and a bank in Singapore.[19]

2. *NASDAQ (2006–2012)*: 161 million credit and debit card numbers were stolen. The estimated cost to the companies that were affected was $300 million. Five Eastern European men eventually breached access to the sensitive NASDAQ system by using SQL to infiltrate password screens. It took these individuals many months to gain access. One of the individuals involved was the mastermind behind the TJX data breach.[20]

3. *eBay (2014)*: 145 million accounts compromised. The estimated cost included $200 million in class-action lawsuits. Hackers were able to use three corporate employee's e-mails and passwords to infiltrate the network and obtain personal data of consumers.[21]

4. *Equifax (2017)*: 143 million accounts were breached. Hackers gained access to consumer's financial data through gaining illegal access to a server in Atlanta. Financial data included Social Security numbers, birth dates, and addresses. The hack was elaborate, which has made it hard for the Federal Bureau of Investigation (FBI) to pinpoint the exact individuals who performed this breach.[22]

5. *Target (2013–2014)*: A total of around 140 million accounts were hacked beginning in late 2013. The estimated cost for Target was around $162 million. This occurred because Target was not effectively protecting user data from the rest of the network.[23]

6. *Heartland Payment Systems (2009)*: The company revealed that tens of millions of transactions might have been compromised. The company's computers were infected with malware. "108 million debit and credit cards affected; estimated cost included $110 million in payments to Visa and Mastercard."[24]

7. Sony (2011): "100 million accounts breached; estimated cost includes 65 class-action lawsuits totaling between $171 million and $1.5 billion." Hackers stole credentials from a system administrator and then planted malware when they were in the network.[25]

8. *TJX (2007)*: "Thieves had stolen information on possibly tens of millions of credit and debit cards. The company first thought its systems had been compromised for about eight months, but it turned out the vulnerability might have lasted for almost a year longer than that. The incident wound up costing TJX millions of dollars paid to the Federal Trade Commission (FTC), credit card companies, banks, and customers. Eleven hackers were eventually arrested for the break-in. Security breaches have only increased in scope and frequency in recent years, as more businesses store their data in digital files and thieves become increasingly sophisticated in how they gain access to those files."[26]

9. *JP Morgan Chase (2014)*: 83 million personal and small business accounts hacked. Hackers were able to penetrate the system because of "a giant security hole left open by a failure to switch on two-factor authentication on an overlooked server."[27]

10. *Home Depot (2014)*. 56 million customers' personal data compromised; the company said it cost them an estimated $33 million."[28] Malware injected into Home Depot's system caused the breach.

Free-Market Theory and Corporate Social Responsibility

Free-market theory holds that the primary aim of business is to make a profit. As far as business obligations toward consumers, this view assumes an equal balance of power, knowledge, and sophistication of choice in the buying and selling of products and services. If businesses deliver what customers want, customers buy. Customers have the freedom and wisdom to select what they want and to reject what they do not want. Faulty or undesirable products should not sell. If businesses do not sell their products or services, it is their own fault. The marketplace is an arena of arbitration. Consumers and corporations are protected and regulated—according to this view—by Adam Smith's (one of the modern founders of capitalism) notion of the "invisible hand." What would have happened to TJX customers without regulation?

Several scholars argue that the "invisible hand" view is not completely oriented toward stockholders. For example, Eugene Szwajkowski argues that "Smith's viewpoint is most accurately positioned squarely between those who contend firms should act out of self-interest and those who believe corporations should be do-gooders. This middle ground is actually the stakeholder perspective. That is, stakeholders are in essence the market in all its forms. They determine what is a fair price, what is a successful product, what is an unacceptable strategy, what is intolerable discrimination. The mechanisms for these determinations include purchase transactions, supplier contracts, government regulation, and public pressure."[29] Szwajkowski continues, "Our own empirical research has clearly shown that employee relations and product quality and safety are the most significant and reliable predictors of corporate reputation."[30]

Economist and free-market advocate Milton Friedman is noted for a philosophical view summarized in the following quote: "The basic mission of business [is] thus to produce goods and services at a profit, and in doing this, business [is] making its maximum contribution to society and, in fact, being socially responsible."[31] Friedman also stated that even with the corporate scandals, the market is a more effective way of controlling and deterring individual wrongdoers than are new laws and regulations.[32]

Free markets require certain conditions for business activity to help society. These conditions include (1) minimal moral restraints to enable businesses to operate and prevent illegal activities such as theft, fraud, and blackmail; (2) full competitiveness with entry and exit; (3) relevant information needed to transact business available to everyone; and (4) accurate reflection of all production costs in the prices that consumers and firms pay (including the costs of job-related accidents, injuries from unsafe products, and externalities, which are spillover costs that are not paid by manufacturers or companies but that consumers and taxpayers often pay, such as pollution costs). Legal and ethical problems arise when some or all of these conditions are violated, as in this chapter's opening case.

Problems with the Free-Market Theory

Although the free-market theory continues to have its advocates, controversy also exists regarding its assumptions about stakeholders and consumer–business relationships. Examples of free-market failures include the deregulation of the cable industry (rates have skyrocketed since 1996) and environmental issues caused by oil drilling and other production. (Refer to the BP *Deepwater Horizon*, Case 7 in this book, or consider the *Exxon Valdez* case.[33]) For example, consider these arguments:

1. Most businesses are not on an equal footing with stakeholders and consumers at large. Large firms spend sizable amounts on research aimed at analyzing, creating, and—some argue—manipulating the demand of certain targeted buyers and groups. Children and other vulnerable groups, for example, are not aware of the effects of advertising on their buying choices.

2. It has been questioned as to whether many firms' advertising activities truthfully inform consumers about product reliability, possible product dangers, and proper product use. A thin line exists between deceit and artistic exaggeration in advertising.

3. The "invisible hand" is often nonexistent for many stakeholders and, in particular, for consumers in need of protection against questionable, poorly manufactured products that are released to market. One reason a stakeholder view has become a useful approach for determining moral, legal, and economic responsibility is that the issues surrounding product safety are complex and controversial.

4. Economic instability occurs because of greed and overproduction from some of the larger corporations. This can lead to successful and prosperous economic eras or times of recessions. Moreover, the wealthy account for a small percentage of society with the free-market theory, where there is a large gap between what they make and what the poor make.[34]

Another important argument against free-market theory is based on what economists refer to as "imperfect markets"—that is, markets in which competition "is flawed by the ability of one or more parties to influence prices."[35]

Intermediaries: Bridging the Disclosure Gap

Inequality of information available to companies and stakeholders is attributable in part to imperfect markets. Investors, for example, rarely have access to complete information to make investment decisions. They must settle for incomplete and/or inaccurate information. The presence of "intermediaries" can help managers and other designated officers obtain accurate information that might otherwise be willfully withheld and/or manipulated for personal gain or misplaced and lost from neglect.

Two general types of intermediaries are financial and information. *Financial intermediaries* include venture capitalists, banks, and insurance companies; *information intermediaries* include auditors, analysts, rating agencies, and the press. These intermediaries obtain information to provide stakeholders with a more complete and accurate financial picture of the company's position in markets. Intermediaries can prevent leaders and managers of companies from taking unfair advantage of imperfect markets by intentionally failing to disclose information to relevant stockholders and stakeholders. Lehman Brothers, for example, used what is called a "Repo 105" scheme to falsely increase the company's balance sheet by billions of dollars, thereby misleading stakeholders in 2007. This scheme involved repurchase agreements, in which Lehman Brothers entered into agreements to "sell" and then "buy back" toxic assets from other banks. This secretive process misled investors since the company recorded the agreements as sales and removed the bad assets from the financial statements, thus showing stakeholders incorrect and misleading information about the company's financial performance. Lehman had more information than its stakeholders and intentionally chose not to disclose its complete and accurate books.[36] Shortly after this scandal, the company filed for bankruptcy in September 2008. At the time of its downfall, Lehman Brothers was the fourth-largest investment bank in the United States.[37]

Another example of imperfect and skewed market power occurs in Africa, "where a few pharmaceutical companies effectively control the availability of several key drugs. In effect, they are beyond the financial means of millions of Africans or their governments. When a few dominating companies cut the prices of several key ingredients of the AIDS cocktail, they demonstrated this power. But this also revealed a further imperfection in the real market, where only rickety systems, if any, exist to deliver the drugs to patients requiring sophisticated and continuous follow-up care."[38]

Mixed-Market Economies

The debate regarding free markets, imperfect markets, and other forms of social organization is interesting but not always helpful in describing how these systems actually work in the marketplace. The free-market system has been more accurately described by economist Paul Samuelson as a "mixed economy."[39] Mixed economies include a balance between private property systems and government laws, policies, and regulations that protect consumers and citizens. In mixed economies, ethics becomes part of legal and business debates. Principles of justice, rights, and duty coexist with utilitarian and market principles.

A realistic approach to managing social responsibility in a mixed-market economy is the stakeholder management approach. Instead of separating profit-making from social and ethical goals, corporate leaders can accomplish both, as the following sections show.

POINT/COUNTERPOINT

Too Big to Fail

The "theory" behind "too big to fail" (TBTF) institutions was invoked during the 2008 U.S. financial crisis. Government assistance to large failing financial institutions, mainly some of the largest banks, was necessary because their failure would have been catastrophic for the United States and even global economies. The idea was and is unpopular in part because it justifies subsidizing the Wall Street institutions that played a significant part in that near meltdown. Since banks and these larger financial institutions are returning to their previous practices, the next major meltdown may be closer than previously believed possible.

On the other hand, some progress has been made. The Federal Deposit Insurance Corp. claims it is now prepared to take over the parent companies of large failing lenders, if necessary. Making banks safer for the economy means opening more capital to facilitate investments and loans. Banks have to be able to invest to survive and thrive. The financial health of the four TBTF banks (Bank of America, Citigroup, JPMorgan, Wells Fargo) is central to the U.S. economy as this country faces continued debate on the debt ceiling and the failed monetary policy. The larger a firm's capital is at any time, the larger the shrinkage in asset values it can suffer before becoming insolvent. It seems obvious that the purpose of helping a large bank and financial institution gain safety and protection from failure is to raise its capital requirements, so it can take any shock to the value of its assets.

Also consider that TBTF helps large banks and in other ways monopolizing firms such as Walmart and Amazon at the expense of smaller and midsize community businesses that are also essential to our economies and individual lives. By making failure less common, in the case of big banks, in particular, it creates "moral hazard" (the subsidization of bad behavior) in our financial system. To avoid another 2008 near meltdown, a robust plan to take over a failing financial firm is needed, and market participants need to understand that they—not taxpayers—have to absorb their own losses. Investors have to believe that banks are "too big to bail." On the other hand, shareholders, creditors, and the parent company would have to take the pain—even to the point of going out of business. Shareholders would be out of business, creditors would sustain huge losses, and top executives probably would be fired.

Instructions: Each student individually adopts *either* the Point *or* Counter-Point argument below, justifying their reasons (using arguments from this case and other evidence/opinions). Then, either in teams or designated arrangements, each shares their reasons. Afterward, the class is debriefed and share insights.

POINT: With the case of the big banks, let them fail if they bring it on themselves and everybody else. Look what happened to Wells Fargo—it almost wrecked itself from illegal and immoral sales practices. Also, the Wall Street titans, risky bankers, and investors who seek only financial gain have forgotten the original mission of banks and financial investment firms: to help small businesses, individual investors, and families needing mortgages to get those funds. This is what growing and sustaining a middle class, a democratic society, and a socially responsible business environment is all about. The U.S. stock market and business system is based on honest yet "competitive enough" strategies and practices. Consider that "in the 1980s, half of retail shopping took place in independent stores; today, it is less than one-quarter. From 2002 to 2017, Home Depot and Lowes almost doubled their joint share of the home-improvement retail market, from 42 to 81 percent. Even before the coronavirus struck, in 43 metropolitan areas more than half of all groceries were bought at Walmart" (Kwak, 2020). Size matters, but for whom and at what costs? (Especially when you and I are paying!)

COUNTERPOINT: Large financial institutions and banks must be supported to compete with global rivals and to protect the U.S. standard of living and way of life. Such institutions are large but require support.

It is naive to believe that small banks and financial institutions, in particular, can finance multimillion-dollar real estate and other projects that support the economic and social growth that sustains the standard of living of Americans and other global citizens. Enabling banks to grow capital to protect their assets during downtimes is one of the only ways to permit them to survive; otherwise, the government and taxpayer dollars will be needed. The United States is not a socialist or government-run society; rather, it is based on free enterprise where there are no artificial ceilings for growth. So, without large, stable companies—like banking and retail—the economy and many people's livelihood would be, and have been, further jeopardized during Covid-19.

SOURCES

Guerrera, Francesco. (2013, September 30). Too big to bail appears to take hold. *MoneyBeat (blog). WSJ.com.* http://blogs.wsj.com/moneybeat/2013/09/30/too-big-to-bail-appears-to-take-hold/.

Guttentag, J. M. (2013, October 16). Is the "too big to fail" problem too big to solve? Part II. *HuffingtonPost.com.* http://www.huffingtonpost.com/jack-m-guttentag/is-the-too-big-to-fail-problem_b_4101117.html.

Heineman, B. W., Jr. (2013, October 3). Too big to manage: JP Morgan and the mega banks. *HBR Blog Network.* http://blogs.hbr.org/2013/10/too-big-to-manage-jp-morgan-and-the-mega-banks/.

Kwak. J. (2020, July 9). The end of small business. *Washington Post.* https://www.washingtonpost.com/outlook/2020/07/09/after-covid-19-giant-corporations-chains-may-be-only-ones-left/?arc404=true.

Shah, N. (2013, October 16). How to deal with "too big to fail." *Economics (blog). WSJ.com.* http://blogs.wsj.com/economics/2013/10/16/how-to-deal-with-too-big-to-fail/.

Simon, A. (2013, October 21). How to fix too big to fail. *National Review Online.* http://www.nationalreview.com/article/361719/how-fix-too-big-fail-ammon-simon.

Ethical Insight 4.2 asks you to identify the types of capitalism that underlie your decisions.

Ethical Insight 4.2

State, Stakeholder, or Stockholder Capitalism?

State capitalism is a form of capitalism in which "the most important stakeholder [the state] retains power over individual shareholders. The government achieves its dominant role in at least three ways. First, it keeps a strong hand in the distribution of both resources and opportunities. Second, it can intervene in virtually any industry. And third, it can direct the economy by means of large-scale infrastructure, research and development, and education, health care, or housing projects." Shareholder capitalism "is the form of capitalism in which the interests of one stakeholder, the shareholder, dominates over all others. Companies operate with the sole purpose of maximizing profits and returning the highest possible dividends to shareholders." Stakeholder capitalism is "a form of capitalism in which companies seek long-term value creation by taking into account the needs of all their stakeholders, and society at large" (Schwab and Vahnam, 2021). Each of these types of capitalism can also be considered ideologies and even mind-sets that decision makers and individuals hold, consciously or not. Take a look at the characteristics of each type of capitalism in the table below, then answer the questions that follow.

Types of Capitalism	State Capitalism	Shareholder Capitalism	Stakeholder Capitalism
Key Stakeholder	**Government**	**Company Shareholders**	**All stakeholders** matter equally
Key Characteristic	**Government** steers the economy, can intervene where necessary	The social responsibility of **business** is to increase its profits	**Society**'s goal is increase the well-being of people and the planet
Implication for Companies	Business interests are **subsidiary** to state interests	**Short-term profit maximization** as highest good	Focus on **long-term value creation** and ESG measures
Advocated by		**Milton Friedman ('70)** «Shareholder Theory»	**Klaus Schwab ('71)** «Davos Manifesto» ('73)

Source: Table from Schwab, K., with Vanham, P. (2021). *Stakeholder Capitalism: A Global Economy that Works for Progress, People and Planet.* Hoboken, NJ: Wiley & Sons, cited in Schwab, K., and Vanham, P. (2021, January 26). What is the difference between stakeholder capitalism, shareholder capitalism and state capitalism? World Economic Forum. https://www.weforum.org/agenda/2021/01/what-is-the-difference-between-stakeholder-capitalism-shareholder-capitalism-and-state-capitalism-davos-agenda-2021/#:~:text=It%20is%20the%20form%20of,highest%20possible%20dividends%20to%20shareholders.

Questions for Discussion

1. Which type of capitalism do you find most defines your thinking—and voting (if you vote)? Explain.
2. Which type of capitalism describes members of your family's thinking and voting? Explain.
3. Which type of capitalism describes the president or person in power in your country of origin's system? Explain.
4. Which type would be most effective in your country of origin? Explain.

Source: Schwab, K., and Vahnam, P. (2021, January 26). What is the difference between stakeholder capitalism, shareholder capitalism and state capitalism? World Economic Forum. **https:// www.weforum.org/agenda/2021/01/what-is-the-difference-between-stakeholder -capitalism-shareholder-capitalism-and-state-capitalism-davos-agenda-2021/#:~: text=It%20is%20the%20form%20of,highest%20possible%20dividends%20to%20share holders.**

4.2 Managing Corporate Responsibility with External Stakeholders

The Corporation as Social and Economic Stakeholder

The stakeholder management approach views the corporation as a legal entity and also as a collective of individuals and groups. The CEO and top-level managers are hired to maximize profits for the owners and shareholders. The board of directors is responsible for overseeing the direction, strategy, and accountability of the officers and the firm. To accomplish this, corporations must respond to a variety of stakeholders' needs, rights, and legitimate demands. From this perspective, the corporation has primary obligations to the economic mandates of its owners; however, to survive and succeed, it must also respond to legal, social, political, and environmental claims from stakeholders. Figure 4.1 illustrates the moral stakes and corporate responsibilities of firms' obligations toward their different stakeholders.

One study has argued that "using corporate resources for social issues not related to primary stakeholders may not create value for shareholders."[40] This finding does not suggest that corporations refrain from philanthropic activities; rather, "the emphasis on shareholder value creation today should not be construed as coming at the expense of the interests of other primary stakeholders."[41]

Shareholder value obsession began in 1976, when it was argued that the owners of companies were not getting full, open, and honest disclosure from professional managers.[42] A major problem was and is not with placing the emphasis on "shareholder value," but on "the use of short-term increases in a firm's share price as a proxy for it." "Ironically, shareholders themselves have helped spread this confusion. Along with activist hedge funds, many institutional investors have idolized short-term profits and share-price increases rather than engaging recalcitrant managers in discussions about corporate governance or executive pay. Giving shareholders more power to influence

Figure 4.1

External Stakeholders, Moral Stakes, and Corporate Responsibilities

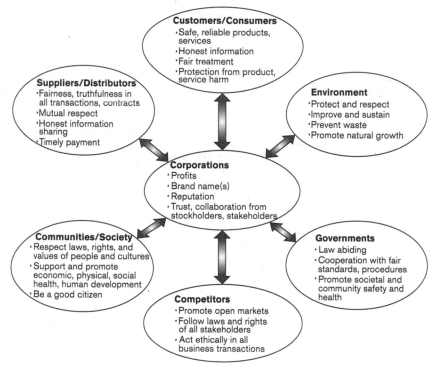

Source: Based on Caux Round Table. (n.d.). Principles for responsible business. *CauxRoundTable.org.* Accessed March 26, 2021, https://www.cauxroundtable.org /principles/.

management (especially in America) and encouraging them to use it should prompt them and the managers they employ to take a longer view."[43]

Critics have not identified a realistic alternative measure of success to shareholder value. Critics of the shareholder model endorse a "stakeholder" model as described and used in this text.[44] "For capitalism to thrive, it urgently needs reform in three areas: shifting from a narrow focus on shareholders to a broader community of stakeholders; adopting an owner-based governance model aimed at building companies with high longevity; and moving from quarterly measures of performance to much longer timeframes."[45]

Corporations are economic *and* social stakeholders. This is not a contradiction but a leadership awareness and choice that requires balancing economic and moral priorities. In the discussion below, we explore the ethical basis on which the relationships between corporations and their stakeholders are grounded. We then turn to the external compliance and legal dimension of stakeholder management, which is also required for effectively dealing with external constituencies.

The Social Contract: Dead or Desperately Needed?

The stakeholder management approach of the corporation is grounded in the concept of a social contract. Developed by early political philosophers, a social contract is a set of rules and assumptions about behavior patterns among the various elements of society. Much of the social contract is embedded in the customs of society. Some of the "contract provisions" result from practices between parties. Like a legal contract, the social contract often involves a quid pro quo (something for something) exchange. Although globalization, massive downsizing, and related corporate practices continue to pressure many employer–employee relationships, the underlying principles of the social contract, like mutual trust and collaboration, remain essential. Reputation of a firm, as well as for leaders, managers, and professionals, is still a foundation for business as well as social exchanges, contracts, and practices. With the Covid-19 pandemic, government assistance was once again, as in past historical disasters, needed and called on to support individuals, families, industries, and businesses of *all* sizes. The government responded, lives were saved, and employment rose.

The social contract between a corporation and its stakeholders is often based on implicit as well as explicit agreements. For example, as Figure 4.1 indicates, when corporations and stakeholders base their negotiations and provisions of services and products on moral standards as well as production-oriented metrics, the success of the business and the satisfaction of the stakeholders increase, and the public's confidence in the businesses also is enhanced. A loss of public confidence can be detrimental to the firm and to its investors. One way to retain and to reinforce public confidence is by acting in an ethical manner that shows a concern for the investing public and the customers of the firm.[46] The question is not really whether a social contract between a corporation and its stakeholders exists, but what the nature of the contract is and whether all parties are satisfied with it. Are customers satisfied with the products and services and how they are treated by a company's representatives? Are suppliers, distributors, and vendors all satisfied by the contractual agreements with the corporation? Do members of the communities a company is located in and serves believe the company is a responsible and responsive citizen? Does the company pay its fair share of taxes? Do employees believe they are paid a fair wage, have adequate working conditions, and are being developed? Do the current political divisions and cultural divisiveness in the United States and certain other nations undermine the social contract between government and citizens, citizens and citizens, within families, states and states?

Balance between Ethical Motivation and Compliance

Ethics programs, as part of the social contract, are essential motivators in organizations. Studies suggest that ethics programs matter more than compliance programs on several dimensions of ethics—for example, awareness of issues, search for advice, reporting violations, decision making, and commitment to the firm.[47] Business relationships based on mutual trust and ethical principles combined with regulation result in long-term economic gains for organizations, shareholders, and stakeholders.[48] If corporate leaders and their firms commit illegal acts, taxpayers end up paying these costs. Corporate leaders and their stakeholders, therefore, have an interest in supporting their implicit social contract as well as their legally binding obligations.

There is a balance to be maintained between external regulation and self-regulation based on the public's trust in corporations. The reputable Edelman Trust Barometer presented its findings in an online survey in 27 markets with 33,000+ respondents, reporting that "78 percent say how a company treats its employees is one of the best indicators of its level of trustworthiness. . . . Fifty-eight percent of the general employees population depend on their employers to be . . . a trustworthy source of information about contentious societal issues." Over three-quarters (76 percent) reported that they "want CEOs to not only address issues, but actually take the lead on change instead of waiting for government to impose it." Interestingly, 67 percent of employees surveyed said they have an expectation that their employers "will join them in taking action on societal issues." That compares with 74 percent who have as high an expectation for their of personal empowerment and job opportunity (80 percent). The report interprets these results, stating that "employees are looking for certainty in an uncertain world, business has an opportunity, even an obligation, to take a stand on issues and to drive informed conversations." Moreover, one in four employees stated that "they would never work for an organization that lacks greater purpose or fails to deliver meaningful societal impact. . . ." And "42 percent say they would need to be paid significantly more to work for an organization that didn't offer these elements of shared action." The report concludes by stating that these results show that "employees want to work for a company that offers leadership, one that stands up for them and their shared values. Without these trust-building efforts, employers will lose out on top talent and be forced to over compensate for the talent that's left."[49]

Covenantal Ethic

The covenantal ethic concept is related to the social contract and is also central to a stakeholder management approach. The covenantal ethic focuses on the importance of relationships—social as well as economic—between businesses, customers, and stakeholders. Relationships and social contracts (or covenants) between corporate managers and customers embody a "seller must care" attitude, not only "buyer beware."[50] A manager's understanding of problems is measured not only over the short term, in view of concrete products, specific cost reductions, or even balance sheets (though obviously important to a company's results), but also over the long term in view of the quality of relationships that are created and sustained by business activity.[51] It may also be helpful to understand the concept of a covenantal ethic in an organizational context by pointing out how great leaders are able to attract and mobilize followers to a vision and beliefs based on the relationship they develop with those being led. Classic leaders like Franklin Roosevelt, John F. Kennedy, and Martin Luther King Jr. instilled an enduring trust and credibility with their followers. The point is that corporate leaders still inspire and motivate followers through their vision, purposive mission, and leading by example, which results in a type of social contract. Warren Buffett, Bill Gates, and Richard Branson are such examples.

The Moral Basis and Social Power of Corporations as Stakeholders

Keith Davis argues that the social responsibility of corporations is based on social power, and that "if a business has the power, then a just relationship demands that business also bear responsibility for its actions in these areas." He terms this view the "iron law of responsibility" and maintains that "in the long run, those who do not use power in a manner in which society considers responsible will tend to lose it." Davis discusses five broad guidelines or obligations that business professionals should follow to be socially responsible:

1. Businesses have a social role of "trustee for society's resources." Since society entrusts businesses with its resources, businesses must wisely serve the interests of all their stakeholders, not just those of owners, consumers, or labor.
2. Business shall operate as a two-way open system with open receipt of inputs from society and open disclosure of its operations to the public.
3. "Social costs as well as benefits of an activity, product, or service shall be thoroughly calculated and considered in order to decide whether to proceed with it." Technical and economic criteria must be supplemented with the social effects of business activities, goods, or services before a company proceeds.
4. The social costs of each activity, product, or service shall be priced into it so that the consumer (user) pays for the effects of his consumption on society.
5. Business institutions as citizens have responsibilities for social involvement in areas of their competence where social needs exist.[52]

The above guidelines provide a foundation for creating and reviewing the moral bases of corporate stakeholder relationships. The public is intolerant of corporations that abuse this mutual trust. For example, a Pew Research Center 2020 Poll found that, "overall, 72% of U.S. adults say social media companies have too much power and influence in politics today, according to the June 16–22 survey. Far fewer Americans believe the amount of political power these companies hold is about the right amount (21%) or not enough (6%)."[53]

MSN Money and *24/7 Wall Street* publish lists of their Customer Service Hall of Fame and Shame (or "best" and "worst" companies) on an ongoing basis. While the company names change, it is interesting to note the positive effects that the transparency effect can have such lists. Glassdoor.com is a job and recruiting company that also provides "greater workplace transparency" and publishes online reviews of different "Best places to work" as well as candid reviews of employee experiences and evaluations.[54]

As Covid-19 has clearly demonstrated, natural environmental, as well as other factors, affect customers' and employees' satisfaction and survival within companies and industries. While rankings as those listed above are important, the next wave of changes will be based on how well companies recover and employees adapt. One survey (2021) of business leaders found that a wake-up call for most companies, stakeholders, and stockholders will be based on "digital transformation (76%), workforce management (74%) and customer engagement (73%).[55] We also add social justice shown in boardrooms, executive suites, and employee engagement.

Corporate Philanthropy

Corporations practice social responsibility in several ways through "external engagements," which means the efforts a company makes to manage its relationships with stakeholders and groups and institutions in need of assistance. These relationships can and should include a wide variety of activities: not just corporate philanthropy, community programs, and political lobbying, but also aspects of product design, recruiting policy, and project execution. "In practice, however, most companies have relied on three tools for external engagement: a full-time CSR team in the head office, some high-profile (but relatively cheap) initiatives, and a glossy annual review of progress."[56]

Such activities are often measured through the impact of corporate philanthropy by counting the number of individuals who are helped by a particular program. Philanthropy, however, can also reduce business risk, open up new markets, engage employees, build the brand, reduce costs, advance technology, and deliver competitive returns. "Corporate philanthropy is usually defined in contrast to various 'shared' or 'blended' value approaches to corporate social responsibility . . . in which companies seek to do well by doing good." It is more helpful to view corporate philanthropy as a discovery phase in investment in a social issue. Such philanthropic investments can serve as incubators for promising ideas and mechanisms for learning both community and corporate needs. "Much like R&D, philanthropy allows companies to make thoughtful investments in sectors where the return profile is typically more speculative. Of course, philanthropy is not the only strategy for companies to play meaningful corporate-citizenship roles. Business leaders should use every tool in their CSR portfolio to help create economic value that can help address relevant societal issues."[57]

A corporation's social responsibility also includes certain types of philanthropic responsibilities, in addition to its economic, legal, and ethical obligations. Corporate philanthropy is an important part of a company's role as "good citizen" at the global, national, and local levels. The public expects, but does not require, corporations to contribute and "give back" to the communities that support their operations. Procter & Gamble's reputation has been enhanced by its global contributions. Some of the greatest recent corporate philanthropists include Warren Buffett, Bill and Melinda Gates, and Mark Zuckerberg. Buffett pledged 12,220,852 shares of Berkshire Hathaway class "B" stock, valued at more than $1 billion, to each of his three children's foundations. The Howard G. Buffett Foundation has contributed funds to agricultural development, clean-water projects, and programs working to fight poverty.[58]

Managing Stakeholders Profitably and Responsibly: Reputation Counts

Globalization and the shifting centers of financial power and influence, the ongoing diffusion of information technology, and the threat of other Enrons continue to pressure corporate competition, along with increasingly wider shareholder activism. "The result is that many employees, investors, and consumers are seeking assurances that the goods and services they are producing, financing, or purchasing are not damaging to workers, the environment, or communities by whom and where they are made."[59] There is, consequently, renewed interest in the area of CSR; that is, how a business respects and responds responsibly to its stakeholders and society as well as to its stockholders.[60] Ethical Insight 4.3 illustrates and asks you to respond to other trends affecting employees post–Covid-19.

Ethical Insight 4.3

Trends That Will Shape Work in 2021 and Beyond

- Employers are changing from managing the employee experience to managing the life experience of their employees.
- Companies are taking stances on current societal and political debates.
- Gender-wage gap continued to increase with returning employees offices.
- New regulations will limit employee monitoring.
- Flexibility shifts from physical locations to time.
- Supports mental health is the new normal.
- Employers will begin to "rent" talent to fill skills gaps.
- States will compete to attract individual talent rather than having companies relocate.

Questions for Discussion

1. In which of these trends, if any, do you see ethical issues occurring?
2. Identify the ethical issues that may arise from some of these trends.
3. Which of these trends could or will affect you? Explain.

Source: Kropp, B. (2021, January 14). 9 Trends That Will Shape Work in 2021 and Beyond. *Harvard Business Review.* https://hbr.org/2021/01/9-trends-that-will-shape-work-in-2021-and-beyond

Most executives and professionals are interested in their stakeholders and are law-abiding. Reputation remains one of the most powerful assets in determining the extent to which a company manages its stakeholders effectively. There is also evidence that socially responsible corporations have a competitive advantage in the following areas:

1. Reputation[61]
2. Successful social investment portfolios[62]
3. Ability to attract quality employees[63]

The organization Business Ethics ranks the top-100 socially responsible corporations in terms of citizenship. Business Ethics uses its own collected data, including the Domini 400 Social Index (which also tracks, measures, and publishes information on companies that act socially responsible). The Standard & Poor's 500 (S&P 500) plus 150 publicly owned companies are ranked on a scale that measures stakeholder ratings. Harris Interactive, Inc. and Reputation Institute, a New York–based research group, conducted an online nationwide survey of 10,830 people to identify the companies with the best corporate reputations among Americans at the turn of the millennium.[64] The Reputation Quotient (RQ) is a standardized instrument that measures a company's reputation by examining how the public perceives companies based on 20 positive attributes, including emotional appeal; social responsibility; good citizenship in its dealings with communities, employees, and the environment; the quality, innovation, value, and reliability of its products and services; how well the company is managed; how much the company demonstrates a clear vision and strong leadership; and profitability, prospects, and risk.

The executive director of the Reputation Institute, Anthony Johndrow, noted, "Reputation is much more than an abstract concept; it's a corporate asset that is a magnet to attract customers, employees, and investors."[65] Google took top place in the Reputation Institute's annual Global Pulse U.S. 2011 study, with Apple and The Walt Disney Company following at second and third place. The study measures an "analysis of the world's 100 top-rated companies based on input from over 55,000 consumers in 15 countries." The following trends were discovered as a result of this study:

- Fifty-eight percent of people's willingness to recommend a company is driven by their perception of the company; only 42 percent depends on perceptions of the company's products and services.
- Two-thirds of C-suite executives at the 150 largest U.S. companies believe we have already entered the Reputation Economy.
- Among the 150 largest companies in the United States, 25 percent now coordinate their reputation strategy and enterprise story through the CEO's office.
- Companies with excellent reputations are two and a half times more likely to have CEOs setting the strategy for enterprise positioning than those with weaker reputations."[66]

Table 4.1
10 Most and Least Reputable Companies in America (2019)

10 most reputable brands	10 least reputable brands
1. Wegmans Food Market	51. Comcast
2. Amazon	52. Bank of America
3. Patagonia	53. The Goldman Sachs Group
4. LL Bean	54. Facebook
5. Walt Disney	55. Dish Network
6. Publix	56. Wells Fargo
7. Samsung	57. Sears Holding Corp
8. Procter & Gamble	58. The Trump Organization
9. Microsoft	59. Philip Morris
10. Sony	60. U.S. Government

Source: Desjardins, J. (2019, July 30). Ranked: The 10 Organizations with the Best (and Worst) Reputations. *Visual Capitalist.* https://www.visualcapitalist .com/organizations-best-and-worse-reputations/.

Brands are among companies' most—if not *the* most—valued assets because they reflect and are an integral part of their reputations and identities. The top-10 most and least reputable brands in America for 2019 are listed in Table 4.1. (Note that since 2019, a few of these companies have experienced ethical and legal issues in their leadership and operations.)

The Harris Poll RQ ranks companies' reputations on six dimensions: social responsibility; vision and leadership; emotional appeal; products and services; financial performance; and workplace environment. The general public rates companies by completing online surveys that are analyzed and used in marketing and policy decisions. You can score your own organization's reputation in Ethical Insight 4.4, "Rank Your Organization's Reputation."

4.3 Managing and Balancing Corporate Governance, Compliance, and Regulation

While leaders and their teams build the reputations of their corporations through high productivity, trust, and good deeds shown toward their stakeholders while satisfying competitive demands of the marketplace, it is also true that laws and regulations set standards for acceptable and unacceptable business practices and behaviors. Just as the market is not entirely "free," neither are all stakeholders and constituencies honest, fair, and just in their motives and business transactions. Corporate scandals discussed throughout this text demonstrated that entire corporations can be brought down by top-level executives and their teams. Lessons from the scandals also showed that corporate boards of directors, CEOs, chief financial officers (CFOs), and other top-level administrators require legal constraints, compliance rules, regulation, and the threat and provision of punishment when crimes are committed. Wrongdoers inside and outside corporations must have boundaries set and disciplinary actions applied

Figure 4.2

Corporate Social Responsibility and Stakeholder Management: Balancing the "Carrot" and "Stick" Approaches

not only to protect the innocent, but also to enable businesses to exist and succeed. The rule of law protects capitalism and democracies against despotic rule and chaos. Research also shows that both "carrot" (motivational, ethical incentives) and "stick" (legal compliance and potential disciplinary action) approaches are necessary for workforces and leaders to be productive and law-abiding. Figure 4.2 illustrates a "carrot and stick" balancing approach that effective corporations use in providing both a legal and ethical culture and transactions, internally and with external stakeholders.

Ethical Insight 4.4

Rank Your Organization's Reputation

Score a company, college, or university at which you worked or studied on the following characteristics. Be objective. Answer each question based on your experience and what you objectively know about the company, college, or university.

1 = very low; 2 = somewhat low; 3 = average; 4 = very good; 5 = excellent

____ Emotional appeal of the organization for me

____ The social responsibility of the organization

____ The organization's treatment of employees, community, and environment

____ The quality, innovation, value, and reliability of the organization's products and/or services

____ The clarity of vision and strength of the organization's leadership

____ The organization's profitability, prospects in its market, and handling of risks

____ Total your score

Interpretation: Consider 30 a perfect score, 24 very good, 18 average, 12 low, and 6 very low.

Questions for Discussion

1. How did your organization do on the ranking? Explain.
2. Explain your scoring on each item; that is, give the specific reasons that led you to score your organization as you did.
3. Suggest specific actions your organization could take to increase its Reputation Quotient.

   3a. Of the 10 most reputable companies (see Table 14.1), which would you want your organization to be more like? Explain.

In this section, we discuss the "stick" approach (legal compliance and regulation) in more detail. With our focus here on the corporation and external stakeholders, we limit our discussion of laws to (1) the Sarbanes-Oxley Act, with a brief overview of the (2) Federal Sentencing Guidelines for Organizations; and then discuss (3) laws regulating competition, consumer protection, employment discrimination/pay/safety, and the environment.

Most corporations effectively govern themselves, to a large extent, through their own control systems and stakeholder precient relationships. A public corporation's federal and state charter provides the legal basis for its board of directors, stockholders, and officers to govern and operate the company. However, as Enron and other corporate scandals have demonstrated, self-governance cannot be counted on to work well alone. A question often repeated from the scandals is, "Where were the boards of directors when the widespread fraud, deception, and abuse of power occurred?"

A 2013 *Time* magazine cover referring to the subprime lending crisis read, "How Wall Street Won: Five Years after the Crash, It Could Happen All Over Again."[67] Ironically, with Covid-19 and dangerous political attacks, this warning came close to being fulfilled. The article makes five recommendations for preventing another financial crisis in subprime mortgage lending, based on the author's research and interviews with leading experts from financial and university institutions: (1) fix the too-big-to-fail problem, (2) limit the leverage (of banks), (3) expose weapons of mass financial destruction ("derivatives" trading), (4) bring shadow banking into the light, and (5) reboot the culture of finance. In summary, these five recommendations argue that some of the largest banks in the United States need closer self-regulation and government regulation in their lending and investing practices in order to stop certain derivatives and high-risk investing from wrecking the economy again. Steps toward this goal include reinstating the former Fed chairman Paul Volcker's rule to "separate government-insured commercial lending from risky trading operations." Reinstating and implementing provisions of the 1933 Glass-Steagall Act, which separates commercial from risky lending practices by banks, along with the Dodd-Frank legislation, would also address this problem. Again, some of these steps have been implemented, and as of 2021, have proven to be stabilizing forces through Covid-19 in particular.

Other suggestions include limiting the leverage larger banks and mortgage companies have to make risky loans. Leverage means the ability "to borrow more money than they can immediately repay." Too much leverage gives banks incentives to overinvest more funds than they have to meet their operating obligations. Also, making "shadow banking"—hiding the amount and types of investments made—more transparent would expose those financiers who put banks, customers' money, and the economy at risk. Finally, "rebooting the culture of finance" in the United States is necessary. The United States suffers from the Wall Street–driven "financialization" of the economy. The original purpose and mission of banks is to lend to real people and businesses, not using customers' and small businesses' money to bankroll high-risk investing, especially when the larger banks limit access to credit to small banks and individuals. Also, the credit ranking system of banks that pays professionals in that system to rank them must change. This system is self-defeating; the credit ratings do not change banking practices, and large-scale questionable investment banking practices could lead to further meltdowns of the economy.[68]

There are a number of other reasons why many of the larger, prominent corporate boards of directors in different industries, not only banking, did not execute their mandated legal and ethical responsibilities during the past financial meltdown and crisis. These include lack of independence, insider roles and relationships, conflicts of interest, overlapping memberships of board members with other boards, decision-making-by-committees, well-paid members with few responsibilities, and lack of financial expertise and knowledge about how companies really operate.[69] There are, however, improvements being made legislatively and in business and board practices.

Best Corporate Board Governance Practices

Most corporate boards act responsibly toward their stakeholders and in the best interests of shareholders. The wake of the large corporate scandals of the early 2000s has led to several best practices for a board of directors. "The Board of Directors must be committed to its functions, be functional, and make informed decisions."[70] This can be achieved through greater objectivity, independence, and oversight by all board members.[71]

With very few exceptions, governance activists have achieved most of the reforms they have sought to effectuate. According to Spencer Stuart's 2020 U.S. Board Index, 89 percent of S&P 500 companies have adopted a majority voting standard when it comes to director's resignation, 90 percent have annually elected boards, and 85 percent of their directors are independent—to name but a few of the more trendy governance issues in recent years.[72] However, those who make their living in the corporate governance industry will undoubtedly continue to push these proposals at smaller companies and come up with additional requirements and heightened standards to propose with each new proxy season. By way of example, Spencer Stuart's 2013 corporate governance policy updates tighten its board responsiveness policy and recommend that shareholders vote "against" or "withhold" their votes for incumbent directors who fail to act on a shareholder proposal that received the support of a majority of votes cast in the previous year, as compared to ISS's prior standard, which looked at whether the proposal received a majority of outstanding shares the previous year or the support of a majority of votes cast in both the last year and one of the two prior years.[73]

The following section discusses the two laws best known for defining the regulations and best practices for companies and their boards of directors.

Sarbanes-Oxley Act

While the 2002 Sarbanes-Oxley Act (SOX) may seem like ancient history now, it was a direct regulatory response by Congress to corporate scandals, and stands as a foundational safeguard against corporate corruption. (Pricewaterhouse-Coopers called this law the most important legislation affecting corporate governance, financial disclosure, and public accounting practice since the 1930s.)[74] The "carrot" approach, or corporate self-regulation, did not work for Enron and other firms involved in scandals; Congress realized that a "stick" approach (laws, regulations, disciplinary actions) was also required. A summary of SOX shows that federal provisions were established to provide oversight, accountability, and enforcement of truthful and accurate financial reporting in public firms. Some of the major issues included (1) a lack of an independent public company accounting board to oversee audits, (2) conflicts of interest in companies serving as auditors and management consultants to companies, (3) holding top-level officers (CEOs and CFOs) accountable for financial statements, (4) protecting whistle-blowers, (5) requiring ethics codes for financial officers, and (6) other reforms as the list below shows. Note that with specific reference to publicly traded companies that are subject to SOX Section 404 compliance requirements, most have adopted the Internal Control Integrated Framework published in 1992 by the Committee of Sponsoring Organizations of the Treadway Commission (COSO).[75] This document explains the principles, rationale, and steps for meeting SOX compliance standards.

The key aspects of SOX can be summarized as follows:

- Establishes an independent public company accounting board to oversee audits of public companies.
- Requires one member of the audit committee to be an expert in finance.
- Requires full disclosure to stockholders of complex financial transactions.
- Requires CEOs and CFOs to certify in writing the validity of their companies' financial statements. If they knowingly certify false statements, they can go to prison for 20 years and be fined $5 million.
- Prohibits accounting firms from offering other services, like consulting, while also performing audits. This constitutes a conflict of interest.
- Requires ethics codes for financial officers of companies that are registered with the Securities and Exchange Commission (SEC).
- Provides a 10-year penalty for wire and mail fraud.
- Requires mutual fund professionals to disclose their vote on shareholder proxies, enabling investors to know how their stocks influence decisions.

• Provides whistle-blower protection for individuals who report wrongful activities to authorities.
• Requires attorneys of companies to disclose wrongdoings to senior officers and to the board of directors, if necessary; attorneys should stop working for the companies if senior managers ignore reports of wrongdoings.[76]

In addition, SOX defines several reforms aimed at improving problems of boards of directors. There are other "best practices" guidelines for boards, including:

1. Separating the role of chairman of the board when the CEO is also a board member
2. Setting tenure rules for board members
3. Regularly evaluating itself and the CEO's performance
4. Prohibiting directors from serving as consultants to the companies they serve
5. Compensating directors with both cash and stock
6. Prohibiting retired CEOs from continuing board membership
7. Assigning independent directors to the majority of members who meet periodically without the CEO[77]

The July/August 2012 cover story of *Financial Executives International* was titled "Sarbanes-Oxley—A Decade Later" and summarized the impact of SOX as follows:

> The act created the Public Company Accounting Oversight Board to police the accounting profession and set auditing standards. It shored up the role of the audit committee, making it independent and responsible for hiring, firing, and overseeing external auditors, removing that authority from management.
>
> Under Section 404, companies were required to establish internal controls and procedures for financial reporting. Another section mandated that both the chief executive and chief financial officers personally attest that they have reviewed the auditors' report and that it "does not contain any material with untrue statements or material omission" or anything that could be "considered misleading."
>
> Sarbanes-Oxley also instituted "clawback" provisions requiring CEOs and CFOs to return ill-gotten gains to their employer. In one notable case, Ian McCarthy, former CEO at Atlanta-based Beazer Homes USA Inc., and former CFO James O'Leary both agreed to return all of their cash bonuses, incentive, and equity-based compensation for 2006. McCarthy had to relinquish more than $5.7 million in cash plus $772,232 in stock sale profits, along with some 120,000 in restricted stock shares; O'Leary returned $1.4 million.[78]

But Congress has been moving in the opposite direction. Two recent laws—the Dodd-Frank Wall Street Reform and Consumer Protection Act of 2010 and 2013's Jumpstart Our Business Startups Act (the JOBS Act)—have largely served to weaken SOX. Dodd–Frank exempted public companies with a "public float" below $75 million, thereby removing 42 percent of public companies.[79] The letter implored both the chairman and ranking members of the House Financial Services Committee to not further reduce safeguards, to no avail. In recent years, SOX has been altered. To include the Supreme Court ruling that the Consumer Financial Protection Bureau's single-director structure is unconstitutional, the Senate increased the threshold for banks qualifying for enhanced prudential standards to $250 billion.[80] A broad range of investor-protection groups and regulators have expressed alarm that the JOBS Act, signed into law by President Barack Obama in early April, "guts" SOX. Among other things, it exempts newly public "emerging growth companies" from meeting Section 404 obligations for five years following an initial public offering.[81] A new version of the JOBS Act passed the House of Representatives with only four no votes. However, since mid-2019 the new version of the JOBS Act has not passed the Senate.[82]

Pros and Cons of Implementing the Sarbanes-Oxley Act

Critics opposed to SOX have argued against the implementation and maintenance of the law for the following reasons:

1. It is too costly. One estimate from a survey by Financial Executives International stated that firms with $5 billion in revenue could expect to spend on average $4.7 million implementing the internal controls required, then $1.5 million annually to maintain compliance.[83] An average first-year cost for complying with Section 404 of the Act (i.e., creating reliable internal financial controls and having management and an independent auditor confirm the reliability) was estimated at $4.36 million.[84] Others argue that the costs exceed the benefits, especially for small firms. "Smaller companies that are audited by the Big Four will have to pay higher audit fees even if they are not subject to Sarbanes-Oxley as the additional audit requirements of Sarbanes-Oxley creep into their methodologies. Many private companies and smaller public companies are realizing that the Big Four have designed their audits to serve the *Fortune* 500 companies and that this model is slow and expensive."[85]

2. It impacts negatively on a firm's global competitiveness. This argument is also based on the costs of keeping internal operations compliant with the act. Critics argue that other companies around the globe do not have this expense, so why should U.S. public firms?

3. Government costs also increase to regulate the law.

4. CFOs are overburdened and pressured by having to enforce and assume accountability required by the law.

5. Critics claim that implementing SOX requirements throughout an organization is too costly and wasteful for small and midsize firms wishing to go public.

6. SOX reduces the willingness of corporations to take risks.

7. Accrual accounting is seen as being more "expensive" under SOX, as certain expenses like R&D must be expensed when incurred, reducing cur-

rent earnings. This may make earnings management a more attractive and "cheap" option for management.

8. SOX is sometimes faulted for not preventing the financial crisis and the Great Recession of 2008–2009, from which the U.S. economy has yet to recover.[86]

Paul Volcker and Arthur Levitt, two widely respected experts previously from the Federal Reserve and SEC, respectively, offered the following counterclaims to some of the previous criticisms:[87]

1. The costs of implementing SOX are minimal compared to the costs of not having it—recall the $8 trillion in stock losses alone during the Great "Recession" and banking crisis of 2008 and the near collapse of the global economy, not counting the damage done to employee families and effects on the economy at large.

2. "Companies have better internal control environments as a result of Sarbanes-Oxley. This will lead to more accurate information being available to investors who are more confident in making investing decisions. All participants in financial reporting have increased responsibilities and consequences for not living up to those responsibilities."[88]

3. The changes required to implement this law are difficult; however, a 2009 *Corporate Board Member* magazine survey found that more than 60 percent of 153 directors of corporate boards of directors believe the effect of SOX has been positive for their firms, and that more than 70 percent viewed the law as also positive for their boards.[89]

4. The data does not support the argument that this law presents a competitive disadvantage to global firms. The NASDAQ stock exchange added six international listings in the second quarter of 2004. A survey by Broadgate Capital Advisors and the Value Alliance found that only 8 percent of 143 foreign companies that issue stocks that trade in the United States claimed that SOX would cause them to rethink entering the U.S. market.[90]

5. If a company uses SOX as a reason to not go public, the firm should not go public or use investors' funds. U.S. markets are among the most admired in the world because they are the best regulated.

6. Financial officers who complain about the requirements of SOX may in fact be suffering from the lack of internal controls they had before. In 2003, 57 companies of all sizes said they had material weaknesses in their controls, after their auditors, who were paid to test financial controls, were terminated. These same auditors decreased their testing of internal controls because they faced pressures to cut their fees.

7. Requiring top executives and financial officers to personally sign off on and take personal ownership of the books is an initial deterrent of fraud and improves organizational culture.

8. SOX has resulted in improvements in the accounting industry in the wake of the fall of former accounting giant Arthur Andersen, at the hand of the Public Company Accounting Oversight Board (PCAOB).

9. Ernst & Young's Les Brorsen sees the creation of the PCAOB to police the auditing profession, coupled with corporate governance rules putting a public company's board-level audit committee, rather than company management, in charge of the auditing process, as "the top two fundamental changes" brought about by the act. "It's fair to say that the largest single impact of Sarbanes-Oxley was to end 100 years of self-regulation," he says. Related to that, Brorsen adds, "improved corporate governance is one of the hallmarks of the legislation."[91]

The costs and benefits of implementing SOX continue to be debated. Still, Volcker and Levitt have argued that, "While there are direct money costs involved in compliance, we believe that an investment in good corporate governance, professional integrity, and transparency will pay dividends in the form of investor confidence, more efficient markets, and more market participation for years to come." Certainly guidelines and specific ways to simplify, decrease unnecessary costs, and streamline implementation of this law must be addressed as companies strive to compete locally, nationally, and especially globally. We note that in 2021, SOX is not only currently relevant, but that many of its previously contested requirements are not widely used in corporations.[92]

The Federal Sentencing Guidelines for Organizations: Compliance Incentive

Before the 2002 SOX, the 1991 Federal Sentencing Guidelines for Organizations (FSGO) were passed to help federal judges set and mitigate sentences and fines in companies that had a few "bad apples" who had committed serious crimes. The FSGO were also designed to alleviate sentences on companies that had ethics and compliance programs. Under the FSGO, a corporation (large or small) receives a lighter sentence and/or fine—or perhaps no sentence or probation—if convicted of a federal crime, provided that the firm's ethics and compliance programs were judged to be "effective." The FSGO changed the view of corporations as entities that were legally liable and punishable for criminal acts committed within their boundaries to the view of the corporation as a moral agent responsible for the behavior of its employees. As a moral agent, the corporation could be evaluated and judged on how effective the leaders, culture, and ethics training programs were toward preventing misconduct and crime.[93]

Companies that acted to prevent unethical and criminal acts would, under the FSGO, be given special consideration by judges when being fined or sentenced. A points system was established to help mitigate the fine and/or sentence if the company displayed the following seven criteria:

1. Established standards and procedures capable of reducing the chances of criminal conduct
2. Appointed compliance officer(s) to oversee plans
3. Took due care not to delegate substantial discretionary authority to individuals who are likely to engage in criminal conduct
4. Established steps to effectively communicate the organization's standards and procedures to all employees

5. Took steps to ensure compliance through monitoring and auditing
6. Employed consistent disciplinary mechanisms
7. When an offense was detected, took steps to prevent future offenses, including modifying the compliance plan, if appropriate[94]

The FSGO have been revised to reflect the post-Enron corporate environment. The revisions add specificity to the 1991 version, include top-level officers' accountability, and attempt to increase the effectiveness and integration of a company's ethics and compliance programs with its culture and operations. Ed Petry, former director of the Ethics Officer Association (EOA), served on the federal committee that revised the FSGO. Petry summarized some of the prominent revisions as follows:[95]

- Compliance and ethics programs (C&EP) are now described in a stand-alone guideline.
- The connection between effective compliance and ethical conduct is stressed.
- Organizations are required to "promote an organizational culture that encourages ethical conduct and a commitment to compliance with the law."

In 2010, the FSGO were revised again. The most notable change promoted the practice of opening a direct line of communication from the chief compliance officer, or those with "operational responsibility for the compliance and ethics program," directly to the governing body on any concerns involving actual or potential criminal conduct.[96] SOX and the Revised Federal Sentencing Guidelines for Organizations (RFSGO) serve as constraints and deterrents to immoral and criminal corporate conduct that ultimately affects stakeholders and stockholders.

Table 4.2 shows RFSGO. SOX is an attempt by the U.S. federal government to provide stricter compliance guidelines and disciplinary actions to corporations in the wake of corporate scandals. The RFSGO add incentives to companies to self-regulate while following laws aimed at protecting the interests of shareholders and stakeholders, including the public. The next section gives an overview of the role that laws and congressional agencies play in protecting the public, consumers, and other stakeholders.

4.4 The Role of Law and Regulatory Agencies and Corporate Compliance

Government at the federal, state, and local levels also regulates corporations through laws, administrative procedures, enforcement agencies, and courts. Regulation by the government is necessary in part because of failures in the free-market system discussed earlier. There are also power imbalances between corporations, individual consumers, and citizens. Individual citizens and groups in society need a higher authority to represent and protect their interests and the public good.[97]

Table 4.2
Revised Federal Sentencing Guidelines for Organizations (2004)

1. Exercise **due diligence** to prevent and detect criminal conduct.

2. Promote an **organizational culture** that encourages ethical conduct and a commitment to compliance with the law.

3. The organization shall use reasonable efforts **not to include within the substantial authority personnel** of the organization **any individual whom the organization knew**, or should have known through the exercise of due diligence, **has engaged in illegal activities** or other conduct **inconsistent with an effective compliance and ethics program.**

4. (A) The organization shall take reasonable steps to **communicate periodically and in a practical manner its standards and procedures,** and other aspects of the compliance and ethics program, to the individuals referred to in subdivision (B) by **conducting effective training programs** and otherwise **disseminating information appropriate to such individuals' respective roles and responsibilities.**
   (B) The individuals referred to in subdivision (A) are the members of the governing authority, high-level personnel, substantial authority personnel, the organization's employees, and, as appropriate, the organization's agents.

5. The organization shall take reasonable steps:
   (A) to ensure that the organization's compliance and ethics program is followed, including monitoring and auditing to detect criminal conduct;
   (B) to evaluate periodically the effectiveness of the organization's compliance and ethics program;
   (C) to have and **publicize a system,** which may include mechanisms that **allow for anonymity or confidentiality,** whereby the **organization's employees and agents** may report or seek guidance regarding potential or actual criminal conduct without fear of retaliation.

6. The **organization's compliance and ethics program shall be promoted and enforced consistently throughout the organization** through (A) appropriate incentives to perform in accordance with the compliance and ethics program; and (B) appropriate disciplinary measures for engaging in criminal conduct and for failing to take reasonable steps to prevent or detect criminal conduct.

7. After criminal conduct has been detected, the organization shall take reasonable steps to respond appropriately to the criminal conduct and to prevent further similar criminal conduct, including making any necessary modifications to the organization's compliance and ethics program.

Source: 2004 Federal Sentencing Guidelines, chapter 8, part B: Remedying harm from criminal conduct, and effective compliance and ethics programs excerpted from §8B2.1. Effective Compliance and Ethics Program of the 2004 Federal Sentencing Guidelines. http://www.ussc.gov/Guidelines/2004_guidelines/Manual/gl2004.pdf.

The role of laws and the legal regulatory system governing business serves five purposes:

1. Regulate competition.
2. Protect consumers.
3. Promote equity and safety.

4. Protect the natural environment.
5. Apply ethics and compliance programs to deter and provide for enforcement against misconduct.[98]

The corporate scandals again exemplified a failure of internal corporate governance and self-regulation by all parties (internal and external to corporations) involved. Individual leaders' greed, ineffective boards, investment banks, and financial companies and traders all conspired with Enron and other companies in the scandals to commit fraud, theft, and deceit (see Case 2). Corporate scandals cannot be initiated and sustained without the direct or indirect assistance and/or negligence from the SEC, banks, investment traders and managers, media, Wall Street, federal legislators, and other players.[99] The subprime-lending crisis also showed how an entire system of stakeholders in the financial, banking, credit and lending system, and government can be involved in a crisis that has been attributed in large part to "predatory lending" practices. As with the corporate scandals, in the subprime crisis one asks, "Where were the federal, state, and local governmental and congressional regulators?" Still, the justice system did serve sentences to executives in the corporate scandals. Starting with Enron and followed by WorldCom, Qwest, Tyco, HealthSouth, and others, more than $7 trillion in stock market losses were accrued. These losses also cost American employees and families more than 30 percent of their retirement savings.[100] More recent scandals such as Volkswagen, Wells Fargo, Equifax, and others will also be added to the following now infamous list. A quick summary will illustrate the aftermath of some of the major scandals.

- *Enron Corporation*: Former chairman and CEO Ken Lay died before being tried and sentenced. Jeffrey Skilling, a former executive, was fined $45 million and received a 24-year, 4-month prison sentence at the Federal Correctional Institution in Waseca, Minnesota.[101] On June 21, 2013, Skilling succeeded in getting his prison sentence reduced by 10 years as part of a court-ordered reduction. With court action, victims of Skilling's crimes will finally receive more than $40 million that he owes.[102] The former CFO, Andrew Fastow, is currently serving a six-year prison sentence at the Federal Detention Center in Oakdale, Louisiana. His wife, former Enron assistant treasurer Lea Fastow, was sentenced to one year in federal prison and one year of supervised release in a halfway house.[103] Since leaving prison in 2011 and resuming life with his wife, Lea, and two sons in Houston, where Enron was based, Fastow has kept a low profile. He reportedly now works nine to five as a document-review clerk at the law firm that represented him in civil litigation.[104]

- *WorldCom, Inc.*: Former CEO Bernard Ebbers pleaded not guilty to fraud and conspiracy charges for allegedly leading an accounting fraud estimated at more than $11 billion. A 2002 class-action civil lawsuit against Ebbers and other defendants resulted in a settlement worth over $6 billion to be distributed to over 830,000 individuals. Ebbers is currently serving 25 years at a federal prison in Louisiana.[105] Scott Sullivan, former CFO, pleaded guilty to fraud charges, testified against Ebbers, and received a five-year prison sentence. Sullivan is currently serving his sentence at the federal prison in Jessup, Georgia.[106]

- *Tyco International Ltd.*: Former CEO Dennis Kozlowski and CFO Mark Swartz were accused of stealing $600 million from the company. A New York state judge declared a mistrial in the case because of pressure on a jury member. Kozlowski received a sentence of eight and a third to 25 years in prison. Both Kozlowski and Swartz could be eligible for parole after six years, 11 months. Kozlowski is currently serving at least eight years and four months at the Mid-State Correctional Facility in Marcy, New York. Swartz was sentenced to at least eight years and four months of prison and ordered to pay $72 million in fines and restitution.[107] On September 23, 2013, both men left a minimum-security prison in Harlem for steady clerical jobs and overnights in apartments following their headline-grabbing $134 million corporate fraud convictions.[108]

- *Adelphia Communications Corporation*: Founder John Rigas was convicted and sentenced to 12 years and has since been released. At age 88, Rigas could be a poster child for inmates who might seek early release from prison because of the hazards of advanced aging. His son Timothy received 17 years for conspiracy and bank and securities fraud. Rigas's other son Michael was acquitted of conspiracy charges.[109]

- *Credit Suisse First Boston*: Frank Quattrone, a former investment banking executive who made millions of dollars helping Internet companies go public during the dot-com boom, was convicted of obstruction of justice and sentenced to 18 months. His first trial in 2003 ended in a hung jury. Quattrone now runs Qatalyst Partners, a San Francisco–based investment bank focused on advising technology companies on mergers and acquisitions. The University of Pennsylvania has received a $15 million gift to examine the U.S. criminal justice system from someone who has had some experience with it: Quattrone himself. The justice center will be housed at the law school of the Ivy League university in Philadelphia.[110]

- *HealthSouth Corporation*: Former CEO Richard Scrushy was federally charged with leading a multibillion-dollar scheme that inflated HealthSouth earnings to show the company was meeting Wall Street forecasts. Sixteen former HealthSouth executives were charged as part of a conspiracy to inflate company earnings. Scrushy is the only executive who has not pleaded guilty and is not cooperating with investigators. Interestingly, in May 2020, Episode 4 of Netflix's *Trial by Media* followed the case of Richard Scrushy, who was accused of financial fraud and was acquitted in a federal criminal trial related to the alleged $2.7 billion fraud. At a civil trial in Jefferson County Circuit Court in 2009, however, Scrushy was found liable for the accounting fraud and ordered to pay HealthSouth nearly $2.9 billion in damages. In an unrelated case, in 2006 Scrushy and former Alabama governor Don Siegelman were convicted of bribery and honest services fraud. Prosecutors alleged Scrushy bought a seat on a hospital regulatory board by arranging $500,000 in donations to Siegelman's 1999 campaign to establish a state lottery. Scrushy, who was released from prison in 2012, recently lost the appeal of that conviction to the 11th Circuit Court of Appeals. HealthSouth asserts Scrushy has not paid his debt to the company and its shareholders because he owes them $2.8 billion, not counting the rapidly mounting daily interest, according to Scrushy's filing.[111]

• *Martha Stewart*: The founder of Martha Stewart Living Omnimedia was convicted of conspiracy, obstruction of justice, and lying about her personal sale of ImClone Systems shares. She was refused a new trial on perjury charges against a government witness. Stewart was sentenced to five months in prison. Her broker, Peter Bacanovic, was fined $2,000.[112]

• Samuel D. Waksal, founder and former CEO of ImClone Systems, was sentenced to seven years in prison for securities fraud, perjury, and other crimes he committed with ImClone stock trades to himself, his father, and his daughter at the end of 2001. Waksal founded Kadmon in 2010 as the successor to ImClone, the company that developed the cancer drug Erbitux and was acquired by Indianapolis-based Eli Lilly in 2008. This new company is also working on cancer medicines and drugs for hepatitis C, inflammatory disorders, and genetic diseases. It's in the same building, along Manhattan's East River, as ImClone. Despite the well-known travails, ImClone was able to bring a very successful drug to market and then get itself acquired. By Wall Street standards, that's a success.[113] It was reported in April 2021 that Waksal agreed to a partial resolution of the insider trading case brought against him by the Securities and Exchange Commission. "In documents filed today [April 17, 2021] with the federal court in Manhattan, Waksal, without admitting or denying the allegations, consented to pay more than $800,000 from the unlawful sales including prejudgment interest, be barred from acting as an officer or director for public companies, and accept other relief."[114]

• *Qwest Communications International, Inc.*: Denver federal prosecutors did not win a conviction against four former midlevel executives accused of scheming to deceptively book $34 million in revenue for the company. Grant Graham (former CFO for Qwest's global business unit), Bryan Treadway (former assistant controller), Thomas Hall (former senior vice president), and John Walker (former vice president) were all found not guilty on 11 charges of conspiracy, securities fraud, wire fraud, and making false statements to auditors. Hall received probation and paid a $5,000 fine.[115]

• *American International Group (AIG)*: Former vice president Christopher Milton received a four-year sentence in 2009 for his role in a $500 million fraud case. He was convicted of conspiracy, mail fraud, securities fraud, and making false statements to the SEC,[116] and the company was later removed from "too big to fail."[117]

• *Bernard L. Madoff Investment Securities LLC*: In 2009, Bernard Madoff was sentenced to 150 years in prison for his elaborate and long-running Ponzi scheme. Madoff pled guilty to 11 counts of financial crimes.[118] Madoff died April 14, 2021, while serving a prison sentence in the Federal Medical Center, Butner, in North Carolina. He had suffered a chronic kidney disease.

- *Fannie Mae*: As a result of the Fannie Mae fraud and the subprime mortgage crisis, Leib Pinter, a former executive of Olympia Mortgage Corporation, was sentenced to 97 months in prison on charges of conspiracy to commit wire fraud. He was ordered to pay $43 million in restitution. In December 2011, the SEC charged six former top executives of Fannie Mae and Freddie Mac with securities fraud.[119]

Why Regulation?

Although governmental legislation and oversight of corporations is an imperfect system, one can always ask: Would you rather live in a system where these laws and controls did not exist? It is also important to note here, as Figure 4.2 shows, that laws are designed to protect and prevent crime and harm, monopolies, and the negative ("externalities") effects of corporate activities (pollution, toxic waste) and also to promote social and economic growth, development, and the health, care, and welfare of consumers and the public. Laws provide a baseline, boundaries, and minimum standards for distinguishing acceptable from unacceptable business practices and behaviors. Values, motivations, beliefs, and incentives to do what is right are also necessary in corporations, as they are in other institutions and society in general. The legal and regulatory system is necessary in society and business to establish ground rules and boundaries for transactions. It is not, however, sufficient alone to accomplish this task. The second observation to keep in mind in this discussion is that even with federal, state, and local laws, governmental regulatory agencies in contemporary capitalist democracies are part of political systems—where lobbyists and interest groups compete for resources, influence, and programs for their own ends. In such systems, the legislative and judicial branches of government are designed to provide arbitration and conflict resolution with law enforcement. The following regulatory agencies serve educational as well as legal purposes for corporations serving consumers in the marketplace.

Laws and U.S. Regulatory Agencies

The U.S. administration from 2016 to 2020 decreased, and in some cases ceased, the enforcement of some of the major laws promoting and prohibiting corporate competition. Among them:

- Sherman Antitrust Act, 1890: Prohibits monopolies (as the case of Microsoft illustrates)
- Clayton Act, 1914: Prohibits price discrimination, exclusivity, activities restricting competition
- Federal Trade Commission (FTC) Act, 1914: Enforces antitrust laws and activities
- Consumer Good Pricing Act, 1975: Prohibits price agreements in interstate commerce between manufacturers and resellers
- Antitrust Improvements Act, 1976: Supports existing antitrust laws and empowers Department of Justice investigative authority

- FTC Improvements Act, 1980: Empowers the FTC to prohibit unfair industry activities
- Trademark Counterfeiting Act, 1980: Gives penalties for persons violating counterfeit laws and regulations
- Digital Millennium Copyright Act, 1998: Protects digital copyrighted material such as music and movies
- Trademark Modernization Act of 2020: Restores rebuttable presumption of irreparable harm to obtain injunctive relief for a trademark violation and amends Lanham Act

Laws Protecting Consumers

Consumers require information and protection from products that may be unsafe, unreliable, and even dangerous. Tobacco (now also "smokeless" tobacco), alcohol, and more recently cocaine, along with other so-called dangerous products, continue to be marketed. The consumer laws and regulatory agencies addressing these products that you may have heard or read about have a long history, too:

- Pure Food and Drug Act, 1906: Prohibits adulteration (ruining) and mislabeling on food and drugs in interstate commerce
- FTC Act, 1914: Created the FTC to govern trade and competitive practices
- Federal Food, Drug, and Cosmetic Act (FDCA), 1938: Amends the Pure Food and Drug Act of 1906 to protect consumers from adulterated and misbranded items and charged the Food and Drug Administration (FDA) with the safety of publicly marketed drugs
- Federal Hazardous Substances Act, 1960: Controls labels on hazardous substances and products used in households
- Truth and Lending Act, 1960: Requires full disclosure of credit terms to buyers
- Consumer Product Safety Act, 1972: Establishes safety standards and regulations of consumer products and created the Consumer Product Safety Commission (CPSC)
- Fair Credit Billing Act, 1974: Requires accurate, current consumer credit reports
- Equal Credit Opportunity Act (ECOA), 1974: Prohibits credit discrimination on the basis of race, gender, religion, age, marital status, national origin, or color
- Fair Debt Collection Practices Act, 1978: Prohibits abusive debt collection practices and allowed consumers to dispute and/or validate debt information
- Nutrition Labeling and Education Act, 1990: Requires food labels to include standard nutritional facts
- Telephone Consumer Protection Act, 1991: Issues procedures to avert undesired telephone solicitations

- Children's Online Privacy Protection Act, 1998: Requires the FTC to make rules to collect online information from children under the age of 13
- Gramm-Leach-Bliley Act, 1999: Allows commercial banks, investment banks, insurance companies, and securities firms to consolidate
- Do Not Call Implementation, 2003: Coordinates the FTC and the Federal Communications Commission (FCC) to provide consistent rules on telemarketing practices
- Fair and Accurate Credit Transactions Act (FACT), 2003: Requires credit agencies to provide a free annual copy of credit reports and created a national system for identity theft fraud alerts

Laws Protecting the Environment

Mercury from China, dust from Africa, smog from Mexico—all of it drifts freely across U.S. borders and contaminates the air millions of Americans breathe, according to recent research from Harvard University, the University of Washington, and many other institutions where scientists are studying air pollution. There are no boundaries in the sky to stop such pollution, no Border Patrol agents to capture it.[120]

The environment is seen less as an inexhaustible free source of clean air, water, soil, and food, and more as a valued resource that requires protection—globally, regionally, and locally. As the sample of environmental laws below indicates, the environment constitutes sources of human, food, vegetation, and animal life.

- Federal Insecticide, Fungicide, and Rodenticide Act (FIFRA), 1947: Regulated the use of pesticides and herbicides. The 1996 amendments facilitate registration of pesticides for special (so-called minor) uses, reauthorize collection of fees to support reregistration, and require coordination of regulations implementing FIFRA and the FDCA.[121]
- Clean Air Act, 1970: Designates air-quality standards; state implementation plans are, however, required for enactment of policies under this Act. In 1990 several progressive and creative new themes were embodied in amendments to the Act, themes necessary for effectively achieving the air-quality goals and regulatory reform expected from these far-reaching amendments.[122] The Clean Air Act:
  - Encourages the use of market-based principles and other innovative approaches, like performance-based standards and emission banking and trading
  - Provides a framework from which alternative clean fuels will be used by setting standards in the fleet and California pilot program that can be met by the most cost-effective combination of fuels and technology
  - Promotes the use of clean low-sulfur coal and natural gas, as well as innovative technologies to clean high-sulfur coal through the acid-rain program

- ○ Reduces enough energy waste and creates enough of a market for clean fuels derived from grain and natural gas to cut dependency on oil imports by 1 million barrels/day
- ○ Promotes energy conservation through an acid-rain program that gives utilities flexibility to obtain needed emission reductions through programs that encourage customers to conserve energy
- National Environmental Act, 1970: Establishes policy goals for federal agencies and enacts the Council on Environmental Quality to monitor policies (amended in 1986)
- Federal Water Pollution Control Act, 1972: Prevents, reduces, and eliminates water pollution (amended in 1990)
- Marine Protection, Research, and Sanctuaries Act, 1972: Regulates the dumping of materials into the ocean (amended in 1992)
- Noise Pollution Act, 1972: Controls noise emission of manufactured products
- Endangered Species Act, 1973: Provides a conservation program for threatened and endangered plants and animals and their habitats
- Safe Drinking Water Act, 1974: Protects the quality of drinking water in the United States, sets safety standards for water purity, and requires owners and operators of public water to comply with standards
- Toxic Substances Act, 1976: Requires testing of certain chemical substances and restricts use of certain substances (amended in 1992)
- Oil Pollution Act, 1990: Establishes penalties for oil spills and damage
- Food Quality Protection Act, 1996: Requires a new safety standard that must be applied to all pesticides used on foods (reasonable certainty of no harm)
- Energy Policy Act, 2005: Addresses energy production in the United States and provides loans to grantees developing energy technologies that avoid the emission of greenhouse gases
- Energy Independence and Security Act, 2007: Increased U.S. energy independence and security while increasing production of clean fuels
- Update on Toxic Substances Act, 2016: Increased public transparency regarding chemicals and mandated EPA evaluate existing chemicals with enforceable and clear deadlines

Taken together, these laws (and others discussed in Chapter 7) are aimed at protecting stakeholders, the public, and the system in which business is conducted. They also indicate the complexity of transactions, responsibilities, and the number of stakeholders with which corporations do business. Business ethics and social responsibility can arguably be seen not as a luxury and/or dichotomy, but as a necessity in providing for and protecting the common good. This point should become even more evident in the concluding section of this chapter, which illustrates classic cases of corporate crises in which stakeholder relationships were not well managed.

■ 4.5 Managing External Issues and Crises: Lessons from the Past (Back to the Future?)

Companies have made serious mistakes as the result of poor self-regulation. As several contemporary corporate crises and now-classic environmental and product- and consumer-related crises illustrate, corporations have responded and reacted slowly and many times insensitively to customers and other stakeholders. The Internet may decrease the time executives have to respond to potential and actual crises.

We conclude this chapter by reviewing some of the major crises from the 1970s to the present, since several of them are only now being resolved. These cases also serve to remind corporate leaders and the public that there is a balance between legal regulation and corporate self-regulation. When corporations fail to regulate themselves and to provide just and fair corrective actions to their failures, government assistance is needed.

Issues and crisis management should be part of a company's management strategy and planning process. Failure to effectively anticipate and respond to serious issues that erupt into crises have been as damaging to companies as the crises themselves. Before the BP *Deepwater Horizon* oil rig explosion and spill, the *Exxon Valdez* oil spill was biggest U.S. environmental disaster. The Manville Corporation's asbestos crisis is another, almost forgotten disaster that is also summarized in the feature boxes on the following pages. As the philosopher George Santayana is noted for saying, "Those who do not remember the past are condemned to repeat it." A sample of other classic crises includes the following:

- In June 2001, Katsuhiko Kawasoe, Mitsubishi Motor Company's president, apologized for that firm's 20-year cover-up of consumer safety complaints. (The company also agreed in 1998 to pay $34 million to settle 300 sexual harassment lawsuits filed by women in its Normal, Illinois, plant. This is one of the largest sexual harassment settlements in U.S. history.)

- By the end of 2001, the American Home Products Corporation paid more than $11.2 billion to settle about 50,000 consumer lawsuits related to the diet-drug combination of fenfluramine and phentermine, commonly known as "fen-phen." In addition, the company put aside $1 billion to cover future medical checkups for former fen-phen users and $2.35 billion to settle individual suits.

- Between 1971 and 1974, more than 5,000 product liability lawsuits were filed by women who had suffered severe gynecological damage from A. H. Robins Company's Dalkon Shield, an intrauterine contraceptive device. Although the company never recalled its product, it paid more than $314 million to settle 8,300 lawsuits. It also established a $1.75 billion trust to settle ongoing claims. The firm avoided its responsibility toward its customers by not considering a recall for nine years after the problem was known.

- Procter & Gamble's Rely tampon was pulled from the market in 1980 after 25 deaths were allegedly associated with toxic shock syndrome caused by tampon use.

- Firestone's problems first came to light in 1978, when the Center for Auto Safety said it had reports that Firestone's steel-belted radial TPC 500 tire was responsible for 15 deaths and 12 injuries. In October 1978, after attacking the publicity this product received, Firestone executives recalled 10 million of the 500-series tires. Firestone recently paid $7.5 million in addition to $350,000 to settle the first case in the Bridgestone/Firestone Ford Explorer crisis; since the recall, 200 injury and death lawsuits have been settled, and it is estimated that it will cost $50 million to settle the lawsuits.

- A federal bankruptcy judge approved Dow Corning Corporation's $4.5 billion reorganization plan, with $3.2 billion to be used to settle claims from recipients of the company's silicone gel breast implants, and the other $1.3 billion to be paid to its commercial creditors. A jury had already awarded $7.3 million to one woman whose implant burst, causing her illness. The company is alleged to have rushed the product to market in 1975 without completing proper safety tests and to have misled plastic surgeons about the potential for silicone to leak out of the surgically implanted devices. More than 600,000 implants were subsequently performed.

Johns Manville Corporation Asbestos Legacy: Still Paying, 2013

If you think the asbestos issues and victims are ancient history, think again (Strand, 2021). "As of 2019, there are over 940,000 active claims pending against the trust" (Strand 2021). "They'll be following in our footsteps," said Robert A. Falise, chairman of the Manville Personal Injury Settlement Trust, which was created by the bankruptcy court to ensure a steady source of money to pay claims filed against Johns Manville Corporation (JM) by workers exposed to asbestos in their workplaces. The company will be responding to outstanding claims by asbestos victims and their families for several decades. In fact, "as of the first quarter of 2012, the trust had paid 773,990 claims in the amount of approximately $4.3 billion, and the trust expects to receive more claims" (Gross 2001).

In June 2000, the company was sold to Warren Buffett for $1.9 billion in cash and the assumption of $300 million in debt. The asbestos-related trust, created to pay claimants, received $1.5 billion. As of March 2001, the trust had paid more than $2.5 billion to 350,000 beneficiaries. There are still more than a half million claimants and another half million expected to file. Looking back, reviews of JM's social responsibility management of the complex web of issues surrounding its asbestos production are mixed.

Asbestosis, mesothelioma, and lung cancer—all life-threatening diseases—share a common cause: inhalation of microscopic particles of asbestos over an extended period of time. The link between these diseases and enough inhaled asbestos particles is a medical fact. JM is a multinational mining and forest product manufacturer, and it was a leading commercial producer of asbestos. As of March 1977, 271 asbestos-related damages suits were filed against the firm by workers. The victims claimed the company did not warn them of the life-threatening dangers of asbestos. Since 1968, the company has paid more than $2.5 billion in such claims. And since the 1950s, it has faced hundreds of lawsuits from workers: their estimated value is more than $1 billion. By 1982, JM was facing more than 500 new asbestos lawsuits filed each month. Consequently, in August 1982, the company filed for Chapter 11 bankruptcy in order to reorganize and remain solvent in the face of the lawsuits; the firm was losing more than half the cases that reached trial. The reorganization was approved, and a $2.5 billion trust fund was set up to pay asbestos claimants. Shareholders surrendered half their value in stock, and it was agreed that projected earnings over 25 years would be reduced to support the trust.

JM devised a settlement that gave the Manville Personal Injury Settlement Trust enough cash to continue meeting claims filed by asbestos victims. Under the settlement, the building products division stated it would give the trust 20 percent of Manville's stock and would pay a special $772 million dividend in exchange for the trust's releasing its right to receive 20 percent of Manville's profits. After the transaction, the trust would own 80 percent of Manville and have $1.2 billion in cash and marketable securities, plus $2.3 billion in assets. This transaction enabled JM to rectify its balance sheet. Also, it changed its name to Schuller Corporation.

After JM spent several years operating under Chapter 11 of the U.S. Bankruptcy Code, the company emerged with $850 million in cash, 50 percent of its common stock, a claim on 20 percent of the company's consolidated profits, and bonds with a face value of $1.3 billion. The trust is expected to pay 10 percent of an estimated $18 billion in present and future asbestos claims to 275,000 victims who already have filed claims (Johns Manville n.d.)

JM's social responsibility toward its workers, the litigants, the communities it serves, and society has, at best, been uneven. Since 1972, the company has been active and cooperative with the U.S. Department of Labor and the American Federation of Labor and Congress of Industrial Organizations (AFL–CIO) in developing standards to protect asbestos workers. However, Dr. Kenneth Smith—the medical director of one of the firm's plants in Canada—refused in the 1970s to inform JM workers that they had asbestosis.

There is also the complication and confusion of evolving and changing legislation on asbestos. The U.S. Supreme Court, as stakeholder, has not taken a stand on who is liable in these situations: Are insurance firms liable when workers are initially exposed to asbestos and later develop cancer, or are they liable 20 years later? Also, right-to-know laws are not definitive in state legislatures. Does that leave JM and other corporations liable for the government's legal indecision?

Of the original 16,500 personal injury plaintiffs, 2,000 have died since the reorganization in 1982. With Warren Buffet's purchase of the company and the asbestos trust solidified, the management of this issue for the company is over.

Note that companies continue to settle asbestos lawsuits. The Mesothelioma Reporter website (www.mesotheliomareporter.org) tracks and reports these settlements. For example, a recent settlement was reported for Pfizer subsidiary Quigley Co. and others who were defendants in a trial "that alleged that they caused personal injury by exposure to asbestos. The asbestos sometimes caused mesothelioma." According to the website, *ABC News* reported that "Pfizer will establish a trust for the payment of pending claims as well as any future claims. It will contribute $405 million to the trust over 40 years through a note, and about $100 million in insurance. Pfizer will also forgive a $30 million loan to Quigley" (National Mesothelioma Claims). As with other corporate crises, the aftermath continues.

SOURCES

Gross, D. (2001, April 29). Recovery lessons from an industrial phoenix. *New York Times*. http://www.nytimes.com/2001/04/29/business/business-recovery-lessons-from-an-industrial-phoenix.html. Updates can also be found at www.asbestos.com, www.claimsres.com, and www.law360.com/companies/johns-manville-corp.

Johns Manville (n.d.). *Asbestos.com*. http://www.asbestos.com/companies/johns-manville.php.

National Mesothelioma Claims. *National Mesothelioma Claims Center*. Accessed April 27, 2021. https://www.nationalmesotheliomaclaims.com/?kw=meso thelioma%20payouts%22?c=google&gclid=Cj0KCQjwyZmEBhCpARIs ALIzmnKdI-VD0Vou09L8oPiTrq7zLv36utriO6tMohinu2IBIlq0fJHyt1QaArfE EALw_wcB.

Pfizer to pay $430 million to settle asbestos claims. (2004, September 3). *Mesothelioma Reporter*.

Strand, T. (2021, March 10). Johns-Manville Asbestos Trust Fund. https://www.mesothelioma.com/asbestos-exposure/companies/johns-manville/

QUESTIONS FOR DISCUSSION

1. Should asbestos victims' claims be the liability of Johns Manville or of the decision makers who authorized the work policies and orders?
2. Who was or is to blame for the asbestos-related deaths and injuries in this case?
3. Is the declaration of Chapter 11 bankruptcy and the creation of a trust the best or only solution in this case? Who wins and who loses with this type of settlement? Why?
4. What ethical principle(s) did Johns Manville's owners and officers use regarding this type of settlement? What principle(s) do you believe they should have used? Explain.

The *Exxon Valdez*, Second Worst Oil Spill in U.S. History: 25 Years Later, Exxon Still Hasn't Paid for Long-Term Environmental Damages

"A year after the *Exxon Valdez* ripped open its bottom on Bligh Reef [off the Alaskan coast] and dumped 11 million gallons of crude oil, the nation's worst oil spill is not over. Like major spills in the past, this unnatural disaster sparked a frenzy of reactions: congressional hearings, state and federal legislative proposals for new preventive measures, dozens of studies, and innumerable lawsuits." The grounding of the oil tanker on March 24, 1989, spread oil over more than 700 miles. Oil covered 1,300 miles of coastline and killed 250,000 birds, 2,800 sea otters, 300 seals, 250 bald eagles, and billions of salmon and herring eggs, according to the *Exxon Valdez* Oil Spill Trustee Council, which manages Exxon settlement money. Sounds somewhat like the BP oil disaster, doesn't it?

Fast-forward to 2013 and note the following: "Today, government studies confirm that most of the populations and habitats injured by the spill have not fully recovered, and some are not recovering at all. Despite this, the government's reopener claim focuses solely on remediating intertidal oil. Government studies report thousands of gallons of *Exxon Valdez* oil [are] still in beaches today, that this oil is still 'nearly as toxic as it was the first few weeks after the spill,' that 'the remaining oil will take decades and possibly centuries to disappear entirely,' and that tests on nearshore animals 'indicate a continuing exposure to oil.'"

Exxon's failure to pay the $5 billion in assessed damages is noteworthy. "After 14 years of appeals, in 2008 the U.S. Supreme Court (invoking a peculiar 1818 maritime ruling) reduced the punitive judgment to only $507 million, with the appeals court adding another $470 million in interest.... Although Exxon has not paid the claim, the government spill account today has $195 million, much of which can be used to fund beach remediation work, in expectation that this will be reimbursed if and when Exxon finally pays the claim."

A grand jury indicted Exxon in February 1990. At that time, the firm faced fines totaling more than $600 million if convicted on the felony counts. More than 150 lawsuits and 30,000 damage claims were reportedly filed against Exxon, and most had not been settled by July 1991, when Exxon made a secret agreement with seven Seattle fish processors. Under that arrangement, Exxon agreed to pay $70 million to settle the processors' oil spill claims against Exxon. However, in return for the relatively quick settlement of those claims, the processors agreed to return to Exxon most of any punitive damages they might be awarded in later Exxon spill-related cases.

Exxon paid about $300 million in damages claims in the first few years after the spill. However, "lawyers for people who had been harmed called that a mere down payment on losses that averaged more than $200,000 per fisherman from 1990 to 1994." Twenty-five years after the disaster, "the U.S. Justice Department and State of Alaska say they are still waiting for long overdue scientific studies before collecting a final $92 million claim to implement the recovery plan for unanticipated harm to fish, wildlife and habitat."

The charge that the captain of the *Exxon Valdez,* Joseph Hazelwood, had a blood-alcohol content above 0.04 percent was dropped, but he was convicted of negligently discharging oil and ordered to pay $50,000 as restitution to the state of Alaska and to serve 1,000 hours cleaning up the beaches over five years. Exxon executives and stockholders have been embroiled with courts, environmental groups, the media, and public groups over the crisis. Exxon has paid $300 million to date in nonpunitive damages to 10,000 commercial fishermen, business owners, and native Alaskan villages.

In 1996, a grand jury ordered Exxon to pay $5 billion in punitive damages to the victims of the 1989 oil spill. At the time that the fish processors had entered the secret agreement with Exxon, they did not know the Alaskan jury would slap the company with the $5 billion punitive damages award. One of the judges claimed that had the jury known about this secret agreement, it would have charged Exxon even more punitive damages. As of 2001, Exxon had not paid any of these damages. It is also estimated that with Exxon's reported rate of return on its investments, it makes $800 million every year on the $5 billion it does not pay. (The company would have made back the $5 billion it refused to pay with accrued interest by 2002.) Brian O'Neill, the Minneapolis lawyer who represents 60,000 plaintiffs in the suit against Exxon, stated, "I have had thousands of clients that have gone bankrupt, got divorced, died, or been down on their financial luck" while waiting for the settlement. Looking back on this case, the November 2001 federal appeals court ruling opened the way for a judge to reduce the $5 billion punitive verdict. (However, the 1994 jury award of $287 million to compensate commercial fishermen was not reduced.)

In 2004, the Environmental News Network (ENN) reported that local residents and several government scientists are still at odds as to "whether Exxon Mobil Corporation should be forced to pay an additional civil penalty for the spill.... The landmark $900 million civil settlement Exxon signed in 1991 to resolve federal and state environmental claims included a $100 million reopener clause for damages that 'could not reasonably have been known' or anticipated."

EPILOGUE

On June 25, 2008, the Supreme Court reduced the previously determined $5 billion punitive damages award against ExxonMobil to $507.5 million. Since Justice Samuel A. Alito Jr. owns Exxon stock, he did not participate in the final decision. With regard to whether Exxon should be held accountable for Captain Hazelwood's irresponsibility in the case, the court split 4-to-4. "The effect of the split was to leave intact the ruling of the lower court, the United States Court of Appeals for the Ninth Circuit, which said Exxon might be held responsible."

Justice David Souter hinted in his last paragraph on behalf of the 5-to-3 majority that this decision reflected the rule he was announcing for federal maritime cases in the Exxon case, "a rule that generally dictates a maximum 1:1 ratio between a punitive damages award and a jury's compensatory award." In effect, by reducing the *Exxon Valdez* verdict to $500 million, the court set a 1:1 ratio by passing the $507.5 million compensatory damage portion of the jury's award in this case. Stakeholders were divided on the outcome of the case. It should be recalled that Exxon had previously paid over $2 billion during the past 19 years on environmental cleanup and $1.4 billion in fines and compensation to thousands of fishermen and cannery workers.

Former Exxon chairman and CEO Rex Tillerson stated that "we have worked hard over many years to address the impacts of the spill and to prevent such accidents from happening in our company again." A different reaction came from the hard-hit Alaskan town of Cordova, where fishermen and local businesses suffered bankruptcies and even suicides in the long aftermath of the crises: "The punitive damages claim 'was about punishing [Exxon] so they wouldn't do it somewhere else,' said Sylvia Lange, who owns a hotel and bar frequented by fishermen. 'We were the mouse that roared, but we got squished.'" As a result of the June 2008 Supreme Court decision, fishermen and others hurt by the disaster will receive about $15,000 instead of $75,000. Note that in 2007, ExxonMobil earned a record $40.6 billion in profits. The company could pay the punitive award with four days profits.

LaRue Tone Hosmer, a noted ethicist, stated, "The most basic lesson in accident prevention that can be drawn from the wreck of the *Exxon Valdez* is that management is much more than just looking at revenues, costs, and profits. Management requires the imagination to understand the full mixture of potential benefits and harms generated by the operations of the firm, the empathy to consider the full range of legitimate interests represented by the constituencies of the firm, and the courage to act when some of the harms are not certain and many of the constituencies are not powerful. The lack of imagination, empathy, and courage at the most senior levels of the company was the true cause of the wreck of the *Exxon Valdez*." Kiley Kroh, deputy editor of the *Climate Progress* blog, stated that "critics of the delay say the ongoing struggle to hold Exxon accountable for unanticipated environmental damages in Alaska offers clear lessons to be learned regarding the continuing process of determining BP's long-term liability for the *Deepwater Horizon* catastrophe, a spill that was 20 times larger than *Exxon Valdez*."

SOURCES

Allen, S. (1999, March 7). Deep problems 10 years after *Exxon Valdez*: Worst oil spill in US has lingering effects for Alaska, industries. *Wall Street Journal*, A1.

Dumanoski, D. (1990, April 2). One year later—the lessons of Valdez. *Boston Globe*, 29.

Exxon Valdez fine excessive, court says. (2001, November 8). *USA Today*, 6A.

Hosmer, L. (1998). Lessons from the wreck of the *Exxon Valdez:* The need for imagination, empathy, and courage. *Business Ethics Quarterly*, 122.

Kroh, K. (2013). 25 years after *Exxon Valdez* oil spill, company still hasn't paid for long-term environmental damages. *ThinkProgress.org*.

Liptak, A. (2008, June 26). Damages cut against Exxon in *Valdez* case. *NYTimes.com*. http://www.nytimes.com/2008/06/26/washington /26punitive.html?_r=0.

McCoy, Charles. (1996, June 13). Exxon's secret *Valdez* deals anger judge. *Wall Street Journal*, A3.

Parloff, R. (2008, June 25). Supreme Court slashes $2.5B *Exxon Valdez* award. *Fortune.com*. https://fortune.com/2008/06/25/supreme-court-slashes-2 -5b-exxon-valdez-award/.

Rawkins, R. (1990, February 28). U.S. indicts Exxon in oil spill. *Miami Herald*, 5.

Savage, D. (2008, June 26). Punitive damages against Exxon in oil spill case slashed by 80%. *LATimes.com*.

Steiner, R. (2013, August 26). Exxon spill case still unresolved. *JuneauEmpire.com*.

QUESTIONS FOR DISCUSSION

1. Who was at fault in this case, and why?
2. Should Captain Hazelwood have been convicted of criminal drunkenness in this case? If so, how would that have changed the outcome of the settlement? If not, why?
3. Did Captain Hazelwood settle his "debt" in this case by agreeing to serve 1,000 hours in cleanup time in Alaska? Explain.
4. Describe Exxon's ethics toward this disaster based on what it had paid over the years up to the June 15, 2008, Supreme Court decision.
5. How much should the 33,000 commercial fishermen, Alaska Native peoples, landowners, businesses, and local governments have been paid as compensation, and why?
6. Respond to the statement by ethicist LaRue Tone Hosmer. Do you believe this sentiment applies to all responsibilities of senior executives in corporations; that is, do they need to show imagination, empathy, and courage toward all their constituencies? Explain your answer.

Chapter Summary

Managing corporate social responsibility (CSR) from the corporate board of directors to the marketplace requires commitment and significant time, effort, and resources from organizations, especially during these unprecedented times following the national turmoil after George Floyd was killed in police custody, the attack on the U.S. Capitol, Covid-19, and voter suppression laws. Corporations are being pressured to publicly identify their ethical positions. At stake is a company's reputation, and even its survival. External regulation is also required to help define guidelines and practices for companies to act responsibly toward their stakeholders, communities, and society.

The corporation as social and economic stakeholder was presented from the perspectives of the social contract and covenantal ethic. Corporate social responsibility was also discussed from legal, ethical, philanthropic, and pragmatic viewpoints. Managing and balancing legal compliance with ethical motivation was illustrated by the Sarbanes-Oxley Act and the Revised Federal Sentencing Guidelines for Organizations. Corporations are being pressured to recognize diversity, equity, and inclusion issues and needs in their policies, procedures, and practices. A section on legal and regulatory laws and compliance presented the complexity of areas in which corporations must navigate with federal, state, and local agencies before creating and distributing their products and services. A summary of recent corporate scandals was given to demonstrate the need for legal compliance in corporations. Arguments were offered to explain that legal compliance legislation and programs alone are necessary but not sufficient enough to motivate ethical and legal behavior in organizations.

Corporate responsibility toward consumers was presented by explaining these corporate duties: (1) the duty to inform consumers truthfully, (2) the duty not to misrepresent or withhold information, (3) the duty not to unreasonably force consumer choice or take undue advantage of consumers through fear or stress, and (4) the duty to take "due care" to prevent any foreseeable injuries. The use of a utilitarian ethic was discussed to show the problems in holding corporations accountable for product risks and injuries beyond their control.

The free-market theory of Adam Smith was summarized by way of explaining the market context governing the exchange of producers and buyers. Several limits of the free market were offered: that imperfect markets exist; the power between buyers and sellers is not symmetrical; and the line between telling the truth and lying about products is very thin. Economist Paul Samuelson's "mixed economy" was introduced to offer a more balanced view of free-market theory and of the unrealistic demands often placed on corporations in marketing new products.

An overview of two classic business ethics cases, Johns Manville Corporation and the *Exxon Valdez* oil spill, were presented to illustrate how legal and regulatory agencies are part of a much broader stakeholder system involving communities and groups in the marketplace. Laws and regulations, as mentioned earlier, are necessary but not sufficient enough forces that corporate leaders must adhere to in order to act fairly toward their constituencies while being profitable.

Questions

1. Identify a company or organization in the media or with which you are familiar that operates ethically. What are the reasons this company/organization is

ethical? (You may refer to the leadership, management, products, or services of the organization.)

2. Do you believe that the Sarbanes-Oxley Act is *not* now needed? Explain or offer a different argument.

3. Are the 2004 Revised Federal Sentencing Guidelines, in your opinion, helpful to organizational leaders and boards of directors in promoting more ethical behavior? Explain. What other actions, policies, or procedures would you recommend?

4. Which of the corporate crises summarized at the end of the chapter were you unfamiliar with? Do you believe these crises represent "business as usual" or serious breakdowns in a company's system? Why?

5. After reading the Johns Manville and *Exxon Valdez* summaries, identify some ways these crises could have been (1) avoided and (2) managed more responsibly after they occurred.

6. What was your score on the "Rank Your Organization's Reputation" quiz in Ethical Insight 4.4? After reading previous chapters in this book, how would you describe the "ethics" of your organization, university, or college toward its customers and stakeholders? Explain.

7. Do you believe the covenantal ethic and social contract views are realistic for large organizations like Bank of America, JPMorgan, ExxonMobil, and Citibank, or federal agencies like the FTC and the Department of Defense? Why or why not? Explain.

8. What is the free-market theory of corporate responsibility, and what are some of the problems associated with this view? Compare this view with the social contract and stakeholder perspectives of CSR.

9. If you had to select either the legal/compliance ("stick") approach or the voluntary/ethical compliance ("carrot") approach toward running a corporation, which would you choose, and why? What would be likely consequences (positive and negative) of your choice? Explain.

Exercises

1. In this chapter's opening case, why do you think it took such a large-scale security breach for TJX to start a serious corporate "ethics" program? Have things changed in 2021 in corporations?

2. Outline some steps you would recommend for preventing future corporate scandals like Wells Fargo, Volkswagen, Boeing MAX, Enron, WorldCom, and the subprime-lending crisis, based on the contents of this chapter.

3. If you were consulting with a large corporation's executive team and were asked to talk about how that team could think about a social contract including stakeholder management reasoning, what would you recommend? Write down your advice.

4. You have been invited as a student who has studied business ethics to present a case to a CEO, CFO, and ethics officer of a midsize firm wanting to be Sarbanes-Oxley compliant. You have been asked to discuss and help them ar-

gue the pros and cons of implementing this law. Lay out your approach and arguments and be ready to tell them what you would recommend they do and why.

5. A large company has invited you to join in a discussion with its legal and human resources officers about integrating ethics, diversity, equity, and inclusion into and between their departments. They want your ideas. Use Figure 4.2 and any other ideas from this and previous chapters to outline what you would contribute. Write up a paragraph to share with your class/group.

6. Find a recent article discussing an innovative way in which a corporation is helping the environment. Explain why the method is innovative and whether you believe the method will actually help the environment or simply help the company promote its image as a good citizen. Use parts of this chapter to evaluate your answer.

Real-Time Ethical Dilemma

My job requires that I lie every day I go to work. I work for a private investigation agency called XRT. Most of the work I do involves undercover operations, mobile surveillances, and groundwork searches to determine the whereabouts of manufacturers that produce counterfeit merchandise.

Each assignment I take requires some deception on my part. Recently I have become very conscious of the fact that I frequently have to lie to obtain concrete evidence for a client. I sometimes dig myself so deeply into a lie that I naturally take it to the next level, without ever accomplishing the core purpose of the investigation.

Working for an investigative agency engages me in assignments that vary on a day-to-day basis. I choose to work for XRT because it is not a routine nine-to-five desk job. But to continue working for the agency means I will constantly be developing new, untruthful stories. And the longer I decide to stay at XRT, the more involved the assignments will be. To leave would probably force me into a job photocopying and filing paperwork once I graduate from college.

Recently I was given an assignment that I believed would lead me to entrap a subject to obtain evidence for a client. The subject had filed for disability on workers' compensation after being hit by a truck. Because the subject refused to partake in any strenuous activity because of the accident, I was instructed to fake a flat tire and videotape the subject changing it for me. Although I did not feel comfortable engaging in this type of act, my supervisors assured me that it was ethical practice and not entrapment. Coworkers and other supervisors assured me that this was a standard "industry practice" and that we would go out of business if we didn't "fudge" the facts once in a while. I was told, "Do you think every business does its work and makes profits in a purely ethical way? Get real. I don't know what they're teaching you in college, but this is the real world." It was either do the assignment or find myself on the street—in an economy with no jobs.

Questions

1. What is the dilemma here, or isn't there one?
2. What would you have done in the writer's situation? Explain.
3. React to the comment, "Do you think every business does its work and makes profits in a purely ethical way? Get real. I don't know what they're teaching you in college, but this is the real world." Do you agree or disagree? Why?
4. Describe the ethics of this company.
5. Compare and contrast your personal ethics with the company ethics revealed here.

Cases

Case 10

Conscious Capitalism: What Is It? Why Do We Need It? Does It Work?

Introduction

Conscious Capitalism: Liberating the Heroic Spirit of Business (2013) is a best-selling book written by John Mackey, former CEO of Whole Foods (now acquired by Amazon); and Rajendra Sisodia, a management professor at Babson College. A major tenet of the book states, "Conscious capitalism is an evolving paradigm for business that simultaneously creates multiple kinds of value and well-being for all stakeholders: financial, intellectual, physical, ecological, social, cultural, emotional, ethical and even spiritual. This new operating system for business is in far greater harmony with the ethos of our times and the essence of our evolving beings" (Sisodia, et al., 2014). The four core tenets underlying the business practices of conscious capitalism include "higher purpose and core values, stakeholder integration, conscious leadership and conscious culture and management" (ibid.). Mackey's, and now Amazon's, Whole Foods business still strives to embody these principles, as do several other selected companies that the book exemplifies. This case presents the purpose, goal, and need for conscious capitalism that, since the publication of the book, has now become a movement.

Why Conscious Capitalism?

Mackey and Sisodia's book is not the first to initiate a change in the ways businesses should change. In his review of *Conscious Capitalism*, Alan Murray states that "capitalist guilt is nearly as old as capitalism itself, but it has seen a resurgence since the financial crises of 2007." Bill Gates called for a new system of "creative capitalism" in 2008 at a World Economic Forum in Davos, Switzerland. He was upset that pharmaceuticals paid more attention to baldness than curing global diseases like malaria. Michael Porter, a Harvard Business School professor, in 2011 called for "shared value capitalism," arguing that business leaders were too occupied by short-term financial profits, more so than "the well-being of customers, the depletion of natural resources, the viability of suppliers, and the concerns of the communities in which they produce and sell." Mackey and Sisodia continue in this tradition, writing that "with few exceptions, entrepreneurs who start successful businesses don't do so to maximize profits. Of course they want to make money, but that is not what drives most of them. They are inspired to do something that they believe needs doing. The heroic story of free-enterprise capitalism is one of entrepreneurs using their dreams and passion as fuel to create extraordinary value for customers, team members, suppliers, society, and investors."

Since the fall of the Berlin Wall in 1989, it has been undisputed in business circles that capitalism and free markets are the best way to promote prosperity and grow economies internationally. Significant progress has been made since the inception of free-enterprise capitalism. Many believe that most of the world's problems today, such as poverty, education inequality, and problems in undeveloped nations, can be solved through innovations brought about by free markets and free-enterprise capitalism. The poorest nations might be encouraged to embrace the ideas of free-enterprise capitalism to achieve similar successes as the developed countries, such as the United States, Japan, and others.

Free-enterprise capitalism is approximately 200 years old. Below is a partial list of accomplishments during the past two centuries, attributed to free-enterprise capitalism.

- Average income per capita on a global level has increased by over 1,000 percent since 1800.
- Average life expectancy globally has increased to 68 years, much greater than the historical average of 30 years.
- Two hundred years ago, 85 percent of the world's population lived on less than $1 a day in today's terms. Today that number is 16 percent.
- In just the last 40 years, undernourished people globally have decreased from 26 percent to 13 percent; if the current trend continues, it is estimated hunger will be virtually eliminated in the twenty-first century.
- Two hundred years ago, the world was almost completely illiterate; today, 84 percent of adults have the ability to read.
- With economic freedom has come political freedom: 53 percent of people currently live in countries that have democratic governments elected by universal suffrage, compared to zero people 120 years ago.
- Two key factors that have led to the success of free-enterprise capitalism have been entrepreneurship and innovation, combined with the freedom and dignity of those transacting business. Both are necessary for capitalism's continued progress going forward. Entrepreneurs are also to be admired in an economy devoted to free-enterprise capitalism because they are the drivers of innovation that improve our lives, companies' competitive positions, and economies.

Why Is Capitalism under Attack?

Despite the achievements of free-market capitalism, it is criticized by many around the world. Capitalism has a branding problem, in which its image has been tarnished for various reasons. Entrepreneurs driving capitalism should be admired, yet so many are vilified. Capitalism by many around the world is depicted as a zero-sum game, in which workers are exploited and consumers are cheated by business owners. Critics of capitalism argue that this alleged, intentional process results in greater inequality between the rich and the poor, fragmentation among communities, and environmental degradation, all with the motivation of making a profit. In this portrayal, business owners and entrepreneurs are depicted as being motivated by greed, seeking profit maximization as a way of doing business, since ethical theory claims that people will only pursue their self-interest at the expense of others.

Underlying reasons of capitalism's branding problem stem, in part, from the corporate scandals that rocked the United States in the 2000–2002 period. Some of the more well-known scandals include Enron, WorldCom, Tyco, and Adelphia Cable, all of which involved executive mischief, causing widespread losses for investors, partners, and communities alike. The latest widespread scandal in the United States—the subprime-lending crisis in 2008—led to the longest recession since the Great Depression. This crisis was caused by illegal and unethical actions of large corporations and companies across all levels of the financial sector. Many of the major banks were lending to those who did not qualify, and then securitizing those loans for sale to other banks and consumers. The rating agencies, which were getting paid fees by the major banks, evaluated all of these securitized mortgage products as AAA (risk-free). Consumers during that time were overwhelmed by debt that they could not afford. These actions resulted in a continuing widespread financial crisis that further divided Main Street from Wall Street, and society in general from capitalism.

Mackey and Sisodia believe there are several reasons for the attacks on capitalism. First, they argue that there has been an intellectual hijacking of capitalism by economists and critics. These parties have placed capitalism in a narrow, self-serving identity helping to paint capitalism as a profit-maximizing machine. Second, many businesses are operating at a low level of consciousness regarding their purpose and the large impact they have on the world. Third, the industrial era that gave rise to a mechanistic view of business, in which employees were seen as resources of production, embraced the goal of receiving the most output from as little input as possible. And finally, expanding regulations and the size of the government has produced a mutant form of capitalism, dubbed "crony capitalism."

This biased thinking is prevalent in the consciousness of many today. Wall Street analysts must meet quarterly earnings projections for all public companies. Many of these analysts tend to view any stakeholder (other than stockholders) as net drainers of value; that is, if you pay employees more, you will earn less in profits. This is a misunderstanding among many today about business in general, which dates back to the turn of the twentieth century when so-called robber barons wielded vast sums of wealth and were not ashamed to flaunt it. For example, Cornelius Vanderbilt, when he was warned about violating the law, was alleged to have said: "Law? Who cares about the law? Hain't I got the power?"

This dated way of thinking, although seemingly still practiced by some (as evidenced in the corporate scandals between 2000 and 2002), shows a low consciousness and moral concern for stakeholders, which can lead to unintended consequences that affect stockholders as well as stakeholders—and, in fact, the entire global economy. This zero-sum concept leads to short-term thinking and can inadvertently support reckless risk-taking among those driven only by short-term profits. If a company seeks only or mainly to maximize profits, it will pressure its entire supply chain to disregard real-time data and constraints. For example, suppliers who are continually dictated to provide product and services to meet unrealistic goals may be rewarded for a few quarters, but in the long-term, such suppliers will do one of three things: go out of business, do business elsewhere, or provide products of lower quality, all of which cause havoc to a company's supply chain. Other consequences, such as disregard for the environment and low employee engagement, have led to the public perception of corporations as greedy, selfish, exploitative, and untrustworthy. Mackey and Sisodia write that "business is good because it creates value, it is ethical because it is based on voluntary exchange, it is noble because it lifts people out of poverty and creates prosperity." Capitalism is therefore challenged to become more "conscious" of its heroic nature.

In 2002, a Gallup poll delineated problems with the perceptions of corporations. The poll found that "90 percent of Americans felt that people running corporations could not be trusted to look after the interests of their employees, and only 18 percent thought that corporations looked after their shareholders. Forty-three percent believed senior executives were only in it for themselves." The *New York Times* was also quoted, stating "the majority of the public . . . believes that executives are bent on destroying the environment, cooking the books, and lining their own pockets." One reason for distrust of executives, in addition to the 2000–2002 scandals, is exorbitant executive pay. The Institute of Policy Studies showed that the ratio of CEO to average employee salaries in 1980 was 42 to 1; in 1990 it was 107 to 1; and in 2000 it was 525 to 1. In recent years, the ratio has declined to 325 to 1, but the discrepancy is still too large, even outrageous compared to all other professional pay-scale comparisons.

The public image spurred by corporate crises such as Enron and large banks "too big to fail"—crises caused by greed and reckless practices—have tainted trust of businesses and even capitalism. Chris Meyer and Julia Kirby stated the following in a keynote address at Bentley University (Waltham, Massachusetts) on the future of capitalism: "We capitalists are stuck in two deep ruts right now. One of those ruts is an overemphasis on return on equity, as it has become one of the primary (if not *the* primary) barometer of success for a company." Meyer and Kirby argue that a fixture on return on equity alone is not an appropriate proxy of the value a company provides, and that by fixating on a single metric, business is committing social suicide. Meyer and Kirby also assert that businesses in general are obsessed with competition, which can be just as harmful as helpful. Competition in free markets has driven innovation in the past, as companies seek out competitive advantages with new products and ways to improve the world; but an infatuation with competition, simply for its own sake, will not help drive the innovation needed if people and companies are hindered from being collaborative and inspiring productive change. Former Dupont CEO Charles Holliday has stated that "Dupont's long history has shown us that no company, however strong and competitive, can go it alone. Involvement in outside organizations and endeavors is a way of learning and leading."

So, where do we go from here? Jack Immelt, one-time CEO of General Electric, is quoted in Rajendra Sisodia's book *Firms of Endearment* as saying, "To be a great company today, you have to be a good company." Under conscious capitalism, good businesses make money by creating value for others, not only by maximizing profits. It is essential for free-enterprise capitalism to be grounded in an ethical system based on shared value creation for all stakeholders. To prosper, companies will have to shift mind-sets and practices by listening to and learning from today's customers. This shift represents a change not only in what people want but also in how products should be designed both aesthetically and functionally. For businesses to reach full potential, a new paradigm must be created to move beyond the simplistic models toward a higher purpose and value creation for all parties. Conscious capitalism is one step in that direction.

What Is Conscious Capitalism?

Doug Rauch, former CEO of Trader Joe's and current CEO of Conscious Capitalism, Inc., defines conscious capitalism as "recognition that we are interconnected and interrelated. That business at its core is a story of us." Jack Canfield, one of my company's advisory board members, describes the conscious capitalism process as building "sustainable, trusting partnerships with people and the earth, adhering to the core values of respect, integrity, and ethics."

A distinction must be made, however, between conscious capitalism and corporate social responsibility (CSR). Some believe they are one and the same. CSR is generally defined as a company's efforts that go beyond what is required by regulators in terms of societal and environmental impacts. To further delineate the distinctions between conscious capitalism and CSR, Edward Freeman, a thought leader on stakeholder relationship management, has stated:

> Assume you are CEO and you are asked the following: Your company's products improve lives. Suppliers want to do business with your company because they benefit from this relationship. Employees really want to work for your company, and are satisfied with their remuneration and professional development. And you're a good citizen in the communities where you are located; among other things, you pay taxes on the profits you make. You compete hard but fairly. You also make an attractive return on capital for shareholder and other financiers. However, are you socially responsible? (Freeman, et al., 2006, 4)

Freeman notes that CSR, although intended to be beneficial, actually helps to reinforce the "separation thesis" that business and society are two distinct entities. At its worst, the separation thesis can generate a destructive idea of capitalism, in which CSR becomes an add-on to business to help lessen the harsh consequences of doing capitalistic business. This style of thinking fails to recognize the central role business plays in the global improvement in the well-being and prosperity of mankind. CSR is generally seen as beneficial to and contributing positive impacts on societies. However, because of the separation thesis, people may still view capitalism as harmful and interpret CSR as an extension of business—not integral to corporations' actual functioning.

Freeman has therefore developed his own version of CSR that breaks down the separation thesis and describes business as an enterprise with moral ramifications, not needing the arm of social responsibility. In this view, capitalism is a system of social cooperation working together to create value that could not be created by individuals. From Freeman's perspective, the idea of corporate social responsibility is unnecessary and the baseline for conscious capitalism (i.e., a stakeholder approach) is set.

The Four Tenets of Conscious Capitalism

The base of conscious capitalism lies in four tenets: higher purpose, stakeholder integration, conscious leadership, and conscious culture and management. To fully understand the tenets, further delineation is necessary. The tenet of higher purpose depicts the powerful and broad impacts business has on the world. These impacts can be much greater when business is based on a higher purpose that goes beyond just generating profits and shareholder value. Purpose is the reason a company exists. Yes, all companies need to make money to survive, but they do not survive to make money. Professions such as lawyers, doctors, and teachers, as examples, put an emphasis on public good and have purposes beyond self-interest; so should business. When entrepreneurs originally create their companies, the majority create them for a purpose, to fill a need in society. Having a higher purpose helps to create a high degree of engagement among all stakeholders, rallying around a singular idea. This helps catalyze creativity, innovation, and organizational commitment—all benefits of pursuing a higher purpose beyond profits.

The second tenet of conscious capitalism is stakeholder integration. This tenet is rather similar to the Freeman style of management discussed earlier. A stakeholder is considered to be an entity that impacts or is impacted by a business. Stakeholders include employees, suppliers, the environment, investors, and more. Conscious businesses recognize that stakeholders are interdependent and that their business must be organized to provide optimal value creation for all parties. Stakeholders cannot be treated as individuals because business is a world of interconnected parties. Optimizing value creation for all stakeholders enables the whole system to flourish, not just the company at the center. It also helps to create a harmony of interests among the interdependent stakeholders so that each party knows it is part of a much larger ecosystem.

To achieve a commitment to the stakeholder approach, we revisit Freeman and his version of CSR, in which he states there are four levels of commitment. Level 1 is a basic value proposition, in which a company must ask itself how it makes its stakeholders better off and what the company stands for. Level 2 involves sustained cooperation among stakeholders, in which the principles and values are established to base everyday engagement between the parties. Level 3 deals with understanding broader societal issues. At this level, companies must ask themselves how the basic value proposition staged in level 1 and the principles of level 2 either fit or contradict key trends and opinions in society. Level 4 deals with ethical leadership, which falls under the third tenet of conscious capitalism.

The third tenet of conscious capitalism is conscious leadership. Every conscious business needs a conscious leader; it is nearly (if not fully) impossible to have a conscious business without a leader at the helm who shares the values of the firm and its higher purpose. To be a conscious leader, one must be motivated first and foremost by service to the higher purpose of the firm and creating value for all stakeholders. Conscious leaders reject the old model of fear-based command-and-control leadership and accept the "carrot and sticks" model as primary motivational tools. This model seeks to mentor, motivate, and inspire people into accomplishing their tasks and seeks to stimulate innovation and creativity over fear. Conscious leaders must also know what values and principles inform their leadership, their individual sense of purpose, and what they stand for as a leader. With conscious leadership in place, the fourth tenet of conscious capitalism becomes easier to achieve.

That fourth tenet of conscious capitalism is conscious culture and management. In a conscious business, the culture within the firm is a tremendous source of strength and continuity. This type of culture naturally evolves from the firm's and management's commitments to higher purpose, stakeholder interdependence, and conscious leadership. A pure focus on the first three tenets of conscious capitalism should ultimately lead to a conscious culture inspired by commitment, innovation, and creativity. Some may ask why culture is so important. A 2005 study by the Economist Intelligence Unit found that 56 percent of U.S. executives felt that the single greatest obstacle to growth for their firm was corporate culture. Conscious businesses, because of their culture, do not face these obstacles on their path to growth. The key to establishing conscious culture and achieving the fourth tenet is to understand the connection between management and culture.

For conscious businesses to thrive, a conscious culture is necessary that entails management promoting a different type of leadership style. The type of management approach to leadership can either magnify or depress the human need to care. Emphasizing a leadership style that connects what people feel and value to how people work promotes achievement beyond the ordinary scope of traditional businesses. The leadership style found in conscious businesses focuses on decentralization, empowerment, and collaboration. This style of management leads to an amplified ability of the firm to continuously innovate and create multiple kinds of value and wealth (not just financial) for all stakeholders, as described by the flowchart in Figure 1, which illustrates the interconnectedness required between culture and management in conscious capitalism firms.

Firms of Endearment (FoEs)

So what exactly is an FoE? It is a "company that endears itself to stakeholders by bringing the interests of all stakeholder groups into strategic alignment. No stakeholder benefits at the expense of any other stakeholder group and each prospers as the others do." FoEs embrace a different idea than most companies. When looking at customers, they strive for share of heart, and not share of wallet. The theme with this form of thought is if you earn a share of the customer's heart, customers will gladly offer you a bigger share of their wallet; do the same

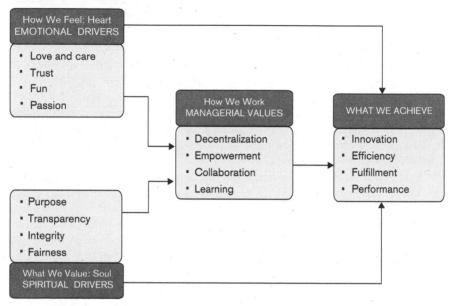

Figure 1

Culture and Management Must Connect

Source: Based on a presentation given by R. Sisodia at the 2012 Conscious Capitalism Conference at Bentley University, Waltham, MA.

for an employee and that employee will give back with substantial increases in productivity and overall work quality. FoEs define the conscious capitalism movement and are at the forefront of conscious business practices, leading the business world into its much-needed evolution. FoEs include Amazon, Honda, Southwest, BMW, IDEO, Starbucks, CarMax, IKEA, Timberland, Caterpillar, Jet-Blue, Toyota, Commerce Bank, Johnson & Johnson, Trader Joe's, The Container Store, Jordan's Furniture, UPS, Costco, LL Bean, Wegmans, eBay, New Balance, Whole Foods, Google, Patagonia, Harley-Davidson, and REI.

FoEs have a distinct set of core values that help differentiate them from competitors. Some of the values have already been mentioned, such as aligning stakeholder interests. There is a laundry list of values distinct to FoEs, and it is pertinent to point out a few here. First, employee compensation and benefits are significantly greater than the standard for the company's category/industry, while executive salaries are modest, leading to a smaller ratio of CEO pay to average pay. FoEs also devote larger amounts of time to employee training than their competitors, part of the reason for lower FoE employee turnover than the industry average. FoEs consider corporate culture to be their greatest asset and therefore their primary source of competitive advantage. They seek to keep it that way by humanizing the company experience for customers and employees alike, by projecting a genuine passion and connecting emotionally.

From an FoE perspective, stakeholders are understood through the acronym SPICE, which stands for society, partners, investors, customers, and employees. Society is part of the local communities in which FoEs are embedded, as well as larger communities in need of resources for societal improvement. FoEs include governments and nongovernmental organizations (NGOs) as well. Partners include upstream suppliers, as well as downstream partners such as retailers, thus representing the broad spectrum of what businesses would consider partners. Investors as a stakeholder include both individual and institutional shareholders, as well as lenders who have helped finance the company. Customers include both individual and organizational (business) customers but extend beyond the current customer. FoEs view customers past, present, and future with equal affection and seek for a share of heart from all. This is a similar viewpoint to how FoEs view employees. Employees past, present, and future are all stakeholders. Families are also included in their consideration of employees as stakeholders. All in all, FoEs have an extremely broad view of stakeholders and take each into equal consideration when planning firm strategy.

The best way to understand a FoE is to understand how one operates. For our purposes, we will focus on Whole Foods as an example of an FoE. Mackey defines the values and concepts that have helped Whole Foods establish and maintain its conscious culture, as well as its competitive advantage against other grocers. For Mackey, purpose involves businesses needing to shift from profit maximization to purpose maximization in an effort to resurrect the brand of business. *Purpose maximization* is a powerful concept in that it drives everything the firm does. It aligns stakeholders by focusing on a purpose, and ironically, it typically results in making more money than one ever thought possible (even more than profit maximization). Mackey further delineates Whole Foods' culture by discussing the concept of decentralization, which involves having 8 to 10 teams within each store and each team being self-managed. The teams are responsible for the operations of their specific store. They make decisions regarding hiring, product selection, merchandising, compensation, and more. Teams are rewarded through gain-sharing and not individual performance; 92 percent of Whole Foods stock options are granted to nonexecutives, whereas in a typical corporation, 75 percent of options will go to the top-five executives. The key to this type of decentralization is that it empowers employees to make their own decisions. By allowing the teams to make decisions on their own, empowerment is greatly increased, which helps lead to greater loyalty. Mackey claims that without empowerment, decentralization is useless.

Not only does Whole Foods focus on decentralization, but they also focus on authenticity and transparency, both of which foster trust. The current system of information-sharing in business is "need to know," which depresses trust within an organization. FoEs focus on being transparent with all stakeholders. Whole Foods accomplishes this by sharing all relevant financial information with team members, including compensation. Another FoE, The Container Store, is a private company and therefore has no obligation to share its financial information, and yet the store shares all of its financial statements with all of its employees every year. Whole

Foods also seeks to promote love and care within its organization. One way of doing so is through "Appreciations." Every meeting at Whole Foods is ended by one employee voluntarily expressing an appreciation for another employee, thus helping to shift the culture from judgment to love. All of this leads to continuous innovation, which is the key to having a sustainable competitive advantage. Last, Whole Foods is committed to collaboration because innovation without collaboration is far less valuable. Collaboration is part of the recipe for success with Whole Foods and many FoEs, making them the truly great firms they are.

Conscious Capitalism: A Different View

The theme of this section has been touched on throughout the case, but it is important for readers to remain focused on how conscious capitalism is an evolution and improvement of the current U.S. system of capitalism. Conscious capitalism opens up a different mind-set. The trade-off thinking of the current system creates an "if/then" mind-set leading to restricted options for managers. Conscious capitalism creates "both/and" thinking, which allows managers, entrepreneurs, and ambassadors of capitalism to open their minds to seemingly contradictory conditions, such as paying employees higher wages than industry averages and yet having higher profit margins than industry averages. Furthermore, "if/then" thinking leads to a zero-sum mind-set, in which one stakeholder can only benefit at the expense of another; this system is becoming unsustainable for reasons illustrated previously. In order for value to be created by capitalism, each participant must make a profit; that is, each stakeholder must receive back more value than they originally invested. If stakeholders do not receive value from taking part in the system, they will eventually drop out. The exclusive pursuit of profit maximization has done enormous damage to this system and the reputation of capitalism because profit maximization, by definition, means giving as little and getting as much as possible. The conscious capitalism system of shared value creation increases opportunities by an order of magnitude as the mind breaks free of zero-sum, profit-maximization thinking.

The heroic story of free-enterprise capitalism is not one of profit maximization; it is one of entrepreneurs using their passion as fuel to create extraordinary value for customers, team members, suppliers, investors, and society. Business is far greater than just the sum of the individual stakeholders. Business is the interrelationship, interconnection, shared purpose, and shared values that various stakeholders of the business cocreate and coevolve together. FoEs and proponents of conscious capitalism do not view stakeholders as competing claimants on the value pool, but rather as active contributors to it. Overall, conscious capitalism creates a better environment than the current system. Companies motivated by higher purposes create sustained wealth for investors (see Figure 2); improve the lives of customers by satisfying their needs; elevate human satisfaction through fulfilling work; and build the social, cultural, infrastructural, and ecological wealth of society.

Conscious capitalism is, then, a revolution of traditional free-enterprise capitalism that opens up thinking to shared value creation for all stakeholders. Companies that follow this model are given the title "Firm of Endearment" and base their business models off trust, authenticity, innovation, and more. These firms tend to pay employees more, work with suppliers to strengthen both firms, and have lower executive pay than most businesses today. The brand of business that needs rejuvenation and conscious capitalism is at the forefront of revitalizing the natural good that business creates. But does conscious capitalism's business model provide financial success?

Conscious Companies

Critics of conscious capitalism argue that if employees are paid more and suppliers are treated well and paid a fair price, these numbers should ultimately hit the bottom line of the conscious firms, thus affecting their stock price. Research has been done on this subject and provides amazing results.

Presentation of Original Research

Studies on those firms that Mackey and Sisodia select and label as FoEs found that those companies generally earn higher shareholder returns, have premium price-to-earnings ratios, and earn a premium return on equity, all while incurring no more risk than the overall stock market. Over a 10-year time period, FoEs produced a cumulative return of 1,026 percent, while the S&P 500 managed only 122 percent. There was also another series of firms called "Good to Great," based on the James Collins book by the same title, with most of these firms focused strictly on profits. These firms also outperformed the S&P 500 but dramatically underperformed FoEs with a cumulative return of 331 percent, as seen in Figure 2. Note the comparison of cumulative 10-year stock market performance for FoEs (1,026 percent) with the exemplary company sample in *Good to Great* (331 percent), and to the S&P 500 (122 percent) for that same period.

Additionally, FoEs had an average price-to-earnings ratio of 26.8, while the S&P 500's was 18.4, and Good to Great companies had a price-to-earnings ratio of 16.8. Sisodia and his coauthors examined the average beta of these firms. Beta is the tendency of a security's returns to respond to swings in the market and is commonly used as a measure of risk. The average beta is that of the market (S&P 500), which is 1. A beta under 1 suggests that a stock, or group of stocks, is less risky than the overall market. Sisodia and his coauthors found that FoEs had an average beta of 0.92, thus leading to the conclusion that FoEs produce superior returns with less risk than the overall market, the ideal risk-return relationship for investors.

Updated Financial Analysis of FoEs

The research presented above was published in 2004 and included 17 public companies. An updated 2012 analysis consisted of 75 public companies split into four different tiers: highly conscious (elite), conscious, nearly conscious, and international. The "highly conscious" tier consists of 10 companies that embrace the four tenets of conscious capitalism. The "conscious" tier has 35 companies that embrace most aspects of conscious capitalism. These firms could improve one or two of the conscious capitalism tenets in order to be considered highly conscious

Figure 2

10-Year FoE Performance

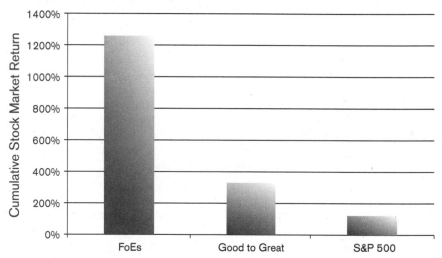

Source: Sisodia, R., Wolfe, D., and Sheth, J. (2007). *Firms of endearment: How world-class companies profit from passion and purpose.* Upper Saddle River, NJ: Wharton School Publishing, 137.

companies. The "nearly conscious" tier consists of 12 firms that had one or two larger issues in their performance and record of conduct, indicating issues they had with at least one important stakeholder group. Finally, the "international" tier consists of 18 companies with headquarters and operations located outside the United States. Represented countries include India, Germany, the United Kingdom, and Canada.

Method of Analysis in Updated Study

The analysis used the four tiers noted above, comparing each tier individually to the S&P 500, Dow Jones Industrial Average (DJIA), and the Russell 3000. An analysis was also performed combining the firms in the "conscious" and "highly conscious" tiers, comparing them to the same three indices. The analysis dates back to 1997, with separate analyses done on the 3-, 5-, 10-, and 15-year stock price performance of the selected firms. The study focused on the stock prices and beta of the selected firms, with the objective of duplicating the results found previously using a larger sample size and also showing the effects that different levels of consciousness have on the financial performance of a company. Essentially, the hypothesis is that FoEs provide superior returns than the overall market with less risk.

The stock price and dividend data was pulled from Bloomberg terminals and was used to calculate quarterly holding period returns from December 31, 1997, to December 31, 2012. For firms that have been publicly traded for less than 15 years, they were simply added into the analysis once public stock price data became available. This was done so that not having a stock price (return would be zero) would not drag down the returns for overall index. The quarterly returns were then averaged together to create an index for each tier of firms. The quarterly returns for the index were then compounded to account for reinvesting dividends. The betas were also pulled from Bloomberg for the individual firms using a linear stock price regression from December 31, 1997, to December 31, 2012, and then averaged together to create an index beta for each tier of firms.

Results of the Analysis

The results of the financial analysis affirmed the previously published results regarding FoEs, even with the expansion to a larger number of firms including international firms. Figures 3 and 4 illustrate the cumulative and annualized performance of each tier of the firms explained above, in comparison to the S&P 500, DJIA, and Russell 3000. It is interesting to note that the "elite FoEs" have the best performance of all the firms, with the "conscious" (second tier) firms lagging the first tier but vastly outperforming the major stock indices. Finally, the "nearly conscious" firms still triple the performance of the major indices.

Another interesting observation is that the "conscious international" firms also vastly outperform the market as a whole, validating that the model works

Figure 3

Results of Cumulative Performance of Tiered Firms

Cumulative Performance	15 Years	10 Years	5 Years	3 Years
Elite FoEs	2282.42%	498.81%	113.97%	98.40%
Conscious FoEs	1017.64%	305.03%	53.90%	47.94%
Combined FoEs	1271.90%	351.37%	67.69%	58.91%
Nearly Conscious	327.92%	195.30%	33.25%	45.41%
International FoEs	1109.64%	836.25%	39.20%	30.39%
S&P 500	98.11%	98.24%	8.55%	36.20%
DJIA	133.11%	102.31%	13.76%	36.14%
Russell 3000	106.96%	109.72%	10.61%	37.43%
Annualized Performance	**15 Years**	**10 Years**	**5 Years**	**3 Years**
Elite FoEs	23.54%	19.60%	16.43%	25.66%
Conscious FoEs	17.46%	15.01%	9.01%	13.95%
Combined FoEs	19.08%	16.27%	10.89%	16.69%
Nearly Conscious	10.18%	11.44%	5.91%	13.29%
International FoEs	18.08%	25.07%	6.84%	9.25%
S&P 500	4.66%	7.08%	1.65%	10.85%
DJIA	5.80%	7.30%	2.61%	10.83%
Russell 3000	4.97%	7.69%	2.04%	11.18%

Source: Sisodia, R., DWolfe, D., and Sheth, J. (2014). Firms of Endearment, 2nd ed. Upper Saddle River, NJ: Pearson Education.

internationally as well as domestically. It is also important to note the differences in returns over the different time periods. In the 3-year analysis, while the selected firms still outperform the major indices, they do so by a smaller margin than the 5-, 10-, and 15-year analyses, with the gaps widening the longer the analysis is performed. This further supports the argument that the conscious business model is effective over the long-term performance of a company, both financially and socially.

The paradox of profits holds true, as these firms do not pursue profit as their objective for being, as indicated previously, but rather pursue a higher purpose, enabling a more holistic view of what business can be. The argument that these firms cannot succeed financially is simply a fallacy, as evidenced by the analysis presented here, as ultimately all financial performance is enveloped in the stock price of a firm.

In the updated beta analysis, there is a slight diversion from the research presented previously. The FoEs analyzed in *Firms of Endearment* had a beta of 0.92, while the firms in the updated analysis have betas slightly higher than 1, as shown in Figure 5.

Figure 4

Cumulative Performance Summary Comparing Fund Indices

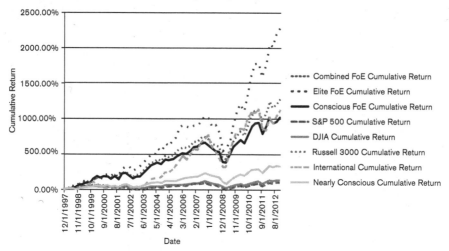

Figure 5

Beta of Indices

Elite FoEs	1.08
Conscious FoEs	1.05
Combined FoEs	1.07
Nearly Conscious	1.00

Source: John Warden's analysis.
Data from Bloomberg.

Although the betas of the firms are higher than the market average of 1, they are only slightly higher, and with their vast outperformance of the market, it is fair to say that investors in these firms will tolerate slightly higher volatility. Also, the beta is only one measure of risk, measuring volatility. A long-term investor seeking firms that outperform the market over 3, 5, and 10 years or more is not as concerned with volatility as a Wall Street trader seeking to take advantage of day-to-day price movements. Essentially the point to be made is that these firms carry little to no extra risk in comparison to the overall market and yet vastly outperform the market over the long term.

Conclusion

Conscious capitalism's business model is timely, even long overdue. Businesses should not be solely focused on profits but should adopt a more holistic approach to doing business. Conscious capitalism integrates all stakeholders, creating a greater pool of wealth for all involved in the ecosystem. Embracing conscious capitalism has proved to bode well for the companies that choose to do so. Conscious firms are healthy, growing businesses able to survive in the long term, outperform competitors, and generate outstanding returns in the stock market. Through the free markets and competition mechanisms of free-enterprise capitalism, it is my belief that firms embracing conscious capitalism will rise further to the top, and more companies will embrace the model as it becomes the only way to compete in the marketplace with shifting dynamics, wants, and needs. Conscious capitalism is the future of business.

Questions for Discussion

1. What are the reasons conscious capitalism resurfaced as an important topic in the press?
2. What are the basic principles and tenets of Mackey and Sisodia's book and the conscious capitalism movement that make it different from other related movements and similar topics?
3. What does ethics have to do with conscious capitalism as presented by Mackey and Sisodia?
4. Why is conscious capitalism not just a theory?
5. What do research results from the updated study in the article show?

Sources

This case was developed from material contained in the following sources:

Collins, J. (2001). *Good to Great*. New York: HarperCollins.

EdSitement. (n.d.). The Industrial Age in America: Robber barons and captains of industry. http://edsitement.neh.gov/lesson-plan/industrial-age-america-robber -barons-and-captains-industry.

Freeman, R. E., Velamuri, S. R., and Moriarty, B. (2006). Bridge Paper. *Company stakeholder responsibility: A new approach to CSR*. Business Roundtable Institute for Corporate Ethics. Charlottesville, Virginia. https://rise-leaders.com/wp-content /uploads/2018/11/stakeholder-responsibility-white-paper-3.8.0-2015.06.02-14 .58.51.pdf.

Mackey, J. (2007). Conscious capitalism: Creating a new paradigm for business. *WholeFoodsMarket.com*. https://www.wholefoodsmarket.com/tips-and-ideas/archive/conscious-capitalism-creating-new-paradigm-for-c2-a0business.

Mackey, J. (2012, May 22–23). Whole Foods Market's conscious culture (Keynote address). Conscious Capitalism Institute. Bentley University, Waltham, MA, 21.

Meyer, C., and Kirby, J. (2012, May 22–23). Standing on the sun: The future of capitalism (Keynote address). Conscious Capitalism Institute. Bentley University, Waltham, MA.

Murray, A. (2013, January 16). Chicken soup for a Davos soul. *WSJ.com*. http://online.wsj.com/news/articles/SB10001424127887324235104578243673073627726.

Sadar, A. (2013). Book review: Conscious capitalism. *Washington Times*. http://www.washingtontimes.com/news/2013/mar/20/book-review-conscious-capitalism/.

Sisodia, R. (2012, May 22–23). Conscious cultures: Building a flourishing business on love and care (Keynote address). Conscious Capitalism Institute. Bentley University, Waltham, MA.

Sisodia, R., and Mackey, J. (2013). *Conscious capitalism: Liberating the heroic spirit of business*. Cambridge, MA: Harvard Business Press.

Sisodia, R., Wolfe, D. B., and Sheth, J. (2007). *Firms of endearment: How world-class companies profit from passion and purpose*. Upper Saddle River, NJ: Prentice Hall.

Case 11

Uber and the Ride-Sharing Economy

In just over 11 years since its founding in March 2009, Uber transformed from a start-up to a company that has $65.6 billion in market cap as of October 9, 2020. Uber used technological innovation to create a new economy in ride-sharing, allowing drivers to earn more money on the side by being able to work their own hours and riders to go through a more efficient process in finding a ride from point A to point B. The creation of the Uber app to connect drivers and riders permanently disrupted the taxi industry, and also added value to society as a whole.

Stakeholder Analysis

Key stakeholders at Uber include the drivers (employees), riders (customers), investors, regulators, and competitors, which include traditional taxicab services and other ride-share companies like Lyft. The drivers are directly affected by rate changes dictated by the corporate office and also make the company what it is today. Without the sheer number of people willing to sign up to be drivers, it would be impossible for Uber to exist. The next group of stakeholders are the riders or customers who pay for Uber's services. Without the riders, Uber would not be able to operate; riders/customers determine the demand of the market. The riders are also directly impacted by the decisions that Uber makes, such as rate increases per ride and surge pricing. Thirdly, the local economies benefit from the service of Uber because it is a source of additional income for drivers, especially those who are lower-middle to middle class. Additionally, the customers stimulate the economy by paying for Uber rides.

Regulators are responsible to enforce the rules and regulations that Uber must follow. There are entire divisions of government tied to Uber, or more generally the ride-sharing industry, and how Uber performs. These are the groups that are fighting to classify drivers as employees and to make sure that Uber is following the safety regulations needed to be in the public transportation space.

Next, the investors and corporate employees of Uber are important stakeholders. The investors can be considered the original stakeholders because they provide capital to the firm to keep it liquid enough; their only concerns are making a profit on their returns. Substantial investors have a voice in making management decisions to ensure that the company is going in the right direction.

Corporate employees are stakeholders because they make these management decisions and handle the day-to-day operations. There are many different departments in charge of updating the app, providing cybersecurity, doing financial analysis for the investors, and providing customer support. These two groups of people have a direct stake in the success of Uber.

Finally, Uber's last stakeholder is its competitors, specifically Lyft and the taxi industry. The competition is directly tied to its performance, but in different ways. Although Uber holds the leading market share of 71 percent (as of August 2020), Lyft is the main competitor in this industry. Lyft tries to emulate and improve on what Uber was able to do, so Uber must constantly be aware of news from Lyft.

Because both Lyft and Uber operate in the same ride-share industry, the state of this industry determines its overall performance. Even though they are competing for market share, they both need this industry to be successful. The taxi industry is also looking to update its business model and take back its share. The taxi industry failed and did not act fast in integrating technology, which ultimately led to its decline. If taxicab operators do not find a way to lower their prices to compete with the ride-share services, Uber and Lyft will run them out of business. The taxi industry can be viewed as a stakeholder of Uber because it needs to conduct a competitive analysis of Uber to be able to compete.

Ride-Sharing Industry Issues

As successful as Uber has been so far, it has not come without controversy. Two very big issues that plague not only Uber but the industry itself are employee rights and surge pricing. First, Uber and the industry overall have been criticized for the treatment of their drivers. Drivers are technically classified as independent contractors instead of employees, and as such they are not eligible for benefits, including health care or paid time off. "Uber has affirmed that all drivers on its platform are partners and must be considered as independent contractors. However, the company has faced various legal proceedings across the world wherein authorities belonging to different legal fields have argued that the drivers should be qualified as employees" (Reis and Chand, 2020). There have also been cases brought forward by drivers who have stated they earn less than minimum wage and are ultimately not being compensated properly for their time. "Under new rules, which [went] into effect in January 2019, companies are required to pay drivers $26.51 an hour in gross pay, or $17.22 after expenses. This may be slightly higher than the $15 minimum wage that (New York City) requires all employers to adhere to by the end of next year, but is still considered to be as equivalent because drivers are independent contractors. About 85 percent of ride-hailing drivers currently make less than the minimum."

Second, the ride-sharing industry has come under fire for "surge pricing," which is when pricing is determined based on the number of drivers available and the number of riders requesting rides. During times of low supply of drivers, such as New Year's Eve or during a hurricane, prices have been known to skyrocket for the riders. While some people have argued that this is a supply-and-demand issue, others are opposed to this pricing strategy because of the greed behind it.

Controversy at Uber

There has been no shortage of ethical and legal issues that Uber has faced. Since 2013, Uber had had at least one major ethical scandal every year related to passenger safety, security of drivers, and privacy issues. The first scandal was in 2013, only four years after the company was founded. In September 2013, a passenger accused an Uber driver of choking her. The driver was accused of grabbing her out of the car by her throat because she was kissing her husband (Moss, 2013). In 2014, an Uber driver who was accused of assault was found to have a criminal record. The driver had felony and misdemeanor charges and at least one felony conviction involving prison time (Taylor, Kate). These two examples bring into question the validity of Uber's background checks as the company is potentially putting passengers at risk.

In 2015, French taxi drivers slammed Uber as "economic terrorism" because Uber's low prices and flexible hours were not in line with French law (Taylor, Kate). When operating in other countries, it is important to understand their laws and regulations and act in a way that does not violate their laws. In 2016, Uber paid $28.5 million to end a lawsuit about safety ads (Taylor, Kate). Uber was accused of misleading customers about safety practices and agreed to refrain from using superlatives when describing background checks. In 2017, a female engineer who used to work at Uber published a blog post about sexual harassment and gender inequality at the company, and Travis Kalanick—the original cofounder and CEO of Uber—was caught fighting with an Uber driver on camera (Taylor, Kate). Here, the CEO's bad behavior is setting up a bad culture for the rest of the organization. When employees cannot look up to their CEO and other leaders in the company, they are less likely to follow company rules and regulations, creating a toxic work environment for all. In 2018, an Uber self-driving car killed a pedestrian, and over 100 U.S. Uber drivers had been accused of sexual assault or abuse of passengers (Taylor, Kate). Over the years the accusations of the sexual assault cases have been rising, which makes one question how much Uber is doing to protect its drivers and its riders. These sexual harassment and assault cases may have been due to the leadership of Kalanick at the time.

Uber addressed its social responsibility and its environmental impact by creating Uber Pool. Uber Pool allows people to share rides for a discount. These shared trips means less environmental impact per person while creating affordable means of transportation for people. Also, Uber is working on a pilot project to go green by offering rides in all-electric or hybrid cars in Paris and Lisbon by 2025 (Uber.com, Sustainability). These are two ways in which Uber is acting toward the betterment of the community.

Uber specifically found itself in the middle of a corporate scandal back in 2017 when the sexual harassment allegations came to light. These claims then shed light on a number of other issues happening at Uber, highlighting deep problems of company culture at the firm. All of these complaints ended up with employees being fired, as well as the forced resignation of the CEO and a few other executives. Uber faced a huge backlash from the public, who started a movement called #DeleteUber. "Hundreds of thousands of customers deleted the ride-hailing app and deactivated their accounts 'within days' of the campaign's launch across social media." This brings into consideration some of the challenges that firms are beginning to experience with the pressure to be ethically responsible in this age of technology. Because technology allows information to be spread rapidly, companies are constantly being monitored by the public.

Uber has always classified its drivers as contractors, which excludes them from being eligible to receive benefits such as health care or retirement funds.

This, in turn, allows the company to save tremendous amounts of money. Uber also pushes all of the cost of owning and insuring the vehicle out onto the driver as well. As a defense to this strategy, Uber has continually claimed that it is just connecting riders with drivers and taking a fee for doing so. In previous cases, after factoring in depreciation on the vehicle, it has been said that drivers are earning less than minimum wage without the possibility of benefits.

Additionally, Uber was accused of entering new markets and testing local governments to see if the company will be shut down or intentionally trying to stall new regulation. The following is an extended quote from a news article in 2017 that I believe summarizes the issue. "On September 22, Uber . . . hit a major roadblock in Britain. Transport for London [TfL], the capital's main transportation agency, which regulates the taxi cab industry, refused to renew the license that allowed Uber to operate in the metropolitan area. In a statement, TfL said that Uber demonstrates a 'lack of corporate responsibility in relation to a number of issues which have potential public safety and security implications.'" Additionally, the taxi industry has stated that Uber is using a loophole to avoid regulations, and the drivers are operating illegal taxi cabs. This, in turn, has driven down the cost of the medallions for cabs and even forced some of them into bankruptcy. Finally, after all of the scandals Uber has faced and after Travis Kalanick resigned as CEO, Dara Khosrowshahi became the new CEO in 2017. Khosrowshahi knew that he needed to make major changes to the corporate culture and work to fix its unethical image. So the issue then stands: Has Uber been able to rebrand the company toward prioritizing corporate social responsibility since then?

Covid-19 Impact

Uber still faces numerous ethical and legal problems. Uber drivers have made some headway in the UK. On March 17, 2021, the UK court told Uber it has to classify drivers as workers and give pension and holiday pay. In 2019, California passed the AB5 law, which requires the "gig companies," including Uber, to re-classify them as employees.

Furthermore, COVID-19 especially affected the ride-sharing economy, as fewer people were requesting rides "On May 7, [2020] Uber reported a $2.9 billion loss during the pandemic in the first quarter, a per-share loss of $1.70" (Goldstein, 2020). In response to the pandemic, ride-sharing companies already took steps at the beginning of the pandemic to control their costs and deal with the decrease in users across the board. "Due to the decline in customers, Uber announced that it will lay off 3,700 employees, which represents roughly 14 percent of its workforce, and enacted a hiring freeze. Lyft laid off about 1,000 people and placed 288 employees on furlough." If this trend continues, it could spell disaster for all stakeholders involved. Drivers may be less willing to let strangers into their cars, and riders may be less willing to get into a stranger's car. Local economies will suffer as folks have less disposable income because they have to pay more money now to get around or they have to drive themselves (e.g., if someone who lives downtown had to buy a car). Regulators would no longer have anything to regulate, and the competition would be under similar pressure to stay alive. Investors and corporate employees would suffer due to devaluation in the firm and continued layoffs affecting their livelihoods.

Uber and the ride-sharing industry are going to have to adapt in the coming years to keep their business models alive. Predictions for Uber and Lyft in the post-Covid-19 world are split. Some prognosticators see signs that these companies will make a roaring comeback from pent-up demand. Other business observers see a continuing legal battle between drivers and their bosses. In the long term, it may also be that driverless cars send this industry into history.

Questions for Discussion

1. What are the sources of Uber's continuing problems to "normalize" into a respectable company?
2. Who are Uber's stakeholders, and what are the main issues each faces?
3. Describe Uber's issues from an ethical perspective.
4. What does it mean for Uber to be a "sharing economy" company, and how does this type of company have any responsibilities to be ethical beyond what other companies have? Explain.

Sources

This case was developed from material contained in the following sources:

Bloodworth, J. (2017, October 7). How Uber stalled in London. *The New York Review of Books*. https://www.nybooks.com/daily/2017/10/07/how-uber-stalled-in -london/.

Brustein, J. (2018, December 4). New York sets nation's first minimum wage for Uber, Lyft drivers. *Bloomberg*. https://www.bloomberg.com/news/articles/2018-12-04 /new-york-sets-nation-s-first-minimum-wage-for-uber-lyft-drivers.

Chand, V., and Reis, A. (2020, April 3). Uber drivers: employees or independent contractors? *Wolters Kluwer International Tax Blog*. http://kluwertaxblog.com /2020/04/03/uber-drivers-employees-or-independent-contractors/?doing_wp_ cron=1594061643.4539089202880859375000#:~:text=Uber%20has%20 affirmed%20that%20all,should%20be%20qualified%20as%20employees.

Goldstein, M. (2020, July 27). What is the future for Uber and Lyft after the pandemic? *Forbes*. https://www.forbes.com/sites/michaelgoldstein/2020/07/27 /what-is-the-future-for-uber-and-lyft--after-the-pandemic/?sh=149d47ac3bc8.

Helling, B. (2020, June 22). Uber surge pricing: How it works and how to avoid it. *Ridester*. https://www.ridester.com/surge-pricing-explained/#:~:text=On%20 the%20average%20weekday%2C%20Uber,Holidays%20can%20also%20 increase%20demand.

Iqbal, M. (2020, July 8). Uber revenue and usage statistics (2020). *Business of Apps*. https://www.businessofapps.com/data/uber-statistics/.

Kelly, J. (2020, May 8). Uber and Lyft are on a collision course with the effects of Covid-19 and new California lawsuit that could crush their business model. *Forbes*. https://www.forbes.com/sites/jackkelly/2020/05/08/uber-and-lyft-are-on-a -collision-course-with-the-effects-of-covid-19-and-new-california-lawsuit-that -could-crush-their-business-model/#dd8b47a20d41.

Leskin, P. (2019, April 11). Uber says the #DeleteUber movement led to "hundreds of thousands" of people quitting the app. *Business Insider*. https://www.business

insider.com/uber-deleteuber-protest-hundreds-of-thousands-quit-app-2019
-4#:~:text=In%20its%20paperwork%2C%20Uber%20said,campaign's%20
launch%20across%20social%20media.&text=The%20%23DeleteUber%20
movement%20took%20social,Trump%20announced%20his%20travel%20ban.

Moss, C. (2013). Uber CEO defends his company after a driver is accused of assault-
ing a passenger. https://www.businessinsider.com/ubers-ceo-travis-kalanick
-defends-driver-in-assault-2013-9.

Reis, A., and Chand, V. (2020). Uber drivers: Employees or independent contractors?
Kluwer International Tax Blog. http://kluwertaxblog.com/2020/04/03/uber-drivers
-employees-or-independent-contractors/.

Uber.com. (n.d.). Sustainability. https://www.uber.com/us/en/about/sustainability/.

Case 12

The Crisis at Wells Fargo Bank: Then and Now

Charles Scharf, the third chief executive of Wells Fargo in just four years since the firm's 2016 crisis, told Congress in March 2020 that "there's much the bank needs to do to fix its cultural problems, and isn't expecting it to be done until 2021" (Marketwatch, 2020). The company paid $3 billion in February 2020 for past illegal sales practices, in addition to $1.2 billion in fines also previously paid. Moreover, the company was still restricted by the Federal Reserve to grow past a $1.95 trillion asset cap until it fixed its cultural problems (Truong, 2020). What happened at Wells Fargo in 2016, and before, and why are issues still lingering with this once name-brand firm?

Wells Fargo: Flashback

Wells Fargo was founded in 1852, offering banking and express services to individuals in California. By 1905, banking had been established as a separate division within the company. Wells Fargo continued to grow throughout the decades by acquiring other banks in the United States. In 2015, the company was a diversified banking and financial services firm with over $1.8 trillion in assets.

Wells Fargo had a reputation for sound management. In 2013, American Banker named then Wells Fargo CEO John Stumpf as "Banker of the Year," and Carrie Tolstedt, head of the retail division, was named to the "Most Powerful Woman in Banking" list. In addition to its strong management, Wells Fargo was also known for allowing collective decision making among senior leaders. One former executive even stated that "no one person runs Wells Fargo and no one person ever will" (Tayan, 2019). Although Wells Fargo used collective decision making, all senior leaders were individually responsible for ensuring that proper practices were followed in their divisions.

The Vision and Shortsightedness

Wells Fargo's vision is to "satisfy our customers' needs and help them succeed financially" (Tayan, 2019). According to CEO Stumpf, vision is key to its culture: "[Our vision] is at the center of our culture, it's important to our success, and frankly, it's been probably the most significant contributor to our long-term performance" (Gujarathi and Barua, 2017).

However, in 2013, rumors circulated that Wells Fargo employees in Southern California were engaging in aggressive tactics to meet their daily cross-selling targets (Tayan, 2019). Cross-selling was how the firm deepened relationships in the community. The practice consisted of selling other financial services and products to existing customers rather than recruiting new ones. Cross-selling was cheaper than recruiting new customers and allowed Wells Fargo to increase its current customer retention rate.

Richard Kovacevich, the CEO of Wells Fargo before Stumpf, referred to cross-selling as "needs based selling" and said that it was Wells Fargo's most important strategy. When Stumpf became CEO, he continued to place emphasis on cross-selling and developed incentives to do so. Financial incentives offered to employees for cross-selling were significant. Branch employees could earn up to $2,000 per quarter while district managers could receive up to $20,000 a year in bonuses (Gujarathi and Barua, 2017).

Senior management had placed so much emphasis on cross-selling that quotas were implemented for the number and type of products to be sold by employees (Gujarathi and Barua, 2017). To ensure that cross-selling quotas were met, branch managers pushed down hourly quotas to employees and routinely monitored their progress to meet those quotas. Failure to meet goals could and did result in employees being publicly chastised by senior leaders. Widespread pressures to meet unrealistic sales targets that were adopted and enforced in financial statements by senior managers contributed to Wells Fargo's crisis. An employee wrote to the chief executive's office and another senior leader in 2013, saying, "I was in the 1991 Gulf War. . . . This is sad and hard for me to say, but I had less stress in the 1991 Gulf War than working for Wells Fargo" (Merle, 2020).

The Sales Strategy Unravels

In later court filings, prosecutors revealed that the bank hid the problem from investors by changing the public description of its sales practices over several years, with the intention of not letting investors know about the problems with cross-selling strategy that senior executives had uncovered (Flitter, 2020).

Wells Fargo's "Sales Quality Manual" stated that customer consent was needed for each service offering and that splitting customers' deposits and opening multiple accounts was a violation of sales integrity (Gujarathi and Barua, 2017). Even with written standards in the firm's quality manual, senior management continued to push unrealistic quotas to branch managers. Not only was the "tone at the top" corrupt in supporting the adoption and enforcement of these draconian sales targets and policies, but reporting false results to shareholders and treating clients with disdain was common practice. Several employees further down the organization also suffered.

Former employees claimed that despite a no-retaliation policy, they were dismissed after reporting unethical behavior and practices. For example, one employee, Yesenia Guitron, reported on the firm's ethics hotline that unrealistic sales quotas encouraged forgery. She was later terminated for insubordination. Another employee, Mr. Bado, a former Wells Fargo banker in Pennsylvania, called the ethics hotline to report unethical sales and was terminated for tardiness. Still another, Mr. Johnson, reported that his manager asked him to open accounts for members of his family without their knowledge. Mr. Johnson was also later terminated for not meeting expectations (Gujarathi and Barua, 2017). Other findings of such practices showed that Ms. Toldstedt, a Wells Fargo officer during that period, ignored concerns that other executives had raised about cross-selling, lied to regulators and Wells Fargo's board, and tightly controlled the bank's public disclosures (Flitter, 2020).

The Fraud Finally Exposed

A timeline of the fraud showed the following: On December 13, 2013, a *Los Angeles Times* investigation revealed—using then employees' internal bank documents, court records, and interviews—the effects their supervisors' pressure had on them to start unnecessary "checking, savings and credit card accounts without customers' permission and forged signatures" (Dwyer, 2017).

On May 4, 2015, again this newspaper's investigation revealed that then-Los Angeles City Attorney Mike Feuer filed a lawsuit in civil court after his search into the issues. A domino effect occurred when the Consumer Financial Protection Bureau and the Office of the Comptroller of the Currency started their probes that showed Wells Fargo had fired 1,500 employees for opening 2 million unauthorized accounts.

On September 8, 2016, Wells Fargo agreed to pay $185 million in fines to regulators and $5 million in refunds to customers; on September 16, 2016, a class action lawsuit was filed in the U.S. District Court in Utah, charging Wells Fargo bank with invasion of privacy, fraud, negligence, and breach of contract. Several days later on September 27, 2016, "six former Wells Fargo employees file a class action lawsuit in federal court, seeking $7.2 billion for those who they say were fired or demoted after refusing to open fake accounts. Louis Supina, of Lower Macungie, says he and his wife, Mary, were among the thousands of unwitting consumers who had bank accounts secretly opened in their names by Wells Fargo" (Dwyer, 2017). On July 10, 2017, in San Francisco, a U.S. District Court judge approved a settlement that would compensate those customers who had unauthorized accounts created in their name.

Wells Fargo CEO John Stumpf resigned on October 12, 2016, and was replaced by Timothy J. Sloan, "an insider who was named president of the company in 2015" (Dwyer, 2017). The bank then settled a class action lawsuit totaling $142 million, with additional claims in 10 other class action lawsuits, designed to compensate customers with unauthorized accounts from May 2002 (Dwyer, 2017).

The Senate Hearing

During the U.S. Senate hearing, no leader from Wells Fargo took ownership of the cross-selling scandal. Stumpf seemed pleased that only 1 percent of employees were terminated because of the scandal, seemingly happy that 99 percent were doing the right thing. Chief financial officer Tim Sloan stated: "I'm not aware of any overbearing sales culture." Another executive stated: "The story line is worse than the economics at this point" (Tayan, 2019).

Following the hearing, some changes were made at Wells Fargo. The CEO and board member positions were separated. An independent investigation was conducted and resulted in John Stumpf resigning and Tim Sloan being named the new CEO. In addition, $47.3 million in outstanding stock options were taken back from Tolstedt, and $28 million from Stumpf were also clawed back. These changes had little effect on the culture inside Wells Fargo.

In 2017, Wells Fargo increased its estimate of the number of potentially un-authorized consumer accounts to 3.5 million. In 2018, the Federal Reserve Board put a strict limit on the company's assets because of widespread consumer abuses. Timothy Sloan abruptly stepped down as CEO; and Charles Scharf, an outsider, was Sloan's replacement.

Wells Fargo continues to stay in the headlines for all the wrong reasons. In 2020, the Treasury Department released a report and said that the community bank business model "imposed intentionally unreasonable sales goals and unrea-sonable pressure on its employees to meet those goals and fostered an atmo-sphere that perpetuated improper and illegal conduct" (Peters, 2020). The bank was fined $25 million, and Stumpf was fined $17.5 million and agreed to a lifetime ban from working in banking. Civil cases have been filed against five other employ-ees, including Toldstedt, who was fined $25 million (Merle, 2020). Since the alle-gations came to light, the bank has also admitted to charging mortgage customers unnecessary fees and forcing auto loan borrowers to buy insurance they did not need (Flitter, 2020). "As part of the settlements, the former executives did not ad-mit or deny wrongdoing, but agreed to cooperate with the OCC [Office of the Comptroller of the Currency] in any investigation, litigation or administrative pro-ceeding related to sales practices misconduct at the bank" (Truong, 2020). Three separate cities sued the bank for giving unfavorable mortgage terms to Black and Latino voters, and in 2020, current CEO Charles Scharf told employees that the bank had failed to diversify its executive core because "the unfortunate reality is that there is a very limited pool of Black talent to recruit from" (Peters, 2020).

Next Steps

In order to right the stagecoach, Wells Fargo needs to change the culture as well as the perception of the company. Since culture is a strong indicator of future performance, it is a leader's responsibility to promote a cohesive culture that will position the organization for future success. The leader will need to be coura-geous, establish a sense of urgency, and be able to articulate the vision for the future. In Wells Fargo's case, the progress of repairing its image has been slowed by the company's recent admission of mistakenly foreclosing on hundreds of cli-ents and repossessing the cars of thousands of others (Merle, 2020).

The sense of urgency for creating change must start at the top. Although there is no indication that the board of directors knew about the cross-selling scam, they were tasked with the duty of providing oversight and failed to do so. The board should not be able to hide behind their statements that they were misled. Keeping the board intact or with only superficial changes will prohibit the neces-sary lasting change that Wells Fargo needs.

The culture that permeated throughout the bank went through many levels. By default, any senior-level executive who was with the company during the scan-dal will not have the trust of associates to change the culture. A transformational outside leader is needed to lead the change.

Finally, Wells Fargo needs to acknowledge and admit to wrongdoing and un-ethical behavior. From the Senate hearings to recent events, Wells Fargo is giving the perception that the company did not do anything wrong; it was just a few bad apples who were eventually terminated. Without the acknowledgment of wrongdoing, employees and the public will not believe in any actions the company wishes to take.

It has yet to be seen if Charles Scharf is the transformational leader needed to right the stagecoach. In January 2020, Scharf told analysts that he is spending nearly all of his time addressing the regulatory headaches that have dogged Wells Fargo. "We are committing all necessary resources to ensure that nothing like this happens again, while also driving Wells Fargo forward" (Merle, 2020). Considering his comments about the recruitment of Black executives, Scharf is continuing to tarnish the reputation of the company instead of galvanizing the workforce. A Wells Fargo spokeswoman said in a statement, "We are consistent with our belief that we should hold ourselves and individuals accountable and that significant parts of the operating model of our Community Bank were flawed at that time. At the time of the sales practices issues, the company did not have in place the appropriate people, structure, processes, controls, or culture to prevent the inappropriate conduct." She continued, "Over the past four years, the bank has made fundamental changes in its business model, compensation programs, leadership, and governance. We are committing all necessary resources to ensure that we operate with the strongest business practices and controls, maintain the highest level of integrity, and have in place the appropriate culture. The company is different today, and we are doing what's necessary to regain the trust of all stakeholders" (Truong, 2020).

Concluding Comments

The brand of Wells Fargo was once associated with possibility, strength, community, and heritage. Today it is still associated in part with scandal. While the company's stock shares have almost kept pace with its peers, Citi and JPMorgan, as of April 2021, its "executive pay plan won approval . . . from a scant 57% of shareholders, based on a preliminary count at the lender's annual meeting—a level so low that it's tantamount to failure" (Foley, 2021). Rebuilding trust will take time, but without company cultural and operational transformation and real changes in its leadership and daily practices, its reputation remains at risk.

Questions for Discussion

1. What went wrong at Wells Fargo that led to the crisis that was exposed?
2. Who was to blame, and why?
3. What was "unethical" as well as illegal about the practices of Wells Fargo's officers?
4. What changes were recommended to get the company back on track?

Sources

This case was developed from material contained in the following sources:

Downdector.com. (2020, December 1). Problems at Wells Fargo. https://downdetector.com/status/wells-fargo/news/351455-problems-at-wells-fargo/.

Dwyer, K. (2017, August 2). Timeline: How the Wells Fargo scandals unfolded. *The Morning Call*. https://www.mcall.com/business/mc-biz-wells-fargo-timeline -20170802-story.html.

Flitter, E. (2020, February 21). The price of Wells Fargo's fake account scandal grows by $3 billion. *New York Times*. https://www.nytimes.com/2020/02/21/business /wells-fargo-settlement.html.

Foley, J. (2021, April 27). Running Wells Fargo just got even more thankless. *Reuters*. https://www.reuters.com/breakingviews/running-wells-fargo-just-got-even-more -thankless-2021-04-27/.

Gujarathi, M. R., and Barua, S. (2017, Spring). Wells Fargo: Setting the stagecoach thundering again. *North American Case Research Association*, *37(2)*.

Marketwatch. (2020, March 10). New Wells Fargo CEO says the bank's issues won't be fixed until 2021. https://www.marketwatch.com/story/new-wells-fargo-ceo-says -the-banks-issues-wont-be-fixed-until-2021-2020-03-10.

Merle, R. (2020, February 21). Wells Fargo reaches $3 billion settlement with DOJ, SEC over fake-accounts scandal. *Washington Post*. https://www.washingtonpost .com/business/2020/02/21/wells-fargo-fake-accounts-settlement/.

Peters, J. (2020, November 28). How Wells Fargo became synonymous with scandal. *Slate*. slate.com/business/2020/11/wells-fargo-scandal-history-karen-attiah.html.

Reuters. (2020, April 1). Prosecutors probe former Wells Fargo exec over scandal: sources. *Business Insurance*. https://www.businessinsurance.com/article /20200401/NEWS06/912333810/Prosecutors-probe-former-Wells-Fargo-exec -over-scandal-sources-Carrie-Tolstedt#:~:text=Tolstedt.-,Ms.,one%20of%20 the%20sources%20said.

Tayan, B. (2019, January 8). The Wells Fargo cross-selling scandal. SSRN, papers. ssrn.com/sol3/papers.cfm?abstract_id=2879102.

Truong, K. (2020, September 23). Three more Wells Fargo execs fined, one banned in fake accounts scandal. *San Francisco Business Times*. https://www.bizjournals .com/sanfrancisco/news/2020/09/23/wells-fargo-occ-fake-accounts -settlement.html.

Notes

1. Popper, N. (2020, February 2). Ransomware attacks grow, crippling cities and businesses. *New York Times*. https://www.nytimes.com/2020/02/09/technology/ransomware-attacks.html?auth=login-email&login=email.

2. TJX's *V.A.L.U.E: Corporate social responsibility report 2013* is available at https://www.tjx.com/docs/default-source/default-document-library/TJX2013_CSR_online.pdf. See also Dividend Channel. (2013). TJX Companies, now #95 largest company, surpassing Capital One Financial. *Forbes.com*. http://www.forbes.com/sites/dividendchannel/2013/09/18/tjx-companies-now-95-largest-company-surpassing-capital-one-financial/.

3. The TJX Companies, Inc. victimized by computer systems intrusion; provides information to help protect customers. (2007, January 17). *Business Wire News*.

4. Visa fines TJX credit card processor. (2007, October 29). *SC Magazine*.

5. Lemos, R. (2007, March 30). TJX theft tops 45.6 million card numbers. *SecurityFocus*. http://www.securityfocus.com/news/11455.

6. Haggerty, N.R.D., and Ramasastry, C. S. (2008, March 12). *Case analysis: Security breach at TJX*. Harvard Business Publishing.

7. Kerber, R. (2008, August 21). Suspect named in TJX credit card probe. *Boston.com*. http://www.boston.com/business/personalfinance/articles/2007/08/21/suspect_named_in_tjx_credit_card_probe/.

8. Goodin, D. (2008, May 13). TJX credit card heist suspect, 2 others, accused of new scam. *Register*. http://www.theregister.co.uk/2008/05/13/trio_accused_in_carding_scam/.

9. Haggerty and Ramasastry (2008).

10. The TJX Companies, Inc. reports strong second quarter FY08 operating results; Estimates liability from computer systems intrusion(s). (2007, August 14). *Business Wire News*.

11. Luna, T. (2015, October 7). TJX CEO Carol Meyrowitz is exiting in style. *Boston Globe*. https://www.bostonglobe.com/business/2015/10/07/tjx-says-herrman-succeed-meyrowitz-chief-executive-officer/y4dEENIWTipCPmRe4nyOvJ/story.html.

12. Bangemen, E. (2007, May 6). Blame for record-breaking credit card data theft laid at the feet of WEP. *Ars Technica*. http://arstechnica.com/news.ars/post/20070506-blame-for-record-breaking-credit-card-data-theft-laid-at-the-feet-of-wep.html.

13. Lemos (2007), op. cit.

14. Anderson, M. and Chapman, M. (2009, June 23). TJX reaches settlement with states on data theft. *ABC News*. https://abcnews.go.com/Technology/story?id=7912705&page=1.

15. The TJX Companies, Inc. (n.d.). Code of ethics for TJX executives. http://www.tjx.com/files/pdf/corp_resp/Code%20of%20Ethics%20for%20TJX%20Executives.pdf.

16. Quotation from Komiya, K. (2020). A majority of consumers expect brands to take a stand on issues before purchasing, survey finds. https://www.barrons.com/articles/a-majority-of-consumers-expect-brands-to-take-a-stand-on-issues-before-purchasing-survey-finds-51594143666; Schooley, S. (2021, March 18). What is corporate social responsibility? *Business News Daily*. https://www.businessnewsdaily.com/4679-corporate-social-responsibility.html.

17. HRM's role in corporate social and environmental sustainability. (n.d.). Society for Human Resource Management. https://www.shrm.org/hr-today/trends-and-forecasting/special-reports-and-expert-views/Documents/Corporate-Social-Environmental-Sustainability.pdf, accessed March 26, 2021.

18. Widman, J. (2011, March 12). 10 massive security breaches. *InformationWeek IT Network Dark Reading*. https://www.darkreading.com/attacks-and-breaches/10-massive-secu-rity-breaches/d/d-id/1096539?piddl_msgorder=thrd&page_number=8.

19. Krebs on Security. (2020, August 26). Confessions of an ID theft kingpin: Part 1. https://krebsonsecurity.com/tag/court-ventures/.

20. Goodin, D. (2013, July 25). "NASDAQ is owned." Five men charged in largest financial hack ever. *Ars Technica*. https://arstechnica.com/information-technology/2013/07/nasdaq-is-owned-five-men-charged-in-largest-financial-hack-ever.

21. Finkle, J., and Seetharman, D. (2014, May 27). Cyber thieves took data on 145 million eBay customers by hacking 3 corporate employees. *Business Insider*. https://www.businessinsider.com/cyber-thieves-took-data-on-145-million-ebay-customers-by-hacking-3-corporate-employees-2014-5.

22. Riley, M., Robertson, J., and Sharpe, A. (2017, September 29). The Equifax hack has the hallmarks of state-sponsored pros. *Bloomberg Businessweek*. https://www.bloomberg.com/news/features/2017-09-29/the-equifax-hack-has-all-the-hallmarks-of-state-sponsored-pros.

23. Vijayan, J. (2014, February 6). Target breach happened because of a basic network segmentation error. *Computer World*. https://www.computerworld.com/article/2487425/target-breach-happened-because-of-a-basic-network-segmentation-error.html.

24. Payments Next. (n.d.). 17 biggest payments industry data breaches with highest impact. https://paymentsnext.com/17-biggest-payments-industry-data-breaches-with-highest-impact/, accessed February 1, 2021.

25. Payments Next. (n.d.), op. cit. See also Bort, J. (2014, December 19). How the hackers broke into Sony and why it could happen to any company. *Business Insider*. https://www.businessinsider.com/how-the-hackers-broke-into-sony-2014-12.

26. Chickowski, E. (2016, May 3). 10 biggest mega breaches of the past 10 years. TJX. Dark Reading. https://www.darkreading.com/endpoint/10-biggest-mega-breaches-of-the-past-10-years/d/d-id/1325374?image_number=3

27. Leyden, J. (2014, December 23). JPMorgan Chase mega-hack was a simple two-factor auth fail. *The Register*. https://www.theregister.com/2014/12/23/jpmorgan_breach_probe_latest/#:~:text=Bank%20bods%20didn't%20follow%20security%20101%2C%20mayhem%20happened&text=Hackers%20broke%20into%20JPMorgan's%20network,authentication%20on%20an%20overlooked%20server.

28. Payments Next. (n.d.), op. cit.

29. Szwajkowski, E. (2000, December). Simplifying the principles of stakeholder management: The three most important principles. *Business and Society, 39(4)*, 381. Other advocates of this interpretation of Smith's views include Bishop, J. (1995). Adam Smith's invisible hand argument. *Journal of Business Ethics, 14*, 165; Rothchild, E. (1994). Adam Smith and the invisible hand. *AEA Papers and Proceedings, 8(2)*, 312–322; and Winch, D. (1997). Adam Smith's problems and ours. *Scottish Journal of Political Economy, 44*, 384–402.

30. Szwajkowski (2000), op. cit., 381.

31. Friedman, M. (1970, September 13). Social responsibility of business is to increase its profits. *New York Times Magazine*. 122–136.

32. Ibid.

33. See Seabury, C. (2020, February 8). The cost of free markets. *Investopedia*. https://www.investopedia.com/articles/economics/08/free-market-regulation.asp.

34. Ibid.

35. Bell, C. (2001, April 3). Testing reliance on free market. *Boston Globe*, C4.

36. Palepu, K., and P. Healy, (2008). *Business analysis and valuation*. Mason, OH: Thomson South-Western. See also Hicks, B. (2010, March 15). Lehman Brothers' 'Repo 105' accounting scandal. *WealthDaily.com*. http://www.wealthdaily.com/articles/lehman-brothers-enron-accounting-gimmicks/2375.

37. Lioudis, N. (2021, January 30). The Collapse of Lehman Brothers: A case study. *Investopedia.* https://www.investopedia.com/articles/economics/09/lehman-brothers-colla pse.asp.

38. Palepu and Healy (2008), op. cit.; Hicks (2010, March 15), op. cit.

39. Samuelson, P. (1973). *Economics*, 9th ed. New York: McGraw-Hill, 345. This discussion is also based on Velasquez, M. G. (1998). *Business ethics: Concepts and cases*, 4th ed. Englewood Cliffs, NJ: Prentice Hall, 166–200.

40. Hillman, A., and G. Keim, (2001). Shareholder value, stakeholder management, and social issues: What's the bottom line? *Strategic Management Journal, 22*, 125.

41. Ibid., 136. Also note that D. Gelles and D. Yaffe-Bellany wrote the following: "Nearly 200 chief executives, including the leaders of Apple, Pepsi and Walmart . . . issued a statement on 'the purpose of a corporation,' arguing that companies should no longer advance only the interests of shareholders. Instead, the group said, they must also invest in their employees, protect the environment and deal fairly and ethically with their suppliers." Gelles, D., and Yaffe-Bellany, D. (2019, August 19). Shareholder value is no longer everything, top C.E.O.s say, *New York Times,* https://www.nytimes.com/2019/08 /19/business/business-roundtable-ceos-corporations.html.

42. Shareholders v stakeholders: A new idolatry. (2010, April). *Economist.* https://www .economist.com/business/2010/04/22/a-new-idolatry.

43. Ibid.

44. Schumpeter: The pursuit of shareholder value is attracting criticism—not all of it foolish. (2012, November). *Economist.* http://www.economist.com/news/business/21567 062-pursuit-shareholder-value-attracting-criticismnot-all-it-foolish-taking-long.

45. Barton, D. (2013, May 15). The city and capitalism for the long term. The Tomorrow's Value Lecture. *McKinsey & Company.* https://www.mckinsey.com/~/media/McKinsey %20Offices/United%20Kingdom/PDFs/The_city_and_capitalism_for_the_long_term .ashx.

46. Torabzadeh, K., Davidson, D., and Assar, H. (1989). The effect of the recent insider-trading scandal on stock prices of securities firms. *Journal of Business Ethics, 8,* 303.

47. Thomas, T., Schermerhorn, J., Jr., and Dienhart, J. (2004). Strategic leadership of ethical behavior in business. *Academy of Management Executive, 18(2)*, 56–66; Trevino, L. K., Weaver, G. R., Gibson, D. G., and Toffler, B. L. (1999). Managing ethics and legal compliance: What works and what hurts. *California Management Review, 41(2)*, 131–151.

48. Trevino et al. (1999), op. cit.

49. Edelman Trust Barometer. (2019). Trust at work, implications for employers. https://www.edelman.com/sites/g/files/aatuss191/files/2019-05/2019_Edelman_Trust _Barometer_Implications_for_Employee_Experience.pdf?utm_source=downloads& utm_campaign=trust_barometer.

50. Kagan, J. (2020, August 1). What is caveat emptor? *Investopedia.* https://www .investopedia.com/terms/c/caveatemptor.asp. "Caveat emptor is a Latin phrase that can be roughly translated in English to "let the buyer beware." While the phrase is sometimes used as a proverb in English, it is also sometimes used in legal contracts as a type of disclaimer. In many jurisdictions, it is the contract law principle that places the onus on the buyer to perform due diligence before making a purchase."

51. Nash, L. (1990). *Good intentions aside: A manager's guide to resolving ethical problems.* Boston: Harvard Business School, 101.

52. See Davis, K. (1973). The case for and against business assumption of social responsibilities, *Academy of Management Journal, 1*, 312–322.

53. Anderson, M. (2020). Most Americans say social media companies have too much power, influence in politics. https://www.pewresearch.org/fact-tank/2020/07

/22/most-americans-say-social-media-companies-have-too-much-power-influence-in
-politics/.

54. Stebbins, S., Sauter, M. B., and Comen, E. (2017, August 24). Customer service hall of fame. *MSN.com*. https://www.msn.com/en-us/money/other/customer-service-hall
-of-fame/ar-AAqEJ1v.

55. EY Americas. (2021, February 23). 2020 wake-up call: US business leaders take bold action to recover from pandemic and accelerate growth with digital transformation. Press Release. https://www.ey.com/en_us/news/2021/02/2020-wake-up-call-us-busi
ness-leaders-take-bold-action-to-recover-from-pandemic-and-accelerate-growth-with
-digital-transformation.

56. Browne, J., and Nuttall, R. (2013, March 1). Beyond corporate social responsibil-ity: Integrated external engagement. *McKinsey & Company*. https://www.mckinsey.com
/business-functions/strategy-and-corporate-finance/our-insights/beyond-corporate
-social-responsibility-integrated-external-engagement#.

57. Conant, D. (2013, September 26). Why philanthropy is R&D for business. *CECP: Chief Executives for Corporate Purpose* (News release). https://www.3blmedia.com/News
/Why-Philanthropy-R-D-Business.

58. Dolan, K. (2014, January 1). Billionaires, led by Zuckerberg, dig a bit deeper with 10 biggest charitable gifts of 2013. *Forbes.com*. http://www.forbes.com/sites/kerryad
olan/2014/01/01/billionaires-led-by-zuckerberg-dig-deep-with-10-biggest-charitable
-gifts-of-2013/.

59. Mento, M. D. (2013, February 10). No. 1: Warren Buffett. *Chronicle of Philanthropy*.

60. Carroll, A. (1991). The pyramid of corporate social responsibility: Toward the moral management of organizational stakeholders. *Business Horizons, 34(4)*, 39–48; CSR has gained credibility as being important as operational effectiveness. The International In-stitute for Sustainable Development (IISD) is considering the creation of ISO standards for corporation social responsibility; see ISO CSR standards: What should an ISO stan-dard on social responsibility look like? (2012, July 18). *IISD.org*.

61. Albinger, H., and Freeman, S. (2000). Corporate social performance and attrac-tiveness as an employer to different job seeking populations. *Journal of Business Ethics, 28(3)*, 243–253; Fombrun, C., and Shanley, M. (1990). What's in a name? Reputation building and corporate strategy. *Academy of Management Journal, 33*, 233–258. For current articles on corporate reputation, see the *Corporate Reputation Review* at https://www.palgrave.com
/gp/journal/41299.

62. See the current *Trends report* at the Social Investment Forum's website, http://www
.socialinvest.org.

63. Turban, D., and Greening, D. (1997). Corporate social performance and orga-nizational attractiveness to prospective employees. *Academy of Management Journal, 40*, 648–672. See also Orlitzky, M., Schmidt, F. L, and Rynes, S. L. (2003, May–June). Corpo-rate social and financial performance: A meta-analysis. *Organizational Studies, 24*, 403–442.

64. Alsop, R. (2001). Corporate reputations are earned with trust, reliability, study shows. *Wall Street Journal*. http://webreprints.djreprints.com/0000000000000000012710003.html.

65. Reputation Institute. (2011). *The Global RepTrak 100: A study of the world's most repu-table companies in 2011*. http://www.reputationinstitute.com/thought-leadership/compli
mentary-reports-2011.

66. Alsop (2001), op. cit.

67. Foroohar, R. (September 23, 2013). How Wall Street won: Five years after the crash, it could happen all over again. *Time*, 30–35.

68. Ibid.

69. Krantz, M. (2002, November 24). Web of board members ties together corporate America. *USA Today.* http://www.usatoday.com/money/companies/management/2002 -11-24-interlock_x.htm; Dallas, L. (1997). Proposals for reform of corporate board of directors: The dual board and board ombudsperson. *Washington and Lee Law Review, 54(1),* 91–148; Daily, C., and Dalton, D. (2003). Conflicts of interest: A corporate governance pitfall. *Journal of Business Strategy, 24(4),* 7.

70. Lopez-de-Silanes, F. (2002, April 9). The code of best practices and the board of directors. International Institute for Corporate Governance (Yale University presentation). http://www.oecd.org/dataoecd/45/14/2086004.ppt.

71. Ibid.; Lipton, M. (2012, December 31). Some thoughts for boards of directors in 2013. *Harvard Law School Forum on Corporate Governance and Financial Regulation.* http://blogs.law .harvard.edu/corpgov/2012/12/31/some-thoughts-for-boards-of-directors-in-2013/.

72. Spencer Stuart. (2020). U.S. Spencer Stuart Board Index. https://www.spencerstuart .com/-/media/2020/december/ssbi2020/2020_us_spencer_stuart_board_index.pdf.

73. Ibid.

74. Lawrence, A., Weber, J., and Post, J. E. (2005). *Business and society,* 11th ed. Boston: McGraw-Hill, 305; Ferrell, O., Fraedrich, J., and Ferrell. (2005). *Business ethics,* 6th ed. Boston: Houghton Mifflin. See also *Sarbanes Oxley Corporate Governance Forum.* http:// www.sarbanes-oxley-forum.com.

75. McNally, J. S. (2013, June). The 2013 COSO Framework and SOX Compliance. Strategic Finance. https://www.coso.org/documents/COSO%20McNallyTransition%20 Article-Final%20COSO%20Version%20Proof_5-31-13.pdf.

76. *The Sarbanes-Oxley Act Community Forum.* http://www.sarbanes-oxley-forum.com; *Sarbanes-Oxley.* http://www.sarbanes-oxley.com; Lawrence, A., et al. (2005). *Business and society,* 14th ed. Boston: McGraw-Hill, 305; Ferrell, O., Fraedrich, J., and Ferrell. (2005). *Business ethics,* 6th ed. Boston: Houghton Mifflin Company.

77. PricewaterhouseCoopers. (2003, March). Navigating the Sarbanes-Oxley Act of 2002. http://www.pwc.com/en_US/us/sarbanes-oxley/assets/so_overview_final.pdf.

78. Sweeney, P. (2012, July/August). Sarbanes-Oxley—A decade later. *Financial Executives International.*

79. U.S. Securities Exchange Commission. (2011, April). *Study Recommendations on Section 404(b) of the Sarbanes-Oxley Act of 2002 for Issuers with Public Float Between $75 and $250 Million.* https://www.sec.gov/files/404bfloat-study.pdf, accessed May 6, 2021.

80. Sweeney, P. (2012, July/August). Sarbanes-Oxley—A decade later. *Financial Executives International.*

81. Adler, J. (2020, July 13). Dodd-Frank at 10: How regulation has (and hasn't) changed since law's passage. *American Banker.* https://www.americanbanker.com/list/dodd -frank-at-10-how-regulation-has-and-hasnt-changed-since-laws-passage.

82. Sweeney (2012, July/August), op. cit.

83. Pollner, G., Ising, E., and Hamlette, T. (2018, August 6). JOBS Act 3.0. *Harvard Law School Forum on Corporate Governance.* https://corpgov.law.harvard.edu/2018/08/06 /jobs-act-3-0/.

84. Volcker, P., and Levitt, A., Jr. (2004, June 14). In defense of Sarbanes-Oxley. *Wall Street Journal,* A16.

85. Sarbanes-Oxley act improves investor confidence, but at a cost. (2005, October). *CPA Journal.*

86. Hazels, D. (2007, May 4). What are the biggest pros and cons of Sarbanes-Oxley legislation? *Kansas City Business Journal.* http://kansascity.bizjournals.com/kansascity /stories/2007/05/07/focus3.html.

87. Volcker and Levitt (2004, June 14), op. cit.; Lys, T. (2009, November). Beneficial or detrimental legislation? *Kellogg Insight.* https://insight.kellogg.northwestern.edu/article /beneficial_or_detrimental_legislation.

88. Hazels (2007), op. cit.

89. Volcker and Levitt (2004), op. cit.

90. Ibid.

91. Ibid.

92. Ibid.; Tunggal, A. (2021). What is SOX compliance? 2021 requirements, controls and more. https://www.upguard.com/blog/sox-compliance.

93. Volcker and Levitt (2004), op. cit.

94. United States Sentencing Commission. (2003, January). 2003 report to Congress: Increased penalties under the Sarbanes-Oxley Act of 2002. https://www.ussc.gov/research /congressional-reports/2003-report-congress-increased-penalties-under-sarbanes-oxley -act-2002; Lies, M., II. (2004). Create a corporate compliance program. George S. May International Company. http://law.georgesmay.com; Hartman, L. (2004). *Perspectives in business ethics*, 3rd ed. Boston: McGraw-Hill; Ferrell et al. (2005), op. cit., 172.

95. Lies (2004), op. cit.

96. Petry, E. (2004, June). Effective compliance and ethics programs: 2004 amendments to the U.S. sentencing guidelines for organizations. DII Signatory Workshop/Best Practices Forum.

97. Jones, E. M., III. (2011, November 9). A blue-ribbon panel commissioned by the ethics resource center makes bold suggestions to improve the federal sentencing guidelines for organizations. *Littler.* http://www.littler.com/publication-press/publication /blue-ribbon-panel-commissioned-ethics-resource-center-makes-bold-sugge.

98. Carroll, A., and Buchholtz, A. (2003). *Business and society*, 5th ed. Mason, OH: South-Western/Thomson, 320.

99. Ferrell et al. (2005), op. cit., 54.

100. Joshua Kennon. (2020). The Worldcom Scandal explained. https://www .thebalance.com/worldcom-s-magic-trick-356121

101. Caruso, K. (2004, Spring). Restoring public trust in corporate America: A legislative or a principled solution? *Southern New Hampshire University Journal*, 36–51; Heffes, E. M. (2003, June). Restoring corporate integrity and public trust. *Financial Executive*, 18–20.

102. Former Enron CEO Skilling gets 24 years. (2006, October 23). *NBCNews.com.* http://www.nbcnews.com/id/15389150/#.UmaxvtJwqTI.

103. Wilbanks, C. (2013, June 21). Ex-Enron CEO Jeff Skilling to leave prison early. *CBS News.* http://www.cbsnews.com/8301-505123_162-57590496/; Jeffrey Skilling biography. (n.d.). *Biography.com.* https://www.biography.com/crime-figure/jeffrey-skilling.

104. Andrew Fastow explained. (n.d.). http://everything.explained.today/Andrew _Fastow/, accessed May 7, 2021.

105. Elkind, P. (2013, July 1). The confessions of Andy Fastow. *Fortune.* https://fortune .com/2013/07/01/the-confessions-of-andy-fastow/.

106. Seelye, K. Q., and Victor, D. (2020, February 3). Bernard J. Ebbers, WorldCom chief jailed in fraud, dies at 78. *New York Times.* https://www.nytimes.com/2020/02/03 /business/bernard-ebbers-dead.html

107. Sorkin, A. R. (2005, September 20). Ex-Tyco executives get 8 to 25 years in prison. *New York Times.* https://www.nytimes.com/2005/09/20/business/extyco-executivesget -8-to-25-years-in-prison.html.

108. Percelay, B. A. (2020, June 26). The fall & rise of Dennis Kozlowski. *N.* https://n-magazine.com/the-fall-rise-of-dennis-kozlowski/.

109. Voreacos, D. (2012, January 26). Adelphia's John and Tim Rigas win dismissal of U.S. tax case. *Bloomberg Businessweek.* https://www.bloomberg.com/news/articles/2012-01-26/adelphia-s-rigases-tax-case-should-be-tossed-u-s-says-after-6-year-fight.

110. Matheson, K. (2013, May 28). Frank Quattrone endows $15 million criminal justice center at Penn. *San Jose Mercury News.* http://www.mercurynews.com/ci_23338398/frank-quattrone-endows-15-million-criminal-justice-center.

111. Faulk, K. (2013, August 8). Richard Scrushy fires back at HealthSouth and SEC in his quest to lead new company (Alabama local news). *AL.com.* http://blog.al.com/spotnews/2013/08/richard_scrushy_fires_back_at.html.

112. Why did Martha Stewart go to jail? (n.d.). *Your Dictionary.* https://biography.yourdictionary.com/articles/why-did-martha-stewart-go-to-jail.html, accessed April 23, 2021.

113. Tirrell, M. (2013, September 3). ImClone's Waksal back in biotech with plans for spinouts. *Bloomberg.com.* http://www.bloomberg.com/news/2013-09-03/imclone-s-waksal-back-in-biotech-with-plans-for-spinouts.html.

114. ArtDaily. (n.d.). Samuel D. Waksal agrees to $800,000 fine. *ArtDaily.* https://artdaily.cc/news/4527/Samuel-D--Waksal-Agrees-to--800-000-Fine#.YIeXqrVKg2w, accessed May 7, 2021.

115. Cook, D. (2004, April 19). Qwest prosecutors end up empty-handed. *CFO.com.* https://www.cfo.com/risk-compliance/2004/04/qwest-prosecutors-end-up-empty-handed/; Taub, S. (2005, February 11). No prison time for Qwest convictions. *CFO.com* http://www.cfo.com/accounting-tax/2005/02/no-prison-time-for-qwest-convictions/.

116. Haigh, S. (2009, January 27). AIG executive sentenced to 4 years in prison for fraud. *San Diego Union-Tribune.* https://www.sandiegouniontribune.com/sdut-gen-re-aig-trial-012709-2009jan27-story.html.

117. Amadeo, K. (2020, November 16). AIG bailout, cost, timeline, bonuses, causes, effects. *The Balance.* https://www.thebalance.com/aig-bailout-cost-timeline-bonuses-causes-effects-3305693.

118. Henriques, D. (2009, June 29). Madoff is sentenced to 150 years for Ponzi scheme. *NYTimes.com.* http://www.nytimes.com/2009/06/30/business/30madoff.html?adxnnl=1&pagewanted=all&adxnnlx=1329339911-bW9pNrjzCf/eKS4iuYvgkQ.

119. Barris, M. (2013). Ex-Brooklyn mortgage executive sentenced in $43 million Fannie fraud. *ADVFN.com.* http://www.advfn.com/news_Ex-Brooklyn-Mortgage-Executive-Sentenced-In-43-Million-Fannie-Fraud_36948846.html; Neumeister, L. (2013, May 12). Compassionate release review buoys old US inmates, *Yahoo! News.* http://news.yahoo.com/compassionate-release-review-buoys-old-us-inmates-165151425.html.

120. Watson, T. (2005, March 14). Air pollution from other countries drifts into USA, emissions that cross borders could cancel out U.S. efforts. *USA TODAY.* http://usatoday30.usatoday.com/educate/college/healthscience/articles/20050320.htm

121. Congressional Research Service. (2011, December 7). Federal Insecticide, Fungicide and Rodenticide Act, United States. *Encyclopedia of Earth.* http://www.eoearth.org/view/article/152745.

122. U.S. Environmental Protection Agency. (n.d.). 1990 Clean Air Act Amendments Summary. https://www.epa.gov/clean-air-act-overview/clean-air-act-highlights-1990-amendments.

5

CORPORATE RESPONSIBILITIES, CONSUMER STAKEHOLDERS, AND THE ENVIRONMENT

OPENING CASE

"The United States is the world's largest economy and the world's largest consumer market. In 2020, American residents will spend around $12.5 trillion on durable and nondurable goods and services. This is more than half a trillion less than last year."[1]

Major ethical stakeholder issues in this chapter deal with the use and abuse of the environment, and the health and rights of consumers with regard to products and advertising. While the current and historical costs of Covid-19 and its aftereffects will significantly raise health care costs internationally, we do not cover this natural disaster topic here. Globally, the other three top public health threats are climate change, obesity, and infectious diseases stemming from antibiotic and antimicrobial bacteria, which kill 23,000 million persons annually.[2]

"Under current law, national health spending is projected to grow at an average rate of 5.5 percent per year for 2018–27 and to reach nearly $6.0 trillion by 2027," according to the Centers for Medicare & Medicaid Services. U.S. health care spending related to obesity in 2020 was $190.2 billion. The newly released United Nations (UN) report on global nutrition does not make for very uplifting reading: amid an already-floundering global economy, the reality of a fattening planet is dragging down world productivity rates, while increasing health insurance costs to the tune of $3.5 trillion per year—or 5 percent of global gross domestic product (GDP).[3] Obesity in the workforce leads to expensive health care, interruptions in productivity, and days absent from work. Obesity and overall weight gain in Americans changed from a problem to a crisis when it was made an issue of public concern by the Food and Drug Administration (FDA) and the National Center for Health Statistics (NCHS). A survey conducted from 2007 to 2009, and updated in 2019, indicated that 42 percent of the U.S. adult population was overweight or obese.[4] Children's obesity prevalence was "13.4% among 2- to 5-year-olds, 20.3% among 6- to 11-year-olds, and 21.2% among 12- to 19-year-olds. Childhood obesity is also more common among certain populations. . . . Hispanic children, 24.2% among non-Hispanic Black children, 16.1% among non-Hispanic White children, and 8.7% among non-Hispanic Asian children." The CDC (Centers for Disease Control and Prevention) found that all U.S. states and territories had more than 20 percent of adults with obesity.[5] Carrying excess weight causes an increased risk for medical conditions, including coronary heart disease, stroke, hypertension, sleep apnea, and some forms of cancer. The rise in obesity comes despite efforts by former first lady Michelle Obama to promote healthy eating and onetime New York mayor Michael Bloomberg's plan to restrict the size of sugary drinks. The problem has become so profound that the U.S. Health and Human Services Department actually declared obesity a disease. On June 18, 2013, the nation's largest physicians' group classified obesity as a medical "disease," despite the recommendations of a committee of experts who studied the issue for a year.[6]

In a 2006 survey of 1,000 households, conducted for *Medicine & Law Weekly,* results showed that 51 percent of the households would like to see fast-food restaurants regulated by the government, while only 37 percent were opposed to such an action.[7] Consumers are suggesting that they are looking for more regulations to be placed on the fast-food industry to provide them with a wider variety of healthier meal options. This is an understandable request given that a Rand study showed that a "food ban [on fast-food restaurants] may have symbolic value, but it has had no measurable impact in improving diets or reducing obesity"[8] in the Los Angeles area.

Another reason cited for the overall increase in overweight and obese individuals in the United States is the ease of selecting calorie-packed foods and the high cost associated with eating healthy. The CDC has pointed out that the availability of foods that are high in fat, sugar, and calories has made it increasingly more convenient for consumers to select those foods.[9] Availability is not the only factor at play. A downward trend in the cost of calories, combined with a downward trend in physical exertion at work, has also contributed significantly to the rise in obesity.[10]

Fast-food chains have reacted to consumers' demand for healthier menus by making changes to their menus and marketing strategies. McDonald's has a new "Go Active" campaign, featuring healthy menu items such as salads topped with chicken and a new fruit and walnut salad. Many of these changes have been targeted at children's nutrition. The "What's Hot in 2012" survey from the National Restaurant Association revealed the top-10 menu trends for 2012, which are relevant in 2021:

1. Locally sourced meats and seafood
2. Locally grown produce
3. Healthful kids' meals
4. Hyper-local items
5. Sustainability as a culinary theme
6. Children's nutrition as a culinary theme
7. Gluten-free/food allergy-conscious items
8. Locally produced wine and beer
9. Sustainable seafood
10. Whole-grain items in kids' meals[11]

Other sources have noted that because of the Covid-19 virus, there is a growing interest in protecting one's immune system (healthline.com). Plant-based, nonprocessed foods; herbal and botanical extracts; kelp, chickpeas, and microgreens are trending.

Previous studies show that all children need protection from unhealthy food marketing. A large body of research since the 1970s "clearly demonstrates that young children do not have the cognitive ability to understand the persuasive intent of advertising, leading the Federal Trade Commission (FTC) to conclude that advertising to children under age six is unfair and deceptive. The American Psychological Association endorses restrictions on all advertising directed to children younger than eight years old. More recent research finds that before age 12, children cannot effectively defend against unwanted advertising influence, raising further concerns about their exposure to advertising for unhealthy products."[12]

The FDA has also joined the fight against obesity by initiating programs to "count calories." Its goals include pressuring fast-food companies to provide more detailed and accurate information about nutrition content to their diners as well as educating consumers. With the partnership between the fast-food chains and the FDA, consumers stand to be better informed about their options to become and remain healthy. Restaurants and company websites now provide consumers with nutritional information for menu items. Restaurants have teamed up with nutritionists who can offer helpful suggestions. When presented with healthier options, it's in the hands of consumers to make the right choices to improve their health.

■ 5.1 Corporate Responsibility toward Consumer Stakeholders

As the largest national economy in the world, the United States produced $21.4 trillion worth of goods and services (measured in GDP) in 2019. China's growing economy earned it the second place slot, with a GDP of $14.3 trillion in 2019.[13] Consumer spending in the United States accounts for about two-thirds of total economic activity. Consumers may be the most important stakeholders of a business. If consumers do not buy, commercial businesses cease to exist. The late management guru Peter Drucker stated that the one true purpose of business is to create a customer.[14] Consumer confidence and spending are also important indicators of economic activity and business prosperity. Consumer interests should be foremost when businesses are designing, delivering, and servicing products. Unfortunately, this often is not the case. As this chapter's opening case shows, giving customers what they want may not be what they need; also, not all products are planned, produced, and delivered with consumers' best health or safety interests in mind. Many companies have manufactured or distributed unreliable products, placing consumers at risk. The effects (and side effects) of some products have been life-threatening and have even led to deaths, with classic cases being the alleged effects of the Merck drug Vioxx, the Bridgestone/Firestone tires on the Ford Explorer, tobacco products and cigarettes that contain nicotine, the Ford Pinto, lead-painted toys, and numerous other examples. At the same time, the majority of products distributed in the United States are safe, and people could not live the lifestyles they choose without products and services. What, then, is the responsibility of corporations toward consumer stakeholders?

Corporate Responsibilities and Consumer Rights

Two landmark books that inspired the consumer protection movement in the United States were Upton Sinclair's *The Jungle* (1906), which exposed the unsafe conditions at a meat-packing facility; and Ralph Nader's *Unsafe at Any Speed* (1965), which created a social expectation regarding safety in automobiles. Then *Fast Food Nation: The Dark Side of the All-American Meal* (2001) by Eric Schlosser, followed by *The Carnivore's Dilemma* (2008) by Tristram Stuart, and Robert Kenner's 2008 documentary *Food, Inc.*, investigated the nature, source, production, and distribution of food in the United States in particular. George Ritzer's *The McDonaldization of Society* (2011) drew attention to the pervasive influence of fast-food restaurants on different sectors of American society, as well as on the rest of the world. In providing "bigger, better, faster" service and questionable food products, McDonald's has been the leader in creating—or reinforcing—a lifestyle change that, as the opening case shows, contributes to obesity. Morgan Spurlock's 2004 documentary, *Super Size Me*, also explored the fast-food industry's corporate influence and encouragement of poor nutrition for profit.

Chase Purdy's book *Billion Dollar Burger* (2020) claimed that "cell-cultured meat is the best hope for sustainable food production, a key to fighting climate change, a gold mine for the companies that make it happen." The book asserts that "the trillion-dollar meat industry is one of our greatest environmental hazards; it pollutes more than all the world's fossil-fuel-powered cars. Global animal agriculture is responsible for deforestation, soil erosion, and more emissions than air travel, paper mills, and coal mining combined. It also, of course, depends on the slaughter of more than 60 billion animals per year, a number that is only increasing as the global appetite for meat swells."[15]

As Steven Fink's issues evolution framework in Chapter 3 illustrated, a "felt need" arises from books, movies, events, and advocacy groups and builds to "media coverage." This then evolves into interest-group momentum, from which stakeholders develop policies and later legislation at the local, state, and federal levels. This same process has occurred and continues to occur with consumer rights. The books and documentaries mentioned here have contributed to articulating and mobilizing the issues of obesity, unsafe cars, and quality of life to the public.

The following universal policies were adopted in 1985 by the UN General Assembly to provide a framework for strengthening national consumer protection policies around the world. Consider which policies apply to you as a consumer:

1. *The right to safety:* to be protected against products, production processes, and services that are hazardous to health or life
2. *The right to be informed:* to be given facts needed to make an informed choice, and to be protected against dishonest or misleading advertising and labeling
3. *The right to choose:* to be able to select from a range of products and services, offered at competitive prices, with an assurance of satisfactory quality
4. *The right to be heard:* to have consumer interests represented in the making and execution of government policy, and in the development of products and services
5. *The right to satisfaction of basic needs:* to have access to basic essential goods and services, adequate food, clothing, shelter, health care, education, and sanitation
6. *The right to redress:* to receive a fair settlement of just claims, including compensation for misrepresentation, shoddy goods, or unsatisfactory services

7. *The right to consumer education:* to acquire knowledge and skills needed to make informed, confident choices about goods and services while being aware of basic consumer rights and responsibilities and how to act on them
8. *The right to a healthy environment:* to live and work in an environment that is nonthreatening to the well-being of present and future generations[16]

From an ethical perspective, corporations have certain responsibilities and duties toward their customers and consumers in society:

- *The duty to inform* consumers truthfully and fully of a product or service's content, purpose, and use
- *The duty not to misrepresent or withhold information* about a product or service that would hinder consumers' free choice
- *The duty not to force or take undue advantage* of consumer buying and product selection through fear or stress or by other means that constrain rational choice
- *The duty to take "due care" to prevent any foreseeable injuries or mishaps* a product (in its design and production or in its use) may inflict on consumers[17]

Although these responsibilities seem reasonable, there are several problems with the last responsibility, known as "due care" theory. First, there is no straightforward method for determining when "due care" has been given. What should a firm do to ensure the safety of its products? How far should it go? A utilitarian principle has been suggested, but problems arise when use of this method adds costs to products. Also, what health risks should be measured, and how? How serious must an injury be? The second problem is that "due care" theory assumes that a manufacturer can know its products' risks before injuries occur. Certainly, testing is done for most high-risk products; but for most other products, use generally determines product defects. Who pays the costs for injuries resulting from product defects unknown beforehand by consumer and manufacturer? Should the manufacturer be the party that determines what is safe and unsafe for consumers? Or is this a form of paternalism? In a free market (or at least a mixed economy), who should determine what products will be used at what cost and risk?[18]

Related to the rights presented above, consumers also have in their implied social contract with corporations (discussed in Chapter 4) the following rights:

- *The right to safety:* to be protected from harmful commodities
- *The right to free and rational choice:* to be able to select between alternative products
- *The right to know:* to have easy access to truthful information that can help in product selection
- *The right to be heard:* to have available a party who will acknowledge and act on reliable complaints about injustices regarding products and business transactions

- *The right to be compensated:* to have a means to receive compensation for harm done to a person because of faulty products or for damage done in the business transaction[19]

These rights are also constrained by free-market principles and conditions. For example, "products must be as represented: Producers must live up to the terms of the sales agreement; and advertising and other information about products must not be deceptive. Except for these restrictions, however, producers are free, according to free-market theory, to operate pretty much as they please."[20]

"Buyer Beware" and "Seller Take Care"

The age-old principle of "Let the buyer beware" plays well according to free-market theory because this doctrine underlies the topic of corporate responsibility in advertising, product safety, and liability. In the 1900s, the concept of "Let the seller take care" placed responsibility of product safety on corporations[21] (which we discuss later in this chapter under product liability doctrines). Several scholars argue that Adam Smith's "invisible hand" view is not completely oriented toward stockholders.

Consumer Protection Agencies and Law

Because of imperfect markets and market failures, consumers are protected to some extent by federal and state laws in the United States. Five goals of government policy makers toward consumers are:

1. Providing consumers with reliable information about purchases
2. Providing legislation to protect consumers against hazardous products
3. Providing laws to encourage competitive pricing
4. Providing laws to promote consumer choice
5. Protecting consumers' privacy[22]

Some of the most notable U.S. consumer protection agencies include:

1. *Federal Trade Commission (FTC)*: deals with online privacy, deceptive trade practices, and competitive pricing
2. *Food and Drug Administration (FDA)*: regulates and enforces the safety of drugs, foods, and food additives and sets standards for toxic chemical research
3. *National Highway Traffic Safety Administration (NHTSA)*: deals with motor vehicle safety standards
4. *National Transportation Safety Board (NTSB)*: handles airline safety
5. *Consumer Product Safety Commission (CPSC)*: sets and enforces safety standards for consumer products
6. *Department of Justice (DOJ)*: enforces consumer civil rights and fair competition

Governmental and international agencies also work to protect consumers' legal rights. The Consumer World website (www.consumerworld.org) has an extensive list of consumer protection agencies that includes the United States and other countries, including India, Hong Kong, Korea, Mexico, Canada, Estonia, and other European countries. The strategic vision of the European Union (EU) consumer policy "aims to maximise consumer participation and trust in the market. Built around four main objectives the European Consumer Agenda aims to increase confidence by: reinforcing consumer safety; enhancing knowledge; stepping up enforcement and securing redress; aligning consumer rights and policies to changes in society and in the economy."[23]

■ 5.2 Corporate Responsibility in Advertising

U.S. revenue from advertising is estimated to reach 242 billion U.S. dollars. During the last 10 years, with the exception of 2020—Covid-19—revenue from ads in the United States was expanding.[24] The extent to which advertising is effective is debatable, but because consumers are so frequently exposed to ads, it is an important topic of study in business ethics. The purpose of advertising is to inform customers about products and services and to persuade them to purchase them. Deceptive advertising is against the law. A corporation's ethical responsibility in advertising is to inform and persuade consumer stakeholders in ways that are not deceitful. This does not always happen, as the tobacco, diet, and fast-food industries, for example, have shown.

Ethics and Advertising

At issue, legally and ethically for consumers, is whether advertising is deceptive and creates or contributes to creating harm to consumers. Although advertising is supposed to provide information to consumers, a major aim is to sell products and services. As part of a selling process, both buyer and seller are involved. As discussed earlier, "Buyer beware" imparts some responsibility to the buyer for believing and being susceptible to ads. Ethical issues arise whenever corporations target ads in manipulative, untruthful, subliminal, and coercive ways to vulnerable buyers such as children and minorities. Also, inserting harmful chemicals into products without informing the buyer is deceptive advertising. The tobacco industry's use of nicotine and addictive ingredients in cigarettes was deceptive advertising.

The American Association of Advertising (AAA) has a code of ethics that helps organizations monitor their ads. The code cautions against false, distorted, misleading, and exaggerated claims and statements, as well as pictures that are offensive to the public and minority groups. The following questions can be used by both advertising corporations and consumers to gauge the ethics of ads:

1. Is the consumer being treated as a means to an end or as an end? And what and whose end?

2. Whose rights are being protected or violated intentionally and inadvertently? And at what and whose costs?
3. Are consumers being justly and fairly treated?
4. Are the public welfare and the common good taken into consideration for the effects as well as the intention of advertisements?
5. Has anyone been or will anyone be harmed from using this product or service?

The Federal Trade Commission and Advertising

The FTC and the Department of Labor (DOL) are the federal agencies in the United States appointed and funded to monitor and eliminate false and misleading advertising when corporate self-regulation is not used or fails. Following is a sample of the FTC's guidelines:

> The FTC Act allows the FTC to act in the interest of all consumers to prevent deceptive and unfair practices. In interpreting Section 5 of the act, the Commission has determined that a representation, omission, or practice is *deceptive* if it is likely to:
>
> • mislead consumers
> • affect consumers' behavior or decisions about the product or service
>
>   In addition, an act or practice is *unfair* if the injury it causes, or is likely to cause, is:
>
> • substantial
> • not outweighed by other benefits
> • reasonably avoidable

The FTC Act prohibits unfair or deceptive advertising in any medium. A claim can be misleading if relevant information is left out or if the claim implies something that's not true. For example, a lease advertisement for an automobile that promotes "$0 down" may be misleading if significant and undisclosed charges are due at lease signing. In addition, claims must be *substantiated*, especially when they concern health, safety, or performance. The type of evidence may depend on the product, the claims, and what experts believe is necessary. If your ad specifies a certain level of support for a claim (e.g., "tests show X"), you must have at least that level of support.

Sellers are responsible for claims they make about their products and services. Third parties—such as advertising agencies or website designers and catalog marketers—also may be liable for making or disseminating deceptive representations if they participate in the preparation or distribution of the advertising or know about the deceptive claims.[25]

Pros and Cons of Advertising

Advertising is part of doing business, and not all advertising is deceptive or harmful to consumers. The arguments, both for and against advertising, raise awareness that provides information to both companies and consumers in their production and consumption of information and transactions. General ethical arguments for and against advertising are summarized below. Ethical Insight 5.1 offers signs of particular types of prevalent loan scams with suggested consumer cautions.

Ethical Insight 5.1

Signs of an Advance-Fee Loan Scam: "Red Flags" from the FTC

- A lender who isn't interested in your credit history—A lender who doesn't care about your credit record should give you cause for concern. Ads that say "Bad credit? No problem," or "We don't care about your past. You deserve a loan," or "Get money fast," or even "No hassle— guaranteed" often indicate a scam.
- Fees that are not disclosed clearly or prominently—Any up-front fee that the lender wants to collect before granting the loan is a cue to walk away, especially if you are told it's for "insurance," "processing," or just "paperwork." Legitimate lenders often charge application, appraisal, or credit report fees. It is also a warning sign if a lender says they won't check your credit history yet asks for your personal information, such as your Social Security number or bank account number.
- A loan that is offered by phone—It is illegal for companies doing business in the United States by phone to promise you a loan and ask you to pay for it before they deliver.
- A lender who uses a copycat or wannabe name—Crooks give their companies names that sound like well-known or respected organizations and create websites that look slick.
- A lender who is not registered in your state—Lenders and loan brokers are required to register in the states where they do business. To check registration, call your state attorney general's office or your state's Department of Banking or Financial Regulation.
- A lender who asks you to wire money or pay an individual is not a legitimate lender—Do not use a wire transfer service or send money orders for a loan. You will have little recourse if there's a problem with a wire transaction, and legitimate lenders don't pressure their customers to wire money.

Source: Federal Trade Commission. (2012). Consumer information, advance-fee loans. http://www.consumer.ftc.gov/articles/0078-advance-fee-loans.

Arguments for Advertising

Arguments that justify advertising and the tactics of puffery and exaggeration include:

1. Advertising introduces people to and influences them to buy goods and services. Without advertising, consumers would be uninformed about products.

2. Advertising allows companies to be competitive with other firms in domestic and international markets. Firms across the globe use advertisements as competitive weapons.

3. Advertising helps a nation maintain a prosperous economy. Advertising increases consumption and spending, which in turn creates economic growth and jobs, which in turn benefits all. "A rising tide lifts all ships."

4. Advertising helps a nation's balance of trade and debt payments, especially in large industries, such as food, automobiles, alcoholic beverages, and technology industries, whose exports help the country's economy.

5. Customers' lives are enriched by the images and metaphors advertising creates. Customers pay for the illusions as well as the products that advertisements promote.

6. Consumers are not ignorant. Buyers know the differences between lying, manipulation, and colorful hyperbole aimed at attracting attention. Consumers have freedom of choice. Ads try to influence desires already present in people's minds. Companies have a constitutional right to advertise in free and democratic societies.[26]

Arguments against (Questionable) Advertising

Critics of questionable advertising practices argue that advertising can be harmful for the following reasons. First, advertisements often cross that thin line that exists between puffery and deception. For example, unsophisticated buyers, especially youth, are targeted by companies. David Kessler, former commissioner of the FDA, referred to smoking as a pediatric disease, since 90 percent of lifelong smokers started when they were 18 years old, and half began by the age of 14. Nearly 9 out of 10 adults who smoke cigarettes daily first try smoking by age 18, and 99 percent first try smoking by age 26.[27]

Another argument is that advertisements tell half-truths, conceal facts, and intentionally deceive with profit, not consumer welfare, in mind. For example, the $300 billion to $400 billion food industry is increasingly being watched by the FDA for printing misleading labels that use terms such as "cholesterol free," "lite," and "all natural." Consumers need understandable information quickly on how much fat (a significant factor in heart disease) is in food, on standard serving sizes, and on the exact nutritional contents of foods. This is increasingly relevant as food-marketing efforts increase. In 2019, total retail and food service sales reached over 6 trillion U.S. dollars for the first time in the United States.[28]

One of the great paradoxes of Americans today is their obsession with diet and health while having one of the worst diets in the world. Also noted earlier, more than two-thirds of adults and more than one-third of children in the United States are obese or overweight. Food industry executives say that customers ask for low-fat food but rarely buy it. For many Americans, the problem is not just that they are consuming so much fat, it is that they don't know what they are eating. On average, recommended daily caloric intake is 2,000 calories a day for women and 2,500 for men. Many Americans far exceed those recommendations, in part because of their increasing reliance on restaurant food.[29]

POINT/COUNTERPOINT

How Free Is Free Speech?

POINT: You can't really trust labels on almost any product. Companies print the ingredients on most products so small that you can't read them; also, what they don't print matters as much if not more as what they do. Note that on so many websites you're also agreeing to something five pages long in order to continue. So, if I really want something, I just sign it.

COUNTERPOINT: Free speech isn't free when someone, person or establishment, harms others to get what they want, or when speech is used for force, fraud, or defamation. Even with labels, contracts, and agreements, it's best to know as much as you can about what you're giving up; and, if you don't understand or agree, turn away—including a click on a website.

SOURCES

Don't let the claims on the front fool you. (n.d.) *Healthline.com.* Accessed March 24, 2021,https://www.healthline.com/nutrition/how-to-read-food
-labels#look-on-the-back.

Kapczynski, A. (2019, December 5). Free Speech, Incorporated. *Boston Review.* http://bostonreview.net/law-justice/amy-kapczynski-free-speech
-incorporated.

Advertising and Free Speech

Because ads are often ambiguous, sometimes misleading, and can omit essential facts, the legal question of "free speech" enters more serious controversies. In commercial speech cases, there is no First Amendment protection if it can be proved that information was false or misleading. In other types of free speech cases, people who file suit must prove either negligence or actual malice.[30]

Should certain ads by corporations be banned or restricted by courts? For example, should children be protected from accessing pornography ads on the Internet? Should companies that intentionally mislead the public when selling their products be denied protection by the court?[31] The U.S. Supreme Court has differentiated commercial speech from pure speech in the context of the First Amendment (see *Central Hudson Gas and Electric Corporation v. Public Service Commission*, 1980, and *Posadas de Puerto Rico Associates v. Tourism Company of Puerto Rico*, 54 LW 4960). Pure speech is more generalized, relating to political, scientific, and artistic expression in marketplace dealings. Commercial speech refers to language in ads and business dealings. The Supreme Court has balanced these concepts against the general principle that freedom of speech must be weighed against the public's general welfare. There is a four-step test developed by Justice Lewis F. Powell Jr. and used to determine whether commercial speech in advertisements can be banned or restricted:

1. Is the ad accurate, and does it promote a lawful product?
2. Is the government's interest in banning or restricting the commercial speech important, nontrivial, and substantial?
3. Does the proposed restriction of commercial speech assist the government in obtaining a public policy goal?
4. Is the proposed restriction of commercial speech limited only to achieving the government's purpose?[32]

For example, do you agree or disagree with the conservative plurality on the Supreme Court that has argued in the tobacco smoking controversy to give more free speech rights to tobacco companies? This has been suggested by Lawrence Gostin:

> The [Supreme] [C]ourt has held that the FDA lacks jurisdiction to regulate cigarettes. The court observed that Congress, despite having many opportunities, has repeatedly refused to permit agency regulation of the product. Thus, Congress has systematically declined to regulate tobacco but has also preempted state regulation. Moreover, the Supreme Court's recent assertion of free speech rights for corporations prevents both Congress and the states from meaningfully regulating advertising. To the extent that commercial speech becomes assimilated into traditional political and social speech, it could become a potent engine for government deregulation. And, perhaps, that is the agenda of the court's conservative plurality.[33]

The commercial speech doctrine remains controversial. The Supreme Court has turned to the First Amendment to protect commercial speech (which is supposedly based on informational content). Public discourse is protected to ensure the participation and open debate needed to sustain democratic traditions and legitimacy. The Supreme Court has ultimate jurisdiction over decisions regarding the extent to which commercial speech—in particular, ads—and cases meet the previous four standards.

Recent judicial decisions regarding a number of areas—including consumer privacy, spam, obesity, telemarketing, tobacco ads, casino gambling advertising, and dietary supplement labeling (see *Greater New Orleans Broadcasting Association Inc. v. United States* and *Pearson v. Shalala*)—have sent the message that "the government's heretofore generally accepted power to regulate commercial speech in sensitive areas has been restricted." Regulators have prohibited certain advertisements and product claims based on the government's authority to protect public safety and the common good. The courts have sent the government (namely, the FDA) "back to the drawing board" to write disclaimers for claims it had argued to be inconclusive. The FDA's regulatory power has currently been curtailed.[34] For a clear, straightforward summary of the limits of "free speech" and the First Amendment, see Elizabeth Smith, Johanna Zelman, and FordHarrison (2021, January 12). The First Amendment: Where it is implicated, and where it is not. https://www.jdsupra.com/legalnews/the-first-amendment-where-it-is-3482126/.

Paternalism, Manipulation, or Free Choice?

Moral responsibility between corporate advertisers and consumers can also be viewed along a continuum. At one end of a spectrum is *paternalistic control;* that is, "Big Brother" (the government, for example) regulates what consumers can and should hear and see. Too much protection can lead to arbitrary censorship and limit free choice. This is generally not desirable in a democratic market economy. At the other end of the continuum is *free choice* and *free speech* that are not regulated by any external government controls. Vulnerable groups—children, youth, the poor, for example—may be more at risk from predatory advertisements, unregulated pornography, and scam advertising. Between these extremes, corporations develop ads to both create and meet consumer demand to buy products and services. The moral and commercial control corporations have in this space can constrain free choice through researched ads that range between puffery, ambiguity, exaggeration, half-truths, and deception to serve corporate interests. Ideally, corporations should seek to inform consumers fully and truthfully while using nonmanipulative, persuasive techniques to sell their products—assuming the products are safe and beneficial to consumer health and safety.

Enforcement of advertising can also be viewed along this continuum. Outright bans on ads can result in court decisions that determine a corporation's right to free speech under the Constitution. The latest such complaint comes from Columbia law professor (and former senior adviser to the Federal Trade Commission) Tim Wu in the *New Republic* article, "The Right to Evade Regulation: How Corporations Hijacked the First Amendment."

Wu criticizes court decisions protecting commercial speech rights as a return to the discredited Lochner era of the early twentieth century, when some judges began interpreting the Due Process Clause as a license that allowed them to overturn economic legislation based on their own economic policy preferences.[35] At the other end of the spectrum, when actual harm and damage can be shown to have occurred as a result of and/or related to deceptive advertisements, the legal system intervenes. As moral and legal disputes occur over specific ads on the paternalism versus manipulation continuum, debate also continues as a matter of perception and judgment from different stakeholder views. In the following section, specific controversial issues of advertising online, children and youth as targets of advertising, and tobacco and alcohol ads are discussed.

5.3 Controversial Issues in Advertising: The Internet, Children, Tobacco, and Alcohol

Advertising and the Internet

Advertising on the Internet and cell phones presents new opportunities and problems for consumers. The ubiquity of Internet and cell phone communication and advertising is evident from these growing indicators:

- Facebook leads its competitors as the first social network to surpass 1 billion registered accounts and as of this writing has more than 2.6 billion monthly active users.
- YouTube's 2021 user base in the world is approximately 2,240.0 million users. That number of global YouTube users is projected at 2,854.1 million users by 2025.
- Total advertising spending worldwide will fall to 517 billion U.S. dollars in 2020, a decline of 11.8 percent compared with the previous year.[36]

The ubiquity of ads on the Web continues to cause ethical problems, particularly for parents and those who wish to protect youth from a host of mobile media instant access via cell phones and pop-up ads, and exposure to websites and advertisements dealing with sex, pornography, violence, drinking, and tobacco. "Two-thirds of parents in the U.S. say parenting is harder today than it was 20 years ago, with many citing technologies—like social media or smartphones."[37]

Seventy-one percent of parents with a child 12 years old or younger report that they are somewhat concerned that their child is spending too much time in front of screens and other devices, including smartphones—and this was before the outbreak of Covid-19. Moreover, it is reported that parents are also concerned about "the impact of digital technology (26%), the rise of social media (21%) and how access to technology exposes children to things at a young age (14%). Other commonly cited reasons for parenting growing more difficult include changing morals and values and the costs associated with raising a child"[38]

The Thin Line between Deceptive Advertising, Spyware, and Spam

The U.S. House of Representatives Judiciary Committee passed the Internet Spyware Prevention Act of 2004, predicting that the problem of spyware would be solved. The act carries penalties of up to five years in prison for using spyware that leads to identity theft. The Department of Justice was given $10 million to find ways to fight spyware and phishing—the act of sending e-mail to a user falsely claiming to be an established legitimate enterprise. There have been other bills introduced by Congress to curb spyware and related Internet crimes.

The debate continues over whether or not congressional legislation and laws can stop Internet spyware and spam. Critics of congressional action alone argue that both industries and government must work to end spam and spyware.[39] Europe, also involved in solving cybercrime as well as daily scamming, takes a wider stakeholder involvement approach that includes legal enforcement and educating industry representatives and consumers. The European Cybercrime Convention, sponsored by the Council of Europe, provides a treaty for combating global cybercrime. The cybercrime convention was approved by 30 countries, including Canada, Japan, South Africa, and the United States, and has been ratified by eight countries.[40] In December 2010, Canada's government passed the Canadian Anti-Spam Law (CASL), designed to regulate specific areas of electronic commerce, including what are known as commercial electronic messages (CEMs). These encompass short messaging service (SMS) texts, social media messaging, and e-mail communications. Although the enforcement date has not yet been set, enforcement is expected to begin in 2014.[41]

Figure 5.1 shows the seriousness of Internet spam, spyware, and data breach statistics by industry. In addition, over 600,000 Facebook accounts are hacked

Figure 5.1

Internet Spam, Spyware, and Crime

Data Breach Statistics by Industry	
Industry	Stats
Medical/Health Care	9,710,520 health care records were exposed in breaches—348.07% more than August.
Business	Between January and September 2019, there were over 7.9 billion data records exposed—a 33% increase from the same time in 2018.
Educational	Schools are the #2 target for ransomware attacks.
Government/Military	17 million **government** records were leaked during 2020—a 278% increase compared with the first quarter of 2019.
Banking/Credit/Financial	In 2017, banks were the target of 47% of financial data breaches.
Top-Five Types of Identity Theft, 2019	
Credit card fraud—new accounts	246,763 reports
Miscellaneous identity theft	166,875 reports
Mobile telephone—new accounts	44,208 reports
Business or personal loan	43,919 reports
Auto loan or lease	38,561 reports

Sources:
1. *HIPAA Journal.* (2020, October 22). September 2020 healthcare data breach report: 9.7 million records compromised.
2. Bekker, E. (2020, January 3). 2020 data breaches: The most significant breaches of the year. IdentityForce.
3. Coker, J. (2020, April 15). 278% rise in leaked government records during q1 of 2020. *Info Security Magazine.*
4. Dautovic, G. (2020, September 30). Top 25 financial data breach statistics (2020 update). *Fortunly.*
5. Impact. (2020, October 21). 10 cybersecurity in education stats you should know for 2020. https://www.impactmybiz.com/blog/cybersecurity-in-education-stats-2020/.
6. Insurance Information Institute. (2020). Facts + statistics: Identity theft and cybercrime. https://www.iii.org/fact-statistic/facts-statistics-identity-theft-and-cybercrime.

each day; 15 percent of social network users reported that their profiles were hacked; and 10 percent of social network users said they were victims of a scam or false link on social networks.

The FTC has extensive guidelines for online advertising. For example, this government agency offers "Clear and Conspicuous Disclosures in On-line Advertisements." From the FTC website, when it comes to online ads, the basic principles of advertising law apply:

1. Advertising must be truthful and not misleading.
2. Advertisers must have evidence to back up their claims ("substantiation").
3. Advertisements cannot be unfair.[42]

The FTC's website further identifies other factors it considers in deter-mining whether a particular disclosure is clear and conspicuous:

• The placement of the disclosure in an advertisement and its proximity to the claim it is qualifying
• The prominence of the disclosure
• Whether items in other parts of the advertisement distract attention from the disclosure
• Whether the advertisement is so lengthy that the disclosure needs to be repeated
• Whether disclosures in audio messages are presented in an adequate volume and cadence and visual disclosures appear for a sufficient duration
• Whether the language of the disclosure is understandable to the intended audience[43]

The following section presents specific advertisement issues in the areas of children and youth (as targets) and tobacco and alcohol.

Advertising to Children

It is estimated that half of American children have a television in their bed-room, and "one study of third graders put the number at 70 percent. And a growing body of research shows strong associations between TV in the bed-room and numerous health and educational problems." With the advent of mobile phones, gaming consoles, tablets, laptops, smart TVs, and e-readers, children are exposed at early ages to access to the Internet. Microsoft asked 1,000 adults who were nonparents and parents, "How old is too young for kids to go online unsupervised?" In 2018, some 94 percent of kids ages 3 to 18 had home Internet access: 88 percent had access through a computer, and 6 percent had access only through a smartphone.[44] Ariel Hochstadt, ex-Google, International tech speaker, provides detailed guidance for parents, adults, and caretakers of children watching and accessing the Internet in "The

Ultimate Guide to Protecting Your Child Online in 2021," (2021, March 17, https://www.vpnmentor.com/blog/the-ultimate-parent-guide-for-child -internet/).

This is a disturbing number given the unlimited availability of and exposure to explicit sexual, pornographic, and other questionable content in ads and on websites, mixed with carefully crafted entertainment that is enhanced by new technologies. Should children and youth be exposed to the uncontrolled Internet through mobile phones and be able to log on from their computers or from computers in libraries and cyber cafés to websites showing explicit sexual and pornographic pictures and videos? At issue is both how much protection can and should parents and guardians exert over children, and how much government protection through censorship does the public want? Although many telecom providers offer controls for parents, as do private firms through products such as Qustodio, Kaspersky Safe Kids, Norton Family, and Mobicip.

Net Nanny, a parental control app that filters and blocks questionable content from children, also raises the question: How much regulation interferes with free speech for all? Moreover, file-sharing technologies and availability of pornography and other questionable content for children provide opportunities not only for users to see explicit material, but to share the content instantly.

Another ethical problem involves companies targeting children at too early an age—between eight and nine years old—with ads. The phenomenon known as *age compression*—KGOY ("kids getting older younger")—refers to "tweens" (between childhood and teenage years). This market is targeted by such companies as Nike, Lululemon, Under Armour, and The North Face. The tween market was estimated at $143 billion a year excluding their influence on household buying decisions. "Roughly a quarter of the population is under 20 years old, and teens spend a majority of their income on clothing.[45] The American Academy of Pediatrics offers realistic guidance for children's, tweens', and teens' uses and viewing of Internet, mobile phones, and other digital devices in "Beyond Screen Time: A Parent's Guide to Media Use" (https://pediatrust.com/The -Media-and-Your-Family-Television-and-Other-Scr-1).

Protecting Children

European, Asian, African, and North American countries are addressing issues of advertising to children. The Children's Online Privacy Protection Act (COPPA) and the FTC's implementing rule took effect April 21, 2000. Commercial websites directed to children younger than 13 years old, or general audience sites that are collecting information from a child, must obtain parental permission before collecting such information. The FTC also launched a special site to help children, parents, and the operators understand the provisions of COPPA and how the law will affect them.[46] In 1974, the Children's Advertising Review Unit (CARU) of the National Advertising Division of the Council of Better Business Bureaus was created to develop guidelines for self-regulating children's advertising. CARU approaches companies that violate

COPPA. In May 2008, CARU recommended and received approval from the operator of the website Stardoll.com to "modify the site to assure it is in compliance with CARU's guidelines and the federal COPPA." CARU observed that the Stardoll website presented "a virtual world where visitors can design fashions for paper dolls and play other dress-up games." When registering for basic membership on the site, visitors must first select one of the following two options: "12 year [sic] and under" or "13 year [sic] and under." Potential members who clicked on the "12 year and under" link were asked to enter their gender and a username, password, and e-mail address. Once that information was submitted, the next screen asked for a parent's e-mail address. After CARU requested changes to the website, Stardoll decided to implement a neutral age-screening process and tracking mechanism.[47]

Advertising and media companies are also working with government agencies to change media strategies.[48] For example, the Media Monitoring Project (MMP) was created in South Africa because of increasing rates of obesity in children. The European Advertising Standards Alliance and the European Sponsorship Association joined together in January 2008 to form the Joint Arbitration Panel that will review "and adjudicate on consumer complaints about event sponsorship, an issue that is generally not covered in the ethical codes of most self-regulatory organisations (SROs) in Europe."[49]

Tobacco Advertising

Critics argue that tobacco and alcohol companies, in particular, continue to promote products that are dangerously unhealthy and that have effects that endanger others. According to the World Health Organization (WHO), cigarettes are "the only legal product that kills half of its regular users when consumed as intended by the manufacturer."[50]

Studies show that "15 of every 100 adult men and 13 of every 100 adult women smoke, with higher figures for certain racial and ethnic groups. Rates of smoking tend to increase as annual household income declines. (Compare a figure of 21 smokers per 100 adults earning less than $35,000 per year, to 7 smokers per 100 adults earning more than $100,000 per year.)" Moreover, education levels show that 35 adults smoke for every 100 adults with their highest education level being a GED; compared with those who have a graduate degree, only 4 smokers for every 100 adults were smokers.[51] The FTC (Federal Trade Commission) reported that the major manufacturers of smokeless tobacco products in the U.S. spending decreased from $658.5 million in 2018 to $576.1 million in 2019, and that cigarette "price discounts made up the two largest spending categories, with $285.6 million paid to retailers and $90.4 million paid to wholesalers. Combined spending on price discounts totaled $376.0 million—or 65.3 percent of all spending in 2019, down from the $413.2 million spent in 2018."[52]

The Marlboro man, the infamous and now-defunct Old Joe Camel, and other cigarette brands linked adventure, fun, social acceptance, being "cool," and risk-taking to smoking. Several new tobacco products have been produced to entice youth and smokers. "Cigarettes, smokeless tobacco, and cigars have been introduced in an array of candy, fruit, and alcohol flavors. R. J. Reynolds' Camel cigarettes, for example, have come in more than a dozen flavors, including lime, coconut and pineapple, toffee, and mint. Flavorings mask the harshness of the products and make them appealing to children; new smokeless tobacco products have been marketed as ways to help smokers sustain their addiction in the growing number of places where they cannot smoke. In addition to traditional chewing and spit tobacco, smokeless tobacco now comes in teabag-like pouches and even in dissolvable candy-like tablets. . . . New products and marketing have been aimed at women, girls, and other populations. The most recent example is R. J. Reynolds' Camel No. 9 cigarettes, a pink-hued version that one newspaper dubbed 'Barbie Camel' because of marketing that appealed to girls."[53]

Despite the fact that cigarette brand product placement in movies was banned by the 1998 Tobacco Master Settlement Agreement, cigarettes appeared in two out of three top-grossing movies in 2005. More than one-third of the movies were youth-rated films. The number of movies with tobacco-related scenes has gone down since 2005, but in 2010 more than 30 percent of top-grossing movies rated G, PG, and PG-13 had tobacco scenes. And studies show that young people who see smoking in movies are more likely to start smoking.[54] Note that in March 2020, the U.S. FDA "issued a final rule using its authority under the Family Smoking Prevention and Tobacco Control Act to require color graphic warnings on cigarette packages. Noting that 'existing Surgeon General's warnings [on tobacco products] . . . go unnoticed and are effectively "invisible,"'" the FDA designed thirteen graphic warnings depicting tobacco-induced ailments from chronic obstructive pulmonary disease (COPD) to cataracts and bladder cancer, among others."[55]

The Tobacco Controversy Continues

The tobacco controversy continues in 2021 in the United States. The American Lung Association and groups supporting anti-smoking and anti-tobacco uses call for a complete ban on tobacco. Lawsuits for and against tobacco use, as with firearms, use courts, public opinion, and lobbyists to make their cases. The WHO (World Health Organization) recently stated that "nicotine contained in tobacco is highly addictive and tobacco use is a major risk factor for cardiovascular and respiratory diseases, over 20 different types or subtypes of cancer, and many other debilitating health conditions. Every year, more than 8 million people die from tobacco use. Most tobacco-related deaths occur in low- and middle-income countries, which are often targets of intensive tobacco industry interference and marketing."[56]

Alcohol Advertising

The NIAAA (National Institute on Alcohol Abuse and Alcoholism) reported that in 2019, alcohol use in the United States showed that "25.8 percent of people ages 18 and older (29.7 percent of men in this age group and 22.2 percent of women in this age group) reported that they engaged in binge drinking . . . and 6.3 percent (8.3 percent of men in this age group and 4.5 percent of women in this age group) reported that they engaged in heavy alcohol use in the past month."[57]

Several 2020 studies also show that alcohol is a factor in the deaths of thousands of people younger than age 21 in the United States each year. This includes 1,072 from motor vehicle crashes; 1,000 from homicides; 208 from alcohol overdose, falls, burns, and drowning; 596 from suicides.[58]

The Centers for Disease Control and Prevention report that "alcohol is the most commonly used and abused drug among youth in the United States, more than tobacco and illicit drugs. Over 90 percent of this alcohol is consumed in the form of binge drinking. On average, underage drinkers consume more drinks per drinking occasion than adult drinkers.

Alcohol ads also raise problems for consumers. Critics of alcohol ads argue that youths continue to be targeted as primary customers, enticed by suggestive messages linking drinking to popularity and success. Anheuser-Busch has been castigated for advertising its alcohol-heavy Spykes "Liquid Lunchables," which come in a colorful, two-ounce container in "kid-friendly flavors like Spicy Mango, Hot Melons, Spicy Lime, and Hot Chocolate." As the watchdog consumer nonprofit Center for Science in the Public Interest (CSPI) noted, "these so-called Spykes aren't juiceboxes, they're malt liquor with more than twice the alcohol concentration of beer."[59] Ethical Insight 5.2 raises the question of who is liable for those who are underage, drink, and get into legal trouble.

Ethical Insight 5.2

Are Minors (Individuals under the Legal Drinking Age) Personally Responsible for Their Voluntary Choices? Should Minors Be Punished as Adults?

"In the U.S., federal law establishes 21 as the national minimum drinking age. Underage drinking is also governed by state laws, which vary by state. In some states, it is a civil offense and in some states it is a criminal offense"(American Addiction Centers, 2021). But who's liable for those under the age of federal and state law?

On November 13, 2003, Ayman Hakki filed a lawsuit in Washington, DC, against several alcohol producers. The suit claimed that in an effort to create brand loyalty in the young, the defendants had deliberately targeted their television and magazine advertising campaigns at consumers under the legal drinking age for more than two decades.

Hakki asked for damages that included all of the profits the defendants had earned since 1982 from the sale of alcohol to minors. He also sought class-action status for his suit. The plaintiff class consisted of all parents whose underage children had purchased alcohol in the last 21 years.

What is your opinion regarding the following quote? "Suits against tobacco and alcohol companies for targeting youthful purchasers reflect a particular philosophy regarding people under the legal drinking or smoking age: they are too immature to take full responsibility for their actions. This philosophy is in serious tension with the approach that has increasingly come to dominate our society's approach to juvenile criminal justice: when minors commit crimes, they ought to be held accountable and punished as adults."

Sources: American Addiction Centers. (2021). Underage Drinking. https://www.alcohol.org /laws/underage-drinking/. Colb, S. F. (2003, December 3). A lawsuit against "big alcohol" for advertising to underage drinkers. *FindLaw.com.* https://supreme.findlaw.com/legal-commentary /a-lawsuit-against-big-alcohol-for-advertising-to-underage-drinkers.html; Social host liability. (2018, November 30). *FindLaw.com.* http://injury.findlaw.com/accident-injury-law/social -host-liability.html.

Product labeling and packaging are also two critical issues that are related to advertising. The national FDA is seeking ways to enhance the quality, usefulness, and clarity of the information to be collected on food labeling for consumers. For example, such labeling terms on food products as "healthy" and "natural" are under review. Specifically, the FDA's Nutrition Innovation Strategy NIS is aimed at "reducing the burden of nutrition-related chronic diseases, which are experienced at a disproportionately higher rate by communities of color. One of the elements of the NIS is to modernize claims, which serve as quick signals for consumers about what benefits a food or beverage they choose might have. Claims and symbols can also help consumers better understand nutrition information and can encourage companies to reformulate products to improve their nutritional value."[60] The USDA (2020–2025) has issued a completely revamped set of dietary guidelines for American consumers at https://www.dietaryguidelines.gov/sites/default/files /2020-12/Dietary_Guidelines_for_Americans_2020-2025.pdf.

5.4 Managing Product Safety and Liability Responsibly

Managing product safety should be priority number one for corporations. As a sign in one engineering facility reads, "Get it right the first time or everyone pays!" Product quality, safety, and liability are interrelated topics, especially when products fail in the marketplace. As new technologies are used in product development, risks increase for users.

How Safe Is Safe? The Ethics of Product Safety

Each year, thousands of people die and millions are injured from the effects of smoking cigarettes and using diet drugs, silicone breast implants; and consumer products such as toys, lawn mowers, appliances, power tools, and household chemicals, according to the Consumer Product Safety Commission (CPSC). But how safe is safe? Few, if any, products are 100 percent safe. Adding the manufacturing costs to the sales price to bolster safety features would, in many instances, discourage price-sensitive consumers. Just as companies use utilitarian principles when developing products for markets, consumers use this logic when shopping. Risks are calculated by both manufacturer and consumer. However, there are enough serious instances of questionable product quality and lack of manufacturing precautions taken to warrant more than a simple utilitarian ethic for preventing and determining product safety for the consuming public. This is especially the case for commercial products such as air-, sea-, and spacecrafts, over which consumers have little, if any, control.

Are cigarettes safe or "dangerous" products? Adverse health effects from tobacco use cause over 480,000 deaths annually.[61] Are other types of drugs safer than nicotine and additives in cigarettes? A meta-analysis (i.e., "the first comprehensive scientific review of both published studies and unpublished data that pharmaceutical companies have said they own and have the right to withhold") by the British medical journal the *Lancet* found that "most antidepressants are ineffective and may actually be unsafe for children and adolescents." This is an interesting finding in light of a recent Mayo Clinic study that found nearly 70 percent of Americans are on at least one prescription drug, and more than half receive at least two prescriptions—many of which are antidepressants.[62] Another concern has been with depression among youth and antidepressant drugs prescribed.

While Covid-19 may be subsiding, over the past year it has also increased tensions, anxieties, and even depression among those youth who have been isolated, out of school, experienced increased pressures in families, and deprived of activities. One 2021 study showed that use of social media helped decrease some of those tensions. Authors of the study concluded that "we have an entire generation of teens and young adults who are significantly affected by COVID-19. . . . The research is clear that our youth are suffering, and any road map for COVID recovery has to center on their mental well-being. But this report also shows that young people are using technology to take control of their mental health, and it would be wise for tech companies to do more to support them where they are."[63]

The use of antidepressants with youth still poses challenges. A meta-analysis study reported that youth (ages 5–18) should avoid certain antidepressants—Paxil, Zoloft, Effexor, and Celexa—because of the risk of suicidal behavior with no benefit from taking the drug. Prozac was found to be an effective drug for depressed children and had no increased suicide risk.[64] Doctors signed more than 164 million prescriptions for antidepressants in 2008, according to IMS Health, making antidepressants one of the most prescribed drugs in the United States.[65] It is interesting to note that, according to the study, the British government recommended against the use of most antidepressants for children, except for Prozac. EU regulators have recommended against Paxil being given to children, and the U.S. FDA has requested that drug manufacturers warn more strongly on their labels about possible links between the drugs taken by adolescents and "suicidal thoughts and behaviors."

Consumers also value safety and will pay for safe products up to the point where, in their own estimation, the product's *marginal value equals its marginal cost*—that is, people put a price on their lives whether they are rollerblading, sunning, skydiving, drinking, overeating, or driving to work.[66]

Product Safety Criteria: What Is the Value of a Human Life?

The National Commission on Product Safety (NCPS) notes that product risks should be reasonable. Unreasonable risks are those that could be prevented or that consumers would pay to prevent if they had the knowledge and choice, according to the NCPS. Firms can use three steps to assess product safety from an ethical perspective:[67]

1. How much safety is technically attainable, and how can it be specifically obtained for this product or service?
2. What is the acceptable risk level for society, the consumer, and the government regarding this product?
3. Does the product meet societal and consumer standards?

These steps, of course, do not apply equally to commercial aircraft and tennis shoes.

Regulating Product Safety

Because of the number of product-related casualties and injuries annually and because of the growth of the consumer movement in the 1960s and 1970s, Congress passed the 1972 Consumer Product Safety Act, which created the CPSC, the federal agency empowered to protect the public from unreasonable risks of injury and death related to consumer product use. The five members of the commission are appointed by the president. The commission has regional offices across the country. It develops uniform safety standards for consumer products; assists industries in developing safety standards; conducts research on possible product hazards; educates consumers about comparative product safety standards; encourages competitive pricing; and works to recall, repair, and ban dangerous products. Each year the commission targets potentially hazardous products and publishes a list with consumer warnings. It recently targeted Costco for the faulty product design of children's products. The death of an 11-month-old in July 1988 in a Costco-designed crib was never reported by the company, even though the company began to redesign the product. Costco was forced to pay a record $1.3 million in civil penalties to settle charges that it violated federal law by failing to report hundreds of injuries and the death.[68]

The CPSC is constrained in part by its enormous mission, limited resources, and critics who argue that the costs for maintaining the agency exceed the results and benefits it produces. Nevertheless, under U.S. president Biden's administration, an overall of certain product safety laws and regulations is underway. The aim is disclosure of meaningful information on the safety of products for consumer stakeholders, such as data on consumer deaths and injuries of products. The CPSC in 2021 is issuing procedural steps before publicly disclosing information from which "the identity of a manufacturer of a product can be readily ascertained. Those include taking reasonable steps to ensure that the information to be disclosed publicly is fair, accurate, and reasonably related to effectuating the purpose of the product safety laws. Practically speaking, this means notifying the manufacturer of the potential disclosure, providing either a summary of what the agency intends to disclose, or the actual disclosure itself, and providing the company with the opportunity to comment, typically 15 days, though that time period can be shortened by the CPSC with a 'public health and safety finding.'"[69]

Consumer Affairs Departments and Product Recalls

Many companies aggressively and voluntarily recall defective products and parts when they discover them or are informed about them. Mattel recalled over 700,000 toys in 2007 because of lead-paint issues. When unsafe products are not voluntarily recalled, the Environmental Protection Agency (EPA), National Highway Traffic Safety Administration (NHTSA), FDA, and CPSC have the authority to enforce recalls of known or suspected unsafe products. Recalled products are usually repaired. If not, the product or parts can be replaced or even taken out of service. American automobiles are frequently recalled for replacement and adjustment of defective parts. Amitai Etzioni, a noted business ethicist, argues that "there is, of course, no precise way of measuring how much more the public is willing to pay for a safer, healthier life via higher prices or taxes, or by indirect drag on economic growth and loss of jobs. In part this is because most Americans prefer to deal with these matters one at a time rather than get entangled with highly complex, emotion-laden general guidelines. In part it is also because the answer depends on changing economic conditions. Obviously, people are willing to buy more safety in prosperity than in recession."[70]

Product Liability Doctrines

Who should pay for the effects of unsafe products, and how much should they pay? Who determines who is liable? What are the punitive and compensatory limits of product liability? First, it is important to note that there is "no uniform product liability statute or common law exists in the United States—each state defines product liability law under its own standards. However, product liability claims are generally brought under the scope of strict product, tort (negligence or fraud) and warranty," as discussed in this section.[71] A brief overview of some litigation over product liability cases may be helpful.

> The ABA (American Bar Association) recently announced online that "The COVID-19 pandemic created an environment in which many companies are fighting unprecedented constraints to assist customers and keep their businesses alive. As they tackle new demands daily—on their businesses and capabilities to operate in the 'new normal'—companies should not overlook how their actions will affect potential exposure to product liability claims related to COVID-19."[72]

In the aftermath and even during Covid-19, "manufacturers, product distributors, parts or component suppliers, sales representatives, and others should not be surprised to see their names in a product liability lawsuit. Depending on the jurisdiction, claims may be brought against parties in the chain of commerce."[73] Such claims could be issued by individuals, companies, or in a "mass tort suit or class action by groups such as healthcare workers, employees, and consumers. For example, plaintiffs' attorneys are filing and advertising for product claims related to "failing to warn about the presence of COVID-19 in manufacturing or distribution facilities; sanitizers, protective gear, and disinfectants misrepresenting the protection against viruses, germs, and bacteria; products claiming to protect against COVID-19; dietary supplements and other foods allegedly curing, treating, or mitigating COVID-19 and its symptoms; drugs and vaccines claiming to treat COVID-19 or lessen its impact . . ." to name a sample.[74]

A brief historical review illustrates the impact of litigation and lawsuits on companies that had allegedly hurt consumers (e.g., the payout in 2001 in litigation and settlements in diet-pill cases alone totaled $7 billion). Merck settled its Vioxx case and approximately 50,000 lawsuits with a $4.85 billion payout, with payouts beginning in August 2008. An additional $950 million was paid, and a guilty plea made to a criminal misdemeanor charge of illegally marketing Vioxx, in November 2011. The $950 million includes a "$321.6 million criminal fine and $628.3 million to resolve civil claims that Merck sold its painkiller Vioxx for unapproved uses and made false statements about its cardiovascular safety." In 2013 Merck agreed to pay $23 million to settle claims it duped consumers into buying the drug.[75]

The doctrine of product liability has evolved in the court system since the early twentieth century, when the dominant principle of *privity* was used. Until the decision in *MacPherson v. Buick Motor Company* (1916), consumers injured by faulty products could sue and receive damages from a manufacturer if the manufacturer was judged to be negligent. Manufacturers were not held responsible if consumers purchased a hazardous product from a retailer or wholesaler. In *MacPherson,* the defendant was ruled liable for harm done to Mr. MacPherson. A wheel on the car had cracked. Although MacPherson had bought the car from a retailer and although Buick had bought the wheel from a different manufacturer, Buick was charged with negligence. Even though Buick did not intend to deceive the client, the court ruled the company responsible for the finished product (the car) because—the jury claimed—it should have tested its component parts.[76] The doctrine of *negligence* in the area of product liability was thus established. The negligence doctrine means that all parties, including the manufacturer, wholesaler, distributor, and sales professionals, can be held liable if reasonable care is not observed in producing and selling a product.

The doctrine of *strict liability* is an extension of the negligence standard. Strict liability holds that the manufacturer is liable for a person's injury or death if a product with a known or knowable defect goes to market. A consumer has to prove three things to win the suit: (1) an injury happened, (2) the injury resulted from a product defect, and (3) the defective product was delivered by the manufacturer being sued.[77]

Absolute liability is a further extension of the strict liability doctrine. Absolute liability was used in *Beshada v. Johns Manville Corporation* (1982). Employees

sued Johns Manville for exposure to asbestos. The court ruled that the manufacturer was liable for not warning of product danger, even though the danger
was scientifically unknown at the time of the production and sale of the product.[78] Medical and chemical companies, in particular, whose products could
produce harmful but unknowable side effects years later, would be held liable
under this doctrine.

Legal and Moral Limits of Product Liability

Product liability lawsuits have two broad purposes. First, they provide a level
of compensation for injured parties; and second, they act to deter large corporations from negligently marketing dangerous products.[79] A California jury
awarded Richard Boeken, a smoker who had lung cancer, a record $3 billion
in a suit filed against Philip Morris in 2001. In 2007, a Los Angeles judge
ruled for Boeken's 15-year-old son on an issue related to his lawsuit against
Philip Morris, which he argued was liable for the death of his father. The
$3 billion suit awarded earlier had been reduced to $55 million. Boeken (age 57)
died in January 2002, seven months after the verdict. The disease had spread
to his spine and brain.[80] The legal and moral limits of product liability suits
evolve historically and are, to a large degree, determined by political as well
as legal stakeholder negotiations and settlements. Consumer advocates and
stakeholders (e.g., the Consumer Federation of America, the National Conference of State Legislators, the Conference of State Supreme Court Justices,
and activist groups) lobby for strong liability doctrines and laws to protect consumers against powerful firms that seek profits over consumer safety. In contrast, advocates of product liability law reform (e.g., corporate stockholders,
Washington lobbyists for businesses and manufacturers, and the President's
Council on Competitiveness) argue that liability laws in the United States have
become too costly, routine, and arbitrary. They claim liability laws can inhibit companies' competitiveness and willingness to innovate. Also, insurance
companies claim that all insurance-paying citizens are hurt by excessive liability laws that allow juries to award hundreds of millions of dollars in punitive damages because insurance rates rise as a result.

However, a two-year study of product liability cases concluded that punitive damages are rarely awarded, more rarely paid, and often reduced after
the trial.[81] The study, partly funded by the Roscoe Pound Foundation in
Washington, DC, is the most comprehensive effort to date to show the patterns of punitive damages awards in product liability cases over the past 25 years.
The results of the study are as follows:

1. Only 355 punitive damages verdicts were handed down by state and federal
   court juries during this period. One-fourth of those awards involved
   a single product—asbestos.
2. In the majority of the 276 cases with complete posttrial information
   available, punitive damages awards were abandoned or reduced by the
   judge or the appeals court.

3. The median punitive damages award for all product liability cases paid since 1965 was $625,000—a little above the median compensatory damages award of $500,100. Punitive damages awards were significantly larger than compensatory damages awards in only 25 percent of the cases.
4. The factors that led to significant awards—those that lawyers most frequently cited when interviewed or surveyed—were failure to reduce risk of a known danger and failure to warn consumers of those risks.

A separate Cornell study reported similar findings.[82]

Furthermore, an earlier federal study of product liability suits in five states showed that plaintiffs won less than 50 percent of the cases; a Rand Corporation study that surveyed 26,000 households nationwide found that only 1 in 10 of an estimated 23 million people injured each year thinks about suing; and the National Center for State Courts surveyed 13 state court systems from 1984 to 1989 and found that the 1991 increase in civil caseloads was for real-property rights cases, not suits involving accidents and injuries.[83]

Contrary to some expectations, another study found that "judges are more than three times as likely as juries to award punitive damages in the cases they hear." Plaintiffs' lawyers apparently mistakenly believe that juries are a soft touch, and "they route their worst cases to juries. But in the end, plaintiffs do no better before juries than they would have before a judge." The study also found that the median punitive damages award made by judges ($75,000) was nearly three times the median award made by juries ($27,000).[84]

Product Safety and the Road Ahead

Covid-19, as noted earlier, has posed challenges and constraints on companies, organizations, institutions, and individuals. At the same time, outsourcing practices continue and new technologies are increasingly used in products, problems for both corporations and consumers will persist. Corporations face issues of cutting costs and increasing quality to remain competitive, while at the same time sacrificing some control over their manufacturing processes through outsourcing. Consumers must trust corporations' ability to deliver safe and healthy products, including food, drugs, toys, automobiles, and medical products. Consumer stakeholders must rely on government agencies such as the FDA and the CPSC to monitor and discipline corporations that violate basic safety standards and practices. Consumers can also use the many watchdog nonprofit groups that monitor and advise on the quality of different projects. Consumer Reports (www.ConsumerReports.org) is one such organization.

■ 5.5 Corporate Responsibility and the Environment

There was a time when corporations used the environment as a free and unlimited resource. That time is ending, in terms of international public awareness and increasing legislative control. The magnitude of environmental abuse, not only by industries but also by human activities and nature's processes, has awakened an international awareness of the need to protect the environment. At risk is the most valuable stakeholder, the earth itself. The depletion and destruction of air, water, and land are at stake. Consider the destruction of the rain forests in Brazil; the thinning of the ozone layer; climatic warming changes from carbon dioxide (CO_2) accumulations; the smog in Mexico City, Los Angeles, and New York City; the pollution of the seas, lakes, rivers, and groundwater as a result of toxic dumping; and the destruction of Florida's Everglades National Park. At the human level, environmental pollution and damage cause heart and respiratory diseases and skin cancer. The top environmental concerns with regard to climate change include deforestation (each year the U.S. population adds over 1,700,000 people); air pollution (while air quality has improved greatly in the last 50 years, it still remains an issue in many major cities with large populations); global warming; water pollution, and natural resource depletion.[85]

We will preview and summarize some of the issues to indicate the ethical implications. The purpose here is not to present in great detail either the scientific evidence or all the arguments for these problems. Rather, our aim is to highlight some issues and suggest the significance for key constituencies from a stakeholder and issues management approach and related ethical implications and concerns.

The Most Significant Environmental Problems

Toxic Air Pollution

More people are killed, it is estimated, by air pollution (automobile exhaust and smokestack emissions) than by traffic crashes. The so-called greenhouse gases are composed of the pollutants carbon monoxide, ozone, and ultrafine particles called particulates. These pollutants are produced by the combustion of coal, gasoline, and fossil fuels in cars. A 2013 American Lung Association report noted that "still, over 131.8 million people—42 percent of the nation—live where pollution levels are too often dangerous to breathe," and "roughly half the people (50.3 percent) in the United States live in counties that have unhealthful levels of either ozone or particle pollution." In 2021, the most polluted cities in the world were Ghaziabad, India; Hotan, China; and Gujranwala, Pakistan. The top-five most polluted U.S. cities in 2020, in terms of year-round particle pollution, were all in California: Bakersfield, Fresno-Madera-Hanford, Visalia, Los Angeles-Long Beach, and San Jose-San Francisco-Oakland.[86]

Air pollution and greenhouse gases are linked to global warming, as evidenced by:

- The five-degree increase in Arctic air temperatures, as the earth becomes warmer today than at any time in the past 125,000 years
- The snowmelt in northern Alaska, which comes 40 days earlier than it did 40 years ago

Figure 5.2

America's Top-Five Global Warming Polluters

Carbon Dioxide Emissions from Company Owned or Operated Power Plants	
Company	Toxic score (pounds released x toxicity x population exposure)
LyondellBasell	29,231,718
Boeing	20,061,951
Huntsman	14,244,096
BASF	11,936,031
Dow Inc.	10,641,781

Source: Baylor, M. (2020). Toxic 100 air polluters index. Political Economy Research Institute. https://www.peri.umass.edu/toxic-100-air-polluters-index-current. The 2020 report is based on 2018 data.

- The sea-level rise, which, coupled with the increased frequency and intensity of storms, could inundate coastal areas, raising groundwater salinity
- The atmospheric CO_2 levels, which are 31 percent higher than pre-industrial levels 250 years ago[87]

Nationally, carbon dioxide emissions are a major source of air pollution. America's top-five warming polluters (by CO_2 emissions from company-owned or -operated power plants) are listed in Figure 5.2. These companies had estimated annual CO_2 emissions of 70 million tons and reported 2003 revenues of $4.4 billion.[88] Internationally, greenhouse gas emission statistics show that Spain had the largest increase in emissions, followed by Ireland, the United States, Japan, the Netherlands, Italy, and Denmark. The EU, Britain, and Germany had emission decreases during this period (see Figure 5.3).

Greenhouse gas emissions **can** be reduced by making power on-site with renewables and other **climate**-friendly energy resources. Examples include rooftop solar panels, solar water heating, small-scale wind generation, fuel cells powered by natural gas or renewable hydrogen, and geothermal energy.[89]

Water Pollution and the Threat of Scarcity

Approximately 1 billion people worldwide lack access to improved water sources. This lack of access comes with a heavy price. Some 2 million deaths a year worldwide are attributable to unsafe water and to poor sanitation and hygiene, mainly through infectious diarrhea. Cholera is still reported to the WHO by more than 50 countries, and about 260 million people are infected with schistosomiasis. Unsafe levels of arsenic and fluoride in water supplies have exposed millions to cancer and tooth damage. The "increasing use of

Figure 5.3

Global Non-CO$_2$ Percent Emissions Change in Six Regions

Region	1990–2000	2000–2010	2010–2020	2020–2030	40-Year Total
OECD[1]	1.2%	2.3%	14.6%	15.8%	37.3%
Non-OECD	12.1%	26.9%	17.2%	29.1%	115.2%
Europe and Eurasia (Non-OECD)	−30.2%	9.8%	11.1%	9.8%	−6.5%
Africa	0.6%	20.5%	10.5%	11.5%	49.2%
Central and South America	10.2%	19.8%	10.1%	9.2%	58.8%
Middle East	47.0%	24.9%	15.6%	18.4%	151.3%
Total	1.5%	16.3%	14.0%	18.5%	59.4%

1. OECD: The Organisation for Economic Co-operation and Development (OECD) is an international organization that works to build better policies for better lives.

Source: Adapted from Office of Atmospheric Programs Climate Change Division, U.S. Environmental Protection Agency. (2012). Summary report: Global anthropogenic non-CO$_2$ greenhouse gas emissions: 1990–2030. https://www.epa.gov/sites/production/files/2016 -08/documents/summary_global_nonco2_projections_dec2012.pdf.

wastewater in agriculture is important for livelihood opportunities, but also associated with serious public health risks. Almost one-tenth of the **global disease burden could be prevented by improving water supply, sanitation, hygiene** and management of **water** resources."[90]

Water pollution is a result of industrial waste dumping, sewage drainage, and runoff of agricultural chemicals. The combined effects of global water pollution are causing a noticeable scarcity. Water reserves in major aquifers are decreasing by an estimated 200 trillion cubic meters each year. The problem stems from the depletion and pollution of the world's groundwater. "In Bangladesh, for instance, perhaps half the country's population is drinking groundwater containing unsafe levels of arsenic. By inadvertently poisoning groundwater, we may turn what is essentially a renewable resource into one that cannot be recharged or purified within human scales, rendering it unusable."[91] It is estimated that the United States will have to spend $1 trillion over the next 30 years to begin to purify thousands of sites of polluted groundwater. An EPA report estimated that it could cost between $900 million and $4.3 billion annually to implement one of the tools under the Clean Water Act for cleaning up the nation's waters.[92] It will require an integrated global effort of public and private groups, of individuals and corporations, to begin planning and implementing massive recycling, including agricultural, chemical, and other pollution controls to address water protection and control. Many companies have already begun conservation efforts. Xerox has halved its use of dichloromethane, a solvent used to make photoreceptors. The firm also reuses 97 percent of the solvent and will replace it with a nontoxic solvent. The Netherlands has a national goal of cutting wastes between 70 percent and 90 percent.

Causes of Environmental Pollution

Some of the most pervasive factors that have contributed to the depletion of resources and damage to the environment include:

1. *Consumer affluence.* Increased wealth—as measured by personal per capita income—has led to increased spending, consumption, and waste.
2. *Materialistic cultural values.* Values have evolved to emphasize consumption over conservation—a mentality that believes in "bigger is better," "me first," and a throwaway ethic.
3. *Urbanization.* Concentrations of people in cities increase pollution, as illustrated by Los Angeles, New York City, Mexico City, São Paulo, and Santiago, to name a few.
4. *Population explosion.* Population growth means more industrialization, product use, waste, and pollution.
5. *New and uncontrolled technologies.* Technologies are produced by firms that prioritize profits, convenience, and consumption over environmental protection. Although this belief system is changing, the environmental protection viewpoint is still not mainstream.
6. *Industrial activities.* Industrial activities that, as stated earlier, have emphasized depletion of natural resources and destructive uses of the environment for economic reasons have caused significant environmental decay.[93]

Enforcement of Environmental Laws

A number of governmental regulatory agencies have been created to develop and enforce policies and laws to protect the general and workplace environments. The Occupational Safety and Health Administration (OSHA), CPSC, EPA, and the Council on Environmental Quality (CEQ) are among the more active agencies that regulate environmental standards. The EPA, in particular, has been a leading organization in regulating environmental abuses by industrial firms.

In the 1970s, the EPA's mission and activities concentrated on controlling and decreasing toxic substances, radiation, air pollution, water pollution, solid waste (trash), and pesticides. The EPA has since used its regulatory powers to enforce several important environmental laws such as:

- *The Clean Air Act of 1970, 1977, 1989, and 1990:* The latest revision of this law includes provisions for regulating urban smog, greenhouse gas emissions, and acid rain, and for slowing ozone reduction. Alternative fuels were promoted and companies were authorized to sell or transfer their right to pollute within same-state boundaries; before, pollution rights could be bought, sold, managed, and brokered like securities.

- *The Federal Water Pollution Control Act of 1972*: Revised in 1977, this law controls the discharge of toxic pollutants into the water.

- *The Safe Drinking Water Act of 1974 and 1996*: Established national standards for drinking water.

- *The Toxic Substances Control Act of 1976*: Created a national policy on regulating, controlling, and banning toxic chemicals where necessary.

- *The Resource Conservation and Recovery Act (RCRA) of 1976*: This legislation provides guidelines for the identification, control, and regulation of hazardous wastes by companies and state governments. The $1.6 billion Superfund was created by Congress in 1980. It provides for the cleanup of chemical spills and toxic waste dumps. Chemical, petroleum, and oil firms' taxes help keep the Superfund going, along with U.S. Treasury funds and fees collected from pollution control. One in four U.S. residents lives within four miles of a Superfund site. It is estimated that 10,000 sites still need cleaning, and it may cost $1 trillion and take 50 years to complete this work.[94]

- *Chemical Safety Information, Site Security, and Fuels Regulatory Relief Act of 1999*: Created standards for storing flammable fuels and chemicals.

The Ethics of Ecology

Advocates of a new environmentalism argue that when the stakes approach the damage of the earth itself and human health and survival, the utilitarian ethic alone is an insufficient logic to justify continuing negligence and abuse of the earth. For example, Mark Sagoff argues that cost–benefit analysis can measure only desires, not beliefs. In support of corporate environmental policies, he asks, "Why should we think economic efficiency is an important goal? Why should we take wants and preferences more seriously than beliefs and opinions? Why should we base public policy on the model of a market transaction rather than the model of a political debate? Economists as a rule do not recognize one other value, namely, justice or equality, and they speak, therefore, of a 'trade-off' between efficiency and our aesthetic and moral values. What about the trade-off between efficiency and dignity, efficiency and self-respect, efficiency and the magnificence of our natural heritage, efficiency, and the quality of life?"[95]

This line of reasoning raises questions such as these: What is a "fair market" price or replacement value for Lake Erie? The Atlantic Ocean? The Brazilian rain forest? The stratosphere?

Consider these five arguments from those who advocate corporate social responsibility from an ecology-based organizational ethic:

1. Organizations' responsibilities go beyond the production of goods and services at a profit.
2. These responsibilities involve helping to solve important social problems, especially those they have helped create.

3. Corporations have a broader constituency than stockholders alone.
4. Corporations have impacts that go beyond simple marketplace transactions.
5. Corporations serve a wider range of human values than just economics.[96]

Although these guidelines serve as an ethical basis for understanding corporate responsibility for the environment, utilitarian logic and cost–benefit methods will continue to play key roles in corporate decisions regarding their uses of the environment. Also, judges, courts, and juries will use cost–benefit analysis in trying to decide who should pay and how much when settling case-by-case environmental disputes. Some experts and industry spokespersons argue that the costs of further controlling pollutants such as smog outweigh the benefits. For example, it is estimated that the cost of controlling pollution in the United States has exceeded $160 billion. It costs the EPA $7 billion a year to regulate air pollution, and the benefits range from $19 billion to $167 billion. These benefits will be achieved as a result of the Clean Air Act amendments and regulatory compliance actions estimated to cost $65 billion in 2020.[97] A WHO study has estimated that air pollution will cause 8 million deaths worldwide by 2020.

How many lives would justify spending $160 billion annually? Although some benefits of controlling pollution have been identified, such as the drop in emissions, improvement of air and water quality, cleanup of many waste sites, and growth of industries and jobs related to pollution control (environmental products, tourism, fishing, and boating), it is not clear whether these benefits outweigh the costs.[98] In wealthier nations, the benefits of pollution control do outweigh the costs. The Lancet Commission on Pollution and Health reports that "the global financial costs of pollution are huge, totaling $4.6 trillion per year—6.2 percent of global economic output. . . . Since 1970 the U.S. has invested about $65 billion in air pollution control and received about $1.5 trillion in benefits."[99] Another question sometimes asked is: Would the environment be better off *without* the environmental laws and protection agencies paid by tax dollars?

Green Marketing, Environmental Justice, and Industrial Ecology

An innovative trend in new ecology ethical thinking is linking the concepts of green marketing, environmental justice, and industrial ecology.[100] Green marketing is the practice of "adopting resource conserving and environmentally-friendly strategies in all stages of the value chain."[101] The green market was estimated at 52 million households in the United States in 1995.

One study identified trends among consumers who would switch products to green brands: 88 percent of consumers surveyed in Germany said they would switch, as would 84 percent in Italy, and 82 percent in Spain. Nearly 70 percent of respondents across the globe said they were somewhat to very willing to spend more on a green product, compared to the same product without green features. Only 11 percent of respondents were not willing at all to spend more money for green features. In open-ended comments, many analysts noted that the economy heavily influences their buying decisions, and cutting costs seems more important to the average consumer than purchasing green products. Respondents would, however, buy green products if the price were not significantly higher. In write-in responses, some respondents expressed concern that green products are not necessarily healthier or better for the environment, even though they claim to be. According to one respondent from the EU, "It's sometimes hard to know how much of that is just marketing and how sustainable green products are in the longer term rather than just being good to someone's conscience."[102]

Companies are, however, adopting green marketing as a competitive advantage and are also using green marketing in their operations—for example, packaging materials that are recyclable, pollution-free production processes, pesticide-free farming, and natural fertilizers.

Environmental justice is "the pursuit without discrimination based on race, ethnicity, and/or socioeconomic status concerning both the enforcement of existing environmental laws and regulations and the reformation of public health policy."[103] Linking environmental justice to green marketing involves identifying companies that would qualify for visible, prestigious awards—such as the Edison Award—for producing the best green products. To win the award, companies need to demonstrate that they had, for example, (1) produced new products and product extensions that represented an important achievement in reducing environmental impact, (2) indicated where and how they had disposed of industrial and toxic materials, and (3) incorporated recycling and the use of less toxic materials in their strategies and processes.

The green marketing and environmental justice link to industrial ecology is made in the long-range vision and practice of companies' integrating environmental justice into sustainable operational practices on an industry-wide basis. Industrial ecology is based on the principle of operating within nature's domain—that is, nothing is wasted; everything is recycled.

Rights of Future Generations and Right to a Livable Environment

The ethical principles of rights and duties regarding the treatment of the environment and multiple stakeholders are (1) the rights of future generations and (2) the right to a livable environment. These rights are based on the responsibility that the present generation should bear regarding the preservation of the environment for future generations. In other words, how much of the environment can a present generation use or destroy to advance its own economic welfare? According to ethicist John Rawls, "Justice requires that we hand over to our immediate successors a world that is not in worse condition than the one we received from our ancestors."[104]

The right to a livable environment is an issue advanced by William T. Blackstone.[105] The logic is that each human being has a moral and legal right to a decent, livable environment. This "environmental right" supersedes individuals' legal property rights and is based on the belief that human life is not possible without a livable environment. Therefore, laws must enforce the protection of the environment based on human survival. Several landmark laws have been passed that are based more on the logic related to Blackstone's "environmental right" than on a utilitarian ethic.

Recommendations to Managers

Boards of directors, business leaders, managers, and professionals should ask four questions regarding their actual operations and responsibility toward the environment:

1. How much is your company really worth? (This question refers to the contingent liability a firm may have to assume depending on its practices.)
2. Have you made environmental risk analysis an integral part of your strategic planning process?
3. Does your information system "look out for" environmental problems?
4. Have you made it clear to your officers and employees that strict adherence to environmental safeguarding and sustainability requirements are a fundamental tenet of company policy?[106]

Using the answers to these questions, an organization can determine its stage on the corporate environmental responsibility profile. The stages range from Beginner (one who shows no involvement and minimal resource commitment to responsible environmental management) to Proactivist (someone who is actively committed and involved in funding environmental management).

Finally, managers and professionals can determine whether their company's environmental values are reflected in the following ethical principles presented in R. Edward Freeman and Joel Reichart's article, "Toward a Life Centered Ethic for Business."[107]

The Principle of Connectedness. Human life is biologically dependent on other forms of life, and on ecosystems as a whole, including the nonliving aspects of ecosystems. Therefore, humans must establish some connection with life and respect that it exists because living things exist in some state of cooperation and coexistence.

The Principle of Ecologizing Values. Life exists in part because of the ecologizing values of linkage, diversity, homeostatic succession, and community. There is a presumption that these values are primary goods to be conserved.

The Principle of Limited Competition. "You may compete [with other living beings] to the full extent of your abilities, but you may not hunt down your competitors or destroy their food or deny them access to food. You may compete but may not wage war."

Chapter Summary

The ethical principles related to corporate responsibility toward consumers include: (1) the duty to inform consumers truthfully, (2) the duty not to misrepresent or withhold information, (3) the duty not to unreasonably force consumer choice or take undue advantage of consumers through fear or stress, and (4) the duty to take "due care" to prevent any foreseeable injuries. The use of a utilitarian ethic was discussed to show the problems in holding corporations accountable for product risks and injuries beyond their control. These principles continue to apply in contemporary advertising online, through cell phones and digital media.

Businesses have legal and moral obligations to provide their consumers with safe products without using false advertising and without doing harm to the environment. The complexities and controversies with respect to this obligation stem from attempts to define "safety," "truth in advertising," and levels of "harm" caused to the environment. The Federal Trade Commission's guidelines for online marketing show that this agency has considerable power and legitimacy in informing the public about ads; it also serves as a useful watchdog on corporate advertising and product regulation. Arguments for and against advertising were presented, with problematic examples of false advertising from the food and tobacco industries highlighted.

Product safety and liability were discussed through the doctrines of negligence, strict liability, and absolute liability. The legal and moral limits of product liability were summarized. States are now moving to limit punitive damages in product liability cases, and tort reform is predicted to change the direction of product liability litigation toward more protection for manufacturers than for injured consumers.

Corporate responsibility toward the environment was presented by showing how air, water, and land pollution is a serious, long-term problem. Federal laws aimed at protecting the environment were summarized. Increasing concern over the destruction of the ozone layer, the destruction of the rain forests, and other environmental issues has presented firms with another area where economic and social responsibilities must be balanced. Innovative concepts and corporate attitude changes were discussed. Green marketing, environmental justice, and industrial ecology principles are being practiced by a growing number of corporations, particularly in Europe—especially since green products and clean manufacturing processes (and certifications) offer a competitive advantage. An innovative move by some corporations is to include environmental safety practices in the strategic, enterprise, and supply-chain dimensions of industrial activities and practices. A diagnostic enables a company to identify its stage of social responsibility toward the environment.

Questions

1. What advertisements—and where do these appear (TV, Internet, print)—do you find "unethical" but legal? Explain.
2. What ethical principles of advertising apply to consumers in all cultures and countries? Explain.
3. Identify some problems associated with the free-market theory of corporate responsibility (discussed in Chapter 4) for consumers? Compare this view

with the social contract and stakeholder perspectives (also discussed in Chapter 4) of corporate social responsibility.

4. Where does the liability of a company end and the responsibility of consumers begin for products? Explain your answer as you define this question more specifically.

5. What constitutes "unreasonable risk" concerning the safety of a product? Identify considerations that define the safety of a product from an ethical perspective.

6. Do you believe the environment is in trouble from climate change and global warming, or do you believe this is "hype" from the press and scientists? Explain.

7. Evaluate and comment on this statement: "North American and European countries have created waste, pollution, and environmental devastation for decades, even centuries. Is it fair that countries like China and India should have the same sanctions now regarding their use of technologies, fuels, and other polluting devices as North America and Europe?"

Exercises

1. Offer examples relevant to any section(s) of this chapter that happened to you, your family or friends, or that you researched resulting from the Covid-19 pandemic or its aftereffects.

2. Identify a recent example of a corporation accused of false or deceitful advertising. How did it justify the claims made in its ad? Do you agree or disagree with the claims? Explain.

3. In a paragraph, explain your opinion of whether the advertising industry requires regulation.

4. Can you think of an instance when you or someone you know was affected by corporate negligence in terms of product safety standards? If so, did you or the person communicate the problem to the company? Was any action taken regarding the defective product? Explain.

5. Do you believe vaping should be banned from all public places where passive smoking can affect nonsmokers? Explain.

6. Find a recent article discussing the environmental damage caused by a corporation's activities. Recommend methods the firm in the article should employ to reduce harmful effects on the environment.

7. Find a recent article discussing an innovative way in which a corporation is helping the environment. Explain why the method is innovative and whether you believe the method will really help the environment or will only help the company promote its image as a good citizen.

Questionable Conflict of Interest

I am a project manager who supports corporate-citizenship-funded programs for our large insurance company. I am responsible for helping choose proposals to support for environmental, community education, and alumni-related projects. Last year, the division in which I work facilitated 120 sponsorships, engaged 100 employees, and provided nearly 25 speakers to various programs.

We have a set of criteria to guide our decision-making process and to help proposals that demonstrate real need. This focus aligns with the mission of the company. Still, there are many organizations with proposals that are high profile, legacy, and/or supported by executives at our firm. These executive-backed requests sometimes receive preferential treatment over the requests that do meet our needs criteria. Several individuals and groups in the company who are aware of these exceptions either shrug it off or feel comfortably conflicted.

Executives form close ties with some of the groups who receive funding without going through our formal process. A dilemma our group faced last year occurred when one executive pressured us to fund a nonprofit that his sister founded. It was a small nonprofit with an environmental focus in an unassigned area and community in which our program operates. This is not the only time executives have bypassed our company policy, but it is one that smacked of nepotism!

While I hesitate to judge whether or not this particular executive was right or wrong, I continue to have issues with the assumed power and authority that executives in our firm take to trump our mandated mission and decisions with regard to funding needy programs. What more should I have done (should I do) to stand up for my personal and professional beliefs?

My reasoning to execute the sponsorship of that particular program was because I was afraid of the backlash if I did not act. The organization has created a culture where this is acceptable, and even though I am not comfortable with this part of our culture, I cannot do much to change it at this point. I cringe at this particular situation and others since I was raised with an ethic of fairness and acting justly toward others. If all people cannot act in a certain way, then no one should act that way. It is difficult managing this process in the real world because people and organizations inevitably have competing interests, stakes, and power in the hierarchy of a company.

Questions

1. What exactly is the conflict of interest here?
2. Is this a serious conflict of interest or just a "business as usual" situation? Explain.
3. What would you have done in this situation before the executive took a decision to fund the sister's program if you had been this project manager? Explain.
4. Describe the ethical principles (or reasoning) you used in your answer to question 3.

Cases

Case 13

For-Profit Universities: Opportunities, Issues, and Promises

For-profit colleges and universities, compared to their public institutional counter-parts, are governed and operated by private corporations. A National Student Clearinghouse report showed for-profit college enrollment changes during the pandemic: undergraduate enrollment was up 3 percent over last year, and down 9 percent in public community colleges enrollment. However, during and in the early aftereffects of Covid-19, one report stated, "When COVID-19 hit the U.S., many experts warned that America's colleges and universities could be devastated. Some of them predicted enrollment declines of up to 20%. So far, those initial forecasts were worse than what has actually taken place. One month into the fall semester of the 2020–2021 academic year, overall enrollment was only 3% lower than at the same time a year earlier . . . for-profit colleges . . . average enrollment is up by 3%. In contrast, at public and private nonprofit four-year universities, enroll-ment fell by about 1.4% and 2%, respectively"(Ott, 2020). However, the same source states that, "Given the recent presidential election results, I also suspect the increase in for-profit enrollment may be short-lived. Graduates of for-profit col-leges are defaulting on their tuition loans at higher rates, and President-elect Joe Biden has vowed to stop these schools from 'profiteering off of students'" (ibid.).

Competitive advantages of for-profit institutions include "flexible scheduling with year-round enrollment, online options, small class sizes and convenient lo-cations." These characteristics attract a large and growing student population entering the education market. It seems the entrepreneurial wave of for-profits has and continues to serve a niche that traditional universities and institutions of higher learning have not served, and perhaps cannot serve, at least to date.

Trouble in Paradise but Still Surviving

"Under a federal law known as the 90/10 rule, for-profit schools are allowed to derive a maximum of 90 percent of their total revenue from federal student aid. The remaining 10 percent must come from elsewhere, including students' repay-ments on their direct loans from the college"(Butrymowicz and Kolodner, 2021). Moreover, the same report noted that "the International Education Corporation, the company that operates . . . 29 other campuses, was owed $33 million in re-payments in 2018, according to an independent audit submitted to the federal Education Department. The company estimated that $13 million of that–or 40 percent–would never be repaid" (ibid.). Continuing student loan defaults and a new U.S. administration are likely to bring more regulatory pressure on for-profits with regard to previous and present pressures experienced by many graduates of these colleges.

For-profit universities and colleges for higher education entered the eye of the storm on Capitol Hill over the last few years with regard to questionable recruiting practices and use of taxpayer funds that have not resulted in gainful employment and promised results for many students. Although for-profit universities have garnered the favor of Wall Street investors and have formed a powerful lobbying group to promote for-profit interests, questions continue to surface as the boundaries between traditional academia and the business of higher education blur. These institutions still manage to enroll more students than do traditional nonprofit universities and colleges, even during the pandemic. They rely on aggressive advertising and marketing, an established niche in the marketplace, and—interestingly—less red tape and bureaucracy, so there are fewer hurdles that potential students have to overcome to enroll and meet academic standards.

Congressional Investigation

The 2012 report of a two-year investigation into for-profit colleges by the U.S. Senate's Health, Education, Labor, and Pensions Committee, comprised primarily of Democratic Party legislators, revealed staggering statistics that have resulted in intense scrutiny by the federal government, creating a call to action for regulation to monitor for-profit institutions. According to other recent investigations, currently "more than $30 billion in taxpayer funds flow to the [for-profit] schools each year" and "about 60 percent of for-profit colleges receive over 70 percent of their revenue from U.S. government programs." These statistics, combined with some for-profit student testimonies about the "dishonest" and "fraudulent" practices of their educational institutions, have resulted in lawsuits. One such lawsuit reached settlement on July 26, 2013, after a "for-profit college in Richmond, Va., agreed to pay $5 million in a class-action settlement filed by eight former students, who argued that the training/education they received was a sham."

Former senator Tom Harkin of Iowa led the investigation into for-profit schools and stated that "in this report, you will find overwhelming documentation of exorbitant tuition, aggressive recruiting practices, abysmal student outcomes, taxpayer dollars spent on marketing and pocketed as profit, and regulatory evasion and manipulation." He added that "these practices are not the exception—they are the norm. They are systemic throughout the industry, with very few individual exceptions."

The storm has continued to build since 2010 as the pressures for legislation increased, driven by senate investigations, increasing litigation, and courts setting precedents. For-profit education probes began in 2010 when press reports started to "raise questions about the quality of proprietary institutions." "These questions stem from the rapid growth of this industry over the last few years, reported aggressive recruitment of students by such institutions, increased variety in the delivery methods used to provide education to students, and the value of the education provided by such institutions."

College, Inc., PBS, and For-Profit Universities

A Public Broadcasting Service (PBS) documentary filmed in 2010 called College, Inc. profiled the for-profit college industry, its historical roots, certain business practices, investors' interests, and issues surrounding the industry. The film examined the application of "private sector principles" to the education industry. The documentary's profile of Michael K. Clifford, a pioneer for-profit education investor and dealmaker, provided a lens to view for-profit education as an opportunity for investors to realize a financial return on their investment while also achieving so-called philanthropic goals; that is, helping failing U.S. universities and colleges keep their doors open for students. (One of his specialties is buying faltering private U.S. colleges.)

Bringing a combination of what Clifford calls the "Three M's: Money, Management, and Marketing," investors have been able to turn around some of the failing institutions and leverage significant value-adds, such as accreditations, while helping the universities bring in huge profits using an improved profit business model. Although there are concerns about the for-profits' "business model," the PBS documentary points out that "'nonprofit' colleges which pay their leaders executive salaries while operating multibillion-dollar sports franchises have long since ceded the moral high ground when it comes to chasing the bottom line."

Pressures on the For-Profit Sector

These external probes have jolted some in the for-profit educational sector as facts from the investigation and large monetary settlements are highlighted by the media. For-profit supporters, however, continue to focus on the impetus of creating these needed institutions, asserting that they "provide very necessary services for rural people and for people learning certain trades" and primarily "help accommodate the mushrooming demand for higher education." Political supporters, many of whom are Republicans, continue to point out the advantages of for-profit education out of concern about the regulatory legislative framework proposed by the Barack Obama administration that emphasizes the "need to look for ways to improve the bad players, but not cast a wide net over the industry."

Key Issues

The for-profit higher education sector's growth and controversy over its business model and practices have triggered reaction and questioning at the state and federal government levels. Some of the primary issues include: the quality of education of these institutions, the amount of money in scholarships and loans they receive from the federal and state governments, the recruiting tactics they use to attract students, and the failure of their graduates in finding jobs.

The National Conference of State Legislatures noted that "critics of for-profit institutions argue that many schools and programs leave students with large amounts of debt, few employable skills, and at a greater risk of not completing a degree at all. This is of greater concern because of the heavy federal subsidies that for-profit institutions receive. . . . Lawmakers have begun to look for ways to better hold these schools accountable for graduating students that can find gainful employment, not be overburdened with large debt they are unable to pay back, and in this way ensure taxpayers are getting a good return on their investment."

A key concern regarding the business practices of for-profits stems from the previously quoted statistics, which note that "more than $30 billion in taxpayer funds flow to the schools each year," and "about 60 percent of for-profit colleges receive more than 70 percent of their revenue from U.S. government programs." The industry seems fundamentally subsidized by public taxpayers who are the source of the money for these loans. As a consequence, a nervous climate of uneasiness has developed that reflects the same concerns that preceded the recent U.S. subprime-lending and housing crisis.

A June 24, 2010, *New York Times* article titled "Battle Lines Drawn over For-Profit Colleges" pointed out that "one source of contention was the planned appearance at the hearings of Steven Eisman, a hedge fund manager known for having predicted the housing market crash. He has recently compared the for-profit college sector to the subprime mortgage banking industry—arguing that both grew rapidly based on lending to low-income people with little ability to repay the loans." For-profit schools make up nearly half of all student defaults. For-profit schools claim to give students who have been turned away from other institutions the opportunity for a higher education, but the reality is that the wider net they have cast primarily includes lower-income individuals who do not have the propensity to be able to pay back these loans, therefore creating an effective "house of cards" and a predicted "student loan bubble."

Statistics, according to the National Center for Education Statistics, show that "21 percent of students at for-profit colleges graduate within six years. That rate is roughly four times higher at nonprofit colleges and universities on average. And even among the minority of students who do manage to graduate from for-profit programs, research suggests they earn 11 percent less compared to graduates of public universities." In addition, according to the Brookings Institution, "roughly half of students who take on debt to study at a for-profit college default on their loans, compared to 19 percent borrowers at nonprofit private colleges and 18 percent of borrowers at nonprofit public colleges." For-profits also have costs ranging from $20,000 to $33,000 per year for full-time students.

The U.S. Department of Education also showed that for the fiscal year (FY) 2011 two-year period and the official FY 2010 three-year period, "for-profit institutions continue to have the highest average two- and three-year cohort default rates at 13.6 percent and 21.8 percent, respectively. Public institutions followed at 9.6 percent for the two-year rate and 13 percent for the three-year rate. Private nonprofit institutions had the lowest rates at 5.2 percent for the two-year rate and 8.2 percent for the three-year rate." In addition, "the average tuition at for-profit colleges is $14,000 a year, compared with $2,500 at community college and $7,000 in-state tuition at a public four-year college, the report found. . . . Students take out larger loans—and default more often." Given the current economic conditions, "with costs soaring, incomes stagnating and little help from government," it should be no surprise "that total student debt, around $1 trillion, surpassed total credit-card debt. . . ." The findings of the for-profit universities investigations are pressuring states to increase monitoring of those institutions. State legislatures in Connecticut, California, Michigan, Delaware, and Maryland have already implemented criteria related to such monitoring. Recent reports also note that "for-profit colleges only enroll 10 percent of students but they account for half of all student-loan defaults. 71% of students in for-profit colleges borrow federal loans, as compared to only 49% of students in 4-year public schools. The average amount borrowed by students in for-profit colleges is nearly $2,000 higher than the amount borrowed in 4-year public schools. These differences in borrowing can't be explained by demographic differences among the student populations; instead, they are mainly caused by the fact that the average tuition at a for-profit college is over $10,000 higher than at a public community college" (Gelrud Shiro and Reeves, 2021).

Some proposed solutions to address for-profits survivability and viability include the following:

1. " A new "gainful employment rule" should be expanded to account for the outcomes of non-graduates and reinstate a revamped gainful employment rule: This rule is important because it holds institutions accountable for the outcomes of their graduates, which more closely aligns the incentives of students and for-profit colleges. For institutions whose graduates don't meet a certain debt-to-earnings ratio, federal funds should be cut. However, as the rule was written under the Obama administration, it did "not hold institutions accountable for the roughly 40% of students who do not graduate."
2. Amend the 90-10 rule: The 90-10 rule states that no more than 90% of for-profit college revenues can come from Title IV programs. This ensures that institutions are not entirely dependent on federal subsidies and can manage to attract at least some students who are willing to pay the full price of their education without federal aid. However, federal funds that come from the GI Bill and other programs run by the Department of Defense do not count towards the 90% limit for federal revenue. This loophole has led for-profit colleges to aggressively target veterans. An amended 90-10 rule should ensure that funds from the Department of Defense and the Veteran's Affairs subsidy programs are counted as part of the allotted 90% of revenue that can flow from federal programs.
3. Improve the College Scorecard: The College Scorecard has become less transparent over the past 4 years. It should be improved to clearly include data on graduate earnings relative to high school earnings as well as loan repayment rates for each school (which the Trump administration began to add in March). This site is an important tool for consumers and it must be used to combat deceptive marketing strategies.
4. Implement institutional risk-sharing: Many experts argue that institutional risk-sharing policies would better align the incentives of for-profit colleges with those of students. These policies require schools to pay the Education Department a percentage of students' outstanding loan balances with negative outcomes. These policies should be accompanied with incentives for enrolling at-risk students so that the risk-sharing does not have the adverse effect of disincentivizing institutions from taking in higher-risk students" (Gelrud Shiro and Reeves, 2021).

Concluding Comments

It is in the interests of states and the federal government to effectively but fairly regulate for-profit and not-for-profit higher education institutions for all stakeholders. With regard to this case, it is also in the interests of for-profit universities and colleges to legally and ethically attract and recruit students, as well as charge rates similar to comparable competitors; and to produce graduating students who can find gainful employment given their education, skills, and abilities. The role of both the federal and state legislatures is to provide "safeguards and transparency for students, hold schools accountable for providing meaningful degrees, and evaluate allocation of state student aid."

To compete for higher enrollment numbers post-Covid-19, those not-for-profit higher education institutions have several options, some of which have been implemented. first, they can join and merge with some of the more successful for-profits—which is a costly, high-risk venture, one that can be disruptive to cultures, professors, and other stakeholders. Second, they can revamp their highly bureaucratic and stodgy methods and ways of attracting, marketing, and enrolling students. Third, they continue as they have, but with rising tuition and other costs and given what the post-Covid-19 world might bring, this option may be problematic.

How and in what ways for-profits will fit into the mix of a changing education landscape in the United States and internationally remains to be seen—especially given the rise of massive open online curriculum (MOOC) initiatives, rising student debt at all higher educational institutions, and the need for different types of jobs and skills in this century.

Specific policy solutions are available to the Biden administration as summarized in this case. Whether or not and to what extent any or all of all these will be adopted is yet to be seen.

Questions for Discussion

1. What purpose and need do for-profit colleges and universities offer to the U.S. educational system?
2. What are the main issues in this case with the for-profit higher university and college education sector?
3. Watch the online video *College, Inc.* produced by PBS. Evaluate PBS's role in making the video *and* its content. Is this a fair, objective account of for-profits? Why? If not, what additional information is needed in the video? Explain your reasoning.
4. Identify some of the major stakeholders and issues using your answers and findings in the above questions and this case. After reviewing the major stakeholders' interests, arguments, and facts regarding these issues, what did you discover? What and whose arguments and information did you find most compelling to help resolve the controversy? Where do you now stand and why on for-profit university institutions and practices? Explain.

5. Do you know any graduates or enrollees in for-profit colleges or universities? What are their experiences and outcomes? Is any of this case's content relevant to what they say? Explain.

Sources

This case was developed from material contained in the following sources:

Blumenstyk, G. (2012, March 2). For-profit colleges compute their own graduation rates. *Chronicle of Higher Education.* http://chronicle.com/article/For-Profits -Develop/131048/.

Butrymowicz, S., and M. Kolodner. (2021, March 25). Left in the lurch by private loans from for-profit colleges. *New York Times.* https://www.nytimes.com/2021/03/25 /business/for-profit-colleges-private-loans.html.

Carey, K. (2010, May 10). "College, Inc." *Brainstorm (blog). Chronicle of Higher Education.* http://chronicle.com/blogs/brainstorm/college-inc/23850.

Cellini, S. R. (2020, November 2). The alarming rise in for-profit college enrollment. Brookings Institution. https://www.brookings.edu/blog/brown-center-chalkboard /2020/11/02/the-alarming-rise-in-for-profit-college-enrollment/.

Fain, P., and Jaschik, S. (2013). Obama on for-profits. *InsideHigherEd.* http://www .insidehighered.com/news/2013/08/26/obama-speaks-directly-profit-higher -education-noting-concerns-sector#ixzz2iPDydhPh.

Gelrud Shiro, A., and R. Reeves. (2021, January 12). The for-profit college system is broken and the Biden administration needs to fix it. *Brookings.* https://www .brookings.edu/blog/how-we-rise/2021/01/12/the-for-profit-college-system-is -broken-and-the-biden-administration-needs-to-fix-it/.

Hess, A. J. (2020, May 19). "We are aggressively recruiting right now": How for-profit colleges are preparing for next semester. *CNBC.com.* https://www.cnbc.com /2020/05/19/how-for-profit-colleges-are-preparing-for-next-semester.html.

Lewin, Tamar. (2012, July 29). Senate Committee report on for-profit colleges condemns costs and practices. *NYTimes.com.* http://www.nytimes.com/2012/07 /30/education/harkin-report-condemns-for-profit-colleges.html.

Maggio, J., and Smith, M. (2010). *College, Inc.* [Documentary]. Frontline. Boston: WGBH Educational Foundation.

Marklein, M. B. (2013, July 26). For-profit college settles class-action lawsuit. *USAToday.com.* http://www.usatoday.com/story/news/nation/2013/07/26/for -profit-college-settlement/2590877/.

McCracken, H. (2012, March 5). College Completion: Who graduates from college, who doesn't and why it matters. *Chronicle of Higher Education.* https:// hollymccracken.wordpress.com/2012/03/05/college-completion-who-graduates -from-college-who-doesnt-and-why-it-matters/.

National Conference of State Legislatures. (2013, July). For profit colleges and universities. *NCSL.gov.*

Ott, M. (2020, November 17). Why for-profit college enrollment has increased during COVID-19. *The Conversation.* https://theconversation.com/why-for-profit-college -enrollment-has-increased-during-covid-19-148619.

Schouten, F., and Schnaars, C. (2013, July 24). For-profit colleges giving big to helpful House members. *USA Today.com.* http://www.usatoday.com/story/news/politics /2013/07/23/for-profit-colleges-contributions-house-regulations/2579041/.

Stiglitz, J. E. (2013, May 12). Student debt and the crushing of the American dream. *NYTimes.com*. http://opinionator.blogs.nytimes.com/2013/05/12/student-debt-and-the-crushing-of-the-american-dream.

U.S. Department of Education. (2013, September 30). Default rates continue to rise for federal student loans (Press release). *ED.gov*. https://www.ed.gov/news/press-releases/default-rates-continue-rise-federal-student-loans.

Case 14

Fracking: Drilling for Disaster?

President Joe Biden has an interesting balancing act to perform with regard to his commitments on climate change with younger voters and more radically oriented Democrats, and with his support of fracking, given the fact that "since 2008, the United States has become the world's leading producer of oil and gas, largely due to advances in hydraulic fracturing, or fracking." For starters, California's Governor Newsom has recently banned fracking (Consumer Watchdog, 2021).

In a lively 2013 CNN article, "Fears of Quakes and Flammable Tap Water Hit Britain as Fracking Looms," Dan Rivers and Ben Brumfield write, "The fear of fracking has come to Britain, replete with worries about potential earthquakes and tap water tainted with natural gas that bursts into flames at the strike of a match." The lifting in May 2013 of a ban on extracting (drilling) for natural gas found in rock layers deep underground in the town of Balcombe in southern England has several hundred protesters worried. Perhaps they have seen the American documentary *Gasland II* (2013) by Josh Fox, which shows several American homeowners losing the value of their properties and homes to certain energy corporations' drilling and releasing flammable gas in their kitchen sinks.

The debate over this drilling process in the United States and now in England has proponents and opponents stating their claims and arguing for very large stakes. Opponents fear for their homes and property values and potentially may have to leave their residences (many already have) because of the aftereffects and devastation caused. Proponents, including former president Obama, see natural gas on U.S. soil as an energy-independent national strategy. Cuadrilla, the British energy company waiting to drill in Balcombe, "believes there is about 200 trillion cubic feet of gas under the ground just within one of its local license areas. To put that figure into context, the United Kingdom uses about 3 trillion cubic feet of gas a year."

What Is Fracking?

Hydraulic fracturing or "fracking" is a process used to retrieve natural gas that is otherwise inaccessible. This technology was first developed in the late 1940s and involves pumping a mixture of water, sand, and chemicals—the "fracking fluid"—deep underground to break up shale rock formations and release pockets of gas. Fracking usually occurs when a new well is drilled, but wells may be fractured multiple times to increase gas extraction. In its lifetime, a well can be fracked up to 18 times; 90 percent of all oil and gas wells in the United States are "fracked" to boost productivity, according to the Interstate Oil and Gas Commission.

First, a well is drilled until it nears the shale layer, typically 5,000 to 12,000 feet below ground. The bore then changes direction and continues drilling horizontally. After the drill is removed, production casing is inserted, and cement is pumped through and around the casing. The cement is installed to prevent anything from getting into the freshwater aquifers. Explosive charges then puncture the casing and cement on the horizontal portion of the drilled tunnel. A mixture of water, sand, and chemicals is pumped down the well and out of these apertures at high pressures. The fracking fluid is over 99 percent water but contains over 500 different chemicals. As a result, a single "frack job" can require as much as 5 million gallons of water. The mixture fractures the rock and allows the trapped gas to escape into the well bore.

The fracking process not only requires millions of gallons of water but also results in large amounts of toxic waste. Some wastewater comes back up the well and must be collected. This wastewater contains dissolved solids such as sulfates and chlorides, metals, and other potentially hazardous components. Conventional municipal sewage or drinking water treatment plants cannot remove the sulfates and chlorides. Instead, the fracking fluid must be sent to a treatment plant, injected into underground disposal wells, or mixed with fresh water and reused.

Benefits

Experts have known for years that natural gas deposits existed in deep shale formations, but until recently the vast quantities of natural gas in these formations were not thought to be recoverable. Hydraulic fracturing makes the drilling process more efficient and makes available vast new reserves of natural gas across the country. Natural gas plays a key role in meeting the energy demands of the United States, supplying about 22 percent of the total. The Energy Information Administration estimates that there is more than 1,744 trillion cubic feet of technically recoverable natural gas that exists within the United States, 60 percent of which is contained as shale gas, tight sands, and coaled methane. The total amount of this resource is estimated to be able to provide enough natural gas to the United States for the next 90 years. Separate estimates of the shale gas resource extend this supply to 116 years.

Shale formations in the United States containing large quantities of natural gas are concentrated in the Northeast Appalachian range and the Rocky Mountain range of the West. The Marcellus Shale formation, which extends from West Virginia and eastern Ohio through Pennsylvania and into southern New York, could become one of the world's most productive natural gas fields. It is estimated that this area alone possesses 500 trillion cubic feet of gas or more, enough to supply the entire East Coast for 50 years. The majority of "fraccidents" have taken place across Pennsylvania in this Marcellus Shale formation, potentially compromising the Delaware River, Monongahela River, and Susquehanna River. With the help of fracking, natural gas currently satisfies nearly one-quarter of the nation's power needs. At current drilling rates and consumption levels, it's expected to provide more than half the nation's natural gas by 2030, according to an MIT study.

The president of the American Chemistry Council (ACC), Cal Dooley, states that "one of our highest priorities in this country is to establish energy security and to reduce our dependence on imported oil. . . . We see a game-changer here with our ability to capitalize on what is estimated to be a 100-year supply of natural gas in shale deposits." This abundant domestic supply of natural gas has provided the United States with a competitive edge in overseas markets and a source for consumption within the country.

Sara Banaszak, senior economist for the American Petroleum Institute (API), further states, "Developing domestic supplies of natural gas will mean billions of dollars in government revenue and reductions in greenhouse gas emissions." The industry boasts that gas is cleaner than oil or coal, emitting less pollution when burned. In May 2010, an industry-financed study conducted at Pennsylvania State University estimated that gas companies spent $4.5 billion developing the Marcellus Shale formation in Pennsylvania. As a result, it has generated $389 million in state and local tax revenue and more than 44,000 jobs.

Instant Millionaires

The natural gas boom in the United States has resulted in big businesses compensating local individuals for the use of their land to drill. Money is earned in signing bonuses, as well as royalties from the amount of gas extracted. Other landowners cashed in by leasing their mineral rights and allowing gas companies to drill horizontally under their properties. One company, Chesapeake Energy, claims to have contracted with a million American households. This modern-day gold rush has allowed struggling locals to become practically millionaires overnight.

Homeowners are offered anywhere from $350 to $30,000 an acre. With additional royalties, this can be a very tempting offer. Rowena Shager of Louisiana negotiated to lease her land. Within a short time, fracking fluid had polluted her family's drinking water. She states, "If I thought I was putting my family's life in jeopardy, or taking away from the value of my property, I never would have signed." A significant number of families are unaware of the potential risks involved when signing contracts with natural gas companies and have suffered negative consequences as a result.

Environmental and Health Concerns

The fracking process has received significant attention in the threats it poses to the environment and human health, particularly water and air pollution across the country. Regulators say that flushing too much of this wastewater into a river could severely harm animals. In 2009, 16 cattle dropped dead near a Chesapeake Energy drilling site in Louisiana after drinking from a mysterious fluid used by drillers that had flooded off during a storm.

Fracking has also been responsible for well-water contamination, filling a basement with methane and blowing up a house in Ohio, and poisoning 17 crows in Louisiana, according to a statement from U.S. environmental group Sierra Club. The nonprofit organization the Natural Resources Defense Council (NRDC) warns that fracking could also trigger earthquakes in certain areas.

The industry maintains its position that hydraulic fracturing has been safe for decades, yet homeowners are coming forward with an entirely different story. Because fracking takes place thousands of feet below the water table where groundwater settles, local drinking water is at risk for contamination. Residents in six states have documented more than 1,000 cases of water contamination as a result of hydraulic fracturing. In the documentary *Gasland* (2010), Josh Fox traveled across the country meeting families that had been affected by hydraulic fracturing. From these interviews, there is evidence that drinking contaminated water has caused headaches, brain damage, asthma, cancer, arsenic poisoning, and loss of taste and smell.

The small town of Dimock, Pennsylvania, is at the heart of the drilling debate. Cabot Oil drilled over 40 wells in just a few months. Gas then contaminated local drinking wells, making the water so hazardous that families were able to ignite their drinking water and start a fire. In late 2009, a group of 19 Dimock residents sued Cabot in federal court for contaminating their wells and devaluing their real estate. The case was finally settled in December 2010, with Cabot Oil and Gas Corporation agreeing to pay $4.1 million to the families affected by methane contamination attributed to faulty Cabot natural gas wells. The settlement also requires Cabot to offer and pay to install whole-house gas-mitigation devices in each of the affected homes. Once the terms of the agreement have been met, Cabot plans to resume operations in Dimock.

EPA Studies

A 2004 hydraulic fracturing study by the EPA found no evidence of water-table contamination. The study concluded that 80 percent of the chemicals degrade underground or are recovered. Because of criticisms of the study, as well as increased attention on fracking, the agency has recently begun a new two-year study of hydraulic fracturing. In March 2012, the EPA released test results concluding that Dimock's water contamination does not pose any risk to human health. The arsenic levels were deemed safe; however, the water of six homes did contain sodium, methane, chromium, and bacteria. Many residents have lost all trust in their drinking water and say they will never use it again.

The EPA is continuing its tests of the drinking water in Dimock homes. It has asked nine natural gas services providers to voluntarily disclose data on chemicals used in hydraulic fracturing. These gas companies include BJ Services, Complete Production Services, Halliburton, Key Energy Services, Patterson-UTI, PRC, Inc., Schlumberger, Superior Well Services, and Weatherford. The EPA intends to use the data in this study underway to determine whether fracking has an impact on water quality for residents living in the vicinity. By November 2010, Halliburton was the only company that refused to voluntarily submit data. As a result, the EPA has issued a subpoena to Halliburton in order to gain this information.

Congress and Regulation

Congress enacted the Clean Water Act in 1972 and the Safe Drinking Water Act in 1974, giving the EPA the power to set national standards regarding maximum acceptable levels of water-contaminates in public water systems. The Safe Drinking Water Act also authorizes states to create regulations to protect their underground drinking water sources, as long as each state complies with the EPA's minimum requirements and receives EPA approval.

The George W. Bush administration introduced the Energy Policy Act (EPACT) of 2005 that exempted oil and gas companies from certain federal regulations protecting drinking water, amending the Safe Drinking Water Act. Bush's vice president Dick Cheney was chairman and CEO of Halliburton Corporation from 1995 to 2000. His former employment and strong ties to the gas and drilling industry certainly influenced the legislation.

EPACT changed the definition of "underground injection" to exclude "the underground injection of fluids or propping agents (other than diesel fuels) pursuant to hydraulic fracturing operations." This amendment, which came to be known as the "Halliburton Loophole," exempted fracking from federal law and gave jurisdiction and authority over hydraulic fracturing operations to the states. Meanwhile, most state oil and gas regulatory agencies do not require companies to report the volumes or names of chemicals being used in extraction. According to the nonprofit Oil and Gas Accountability Project, one of the country's dirtiest industries enjoys the exclusive right to "inject toxic fluids directly into good quality groundwater without oversight." This is a significant issue because Americans get approximately half of all drinking water from underground sources.

In 2009, U.S. Representative Diana Degette (Democrat, Colorado) introduced a bill called the Fracturing Responsibility and Awareness to Chemical Act (FRAC Act). Under this bill, gas producers would be required to disclose chemical identities of all constituents of the fracturing fluid, making this information available on a website.

This would allow emergency crews and first responders to have access to the chemical identities in the case of an emergency. The bill would also close the Halliburton Loophole. As of 2013, Congress has not passed this bill.

State Legislation

More than 30 states have varying degrees of shale production or exploration. A significant number of states' legislation is based on rules laid down by Colorado following many stakeholder discussions. After documented damage from fracking within the state, Colorado implemented a comprehensive drilling plan, including practices to minimize the negative effects on communities and the environment, drilling at a required distance from homes, and reporting chemical identities.

Drilling in the Northeast is the most recent development, while hydraulic fracturing operations in the southern and western areas of the country are much more established. Drilling into the Marcellus Shale formation has stirred up controversy and resistance. Pennsylvania passed regulations on fracking in November 2010, requiring disclosure of a Material Safety Data Sheet with a list of additives used in drilling. In December 2010, New York tried to place a temporary ban on fracking until May 2011, in order to study environmental impacts. Then-Governor David Paterson vetoed the bill, stating that it would put many people out of work. Instead, he issued an executive order instituting a moratorium that extended until July 1, 2011, beyond the date specified in the original bill. Oil companies are pleased because this executive order makes a distinction between the types of drilling, allowing horizontal drilling but disallowing vertical. Recently the cities of Pittsburgh, Pennsylvania, and Buffalo, New York, have enacted altogether bans on hydraulic fracturing.

New York State will possibly not be allowing fracking anytime soon, with drilling giant Chesapeake Energy reportedly abandoning its fight to retain land leases in portions of the state sitting atop vast natural gas reserves. "We can't speak to what drove Chesapeake's decision. However, it's fundamental that organizations prioritize their resources and make decisions based on the known business climate. They do not embrace uncertainty," said Jim Smith, spokesman for the Independent Oil and Gas Association of New York.

So, going forward, it seems that President Biden may imitate Obama's energy policy—"all of the above." Natural gas is "40 percent more carbon efficient than oil or coal." Depending on the part of his base that truly wants climate change reversed, not stalled, Biden may still try to have it both ways, using fracking as "a step forward until renewables are more widely adopted," or he may more aggressively start moving toward other renewable sources. International countries are somewhat split on this divide as well.

Questions for Discussion

1. Do you think U.S. self-dependence on natural gas is worth the contamination of water supplies?
2. Should fracking be allowed to continue given the risks and damage to the environment? Why or why not?
3. If you were a top executive at Chesapeake Energy or Cabot Oil, for example, how would you persuade homeowners to sell your company the use of their land for drilling? How would your personal and corporate ethics guide you?
4. What role does legislation play in holding fracking companies accountable to ethical behavior?
5. In your opinion, how should fracking companies respond to the new EPA study regarding hydraulic fracturing?

Sources

This case was developed from material contained in the following sources:

City council to weigh stance on tougher fracking regulations. (2013, August 7). *CBSLA.com*. http://losangeles.cbslocal.com/2013/08/07/city-council-to-weigh -stance-on-tougher-fracking-regulations/.

Consumer Watchdog. (2021, April 23). Consumer Watchdog applauds fracking ban, calls for more steps as first quarter 2021 oil permit approvals plunge. *Cision PR Newswire*. https://www.prnewswire.com/news-releases/consumer-watchdog -applauds-fracking-ban-calls-for-more-steps-as-first-quarter-2021-oil-permit -approvals-plunge-301276229.html.

Cupas, A. C. (2009, Winter). The not-so-safe drinking water act: Why we must regulate hydraulic fracturing at the federal level. *William and Mary Environmental Law and Policy Review, 33(2)*, 605–635.

EPA asks gas services firms to voluntarily disclose fracking info. (2010, September 13). *Chemical Week.*

EPA issues subpoena for hydraulic fracturing data. (2010, November 8). *Chemical Week.*

Fox, J. (2010). *Gasland.* [Documentary]. New York: International WOW Company.

Fracking across the United States. (2012). *EarthJustice.org.* http://earthjustice.org/features/campaigns/fracking-across-the-united-states.

"Fracking" for energy in Northeast: boon or doom? (2010, November 11). *NBCNews.com.* http://www.nbcnews.com/id/40135664/ns/us_news-environment/#.UsvAKfQW2So.

Fracturing Responsibility and Awareness of Chemicals Act. (n.d.). *Ballotpedia.org.* Accessed March 26, 2021, https://ballotpedia.org/Fracturing_Responsibility_and_Awareness_of_Chemicals_Act.

Jenkins, H. W., Jr. (2010, October 6). Americans (sort of) love fracking; the Northeast's shale gas boom is being domesticated. *WSJ.com.*

Krauss, C., and Zeller, T. (2010, November 6). When a rig moves in next door. *NYTimes.com.* https://www.nytimes.com/2010/11/07/business/energy-environment/07frack.html.

Legere, L. (2010, December 16). DEP drops Dimock water plans; Cabot agrees to pay $4.1 million to residents. *Times Tribune.* https://www.thetimes-tribune.com/archive/dep-drops-dimock-waterline-plans-cabot-agrees-to-pay-4-1m-to-residents/article_60abb530-7f0d-59d3-b274-e5db84ede66d.html.

Lustgarten, A. (2009, April 30). 16 cattle drop dead near mysterious fluid at gas drilling site. *Propublica.org.* https://www.propublica.org/article/16-cattle-drop-dead-near-mysterious-fluid-at-gas-drilling-site-430.

Martin, S. (2011, January 10). US shale rush poses challenges. *ICIS. Chemical Business, 279 (2)*, 28.

Natural gas "fracking" debate draws hundreds. (2010, September 14). *CBSNews.com.*

Phillips, S. (2012, March 15). EPA's test results show safe drinking water in Dimock. *StateImpact.*

Rivers, D., and Brumfield, B. (2013, August 7). Fears of quakes and flammable tap water hit Britain as fracking looms. *CNN.com.* http://www.cnn.com/2013/08/07/world/europe/uk-fracking/.

Roosevelt, M. (2010, June 18). Gulf oil spill worsens—but what about the safety of gas fracking? *LATimes.com.* http://latimesblogs.latimes.com/greenspace/2010/06/gulf-oil-spill-bp-hydraulic-fracturing-gas-fracking-.html.

Scheer, R., and Moss, D. (2010, December 26). Fracking. *EMagazine.com.*

Shaleionaires. (2010, November 14). *60 Minutes reports on fracking.* Bar-On, S., and Frank, M. (producers). CBS News.

Testimony on Energy and Mineral Resources. (2009, June 4). GWPC [Ground Water Protection Council] testimony to the House Committee on Natural Resources, appendix 15, DEC statements. Division of Mineral Resources, New York State. http://www.dec.ny.gov/docs/materials_minerals_pdf/ogsgeisapp2.pdf.

Varela, V. B. (2020, December 18). What's next for fracking under Biden? Council on Foreign Relations. https://www.cfr.org/in-brief/whats-next-fracking-under-biden.

Wolfgang, B. (2013, August 7). As N.Y. fracking ban drags on, leading energy
    company backs out. *WashingtonTimes.com.* https://www.washingtontimes.com
    /news/2013/aug/7/ny-fracking-ban-drags-leading-energy-company-backs/.
Zeller, T., Jr. (2010, December 11). New York governor vetoes fracking bill. *NYTimes
    .com.* http://green.blogs.nytimes.com/2010/12/11/new-york-governor-vetoes
    -fracking-bill.

Case 15

Neuromarketing

Contemporary consumers have access to millions of products. There was a time when a consumer entered a store looking for a pair of sneakers and had only two options. Those days are over. First, markets have expanded to online as well as physical locations. Second, markets are now saturated with different brands, pricing, and payment options—all competing for consumers' attention. A present challenge for marketers is to determine what consumers want, need, and are likely to buy—both online and in physical locations.

Since almost 90 percent of consumer purchasing decisions take place at what can be considered an "unconscious" or perhaps "subconscious" level, it has not always been easy to accurately identify the drivers of consumers' buying behaviors—until now. *Neuromarketing* is a recent phenomenon that takes this observation into consideration in order to develop marketing strategies corporations can use. The term was coined in 2002 by professor Ale Smidts and refers to a practice that combines neuroscience and marketing to delve into the unconscious minds of consumers.

Neuromarketing technology provides a starting point to understand how consumers react to marketing stimuli, how they make their decisions, and what moves them from a potential customer to a buyer. The application of neuroscience can result in "a better identification and understanding of the cerebral mechanism that fundament the consumer's behavior." It informs researchers of the strengths and weakness of marketing materials and tactics by measuring a person's brain activity (Odekerken, 2018). It yields new information as compared to already-known marketing tactics. That being said, "it is not about what neuromarketing does, but what researchers, marketers, and politicians do with that information" (Odekerken, 2018). It does not force anyone to buy a product by hitting a "buy" button in your brain; it increases the compatibility of products with consumer's preferences (Wieckowski, 2019).

Neuromarketing technology is sub-sectioned into "functional magnetic resonance imaging (fMRI), electroencephalography (EEG), eye tracking, positron emission tomography (PET), and magneto encephalography (MEG)" (Market Research Future, 2020). A main tool used in neuromarketing is fMRI, a technology that allows tracking the brain's responses when exposed to different stimuli. Using an fMRI, brain activity can be recorded noninvasively, without any risks of radiation. This technology is anticipated to increase until 2023 in market share despite concerns of cost and mobility (Market Research Future, 2020). Another technology available to neuromarketers is the EEG test. EEG tests measure electrical activity within the brain and can be used with software to produce several different views of the brain. EEG tests use flashes of red and yellow to show which area of the brain is engaged by the stimuli. This is considerably useful to researchers and marketers, given that each different part of the brain correlates with a different function. In addition to fMRI and EEG tests, neuromarketing also encompasses eye-tracking and galvanic skin response (GSR) tests. Eye-tracking technology can determine exactly where a person is looking; it allows for the monitoring of pupil movement, which gives marketers a means to determine if users are having trouble locating information or navigating through a web page, or if they are failing to see information altogether. Because of its usage by media and advertising companies, eye tracking has become an emerging trend and is anticipated to gain substantial market share in neuromarketing technologies (Market Research Future, 2020). GSR tests, on the other hand, measure the degree of electrical conductance across the surface of skin and can indicate emotional responses.

Since neuromarketing has increased in popularity, several companies have become frontrunners in the market. NeuroFocus is one of the market leaders with a team of neuroscience and marketing experts from the University of California, Berkeley, the Massachusetts Institute of Technology (MIT), Harvard, and Hebrew University. The company was acquired by the Nielsen Company, a worldwide leader in marketing and advertising research, and has numerous Fortune 100 clients ranging from manufacturers of automobiles and consumer packaged goods, as well as major cable television and motion picture studios.

EmSense, another neuromarketing vendor, combines neuroscience experts from MIT, Harvard, and Stanford with marketing experience from Pepsi-Cola, Disney, and Gillette. Like NeuroFocus, EmSense has worked with large companies like Microsoft. The NeuroFocus portfolio offers solutions for advertising, in-store display, videogaming, packaging, and online marketing elements. Sands Research is a company that offers neuroscience-based research. In addition to using technology like EEG tests and eye tracking, Sands has developed its own system of scoring media, the Neuro Engagement Factor (NEF). The NEF ranks marketing elements, like advertisements, on a scale of 1 to 5 based on the level of consumer engagement. The company's technology has attracted clients like Sam's Club and Chevron and has also been used to conduct insightful studies on Super Bowl advertisements.

Hyundai employed EEG technology to test consumer reactions to a 2011 test model of. Using a test group of 15 men and 15 women, Hyundai asked participants to stare at different parts of the model, while monitoring the electrical activity in their brains. A manager of brand strategy, Dean Macko, stated, "We want to know what consumers think about a car before we start manufacturing thousands of them" (Keshav, n.d.). Macko expects the company to make adjustments to the model's exterior based on the EEG reports (Burkitt, 2009).

The Weather Channel (TWC) has also chosen to use neuroscience. In this case, TWC was looking to optimize its on-air promotions for one of its series, "When Weather Changed History." To do this, the company teamed up with NeuroFocus and used three different neuroscience technologies for the study: EEG tests, eye-tracking technology, and GSR. These methods tested viewers' neurological and biophysical responses to three different promotions. The study was aimed at answering four different questions: "Are the spots effective? What about each of them is more or less effective? How well do they convey the intended messages? How do we build the most effective final versions of the spots?" To answer these questions, NeuroFocus recorded metrics like attention, emotional engagement, and memory retention. Each spot was scored based on these metrics, providing valuable insights: "TWC's marketing team welcomed this research, because the information was clear, intuitive, quantitative, and objective. It was also well received because it helped pinpoint how we could improve the effectiveness of our promos."

Uma Karmarkar, a professor of consumer psychology and behavioral economics, cites the example of junk-food giant Frito-Lay, which in 2008 hired a neuromarketing firm to look into how consumers respond to Cheetos, the top-selling brand of cheese puffs in the United States. Using EEG technology on a group of willing subjects, the firm determined that consumers respond strongly to the fact that eating Cheetos turns their fingers orange with residual cheese dust. In her background note, Karmarkar cites an article in the August 2011 issue of *Fast Company*, which describes how the EEG patterns indicated "a sense of giddy subversion that consumers enjoy over the messiness of the product."

Ethical Issues Associated with Neuromarketing

Since the field of neuromarketing is gaining momentum and attention, it has also experienced resistance from those who oppose this type of research based on ethical reasons. Among the most vocal of these opponents is the nonprofit consumer protection group Commercial Alert. This agency is raising awareness about the ethical implications of neuromarketing, namely: Is it ethical to conduct such research and development, since these techniques and activities could open the door to unprecedented and possibly abusive influence over consumers? The following five questions raise additional ethical concerns about neuromarketing.

Ethical Question 1: Does the practice of "reading people's minds"—or at least observing brain scans to get clues on how consumers react to targeted buying practices and objects—give marketers an unfair and potentially harmful advantage over consumers?

Neuromarketing practices could potentially give corporations an unfair advantage over consumers' choices and buying activities. Because marketers could gain access to a consumer's inner thoughts and opinions, some of which the consumer may not even be aware of, this power could easily be misused. However, it is important to note that neuromarketing—and perhaps most forms of marketing—rely on subconsciously influencing consumers. For example "priming," a common marketing tactic, involved subconscious reminders and was first used long before neuromarketing was invented. Neuromarketing explains how and why some priming tactics are more effective influencers than others (Odekerken, 2018). In 2012, Target came under fire for its use of neuromarketing and its predicting ability after it sent ads for pregnancy and baby products to a woman who had not yet told anyone about her pregnancy (Wieckowski, 2019). According to *Fast Company*, "Consumer advocates and other groups have claimed neuromarketers are exploiting people to 'sell us crap we don't need' and creating unhealthy and irresponsible addictions and cravings" (Randall, 2009). Advocacy group Commercial Alert agreed. In a letter sent to then–Senate Commerce Committee chair John McCain in 2004, the group quoted Adam Koval, a neuromarketing pioneer, stating that this new technology "will actually result in higher product sales or in getting customers to behave the way [corporations] want them to behave." These arguments raise an ethical question with regard to whether a company should have this type and amount of power over consumers' buying behavior.

Ethical Question 2: What if neuromarketing is used by politicians or groups with extreme political interests?

Consider the effects of a political party using neuromarketing to influence voter decisions. If these groups have the power to learn from their constituents' thoughts and opinions, they could also have an enormous advantage in persuading them to vote a certain way in elections. Some advocacy groups fear that this power will be abused by politicians. In its letter to Senator McCain, the Commercial Alert group noted that "political consultants have already teamed up with neuroscientists ... to conduct neuromarketing experiments to gauge the effectiveness of political advertising."

The power of neuromarketing could also potentially be exploited by extreme political or social groups to engage in dangerously effective propaganda campaigns. What if extremist regimes had had this technology? Could they have been even more powerful in their anti-Semitic campaign and perhaps faced less resistance from enemies around the world? Writers at *Fast Company* and Commercial Alert even go so far as to suggest that neuromarketing could be used by some politicians or extremist groups to "brainwash" the public into accepting their political or social viewpoints. During earlier uses of the neuromarketing in political campaigns, research focused more on political judgment. Recently, the appearance of political candidates to voters is the focus. A critical question becomes, "What happens when politicians know what 'persona' leads to the most votes?" Or, "How can one deliver a speech that will prime voters to strongly move a candidate into a landslide win?" (Odekerken, 2018).

Ethical Question 3: When does knowing an individual's subconscious thoughts cross the line of privacy invasion?

Since the September 11, 2001, attacks and subsequent Patriot Act legislation, privacy has been a hot topic. The introduction of neuromarketing aggravates issues of individual privacy. People questioned whether recording a person's telephone conversations or tracking Internet activity was an invasion of privacy; gaining access to an individual's subconscious thoughts is far more serious. Consumers generally are concerned about privacy, and many of them seem to know that their purchase behavior is available to the company. Even so, many also believe that their own thoughts are private and protected (Wieckowski, 2019).

Some marketers argue that this technology is advantageous in that it can reveal a consumer's inner feelings or motivations that cannot be obtained through a focus group, either because the person is unaware of them or because people lie about what motivates them. Consumers may consider neuromarketing a breach of their right to privacy, especially when a company may know more about them and their purchasing desires than companies divulge (Wieckowski, 2019).

But shouldn't consumers have the right to disclose only the information that they are conscious of and deem acceptable to share with a corporation? Circumventing the individual's judgment on these matters through the use of neuromarketing could be considered an unfair violation of privacy.

Ethical Question 4: Could increases in marketing effectiveness lead to higher levels of "marketing-related diseases" that are already having harmful effects on American society?

Ethical Question 5: Related to question 4, could neuromarketing be used to irresponsibly target young consumers?

Some marketing practices often and more easily influence the youth in a society. Children and teenagers are known to be the easiest segments to target and persuade through mass-media advertising and other marketing tactics. Consumer protection groups have been formed to fight against corporations that are believed to be unethically targeting children, particularly during children's television programming. Commercial Alert has been a major player in this area, stating that "corporations regularly promote . . . to children and teenagers degraded values and products including materialism, addiction, violence, gambling, pornography, anti-social behavior, etc. Any increase in the effectiveness in the marketing of these values and products could impact the character of millions of Americans." With neuromarketing technology, these organizations will have greater power to influence levels of demand among already-susceptible groups of consumers.

The Stakeholders

The focal stakeholders in this case are the neuromarketing companies, such as NeuroFocus, EmSense, and Sands Research. Other stakeholders include experts in both marketing and neuroscience that invest in neuromarketing companies; experts against neuromarketing; brands that use neuromarketing in their strategy; brands that do not use or support using a form of neuromarketing; neuromarketing competitors (i.e., traditional marketing agencies); consumers; Commercial Alert and other consumer rights groups; political groups; the media; lawyers; and legislatures.

Neuromarketing companies are forming coalitions with marketing and neuroscience experts. Gaining the support of experts supports the argument that neuromarketing is an ethical, efficient, and effective practice. Neuromarketing companies are also forming coalitions with companies such as Frito-Lay, Pepsi-Cola, Microsoft, and Hyundai. However, experts and consumers who are not in agreement about the use of neuromarketing are forming their own coalitions to improve awareness of the ethical implications of neuromarketing. The *New York Times* and *Fast Company*, as noted earlier, have started covering the issue in recent years. Blogs such as Robert Dooley's "Neuromarketing: Where Brain Science and Marketing Meet" (www.neurosciencemarketing.com/blog/) have cropped up to discuss questionable issues about neuromarketing. PBS has also run programming and hosted discussions on the issue on its website. A third-party certification could offer a solution by companies showing that that they received a quality neuromarketing product. Such a certification can also reassure customers that their rights are being protected (Wieckowski, 2019).

Whether and to what extent neuromarketing practices are used in ethically questionable ways remains a topic of debate. Buyer beware and seller take care remain precautions.

Questions for Discussion

1. Do you believe that neuromarketing is unethical or an innovative business practice? Explain.
2. Do all or most companies that market products and services use questionable techniques to influence and persuade customers?
3. Are you personally concerned or bothered by the neuromarketing techniques described in this case? Explain.
4. What moral responsibilities, if any, should marketing companies have—especially those firms using neuromarketing techniques? Explain.

Sources

This case was developed from material contained in the following sources:

Alexander, J. (2009, September 1). Neuromarketing to viewers. *Cablefax*. https://www.cablefax.com/programming/neuromarketing-to-viewers.

Baños-González, M., Fernández, A., and Rajas-Fernández, M. (2020, September). The application of neuromarketing techniques in the Spanish advertising industry: Weaknesses and opportunities for development. *Frontiers in Psychology*. https://www.ncbi.nlm.nih.gov/pmc/articles/PMC7494799/.

Bhatia, K. (n.d.). Neuromarketing: Towards a better understanding of consumer behavior. https://www.academia.edu/11478729/Neuromarketing_Towards_a_better_understanding_of_consumer_behavior.

Boricean, V. (2019, November 15). Brief history of neuromarketing. International Conference on Economics and Administration. https://livrosdeamor.com.br/documents/brief-history-of-neuromarketing-5bcd77e6930c0.

Brain Scientific. (2020, April 9). Neuroscience study finds consumers engage most with "hopeful" and encouraging messaging about Covid-19. *GlobeNewsWire*. http://www.globenewswire.com/fr/news-release/2020/04/09/2014218/0/en/Neuroscience-Study-Finds-Consumers-Engage-Most-with-Hopeful-Encouraging-Messaging-about-COVID-19.html.

Burkitt, L. (2009, November 16). Neuromarketing: Companies use neuroscience for consumer insights. *Forbes*. https://www.forbes.com/forbes/2009/1116/marketing-hyundai-neurofocus-brain-waves-battle-for-the-brain.html?sh=483d99be17bb.

Carmichael, M. (2004, November 9). Neuromarketing: Is it coming to a lab near you? Frontline. *PBS.org*. http://www.pbs.org/wgbh/pages/frontline/shows/persuaders/etc/neuro.html.

Centers for Disease Control and Prevention. (2020, May 21). Smoking and tobacco use. https://www.cdc.gov/tobacco/data_statistics/fact_sheets/index.htm.

Commercial Alert. (2003, November 30). Commercial Alert asks Emory University to halt neuromarketing experiments (Press release). *Commercial Alert.org.*

Commercial Alert. (2004, July 12). Commercial Alert asks Senate Commerce Committee to investigate neuromarketing (Press release). *Commercial Alert.org.*

Elliott, S. (2008, March 31). Is the ad a success? The brain waves tell all. *NYTimes .com.* http://www.nytimes.com/2008/03/31/business/media/31adcol.html.

EyeTracking. (n.d.). What is eye tracking? *EyeTracking.com.* http://www.eyetracking .com/technology/learn/.

Market Research Future. (2020, September). Market synopsis of global neuromarketing technology market. https://www.marketresearchfuture.com/reports /neuromarketing-technology-market-5340.

Nobel, C. (2013, February 1). Neuromarketing: Tapping into the "pleasure center" of consumers. *Forbes.* http://www.forbes.com/sites/hbsworkingknowledge/2013 /02/01/neuromarketing-tapping-into-the-pleasure-center-of-consumers/.

Odekerken, D. (2018, May 28). Ethics of neuromarketing. *Neurofied.com.* https:// neurofied.com/the-ethics-of-neuromarketing/.

Randall, K. (2009, September 15). Neuromarketing hope and hype: 5 brands conducting brain research. *Fast Company.* https://www.fastcompany.com/1357239 /neuromarketing-hope-and-hype-5-brands-conducting-brain-research.

Reda, S. (2008, April). Marketing's next (brain) wave. *SandsResearch.com.* Accessed March 28, 2012, http://www.sandsresearch.com/Stores_Article.aspx.

Wieckowski, A. (2019, January 23). When neuromarketing crosses the line. *Harvard Business Review.* https://hbr.org/2019/01/when-neuromarketing-crosses-the -line.

Case 16

Opioid Crisis in America

The Centers for Disease Control and Prevention (CDC) of the Department of Health and Human Services, reported that more than 130 individuals in the United States do not survive opioid-related overdoses each day (CDC, 2018). Although the daily death rate is severe, the widespread effect of the abuse is more common than expected. In a more quantifiable analysis, misuse of prescribed opioids and illegal use of heroin "affects more than 2 million Americans and an estimated 15 million people worldwide each year. The prevalence of opioid misuse and addiction is rapidly increasing" (Medline, n.d.). The U.S. drug-overdose epidemic is worsening. Almost 90,000 U.S. overdose deaths occurred between September 2019 and September 2020, which is the highest figure since the late 1990s, according to data from the CDC (Smith, 2021).

The Medical History

Dating to the mid-1800s, medics used morphine during the Civil War to aid as an anesthetic during battle, which led to dependency after the war ended (CNN, 2021). The National Institute on Drug Abuse pinpointed the modern-day opioid issue commencing in the late 1990s—namely, when the pharmaceutical companies reassured the medical community that patients would not become addicted to prescription opioid pain relievers, and then health care providers began to prescribe them at greater rates. These events subsequently led to a widespread diversion and misuse of these medications before it became clear that these medications could indeed be highly addictive (National Institute on Drug Abuse, 2019).

The second major increase came in 2010, with rapid development of heroin overdoses. Beginning in 2013, synthetic drugs rapidly increased overdose-induced deaths, mainly from IMF (illicitly manufactured fentanyl). From 1999 through 2017, overdose deaths comprised of both prescription opioids and illicit opioids reached a total of nearly 400,000. In 2017 alone, more than 68 percent of all reported drug overdoses were related to an opioid. In comparison, the opioid-related deaths reported in 2017 were more than six times higher than those reported in 1999, at the start of the crisis (CDC, 2021).

National Side Effects

The CDC quantified the national crisis in dollar figures as costing an estimated $78.5 billion each year due to the misuse of prescription opioids; this amount considers health care costs, loss of productivity, addiction and prevention treatments, as well as criminal justice expenditures (CNN, 2021). Shedding light on recent public policy tactics, the United States government enacted the 21st Century Cures Act in 2016, with the goal of funding treatment and prevention programs. In 2017, the Department of Justice launched an Opioid Fraud and Abuse Detection Unit.

Ex-president Donald Trump made nationwide efforts in October 2018 to introduce opioid legislation. The goal of the SUPPORT for Patients and Communities Act was to fund both research for alternative drugs for nonaddictive pain management and treatments for Medicaid patients with substance abuse disorders. "State legislatures are also introducing measures to regulate pain clinics and limit the quantity of opioids that doctors can dispense" (CNN, 2021).

There are several tiers of major stakeholders affected by this crisis: first and foremost, patients. Since opioids are costly and not readily available, opioid-addicts often turn to a cheaper drug choice—heroin—which leads to another devastating and life-threatening habit. Additionally, families of addicts are affected secondarily. Pharmaceutical companies have a large profit motive in this industry, causing many firms to mislead consumers and prescribing physicians. Taxpayers and regulatory bodies are being relied on to fund and eradicate the crisis. When filling prescriptions, pharmacies such as CVS are able to control and limit the number of days a patient is supplied opioids.

Prevention Tactics

The National Institutes of Health (NIH), part of the Department of Health and Human Services, has several focused priorities in response to the public health crisis and its effects on social and economic welfare, including:

1. Improving access to treatment and recovery services
2. Promoting use of overdose-reversing drugs
3. Strengthening our understanding of the epidemic through better public health surveillance
4. Providing support for cutting-edge research on pain and addiction
5. Advancing better practices for pain management (National Institute on Drug Abuse, 2019)

The United States Surgeon General is considered and endorsed as the nation's doctor and infrequently broadcasts critical issues and warnings. Historically, the Surgeon General has communicated key issues to the public, including the dangers surrounding tobacco usage, skin cancer, and drinking during pregnancy, to name a few. In April 2018, the U.S. Surgeon General advised Americans to carry Naloxone on their persons. Naloxone is a drug used by medical professionals to reverse the effects of an opioid overdose. However, this controversial solution is merely a quick fix and provides a "safety net" for individuals to overdose, be revived, and continue the horrific cycle of addiction and inappropriate drug use. There are many steps that need to be taken to ensure Americans are fully aware of the necessary precautions and, ultimately, the consequences and severity of the opioid crisis.

Stakeholders and Issues

Some of the major stakeholders described include patients, their families, prescribing medical professionals, pharmaceutical companies, taxpayers, pharmacies, and regulatory bodies. Patients are prescribed opioids for purposes of pain management. Oftentimes, patients are prescribed more pills than needed for their injuries and then continue to use them even when they no longer have the initial pain that the medication was intended to provide relief for. The U.S. Department of Health and Human Services (HHS, 2019) noted, in a 2017 National Survey on Drug Use and Health, that 11.4 million people misused prescription drugs throughout the year. The balance between prescribing effective opioid drugs for pain relief and overprescribing the drug is a difficult equilibrium to meet.

Another key issue is that patients are no longer able to maintain their long-term treatment regimens since the risk of abusing opioids and becoming addicted remains a threat. The CDC published a guideline for prescribing opioids for chronic pain, a huge component and side effect of the crisis. The CDC stated that "many Americans suffer from chronic pain. These patients deserve safe and effective pain management. Prescription opioids can help manage some types of pain in the short term. However, we don't have enough information about the benefits of opioids long term, and we know that there are serious risks of opioid use disorder and overdose." The CDC guideline also noted that 249 million prescriptions for opioid pain medication were written by health care providers in 2013 and "enough prescriptions were written for every American adult to have a bottle of pills" with high dosages and long-term use (CDC, n.d.). Patients and their families should be cognizant of the dangers involved with the highly addictive drugs and how to use dosages properly and prevent the likelihood of addiction.

Physicians are integral in prescribing pain management to patients. While many doctors are hearing the public health concern and lowering their prescription supplies per patient, there is still a long way to go. Unfortunately, with the risk of addiction, some doctors are now underprescribing medications for patients who require a longer recovery period, as well as chronic pain patients, discussed previously. The overregulation appears to be backfiring, as the ability for physicians to adequately prescribe medications to those in need is now questioned and, ultimately, insufficient. With many different agencies and regulatory legislations being introduced, physicians are conflicted more than ever between providing evidence-based drug therapy for pain and the risk of overprescribing patients, which could lead to addiction.

Pharmaceutical companies appear to display ethical relativism, a self-interest approach that "holds that no universal standards or rules can be used to guide or evaluate the morality of an act. This view argues that people set their own moral standards for judging their actions. Only the individual's self-interest and values are relevant for judging his or her behavior" (see Chapter 2). The results of a poll conducted in 2019 showed that most Americans blame pharmaceutical companies for the opioid crisis, with a similar number of people blaming drug users themselves as responsible (Stobbe and Swanson, 2019). An individual who took part in the poll supports the notion that users themselves are at fault, stating, "Nobody's forcing them to drugs. Nobody puts it in their hand and puts a gun to the head and says; 'Here, take this.'" There are several steps that could lead to an addiction to opioids, thus it is difficult to pinpoint one sole stakeholder to be blamed for the crisis.

An Ethical Lens: Pharmaceutical Companies and Patients

The principle of utilitarianism is important as we discuss the crisis at hand. Both physicians and pharmaceutical companies are major players; so are those engaged in opioid manufacturing and sales and advocacy groups; it is important to ensure these parties are taking the best course of action for the majority, also described as "the greatest good for the greatest number of people." The utilitarian principle requires that all stakeholders be taken into account and analyzed before any action is taken. Furthermore, the doctors and firms must consider the costs and benefits related to the decision at stake. "Pharmaceutical companies have created many lifesaving drugs over the years, and have helped hundreds of millions of people. However, if a company is perceived to act unethically and violates the public trust, that company stands to face not only more lawsuits, but the loss of customers and the financial resources that help these companies succeed" (Weiss, 2014, 338).

The Common Good doctrine follows a similar thought process, as the interdependency of all stakeholders is highlighted. By including the broader environment, the legislative system, the health care system, and public policy, there is more likelihood that effective practices will be instituted and normalized. "The ethic of the common good calls us to share in a common vision of a society that benefits and is beneficial for all members, while respecting individual differences. Using this ethic in our decision making also calls us to take goals and actions that include others besides ourselves and our own interests into account" (see Chapter 2). By integrating this principle, pharmaceutical companies would evaluate the perspective of shareholders, management, employees as well as patients, doctors, and the treatment population. Evaluating the decision from these additional viewpoints allows for both costs and benefits to be intertwined in the firm's practices.

As patients taking pain relief and management drugs are at-risk for addiction to opioids, there must be responsibility at many levels: by the manufacturing companies, by doctors in making their dosage/treatment length determinations, by regulatory agencies for safety measures, and by the patient themselves. It is quite easy to point the finger, but the individual that reaches an addiction (and perhaps overdoses as a result) needs to be aware and cautious of the risks and decisions being made. The medical community and the U.S. Surgeon General are consistently pushing out publications and communications to the nation in order to bring awareness, enact new legislation, and provide comprehensive prevention programs to help reduce illicit drug use, misuse, and abuse of prescription drugs and, overall, to reduce the commonality of the chronic illness of opioid addiction in the country.

Efforts being made for alternatives to pain relief, drug-prescribing standards, and prevention tactics will help begin to address overdoses from opioid-related causes and make a lasting impact on the crisis and the many stakeholders being affected.

Questions for Discussion

1. What did you learn from this case that you didn't know about opioids in America?
2. Explain if and how using a stakeholder AND an issues management approach can help understand this case better than just reading it?
3. What specific ethical principles and reasoning are relevant to apply in this case?
4. Who is to blame, and why, in this case?
5. Is the opioid crisis in America over? Why or why not? What solution paths would you recommend to help contain, if not eradicate, the crisis?

Sources

This case was developed from material contained in the following sources:

CDC. (n.d.). CDC guideline for prescribing opioids for chronic pain. Accessed March 26, 2021, https://www.cdc.gov/drugoverdose/pdf/guidelines_at-a-glance-a.pdf.

CDC (2018). CDC Wonder database, National Vital Statistics System. https://wonder.cdc.gov. See also CDC Prescription Opioid Data at https://www.cdc.gov/drugoverdose/data/prescribing.html/.

CDC. (2021, March 17). Understanding the epidemic. https://www.cdc.gov/drugoverdose/epidemic/index.html.

CNN. (2021, March 16). Opioid crisis fast fact. *CNN.com*. https://www.cnn.com/2017/09/18/health/opioid-crisis-fast-facts/index.html.

HHS. (2019, January). What is the U.S. opioid epidemic? https://www.hhs.gov/opioids/about-the-epidemic/index.html.

Medline. (n.d.). Opioid addiction. Genetics home reference. Accessed June 25, 2019, https://ghr.nlm.nih.gov/condition/opioid-addiction#statistics.

National Institute on Drug Abuse. (2019, January). Opioid overdose crisis. *DrugAbuse.gov*. https://www.drugabuse.gov/drugs-abuse/opioids/opioid-overdose-crisis#one.

Smith, T. (2021, April 30). 8 keys to end the nation's drug-overdose epidemic. https://www.ama-assn.org/delivering-care/opioids/8-keys-end-nation-s-drug-overdose-epidemic.

Stobbe, M., and Swanson, E. (2019, April 25). AP-NORC poll: Many blame drug firms for opioid crisis. *AP News*. https://www.apnews.com/103530ad684f4941999e99467121b5d6.

Weiss, J. W. (2014). *Business Ethics: A stakeholder and issues management approach*. 6th ed. San Francisco: Berrett-Koehler.

Notes

1. Mitterling, T., Tomass, N. and Wu, K. (2020). The decline and recovery of consumer spending in the US. *Brookings.* https://www.brookings.edu/blog/future-development /2020/12/14/the-decline-and-recovery-of-consumer-spending-in-the-us/.

2. Keck School of Medicine of USC. (2020, February 6). Three global health threats. *Your Public Health (blog).* University of Southern California. https://mphdegree.usc.edu /blog/3-global-public-health-threats/.

3. "Globesity": U.S. junk food industry tips global scales. (2013, September 7). *RT.com.* http://rt.com/usa/us-obesity-food-global-regulation-551/; and Kalaidis, J. (2013, February 25). Should the U.S. adopt a fat tax? *The Week.* https://theweek.com/articles /467316/should-adopt-fat-tax. See also Nath, T. (2019, June 25). The economic cost of an obese society. *Investopedia.* https://www.investopedia.com/articles/personal-finance /041715/economic-cost-obese-society.asp.

4. Hales, C. M., Carroll, M. D., Fryar, C. D., and Ogden C. L. (2020, February). Prevalence of obesity and severe obesity among adults: United States, 2017–2018. National Center for Health Statistics NCHS Data Brief No. 360. https://www.cdc.gov/nchs /data/databriefs/db360-h.pdf; Shields, M., Carroll, M., and Ogden, C. (2011, March). Adult obesity prevalence in Canada and the United States. National Center for Health Statistics Data Brief No. 56. http://www.cdc.gov/nchs/data/databriefs/db56.pdf.

5. Centers for Disease Control and Prevention (CDC). (2019). https://www.cdc.gov /obesity/data/prevalence-maps.html; and https://www.cdc.gov/obesity/data/childhood .html.

6. Wood, L. (2006, January, 30). Obesity has become such a problem that the US Health and Human Services have declared it a disease. Research and Markets (press release). *PRWeb.com.* http://www.prweb.com/releases/2006/01/prweb338077.htm; Americans fatter than ever, obesity officially called a "disease." (2013, June 19). *RT.com,* http://rt .com/usa/obesity-disease-americans-record-957/.

7. Health promotion: Survey finds consumers want healthier fast foods. (2006, February 10). *Medicine & Law Weekly,* 182.

8. Sturm, R., and Hattori, A. (2015, May 25). Diet and obesity in Los Angeles County 2007–2012: is there a measurable effect." *Social Science & Medicine, 133,* 205–211. https:// www.rand.org/pubs/external_publications/EP50830.html.

9. Adult obesity causes and consequences. (n.d.) *CDC.gov.* https://www.cdc.gov /obesity/adult/causes.html.

10. Philipson, T., and Posner, R. (2010, July 30). Fat new world: Technology spawned the obesity plague. It can also provide a cure. *Wall Street Journal.* http://online.wsj.com /news/articles/SB10001424052748703940904575395513421527100.

11. Stensson, A., and Carroll, P. (2012, December 9). Hottest restaurant menu trends in 2012 include healthful kids' meals and locally sourced ingredients, according to National Restaurant Association. *The National Provisioner.* https://www.provisioneronline.com /articles/97445-national-restaurant-association-reveals-hot-menu-trends-for-2012.

12. Harris, J., Heard, A., and Schwartz, M. (2014, January). Older but still vulnerable: All children need protection from unhealthy food marketing. Rudd Brief. Yale Rudd Center for Food Policy and Obesity. http://uconnruddcenter.org/files/Pdfs/Protecting _Older_Children_3_14.pdf.

13. World Bank. (2019). GDP ranking. *World Bank.* http://databank.worldbank.org /data/download/GDP.pdf.

14. Drucker, P. (1973). *Management: Tasks, responsibilities, practices.* New York: Harper & Row, 61.

15. Purdy, C. (2020). *Billion dollar burger: Inside Big Tech's race for the future of food.* New York: Portfolio/Penguin.

16. Consumers International. (2011). What are consumer rights? http://www.consumersinternational.org/who-we-are/consumer-rights.

17. Velasquez, M. (1988, 1998). *Business ethics concepts and cases,* 2nd and 4th eds. Englewood Cliffs, NJ: Prentice Hall.

18. Velasquez, M. (2001). The ethics of consumer protection. In Hoffman, W., Frederick, R., and Schwartz, M. (eds.), *Business ethics,* 4th ed. Boston: McGraw-Hill, 424.

19. Boatright, J. (1999). *Ethics and the conduct of business,* 3rd ed. Englewood Cliffs, NJ: Prentice Hall, 273.

20. Velasquez, M. (2002). *Business ethics: concepts and cases,* 335–344. Upper Saddle River, NJ: Prentice Hall.

21. Buchholz, R. (1991, July/August). Corporate responsibility and the good society: From economics to ecology. *Business Horizons, 34(4),* 19–31; Holloway, R., and Hancock, R. (1973). *Marketing in a changing environment,* 2nd ed. New York: John Wiley and Sons.

22. Bell, C. (2001, April 3). Testing reliance on free market. *Boston Globe,* C4.21.

23. European Commission. (2012, May 22). A new European Consumer Agenda—Boosting confidence and growth by putting consumers at the heart of the Single Market (Press release). http://europa.eu/rapid/press-release_IP-12-491_en.htm.

24. Kelly, L. (2021, April 1). Digital ad sales to top two-thirds of total spend for first time in 2021, Magna forecasts. *Marketing Dive.* https://www.marketingdive.com/news/digital-ad-sales-to-top-two-thirds-of-total-spend-for-first-time-in-2021-m/597685/.

25. Federal Trade Commission (FTC). Privacy and security. *FTC.gov.* https://www.ftc.gov/news-events/media-resources/protecting-consumer-privacy-security.

26. Velasquez (1998). *Business ethics concepts and cases,* 4th ed. Englewood Cliffs, NJ: Prentice Hall, 343–349.

27. Centers for Disease Control and Prevention. (n.d.). Youth and tobacco use. https://www.cdc.gov/tobacco/data_statistics/fact_sheets/youth_data/tobacco_use/index.htm, accessed March 24, 2021; National Center for Chronic Disease Prevention and Health Promotion, Office on Smoking and Health. (2012). *Preventing tobacco use among youth and young adults: A Report of the Surgeon General.* Atlanta: Centers for Disease Control and Prevention.

28. Coppola, D. (2021, February 19). Total retail and food services sales in the U.S. 1992–2019. *Statista.* https://www.statista.com/statistics/197569/annual-retail-and-food-services-sales/.

29. Gould, S. (2017, May). 6 charts that show how much more Americans eat than they used to. *Business Insider.* https://www.businessinsider.com/daily-calories-americans-eat-increase-2016-07.

30. Associated Press. (2003, January 11). Supreme Court to take up Nike free-speech case. *The Olympian.*

31. Biskupic, J. (2004, June 29). High Court upholds block of web porn law. *USAToday.com.*

32. The major source of this "doctrine" can be found in: Kerr, L. (2011). *A Justice's Surprise That Has Stood Its Ground: The Enduring Value of the Commercial Speech Doctrine's Powellian Balance.* https://core.ac.uk/download/pdf/215233537.pdf. The excerpt used here is based on Steiner G. A., and Steiner, Steiner, J. F. (2000). *Business, government, and society,* 9th ed. Boston, MA: McGraw-Hill, 596.

33. Gostin, L. (2002). Corporate speech and the constitution: The deregulation of tobacco advertising. *American Journal of Public Health, 92(3)*, 352–355.

34. Greenhouse, L. (2008, June 19). The Supreme Court case, advertising; Nike free speech case is unexpectedly returned to California. *NYTimes.com*; Cava, A. (2000, Spring). Commercial speech 1999: Significant developments. *Academy of Marketing Science Journal, 28(2)*, 316–317. For more detail and discussion on these issues and other court cases, see Emord, J. (2000, Spring). *Pearson v. Shalala:* The beginning of the end for FDA speech suppression. *Journal of Public Policy & Marketing, 19(1)*, 139–143.

35. Samp, R. (2013, June 11). In attack on commercial speech, law professor sadly supports selective rights. *Forbes.com*. http://www.forbes.com/sites/wlf/2013/06/11/in-attack -on-commercial-speech-law-professor-sadly-supports-selective-rights/2/.

36. Zephoria Digital Marketing. (2020). The top 20 valuable Facebook statistics. https:// zephoria.com/top-15-valuable-facebook-statistics/; Statista. (2021). Worldwide advertising revenues of YouTube as of 4th quarter 2020. Percentage of adults in the United States who use selected social networks as of September 2020. (2021, January). *Statista*. https://www .statista.com/statistics/246230/share-of-us-internet-users-who-use-selected-social -networks/revenues/#:~:text=YouTube's%20worldwide%20advertising%20revenues%20 amounted,accumulated%20over%20100%20million%20subscribers; Cramer-Flood, E. (2020, July 6). Global digital ad spending update Q2 2020. https://www.emarketer.com /content/global-digital-ad-spending-update-q2-2020.

37. Auxier B., M. Anderson, A. Perrin, and E. Turner. (2020). Parenting Children in the Age of Screens. https://www.pewresearch.org/internet/2020/07/28/parenting-children-in -the-age-of-screens/.

38. Ibid.

39. Federal Trade Commission. (2014). Fiscal year 2014 congressional budget justification. See especially the section on privacy, data security, and technology, 9–11. http:// www.ftc.gov/sites/default/files/documents/reports_annual/fy-2014-congressional -budget-justification/2014_cbj.pdf.

40. For planned activities and accomplishments of the European Cybercrime Convention, see Council of Europe. (n.d.). Action against cybercrime. http://www.coe.int/t /DGHL/cooperation/economiccrime/cybercrime/default_en.asp, accessed March 26, 2021.

41. Chang, H. (2014, February 5). Canada: Canada's anti-spam law comes into force on July 1, 2014. *Mondaq.* http://www.mondaq.com/canada/x/291080/international+trade +investment/Canadas+AntiSpam+Law+Comes+into+Force+on+July+1+2014.

42. Federal Trade Commission. (2013, March). How to make effective disclosures in digital advertising. *Dot com Disclosures.* http://www.ftc.gov/sites/default/files/attachments /press-releases/ftc-staff-revises-online-advertising-disclosure-guidelines/130312dot comdisclosures.pdf.

43. Ibid.

44. Children's Internet Access at Home. (2020, May). *The Condition of Education.* National Center for Educational Statistics. https://nces.ed.gov/programs/coe/indicator_cch.asp.

45. Piper Sandler. (2020, Fall). *Taking Stock with Teens.* http://www.pipersandler.com /private/pdf/TSWTs_Fall_2020_Full_Report.pdf.

46. Federal Trade Commission. (n.d.). Children's privacy. https://www.ftc.gov/tips -advice/business-center/privacy-and-security/children%27s-privacy, accessed March 26, 2021.

47. Children's Advertising Review Unit. (2008, May 28). CARU reviews advertising for Stardoll.com website. *CARU.org.*

48. Sikiti da Silva, I. (2007, January 9). Task force on advertising to children in SA. *BizCommunity.com.* http://www.bizcommunity.com/Article/196/11/12890.html.

49. See the European Advertising Standards Alliance website at http://www.easa-alliance.org/.

50. World Health Organization. (2006, May 30). Regulation urgently needed to control growing list of deadly tobacco products (Press release). http://www.who.int/mediacentre/news/releases/2006/pr28/en/index.html.

51. Egan, S. (2003, June 25). Why smoking rates are at new lows. *New York Times.* Karas, L. (2020, December 11). Graphic warnings on cigarettes: Public health vs. corporate speech. *Bill of Health.* https://blog.petrieflom.law.harvard.edu/2020/12/11/graphic-warnings-cigarettes-first-amendment/.

52. Katz, J. (2021, March 30). FTC releases reports on cigarette and smokeless tobacco sales and marketing expenditures for 2019. *Federal Trade Commission.* https://www.ftc.gov/news-events/press-releases/2021/03/ftc-releases-reports-cigarette-smokeless-tobacco-sales-marketing.

53. American Cancer Society. (2013, July 8). Why people start smoking? *Cancer.org.* https://www.cancer.org/healthy/stay-away-from-tobacco/why-people-start-using-tobacco.html.

54. Kaufman, M. (2004, September 19). U.S. racketeering trial against tobacco industry is set to start. *Washington Post,* A14. See also Campaign for Tobacco-Free Kids. (2010, July 1). U.S. racketeering verdict: Big tobacco guilty as charged. *TobaccoFreeKids.org.* https://www.tobaccofreekids.org/what-we-do/industry-watch/doj/faq.

55. Karas (2020, December 11), op. cit.

56. WHO (World Health Organization). (n.d.). Tobacco. https://www.who.int/health-topics/tobacco#tab=tab_1, accessed June 16, 2021.

57. NIH and NIAAA. (2021, June). Alcohol facts and statistics. https://www.niaaa.nih.gov/publications/brochures-and-fact-sheets/alcohol-facts-and-statistics, accessed June 16, 2021.

58. Ibid.

59. Unknown author. (2007, April, 5). Anheuser-Busch condemned for pushing alcohol-heavy Spykes "Liquid Lunchables." *ConsumerAffairs.com.* https://www.consumeraffairs.com/news04/2007/04/spykes.html.

60. FDA (2021, May 6). Constituent update, FDA issues procedural notice on consumer research on "healthy" symbol. https://www.fda.gov/food/cfsan-constituent-updates/fda-issues-procedural-notice-consumer-research-healthy-symbol.

61. FDA. (2019, September 12). Health information. https://www.fda.gov/tobacco-products/public-health-education/health-information.

62. Schleicher, A. (2004, April 26). Most antidepressants deemed unsafe for children. *PBS Online News Hour.*

63. Common Sense. (2021). One year into the pandemic, a new survey reveals that teens and young adults are actively turning to online sources to cope with mental health. *Cision PR Newswire.* https://www.prnewswire.com/news-releases/one-year-into-the-pandemic-a-new-survey-reveals-that-teens-and-young-adults-are-actively-turning-to-online-sources-to-cope-with-mental-health-301248974.html.

64. Ibid. See also Medical News Today. (2021). What is Prozac (fluoxetine)? https://www.medicalnewstoday.com/articles/263773#:~:text=The%20FDA%20requires%20Prozac%20to,decreased%20libido%20and%20sexual%20dysfunction.

65. Ruin, R. (2010, January 5). Study: Antidepressant lift may be all in your head. *USAToday.com.* http://www.usatoday.com/news/health/2010-01-06-antidepressants06

_ST_N.htm; Study shows 70 percent of Americans take prescription drugs. (2013, June 20). *CBSNews.com.* http://www.cbsnews.com/news/study-shows-70-percent-of-americans-take-prescription-drugs/.

66. Lee, D. (2000, December). How government prevents us from buying safety. *Ideas on Liberty, 50(12),* 32–33.

67. DeGeorge, R. (1990). *Business ethics,* 3rd ed. New York: Macmillan, 182, 183.

68. O'Donnell, J. (2001, April 4). Costco's history reads like a recipe for recalls/Company kept quiet. *USA Today,* B1.

69. Falvey, C., M. Cohen, and J. Gilbert. (2021, April 29). New bills seek to repeal controversial provision of Product Safety Act. https://www.retailconsumerproductslaw.com/2021/04/new-bills-seek-to-repeal-controversial-provision-of-product-safety-act/

70. Etzioni, A. (1978). The need to put a price on life. *Communitarian Network.*

71. Shook Hardy & Bacon LLP. (2018, October 25). Product liability in the USA. *Lexology.* https://www.lexology.com/library/detail.aspx?g=3714f105-6d2e-4e33-be4f-17289ae7e547.

72. ABA (American Bar Association). (2021). Product liability claims we expect to see as a result of COVID-19. https://www.americanbar.org/groups/litigation/committees/mass-torts/articles/2021/spring2021-product-liability-claims-we-expect-to-see-as-a-result-of-covid19/.

73. Ibid.

74. Ibid.

75. Feeley, J., and Voreacos, D. (2011, November 23). Merck to plead guilty, pay $950 million in U.S. Vioxx probe. *Bloomberg.com.* http://www.bloomberg.com/news/2011-11-22/merck-agrees-to-pay-950-million-to-settle-u-s-government-s-vioxx-probe.html. Also see, Merck settles Vioxx claims for $4.85 billion. (2007, November 9). *Reuters.* https://www.reuters.com/article/us-merck-settlement/merck-settles-vioxx-claims-for-4-85-bln-idUSWNAS1784200711O9.

76. DesJardins, J., and McCall, J. (eds.) (1990). *Contemporary issues in business ethics.* Belmont, CA: Wadsworth, 255.

77. See Posch, R. (1988). *The complete guide to marketing and the law.* Englewood Cliffs, NJ: Prentice Hall, 3; Sturdivant, F., and Vernon-Wortzel, H. (1991). *Business and society: A managerial approach,* 4th ed. Homewood, IL: Irwin, 305.

78. Carroll, A., and A. Buchholtz. (2000). *Business and Society: Ethics and Stakeholder Management.* Cincinnati, OH: South-Western College, 258; DesJardins and McCall (1990), op. cit., 255.

79. Carroll and Buchholtz. (2000), op. cit., 259.

80. Maljustice in the courts. (2001, June 19). *Boston Globe,* A14.

81. Judge rules in favor of ex-smoker's son against Philip Morris. (2007, July 19). *KNBC News Los Angeles.*

82. Geyelin, M. (1992, January 6). Law: Product suits yield few punitive awards. *Wall Street Journal,* B1.

83. Felsenthal, E. (1996, June 17). Punitive awards are called modest, rare. *Wall Street Journal,* B4.

84. Geyelin (1992), op. cit.

85. Tsui, J. F. (2020, February 24). Five Biggest environmental issues affecting the U.S. *Environmental Protection Magazine.* https://eponline.com/articles/2020/02/24/five-biggest-environmental-issues-affecting-the-us.aspx.

86. American Lung Association (n.d.). Most polluted cities. https://www.stateoftheair.org/city-rankings/most-polluted-cities.html, accessed March 26, 2021.

87. American Lung Association. (2013). State of the air report. *StateofthAair.org*.

88. Ibid.

89. C2ES. (2020, March 26). Climate basics: What we can do. Center for Climate and Energy Solutions. https://www.c2es.org/content/what-we-can-do/#:~:text=Greenhouse%20gas%20emissions%20can%20be,renewable%20hydrogen%2C%20and%20geothermal%20energy.

90. UNESCO WWAP. (2020). Fact 39: Water and health. World Water Assessment Programme. United Nations Educational, Scientific and Cultural Organization. http://www.unesco.org/new/en/natural-sciences/environment/water/wwap/facts-and-figures/all-facts-wwdr3/fact-39-water-and-health/#:~:text=of%20water%20resources-,Almost%20one%2Dtenth%20of%20the%20global%20disease%20burden%20could%20be,status%20in%20a%20sustainable%20way.

91. Sampat, P. (2001, July). The hidden threat of groundwater pollution. *USA Today*, 28–31. See also World Health Organization. (2011). Facts and figures on water quality and health.

92. Woods, R. (2001, August 3). EPA estimates costs of clean water TMDL program (Press release). *Environmental News*, 1.

93. Based on Steiner, G.A., and Steiner, J. F. (1991). *Business and society*, 3rd ed. New York: McGraw-Hill, 591; Steiner and Steiner (2000), op. cit., 484–485; Post et al. (2002), op. cit., 266.

94. Post et al. (2002), op. cit., 266.

95. Sagoff, M., DesJardins, J., and McCall, J. (1990). *Economic theory and environmental law in contemporary issues in business ethics*. Belmont, CA: Wadsworth, 360–364.

96. Buchholz (1991), op. cit., 19.

97. Environmental Protection Agency (EPA). (1990). *Environmental investments: The cost of a clean environment*. Washington, DC: EPA. See also EPA. (2011, April). *The benefits and costs of the Clean Air Act from 1990 to 2020: Final report—Rev. A.* https://www.epa.gov/sites/production/files/2015-07/documents/fullreport_rev_a.pdf.

98. Post et al. (2002), op. cit., 272.

99. Cohen, S. (2017, October 23). The human and financial cost of pollution. Earth Institute, Columbia University. *State of the planet*. https://blogs.ei.columbia.edu/2017/10/23/the-human-and-financial-cost-of-pollution/.

100. This section is based on Oyewole, P. (2001, February). Social costs of environmental justice associated with the practice of green marketing. *Journal of Business Ethics, 29(3)*, 239–251.

101. Johri, L., and Sahasakmontri, K. (1998). Green marketing of cosmetics and toiletries in Thailand. *Journal of Consumer Marketing, 15(3)*, 265–281.

102. Quick Pulse: Green buying—an exploration of "green" consumer trends. (2012, March 12). *Euromonitor International Market Research (blog)*. http://blog.euromonitor.com/2012/03/quick-pulse-green-buying-an-exploration-of-green-consumer-trends.html#sthash.fNpDXbcN.dpuf.

103. See Oyewole (2001), op. cit., 240.

104. Velasquez (1998), op. cit., 292.

105. Blackstone, W. (1974). Ethics and ecology. In Blackstone, W. (ed.), *Philosophy and environmental crisis*. Athens: University of Georgia Press.

106. Bloom, G., and Morton, M. (1991, Summer). Hazardous waste is every manager's problem. *Sloan Management Review*, 83.

107. Freeman, R. E., and Reichart, J. (2000). Toward a life centered ethic for business. *Ruffin Series of the Society for Business Ethics, 2*, 154. Reprinted with permission of the publisher.

6

THE CORPORATION AND INTERNAL STAKEHOLDERS

Values-Based Moral Leadership, Culture, Strategy, and Self-Regulation

OPENING CASE

Two Classic-to-Contemporary Leaders' Ethical Styles: 2021

Warren Buffett, Berkshire Hathaway

"At 90 years of age [Warren] Buffett has never been more of a force (more on that in a bit). . . . Buffett has to be the most impactful nonagenarian in America, if not the world."[1] A fortune of $82 billion makes him the seventh richest citizen of planet Earth. As founder and chief executive officer (CEO) of Berkshire Hathaway—which is, at the time of this writing, is the seventh largest U.S. company—Buffett has taken unprecedented steps in recent years to ensure that his messages about investing, ethics, and philanthropy reach an audience that will survive him. He didn't invent the light bulb, but he's had lots of bright ideas. He didn't devise the mass-production assembly line, but his companies have sold masses of goods. And Warren Buffett didn't originate the concept of money, but he has more of it than most—he has been listed among the top 10 wealthiest business person by *Forbes* for several years.[2] So what will be the Omaha investor's legacy? Or, rather, his legacies? Observers say the 90-year-old's ideas and philosophy of business and life will last far beyond his own. "Somebody from this group will learn something that will affect their lives," Buffett told a group of graduate students during a 2005 visit to Omaha.

"Buffett's emphasis on working with ethical people is already influencing business leaders and business schools, a change that could last far into the future," said Bruce Avolio, director of the University of Nebraska-Lincoln's Leadership Institute. "He buys the culture when he invests in an organization," Avolio said, "valuing a business's human condition as much as its financial condition. That's shifting people's thinking, and it has a huge impact. It's a model that's replicable—treating people fairly. Integrity underlies not only Warren Buffett's investments but also his philosophy of life." Keith Darcy, head of the 1,400-member Ethics and Compliance Officers Association in Waltham, Massachusetts, said Buffett has played a hand in "a flight to integrity" by investors, executives, employees, suppliers, and customers who want to be involved with companies that do business correctly. "It's essential to him to be working with people he trusts," Darcy said. "Without that level of trust, it's not worth doing business. Certainly he has been an exemplar for understanding that when you make investments, character and reputation are everything." In meetings with students, Darcy said, Buffett "speaks from his heart. He certainly is a mythological figure, except he's not a myth, he's real—a man of enormous success who always has believed in investing in companies with inherent value, but in particular the people in those businesses." Darcy believes Buffett will be a role model far into the future. Buffett himself has stated: "I want employees to ask themselves whether they are willing to have any contemplated act appear on the front page of their local paper the next day, to be read by their spouses, children, and friends.... If they follow this test, they need not fear my other message to them: Lose money for the firm, and I will be understanding; lose a shred of reputation for the firm, and I will be ruthless."[3]

Ratan Tata, Former Chairman of the Indian Corporation Tata Group

Ratan Tata retired on his 75th birthday after leading the Indian corporate conglomerate, the Tata Group. He assumed leadership from his uncle in 1991. The so-called House of Tata owns over 100 companies in 80 countries, including the Taj Group of luxury hotels and the exclusive Tata Nano car. The group's holdings exceed those of Walmart or ExxonMobil. The Tata Group was the first Indian company to obtain $100 billion in revenues, half of which is from abroad. Ratan Tata helped acquire significant European enterprises, including Jaguar Land Rover and Corus, the Anglo-Dutch steelmaker. Under his leadership, this group is now "perceived to represent Indian capitalism at its best, enjoying the goodwill of millions of customers, the loyalty of more than 400,000 employees and the investments of 3.8 million shareholders, while also reinvesting a substantial part of its profits into philanthropic work overseen by a set of trusts."[4] He currently owns 66 percent shares of Tata Son—the holding company that controls the salt-to-software conglomerate. His ethical beliefs are embodied in the company's policies, as stated in the company's Article and Rules for Sustaining CSR, Clause No. 10:

> A Tata Company shall be committed to be a good corporate citizen not only in compliance with all relevant laws and regulations but also by actively assisting in the improvement of the quality of life of the people in the communities in which it operates with the objective of making them self-reliant. Such social responsibility would comprise: to initiate and support community initiatives in the field of community health and family welfare, water management, vocational training, education and literacy, and encourage application of modern scientific and managerial techniques and expertise. This will be reviewed periodically in consonance with national and regional priorities. The company would also not treat these activities as optional ones but would strive to incorporate them as an integral part of its business plan. The company would also encourage volunteering amongst its employees and help them to work in the communities. Tata companies are encouraged to develop social accounting systems and to carry out social audit of their operations.[5]

Outstanding Ethically Diverse Leaders

In addition to the two classical contemporary leaders above, we recognize here that many more women and leaders of different genders, nationalities, and specializations are contributing by their ethical accomplishments and examples to business, government, science, and other sectors. To mention only a few: Jacinda Ardern's (Prime Minister of New Zealand 2017–) decisiveness coupled with "empathy, authenticity, tolerance and kindness" was evident in her fast response of locking down New Zealand when Covid-19 first appeared.[6] Tsai Ing-Wen (2016–), the first female president of Taiwan, was reelected in 2020 with over 57 percent of the popular vote. She legalized same-sex marriage in 2019 and defended Taiwan's independence from other countries. In December 2020, under Tsai's leadership, Taiwan had gone more than 200 days without a locally acquired COVID-19 case, and seven deaths since the start of the pandemic.[7] Dr. Kizzmekia Corbett (1987–), a 34-year-old black female scientist, and her team are credited with having rolled out the first stage of clinical trials to a vaccine platform in collaboration with Moderna.[8] Aurora James (1984–), notable innovative fashion designer, is the founder of Brother Vellies and the

15 Percent Pledge. Brother Vellies—the African artisanal shoe and handbag line—is an "ethical and sustainable luxury brand [that] has workshops in South Africa, Ethiopia, Kenya and Morocco, providing jobs for hundreds of traditional handicraft makers." She has recruited retailers, such as Macy's, to dedicate 15 percent of their shelf space to Black-owned brands—"Black people represent roughly 15 per cent of the US population."[9]

■ 6.1 Leadership and Stakeholder Management

Leadership is the ability to influence followers to achieve common goals through shared purposes. While there is no perfect leader, or prescription for ideal leadership characteristics, Buffett, Tata, Arden, Corbett, and James exemplify leaders with strategic market performance, values, and ethical standards.[10] With the onslaught of the Covid-19 pandemic, leaders of diverse gender, nationalities, color, and backgrounds have had to demonstrate crisis skills and capacities. They have also had to be purposeful, empathetic, courageous, and confident, taking time to reflect in the midst of chaos. Some scholars offered tips for leadership, "The coronavirus represents a historic inflection point that is likely to forever change us . . . take stock of your own life. Does your work reflect your values? Have you let some important relationships languish? Did you give up on a dream too soon? You're not going to be a good business leader unless you know how to lead yourself."[11]

Leaders, with the help of followers, are responsible for enacting an organization's vision, mission, and strategies, and for achieving goals in socially responsible ways.[12] Leaders also help define the culture and model the values of organizations that are essential for setting and modeling the legal and ethical tone and boundaries. Warren Buffett, Ratan Tata, and the other leaders introduced above embody the ethical leadership values, characteristics, and actions addressed in this chapter.

The CEO or president, who sometimes is also the chair of the board of directors, is the highest-ranking leader in a company. However, in both for- and not-for-profit organizations, the CEO reports to and is advised by the board of directors, which also serves leadership and governance roles. Leadership is not only limited to a few individuals or teams at the top of organizations. Individuals throughout an organization exert leadership responsibilities and influence in their roles and relationships to direct and guide their organizations.

Leadership also requires active involvement with and alignment of internal and external stakeholder relationships. Business relationships involve transactions and decisions that require ethical choices and, many times, moral courage. Building new strategic partnerships, transformational restructuring and layoffs, consumer lawsuits, environmental crises, bold new "green" initiatives, and turning around corporate cultures damaged by the effects of harmful products are examples of situations that require leadership business and ethical decisions. Leaders are responsible for the economic success of their enterprises and for the rights of those served inside and outside their boundaries. Research on leadership demonstrates that moral values, courage, and credibility are essential leadership capabilities.[13] James Collins's five-year research project on "good to great" companies found that leaders who moved from "good to great" showed what he called "Level 5" leadership. These leaders "channel their ego needs away from themselves and into the larger goal of building a great company. It's not that Level 5 leaders have no ego or self-interest. Indeed, they are incredibly ambitious—*but their ambition is first and foremost for the institution, not themselves*" (emphasis added).[14] Collins also concluded that Level 5 leaders build "enduring greatness through a paradoxical blend of personal humility and professional will"[15]—we would also add leadership characteristics of diverse backgrounds, gender, race, country of origin, age, expertise and experience.

Creating a "purpose-driven organization," as stated, helps "rally the organization behind an authentic higher purpose—an aspirational mission that explains how employees are making a difference and gives them a sense of meaning. If you do that, they will try new things, move into deep learning, and make surprising contributions. The workforce will become energized and committed, and performance will climb"[16]

This chapter focuses on the challenges that values-based leaders face while managing internal stakeholders, strategy, and culture in organizations. From a stakeholder management approach, an organization's leaders are responsible for initiating and sustaining an ethical, principled, and collaborative orientation toward those served by the firm.[17] Leaders model and enforce the values they wish their companies to embody with stakeholders.[18] One of an organization's most prized assets is its reputation, as noted earlier in the text. Reputations are built through productive and conscientious relationships with stockholders and stakeholders.[19]

A stakeholder, values-based leadership approach determines whether or not the organization and culture:

- Are integrated or fragmented
- Tolerate or build relationships
- Respect diversity and embed inclusiveness in cultures
- Isolate the organization or create mutual benefits and opportunities
- Develop and sustain short-term or long-term goals and relationships
- Encourage idiosyncratic dependent implementation based on division, function, business structure, and personal interest and style or encourage coherent approaches, driven by enterprise, visions, missions, values, and strategies

Effective leaders guide the ethical and strategic integration and alignment of the internal organization with the external environment. As the following sections show, competent leaders demonstrate different competencies in guiding and responding to their stakeholders and stockholders.

Figure 6.1

Strategic Alignment Questions

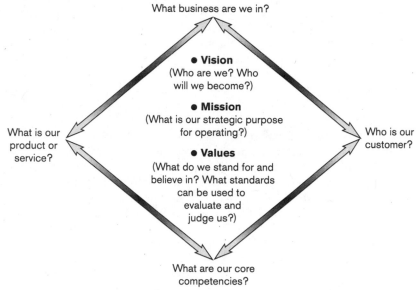

What business are we in?

● **Vision**
(Who are we? Who
will we become?)

● **Mission**
(What is our strategic purpose
for operating?)

● **Values**
(What do we stand for and
believe in? What standards
can be used to
evaluate and
judge us?)

What is our
product or
service?

Who is our
customer?

What are our core
competencies?

Source: Joseph W. Weiss. © 2014.

Defining Purpose, Mission, and Values

Leading an organization begins by identifying and enacting purpose and ethical values that are central to internal alignment, external market effectiveness, and responsibility toward stakeholders. As Figure 6.1 shows, key questions executives must answer before identifying a strategy and leading their firm are centered on defining the organization's vision, mission, and values: *What business are we in? What is our product or service? Who are our customers? What are our core competencies?*

A values-based leadership approach is exemplified by Chester Barnard, who wrote in 1939 that effective leaders and managers "inspire cooperative personal decisions by creating faith in common understanding, faith in the probability of success, faith in the ultimate satisfaction of personal motives, and faith in the integrity of common purpose."[20] In the classic book *Built to Last,*[21] authors James Collins and Jerry Porras state, "Purpose is the set of fundamental reasons for a company's existence beyond just making money. Visionary companies get at purpose by asking questions similar to those posed by David Packard [cofounder of Hewlett-Packard]: 'I want to discuss why a company exists in the first place. . . . Why are we here? I think many people assume, wrongly, that a company exists simply to make money. While this is an important result of a company's existence, we have to go deeper and find the real reasons for our being.'"

JetBlue's founder and former CEO, David Neeleman—who is launching another new airline, Breeze, in 2021 and is part owner of the Brazilian airline, Azul—said:

For our company's core values, we came up with five words: safety, caring, fun, integrity, and passion. We guide our company by them. But from my experience—and I've had a lot of life experiences that were deep religious experiences—I feel that everyone is equal in the way they should be treated and the way they should be respected. I think that I try to conduct myself in that way. I treat everyone the same: I don't give anyone more deference because of their position or their status. Then I just try to create trust with our crewmembers. I know if they trust me, if they know I'm trying to do the best things I think are in their long-term interest, then they'll be happier and they'll feel like this is a better place to work. The top five tips for landing a job at JetBlue include (1) *Do your homework!* Study JetBlue's history and their current happenings and their five core values; (2) *Know your story:* Be prepared for the interview by reviewing your own challenging situations and how you handled them; (3) *Show your passion:* People at JetBlue are very passionate about the company and what they do. Showing passion for the company and role you are applying for is important; (4) *Be open and honest;* and (5) *Be yourself!* "We are a fun company, and we just want you to be you!"[22] [Even though Neeleman was not directly responsible in 2007 when JetBlue passengers were stranded on the JFK tarmac for 8 hours after an ice storm, he was pushed out of his CEO position; afterward he responsibly owned the problem as the founder and leader of the airline. His entrepreneurial reputation and accomplishments remain intact.]

Ethical companies may also include a "social mission" in their formal mission and values statements. A social mission is a commitment by the organization to give back to the community and external stakeholders who make the organization's existence possible. Ben & Jerry's (now a division of the Anglo-Dutch Unilever conglomerate), Lands' End, Southwest Airlines, and many other companies commit to serving their communities through different types of stewardship outreach, facility sharing (e.g., day care and tutoring programs), and other service-related activities.

A starting point for identifying a leader's values is a foundational vision and mission statement of the company. Levi Strauss & Co.'s statement, shown in Figure 6.2, exemplifies an inspirational vision with ethical values.

The classical visionary, "built to last" companies "are premier institutions in their industries, the crown jewels—several are still 'lasting' today—that are widely admired by their peers and have a long track record of making a significant impact on the world around them. . . . Visionary *companies* prosper over long periods of time, through multiple product life cycles and multiple generations of active leaders."[23] Some companies have since had financial issues and loss of competitive issues, even ethical issues, but all left legacies still studied. These included 3M, American Express, Citicorp, Ford, General Electric, Hewlett-Packard, IBM, Johnson & Johnson, Marriott, Merck, Motorola, Nordstrom, Philip Morris, Procter & Gamble, Sony, and Disney. These visionary companies, Collins and Porras discovered, succeeded over their rivals by developing and following a "core ideology" that consisted of core values plus purpose. Core values are "the organization's essential and enduring tenets—a small set of general guiding principles; not to be confused with specific cultural or operational practices; not to be compromised for financial gain or short-term expediency."

Figure 6.2

Levi Strauss & Co. Values and Vision Statement[1]

VALUES

Our values are fundamental to our success. They are the foundation of our company, define who we are and set us apart from the competition. They underlie our vision of the future, our business strategies and our decisions, actions and behaviors. We live by them. They endure.

Four core values are at the heart of Levi Strauss & Co.: Empathy, Originality, Integrity and Courage. These four values are linked. As we look at our history, we see a story of how our core values work together and are the source of our success.

Empathy—Walking in Other People's Shoes

Empathy begins with listening . . . paying close attention to the world around us . . . understanding, appreciating and meeting the needs of those we serve, including consumers, retail customers, shareholders and each other as employees.

Levi Strauss and Jacob Davis listened. Jacob was the tailor who, in the 1870s, first fashioned heavy cotton cloth, thread and metal rivets into sturdy "waist overalls" for miners seeking durable work pants. Levi in turn met Jacob's needs for patenting and mass production of the product, enthusiastically embracing the idea and bringing it to life. The rest is history: The two created what would become the most popular clothing in the world—blue jeans.

Our history is filled with relevant examples of paying attention to the world around us. We listened. We innovated. We responded.

- As early as 1926 in the United States, the company advertised in Spanish, Portuguese and Chinese, reaching out to specific groups of often-neglected consumers.
- In the 1930s, consumers complained that the metal rivets on the back pockets of our jeans tended to scratch furniture, saddles and car seats. So we redesigned the way the pockets were sewn, placing the rivets underneath the fabric.
- In 1982, a group of company employees asked senior management for help in increasing awareness of a new and deadly disease affecting their lives. We quickly became a business leader in promoting AIDS awareness and education.

We believe in empathetic marketing, which means that we walk in our consumers' shoes. In the company's early years, that meant making durable clothes for workers in the American West. Now, it means responding to the casual clothing needs of a broad range of consumers around the world. Understanding and appreciating needs—consumer insight—is central to our commercial success.

Being empathetic also means that we are inclusive. Levi Strauss' sturdy work pants are sold worldwide in more than 80 countries. Their popularity is based on their egalitarian appeal and originality. They transcend cultural boundaries. Levi's® jeans—the pants without pretense—are not just for any one part of society. Everyone wears them.

Inclusiveness underlies our consumer marketing beliefs and way of doing business. We bring our Levi's® and Dockers® brands to consumers of all ages and lifestyles around the world. We reflect the diverse world we serve through the range and relevancy of our products and the way we market them.

Likewise, our company workforce mirrors the marketplace in its diversity, helping us to understand and address differing consumer needs. We value ethnic, cultural and lifestyle diversity. And we depend and draw upon the varying backgrounds, knowledge, points of view and talents of each other.

As colleagues, we also are committed to helping one another succeed. We are sensitive to each other's goals and interests, and we strive to ensure our mutual success through exceptional leadership, career development and supportive workplace practices.

Empathy also means engagement and compassion. Giving back to the people we serve and the communities we operate in is a big part of who we are. Levi Strauss was both a

Figure 6.2 *–continued*

merchant and a philanthropist–a civic-minded leader who believed deeply in community service. His way lives on. The company's long-standing traditions of philanthropy, community involvement and employee volunteerism continue today and contribute to our commercial success.

Originality—Being Authentic and Innovative

Levi Strauss started it and forever earned a place in history. Today, the Levi's® brand is an authentic American icon, known the world over.

Rooted in the rugged American West, Levi's® jeans embody freedom and individuality. They are young at heart. Strong and adaptable, they have been worn by generations of individuals who have made them their own. They are a symbol of frontier independence, democratic idealism, social change and fun. Levi's® jeans are both a work pant and a fashion statement–at once ordinary and extraordinary. Collectively, these attributes and values make the Levi's® brand unlike any other.

Innovation is the hallmark of our history. It started with Levi's® jeans, but that pioneering spirit permeates all aspects of our business-innovation in product and marketing, workplace practices and corporate citizenship. Creating trends. Setting new standards. Continuously improving through change. For example:

- We were the first U.S. apparel company to use radio and television to market our products.
- With the introduction of the Dockers® brand in 1986, we created an entirely new category of casual clothing in the United States, bridging the gap between suits and jeans. A year later, Dockers® khakis had become the fastest growing apparel brand in history. Throughout the 1990s, we were instrumental in changing what office workers wear on the job.
- Our European Levi's® brand team reinvented classic five-pocket jeans in 1999. Inspired by the shape and movement of the human body, Levi's® Engineered Jeans™ were the first ergonomically designed jeans.

Now, more than ever, constant and meaningful innovation is critical to our commercial success. The worldwide business environment is fiercely competitive. Global trade, instantaneous communications and the ease of market entry are among the forces putting greater pressure on product and brand differentiation. To be successful, it is imperative that we change, competing in new and different ways that are relevant to the shifting times.

As the "makers and keepers" of Levi Strauss' legacy, we must look at the world with fresh eyes and use the power of ideas to improve everything we do across all dimensions of our business, from modest improvements to total reinventions. We must create product news that comes from the core qualities of our brands—comfort, style, value and the freedom of self-expression–attributes that consumers love and prefer.

Integrity—Doing the Right Thing

Ethical conduct and social responsibility characterize our way of doing business. We are honest and trustworthy. We do what we say we are going to do.

Integrity includes a willingness to do the right thing for our employees, brands, the company and society as a whole, even when personal, professional and social risks or economic pressures confront us. This principle of responsible commercial success is embedded in the company's experience. It continues to anchor our beliefs and behaviors today, and is one of the reasons consumers trust our brands. Our shareholders expect us to manage the company this way. It strengthens brand equity and drives sustained, profitable growth and superior return on investment. In fact, our experience has shown that our "profits through principles" approach to business is a point of competitive advantage.

(continued)

Figure 6.2 –*continued*

This values-based way of working results in innovation:

- Our commitment to equal employment opportunity and diversity predates the U.S. Civil Rights movement and federally mandated desegregation by two decades. We opened integrated factories in California in the 1940s. In the 1950s, we combined our need for more production and our desire to open manufacturing plants in the American South into an opportunity to make change: We led our industry by sending a strong message that we would not locate new plants in Southern towns that imposed segregation. Our approach changed attitudes and helped to open the way for integration in other companies and industries.
- In 1991, we were the first multinational company to develop a comprehensive code of conduct to ensure that individuals making our products anywhere in the world would do so in safe and healthy working conditions and be treated with dignity and respect. Our Terms of Engagement are good for the people working on our behalf and good for the long-term reputation of our brands.

Trust is the most important value of a brand. Consumers feel more comfortable with brands they can trust. Increasingly, they are holding corporations accountable, not only for their products but also for how they are made and marketed. Our brands are honest, dependable and trusted, a direct result of how we run our business.

Integrity is woven deeply into the fabric of our company. We have long believed that "Quality Never Goes Out of Style." Our products are guaranteed to perform. We make them that way. But quality goes beyond products: We put quality in everything we do.

Courage—Standing Up for What We Believe

It takes courage to be great. Courage is the willingness to challenge hierarchy, accepted practices and conventional wisdom. Courage includes truth telling and acting resolutely on our beliefs. It means standing by our convictions. For example:

- It took courage to transform the company in the late 1940s. That was when we made the tough decision to shift from dry goods wholesaling, which represented the majority of our business at the time, and to focus instead on making and selling jeans, jean jackets, shirts and Western wear. It was a foresighted–though risky–decision that enabled us to develop and prosper.
- In the 1980s, we took a similar, bold step to expand our U.S. channels of distribution to include two national retail chains, Sears and JCPenney. We wanted to provide consumers with greater access to our products. The move resulted in lost business in the short term because of a backlash from some important retail customers, but it set the stage for substantial growth.
- We also demonstrated courage in our workplace practices. In 1992, Levi Strauss & Co. became the first Fortune 500 company to extend full medical benefits to domestic partners of employees. Although controversial at the time, this action foreshadowed the widespread acceptance of this benefit and positioned us as a progressive employer with prospective talent.

With courage and dedication, we act on our insights and beliefs, addressing the needs of those we serve in relevant and significant ways. We do this with an unwavering commitment to excellence. We hold ourselves accountable for attaining the high performance standards and results that are inherent in our goals. We learn from our mistakes. We change. This is how we build our brands and business. This is how we determine our own destiny and achieve our vision of the future.

The story of Levi Strauss & Co. and our brands is filled with examples of the key role our values have played in meeting consumer needs. Likewise, our brands embody many

Figure 6.2 *–continued*

of the core values that our consumers live by. This is why our brands have stood the test of time.

Generations of people have worn our products as a symbol of freedom and self-expression in the face of adversity, challenge and social change. They forged a new territory called the American West. They fought in wars for peace. They instigated counterculture revolutions. They tore down the Berlin Wall. Reverent, irreverent–they all took a stand.

Indeed, it is this special relationship between our values, our consumers and our brands that is the basis of our success and drives our core purpose. It is the foundation of who we are and what we want to become:

Vision
People love our clothes and trust our company.
We will market the most appealing and widely worn
casual clothing in the world.
We will clothe the world.

---

[1] Also see Levi Strauss' current vision and value states at: https://mission-statement.com/levi-strauss/#:~:text=Levi's%20mission%20statement%20is%2C%20%E2%80%9C%20To,and%20superior%20products%20and%20service.

Source: Levi Strauss & Co. Used by permission of Levi Strauss & Co. Reprinted by permission of Levi Strauss & Co.

Purpose is "the organization's fundamental reasons for existence beyond just making money—a perpetual guiding star on the horizon; not to be confused with specific goods or business strategies."[24] Excerpts of core ideologies from some of the classic visionary companies are instructive and are summarized here:[25]

- Disney: "To bring happiness to millions and to celebrate, nurture, and promulgate wholesome American values."
- Walmart: "We exist to provide value to our customers—to make their lives better via lower prices and greater selection; all else is secondary. . . . Be in partnership with employees."
- Sony: "Respecting and encouraging each individual's ability and creativity."
- Motorola: "To honorably serve the community by providing products and services of superior quality at a fair price."

Built-to-last companies "more thoroughly indoctrinate employees into a core ideology than their comparison companies [i.e., those companies in Collins and Porras's study that did not last], creating cultures so strong that they are almost cult-like around the ideology."[26] Visionary companies also select and support senior management on the basis of whether they fit with the core ideology. These best-in-class companies also attain more consistent goals, strategy, and organizational structure alignment with their core ideology than do comparison companies in Collins and Porras's study.[27] Take the assessment in Ethical Insight 6.1 to gauge your present ethical leadership style.

Ethical Insight 6.1

Your Moral Leadership Profile

Using actual situations in which you served in a leadership role, score the following statements with regard to how each statement characterizes your leadership style:

1 = Very little, 2 = Somewhat, 3 = Moderately, 4 = A lot, 5 = Most of the time

1. I act ethically even if my peers disagree with me.   1   2   3   4   5
2. I generally speak out for what I believe is right regardless of pressure from others.   1   2   3   4   5
3. I tell others when I sense there are wrongdoing or hurtful activities about to happen.   1   2   3   4   5
4. I maintain composure when people try to pressure me into saying or doing unjust things.   1   2   3   4   5
5. I do not back down when I know that others are violating just rules and procedures.   1   2   3   4   5
6. I don't go along with the crowd or majority just to get their approval when I know they are wrong and/or acting unethically.   1   2   3   4   5
7. My decisions are generally ethical and based on principles, not on random acts of instant gratification or whim.   1   2   3   4   5
8. I say and do the right thing even if I lose the favor of some friends.   1   2   3   4   5
9. I generally act from my beliefs and ethical principles first, regardless of the approval of my friends.   1   2   3   4   5
10. I go with what's right for a project even though my friends and colleagues may turn against me.   1   2   3   4   5

Your Scores and Interpretation

Add up your scores. Total of 10 statements = _____. If you received 40 or higher, you are considered a courageous leader. A score of 20 or below indicates you avoid conflict and difficult situations that challenge your moral leadership. Examine the items in which you scored highest and lowest. Do these scores and items reflect your moral courage in tough situations generally? Why or why not? What do you need to do to improve or change your moral courage? How do your scores compare to other students?

Source: Adapted from Daft, R. L. (2005) *The leadership experience*, 3rd ed. © 2005, South-Western, a division of Thomson Learning.

Leadership Stakeholder Competencies

Core competencies of responsible leaders include the ability to:

1. Define and lead the social, ethical, and competitive mission of organizations, which includes community-based, social, and environmental stewardship goals that promote being a global corporate citizen.[28]

2. Build and sustain accountable relationships with stakeholders.[29]
3. Dialogue and negotiate with stakeholders, respecting their interests and needs beyond economic and utilitarian dimensions.[30]
4. Demonstrate collaboration and trust in shared decision making and strategy sessions.
5. Show awareness and concern for employees and other stakeholders in the policies and practices of the company.

Effective ethical leaders develop a collaborative approach to setting direction, leading top-level teams, and building relationships with partners and customers. Not all companies live up to their aspirational and sometimes legal and ethical responsibilities. Nevertheless setting socially responsible benchmarks in their mission, values, and company conduct statements can damage leaders' credibility, influence, and even positions by violating those statements. At Johnson & Johnson, one of the seven principles of leadership development states: "People are an asset of the corporation; leadership development is a collaborative, corporation-wide process."[31] The company lives its leadership principles through its Executive Development Program. Figure 6.3 shows the Johnson & Johnson credo. The now-classic "Beliefs of BorgWarner" corporation credo, shown in Figure 6.4, is another example of values that companies should aspire to follow, even though that firm paid a penalty by misstating its financial records between 2012 and 2016.

Organizational leaders are also ultimately responsible for the economic viability and profitability of a company. From a values-based, stakeholder management perspective, leaders must also oversee and implement the following in their organizations:

- Set the vision, mission, and direction.
- Create and sustain a legal and ethical culture throughout the organization.
- Articulate and guide the strategy and direction of the organization.
- Ensure the competitive and ethical alignment of organizational systems.
- Reward ethical conduct.[32]

Herb Kelleher cofounded Southwest Airlines in 1966 on a personal $10,000 investment. He retired on June 19, 2001, with a $200 million stake in the company. Kelleher's principles of management are straightforward and simple:[33]

- Employees come first, customers second.
- The team is important, not the individual.
- Hire for attitude, train for skills.
- Think like a small company.
- Eschew organizational hierarchy.
- Keep it simple.

Figure 6.3

Johnson & Johnson Credo[1]

We believe our first responsibility is to the doctors, nurses, and patients; to mothers and fathers; and all others who use our product and services. In meeting their needs, every-thing we do must be of high quality.

We must constantly strive to reduce our costs in order to maintain reasonable prices.

Customers' orders must be serviced promptly and accurately.

Our suppliers and distributors must have an opportunity to make a fair profit.

We are responsible to our employees, the men and women who work with us throughout the world.

Everyone must be considered as an individual. We must respect their dignity and recog-nize their merit.

They must have a sense of security in their jobs.

Compensation must be fair and adequate, and working conditions clean, orderly, and safe.

We must be mindful of ways to help our employees fulfill their family responsibilities.

Employees must feel free to make suggestions and complaints.

There must be equal opportunity for employment, development, and advancement for those qualified.

We must provide competent management, and their actions must be just and ethical.

We are responsible to the communities in which we work and to the world community as well.

We must be good citizens—support good works and charities and bear our fair share of taxes.

We must encourage civic improvements and better health and education.

We must maintain in good order the property we are privileged to use, protecting the environment and natural resources.

Our final responsibility is to our stockholders.

Business must make a sound profit.

We must experiment with new ideas.

Research must be carried on, innovative programs developed, and mistakes paid for.

New equipment must be purchased, new facilities provided, and new products launched.

Reserves must be created to provide for adverse times.

When we operate according to these principles, the stockholders should realize a fair return.

---

1. Also see the historical progression of this Credo: https://www.jnj.com/our-heritage /timeline-of-johnson-johnson-credo-driven-decisions?utm_source=google&utm_medium =cpc&utm_campaign=GO-USA-ENG-PS-Corporate%20Equity-BC-PH-RN-BRAND_REP _MGMT&utm_content=Credo&utm_term=johnson%20&%20johnson%20credo&ds_rl =1262818&gclid=CjwKCAjwhYOFBhBkEiwASF3KGfLTJrYwWJmbHX6ZLrVl-PytjS2EQnPZ iKV5PJIOi80TC3ANJ1jUrxoCs0AQAvD_BwE&gclsrc=aw.ds, accessed May, 2021.

Source: Johnson & Johnson. Reprinted by permission of Johnson & Johnson.

Kelleher owned and operated Southwest Airlines on these principles. When asked how the company would survive once he stepped down, Kelle-her responded, "The real answer is we have a very strong culture and it has a life of its own that is able to surmount a great deal. If we should, by happen-stance, have someone succeed me who is not interested in the culture, I don't think they would last a long time. The place would just rise up."[34] Kelleher's

Figure 6.4

The Beliefs of BorgWarner: To Reach beyond the Minimal[1]

Any business is a member of a social system, entitled to the rights and bound by the responsibilities of that membership. Its freedom to pursue economic goals is constrained by law and channeled by the forces of a free market. But these demands are minimal, requiring only that a business provide wanted goods and services, compete fairly, and cause no obvious harm. For some companies, that is enough. It is not enough for BorgWarner. We impose upon ourselves an obligation to reach beyond the minimal. We do so convinced that by making a larger contribution to the society that sustains us, we best assure not only its future vitality, but our own.

This is what we believe.

We Believe in the Dignity of the Individual

However large and complex a business may be, its work is still done by dealing with people. Each person involved is a unique human being, with pride, needs, values, and innate personal worth. For BorgWarner to succeed, we must operate in a climate of openness and trust, in which each of us freely grants others the same respect, cooperation, and decency we seek for ourselves.

We Believe in Our Responsibility to the Common Good

Because BorgWarner is both an economic and social force, our responsibilities to the public are large. The spur of competition and the sanctions of the law give strong guidance to our behavior, but alone do not inspire our best. For that we must heed the voice of our natural concern for others. Our challenge is to supply goods and services that are of superior value to those who use them; to create jobs that provide meaning for those who do them; to honor and enhance human life; and to offer our talents and our wealth to help improve the world we share.

We Believe in the Endless Quest for Excellence

Though we may be better today than we were yesterday, we are not as good as we must become. BorgWarner chooses to be a leader—in serving our customers, advancing our technologies, and rewarding all who invest in us their time, money, and trust. None of us can settle for doing less than our best, and we can never stop trying to surpass what already has been achieved.

We Believe in Continuous Renewal

A corporation endures and prospers only by moving forward. The past has given us the present to build on. But to follow our visions to the future, we must see the difference between traditions that give us continuity and strength and conventions that no longer serve us—and have the courage to act on that knowledge. Most can adapt after change has occurred; we must be among the few who anticipate change, shape it to our purpose, and act as its agents.

We Believe in the Commonwealth of BorgWarner and Its People

BorgWarner is both a federation of businesses and a community of people. Our goal is to preserve the freedom each of us needs to find personal satisfaction, while building the strength that comes from unity. True unity is more than a melding of self-interests; it results when values and ideals also are shared. Some of ours are spelled out in these statements of belief. Others include faith in our political, economic, and spiritual heritage; pride in our work and our company; the knowledge that loyalty must flow in many directions; and a conviction that power is strongest when shared. We look to the unifying force of these beliefs as a source of energy to brighten the future of our company and all who depend on it.

---

[1] Current Core Values statement, accessed 2021: https://www.borgwarner.com/careers/who-we-are; http://www.turbos.bwauto.com/en/company/vision.aspx.

Source: BorgWarner Corp. Reprinted by permission of the BorgWarner Corporation.

message is printed in white letters on the black elevator glass in the lobby of Southwest's corporate headquarters: "The people of Southwest Airlines are the creators of what we have become—and what we will be. Our people transformed an idea into a legend. That legend will continue to grow only so long as it is nourished—by our people's indomitable spirit, boundless energy, immense goodwill, and burning desire to excel. Our thanks—and our love—to the people of Southwest Airlines for creating a marvelous family and a wondrous airline."[35] This emphasis is shared with the company's current CEO and chairman Gary C. Kelly, who in relation to culture, is quoted as saying, "It's not one thing, it's everything."[36] Leaders who dare to be different stretch goals while maintaining a moral, values-based approach:

- Seek to revolutionize every strategy and process for optimal results while maintaining the organization's integrity.[37]
- Empower everyone to perform beyond stated standards, while maintaining balance of life and personal values.
- Understand and serve customers as they would themselves.
- Create and reward a culture obsessed with fairness and goodwill toward everyone.
- Act with compassion and forgiveness in every decision toward every person and group.
- Do unto their stockholders and stakeholders as they would have them do to their company.
- Treat the environment as their home.

Example of Companies Using Stakeholder Relationship Management

A 2007 study (updated in 2014) of exemplary companies that have gone beyond traditional business models coined the term "firms of endearment" (FoEs). Leaders of these firms practice "stakeholder relationship management."[38] An FoE is "a company that *endears* itself to stakeholders by bringing the interests of all stakeholder groups into strategic alignment. No stakeholder group benefits at the expense of any other stakeholder group, and each prospers as the others do."[39] The authors' two-year research project started with measures of "humanistic performance—meeting the needs of stakeholders other than shareholders—and worked forward." The authors "asked for nominations from thousands of people all over the world, including business professionals, marketing professionals, MBA students, and about 1,000 consumers."[40] The companies selected underwent further screening using quantitative and qualitative performance of each firm for each stakeholder (societal communities, partners, investors, customers, and employees). The companies studied are not exhaustive, and the authors note that none of the firms are perfect. It was found that "the public FoEs returned 1,026 percent for investors over the 10 years ending June 30, 2006, compared to 122 percent for the S&P [Standard & Poor's] 500 . . . an 8–1 ratio!"[41] The companies in the "final cut" for the most recent release[42] are as follows:

U.S. Public Firms

3M	Cognizant	Schlumberger
Adobe	Colgate Palmolive	Southwest
Amazon	Costco	Starbucks
Autodesk	Disney	T. Rowe Price
Boston Beer Company	FedEx	UPS
CarMax	Nordstrom	Whole Foods
Chipotle	Panera Bread	
Chubb	Qualcomm	

U.S. Private Firms

Barry-Wehmiller	Jordan's Furniture	SAS Institute
Bon Appetit	L.L. Bean	SC Johnson
Clif	Method	Stonyfield Farm
The Container Store	Millennium	TD Industries
Driscoll's	Pharmaceuticals	Timberland
Gore	The Motley Fool	TOMS
GSD&M	New Balance	Union Square
Honest Tea	Patagonia	USAA
IDEO	Prana	Wegmans
Interstate Batteries	REI	

Non-U.S. Firms

BMW	Honda	Novo Nordisk
Cipla	IKEA	Posco
Fabindia	INDITEX	TATA
FEMSA	Mahindra	Toyota
Gemalto	Marico	Unilever

Some of the defining characteristics of FoEs include:

- Competitive advantage through a business model in which all stakeholders add and benefit from gains in value created from a deeper set of resources.
- Possess a humanistic soul. "From the depths of this soul, the will to render uncommon service to all stakeholders flows. These companies are imbued with the joy of service—to the community, to society, to the environment, to customers, to colleagues."[43]
- Leaders who "facilitate, encourage, reward, recognize, and celebrate their employees for being of service to their communities and the world at large, for no reason other than that it is the right thing to do."[44]

Honda, for example, "marries suppliers for life"; the company supports suppliers in improving quality, service, and profits. Costco's CEO Craig Jelinek embodies the stakeholder management approach. His salary for the fiscal year 2017 was $713,462, 5.5 million in stock awards, $192,800 in bonus pay, and an additional 1$180,908; Costco's revenues in its most recent fiscal year rose 9.21 percent to $116.761 billion.[45] (The average CEO compensation of a Forbes

500 company in 2017 was $11.5 million.[46]) Costco's low employee turnover and liberal benefits have created loyalty in an industry that is standard-setting. Southwest Airlines has an elected "Culture Committee" consisting of 200 employees in charge of sustaining the company's humanistic culture. JetBlue's founder, David Neeleman, quickly responded to the post-2007 Valentine's Day crisis when passengers were kept on board planes that had been grounded because of weather conditions. Neeleman instituted "employee cross-training so that all 900 of the corporate employees in JetBlue's Forest Hills, New York, office could assist at nearby JFK airport during any future operational crisis."[47] Neeleman also initiated action on a customer's "Bill of Rights" document. All the FoE companies and their leaders exhibited these types of stakeholder relationship management actions, attributes, and policies.

Ethical Insight 6.2 is a survey among CEOs in 60 countries asking which historical leaders they admired the most.

Ethical Insight 6.2

Global CEO Survey: Leaders CEOs Most Admire

The PricewaterhouseCoopers (PWC) annual survey asked CEOs in 60 countries "to share an example of someone from literature or history who exhibited good leadership, and what the CEOs admired about them." PWC was interested in the types of leaders CEOs named and reasons for naming them. The top-10 people named by CEOs across seven regions and over 60 countries were:

1. Winston Churchill
2. Steve Jobs
3. Mahatma Gandhi
4. Nelson Mandela
5. Jack Welch
6. Abraham Lincoln
7. Margaret Thatcher
8. Ronald Reagan
9. John F. Kennedy
10. Bill Clinton/Napoleon Bonaparte

There was an unusually high degree of agreement on leaders admired across different geographies and cultures. CEOs identified Winston Churchill in 30 countries across six regions. Steve Jobs before his death was identified by CEOs in 37 countries and six regions. PWC also discovered that CEOs named by emerging-market countries tended to identify role models in regions other than their own, even though they gave tribute to local heroes. North American and Western European CEOs were more alike in their choices and chose most admired leaders nearer home. PWC noted this finding indicated that these CEOs might "reflect their markets' dominant economic standing in recent history—but could also be an obstacle to their ability to adapt to different cultural traits that are gaining (or regaining) prominence as the global economy rebalances." Fifteen female leaders were identified, and Margaret Thatcher was the only one in the top 10 who received several mentions. Next most identified were Angela Merkel, Ayn Rand, Mother Teresa, and Queen Elizabeth I. The authors found that "female CEOs were more than four times more likely to select female leaders than male CEOs: 17 percent of women CEOs chose women leaders, with 78 percent choosing male leaders. 4 percent of male CEOs, meanwhile, named female leaders and 95 percent named male leaders." Leaders who had "a strong vision" were most identified. Other characteristics included "motivational, caring, innovative, persistent, and ethical qualities." Respondents seemed to choose leaders who were driven "by the prevailing mood of the time, which could explain why so many CEOs chose leaders who were persistent in the face of adversity—as well as transformational leaders and leaders who did the 'right thing.'"

Questions

1. Who are your most admired leaders?
2. What traits do/did they have?
3. How would you describe and characterize their ethics?
4. How alike and/or different are your choices from your (evolving) leadership style? Explain.

Source: PricewaterhouseCoopers. (2013). Global CEO survey: Leaders CEOs most admire. *PWC.com.* Accessed January 8, 2014, https://www.pwc.com/gx/en/ceo-survey/2013/pdf/us -ceo-survey-2013.pdf.

Note: This particular survey and list has not been updated. However, there is an annual list of both top ranked CEOs from anonymous employees surveys (https://www.comparably.com /news/best-ceos-2020/) and the 10 most admired companies ranked by Human Resources Directors (HRD) 2021 (https://www.hcamag.com/us/specialization/leadership/2021-the -worlds-most-admired-companies/245296).
The 2021 top ranked company list includes:

1. Apple
2. Amazon
3. Microsoft
4. Walt Disney
5. Starbucks
6. Berkshire Hathaway
7. Alphabet
8. JPMorgan Chase
9. Netflix
10. Costco Wholesale

The companies selected in 2021 out-performed their 3,800 rivals "not only in terms of their financial standing but also in other facets of management, from innovation to social responsibility to people leadership, earning them high marks from . . . executives, directors and analysts from a variety of industries." Criteria in the nine ranking criteria included excellence set by researchers, "including product quality, people management, social responsibility and 'soundness of financial position.'" Apple has topped the list for 14 years.
The 2020 top 10 ranked CEOs of large sized companies by employees include:

1. Eric Yuan, Zoom Video Communications, San Jose, CA
2. Brian Halligan, HubSpot, Cambridge, MA
3. Sundar Pichai, Google, Mountain View, CA
4. Satya Nadella, Microsoft, Redmond, WA

mleff:0

5. Shantanu Narayen, Adobe, San Jose, CA
6. Ryan Smith, Qualtrics, Provo, UT
7. Patrick Pacious, Choice Hotels, Rockville, MD
8. Timothy Cook Apple, Cupertino, CA
9. Annette Brüls, Medela, McHenry, IL
10. Vlad Shmunis RingCentral, Belmont, CA

"Comparably (www.comparably.com) is a leading workplace culture and compensation monitoring site that provides the most comprehensive and accurate representation of what it's like to work at companies. The final data set was compiled from 10 million ratings across 60,000 North American companies."

Spiritual Values, Practices, and Moral Courage in Leading

John Kotter of Harvard University has said that "what we call courage is a strong emotional commitment—and the key word is "emotional"—to some ideas. Those ideas could be called a vision for where we're trying to drive the enterprise. They could be called values for what we think is important in life. They could be called principles of what is right and wrong. When people don't just have an intellectual sense that these are logically good, but are deeply committed to them, they're developing courage. When you run up against barriers that keep you from those ideals, the stronger your commitment, the more likely you are to take action consistent with those ideals. Even if it's against your short-term best interests. . . . The bigger the context, the greater the barriers, the more the snake pits . . . the more there will be times for courageous acts."[48]

Moral courage comes from the heart and soul as well as the head. When leaders face extreme dilemmas, where not only their own but their organization's reputation or existence is at stake based on the course of action that must be taken (or not taken), they come to know the meaning of this type of courage. An emerging body of literature describes leadership from just such a spiritual perspective.[49] Spirituality, broadly defined, is the search for "ultimate meaning and purpose in one's life."[50] This dimension of leadership is inherently linked to ethics, in that leaders act as stewards and servants who do "the right thing" for their followers, communities, and society.[51] Spiritual values and practices are also the sources of moral courage, which is the ability to act with wisdom of the soul against fear, greed, conformity, and pressures that work against the common good. Spiritual values originate from a deeper wisdom of having a sense of purpose and "knowing yourself." Some religious traditions, including Christianity, link this deeper knowing to a person's "calling" that is discovered and nurtured from their relationship with community and the source of their spiritual guidance. The following characteristics illustrate leadership from a spiritual perspective:[52]

- Understand and practice reflective "being" as well as "doing." Genuine spirituality must be the willingness to enter into the process of dialogue with oneself and with others, and to try to stay with it over a period of time. "Being is the only reality with integrity; obeying one's conscience brings one into communion with this 'integrity of Being.'"[53]

- Use discernment, prayer, and patience in strategic decision making. Decisions are analyzed within the context of communities.
- See the leadership role as a calling that reveals its presence by the enjoyment and sense of renewed energy in the practice and results yielded.
- Seek to connect with people and connect people to people with meaning and in meaningful ways.
- Create communities, environments, and safe havens for empowerment, mobilization, development, spiritual growth, and nourishment.
- Lead with reflection, choice, passion, reason, compassion, humility, vulnerability, and prayer, as well as courage, boldness, and vision.

Spiritually based values and practices of leaders have been shown to positively affect their stakeholder relationships as well as performance: "The spiritual values of integrity, honesty, and humility, and the spiritual practices of treating others with respect and fairness, expressing caring and concern, listening responsively, appreciating others, and taking time for personal reflection have all been linked to quantifiable positive effects for organizations and individuals. They cause leaders to be judged as more effective by both their peers and their subordinates, and they lead to enhanced performance. They have been proven to be associated with increased worker satisfaction and motivation, greater productivity, greater sustainability, and enhanced corporation reputation, which in turn have all been linked to increases in the bottom line of profits."[54]

Jim Collins's Level 5 leadership, or servant leadership, focuses on ethical behavior through good stewardship. Leaders that act as stewards both empower followers in their decision making and help them gain control over their work. Servant leadership is selfless and involves working alongside followers to achieve shared goals and improve collective welfare. The focus is not on the individual but on the whole. A key component of ethical leadership is the treatment of followers with respect, empowering them to grow both personally and professionally. Servant leaders lead with respect and empowerment.

Leading with stewardship assumes an authority without domination. These leaders sincerely care for their followers' well-being and achievement of personal and professional goals. This kind of effective stewardship results in a team-oriented, cooperative environment. Organizations led by stewardship are often characterized by decentralized decision-making structures. Authority is not centered in a single individual, group, department, or administrative body, distributing power among all stakeholders.

The servant leadership approach implemented by the leaders listed above, among many others, was formulated by Robert K. Greenleaf. Greenleaf saw a strong correlation between leadership and service, stating that "the essential quality that separates servant leaders from others is that they live by their conscience—the inward moral sense of what is right and wrong. That one quality is the difference between leadership that *works* and leadership—like servant leadership—that endures." Stewardship demands that leaders devote themselves to a greater cause, rather than personal accolades. This approach to leadership is characterized by the following attributes:

1. *Placing service before self-interest*: Recognition or financial rewards are not the primary concern of servant leaders.
2. *Listening to others*: Servant leaders do not impose their will on others but listen to the concerns and ideas of all stakeholders. This strengthens relationships, provides an understanding of group dynamics and needs, and allows for more effective allocation of resources.
3. *Inspiring followers through trust*: Servant leaders value trust and are truthful, owing to their strong moral convictions.
4. *Working toward feasible goals*: Problem solving is most often a team effort, and servant leaders work toward solving the most pressing issues.
5. *Helping others whenever possible*: Servant leaders go out of their way to help those around them; often these above and beyond tasks are not an explicit part of their job description.

Stewardship and servant leadership are targeted at empowering followers to become champions. They often evoke strong loyalty and cooperation in and out of the workplace. The ethical style of these leaders is one of universalism, altruism, and pragmatism. They demonstrate James Kouzes and Barry Posner's five dimensions of transformational leadership: ethically modeling the way; inspiring a shared vision; challenging the process; enabling others to act; and encouraging the heart in ways that exceed transactional, transformational, and charismatic leaders.[55] Don DeGraaf, Colin Tilley, and Larry Neal discuss servant leadership as follows:

> The main assumption is that true leadership should call us to serve a higher purpose, something beyond ourselves. One of the most important aspects of leadership is helping organizations and staff identify their higher purpose. The best test of the Servant-Leadership philosophy is whether or not customers and staff grow as persons! Do customers become healthier, wiser, free, more autonomous, more likely themselves to become "servants"? And, what is the effect on the least privileged in society? Will they benefit? Or, at least, not be further deprived? To achieve this higher purpose of public organizations, you, as a leader, must be passionate about your desire to improve your community and yourself! As stakeholders increasingly value social responsibility and broaden its application to business practices, ethical leadership will remain relevant and become an even more significant matter.[56]

Failure of Ethical Leadership

Corporate leaders can and do fail when their decisions, lacking moral courage, throughout this text. It Is worth mentioning that one of the earliest, most notorious lawbreakers and a forerunner to Enron executives was also "Chainsaw Al" Dunlap, former CEO of Sunbeam, who died in 2019. He was fired following a Securities and Exchange Commission investigation of accounting fraud under his watch. Dunlap was known for his ability to achieve profits. To meet Sunbeam's profit projections and appease Wall Street analysts, Dunlap devised a method of selling Sunbeam spare parts (used to fix broken blenders and grills) for $11 million to a company that warehoused the parts. That company valued the parts at $2 million. Dunlap and company pressured the warehouse firm to sign a contract to buy the parts at $11 million, booking $8 million in profit. (The parts were never sold.) Dunlap was instrumental in laying off large numbers of employees and cutting back organizational operations to achieve profitability.[57] Dunlap described his other approaches to doing business in his book *Mean Business: How I Save Bad Companies and Make Good Companies Great*.[58]

Seven symptoms of the failure of ethical leadership provide a practical lens to examine a leader's shortsightedness.[59] (Note: we also add an eighth symptom of failure of ethical leadership below.)

1. Ethical blindness: They do not perceive ethical issues because of inattention or inability.
2. Ethical muteness: They do not have or use ethical language or principles. They "talk the talk" but do not "walk the talk" on values.
3. Ethical incoherence: They are not able to see inconsistencies among values they say they follow (e.g., they say they value responsibility, but reward performance based only on numbers).
4. Ethical paralysis: They are unable to act on their values from lack of knowledge or fear of the consequences of their actions.
5. Ethical hypocrisy: They are not committed to their espoused values. They delegate things they are unwilling to or cannot do themselves.
6. Ethical schizophrenia: They do not have a set of coherent values; they act one way at work and another way at home.
7. Ethical complacency: They believe they can do no wrong because of who they are. They believe they are immune to being unethical.
8. Ethical exclusion and bigotry: They are closed-minded, illogical, and discriminate against individuals whom they view as "different" from them and their values.

Ethical Dimensions of Leadership Styles

Every leadership style has an ethical dimension. An organizational leader's (as well as your own) moral decision-making style can also be evaluated using the continuum shown in Figure 6.5.

The *manipulator* leadership style is based on a Machiavellian principle that views leadership amorally. That is, the end result justifies the means taken to reach it. Power is the driving force behind a manipulator's motives. This is an egotistically and essentially economically motivated moral leadership style. Leaders who lack trust and interest in relationship building and are oriented toward the short term may also be manipulators. Although the motives

Figure 6.5

Moral Leadership Styles

LESS ETHICAL   MORE ETHICAL

| Manipulator (end-justifies-means ethic) | Bureaucratic administrator (rule ethic) | Professional manager (social-contract ethic) | Transforming leader (personal ethic) |

Source: Hitt, W. (1990). *Ethics and leadership: Putting theory into practice.* Columbus, OH: Batelle, 138–174.

underlying this style may be amoral, the consequences could prove immoral. Have you ever worked under someone who used this style?

The *bureaucratic administrator* is a rule-based moral leadership style. Based on the theories of German sociologist Max Weber, the bureaucratic administrator acts on the rational principles embodied in an ideal organizational bureaucracy—that is, fixed rules that explain the purpose and functions of the organization, a hierarchy that shows the chain of command, well-defined job descriptions, professional managers who communicate and enforce the rules, and technically qualified employees who are promoted by expertise and rewarded by rank and tenure. The driving force behind this style is efficiency ("doing things right," functioning in the least wasteful manner) more than effectiveness (producing the intended result or aim, "doing the right things"). Although this leadership style has an admirable aim of basing decisions only on objective, rational criteria, the moral problem with it lies in the "sin of omission." That is, a leader may follow all the rules exactly but hurt someone unintentionally by not attending to legitimate human needs because the option to do so was not included in the rules.

For example, a military captain may follow remote orders of a general by sending a regiment into a battle zone knowing it will lead to disaster, based on available "on the ground" conditions. Nevertheless, rather than risk disobeying orders and the formal consequences, the captain proceeds. Another captain who has a different moral leadership style may choose to risk disobeying orders to save the troops. Rules for overly bureaucratic leaders can become ends in themselves.

Rules cannot address all problems and needs in what we know are imperfect and political organizations. Well-intentioned bureaucratic administrators may try to act amorally, but their efforts could result in immoral and irresponsible consequences. Do you recognize this moral leadership style? Have you ever worked for someone who used it?

The *professional* manager aims at effectiveness and "doing things right." This style is grounded in Peter Drucker's view of managers as professionals who have the expertise and tools for accomplishing work effectively through others.[60] Based on a social contract, this management style relies—like the previous two styles—on amorality for getting work done. For example, professional career managers use rational objectives and their training to accomplish the organization's work. The organization's corporate culture and the social contract—implicit and explicit agreements—made between managers and organizational executives set the ground rules that govern the manager's behavior. However, social contracts are not always ethical.

An ethical problem with this leadership style lies in the real possibility that the collective corporate culture and the dominant governing group may think and act amorally or immorally. *Groupthink* (consensus-dominated decision making, based on uncritical, biased thinking) may occur.[61] The collective may lead itself astray. Professional managers, by training, are still prone to unethical behavior. Do you recognize managers or leaders who act amorally or immorally as "professionals"?

Finally, the *transforming* leadership style, based on James Burns's theory,[62] is grounded in a personal ethic. Transformational leaders base their effectiveness on relationships with followers. Also, this style focuses on the charisma, energy, and excitement the leader brings to relationships. Transformational leaders are involved in the growth and self-actualization of others and view others according to their potential. Such leaders identify and elevate the values of others. They empower, coach, and help promote other leaders. This leadership style is moral because "it raises the level of human conduct and aspirations of both leaders and led, and thus has a transforming effect on both."[63]

William Hitt moved the continuum of moral leadership one step beyond the transformational leader to what he termed an "encompassing approach to leadership," or "the effective leader–manager."[64] The encompassing leader learns from the shortcomings of each of the four leadership styles on the continuum (Figure 6.5) and uses all of their strengths. For example, manipulative leadership does value the effective use of power. However, this style's deceptive and dysfunctional use of power should be avoided. The bureaucratic administrator values the effective use of rules; however, these should not become ends rather than means. The professional manager values results; however, human concerns should be valued more highly than physical and fiscal results. The transformational leader values human empowerment; however, even this characteristic is not the complete job of management.

Socially and morally responsible leaders should observe their obligations to all stakeholders, including their own conscience, and observe in their dealings the ethical principles of rights, justice, and duty—in addition to utilitarian logic). Branson, head of The Virgin Group of companies, continues to emphasize people. "When he won a large case against British Airways, instead of keeping the money he distributed the £500,000 [$689,000 USD] award between his staff. Richard Branson has always believed in the philosophy of training staff so they are good enough to leave but treating them so good that they don't want to."[65] Branson noted in a CNN interview, "I would say . . . most important is how good you are with dealing with people, you know, whether you're a good motivator of people. And I think that, no question, that ethics should play a big part, I think, for a company. If you deal well with people and fairly with people, then people will want to continue to deal with you and come back for more." He continued on a related topic about business ethics: "If we'd wanted to fly to a particular country in this world—and I'm not to talk about America—you know, as a country we desperately wanted to fly to, we'd wanted to fly years ago, and we were willing to slip some money under the table, it would have cost next to nothing to get a license to fly to it. We felt that was wrong. And we just wouldn't do something like that. And, therefore, it took us 10 years before we legitimately got the license. And so I think it's very important that you sleep well at night and that you run your company in an ethical way."[66]

How Should CEOs as Leaders Be Evaluated and Rewarded?

Fair and just compensation systems for executives and professionals are necessary for creating long-term corporate value; and for encouraging active participation in the legal, ethical, and business effectiveness of firms. Pay and compensation are not the only ways organizational leaders, CEOs in particular, are compensated. There are also intrinsic as well as extrinsic rewards that motivate leaders, especially those who follow the servant and stewardship models. However, many CEOs of large, publicly traded firms are selected and evaluated based on their level of pay and compensation.

CEO Pay: Excessive or Earned?

It is important to reiterate that most CEOs, especially in small, medium-size, and even large firms, earn their salaries and benefits from the value they create for their companies. And although many have increased the revenue and market value of their firms many times over, there are, however, a large number of CEOs whose pay and compensation drastically exceeds their firm's performance.

Executive compensation is largely a demonstration of accountability. Increasing scrutiny and pressure has been placed on the topic of CEO compensation following global economic difficulties and corporate scandals. The Economic Policy Institute's 2019 CEO Compensation Study of the top-350 CEOs noted that pay levels were 14 percent higher in 2019 than in 2018, with the average compensation growing from $14.5 million in 2018 to $21.3 million in 2019. In relation to the structure of pay, the study claims, "The composition of CEO compensation is shifting away from the use of stock options and toward the use of stock awards. Vested stock awards and exercised stock options totaled 16.7 million in 2019 and accounted for 78.6 percent of average realized CEO compensation.[67]

CEO Evaluations

The board of directors of a company is technically responsible for disciplining and rewarding the CEO. This is reflected in the increasing number of board evaluations of the CEO—86 percent of public company boards perform an annual CEO evaluation, according to a National Association of Corporate Directors study. "For both nonprofit and investor-owned organizations, appointing the CEO, establishing performance expectations, and assessing the CEO's performance in relation to those expectations are among a governing board's most fundamental and important duties."[68] Evidence shows that "CEO appraisals require a special commitment from the CEO and from the board members" in order for the process to work well and the results to be meaningful. "A CFO magazine survey of 2,000 employees in several large public companies found that only 39 percent believe their performance reviews are effective."[69] However, in many instances, it is the CEO who is also president of the company and chairperson of the board.

Two forces influence the popularity of boards of directors evaluating CEOs. The first is the increased recognition of the critical roles CEOs play and the increased compensation levels received for those roles. The second influential force is pressure from the investment community, which dates back to the beginning of shareholder awareness in the 1980s, when corporate acquisitions and restructuring activities were questioned with regard to the effectiveness of CEOs and their boards, due diligence, and management practices. Still, not all CEOs are formally evaluated with their top-level team members and other employees. For publicly traded companies, such as those listed on the New York Stock Exchange, NASDAQ, and other trading companies, industry analysts constantly score and keep pressure on the performance of CEOs and chief financial officers (CFOs)—by the numbers. Market performance is a major evaluator of these officers' effectiveness. Annual reports and financial audits available to stockholders are another form of assessing leaders.

CEOs are also evaluated by assessing gaps between their stated and enacted strategies and by using customer and employee surveys. Assessments of the organization's systems are also reflections of the leader's overall effectiveness in directing, aligning, and implementing strategy. Finally, leaders must balance and align stakeholder interests with the dominant mission and values of the company. Certainly not all CEOs are overpaid. Still, many critics argue that CEO pay and compensation in the larger, publicly traded companies are not in line with the performance of their firms, especially over the last decade.

6.2 Organizational Culture, Compliance, and Stakeholder Management

The Ethics and Compliance Initiative (ECI) reported on how organizational changes affect the percentage of employees who say they witnessed misconduct. In companies with no organizational changes, 33 percent of employees witnessed misconduct; in organizations with few changes, 60 percent witnessed misconduct; and when there are many organizational changes, 75 percent of employees say they observed wrongdoing. The survey notes the correlation between organizational change and percent of employees witnessing misconduct is most likely attributed to the Covid-19 pandemic as companies had to enact sudden change and increased workplace challenges. Employees with weak leader commitment were three times more likely to be pressured to bend the rules than employees with strong leader commitment.[70]

Misuse of company time, abusive behavior, abuse of company resources, lying to employees, and violating company Internet use policies were the five most frequently observed types of misconduct in another survey on workplace ethics done by the Ethics Research Center (ERC). A major factor in these trends is the influence and use of social media at the workplace. Several drivers are critical in reducing ethics risk: a well-implemented ethics program and a strong ethical culture. If U.S. businesses viewed ethics as building reputational capital—protecting corporate brand and preventing misconduct—ethics risk in the United States would be substantially reduced.[71] The survey reported that ethics risk is reduced when there are lower levels of misconduct, greater awareness of wrongdoing, and a reduction in retaliation of reporting.[72] Interestingly, the same survey found that only 29 percent of U.S. companies actually have strong ethical cultures. On a less than positive note, the survey concluded that these results were "borne out by a wave of major corporate scandals that wiped out whole companies and cost thousands of employees their jobs. Given this history, there is reason to be concerned that the current weakness of ethics cultures could foreshadow a new surge in misconduct."[73]

What is organizational culture, and why is it so important to supporting ethical activities and curtailing unethical actions? According to the ERC, four elements shape ethical culture: (1) ethical leadership, (2) supervisor reinforcement, (3) peer commitment to ethics, and (4) embedded ethical values. Studies on culture generally show that coupled with leadership, organizational culture is central to a firm's overall effectiveness and operating efficiency. As Figure 6.6 illustrates, culture is also the "glue" that holds the other organizational dimensions (strategy, structure, people, systems, and technology) together. Strong organizational cultures are possible only with strong leaders who model, build, and help sustain legal and ethical cultures through well-defined and comprehensively implemented ethics and compliance programs.

Organizational Culture Defined

A corporation's culture is the shared values and meanings its members hold in common, which are articulated and practiced by an organization's leaders. Purpose, embodied in corporate culture, defines organizations.

Corporate culture is transmitted through (1) the values and leadership styles that the leaders espouse and practice, (2) the heroes and heroines that the company rewards and holds up as models, (3) the rites and symbols that organizations value, and (4) the way that organizational executives and members communicate among themselves and with their stakeholders.

Heroes and heroines in corporations set the moral tone and direction by their present and past examples. They are the role models; they define what is successful and attainable; they symbolize the company to outsiders and in-

Figure 6.6

Contingency Alignment Model

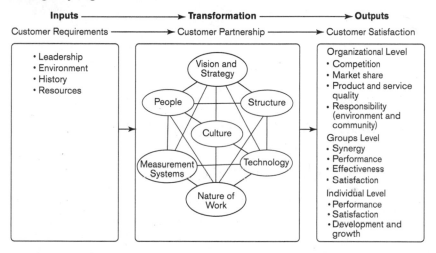

siders; and they preserve the valued qualities of the firm, set standards of excellence, and motivate people. Enduring corporate and organizational cultural heroes include Warren Buffett of Berkshire Hathaway; Herb Kelleher of Southwest Airlines; Ben Cohen and Jerry Greenfield at Ben & Jerry's; Mary Kay at Mary Kay Cosmetics; Angela Merkel, Chancellor of Germany; Melinda Gates, cofounder of the Bill & Melinda Gates Foundation; Abigail Johnson, president-CEO of Fidelity Investments; and Mary Barra, CEO of General Motors. Who are the heroes and heroines in your organization? By what qualities and characteristics are they remembered? Are they moral, immoral, or amoral leaders?

Rituals in companies help define corporate culture and its moral nature. Zappos, a retail shoe and clothing company, has had an interesting, quirky, and creative culture that stresses and balances family with innovation values. The tragic death of their founder has and will have an undetermined impact on the company, but their employees started out and have been close-knit and emphasized caring as well as productivity; they have also been involved in community service.[74]

Corporately sanctioned rituals that bring people together, foster openness, and promote communication can lower stress and encourage moral behavior. Social gatherings, picnics, recognition ceremonies, and other company outings where corporate leaders are present, and where values, stories, problems, accomplishments, and aspirations are shared, can lead to cultures that value people and the company's aims. Does ethics matter for an organization's survival and market effectiveness? The "good management hypothesis" suggests that there is a positive relationship between a corporation's performance and how it treats its stakeholders. Studies confirm this hypothesis.[75]

Observing Organizational Culture

Organizational cultures are both visible and invisible, formal and informal. They can be studied by observation, and by listening to and interacting with people in the culture in the following ways:

- Studying the physical setting
- Reading what the company says about its own culture
- Observing and testing how the company greets strangers
- Watching how people spend time
- Understanding career-path progressions
- Noting the length of tenure in jobs, especially for middle managers
- Observing anecdotes and stories

How ethically is your organizational or company culture using these methods?

Traits and Values of Strong Corporate Cultures

Strong corporate cultures (1) have a widely shared philosophy; (2) value the importance of people; (3) have heroes (presidents and products) that symbolize the success of the company; and (4) celebrate rituals, which provide opportunities for caring and sharing, for developing a spirit of "oneness" and "we-ness."[76] From a stakeholder management view, organizational systems are aligned along the purpose, ethical values, and mission of the company. Also, individuals and teams in ethical cultures demonstrate a tolerance and respect for individual differences, compassion, ability to forgive and accept, and freedom and courage to do the right thing in questionable situations. The authors of the ERC survey referred to earlier state that "by every measure, strong ethics programs and strong ethics cultures produce substantially better outcomes—less pressure, less misconduct, higher reporting, and less retaliation—than in weaker ethical environments."[77] Moreover, the same survey concluded that for employees who felt pressure to bend the rules, the prevalence of misconduct was twice as high. In an earlier version of the study, 30 percent of employees observe misconduct in strong cultural environments as opposed to 89 percent in weaker cultures. Twenty-nine percent of employees working in companies with strong ethical cultures who reported misconduct experienced retaliation as a result, compared to the 46 percent who experienced retaliation in weak cultural environments.[78] As discussed below, fear and retaliation prevent reporting of illegal and unethical acts by employees.

Corporate values and mission statements serve as the economic, political, social, and ethical compasses for employees, stakeholders, and systems. Two classic benchmark values statements and a contemporary example are those of Johnson & Johnson (Figure 6.3), BorgWarner (Figure 6.4), and Patagonia. Patagonia's mission statement is also an example of exemplary ethical corporate values:

Build the best product

Our criteria for the best product rests on function, repairability, and, foremost, durability. Among the most direct ways we can limit ecological impacts is with goods that last for generations or can be recycled so the materials in them remain in use. Making the best product matters for saving the planet.

Cause no unnecessary harm

We know that our business activity—from lighting stores to dyeing shirts—is part of the problem. We work steadily to change our business practices and share what we've learned. But we recognize that this is not enough. We seek not only to do less harm, but more good.

Use business to protect nature

The challenges we face as a society require leadership. Once we identify a problem, we act. We embrace risk and act to protect and restore the stability, integrity and beauty of the web of life.

Not bound by convention

Our success—and much of the fun—lies in developing new ways to do things.[79]

High-Ethics Companies

What would a highly effective values-based organizational culture look like? Mark Pastin studied 25 "high-ethics, high-profit" firms, which at the time included Motorola, 3M, Cadbury Schweppes, Arco, Hilby Wilson, Northern Chemical, and Apple. Although the list of high-ethics firms—like "built to last" firms—changes, the four principles that Pastin used to describe such firms serve as a benchmark for understanding ethically effective organizations:

1. High-ethics firms are at ease interacting with diverse internal and external stakeholder groups. The ground rules of these firms make the good of these stakeholder groups part of the firm's own good.
2. High-ethics firms are obsessed with fairness. Their ground rules emphasize that the other person's interests count as much as their own.
3. In high-ethics firms, responsibility is individual rather than collective; individuals assume responsibility for the firm's actions. The ground rules mandate that individuals are responsible for themselves.
4. The high-ethics firm sees its activities as having a purpose, a way of operating that members of the firm value. And purpose ties the firm to its environment.[80]

Many of the FoEs (firms of endearment) discussed at the beginning of this chapter demonstrate these principles; for example, Amazon, Costco, New Balance, IKEA, L.L. Bean, Wegmans, Patagonia, and REI, to name a few. More recently, Amazon has come under scrutiny and conflict with alleged mistreatment of employees. Although the company won the employee vote not to unionize in 2021, this issue is not likely to subside, especially if the company does not raise wages and improve working conditions going forward.

Weak Cultures

What about companies that are not ethical? Companies that reinforce secrecy, hidden agendas, and physical settings that isolate executives from managers and employees, and emphasize status over human concern, often are cultures in trouble. Troubled corporate and organizational cultures can breed and encourage unethical activities, as seen most recently in 2020–2021 by Wells Fargo, Ferrero USA, Volkswagen, Foxconn, and others. In the first decade of the twenty-first century, the scandals at Enron, WorldCom, Adelphia, and Arthur Andersen were indicative of weak and, in many, corrupt cultures. Figure 6.7 shows results of the ERC's 2011 survey with regard to the observing and reporting of misconduct in strong and weak cultures.

Organizations that also overstress hypercompetition, profit at any cost, and singular economic or introverted self-interest over stakeholder obligations, and

---

Figure 6.7

Ethical Conduct in Strong and Weak Cultures

The Ethics Resource Center states that ethics is a component of culture. The group measured culture through three dimensions:

1. Ethical leadership/tone at the top
2. Supervisor reinforcement of ethical behavior
3. Peer commitment/supporting one another in doing right

Gallup also identified elements of strong organizational cultures as follows:

- diversity and inclusion
- safety
- innovation
- compliance
- high performance

In weaker cultures, misconduct is more prevalent with the following characteristics, as noted by Gallup:

- an eroding identity in the marketplace and within the organization
- declining customer engagement feedback
- the inability to attract world-class talent
- difficulty driving organic growth based on customer-employee interactions
- leadership initiatives stalling out

Sources: Ethics Resource Center. (2012). 2011 National business ethics survey, 20. *Ethics .org.* Gallup. (2018). Gallup's approach to culture. https://www.gallup.com/workplace /232682/culture-paper-2018.aspx?utm_source=google&utm_medium=cpc&utm _campaign=workplace_non-branded_cuture_perspective_paper_download&utm_term =organizational+culture&gclid=CjwKCAjw8cCGBhB6EiwAgORey -N4FFgP5UYlTIa3vDW31o1uOL5E_keT4tzHwYpifTTyeQJaGQh4ihoCybQQAvD _BwE&thank-you-report-form=1.

that have no moral direction, often have cultures in trouble. Signs of cultures in trouble, or weak cultures, include the following:[81]

- An inward focus
- A short-term focus
- Morale and motivational problems
- Emotional outbursts
- Fragmentation and inconsistency (in dress, speech, physical settings, or work habits)
- Clashes among subcultures
- Ingrown subcultures
- Dominance of subculture values over shared company values
- No clear values or beliefs about how to succeed in business
- Many beliefs, with no priorities about which are important
- Different beliefs throughout the company
- Destructive or disruptive cultural heroes, rather than builders of common understanding about what is important
- Disorganized or disruptive daily rituals

In an earlier survey, the ERC found that "severe" ethical risks for businesses with weak cultures included "1. Lying to employees, 2. Abusive behavior, 3. Discrimination, 4. Lying to stakeholders, 5. Misreporting hours worked, 6. Safety violations, 7. Putting own interests ahead of the organization, 8. Improper hiring practices, 9. Sexual harassment, 10. Stealing/ Provision of low quality goods and services, 11. Environmental violations, 12. Internet abuse, 13. Misuse of confidential organization information, and 14. Alteration of financial records."[82]

One of the worst corporate cultures in recent history was Enron's. Malcolm S. Salter, Harvard Business School professor, described Enron's culture the following way:

> Enron is a classic and enduring case that should never be forgotten, about how a team of executives, led by Ken Lay, created an extreme performance-oriented culture that both institutionalized and tolerated deviant behavior. It's a story about a group of executives who created a world that they could not understand and therefore could not control. It's a story about the delinquent society— and I use that phrase intentionally—that grew up around the company, and here I'm referring to the collusion of Enron's various advisors and financial intermediaries. And most importantly, Enron is a story about how fraud is often preceded by gross incompetence: where the primary source of that incompetence is inexperience, naiveté, an ends-justify-the-means attitude toward life, and so on. And most importantly, an inability to face reality when painful problems arise.[83]

A values-based stakeholder management approach would assess an organization's values with these questions: Do the leaders and culture embody "high-ethics" or "in trouble" characteristics in their values, actions, and policies? Are the values written down? Do others know the values? Do the values reflect a concern for and obligation toward the organization's stakeholders? Do the values reflect a utilitarian, just, dutiful, or egotistical ethic? Are the values taken at "face value" only, or are they practiced and implemented by employees? Do the values and communication patterns promote moral, immoral, or amoral behavior?

POINT/COUNTERPOINT

Does Culture or Strategy Affect Employees' Ethical Behavior More?

Argue a case For (Point) and Against (Counterpoint)

POINT: Organizational culture influences employees' ethical (or unethical) behaviors and actions more than strategy. People feel culture.

COUNTERPOINT: Strategy is based on a company's/organization's vision and mission, *which are the first and final guides* for employees' behaviors and actions. Strategies are also tangible and more susceptible and exposed to (un) ethical actions behaviors. Culture is more vague and subjective.

6.3 Leading and Managing Strategy and Structure

If culture is the glue that holds organizations together, strategy maps the direction. The moral dimensions of strategy are also based on ethics. People are motivated to implement strategies that they believe in and are able to enact and that produce results. Strategy and the strategy development process are the domain of organizational leaders. Gary Hamel, a contemporary strategy guru, calls for a "revolution" in leading the strategy innovation process. He states that "you need a set of values that will set you apart from the courtiers and wannabes." Those values include "honesty, compassion, humility, pragmatism, and fearlessness."[84] The strategy-making process also involves stakeholder management. A corporation's strategy is propelled and supported by its people, stakeholders, culture, and moral contributions to its communities, customers, and society. Strategic thinking has evolved from a mechanistic process to a more holistic process, which emphasizes innovation, generation of value for stakeholders and stockholders, involvement and learning with stakeholders, and building customer partnerships and relationships.[85] This section and the next discuss the relationships between corporate strategy, structure, culture, systems, and moral responsibility. How do strategy and structure influence the moral behavior of employees?

Corporate leaders are responsible for orchestrating the development and execution of strategy. An organization's strategy influences legality, morality, innovation, and competitiveness in the following ways:

1. Strategy sets the overall direction of business activities. Enterprise strategy, for example, can emphasize revenue and growth over customer satisfaction or product quality. It can drive technical concern over professional development. Corporate strategy can also direct a firm's activities toward social issues, employee rights, and other stakeholder obligations. It can include or exclude stakeholders and employees. It can innovate recklessly for the short term or in long-term ways that benefit society as well as a few market niches.

2. Strategy reflects what management values and prioritizes. It mirrors management's ethics and morality. It is the message to the messengers. Strategy says: "We care and value your feedback, safety, and concerns," or "We only want your money and participation in our profits."

3. Strategy sets the tone of business transactions inside the organization. Reward and control systems reflect the values of the larger strategic direction. An emphasis on profit at the expense of employee development is usually reflected as rigid and unrealistic incentive and revenue quota systems. Growth and expansion can be made a priority at the expense of talent development and contribution.

Marianne Broadbent, a leading scholar in information technology, offered the following insights about strategy:

> When creating a strategy, I see a number of steps: the aspiration, the big business principles or maxims, then having a number of scenarios or options which are based on a set of strategic assumptions that you constantly, constantly pick to see if they are in sync. And then you use that information to shift and change. At a tactical level, that means rolling out products and services in a very careful, risk-managed way so that you can sense and respond to the marketplace.
>
> Strategy is very much about synchronizing the enterprise with its external environment as much as possible. Think about how increasingly interconnected economies, markets, technology and political situations are. September 11 is a great example of how quickly things can change and how interdependent logistics, for example, is with strategy, with customer service, with the politics of what's going on at the moment. I look at strategy more as synchronization, and that which focuses much more on what we call the market inputs rather than the outputs.[86]

From a values-based stakeholder management approach, the strategy development and implementation process should reflect the vision and mission of the organization. As with the Levi Strauss's values and vision statement (Figure 6.2), the strategy would be reviewed from these statements: "Integrity—Doing the Right Thing. Ethical conduct and social responsibility characterize our way of doing business. We are honest and trustworthy. We do what we say we are going to do. Integrity includes a willingness to do the right thing for our employees, brands, the company and society as a whole, even when personal, professional and social risks or economic pressures confront us. This principle of responsible commercial success is embedded in the company's experience. It continues to anchor our beliefs and behaviors today and is one of the reasons consumers trust our brands. Our shareholders expect us to manage the company this way. It strengthens brand equity and drives sustained, profitable growth and superior return on investment. In fact, our experience has shown that our 'profits through principles' approach to business is a point of competitive advantage."

A firm should identify issues that affect its stakeholder obligations and relationships while developing strategies. From a social and moral perspective, managers should be concerned about fulfilling their internal stakeholder obligations through these strategies. Responsible corporations must be prepared to equitably and justly enable the workforce with new technical skills and integrate aging employees, dual-career families, and new immigrants. Flexible work times, health care programs, and flexible management styles must be implemented to manage this changing workforce responsibly.

Organizational Structure and Ethics

Structure is another organizational dimension, shown in Figure 6.6, along with strategy and culture, that is part of an organization's infrastructural makeup. Ask to see almost any organization's structure and you will be handed a hierarchical set of boxes connected by lines. This so-called pyramid, or functional structure, is one of the oldest forms of depicting arrangements in companies.

Regardless of the specific type of structure, from an ethical, values-based stakeholder management perspective, the key concerns and questions regarding any structure are the same:

- How centralized or decentralized are the authority, responsibility, communication, and information flow?
- How organic (less structured) or mechanistic (more structured) are the systems?
- How tall (more layers of bureaucracy) or flat are the reporting systems?
- How formal or informal are procedures, rules, and regulations?
- How much autonomy, freedom, and discretion do internal stakeholders and decision makers have?
- How flexible, adaptable, and responsive are systems and professionals to responding to internal and external threats, opportunities, and potential crises?

Although there are no absolute guidelines regarding which structure is more immune to or leads to ethical problems, the following overview provides some evidence about how structure relates to ethical behavior. Functionally *centralized* structures can encourage lack of communication, coordination, and increased conflict because each area is typically separated by its own boundaries, managers, and systems. Infighting over budgets, "turf," and power increase the likelihood of unethical, and even illegal, activities. For example, post–September 11, 2001, reports show the overly centralized Central Intelligence Agency (CIA) and Federal Bureau of Investigation (FBI) communicated poorly with each other, with the White House, and with other systems of government.

On the other hand, highly supervised employees in bureaucratic firms may also act more ethically than employees in entrepreneurial, laissez-faire firms because employees tend to think through the risk of getting caught in firms with more supervised structures. A study conducted by renowned ethicists John Cullen, Bart Victor, and Carroll Stephens reported that a subunit's location in the organizational structure affects its ethical climate.[87] At a savings and loan association and also at a manufacturing plant, the employees at the home offices reported less emphasis on laws, codes, and rules than did the employees at the branch offices. Perhaps control by formal mechanisms becomes more necessary when direct supervision by top management is not feasible.

There is evidence that *decentralized* structures can encourage more unethical behavior among employees than more supervised, controlled structures. Wells Fargo was reported to have had a decentralized structure during the time of its ethical and legal crisis. Business unit managers were advised to run their operations as if it were "their own." Citicorp's credit card processing division illustrated the relationships among organizational structure, competitive pressures, and immoral and illegal behavior. The bank fired the president and 11 senior executives of that division because they fraudulently overstated revenue by $23 million for two years. The inflating of revenue by division employees may have been related to the fact that employee bonuses were tied to unrealistic revenue targets. Citicorp centralized its organizational functions. In this case, the decentralized structure left the bank susceptible to potential abuse by employees. On the other hand, some decentralized structures may enable individually responsible and ethical professionals to communicate their beliefs and report errors faster, up and down a more fluid chain of command.

Pressures from upper-level managers who overemphasize unrealistic quarterly revenue objectives and who give unclear policies and procedures to guide ethical decision making may also contribute to immoral behavior in more decentralized structures. There is evidence to support the argument that middle- and lower-level managers, in particular, feel pressured to compromise their personal moral standards to meet corporate expectations.[88] Managers in large firms may compromise their personal ethics to meet corporate expectations for several reasons, which include:

1. Decentralized structures with little or no coordination and central policy and procedures encourage a climate for immoral activities when pressures for profit making increase.
2. Unrealistic short-term and bottom-line profit quotas add pressure on employees to commit unethical actions.
3. Overemphasis on numbers-driven financial incentives encourages shortcuts.
4. Amoral organizational and work-unit cultures can create an environment that condones illegal and immoral actions.

Boundaryless and Networked Organizations

The decentralization of organizations has been accelerated by information technology and the reengineering of business processes. Software applications and Web-enabled intranets and extranets allow the boundaries within organizations and between customers and companies to become more transparent and fluid.[89] These changes are not easy, nor are they isolated from the larger context of the organization. An organizational expert noted that the main reason implementation of major technology changes fails is that "the technology was seen as the solution, without taking into account the complex dynamic of the organization and people. It doesn't matter in which area, whether it's knowledge management or B2B [business to business]. You can't forget that organizations are made of people and technology, and both people and technology will define the success of an organization."[90]

From both an ethics and efficiency perspective, care should be taken by companies implementing digital networks, because one study has reported that digital networks generate both opportunities for and threats to worker autonomy.[91] Major opportunities include increased communication capabilities, "informedness," and "teleworking." Threats to worker autonomy are electronic monitoring, dependence on third-party operators and managers, and task prestructuring, which can reduce individual responsibility and control. These opportunities and problems depend, in part, on the type of organizational structure in place: how open and responsive it is or how closed and vulnerable it may be to unethical activities.

■ 6.4 Leading Internal Stakeholder Values in the Organization

The other internal dimensions of organizations, illustrated in Figure 6.6, should also be aligned in order for the organization to succeed in meeting its goals and social responsibility obligations. In practice, aligning an organization's values and mission with its internal stakeholders, while treating external groups and organizations ethically, is difficult because of competing values of internal stakeholders. The following quote from Carl Anderson illustrates the diversity among stakeholder values:

> An organization in almost all its phases is a reflection of competing value choices. Owners want a return on their investment. Employees want secure jobs and career development. Managers want growth and industry leadership. Government regulators want minimal pollution, safety, work opportunities for a wide variety of groups, and tax revenues. For top managers, this competition comes to a head because they must unravel complex problems whose solutions benefit some groups but have negative consequences for others. Framing these decisions inevitably leads to some crucial dilemmas for managers, who must answer the broad question, "What is a convincing balance among competing value choices?"[92]

Figure 6.8

A Functional Profile of Internal Organizational Stakeholders: Professional Orientations

	Professional Stakeholders				
Orientations	Marketing and Sales	Research and Development (R&D)	Production	Finance and Accounting	Information Systems
Background	Liberal arts; social sciences; entrepreneurial; technical	Electrical engineering; technical	Mechanical engineering; operations	Finance; accounting; auditing; tax	Software "engineers"; data management; programming
Goals and "Stakes"	High product mix; revenue and market competitiveness; customer satisfaction	Market dominance; innovation; competitiveness	Product yield; Quality control	Low-cost capital; efficient borrowing; accountability	Problem solving; organizational integration; systems functioning
Focus and Rewards	Product or service leadership; creative autonomy; bonuses; equity; career mobility	Next "killer" application; resources to innovate; prestige	Product life cycle stability; peace with R&D job security; bonuses	Low costs; high yields; data access; accuracy; cooperation; career advancement	Satisfied users; state-of-the-art technology; career advancement; new skill development
Time Horizon	Short to medium time frame	Medium to long time frame	Short to continuous time frame	Continuous time frame	Continuous time frame

R. Edward Freeman and Daniel Gilbert Jr. argued that we must understand the multiple and competing values underlying stakeholders' actions in order to understand the choices corporations make.[93] Balancing internal stakeholder interests can be difficult because of the diversity of professional and functional backgrounds, training, goals, time horizons, and reward systems. These differences are further influenced by organizational politics, the constraints and pressures of other internal systems, and changing roles and assignments. Figure 6.8 is an example of an organization's internal stakeholders and competing professional value orientations.

Function orientations, such as marketing, research and development (R&D), production, information systems, and finance, have built-in competing values, especially when employees who are under pressure must design, deliver, and service complex products and services for demanding customers. Marketing and sales professionals work with short- to medium-term time horizons and are rewarded on the basis of their results. Sales professionals, in particular, have a very short time horizon and depend on the success of individual and team selling abilities to satisfy, retain, and attract customers. R&D professionals generally have a longer time horizon and are rewarded for their innovations.

The contrast between marketing and sales professionals and R&D professionals is shown in Figure 6.8, and you can see how value differences and role conflicts can occur within cross-functional teams. Competition and conflict can lead to higher productivity and also to unethical decisions and practices, such as producing unsafe products or lying to customers to make a sale.

From a stakeholder management perspective, it is the role of an organization's leaders, with the support of each professional, to ensure that the internal integrity and market effectiveness of a company is based on the types of relationships and values that embody trust, collaboration, and a "win–win" goal for stakeholders and stockholders. Amorally and unethically led and managed organizations with conflicting internal values can, and sometimes do, lead to illegal situations. Interpersonal communication skills, conflict resolution, and collaborative negotiation methods are also needed to help integrate these functional area differences.

Value and innovation are created when the collaborative efforts of an organization's systems create synergy. The organization's vision, values, and mission, which are reinforced by the culture and example of the leaders, are the cornerstone for integrating structures and systems. Following this logic, W. Chan Kim and Renee Mauborgne posed the following research question: "What type of organization best unlocks the ideas and creativity of its employees to achieve this end?"[94] They discovered that "when putting value innovation strategies into action, structural conditions create only the potential for individuals to share their best ideas and knowledge. To actualize this potential, a company must cultivate a corporate culture conducive to willing collaboration."[95]

These authors see "the positively reinforcing cycle of fair process" as one that creates innovative outcomes for companies. As they describe this process, for each success a group has in implementing a "general value innovation strategy" based on fair process, the result strengthens the group's cohesiveness and belief in the process. This, in turn, sustains the collaboration and creativity inherent to value innovation. The four components of that process include:[96]

1. Engagement, explanation, expectation, clarity
2. Idea sharing and voluntary cooperation
3. Value innovation plans and rapid execution
4. Organizational confidence in and respect for colleagues' intellectual and emotional worth.

6.5 Corporate Self-Regulation and Ethics Programs: Challenges and Issues

According to the ethicist Lynn Paine in a *Harvard Business Review* article, a values-based approach in ethics programs should be more effective than a strict, rules-based compliance approach, since a values approach is grounded and motivated in personal self-governance.[97] Employees are more likely to be motivated to "do the right thing" than threatened if they violate laws and rules. A values-based stakeholder management approach assumes that corporations (owners and management) ought to intrinsically value the interests of all stakeholders.[98] In practice, this is not always the case.[99] Later studies suggest that both values-based and compliance ethics programs seem to work effectively together. Without values-based compliance, however, compliance and fear-based programs are less likely to succeed.[100] Responsible self-regulation in companies can enhance entrepreneurship and reduce unnecessary costs of too much bureaucratic control (e.g., it is estimated that the 2002 Sarbanes-Oxley Act costs large public companies $16 million to implement). One study by the Open Compliance Ethics Group (OCEG) found that firms that had an ethics program for 10 or more years did not have "reputational damage" during the last five years. Ethics programs appear to have some intended effect.[101] Complete your company's "Ethical Weather Report" to identify your point of view regarding how ethical your company is.

The Federal Sentencing Guidelines for Organizations (FSGO) were established in 1984 by Congress—which passed a crime bill that instituted the U.S. Sentencing Commission. This commission, made up of federal judges, was empowered with sentencing those found in violation of the guidelines. In 1987, uniform guidelines were created for sentencing individuals in the federal courts. Some federal judges quit the bench in protest of the strictness of the guidelines and the sentences they were required to hand down. In 1991, the commission shifted the emphasis from individual wrongdoers to organizations that might be found guilty for the illegal actions of their employees. The 2015 revised guidelines threaten fines of up to $150 million to companies found guilty of violating the federal guidelines based on a point system.[102] However, those fines can be substantially reduced if an organization implements an "effective program to prevent and detect violations of law." Companies that followed the requirements of the FSGO could find relief from lawsuits that resulted from one or more criminally motivated professionals. However, without active, ethical leadership, there is less likely to be a strong culture, open communication, and support from other organizational systems to support ethics programs.

Ethical Insight 6.3

Ethical Climate of Your Organization

Step 1: Complete the following questionnaire using the organization employing you now or in the recent past. Record the number beside each item from the scale that realistically reflects your experience with and understanding of the organization.

0 = Completely False, 1 = Mostly False, 2 = Somewhat False, 3 = Somewhat True, 4 = Mostly True, 5 = Completely True

_____ 1. In this organization, people can, and often do, follow their own principles and belief systems.

_____ 2. Employees and professionals are expected to do what it takes to achieve the organization's goals and interests.

_____ 3. Individuals and groups generally protect and advance each other's interests.

_____ 4. Dutifully following the organization's rules and decisions are strongly expected.

_____ 5. Everyone protects themselves over others' interests in this organization.

_____ 6. The law, rules, and regulations are first and foremost with authority here.

_____ 7. People are strictly expected to stay within the organization's authoritative rules.

_____ 8. Efficiency is oftentimes more important than effectiveness in this organization.

_____ 9. People are considerate to and for others in this organization.

_____ 10. Professional ethical codes and principles are very important in this organization.

_____ 11. People in this organization are rewarded for promoting the interests of customers and stakeholders.

Step 2: Add your responses to 1, 3, 6, 9, 10, and 11. Write the sum after "Subtotal 1" below. Now reverse the scores on questions 2, 4, 5, 7, and 8 (5 = 0, 4 = 1, 3 = 2, 2 = 3, 1 = 4, 0 = 5). Add these reverse scores (i.e., number value) and write the sum after "Subtotal 2" below. Now add Subtotal 1 with Subtotal 2 for your overall score. The total score ranges between 0 and 55. The higher the score, the more the organization supports ethical behavior.

Subtotal 1 _____ + Subtotal 2 _____ = Overall Score _____

Step 3: Write a statement describing your organization's ethics. Explain why the organization is as you describe it. How does/did the ethical climate affect you, your attitudes, energy, motivation, and ethical orientation?

Step 4: What would you say to the leaders and staff of this organization, if you could, regarding the culture, policies, procedures, and ethical environment? What recommendations would you offer to change the climate and culture of the organization?

Source: Reprinted from Cullen, J. B., Victor, B., and Stephens, C. (1989, Autumn). An ethical weather report: Assessing the organization's ethical climate. *Organizational Dynamics, 18,* 50–62. With permission from Elsevier.

Organizations and Leaders as Moral Agents

Since corporations are charted as citizens of states and nations, they also share the same rights and obligations as citizens. Corporations are not, however, individuals; they are moral agents that must follow laws, rules, and regulations of their local and national settings. When corporations violate such laws, they are also subject to penalties and fines, and can even have their right to exist taken away, depending on judicial findings in criminal acts (as was the case with the then highly prestigious accounting firm, Arthur Andersen). The role of leaders as moral agents has not been emphasized enough as one of the key ingredients in building and sustaining ethics programs. Organizational leaders who lack strong moral character and convictions, even if they are brilliant strategists and execute excellently, leave their firms vulnerable to illegal and unethical acts, as Enron clearly showed.

Ethics Codes

Ethics codes are value statements that define an organization. Leaders' values again play a significant role in shaping the values of the organizations in which they serve. Six core values that researchers have found desirable in such codes include (1) trustworthiness, (2) respect, (3) responsibility, (4) fairness, (5) caring and (6) citizenship.[103] Johnson & Johnson's credo (Figure 6.3) is an outstanding example. Major purposes of ethics codes include:[104]

- To state corporate leaders' dominant values and beliefs, which are the foundation of the corporate culture
- To define the moral identity of the company inside and outside the firm
- To set the moral tone of the work environment
- To provide a more stable, permanent set of guidelines for right and wrong actions
- To control erratic and autocratic power or whims of employees
- To serve business interests (because unethical practices invite outside government, law enforcement, and media intervention)
- To provide an instructional and motivational basis for training employees regarding ethical guidelines and for integrating ethics into operational policies, procedures, and problems
- To constitute a legitimate source of support for professionals who face improper demands on their skills or well-being
- To offer a basis for adjudicating disputes among professionals inside the firm and between those inside and outside the firm
- To provide an added means of socializing professionals, not only in specialized knowledge, but also in beliefs and practices the company values or rejects

Codes of Conduct

An organization's code of conduct is only as credible as the CEO's and leaders' personal and professional codes of conduct. Leaders must "walk the walk" as well as "talk the talk." "An organization's code of conduct, alternatively referred to as 'code of ethics' or 'code of business standards,' is the stated commitment of the behavioral expectations that an organization holds for its employees and agents. Such codes are now commonplace for most corporations and are increasingly shared not only with employees, but also with customers and the public at large. To be successful, a code must be believable by all stakeholders to which it applies. A corporation's leaders must show commitment to communication and fairly enforcing codes of conduct for such documents to be effective. However, how the code is written and what it contains are also important elements regarding whether it has the power to influence not only perceptions, but actions."[105]

One survey of U.S. corporate ethics codes found that the most important topics were general statements about ethics and philosophy; conflicts of interest; compliance with applicable laws; political contributions; payments to government officials or political parties; inside information; gifts, favors, and entertainment; false entries in books and records; and customer and supplier relations.[106] Notable firms go further in detailing corporate obligations. The examples of Johnson & Johnson and BorgWarner (Figures 6.3 and 6.4) define their obligations to various stakeholders. Other exemplary codes include those of KMPG and PricewaterhouseCoopers.

Examples of items in a code of conduct include the following list:[107]

- Financial Integrity & Assurance
- Ethical Principles
- Intellectual Property
- Information Security
- Workplace Violence
- Insider Trading
- Illegal Business Practices
- OSHA (Occupational Safety and Health Administration) guidelines
- Legal & Effective E-mail
- Anti-Money Laundering
- Conflicts of Interest
- Health & Safety
- Harassment
- Record Keeping & Destruction
- Gifts & Gratuities
- Antitrust
- Diversity

Companies looking to buy (acquirers) other companies (targets) perform preacquisition due diligence on the management, finance, technology, services and products, legality, and ethics of the targets. That is, companies looking to purchase other companies need to perform analyses to discover if the targets are telling the truth about their products, finances, and legal records. "Where does one start in uncovering the ethical vulnerability of a target?" The following basic questions are suggested as a starting point:[108]

1. Does the target have a written code of conduct or code of ethics?
2. Does the company provide ethics training or ethics awareness-building programs for management and company employees?
3. Are avenues, such as an ethics office or hotline, available for employees to ask questions about ethical issues?

Problems with Ethics and Conduct Codes

The problems with corporate ethics codes in general are the following:[109]

1. Most codes are too vague to be meaningful; that is, the codes do not inform employees about how to prioritize conflicting interests of

distributors, customers, and the company. What does being a "good citizen" really mean in practice?
2. Codes do not prioritize beliefs, values, and norms. Should profit always supersede concern for customers or employees?
3. Codes are not enforced in firms.
4. Not all employees are informed of codes.
5. Codes do not relate to employee's actual work and ethical "gray" areas.
6. Top-level leaders in organizations usually do not show interest or involvement in the programs.
7. Codes do not inspire or motivate employees to follow laws, rules, and procedures.
8. Codes that are used internationally have sections that are irrelevant or incomplete to other country personnel's experiences and specific areas of concern.

Ethics codes are a necessary but insufficient means of assisting or influencing professionals with managing moral conduct in companies. One study showed that companies that had corporate ethics codes had "less wrongdoing and higher levels of employee commitment."[110] However, the authors explain that "formal ethical codes are one component of a milieu that encourages and supports high standards of ethical behavior; that is, these organizations have formal and informal mechanisms to ensure that ethical conduct becomes 'a way of life.'" Also, employee behavior was not as influenced by the ethics codes because the codes "are not part of the organizational environment." Part of the message here may also be that implementing several organizationally supported and integrated values-based stakeholder management and ethics programs has a better chance of meeting intended goals than does reliance on brochures and printed documents.

Ombuds and Peer-Review Programs

Ombuds and peer-review programs are additional methods that corporations use to manage the legal and moral aspects of potentially problematic activities in the workplace. The International Ombudsman Association provides updates for members, methods, and other information on programs described in this section (International Ombudsman Association, 2021, https://ioa.memberclicks .net/what-is-an-organizational-ombuds). The ombuds approach provides employees with a means of having their grievances heard, reviewed, and resolved. Originating in Sweden, this concept was first tried at Xerox in 1972 and later at General Electric and Boeing. Ombuds individuals are third parties inside the corporation to whom employees can take their grievances. At Xerox, employees are encouraged to solve their problems through the chain of command before seeking out the ombudsperson. However, if that process fails, the employee can go to the ombudsperson, who acts as an intermediary. The ombuds individuals, with the employee's approval, can go to the employee's manager to discuss the grievance. The ombudsperson can continue through the chain of command, all the way to the president of the corporation, if the problem has not been satisfactorily resolved for the employee. Ombudspersons have no power themselves to solve disputes or override managers' decisions. Complaints usually center on salary disputes, job performance appraisals, layoffs, benefits, and job mobility. At General Electric, ombudspersons report that they handle 150 cases every year.

The International Ombudsman Program stated on its website, "The legislative and corporate governance environment has changed in recent years. It is more critical than ever for companies to have a complete system for identifying and resolving ethics problems. Such a system works best if it combines formal channels such as hotlines and compliance policies with the informal channel of an ombuds office, which remains independent of the company's management structure."[111]

An example of an effective ombuds program is that of the International Franchise Association (IFA). Its board of directors adopted a comprehensive self-regulation program that has a clearly and strongly stated ethics code; an investor awareness and education program; a franchise education compliance and training program; a code enforcement mechanism; and an ombudsperson program, which is described as follows: "The ombudsperson program is designed to enable franchisors and franchisees to identify disputes early and to assist them in taking preventative measures . . . facilitating dispute resolution . . . recommending non-legal methods and approaches to resolving disputes, encouraging [both parties] to work together to resolve disputes, providing confidentiality throughout the process, and providing objective and unbiased advice and guidance to all the participants."[112]

A problem with the ombuds approach is that managers may feel their authority is threatened. Employees who seek out ombudspersons also might worry about their managers retaliating against them from fear or spite. Confidentiality also has to be observed on the part of ombudspersons. Ombudspersons are as effective as the support of the program by stakeholders allows them to be. Their success is measured by the trust, confidence, and confidentiality they can create and sustain with the stakeholders. Finally, the ombudsperson's effectiveness depends on the acceptance by managers and employees of the solutions adopted to resolve problems. Ombuds programs, for example, have been successful at IBM, Xerox, General Electric, the U.S. Department of Education, The World Bank, and several major U.S. newspaper organizations.

Peer-review programs have been used by more than 100 large companies to enable employees to express and solve grievances, thus relieving stress that could lead to immoral activities. Employees initially use the chain of command whenever a problem exists. If the supervisors or executives do not resolve the problem, the employee can request a peer-review panel to help find a solution. Two randomly selected workers in the same job classification are chosen for the panel along with an executive from another work unit. The selection must be reviewed in reference to company policy. Peer-review programs work when top management supports such due process procedures and when these mechanisms are perceived as long-term, permanent programs.

Peer-review programs have received positive reviews and have had good results, particularly in the health care and accounting industries. More than 50 percent of the U.S. state boards of accountancy require certified public accountants to participate in a peer-review program to obtain a license to practice.[113] Congress has mandated the use of the Medicare Peer Review Organization since 1982.[114] In England, peer-review accreditation programs have evolved as external voluntary mechanisms that also provide organizational development of health care providers.[115] Ombudsperson and peer-review programs serve as popular mechanisms not only for solving disputes among stakeholders, but also for integrating the interests of diverse stakeholders.

We conclude this chapter by presenting a "Readiness Checklist" organizations can use to determine whether or not their executives and professionals use a values-based stakeholder management approach to create and sustain integrity in the organization. If not, they may review their vision, mission, values statements as well as their ethics and codes of conduct. You may consider applying the checklist to your organization or institution.

Is the Organization Ready to Implement a Values-Based Stakeholder Approach? A Readiness Checklist

A values-based stakeholder readiness checklist can inform and educate (even interest and mobilize) top-level leaders to evaluate the ethics of their business practices and relationships. The following readiness checklist is an example that can be modified and used as a preliminary questionnaire for this purpose:

1. Do the top leaders believe that key stakeholder and stockholder relationship building is important to the company's financial and bottom-line success?
2. What percentage of the CEO's activities is spent in building new and sustaining existing relationships with key stakeholders?
3. Can employees identify the organization's key stakeholders?
4. What percentage of employee activities is spent in building productive stakeholder relationships?
5. Do the organization's vision, mission, and value statements identify stakeholder collaboration and service? If so, do leaders and employees "walk the talk" of these statements?
6. Does the corporate culture value and support participation and open and shared decision making and collaboration across structures and functions?
7. Does the corporate culture treat its employees fairly, openly, and with trust and respect? Are policies employee-friendly? Are training programs on diversity, ethics, and professional development available and used by employees?
8. Is there collaboration and open communication across the organization? Are openness, collaboration, and innovation rewarded?

9. Is there a defined process for employees to report complaints and illegal or unethical company practices without risking their jobs or facing retribution?
10. Does the strategy of the company encourage or discourage stakeholder respect and fair treatment? Is the strategy oriented toward the long or short term?
11. Does the structure of the company facilitate or hinder information sharing and shared problem solving?
12. Are the systems aligned along a common purpose or are they separate and isolated?
13. Do senior managers and employees know what customers want, and does the organization meet customer needs and expectations?

If answers to these questions are mostly affirmative, the internal organization most likely reflects ethical leadership, culture, and practices. If responses are mostly negative, legal and ethical problems may be imminent.

Chapter Summary

Corporate and organizational leaders set the vision, mission, and values of their enterprises, even though leadership, informal and emergent, is dispersed throughout organizations. Leaders also help define the culture of companies that determine their firms' ethical and legal boundaries and contributions. A stakeholder management, values-based approach is central to organizing and aligning internal systems to respond to all stakeholders. There are still many lessons to be found in the classic "built to last" and "good to great" companies, whose fundamental purposes and core values were the foundation for competitive long-term achievement. More recently, highly successful companies referred to as "firms of endearment" exemplify even more of a values-based, stakeholder approach in dealing with customers, employees, suppliers, vendors, and society. This chapter offered numerous examples and evidence of effective values and stakeholder management approaches leaders use in the marketplace.

Leaders define and model the moral character of organizations. Leaders guide the identification of a vision, mission, and values and then serve as ethical role models in their stakeholder and business relationships. Figure 6.1 illustrates a strategic alignment model that leaders can use to guide their strategy development process. James Collins's "Level 5" leader profile was used as an example of successful leaders. A values-based stakeholder management approach was summarized, and it's argued that organizations can be economically successful by being socially responsible and ethical with their stakeholders.

Leadership in organizations can be defined from a values-based approach: Leaders define and model the social and ethical as well as the competitive mission of companies. They build and sustain relationships with stakeholders while demonstrating collaboration and trust. Stakeholder management is the basis for strategic alliances. Former president of Southwest Airlines Herb Kelleher is an example of a successful competitive industry leader who led ethically and spiritually.

Failure of ethical leadership is evidenced by eight symptoms: ethical blindness, muteness, incoherence, paralysis, hypocrisy, schizophrenia, complacency, and ethical exclusion and bigotry. Mickey Monus, former CEO of the Phar-Mor company, failed to lead ethically and was sentenced to 20 years in prison for mail fraud, wire fraud, bank fraud, and theft. "Chainsaw Al" Dunlap, former CEO of Sunbeam, was fired after the SEC found fraudulent activities during his tenure.

The reasonableness of CEO pay and performance was discussed. Not all CEOs are overpaid, but there is a significant number of highly visible CEOs whose high compensation appears unrelated to their firm's performance. This remains a concern of activist shareholders.

Figure 6.6 summarizes an alignment contingency model for understanding the "big picture" of leaders' tasks in defining and implementing effective and ethical strategies, cultures, and structures. Strategies, cultures, structures, and systems are aligned along a vision, mission, and core values. This approach is compatible with the "firms of endearment," "built to last," and "good to great" studies of successful organizations. Customers as key stakeholders are central to an organization's alignment since they are essential to a firm's success.

Strategy must be aligned with markets, values, culture, leadership style, and structure to be effective. Strategy serves both a revolutionary role (to be innovatively competitive) and a more classical role at four levels: enterprise, corporate, business, and function. Strategies influence ethics by the expectations, pressures, motivation, and rewards they create. Overly aggressive strategies, which may also be unrealistic, can create implementation pressures that lead to unethical activities.

Culture, structure, and other systems are internal dimensions that allow leaders and professionals to implement strategy. "High-ethics" company cultures can serve as a benchmark for other organizations' cultures. Such cultures are grounded in well-defined purposes that drive operations. These cultures are also modeled by leaders who are devoted to fairness, interaction with all stakeholders, concern for stakeholder interests, and individual responsibility.

Organizational structures that are overly centralized or decentralized may foster ethical problems. Although there is not "one best way" to structure a company, there are advantages and disadvantages to each type of structure. For example, centralized functional structures discourage open communication and sharing and must be integrated. Decentralized structures, such as networks and project teams with little or no coordination, may create a climate for unethical activities, such as fraud, theft, and unfair pressure of customers and alliance partners. Having leaders who rely on mission-driven ethical values that are communicated, reflected in the culture, and enforced throughout a firm is a necessary part of structural alignment.

Figure 6.8 illustrates the challenge of balancing internal organizational and professional stakeholders' values. Professional stakeholders in marketing, R&D, sales, finance, and production often function within four boundaries: rewards, time horizons, training backgrounds, and resource constraints. A critical task of organizational leaders is to guide internal professionals and focus them on the mission and values of the company.

An overview of self-regulated ethics programs was presented. Ethics programs, codes, ombudspersons, peer reviews, and ethics officers programs are ways in which corporations can attempt to regulate themselves. Johnson & Johnson's "credo" (Figure 6.3) is an example of an outstanding ethics code.

A "Readiness Checklist" for assessing a values-based, stakeholder readiness perspective was offered that enables firms to address the extent to which they use a values-based stakeholder approach in their business practices.

Questions

1. Describe the most ethical leader for whom you have worked. Now describe the least ethical leader. Which leader did you learn valuable lessons from and enjoy working with the most? The least? Why? What role did ethics play in your answers? Explain.
2. Describe an experience you have had (or an experience where you observed a leader) that required moral courage to either make a tough decision or refrain from making a decision that could have had harmful consequences. After describing the experience, answer these questions: (a) What was "moral" about the decision that had to be made? (b) What differentiated this situation and decision from other decisions that were serious but that did not require "moral courage"? Explain.
3. Do you believe leaders in large Fortune 500 companies follow and model their stated visions, missions, and values in everyday business dealings? Explain. Identify a Fortune 500 company and CEO in the news that demonstrates ethical behavior. Is there any evidence that their company's performance is related to ethical leadership behavior? Explain.
4. Do companies have to operate ethically to be financially successful? Explain.
5. Identify some characteristics of a values-based stakeholder approach to leading and running a company. Do you agree or disagree with these characteristics? Explain.
6. Which of the 13 values-based readiness checklist steps would you expect are least practiced in most companies? Which steps on the list do you believe the organization for which you work(ed) practiced least? Why?
7. Do you believe most CEOs in U.S. companies are overpaid and underperform? Explain. What pay or performance criteria do you believe should be used for top-level officers in publicly traded companies?
8. Offer one difference a values-based, ethical stakeholder approach could make in the formulation and implementation of an organization's strategy. Explain.
9. Suggest three differences a values-based, ethical stakeholder perspective could make in forming and building a new organizational culture. Explain.
10. What clues would you look for in identifying ethical and unethical activities by evaluating an organization's structure? Explain.

11. If you were to evaluate the alignment of an organization's strategy, structure, and culture from a values-based stakeholder approach, suggest three criteria you would use and some questions you would ask.
12. Which is most effective for organizational stakeholders: internal self-regulation or government regulation? Defend your points.
13. Explain the strengths and weaknesses of organizational (a) ethics codes, (b) ombuds and peer-review programs, and (c) ethics departments.

Exercises

1. Assume you are an ombudsperson or an ethics officer for a large organization. What problems do you believe you would experience? Why? What contributions do you think you could make in this role? Why?
2. Describe the type of training you would need, and list specific competencies that would help you in the role of ombuds or ethics officer.
3. Draft a brief values statement (or list some major values) of the ideal company for which you would like to work. Compare your list with other students' lists. What similarities and differences did you find? Compare your list to the examples in this chapter. What are the similarities or differences?
4. Briefly describe the leader of an organization in which you work or have worked. Evaluate the moral, amoral, or immoral characteristics of the leader. Refer to the "ethics of leadership styles" and the "seven symptoms of the failure—or success—of leadership" in the chapter.
5. Return to question 4. Suggest specific ways that your leader could improve their leadership competency and ethical style.
6. Briefly describe the culture of an organization in which you work or have worked. Explain how the culture affected a specific business practice. How ethical or unethical were the effects of the culture on that business practice? Explain.
7. Return to question 6. Suggest a few ways in which that organization's culture could be strengthened or changed. Offer a suggestion for the way the strategy formulation or implementation could be changed. Offer a way in which one of the practices or management methods of the system could be changed for improvement.

Values and Leadership at Z Insurance Corp.

"What Would You Do?" I graduated from the University of New England on a beautiful day in May. Graduating cum laude, with a job in my back pocket, I thought that my future was as bright as the sun was that day. However, unlike that beautiful day, blue skies did not lie ahead for me professionally.

During the spring of my senior year, I was busy interviewing for full-time positions after graduation. At one particular campus career fair, I came across the booth for Z Insurance Corp. As a business student, I had a keen interest in financial services. I believed and still believe that it is a noble profession, which helps to give hardworking people the power to be financially stable, save money for retirement, or put their children through college. Because of these interests, I was very curious to see what Z Corp. had to offer in the realm of financial services.

Looking back (with 20/20 hindsight), I believe that I was duped from the beginning. I'll tell you why in the following two actual scenarios.

Scenario One: "How I Learned to Lie to the Elderly"

My grandmother is one of the most caring and wonderful people I know. Recently, my grandfather passed away and left my grandmother with a considerable amount of money, and little financial experience to manage it. She guarded the money very carefully, since it was earned by her best friend and loving husband. Back to Z Corp.

The new "recruits" at Z Corp. have a two-week-long orientation before they can begin their work. During the first couple of days of this orientation, we watched films that illustrated how we would be helping senior citizens protect their life savings. These films had positive messages about America's senior citizens, including how to communicate with them in a respectful manner, cherish their money as if it was ours, and take each question they had with the utmost care. Although I was still a bit shocked by the fact that I was now an insurance salesperson, I was excited by the prospect of making a difference in the lives of America's senior citizens. I was picturing folks, similar to my grandmother, who would trust us to help them protect their life's hard-earned money.

These utopian ideals were soon transformed into harsh realities. Daily, I became increasingly aware of the games that this company was playing with us and the people that we were to "help." On one particular day, we were discussing how we were going to "entice" our customers on the phones so that they would listen to our message about long-term care insurance. Again, we didn't know that we were going to be involved in "cold calling," which was yet another surprise to us. During this meeting, we were given our "communication," which was to be followed very closely, not deviating from any of the scripts. While I was reading over the "communication," something struck me as peculiar. The following is a rough sample of our "communication":

Z Corp. Rep: "Hello, my name is Lea Stern from Z Corp. I am a financial adviser. I am calling in regard to literature that you received in the mail from us. Do you recall receiving this information?" (Usually the response was "No, I don't remember seeing anything from Z Corp.")

Z Corp. Rep: (*chuckling*) "Oh, I am sure you may not have. We all receive so much in the mail these days that you may have thrown it away or may have not read it yet."

After I read this script, I asked the sales manager whether or not these folks actually received something from Z Corp. regarding long-term care insurance. What he said in response to my question still rings clear in my head. So clear, in fact, that I am going to quote it: "These folks are old and confused. Most likely they received something in the mail about 'financial planning.' We are banking on the fact that they will not remember or realize who it was from and will take our word that it was from us."

"Old and confused" is how the sales manager described my loving grandmother. Because of the values that I grew up with and still hold, I could not imagine taking advantage of hardworking seniors in such a twisted, immoral way. With this one statement, I decided that I did not respect my manager or Z Corp. My attitude changed immediately. I knew from that moment that I would find it very hard to work for Z Corp. and almost impossible to work for that manager.

Scenario Two: "Reading the Fine Print"

I have been blessed with a wonderful family who surrounded me with caring people who would never try to take advantage of me. Maybe I am trusting and a bit naive, but I'm not stupid! With the experience I described previously at Z Corp., I learned that this trust could be a double-edged sword. I lived 21 years not realizing how twisted company policies and practices could be; it took only one week at Z Corp. for me to wake up to "corporate realities"—at least in an insurance-sales setting.

At the career fair at the University of New England, I had a wonderful conversation with a sales manager at Z Corp. We discussed the virtues of being a financial adviser, such as recommending appropriate mutual funds based on financial needs, careful investments, and the merits of having Series 6 and 7 licenses. I enjoyed the fact that Z Corp. seemed to be a company that helped folks invest in diversified ways. Never once were insurance sales, cold calling, or no pay for four months mentioned; not during the first, second, or final interview. Only when I signed on and was in training did I find out the truth about this shifty company.

During each of the lunches on that first week of our orientation, the "recruits" discussed what we called the "footnote." We used this term because we felt there was always another footnote regarding pay, customer contact, or office supplies. I felt as if I were employed at a different company, with a completely different position than the one for which I originally interviewed. Some of this may have been my fault. For example, I never asked what the values of this company were or what its mission was. However, important points such as job function and company mission, as well as reimbursement, should be communicated truthfully. I felt as if the people at Z Corp. did not communicate effectively with us at all. A communication channel was not established between the managers and me at Z Corp. Without proper communication, I was taken advantage of and didn't feel comfortable being in the follower role. I didn't know what the company stood for, and most important, I didn't know what I stood for!

Questions

1. What are your general reactions to the two scenarios?
2. Would you react similarly or differently than the writer? Explain.
3. Do you believe the writer is naive and that these scenarios represent the "real world" from which she has been sheltered? Or do you think this company is a single "rotten apple" among the more honest companies in this industry and the writer should react as she did? Explain.
4. Are there any illegal or unethical tactics that the company sales manager/rep is using? Explain.

Real-Time Ethical Dilemma

Whose Values? Whose Decision?

Jim Howard is a sales manager at a software company that produces a search interface for databases with indexed information. The company is an established vendor and has a good reputation in the market for its high-quality products, fast and personal customer support, and strong loyalty to its customers. Part of the values statement of the company includes, "We will treat our customers with respect and dignity."

In his first year with the company, Jim noticed that the sales force was having difficulty acquiring new customers and retaining existing ones. The problem was complex: a shrinking market with continuously increasing buying power, increasing competition, and the emergence of free alternatives from the Internet. These problems started to significantly affect the company's revenue. The company's reaction was to drastically decrease the cost of its products, bundle databases into packages, and start to alter product introductions by including several value-added services that were new to the market.

Jim's boss suggested that Jim take over the responsibility for the yearly renewals of customer subscriptions from the company's secretary, which previously had been regarded as an easy clerical procedure. When he started to check the old accounts and follow up with renewals, he faced a problem that he thought would never have occurred: unfair treatment of old customers in comparison to new customers in terms of the product pricing. Existing customers were offered renewal at triple the price of the same package offered to new customers.

When he asked his boss whether he should inform the old customers that the price had changed and whether the old customers could now benefit from the lowered price, the answer was, "Why don't we try to get this price? If the customer refuses to pay it, then we'll negotiate." An additional difficulty was that, in the last few months, information had been disseminated to all customers that made the company's new pricing strategy visible to customers. Jim shared the fact with his boss that this information was already available to customers and pointed out the contradiction. His boss remained insistent, to the point of shouting, that Jim follow his previous instructions with the sales force.

Jim felt he was betraying the company, the customer, his sales force, and his own professional values. He didn't want to lose his job, and he didn't want to lose any more customer accounts.

Questions

1. If you were Jim, what would you do in this situation?
2. What are the issues here? For whom?
3. Who stands to be hurt the most from following the advice of Jim's boss?
4. What would a values-based stakeholder management approach suggest that you do, if you were Jim? Lay out an action plan and be ready to role-play your suggested approach.
5. Compare your answer to question 1 to your approach in question 4. Any differences? If so, could you still follow what you said in question 4?

Case 17

Corporate Responsibility in the Age of Big Data: Facebook's Obligations to Protect Consumers

A popular adage states that "there is no such thing as a free lunch." Social media platforms such as Facebook, Instagram, Google, TikTok, and LinkedIn offer access to their platforms where users can connect and share information with each other at seemingly no cost. These companies then collect data on consumers, either selling the information itself or using it to target consumers for third-party advertising. This is the business model of the "modern age"; the product is not the services utilized by individual users but rather access for third-party companies to the users themselves and their data. According to Wharton Customer Analytics and a Drexel marketing professor, Elea Feit, "Most companies are collecting data these days on all the interactions, on all the places that they touch customers in the normal course of doing business." The old adage should be updated for modern times to read "If the service is free, you are the product" (Deloitte, 2021).

Facebook is well known for providing users access to third-party-developed applications that enhance the appeal of its platform. Applications (referred to as "apps") come in many forms, from videogame farming simulators to video summaries of the user's past year of photographs and posts and quick quizzes that claim to provide insight into one's personality. One of these apps, Your Digital Life, developed by Aleksandr Kogan of Cambridge University in June 2014, offered users a standard personality quiz experience. The app was downloaded by 270,000 people and installed on their Facebook accounts. The app then provided Kogan access to the data of not only the users who downloaded the app, but their friends' data as well. Such data included posts, status updates, and even private messages. Ultimately the profiles of an estimated 50 million users were downloaded to Kogan's private database.

This information was then provided to Cambridge Analytica, a political data firm, for use in various political initiatives—most famously the 2016 U.S. presidential election. The firm first entered politics that year with the goal of "giving conservatives big data tools to compete with Democrats" (Detrow, 2018). The firm had high-profile conservative activists involved from inception. Wealthy Republican donor Robert Mercer and political strategist Steve Bannon of Breitbart News were on its board, which helped direct its politically driven activities. The firm was comprised of data scientists, psychologists, social media experts, and creative designers. Using the data acquired by Kogan's app, they built psychographic profiles of Facebook users to understand their political leanings and susceptibility to various advertising methods. Cambridge Analytica then build a network of news sites and blogs, interlinked to increase the apparent legitimacy of their claims, and used Facebook's targeted advertising capabilities combined with the profiles built using Kogan's data. Strategies for different user profiles were developed, ranging from misinformation and the warping of the facts to fear campaigns and genuinely conveying information that may be influential. The firm not only claims to have been a major driver in President Donald Trump's surprise victory over Hillary Clinton in the 2016 election, but the Brexit referendum in 2016 as well. In a post-election piece titled "The Data Gurus Who Anticipated the Election Results," Frank Luntz, a political consultant declared, "There are no longer any experts except Cambridge Analytica. They were Trump's digital team who figured out how to win" (Zizal, 2016).

The use of Facebook's marketing capabilities and access to consumer data is at the core of Facebook's business model. Facebook allows companies the opportunity to market to its 2.7 billion monthly active users and boasts an accessible API (application programming interface), which allows third-party developers to build apps that are easy to upload to the Facebook platform. Data collection and utilization was widespread on the platform prior to its inception and is nothing new, and in fact in 2014 Facebook expanded its data protections for consumers. Facebook introduced three restrictions that year. The first was to limit developers from accessing data on consumers' friends who did not download the data-gathering application. Furthermore, if apps were not used for three months, then developers lost access to the user's data. And finally, Facebook developers who had uploaded apps to the platform prior to 2014 had to submit to an audit to confirm that data collected outside of these guidelines was deleted. The consequence of not following these procedures would result in immediate termination from the platform. Facebook's commitment to these audits was minimal. In 2016, Facebook contacted Cambridge Analytica to conduct an audit and inquire if the data collected, against policy, had been deleted. The only proof required was a signed certification that in fact the information had been deleted. As of late, there have been several new updates to Facebook's user privacy practices. In a piece published by Facebook CEO Mark Zuckerberg titled "A Privacy-Focused Vision for Social Networking," he wrote that because "people also want to interact privately, there's also an opportunity to build a simpler platform that's focused on privacy first." His new vision stressed private interactions, encryption, reduction of permanency, safety, interoperability, and secure data storage. Noticeably missing from these core ideas are data sharing and ad targeting, which were what brought Facebook into the spotlight.

The matter gained national attention in March 2018 when Christopher Wylie, a Cambridge Analytica data scientist, publicly revealed the extent to which data was collected without consumers' awareness and the ultimate use of that information for political means, which some would consider manipulation. This resulted in not only media attention but a drop in Facebook users, a drop in share price, outrage from privacy advocates, and investigations by lawmakers. Cambridge Analytica executives had been called before Congress multiple times, but in May 2018 the company closed, saying that "the siege of media coverage has driven away virtually all of the company's customers and suppliers." This left Facebook and its massive stores of user information as an unanswered question for regulators. States such as Vermont and California enacted a range of regulations requiring data brokers to register with the state or requiring companies to allow consumers to opt-out of data gathering. According to the *New York Times*, "the California Consumer Privacy Act grants people in the state the right to opt-out of the sale of their personal information. Apps, websites and other services that exchange personal data for money—or for non-monetary compensation—must prominently display a 'Do Not Sell My Data' notice allowing people to stop the spread of their information" (Cowan and Singer, 2020).

After testifying to Congress, Zuckerberg pledged to take action to prevent a crisis like this from happening in the future. Zuckerberg pledged to restrict developers' data access even further and reduce the data that users provide to apps to just the user's name, profile photo, and e-mail address. Facebook would also require developers to obtain approval from consumers before accessing their posts or private data. The company would also conduct a full forensic audit of suspicious apps and ban developers who do not agree to the increased oversight. Many speculate that Zuckerberg's refusal to accept blame for this scandal, and the consistent blaming of rogue developers, was a way to prepare for a legal defense that might be required later. Investigations by the Federal Trade Commission and Congress, as well as fines in other foreign countries including England and Italy, indicated that Facebook's responsibility for Cambridge Analytica's gathering of user information without consent, and the broader questions the scandal raised, would be far from over.

The Facebook-Cambridge Analytica scandal raises ethical questions about whether Facebook, as the operator of the social network platform, had an obligation to inform users that their data was being collected and whether or not the company should have provided data protection. The scandal is an example of improper collection and misuse of that data. However, data collection is relatively new and unregulated, which creates ethical gray areas. Many firms collect similar data as Cambridge Analytica while informing customers they are doing so. These firms then sell that properly acquired data to third parties who then use it for political action as well. Other organizations purchase data without an understanding of how it was acquired, even if the method was unethical. The data is then used for legitimate advertising purposes. Most large corporations are involved in large-scale data acquisition and analysis. An important lesson learned from this scandal is that the public's eyes were opened to see how detailed their collected information can be and how it can be used without their knowledge or approval.

Epilogue

Facebook consented to pay a £500,000 fine, set by the data-protection watchdog in the United Kingdom, for its role in the Cambridge Analytica scandal. A Facebook lawyer stated that Facebook also enacted changes to restrict app developers' access to information. Facebook also made no admission of liability (Criddle, 2020). While this scandal is over, the issue as indicated earlier remains: large social media companies' "surveillance business models, their increasingly central position in digital society, and the power they now hold as a result" (Cobbe, 2020). For example, the legal and ethical concern persists about how "micro-targeting is used across the political spectrum" with regard to large social media firms allowing political campaigns to "slice and dice the electorate, dividing voters into small groups," thus facilitating the "prospect of campaigns using these tactics to suppress turnout among supporters of other candidates" (Cobbe, 2020).

In fairness to Facebook, it claimed that bad actors and their questionable information cannot always be easily detected. The company walks a fine line between freedom of the press and propagating dangerous propaganda. The firm did tighten its surveillance on political advertising during the 2020 presidential race between Donald Trump and Joe Biden.

Still, critics of large social media companies claim that by their very nature and DNA, they participate in what has been termed "surveillance capitalism" (Zuboff, 2019). That is, their business models—how they make money—are designed to collect, analyze and use private citizens' data to sell to advertisers without the knowledge of users. This practice is, according to this theory, part of "an economic system centered around the commodification of personal data with the core purpose of profit-making" and the "increasing price of data having limited accessibility to the purchase of personal data points to the richest in society" (Surveillance capitalism, n.d.).

With regard to how one group of stakeholders, consumers, feel about the dilemma of using social media firms and individuals' concern for privacy, a Pew Research Center 2018 study concluded that, "on one hand, the rapid growth of the platforms is testimony to their appeal to online Americans. On the other, this widespread use has been accompanied by rising user concerns about privacy and social media firms' capacity to protect their data. All this adds up to a mixed picture about how Americans feel about social media" (Rainie, 2018). Other stakeholders and their stakes also present a more complicated but very important view of this controversy.

Questions for Discussion

1. What role(s) did Facebook have in this case?
2. Did Facebook violate its trust and obligations to consumer stakeholders? Explain.
3. What should Facebook have done differently in this case to be a responsible firm?
4. Was your view and practices using Facebook changed or not in this case? Explain.
5. What would you recommend to Facebook as an ethical and consumer consultant?

Sources

This case was developed from material contained in the following sources:

Ballhous, R., and Gross, J. (2018, May 2). Cambridge Analytica closing operations following Facebook data controversy. *Wall Street Journal*. https://www.wsj.com

/articles/cambridge-analytica-closing-operations-following-facebook-data
-controversy-1525284140.

BBC US and Canada. (2018, March). Facebook's Zuckerberg speaks out over
Cambridge Analytica "breach" BBC *News*. https://www.bbc.com/news/world-us
-canada-43494337.

Cadwalladr, C. (2018, March). Cambridge Analytica whistleblower: "We spent $1m
harvesting millions of Facebook profiles." *The Guardian*. YouTube Video. 40:32.
https://www.youtube.com/watch?v=FXdYSQ6nu-M.

Cobbe, J. (2020, October 15). Behind Cambridge Analytica lay a bigger threat to our
democracy: Facebook. https://www.theguardian.com/technology/commentisfree
/2020/oct/15/cambridge-analytica-threat-democracy-facebook-big-tech.

Cowan, J., and Singer, N. (2020, January). How California's new privacy law affects
you. *New York Times*. https://www.nytimes.com/2020/01/03/us/ccpa-california
-privacy-law.html.

Criddle, C. (2020, October 28). Facebook sued over Cambridge Analytica data
scandal. *BBC News*. https://www.bbc.com/news/technology-54722362.

Deloitte.(2021). Marketing data science trends, How the science of data analytics is
shaping the future of marketing. https://www2.deloitte.com/us/en/pages/deloitte
-analytics/articles/marketing-data-science-trends.html

Detrow, S. (2018, March). What did Cambridge Analytica do during the 2016 election?
NPR. https://www.npr.org/2018/03/20/595338116/what-did-cambridge-analytica
-do-during-the-2016-election.

Granville, K. (2018, March 19). Facebook and Cambridge Analytica: What you need to
know as fallout widens. *New York Times*. https://www.nytimes.com/2018/03/19
/technology/facebook-cambridge-analytica-explained.html.

Hern, A. (2018, December). Italian regulator fines Facebook £8.9m for misleading
users. *The Guardian*. https://www.theguardian.com/technology/2018/dec/07
/italian-regulator-fines-facebook-89m-for-misleading-users.

Hern, A., and Cadwalladr, C. (2018, April). Aleksandr Kogan collected Facebook
users' direct messages. *The Guardian*. https://www.theguardian.com/uk-news
/2018/apr/13/revealed-aleksandr-kogan-collected-facebook-users-direct
-messages.

Lapowsky, I. (2019, March). How Cambridge Analytica sparked the great privacy
awakening. *Wired*. https://www.wired.com/story/cambridge-analytica-facebook
-privacy-awakening/.

Lushner, A. (2018, March). Cambridge Analytica: Who are they, and did they really
help Trump win the White House? *The Independent*. https://www.independent.co
.uk/news/uk/home-news/cambridge-analytica-alexander-nix-christopher-wylie
-trump-brexit-election-who-data-white-house-a8267591.html.

Meyer, R. (2018, March). The Cambridge Analytica scandal, in three paragraphs.
The Atlantic. https://www.theatlantic.com/technology/archive/2018/03/the
-cambridge-analytica-scandal-in-three-paragraphs/556046/.

Newton, C. (2018, March). Facebook's Cambridge Analytica data scandal, explained.
The Verge. YouTube Video. 6:16. https://www.youtube.com/watch?v
=VDR8qGmyEQg.

Ng, A. (2018, May.) Facebook's "proof" Cambridge Analytica deleted that data?
A signature. *CNET*. https://www.cnet.com/news/facebook-proof-cambridge
-analytica-deleted-that-data-was-a-signature.

Rainie, L. (2018, March 27). Americans' complicated feelings about social media in an era of privacy concerns. Pew Research Center, https://www.pewresearch.org/fact-tank/2018/03/27/americans-complicated-feelings-about-social-media-in-an-era-of-privacy-concerns/.

Surveillance capitalism (n.d.). *Wikipedia.org*. Accessed March 26, 2021, https://en.wikipedia.org/wiki/Surveillance_capitalism.

Zizal, A. (2016, November 8). Election 2016: The data game. *Cambridge Analytica*. https://www.linkedin.com/pulse/trump-how-we-did-luncheon-talk-kuala-lumpur-azrin-zizal/

Zuboff, S. (2019). *Age of Surveillance capitalism: The fight for a human future at the new frontier of power*. New York: PublicAffairs.

Zuckerberg, M. (2019, March). A privacy-focused vision for social networking. *Facebook*. https://www.facebook.com/notes/mark-zuckerberg/a-privacy-focused-vision-for-social-networking/10156700570096634/.

Case 18

Boeing: The 737 "MAX-imum" Mistake

"In 2017, the 737 MAX entered service. Since then, 346 people died in two 737 MAX crashes: a Lion Air plane crashed on October 29, 2018, after taking off in Indonesia (189 died); and an Ethiopian Airlines plane crashed after taking off in Ethiopia on March 10, 2019 (157 died)"(*USA Today*, 2020). American Airlines started training its pilots to fly the refurbished aircraft during the first half of 2021; other European carriers are to follow. All aboard?

Background

The Boeing Company has been recognized for its reputation as one of the world's largest firms in the aerospace industry. Present in over 150 countries, Boeing has been able to forge its path through the production of passenger and military aircrafts, defense products, space capsules, rockets, security systems, and more (Boeing, 2019). However, March 10, 2019, was a dark day in the company's history. Only a few moments after takeoff, Ethiopian Airlines Flight 302 crashed, killing all 157 passengers on board. This was the second deadly crash of a Boeing aircraft in a short period of only five months, after Lion Air Flight 610 crashed into the Java Sea in October 2018. The aircraft went down 13 minutes after takeoff and only 5,200 feet of ascent, having reported an unknown control issue two minutes into the flight (Wright and Karmini, 2018). Both aircrafts were Boeing 737 MAX 8 jets.

Brief History

The market in which the Boeing 737 line of aircraft operated was one considered to be "large but narrow." The Boeing 737 and its main competitor, the Airbus A320, comprised about half of the 28,000 commercial airlines in the world (Campbell, 2019). The two companies were married in a quest to stay both cheap and competitive. In an effort to cut costs, the two manufacturers focused on fuel efficiency and ways to "squeeze" even as small as one percentage point of efficiency wherever possible. In 2010, Airbus leveled the playing field, releasing a "new and improved" version of the A320: the A320neo would save airlines thousands of dollars in fuel (Campbell, 2019). Boeing considered taking the financial hit and selling its 737s at a discounted price, as the company was working on designing an entirely new plane. However, after talking with some of its major consumers such as American Airlines, Boeing realized customers would not wait.

Boeing struggled to keep a tight grip on Airbus's new release. To stay relevant and prevent loss of market share, Boeing redesigned its 737 aircraft. Not only was Boeing redesigning the aircraft, but initial plans required getting to market under a strict time schedule of six years (Campbell, 2019). The company based the newest model, the MAX line, off of existing 737 models, which, at the time, were nearly 50 years old. To maintain the Type Certificate issued by the

U.S. Federal Aviation Administration (FAA), which approves planes for flight, Boeing had to redesign the plane to be "cutting edge" but continue to maintain the integrity and "feel and fly" of the original 737 aircrafts from the 1960s (Campbell, 2019). This required engineers to mount the larger, more powerful engine further up on the wing, unlike engines that originally were built for this type of plane. With this alteration, the aerodynamics were also changed and, depending on the situation, the nose of the aircraft could be pushed upward, causing the plane to crash (BBC News, 2019). Staying within the original blueprints would not have jeopardized the certification process.

According to internal document released after the crashes, Boeing employees criticized this move and doubted the plane's ability to fly safely. Some even said that the airplane was "designed by clowns, who in turn are supervised by monkeys" and that the plane had "piss poor design" (Isidore and Levitt, 2020). The MAX line received its Type Certification approximately 5.5 years into the project (Campbell, 2019). Shortly after, pilots began boasting about their ability to fly the aircraft with only two and a half hours of online training and with no simulation testing whatsoever (Campbell, 2019).

At the time of the crisis, the 737 MAX was Boeing's most recently released line of aircraft, one that bolstered Boeing's reputation, contributing to it becoming the fastest-selling aircraft in history with 5,000 orders to over 100 customers across the globe (Boeing, 2019). As a single-aisle jet, it was designed "to offer the greatest flexibility, reliability, and efficiency in the single-aisle market" (Boeing, 2019)." The MAX 8 seats a maximum of 210 passengers, is over 129 feet long, and has a wingspan of 117 feet. The aircraft was operated by over 65 popular airlines, including United Airlines, Southwest Airlines, and American Airlines (Boeing, 2019). Currently, there are approximately 7,300 early versions of the MAX, and almost 20 percent of those are parked (Isidore, 2020).

The Crisis

On October 28, 2019, just one day before the first deadly crash of a 737 MAX 8 jet, an off-duty pilot jumped into action aboard a Lion Air flight to help pilots control a nosedive, believed to have been caused by a "malfunctioning flight-control system" (*Chicago Tribune*, 2019)." This would later be attributed to the MCAS system. Neither the flight manual nor MAX training informed pilots of this stabilization system (Isidore and Levitt, 2020). The first officer and pilot spent the first 15 minutes of flight battling nosedive after nosedive, referencing the aircraft's "quick reference guide" meant for "non-normal" situations, to no avail (Campbell, 2019). The off-duty pilot, who was simply catching a ride to his next shift, offered a suggestion that allowed the pilots to regain control and safely land the aircraft (Campbell, 2019). Per standard procedure, the incident was reported to the airline, followed by an investigation. After inspectors checked the aircraft for major equipment failures, the search revealed no findings, and the aircraft was cleared for flight (Campbell, 2019). This was the same aircraft that went down several minutes post-takeoff the following day, after 28 failed attempts to pull out of recurring nosedives, killing everyone on board.

Following the October Lion Air crash, black-box data revealed to investiga-tors that the cause of the crash seemed to lie within an automatic safety system that forced the plane into an irreversible nosedive (*Chicago Tribune*, 2019). Only five months later, Ethiopian Airlines Flight 302 went down, taking with it the lives of all 157 passengers. Several weeks after the Ethiopian Airline crash, the Ethio-pian Accident Investigation Bureau (AIB) released a preliminary report that con-tained "flight data recorder information indicating the airplane had an erroneous angle of attack sensor input that activated the Maneuvering Characteristics Aug-mentation System (MCAS) function during the flight, as it had during the Lion Air 610 flight" (Boeing, 2019)."

Symptoms of Impending Crisis

In addition to the incident that occurred one day before the Lion Air crash of the same aircraft, there were several factors that pointed to the crisis. Eight days after the first crash, Boeing's internal online portal for pilots posted a bulletin stating, "Boeing would like to call attention to an [angle of attack] failure condition that can occur during manual flight only" (Campbell, 2019)." The bulletin provided no expla-nation for the failure, and pilots searched for answers with no success. Pilots were never made aware of the MCAS system in the first place and were therefore un-aware of how to counteract the system in a crisis. Once fully understood, tests showed that pilots only had 40 seconds to identify and recover when MCAS kicked in to alter the angle of attack of the aircraft (Wichter, 2019). Many pilots were an-gered and felt that information was being withheld from them that contributed to the crisis. This quickly destroyed trust between Boeing and many employees.

Additionally, the expedited launch and production of the line of MAX aircrafts called for new engines in the design plans. The aircrafts used LEAP-1B engines, which were more efficient than those in earlier models of the 737 (Campbell, 2019). Despite their efficiency, they were both larger and heavier pieces of equip-ment. Because of the difference in size, installing engines in the same location was not an option, as it caused clearance issues on takeoff (Campbell, 2019).

The new aircraft design called for mounting engines higher and farther for-ward on the wing, but this led to aerodynamic issues. Out of fear that changes to design plans would affect the status of the line's Type Certificate, MCAS was developed as a solution. The intent was that the system would recognize a steep ascent and regulate the aircraft's position in increments of nine seconds at a time until it reached the appropriate angle of attack (Campbell, 2019).

Boeing disclosed that soon after deliveries of the MAX began, it became aware of a faulty warning light that was to alert crews of sensor issues such as those in the cases of the two crashes (Robison, 2019). When the planes involved in the crashes were purchased, these lights were optional and cost an additional $80,000 per plane to get. Both Lion Air and Ethiopian Airlines did not purchase these sensors (Yglesias, 2019). Boeing made a statement following a round of MAX testing in May 2019, defending its decision not to disclose the faulty warn-ing light at the time because engineers ruled it was not a safety issue (Robison,

2019). This seemingly contradicts later released internal documents that highlight employees apprehension, with someone saying "I really would struggle to defend the [simulator] in front of the FAA next week," and others claiming they would not put their families on board (Isidore and Levitt, 2020).

Months after the crashes, it was revealed that there were more issues than the MCAS system alone. Previously unreported concerns with wiring that helps control the tail were discovered that could lead to short-circuiting. Boeing is investigating this, as the company does not want to change the wiring as it could cause additional damage. In addition, a manufacturing problem that leaves the plane's engines vulnerable during a lightning strike has been unveiled. General Electric and Safran, which manufacture the engines, told the FAA they had discovered a possible weakness in the rotors, which could cause them to shatter (Kitroeff and Gelles, 2020).

The Aftermath: Crisis Response

Boeing stood by its "full confidence" in the line of 737 MAX aircrafts for several days after the incident. On March 13, 2019, three days after the Ethiopian Airline crash, Boeing chose to cooperate with the recommendation of the FAA , the U.S. National Transportation Safety Board (NTSB), and other aviation authorities to suspend the flight of all 737 MAX aircrafts (Boeing, 2019). The grounding of the plane has cost Boeing $18.7 billion in increased production costs, customer compensation, and improvements (Isidore, 2020). Boeing defended its actions by stating the decision was made "out of an abundance of caution" and in support of one of Boeing's core values: safety. Boeing's president, CEO, and chairman of the company, Dennis Muilenburg, stated, "On behalf of the entire Boeing team, we extend our deepest sympathies to the families and loved ones of those who have lost their lives in these two tragic accidents" (Boeing, 2019)." In this statement, he assured the media that "there is no greater priority for our company and our industry, and we are doing everything we can to understand the cause of the accidents in partnership with the investigators, deploy safety enhancements, and help ensure this does not happen again" (Boeing, 2019).

Only a few days later, Muilenburg released an open letter informing the public that the company was working on a software update inclusive of full pilot training (*Chicago Tribune*, 2019). Despite concerted efforts on the part of Boeing and Muilenburg to assure the public of their dedication to reaching a solution, on March 27, 2019, the Boeing Company rejected the call for "broader oversight" (*Chicago Tribune*, 2019). The company continued to defend the safety of the 737 MAX line, denying wrongdoing and "rejecting calls for investigation of the relationship" with the FAA (*Chicago Tribune*, 2019). On June 17, both parties in the senate criticized Steve Dickson, FAA administrator, for his cozy relationship with Boeing (Chokshi and Gelles, 2020).

After the Ethiopian AIB put forth its preliminary report, Boeing agreed to release a software update to the MCAS as well as appropriate pilot training to add "additional layers of protection and prevent erroneous data" from causing the system to fire, giving pilots the option to manually control the aircraft (Boeing, 2019).

Ethical Issues

As in any industry, aircraft companies are on a perpetual quest for both innovation and progress in order to stay competitive. The question becomes, at what point do companies take too much risk or cut costs at the expense of consumer safety? How do firms balance safety and technology without destroying the bottom line? Boeing's expedited timeframe to release the MAX line of aircrafts required blueprints and designs to be brought forward in half the time of a typical aircraft overhaul (Campbell, 2019). With this type of intense time pressure, designs were often submitted with mistakes or "incomplete schematics" (Campbell, 2019)." These actions contradict Dennis Muilenburg when he said "lives depend on what we do, and that demands excellence and the utmost integrity" to the Boeing employees during an ethics training course (Boeing, 2019).

Additionally, the responsibility of the aircraft regulatory body, the FAA, has been brought into question. Despite the fact that the FAA is responsible for the safety of all U.S. aircraft, significant authority is delegated back to manufacturers regarding certificates (Campbell, 2019). The sheer amount of work that the FAA is responsible for, in conjunction with its "perennially understaffed" workforce (Wichter, 2019), would prevent any certificates from being issued if this was not common practice. Individuals from within the FAA state that there was heavy pressure to delegate back to Boeing, which caused incomplete reviews and paperwork as well as rushed work product (Campbell, 2019). Many critics define the relationship between Boeing and the FAA as "symbiotic" and "just too cozy" (Wichter, 2019).

Continuing Issues

As part of the submission to the FAA to receive Type Certificates to fly, a list must be provided describing all of the changes to the aircraft from the previous model. The FAA's list of changes on the 737 MAX line of aircrafts, on record as being over 30 pages long and inclusive of items as small as seatbelt design, never mentioned MCAS (Campbell, 2019). In addition to the failure to disclose MCAS on the list, the original specs called for the system to be able to move the angle of the aircraft by no more than 0.6 degrees; the final model allowed the angle to shift up to 2.5 degrees and was much more powerful than previously anticipated (Campbell, 2019). For the 373 MAX to be deemed safe to fly after these crashes, several days of testing would be done, which would include emergency procedures and flight maneuvers in order to assess if the changes meet FAA standards. After the flights, the FAA would spend over a week preparing reports on its findings. Then Boeing would submit details of the software's design process and tests. Finally, outside experts and the FAA would determine if new training would be required for pilots or issue orders to allow the MAX to fly again (Chokshi and Gelles, 2020).

To cut production costs while the MAX line was in development, Boeing laid off experienced engineers to outsource engineering work to lower-wage employees. These employees were primarily responsible for testing and designing software that went into the MAX; they often worked in countries with inexperienced aerospace industries and had relatively junior backgrounds. Part of the outsourcing contracts included jobs in exchange for MAX aircraft orders in said countries. Last, in Boeing's statement regarding the faulty warning light, the company mentions that senior leadership was "not involved in the review" (Robison, 2019). For a company that has always been well known for its "meticulous designs," many question how it could have made such basic software mistakes (Robison, 2019).

After the release of the MAX aircraft, Boeing's revenue grew by 50 percent to upward of $101 billion, the stock price quadrupled, and profits doubled. Executives even made bonuses based on the fast-paced sales of the aircrafts; however, the incidents with the 737 MAX 8 aircrafts subsequently led to a $25 million decrease in market capitalization (Campbell, 2019). Boeing's most recent financial results revealed $466 million in loss and 7,000 additional layoffs by the end of 2021 (McIntosh, 2020). This fact, coupled with the 436 canceled 373 MAX orders, including those customers that converted to an alternate model, has put Boeing in a difficult financial position, especially during Covid-19, when many passengers are already weary of flying.

Not only is Boeing plagued with lawsuits from the families of victims of the two deadly crashes, but the company owes billions of dollars to suppliers and customers for the grounding of hundreds of flights. Recently, the U.S. Department of Justice began a criminal probe into Boeing to determine how, why, and when such critical decisions were made about the software design (Robison, 2019).

The events that have unfolded regarding the Boeing 737 MAX 8 aircrafts left customers, governments, and regulatory agencies shaken. This issue is rooted deeper than just economic troubles or political quarrels; it has led to the deaths of 346 people, including one child, two babies, and an Iraq War veteran. The social expectation of safety was violated for millions of human beings.

In addition to the loss of life, several other issues exist in this case. Boeing is not limited to the financial, economic, and corporate interests involved in the MAX crashes. This was a deep-seated issue within the heart of the organization, caused by an overemphasis on profit and an underemphasis on ethics. The Boeing case also presents government and regulatory issues dealing with product standards and who regulates whom, technological issues with regard to the development of the faulty software, legal issues regarding consumer protection, and last, it has evolved into an economic issue negatively impacting many stakeholders.

In terms of government and regulatory issues, the Federal Aviation Association regulates the airline industry. The FAA's diversion of responsibility demonstrated lack of regulatory oversight. This prompted bad paperwork, rushed designs, and cut corners such as the failure to include all differences between the original 737 model and the new 737 MAX design. This quickly became a conflict of interest as Boeing found itself acting as the regulatory body for its own product. Various regulatory agencies are in place to prevent similar situations from occurring in many industries, including the airline industry with the development of the FAA. The FAA's demanding workload and lack of sufficient staffing contributed to a fatal mistake.

Pressures were exerted on employees from upper-level management to quickly bring the MAX aircraft to market to compete with Airbus, which suggests the influence of competitive status and financial gain over human concern. A sizable risk of having a weak culture is the occurrence of safety violations. As engineers began to stray from original blueprints and designs and failed to document such changes properly, they began to get lost. The technology used for the MCAS had several flaws that were missed in testing. Once released, the 737 came with minimal to no training or education. Many pilots were completely unaware of the MCAS system. Consumers have a legal right to protection and the social expectation of safety. Both were violated, which led to loss of life.

Following the crash, nearly $30 billion of orders were lost, and Boeing's missteps greatly affected other stakeholders from an economic standpoint. Aside from lawsuits from family members and insurance companies of the human lives lost, the grounding of the MAX aircraft has taken a serious toll on suppliers and other airline carriers. It has caused thousands of flights to be canceled, significant air traffic rescheduling, and millions of lost dollars in customer tickets and rerouting (not to mention, angry customers). It also affects Boeing's supply chain, as operations of the MAX fleet have halted during the investigation. The financial impact of grounding the aircrafts will only continue to grow as issues continue.

A predominant issue in the case was Boeing's crisis response methodology. In situations where lives and safety are compromised, a different approach to crisis management is required. The organization's initial response and statement of ownership is paramount, and failure here allows the powerful stakeholders—in this case, the media—to take over (Matthews, 2019).

CEO Muilenburg's statement on behalf of Boeing was not only defensive, but it came too late. Failure to take ownership led to speculation by powerful stakeholders, only perpetuating the situation.

Reputation is an organization's most valuable asset, and Boeing's mistakes have cost the company more than just money. Since the crash, Boeing's stock price plummeted. A shareholder captured the thoughts of many at the first annual meeting after the March 2019 incident by stating, "We don't have to have 300-plus people die every time to find out that something is unreliable" (Wichter, 2019).

Ironically, when there was still a lack of information regarding the exact cause of the crash, Muilenburg "faced the music," issuing a statement reiterating the company's commitment to safety, despite media backlash, all while other countries were grounding their fleet of MAX aircrafts. This was a defensive approach, as Muilenburg stood by the safety of the aircraft, did not admit fault, and avoided apologizing directly to victims. It signaled a lack of corporate openness and willingness to disclose to and be honest with the media. Lack of communication left the media and the public to fill in the gaps, forcing Boeing to come rearing back in defense when accused of caring "more about money than people" (Matthews,

2019). Powerful stakeholders, such as the media, employees, other airlines, and airplane safety advocates, including the famous Captain Chesley "Sully" Sullenberger, who safely landed a flight in the Hudson, began to publicly voice concerns (Matthews, 2019). The accommodating phase did not occur until after Ethiopian officials released the preliminary report confirming that the cause of the crash was due to the MCAS system. Boeing first refuted the safety issue, and then entered the most agonizing phase, insight. Boeing began to understand the severity of the circumstances when it started putting plans into motion for software updates. However, only once the FAA became involved did Boeing fully begin accommodating stakeholders. Boeing officials addressed the public pressure from the media to reduce consumer anxiety by complying with the FAA's recommendation to ground flights until the root was identified. Boeing presently is beginning to rebound somewhat.

American Airlines even made a statement that the grounding of 737 MAX 8 jets caused the airline to cancel over 7,800 flights since March 2019, which has cost over $185 million. This impact led to fuller planes and an increase in the revenue per available seat mile (Josephs, 2019). The 737 MAX 8 aircrafts make up about 2.6 percent of American Airlines' fleet (Josephs, 2019). Over 380 airline-owned aircrafts are parked on runways across the globe, unused; suppliers have reduced staff to cut down on employee idle times while the planes are grounded (Cameron and Wall, 2019).

The FAA is now under scrutiny for lack of oversight. The constant care and attention that situation required is not helping the FAA's workload or staffing constraints. The government and Department of Justice are now performing a significant internal investigation, which will likely cause more strife for Boeing, owners, stockholders, suppliers, airline operators, and consumers as more safety issues are brought to light.

Whereas some of these stakeholders are only dealing with bits and pieces of the aftermath, Boeing is still trying to navigate the situation. Boeing's stock fell by 18 percent after the Ethiopian Airlines crash in March 2019 (Cameron and Wall, 2019). Boeing saw deliveries decline by over one-third through June 2019.

July marked the third consecutive month during that period after the second crash, with no new MAX orders. Over 150 undelivered aircrafts are sitting idle in the United States alone, draining cash flow and hurting Boeing's dividend payouts and share buybacks (Cameron and Wall, 2019). During this same month, Boeing lost a $5.5 billion Saudi Arabian order for 50 aircrafts to Airbus, which has caused other major customers to threaten cancellation of orders too. In the meantime, Airbus is pushing sales of its A320neo and is expected to deliver a record number of aircrafts (Cameron and Wall, 2019). With billions of dollars in losses already, this number could continue to grow exponentially and threaten the survival of Boeing. Boeing is forced to rely on its other products, such as defense equipment and 787 Dreamliners, to help recover from this blow (Cameron and Wall, 2019).

The first Boeing 737 flew in 1967. Several versions of the aircraft made up the first generation of the fleet. As time continued, improvements were made on the original design and new generations were created. In 2006, discussions began on how the next generation of 737s would be formed. Delayed decision making allowed the company's rival, Airbus, to announce its newest design, the A320neo, before Boeing (Slotnick, 2020). Despite the competitor's announcement, Boeing continued to delay its response. In spring of 2011, Boeing was close to deciding to engineer an entirely new aircraft. However, after Boeing's CEO had a conversation with American Airlines' chief executive, the company switched directions as a deal was in the works between American Airlines and Airbus, despite Boeing and American Airlines' decade-long exclusive partnership (Slotnick, 2020).

Following the method used during transition between the previous generations of 737s, the company shared sufficient similarities between the updated and prior version so that pilots and ground staff could work with the planes without needing additional aircraft certification (Slotnick, 2020). As such, pilots were only required to take a brief course instead of the simulator training that would have otherwise been required. Furthermore, as it was already a certified airframe, the 737 MAX did not have to undergo the lengthy certification process required for a new aircraft (Slotnick, 2020). The desire to keep these similarities and fast-track to market ultimately led to two deadly crashes associated with the 737 MAX.

Because of the larger size and forward position of the 737 MAX's engines, the nose of the plane could tilt upward (BBC News, 2019). To combat this, the MCAS system was designed to push the nose down and stabilize the aircraft (Campbell, 2019). This was to allow pilots to fly the 737 MAX without complex training. Pilots were unaware of this integration. After undergoing test flights and data gathering from the FAA (which Boeing had a comfortable relationship with), the 737 MAX received the FAA's approval and, shortly after, approval from global regulators (Chokshi and Gelles, 2020).

On October 29, 2018, despite problems flying the previous day, Lion Air Flight 610 took off, and after only 12 minutes crashed, killing all 189 passengers. After the first crash, the MCAS system was brought into question, but ultimately the usage of 737s did not stop. The second crash occurred on March 10 the following year, with Ethiopian Airlines Flight 302. After one minute, pilots reported flight-control issues, followed by the activation of the MCAS system. Six minutes after takeoff, Flight 302 crashed into the ground killing all 157 passengers (Slotnick, 2020). Later that day, Ethiopian Airlines grounded its fleet of 737s; that was followed by the Chinese aviation authority ordering the grounding of all 737s in China. The FAA was the last aviation authority to order the grounding of the 737 MAX several days after the crash (Slotnick, 2020).

Despite a predicted relaunch by 2019, the 737 MAX remained grounded. While reviewing the aircraft, the team discovered additional problems. General Electric and Safran, manufacturers of the engines, told the FAA of a possible weakness in the rotors, which could cause them to shatter. Furthermore, a manufacturing error had left the plane's engines vulnerable to a lightning strike (Kitroeff and Gelles, 2020). These additional errors have continued to delay the 737 MAX's approval.

As of late, the FAA has approved test flights of the 737 MAX to demonstrate its ability to fly safely with the new flight-control software. Several days of testing will include emergency procedures and flight maneuvers in order to assess if the changes meet FAA standards. After the flights, the FAA will spend over a week preparing reports on its findings. After, Boeing will submit details of the software's design process and tests. Finally, the FAA along with an outside group of experts will review the contents of the tests and files and determine the approval of the aircraft and what training is required for pilots (Chokshi and Gelles, 2020). Despite the progress Boeing has made in regaining approval for the aircraft, it is fighting countless legal battles related to the crashes and the company's negligence (Slotnick, 2020). These cases have yet to reach conclusions.

Update

While legal and technical issues regarding the 737 have yet to be solved by the FAA and other stakeholders, the 737 MAX is back in service in most of the world, with the current exception (at the time of this writing) of China (Kent, 2021).

Questions for Discussion

1. What went wrong with the Boeing 737?
2. Who was at fault, when, and why?
3. What are the ethical concerns in the case?
4. Present an argument on Boeing's behalf, justifying the return of the 737 to service; then present an argument against returning the plane to service.

Sources

This case was developed from material contained in the following sources:

BBC News. (2019, April 5). Boeing 737 Max: What went wrong? https://www.bbc .com/news/world-africa-47553174.

Boeing. (2019, June 26). 737 Max updates. https://www.boeing.com/737-max -updates/#.

Cameron, D., and Wall, R. (2019, July 9). Airbus poised to overtake Boeing as biggest plane maker. *Wall Street Journal.* https://www.wsj.com/articles/boeing-737-max -grounding-hits-jetliner-deliveries-11562686324.

Campbell, D. (2019, May 2). The many human errors that brought down the Boeing 737 Max. *The Verge.* https://www.theverge.com/2019/5/2/18518176/boeing -737-max-crash-problems-human-error-mcas-faa.

Chicago Tribune. (2019, May 29). Timeline: Boeing 737 Max jetliner crashes and aftermath. https://www.chicagotribune.com/business/ct-biz-viz-boeing-737-max -crash-timeline-04022019-story.html.

Chokshi, N., and Gelles, D. (2020). Boeing gets go-ahead for test flights of its troubled 737 Max. *New York Times.* https://www.nytimes.com/2020/06/28 /business/boeing-737-max-faa.html.

Isidore, C. (2020). Boeing is nearing a long-delayed approval for the grounded 737 Max. *CNN Business.* https://www.cnn.com/2020/10/16/business/boeing-737 -max-approval/index.html.

Isidore, C., and Levitt, R. (2020). "Designed by clowns": Boeing releases flood of troubling internal documents related to. *CNN Business.* https://www.cnn.com /2020/01/09/business/boeing-documents/index.html.

Josephs, L. (2019, July 10). American Airlines says Boeing 737 Max grounding cost it $185 million in the second quarter. *CNBC.* https://www.cnbc.com/2019/07/10 /american-airlines-says-boeing-737-max-cost-185-million-in-the-second-quarter .html.

Josephs, L. (2020, December 29). Boeing 737 Max passenger flights resume in U.S. after nearly two-year ban. *CNBC.* https://www.cnbc.com/2020/12/29/737-max -returns-to-the-us-after-deadly-crashes.html.

Kent, G. (2021, May 5). 2 years after being grounded, the Boeing 737 Max is flying again. *Seattle Times.* https://www.seattletimes.com/business/boeing-aerospace /faa-has-further-questions-on-latest-boeing-737-max-electrical-problem/.

Kitroeff, N., and Gelles, D. (2020, January 5). It's not just software: new safety risks under scrutiny on Boeing's 737 Max. *New York Times.* https://www.nytimes.com /2020/01/05/business/boeing-737-max.html.

LeBeau, P. (2019, July 3). Boeing sets aside $100 million for families of 737 Max crash victims. *CNBC.* https://www.cnbc.com/2019/07/03/boeing-sets-aside-100 -million-for-families-of-737-max-crash-victims.html.

Levin, A. (2020). "We're going to ground the plane": How Boeing's Max was parked. *Bloomberg.* https://www.bloomberg.com/news/articles/2020-10-31/boeing -provided-the-faa-with-the-evidence-it-needed-to-ground-the-737-max.

Matthews, K. (2019, March 25). Analysis: Boeing is doing crisis management all wrong after Max crashes. *The Conversation.* http://theconversation.com/boeing-is -doing-crisis-management-all-wrong-heres-what-a-company-needs-to-do-to-resto re-the-publics- trust-114051.

McIntosh, A. (2020, November 2). Boeing CEO shrugs off threat from China's $8.8B C919 jet—then it flew at a Jiangxi air show. *Puget Sound Business Journal.* https://www.bizjournals.com/seattle/news/2020/11/02/boeing-china-737-max -comac-jets-c919-competition.html.

Robison, P. (2019, June 29). Boeing's 737 MAX software outsourced to $12.80-an -hour engineers. *Sydney Morning Herald.* https://www.smh.com.au/business /companies/boeing-s-737-max-software-outsourced-to-12-80-an-hour-engineers -20190629-p522h4.html.

Slotnick, David. (2020, October 29). The first Boeing 737 Max crash was 2 years ago today. Here's the complete history of the plane that's been grounded since 2 crashes killed 346 people 5 months apart. *Business Insider.* https:// www.businessinsider.com/boeing-737-max-timeline-history-full-details -2019-9.

USA Today. (2020, February 5). What caused two devastating crashes of the 737 MAX airplane? Staff report. https://www.usatoday.com/story/augmented-reality /2020/02/05/interactivestory-experienceid-737/4596125002/.

Wichter, Z. (2019, March 22). What you need to know after deadly Boeing 737 Max crashes. *New York Times.* https://www.nytimes.com/interactive/2019/business /boeing-737-crashes.html.

Wright, S., and Karmini, N. (2018, October 29). Indonesia Lion Air flight with 189 on board crashes into sea. *Chicago Tribune*. https://www.chicagotribune.com/nation -world/ct-indonesia-flight-missing-20181028-story.html.

Yglesias, M. (2019, March 29). The emerging 737 Max scandal, explained. *Vox*. www .vox.com/business-and-finance/2019/3/29/18281270/737-max-faa-scandal -explained.

Notes

1. Serwer, A. with Zahn, M. (2020, April 29). Why Warren Buffett matters more than ever on his 90th birthday. *Yahoo! Finance*. https://www.yahoo.com/lifestyle/why -warren-buffett-matters-more-than-ever-on-his-90th-birthday-115107937.html.

2. Buffett, W. (2021, January 1). Real-time billionaires. *Forbes*. https://www.forbes .com/profile/warren-buffett/?list=rtb/&sh=3bf559c46398.

3. Jordon, S. (2008, May 3). Warren Buffett eager to spread his life's lessons to growing audience. *Omaha.com*. http://www.omaha.com/index.php?u_page=1208&u_sid=10325539.

4. Choudhury, C. (2013). Ratan Tata, India's corporate czar, retires with a $500 billion vision. *BloombergView*. https://www.bloomberg.com/opinion/articles/2013-01-03/ratan -tata-india-s-corporate-czar-retires-with-a-500-billion-vision; Anand, A., Cherian, K., Gautam, A., Majmudar, R., and Raimawala, A. (2013, January 3). Business vs. ethics: The India tradeoff? *Wharton@knowledge.com*. http://knowledge.wharton.upenn.edu/article /business-vs-ethics-the-india-tradeoff/. See also ET NowDigital. (2020, December 27). Ratan Tata's 4-point guide for India heading into 2021. https://www.timesnownews.com /business-economy/economy/article/ratan-tata-s-4-point-guide-for-india-heading-into /699588.

5. Srivastava, A., Gayatri, N., Vipul, M., and Pandey, S. (2012). Corporate social responsibility: A case study of TATA Group. *Journal of Business and Management, 3(5)*, 17–27.

6. Smyth, L. (2021, February 12). 16 most influential women in leadership for 2021. *CEO Magazine*. https://www.theceomagazine.com/business/management-leadership /women-in-leadership-2021/.

7. Ibid.

8. CBS. (2021, January 9). Meet the Black female scientist at the forefront of COVID-19 vaccine development. https://www.cbsnews.com/news/covid-19-vaccine -development-kizzmekia-corbett/.

9. Smyth (2021, February 12), op. cit.

10. Korn Ferry. (2020). The Covid-19 Korn-Ferry leadership guide: Strategies for managing through the crisis. https://www.kornferry.com/content/dam/kornferry/special -project-images/coronavirus/docs/KF_Leadership_Playbook_Global_FINAL.pdf.

11. Tsedal Neely, quoted in Silverthorne, S. (2020, October 6). 18 Tips managers can use to lead through Covid's rising waters. *Harvard Business Review*. https://hbswk.hbs.edu /item/18-tips-managers-can-use-to-navigate-covid-s-rising-waters.

12. Selznick, P. (1983). *Leadership in administration: A sociological interpretation*. Berkeley: University of California Press.

13. Karakas, F., and Sarigollu, E. (2012). The role of leadership in creating virtuous and compassionate organizations: Narratives of benevolent leadership in an Anatolian tiger. *Journal of Business Ethics, 113(4)*, 663–678; Kouzes, J., and Posner, B. (2003). *Credibility: How leaders gain and lose it, why people demand it*, rev. ed. San Francisco: Jossey-Bass; Finkelstein, S. (2003). *Why smart executives fail*. New York: Portfolio; Zauderer, D. (1992, September 22). Integrity: An essential executive quality. *Business Forum*, 12–16.

14. Collins, J. (2001). *Good to great*. New York: HarperCollins, 21.

15. Ibid. It should be noted that the companies and leaders Collins studied achieved their greatness over 15-year time periods that spanned the 1970s, 1980s, and some into the 1990s. Although many of the companies are not currently great, Collins's best practices and principles continue to be widely read and used by corporations.

16. Quinn, R., and Takor, A. (2018). Creating a Purpose-Driven Organization. *Harvard Business Review*. https://hbr.org/2018/07/creating-a-purpose-driven-organization.

17. Waddock, S., and Graves, S. (1997, March–April). Does it pay to be ethical? *Business Ethics*, 14; Waddock, S., and Graves, S. (1997). The corporate social performance–financial performance link. *Strategic Management Journal, 18(4)*, 303–319; Waddock, S., and Graves, S. (1997). Quality of management and quality of stakeholder relations: Are they synonymous? *Business and Society Review, 36(3)*, 250–279; Waddock, S., and Graves, S. (2000). Beyond built to last . . . stakeholder relations in built-to-last companies. *Business and Society Review, 105(4)*, 393–418.

18. For more on this perspective, see Svendsen, A. (1998). *The stakeholder strategy*. San Francisco: Berrett-Koehler; and also Quinn, D., and Jones, T. (1995). An agent morality view of business policy. *Academy of Management Review, 20(1)*, 22–42.

19. Based on Svendsen (1998), op. cit., tables 1 and 2.

20. Barnard, C. (1939). *The functions of the executive,* 259. Cambridge, MA: Harvard University Press. Collins, J., and Porras, J. (1994). *Built to last: successful habits of visionary companies,* 78. New York: HarperCollins.

21. Collins and Porras (1994), op. cit., 78.

22. Ford, R. (2004). David Neeleman, CEO of JetBlue Airways, on people + strategy = growth. *Academy of Management Executive, 18(2)*, 141; A day in the life: Recruiting. (2013, May 8). *JetBlue.com*. http://blog.jetblue.com/index.php/2013/05/08/a-day-in-the-life-recruiting, accessed January 7, 2014.

23. Collins and Porras (1994), op. cit., 78.

24. Ibid.

25. Ibid., 73.

26. Ibid., 70.

27. Based on Svendsen (1998), op. cit., 1–2.

28. Greenleaf, R. (1977). *Servant leadership: A journey into the nature of legitimate power and greatness.* Mahwah, NJ: Paulist Press.

29. Robert Boutilier. (2012). *A stakeholder approach to issues management.* New York: Business Expert Press.

30. Ibid.

31. Fulmer, R. (2001, Winter). Johnson & Johnson: Frameworks for leadership. *Organizational Dynamics, 29(3)*, 219.

32. Trevino, L., Hartman, L., and Brown, M. (2000, Summer). Moral person and moral manager: How executives develop a reputation for ethical leadership. *California Management Review, 42(4)*, 128–142.

33. Brelis, M. (2000, November 5). Herb's way. *Boston Globe*, F1; O'Neill, M. (2001, May 28). The chairman of the board looks back. *Fortune*, 63–76.

34. Brelis (2000, November 5), op. cit., F4

35. Rolfes, R. (n.d.) Southwest banks on culture—literally. *Insigniam Quarterly*. https://quarterly.insigniam.com/corporate-culture/southwest-banks-on-culture-literally/, accessed January 16, 2021.

36. Attributed to Herb Kelleher, Southwest Airlines founder, Brelis, M. (2000, November 5), op. cit., F1; O'Neill, M. (2001, May 28), op. cit.

37. Sisodia, R., Sheth, J., and Wolfe, D. (2014). *Firms of endearment: How world-class companies profit from passion and purpose,* 2nd ed. Upper Saddle River, NJ: Pearson Education.

38. Ibid., 7.

39. Ibid., 13.

40. Ibid., 14.

41. Ibid., 19.

42. Ibid., 24.

43. Macrotrends. (2020). Costco revenue 2006–2020: Cost. https://www.macrotrends .net/stocks/charts/COST/costco/revenue.

44. Equilar. (2017). CEO Pay Study 2017. Associated Press. https://www.equilar.com /reports/48-associated-press-ceo-pay-study-2017.html. Also see Fottrell, Q. (2018, May 19). Fortune 500 CEOS are paid from double to 5,000 times more than their employees. https://www.marketwatch.com/story/fortune-500-ceos-are-paid-from-double -to-5000-times-more-than-their-employees-2018-05-16.

45. Macrotrends. (2020), op. cit.

46. Equilar. (2017, May 23). Associated Press CEO pay study. https://www.equilar.com /reports/48-associated-press-ceo-pay-study-2017.html; Costco CEO's compensation drops 38% in 2011. (2011, December 14). *USA Today Money*; also see DeCarlo, S. (2011, April 13). Show me the money. *Forbes.com*. http://www.forbes.com/2011/04/12/compensation-chief -executive-salary-leadership-ceo-compensation-11-intro.html.

47. Hanna, J. (2008). JetBlue's Valentine's Day Crisis. https://hbswk.hbs.edu/item /jetblues-valentines-day-crisis.

48. Strategies for Influence. (2019, October 11). John Kotter—change management and leadership. https://strategiesforinfluence.com/john-kotter-change-management-and-leader ship/. (Note: This is an approximate source since Kotter has made statements on videos as well as in his written, published works.)

49. Stampatori, R. (2004, September). Everything you wanted to know about courage . . . but were afraid to ask. *Fast Company, 86*, 97–111.

50. Reave, L. (2005). Spiritual values and practices related to leadership effectiveness. *Leadership Quarterly, 16*, 655–687.

51. Frederic, W. (2001, March). Review of Mitroff and Denton's "A spiritual audit of corporate America: A hard look at values in the workplace." *Religion and Society, 40(1)*, 118.

52. Greenleaf, R. (1977), op. cit; Block, P. (1993). *Stewardship: Choosing service over self-interest*. San Francisco: Berrett-Koehler.

53. Brelis (2000, November 5), op. cit., F1

54. Reave, L. (2005), op. cit.

55. Kouzes, J., and Posner, B. (2003), op. cit.

56. DeGraaf, D., Tilley, C., and Neal, L. (2004). Servant leadership characteristics in organizational life. In L. C. Spears and M. Lawrence (eds.), *Practicing servant leadership: Succeeding through trust, bravery, and forgiveness*, 133–166. San Francisco: Jossey-Bass.

57. Byrne, J. (1998). How Al Dunlap self-destructed. *Business Week*, 44–45.

58. Dunlap, A., and Adelman, B. (1996). *Mean business: How I save bad companies and make good companies great*. New York: Simon & Schuster.

59. Driscoll, D. M., and Hoffman, W. (2000). *Ethics matters*. Waltham, MA: Center for Business Ethics, 68; Hitt, W. (1990). *Ethics and leadership: Putting theory into practice*. Columbus, OH: Batelle, 138–174.

60. Drucker, P. (1978). *Management: Tasks, responsibilities, practices*. New York: Harper & Row.

61. Janis, I. (1972). *Groupthink: Psychological studies of policy decisions and fiascoes*. Boston: Houghton Mifflin.

62. Burns, J. (1978). *Leadership*. New York: Harper & Row.

63. Hitt (1990), op. cit., 169.

64. Ibid.

65. Geeknack (2021, January 30). Richard Branson—Leadership style & principles. https://www.geeknack.com/2021/01/30/richard-branson-leadership-style-and-principles/.

66. *Wall Street Journal* and HayGroup. (2010). *Wall Street Journal*/Hay Group 2010 CEO Compensation Study. *HayGroup.com*. http://www.haygroup.com/downloads/ww/misc /wsj_hay_group_2010_study_summary_results.pdf, accessed February 4, 2012. Beck, G. (2007, August 31). Transcript: Honest questions with Sir Richard Branson. *CNN.com*. http://transcripts.cnn.com/TRANSCRIPTS/0708/31/gb.01.html.

67. Deutsch, C. (2008, April 6). A brighter spotlight, yet the pay rises. *New York Times*.

68. Ibid.

69. Ethics and Compliance Initiative. (2020). Global business ethics survey: Pressure in the workplace. *Ethics.org*. https://www.ethics.org/wp-content/uploads/Global-Business -Ethics-Survey-2020-Report-1-Final.pdf.

70. Ethics Resource Center. (2012). 2011 National Business Ethics Survey: Workplace ethics in transition. *Ethics.org*. https://s3.amazonaws.com/berkley-center/120101Nation alBusinessEthicsSurvey2011WorkplaceEthicsinTransition.pdf.

71. Ibid.

72. Ibid.

73. Karakas, F., and Sarigollu, E. (2012), op. cit.; Kouzes, J., and Posner, B. (2003), op. cit.; Finkelstein, S. (2003), op. cit.; Zauderer, D. (1992, September 22), op. cit.

74. Noel, D. (2016, March 31). Zappos celebrates 10 year anniversary of core values. *Zappos.com*. https://www.zappos.com/about/stories/core-value-elevators.

75. Graves, S., and Waddock, S. (2000). Beyond built to last stakeholder relations in "built-to-last" companies. *Business and Society* Review 105(4), 394.

76. Deal, T., and Kennedy, A. (1982). *Corporate culture: The rites and rituals of corporate life*. Reading, MA: Addison-Wesley, 9–12.

77. Ethics Resource Center (2012), op. cit., 35.

78. Ibid., 85.

79. Patagonia. Core values. https://www.patagonia.com/core-values/, accessed June 21, 2021.

80. Pastin, M. (1986). *The hard problems of management: Gaining the ethics edge*. San Francisco: Jossey-Bass, 218–228. 83. Keogh (1988), op. cit., 45.

81. Lagace, M. (2004, July 12). Enron's lessons for managers. *HBS Working Knowledge*. http://hbswk.hbs.edu/item.jhtml?id=4253&t=organizations&nl=y.

82. Ethics Research Center (2012), op. cit., 11.

83. Lagace (2004), op. cit.

84. Hamel, G. (2000). *Leading the revolution*. Cambridge, MA: Harvard Business School Press, 204–205.

85. Cusumano, M., and Markides, C. (eds.). (2001). *Strategic thinking for the next economy*. San Francisco: Jossey-Bass.

86. Broadbent, M. (2002, July). Synchronizing the CIO. *CIO Insight, 15,* 32–35.

87. Cullen, J., Victor, B., and Stephens, C. (1989). An ethical weather report: Assessing the organization's ethical climate. *Organizational Dynamics, 18,* 50–62.

88. Kim, W., and Mauborgne, R. (2001). Strategy, value innovation, and the knowledge economy. In Cusumano, M., and Markides, C. (eds.), *Strategic thinking for the next economy*, 197–228. San Francisco: Jossey-Bass.

89. Ashkeas, R., Ulrich, D., Jick, T., and Kerr, S. (1995). *The boundaryless organization*. San Francisco: Jossey-Bass.

90. Chan, K. (May 21, 2001). From top to bottom. *Wall Street Journal,* R12.

91. Brey, P. (1999). Worker autonomy and the drama of digital networks in organizations. *Journal of Business Ethics, 22(1)*, 15–22.

92. Anderson, C. (1997). Values-based management. *Academy of Management Executive, 11(4)*, 25.

93. Freeman, R. E., and Gilbert D., Jr. (1988). *Corporate strategy and the search for ethics.* Upper Saddle River, NJ: Prentice Hall.

94. Kim and Mauborgne (2001), op. cit.

95. Ibid., 218.

96. Ibid., 222.

97. Paine, L. P. (1994, March–April). Managing for organizational integrity. *Harvard Business Review*, 106–117.

98. Donaldson, T., and Preston, L. (1995). The stakeholder theory of the corporation: Concepts, evidence, and implications. *Academy of Management Review, 20*, 65–91.

99. Ansoff, H. (1965). *Corporate strategy.* New York: McGraw-Hill, 38; Boatright, J. (1999). *Ethics and the conduct of business*, 3rd ed. Upper Saddle River, NJ: Prentice Hall.

100. Weaver, G., Trevino, L., and Cochran, P. (1999, February). Corporate ethics practices in the mid-1990s: An empirical study of the Fortune 1000. *Journal of Business Ethics, 18(3)*, 283–294.

101. How am I doing? (2005, Fall). *Business Ethics*, 11.

102. United States Sentencing Commission. (2015). Chapter eight: sentencing of organizations. https://www.ussc.gov/guidelines/2015-guidelines-manual/2015-chapter-8.

103. Schwartz, M. S. (2002). A code of ethics for corporate code of ethics. *Journal of Business Ethics, 41*, 27–43.

104. Brooks, L. (1989). Corporate Codes of Ethics. *Journal of Business Ethics, 8*, 117–129; Bowie, N. and Duska, R. (1990). *Business Ethics* (2nd ed.). Upper Saddle River, NJ: Prentice Hall.

105. 50 codes of ethics benchmarked—2008 Q2*NYSE Governance Services*. http:// members.corpedia.com/?50cocbench08q2, accessed February 3, 2014. For updates to the nature and application of organizational Codes of Ethics, see SHRM, Society for Human Resource Management (2021). https://www.shrm.org/resourcesandtools/tools -and-samples/policies/pages/code-of-ethics-conduct-policy.aspx.

106. Frankel, M. (1989). Professional codes: Why, how, and with what impact? *Journal of Business Ethics, 8*, 109–115.

107. See Gordon, S. (n.d.). Implementation of effective compliance and ethics programs and the federal sentencing guidelines. *Corporate compliance answer book 2018*. https://legacy .pli.edu/product_files/Titles/2470/%23205998_02_Corporate_Compliance_Answer _Book_2018_P3_20170915151415.pdf.

108. Harrison, J. (1999). Finding the ethics soft spots of a target. *Mergers and Acquisitions, 34(2)*, 8.

109. Frankel (1989), op. cit.

110. Frankel (1989), op. cit.; Somers, M. (2001). Ethical codes of conduct and organizational context: A study of the relationship between codes of conduct, employee behavior, and organizational values. *Journal of Business Ethics, 30*, 194.

111. International Ombudsman Association. (2013). Ethics, HR and the importance of ombuds programs. *Human Capital Strategies, 288*, https://www.ombudsassociation.org /assets/docs/EthicsandOmbuds-HRI.pdf; Somers (2001), op. cit., 194.

112. Franchise association launches ombudsman program as key self-regulation component. (2001, April). *Franchising World*, 33, 36.

113. Bhatia, A., Blackstock, S., Nelson, R., et al. (2000, Fall). Evolution of quality review programs for Medicare: Quality assurance to quality improvement. *Health Care Financing Review, 22,* 69–74.

114. Ibid.

115. Shaw, C. (April 7, 2001). External assessment of health care. *British Medical Journal, 322,* 851–854.

7

EMPLOYEE STAKEHOLDERS AND THE CORPORATION

OPENING CASE

Generational Profiles of a Changing Workforce

Although Covid-19 has overshadowed—and emphasized—many workforce differences, generational values, attitudes, and work habits still matter, even though some may ask, Will generational differences matter post-Covid-19? Ongoing claims about generational differences vary. There are those who argue that such differences do not really matter, only stereotypes do; others state that knowing these differences adds information that helps navigate workplace relationships. We begin by presenting generational changes to help understand stakeholder differences that can lead to ethical dilemmas but also productive relationships.

Gen Z, millennials, and Gen X-ers are three of the latest entrants since the baby boomers to enter a changing workforce. "There are about

72.17 million millennials, born between 1980 and 1995 [others say between 1982 and 2003], and they're rapidly taking over from the baby boomers who are now pushing 60."[1] "We are beginning to see increasingly younger people come in and ask long-term questions; five years down the road, where can I grow in this company? This was not necessarily the case with Gen X, people born between 1964 and 1981, who number 65.17 million. This generation is independent, values work–life balance, is flexible and informal, and technologically adept. X-ers' agility, self-reliance, and good work ethic with higher education levels adds to their propensity for leadership.[2]

Gen Z is the newest group in the workforce. Those born in the late 1990s (67.17 million) are described as a diverse group that defies categorization. Members of Gen Z contradict the previous generation and even defy characterizations among themselves. A brief generalization suggests that this generation is "global, social, visual and technological. They are the most connected, educated, and sophisticated generation ever. They are the up-agers, with influence beyond their years."[3]

Returning to the workforce to join this mix are the baby boomers, the 69.59 million born between 1945 and 1964. For example:

> Shirley Serey is the community college student of the future: 59 years old, MBA, corporate manager, breast cancer survivor—and new teacher of special education, helping fourth and fifth graders with disabilities learn to read. . . . Serey is at the leading edge of tens of millions of baby boomers who are beginning to shift into a new phase of life and work. As many as four out of five people in their 50s and 60s say they expect to continue to work, some because they have to for financial reasons, but many more because they want to, for the social connections, intellectual engagement, and fulfillment of making a difference. Neither old nor young, many are seeking 'encore careers' that combine a renewed commitment with continued income and increased flexibility. . . . Shirley Serey is typical of the target market for such encore colleges. Her story weaves several themes common to boomers managing transitions to this new stage of life—the need for flexibility, the unexpected obstacles in the search for meaning, an impulse to give something back, to help other people, and to make a direct and noticeable impact.[4]

Employers and employees are experiencing a different mix of values, styles, and dilemmas in the changing workplace, as the above scenarios indicate. A review of workforce trends also indicates significant changes at the societal level. For example, "the Department of Labor must work with a wide spectrum of job seekers, including those with special needs such as the disadvantaged, people with disabilities, veterans, disadvantaged youth, and those who have lost their jobs due to foreign competition. Addressing the job seekers' needs is further complicated by the dynamics of the changing workplace. New technologies, increased competition, and changing labor markets have prompted employers to downsize, change employment patterns, and seek alternative labor sources such as qualified foreign workers."[5] A policy summit on America's "workforce mosaic" revealed that "America's workforce is currently being shaped by three converging trends: rapid growth in the non-white population, baby boomers who are staying in the workforce longer, and veterans returning from the ongoing wars in Iraq and Afghanistan." University of North Carolina research shows that "79 million baby boomers will exit the U.S. workforce over the next 20 years." This graying workforce will result in some significant losses of experienced and top-level employees of large companies and a potential shortage of American workers.[6] As of 2020, the workforce is predicted to be tech-savvy and socially conscious; today's workers have a very short attention span, are ambitious, job hoppers, and boomerang employees, meaning "there's no shame in their game for leaving a company only to return to work later."[7]

This chapter addresses the following questions: What is different about today's workforce, and how does this affect the corporation's ethical responsibilities? What, if anything, binds employees to their companies these days as we enter a post-Covid-19 world? What is the changing nature of the employer–employee social and psychological contract in a hybrid-technology, in-person workforce? How has this contract changed historically? What are the boundaries of employee loyalty? When do employees have the right or obligation to "blow the whistle" on a company?

A number of issues that employees and employers face are also presented, such as dating in the workplace, same-sex marriage rights and LGBTQI, types of discrimination, drug testing, Internet use, privacy, and sexual harassment. The rights and responsibilities of both employers and employees are discussed with the aim of offering perspectives on what stakeholders can expect and how ethical dilemmas can be prevented and solved, beginning with an awareness of these issues. Creating a legal and ethical working environment where mutual respect and concern create conditions for productivity and human development is a worthy goal.

▪ 7.1 Employee Stakeholders in the Changing Workforce

The confluence of the Black Lives Matter Movement, the January 6, 2021, attack on the U.S. Capitol coupled with a divided and divisive U.S. electorate, and the coronavirus has significantly affected the workforce's health and working habits. Previous to these tumultuous events, the forces of globalization, deregulation, shareholder activism, and information technology also influenced business practices and processes. Industries and many companies post Covid-19 are now having to reinvent and revive their businesses. Midlevel management layers are being pressured, many diminishing. Functions continue to be outsourced, offshored, eliminated, and replaced by online automation, cheaper international labor, and networked infrastructures. Knowledge workers with technological and people skills must manage processes and themselves in cyberspace with speed, efficiency, and accuracy.

Within the context of this "digital economy," markets that rely on the Internet are growing because of the virus (which has increased work-from-home arrangements) as well as the cost savings. The following changes with employees and professional stakeholders continue to occur:[8]

- An increasing shift to knowledge, along with technology-enabled work, which increases the potential for satisfying work but heightens stress with changing working habits.
- Post-Covid-19, 52 percent of employees in one survey reported that they are more likely to and desire to change jobs that do not accommodate remote work combined with in-person presence.
- Quality of work life is not inherent or guaranteed in the workplace. In one worst-case scenario, Thomas Malone of MIT stated that all work relationships could possibly be mediated by the market, with every employee functioning as a company in shifting alliances and ventures.[9]

POINT/COUNTERPOINT

Instructions: Each student individually will adopt *either* the Point or CounterPoint argument and justify their reasons (with arguments using this case and other evidence/opinions). Then, either in teams or designated arrangements, students share their reasons. Afterward, the class is debriefed and there is further discussion.

POINT: I prefer working from home. It's less hassle, cheaper, gives me more freedom of movement, has less office politics and distractions, and I accomplish more.

COUNTERPOINT: I miss people, interaction, my friends, finding out what's really going on behind the scenes, and not feeling like a robot at the end of the day.

When the coronavirus and the Covid-19 disease emerged throughout the world, almost everyone was forced to work remotely at home to prevent the virus from spreading. This sparked a debate of whether companies would benefit using remote work, which would strongly transition to a more "digital economy." Here are the arguments brought up for and against remote working:[10]

<table>
<tr><td>Pros</td><td>Cons</td></tr>
</table>

Hiring from a wider pool of talent: Companies have the opportunity to look both nationally and internationally for employees.

Productive workforce: Performance improves when employees are permitted to work from home. This is supported by a Stanford study.

Employee satisfaction: Remote workers are typically happier in their jobs due to better work–life balance.

Cutting cost: Having remote workers reduces costs, specifically operating cost (e.g., office supplies).

Finding the right employees: Although there is a diverse pool of people to choose from, it is tough to find people who thrive in a remote work environment.

Communication: There is greater potential for unclear or lack of communication since contact between managers and remote workers may be limited.

Team building: Remote workers struggle to build relationships with coworkers because of limited in-person contact.

Source: Remote Work: The Pros and Cons for Employers. (2020, June 22). *LawDepot.com (blog).* https://www.lawdepot.com/blog/remove-work-pros-and-cons

Change in the workforce and workplace presents ethical tensions and issues that are addressed in this chapter.

The Aging Workforce

According to the Bureau of Labor Statistics (BLS), "The baby-boom generation moves entirely into the 55–years-and-older age group by 2020, increasing that age group's share of the labor force from 19.5 percent in 2010 to 25.2 percent in 2020. The 'prime-age' working group (ages 25 to 54) is projected to drop to 63.7 percent of the 2020 labor force."[11] The share of workers age 55 and older is projected to remain at 25 percent or more through the 2018–2028 decade. Conversely, the labor force participation rate for those ages 16 to 24 is projected to continue to decline, to 51.7 percent.[12] Twenty years ago in 2001, for the first time, the number of workers age 40 and older surpassed the number of those younger than 40. At the same time, those aged 16 to 24—the "baby busters"—made up 16 percent of the workforce, a proportion that continues to decrease, and the seniors older than age 55 represented about 13 percent of the workforce. "Employment is projected to grow by 8.4 million jobs to 169.4 million jobs over the 2018–2028 decade, according to BLS data, and an aging population and labor force (ages 16 to 24) is projected to continue to decline to 51.7 percent will contribute to changes expected over the coming decade, including a continued decline in the labor force participation rate in employment."[13] Japan was the first nation ever with a population in which the average age is 40. By 2040, 20 percent of Japan's workforce is presumed to retire.[14] Combined with generational differences, age differences can aggravate values and work ethic clashes as this chapter's Real-Time Dilemma exemplifies. Does age play a role in that dilemma?

One result of the population growth slowdown is that the number of managerial leadership positions will outstrip available talent. "While the impact will vary in different countries, the aging workforce coupled with declining birth rates in some countries will result in a shrinking talent pool that will require organizations to review and modify their human resource policies to adjust to the changing environment."[15] Older workers will be needed for their skills and experience, and also because of the shortage of younger workers to replace them.[16]

Generational Differences in the Workplace

As this chapter's opening case suggests, generational differences offer challenges to coworkers and managers. As of May 2020, a study shows that approximately 52 percent of organizations consider generational differences at least to a certain extent when designing and delivering task for their employees. However, the same study revealed that only 6 percent of respondents strongly agree that their leaders are equipped to lead a multigenerational workforce efficiently.[17] Generational analysis looks at differences among worldviews, attitudes, and values of generations of Americans. Large differences in the generations from World War II to the present in the U.S. population have had a substantial influence on government, corporate, and workplace policies. This information, although subjective, is used to develop workplace strategies and to evaluate ethical principles and beliefs of different groups in the workforce.[18] The following brief summary of five generations' dominant value orientations highlights some of these differences. As you read the descriptions of generational profiles, turn again to this chapter's Real-Time Dilemma to help explain possible sources of the conflict and potential organizational issues and dilemmas that are about to erupt.

- *GI Generation (born 1901–1925).* This generation survived the Great Depression and served in World War II. Members of this generation are churchgoers and belong to clubs and professional organizations. They express rugged individualism but are members of many groups. They tend to believe in upward mobility, civic virtue, and the American Dream.

- *Silent Generation (born 1926–1945).* This generation was too young to fight in World War II. They were influenced by the patriotism and self-sacrifice of the GI generation, from whom they did not wish to differentiate themselves. Their dominant principles are allegiance to law and order, patriotism, and faith. The silent generation likes memorabilia such as plaques, trophies, and pictures of themselves with important people. Most members are already in some form of retirement (i.e., fully retired or working part-time, occasionally, or seasonally to bring in some additional income).[19] "If nothing else, the title promised a look at an era long gone. The 1950s, that is: the object of knowing derision today buried in clichés about a time when America was the land of happy automatons—a people unthinking, accepting, and repressed. Especially the serious, non-revolutionary, and jobs- and marriage-focused young." This silent generation stood in stark contrast to the "more colorful decades to come—years of riots, bomb-throwing, seizure of the universities, the reign of the Weathermen."[20] This generation is characterized by "giving back and contributing to the collective good."[21]

- *Baby Boomers (born 1945–1964).* They have led and set trends in society. They distinguish themselves from the former generations by assuming debt. Their "buy now, pay later" belief characterizes their instant gratification practices. They can be moralistic, but they question authority and the moral and ethical principles of institutions. They do not "join" or sacrifice personal pleasure for the good of the group or collective. They mix and match religious traditions and avoid the dogma and teachings of single religions. Baby boomers value health and wellness, personal growth, involvement, public recognition, status symbols, first-class travel upgrades, visible roles such as speaking at industry trade shows, and any type of resort or retreat. As employees, they are "process-oriented and relationship-focused."[22] Baby boomers have the lowest level of engagement and the highest level of *active disengagement*—nearly one in four are actively disengaged. Because this generation makes up such a large part of the working population, and many may be in the workforce long past the traditional retirement age, a targeted effort to raise these workers' engagement levels could have important ramifications for companies and the overall U.S. economy.[23] More so than other generations, baby boomers respond to managers who make an extra effort to show that they care. Managers should keep this in mind during day-to-day interactions and find ways to communicate interest in these employees by inquiring about their work and other important aspects of their lives.[24]

- *Generation X (born 1965–1981).* Known as the "baby busters," this generation has 41 million members. Sandwiched between the two larger generations, they feel they are demographically overlooked. They grew up in a time of high national debt and bleak job markets and were labeled as the "McJob" generation—a phrase referring to holders of low- and entry-level jobs. They generally believe that they will get less materially than the boomers. Insecurity is a dominant theme for X-ers, who value close friends and virtual families more than material success. They, like the boomers, are also suspicious of institutions. They experience their journey through life as one that changes rapidly and continuously.

- *Generation Y (born 1982–2003).* The millennial generation (or "echo boomers") numbers about 80 million. They spend $170 billion a year of their parents' and their own money and comprise one-third of the U.S. population. They have grown up with computers, instant messaging, and new digital technologies, just as the boomers grew up with the telephone and television. Y-ers don't want to be associated with X-ers, whom they believe are selfish and complaining and the least heroic generation—a bunch of "slackers." Y-ers grew up with a strong job market. They are ambitious, motivated, extremely impatient and demanding, and have a sense of entitlement.

- *Generation Z (born 1995–2010).* The Gen Z-ers are the youngest generation that is just entering the workforce. Gen Z and millennials have a lot
of things in common. Both generations were born in the digital age, which
has given them skills that are necessary for the future marketplace. But there
are also many things that make Gen Z different from the previous. "Their
desire for work–life balance is deep." They saw how their parents were
struggling financially during the Great Recession. Therefore, it is important for them to have work–life balance as security in work. Inclusion is
one of their priorities in the work environment, but they want to be considered by their own talent rather as a team. One of their greatest abilities
is multitasking. More than millennials, Z-ers have the ability to navigate
through a vast of systems and apps. They grew up connected to the world,
and they are in constant update. It is easier for them to learn new technologies and systems, which could be a big help in the future as frequent change
happens in workplaces. Gen Z-ers also like feedback and view failure as a
great way of learning new and innovative ways of improving their skills.[25]

Millennials place a high priority on workplace culture and desire a work
environment that emphasizes teamwork and a sense of community. They also
value transparency (especially as it relates to decisions about their careers, compensation, and rewards). They want to provide input on their work assignments and want and need the support of their supervisors. Millennials also
are particularly attuned to the world around them, and many want the chance
to explore overseas positions. All of the above statements also are true of non-
millennials, yet not to the same degree as the millennial generation. With
regard to ethics, members of this generation observe fewer boundaries than
previous generations; are more flexible about when and where to apply boundaries; are more open and transparent; are more likely to discuss work activity
with private and public people; are more likely to engage in and tolerate behavior that is others consider unacceptable; are a more at-risk generation than
the others and therefore more likely to observe misconduct and experience
retaliation after reporting it; are more likely than older generations to respond
to ethics and compliance programs that include social interaction and support (training, advice, help lines).[26]

Generation Y is more positive than other employee groups and is more
likely to agree that "senior management communicates a clear vision of the
future direction of my organization." They:

- Have more favorable views on workplace issues, from work–life balance
to performance reviews and having access to their immediate supervisor.
- Value teamwork and fairness and are more critical than other age groups
on issues of fairness and cooperation.
- Want to be challenged at work.
- Are motivated less by money and more by opportunities to advance and
have a life outside of the office.
- Are concerned about tuition reimbursement and flexible spending
accounts for dependent care.

Over half of Generation Y-ers would leave their organization to work for an organization that offered better benefits.[27]

At this point in their careers, millennials are generally more upbeat about all aspects of engagement than are baby boomers or Generation X members, but millennials are particularly more positive about growth and development opportunities. Despite their higher engagement levels, millennials are the most likely of all generations to say they will leave their company in the next 12 months if the job market improves. More than one in four of these young workers strongly agreed with this statement when asked in 2012.[28]

From a manager's perspective, Generation Y employees require "super-high maintenance," since they are "on fast-forward with self-esteem." They often expect office cultures to adapt to them. With these attitudes, they generally require coaching, rigorous feedback, and smaller and more realistic goal setting, with deadlines and increasing responsibility.

From the employer's perspective, integrating individual and group differences in the workforce requires leadership, planning, new policies, and training. In larger, more complex organizations, providing education and training to integrate the workforce is a necessity.[29] With which of these values do you identify? What other values that are not listed here motivate you? Underlying individual values combined with other background factors influence perceptions, beliefs, behaviors, and ethical decisions.

With different generations, generation bias unfortunately exists within certain companies. In a study conducted by an Addison Group of 1,000 people, results showed that while 90 percent of workers were satisfied with the diverse age range, they highlight the presence of generational bias. The same study showed that 35 percent of respondents felt that their company's culture and process favored one generation over another, and 45 percent of workers specifically emphasized that employers are biased toward millennials.[30] Other significant evidence suggested that organizations need to develop and recognize the unique value of each individual, as well as the synergy that can be created between people with different experiences and perspectives.

While most acknowledge the presence of different generations, there are those that who do not believe generational differences are problematic. "Humans naturally seek simplified explanations for their own and others' behavior through a process of sensemaking." A major example of this is the creation and presence of stereotypes as a way to classify people into distinct groups based on certain characteristics. Reasons supporting this view include "no credible scientific evidence that (a) generations exists, (b) that people can be really classified into generational groups, and (c) that there are demonstrable differences between such groups." Those arguing against focusing on generational differences claim that 'such differences are oversimplifications of actual facts.[31] During the pandemic, baby boomers were alleged to be hoarders, asking members of "Gen X" how to properly isolate themselves from others.[32] Instead, researchers should use a more logical, comprehensive theory or explanation to properly explain these behaviors. Overall, studies and interest with regard to generational differences add value to understanding and facilitating workforce leadership, management, and collaboration, while avoiding stereotyping.[33]

Steps for Integrating a Multigenerational Workforce

Generational differences may be only one among several issues that cause conflict and ethical dilemmas in the workplace. Using communication skills and emotional intelligence (managing self, others, and relationships with awareness and sensitivity) are important. Here are steps that employers can use to help diagnose, prevent, and resolve misunderstood generational differences. If you are not a boss, team leader, or supervisor, read these steps as if you were one. Taking this perspective can help you see the larger picture outside of a particular generational lens.[34]

Identify the Problem Areas

Where do I see the problems? Where do I expect to see the problems? Is there resentment about special treatment to senior or younger members in the workplace? Are the problems between individuals or groups from different generations? What are the sources of the problems: value differences, rewards, motivation, work methods, other?

Get to Know the Individuals Inside Their Roles and Positions

For millennials and Gen X-ers, as well as members of other generations, it is important to arrange for conversations to discuss broader topics and subjects that are important to them. Do not wait for employees to come to you; it is important to plan, arrange, and invite individuals to conversations where needs and perceptions can be shared in nonthreatening ways. Being able to listen to the other's views, opinions, and perceived or experienced issues will help you understand the person's issues. These are necessary first steps that lead to problem resolution.

Understand and Anticipate Expectations of Different Generations

"One size (of leadership or management) does not fit all." Although individuals must be recognized and treated as the unique individuals they are, it is also important for managers to seek balance between the employee and the company. Knowing generational members' expectations is important in negotiating this balance between responsibilities and obligations. "This can be achieved when a company (1) does not ask too much of its employees and (2) knows what it's willing to give employees *before* they've been given too much."[35]

Develop a Personal Growth and Development Plan for Each Employee

Millennials and Gen X-ers value and enjoy learning and benefit from their work when they are engaged. Assisting them to develop specific future goals and marketable skills is motivational and will focus their high work ethic and energy toward positive effort and outcomes.

Engage and Communicate

Younger entrants into the workforce are accustomed to being engaged, not mandated to work or reprimanded in an authoritarian way. Seek their input and advice. Conflicts between Gen X-ers and millennials often occur when the former try to take charge over the latter. Neither likes to be told unilaterally what to do. If reprimands or criticisms are necessary, these can best be communicated one-on-one, as soon as a wrong action is done, and as objectively as possible. Reverse mentoring and mutual mentoring are two newer ways that Gen X-ers and previous generational types can learn from younger professionals. These more recent forms of mentoring can be effective ways of sharing and learning different professional values and work ethics. Generation X, millennials, and baby boomers are all most engaged when they have the opportunity to do what they do best every day. Engagement for millennials, Generation X, and baby boomers is connected to having a strong sense of what their organization stands for. Find ways to help these employees verbalize and internalize what the company's mission and purpose means to them.[36]

Be a Leader, Not a Friend

Gen X-ers and millennials are looking for role models in organizations, not buddies in a boss. Both generational members want to be led, since they generally have friends. This does not mean that they want to be led by authoritarian or unreasonable leaders. Character counts. Gen X-ers and millennials move toward bosses who have strong character. They know when they see strong character. For effective managers, character means "Do what you say and say what you do" in a reliable, trustworthy way and "Do the right thing"—although it may not always be comfortable. Ethical Insight 7.1 engages you to identify a mentoring technique you prefer to assist in your career—and/or present position—development.

Ethical Insight 7.1

Bridging Diversity Gaps in the Workplace

Do Companies Use Mentoring Programs, and Why Are They Significant?

"Mentoring benefits an organization by improving job satisfaction and retention, and aids in the personal and professional development of the mentee."[37]

- About 70 percent of Fortune 500 companies have a mentorship program and studies shows positive results:
- Employees who participated in the program were five times more likely to advance in pay grade, and mentors made even more progress.
- Mentees were promoted five times more than those not in the program, and mentors six times more.
- Retention rates were significantly higher for mentees (72 percent) and for mentors (69 percent) than for employees who did not participate (49 percent).
- Cornell University's School of Industry and Labor Relations study found that mentoring programs boost minority representation at the management level.
- Minority representation increased from 9 percent to 24 percent (compared to −2 percent and 18 percent with other diversity initiatives).
- Promotion and retention rates improved for minorities and women (15 percent to 38 percent) compared to nonmentored employees.

New and Changing Types of Mentoring Programs

The old mentoring model assigned a younger professional to a more senior professional for an indefinite time. The following programs reflect new trends:

- *One-on-one:* In a traditional model, usually a senior organizational member works with a newer employee to develop trust, provide consistent support; there is a commitment to work together over time
- *Mentoring circles:* Some companies form mentoring circles to allow intra-departmental networking and growth.
- *Short-term, goal-oriented mentoring:* Mentor/mentee are paired with specific goals that have time limits.
- *Peer-to-peer mentoring:* Young employees are paired together.
- *Speed mentoring:* Mentor/mentee are paired in restricted time-bound sessions for quick-hit information and networking (e.g., one hour).
- *E-mentoring:* E-mail is the medium used for communication between paired mentee and mentor.
- *Reverse mentoring:* Senior executives' mentees are paired with younger professional mentors to help senior executives catch up on new practices.
- *Job-fit-related mentoring:* Particular mentors and mentees are assigned to work on specific jobs.
- *Mutual learning, adaptation, and change:* Mentor and mentee are paired based on a learning partnership aimed at mutual growth and development.

Questions

1. Which of the above types of mentoring programs might help ease the potential ethical dilemmas in this chapter's Real-Time Dilemma?
2. Suggest how one or more of the mentoring programs here might be arranged by Ralph the CEO to help Bill and Lana's working relationship.
3. Would mentoring help your job satisfaction, enrichment, and socially responsible engagement? Which type of mentoring approach would you choose, and why?

Sources: Katz, N. (2007, February). Enhancing effectiveness in mentoring. *Nation's Cities Weekly.*
Mentoring: Current trends. (2007, November 16). *Insala.com.*
Offsteing, E., Morwick, J., and Shah A. (2007, March 22). Mentoring programs and jobs: A contingency approach. *Review of Business, 27(3),* 32–37.
Petrin, R. (2011, June 6). Business mentoring matters. *Management Mentors.*
SmartbizTeam. (2020, April 22). Mentoring in the workplace: Best 6 types of mentoring programs. https://resources.smartbizloans.com/blog/employee-management/mentoring-in-the-workplace-best-types-of-mentoring-programs/.
U.S. Department of Agriculture. (n.d.). Mentoring models. https://www.targetcenter.dm.usda.gov/mentoring/models.

Women in the Workforce

The Families and Work Institute noted, in its National Study of the Changing Workforce, that "the desire for jobs with more responsibility among young women with children is at its highest point." Women have also made educational

Figure 7.1

Does Your Organization Capitalize on Gender Strength?

- What evidence demonstrates that women enjoy working in the organization, and how is this monitored?
- What training and development opportunities are there, and how well are these accessed?
- What mentoring and coaching opportunities exist for women? How are these implemented and monitored?
- Do women have real choices about work–life responsibilities?
- How is women's advancement supported through internal networks?
- Who are the women's visible role models in the organization, and why?
- How does the organization actively attract and position itself with women?
- What do the stats and trends show when it comes to attracting, retaining, and developing women?
- How can women be assured of fair and transparent promotion processes, and accessible dispute mechanisms?
- How are equal pay for equal work, fair rewards, and recognition for women monitored?
- What do the women think about the effectiveness of parental and care support options?
- What external awards and recognitions have the organization (and the female employees) received?

Source: Adapted from Aurora Gender Capital Management's online service for women to research and compare organizations at http://www.wherewomenwanttowork.com.

advances. "American women are more likely to enroll in and complete college than men. In 2015, 72.5 percent of female recent high school graduates were enrolled, compared to 65.8 percent of recent male graduates. In 2017, women made up about 56 percent of students on college campus." Receiving a proper education helped women transition well into the real world.[38] Figure 7.1 suggests questions that leaders and managers can ask to assess whether their organizations are capitalizing on gender diversity.

As of December 2019, women hold more jobs than men. Experts believe this trend will continue because of the economic shift away from so-called traditional male-dominated jobs along with the sectors that historically employ more women are growing. "Women are also highly represented in government service jobs, standing at 58 percent, and holding 56 percent of positions in financial-related roles."[39] Feminists are and have been advocating for women's rights, freedom, and equality to bring changes and promote ideas that women have the ability to hold management, leadership, and CEO-level positions, and that inequality of pay should be based on comparable work done, not on gender and discrimination. Women's active and leadership roles in the workforce have resulted in positive change and growth in the economy.[40] Statistics from a 2018 study indicate that women have made significant leadership progression in the workforce:[41]

- Women are 5 percent of Fortune 500 CEOs.
- Women are 7 percent of top executives in the Fortune 100 companies.
- They hold 19 percent of the Standard & Poor's 1,500 board seats.
- They are 26.5 percent of executive and senior officials and managers, and 11 percent of top earners.

In 2003, Catalyst released a survey on "women in U.S. corporate leadership" to examine "what keeps women from reaching the top."[42] The findings showed the top-five barriers to be:

- Lack of significant general management or line experience (47 percent)
- Exclusion from informal networks (41 percent)
- Stereotyping and preconceptions of women's roles and abilities (33 percent)
- Failure of senior leadership to assume accountability for women's advancement (29 percent)
- Commitment to personal/family responsibilities (26 percent)[43]

In the same study, participants cited the following top-five success strategies they used to reach the top:

- Exceeding performance expectations (69 percent)
- Successfully managing others (49 percent)
- Developing a style with which male managers are comfortable (47 percent)
- Having recognized expertise in a specific content area (46 percent)
- Taking on difficult or highly visible assignments (40 percent)

Do you agree with the top-five barriers women face to "get to the top" of organizations? If not, what factors do you believe account for the lack of advancement of women to more senior-level and corporate board positions?

Same-Sex Marriages, Civil Unions, Domestic Partnerships, and Workforce Rights

The U.S. Supreme Court ruled on June 26, 2013, that Section 3 of the Defense of Marriage Act is unconstitutional.[44] The federal government can no longer discriminate against married lesbian and gay couples with regard to federal benefits and protections.[45] Same-sex couples validly married by December 31, 2013, can file 2013 federal taxes as married couples.[46] Other tax changes were also amended under this law.[47]

In 2004, Massachusetts became the first state to grant same-sex couples the right to marry. Whether or not other states will recognize Massachusetts' same-sex unions is unresolved. How would the benefits be affected, for example, of a same-sex married Boston employee moved by an employer to another state that prohibits gay marriages? "Civil unions" are legally permitted in Colorado, Hawaii, Illinois, Vermont, and New Jersey. "Domestic partnerships" are allowed in California, District of Columbia, Maine, Nevada, Oregon, Washington, and Wisconsin; Hawaii permits "reciprocal beneficiaries," similar to domestic partnership. Connecticut, Delaware, New Hampshire, Rhode Island, and Vermont permit same-sex marriages "and have converted all civil unions into marriages. . . . All of the states that allow for civil unions or domestic partnerships now also allow for same sex marriage, either through statute or court ruling."[48] On June 26, 2015, the Supreme Court ruled gay marriage to be legal nationwide, which means that the states that ban same-sex marriage will no longer be able to enforce those bans. Individuals, then, are protected by Title VII of the 1964 Civil Rights Act from being discriminated against on the basis of sex; Title VII applies to employers with 15 or more employees. Moreover, "some courts have ruled that Title VII also bans discrimination based on sexual orientation or gender identity—such as who are designated as LGBTQ (lesbian, gay, bisexual, transgender, and queer).[49]

Similar domestic partnership systems exist across the globe. Same-sex marriage is now legal in all Canadian provinces. Sweden legalized same-sex marriage in 2009, following Norway in 2008. The Netherlands expanded its definition of marriage in 2001 to include both opposite-sex and same-sex couples. Belgium followed in 2003, and same-sex couples have been allowed to adopt children since 2006. Spain also voted to extend full marriage rights to same-sex couples in 2005. Portugal and Iceland legalized same-sex marriage in 2010,[50] and Denmark followed in June 2012.[51] New Zealand and France legalized it in 2013. In 2019 Austria, Taiwan, and Ecuador legalized marriage equality, with Costa Rica following in 2020. (For a 2021 update on 29 countries, see Marriage Equality around the World.[52])

Some political jurisdictions have special legislation that allows same-sex couples to register their committed relationships and gain some benefits. However, they do not receive all the advantages that opposite-gender couples automatically acquire when they marry.

Six states have adopted civil unions available to both same-sex and opposite-sex couples. Civil unions provide legal recognition of the couples' relationship while providing legal rights to the partners, similar to those accorded to spouses in marriages. From July 1, 2013, civil unions ceased to be offered in Delaware, and Rhode Island followed a month later, after the states' respective same-sex marriage laws took effect. Two states have adopted broad domestic partnerships that grant nearly all state-level spousal rights to unmarried couples. Domestic partnerships are available to both same-sex and opposite-sex couples.[53] Five states recognize civil unions for same-sex couples: Hawaii, Vermont, Colorado, New Jersey, and Illinois. All of the states that allow for civil union or domestic partnerships now also allow for same-sex marriage, either through statute or court ruling.[54]

The Increasing Cultural Mix: Minorities Are Becoming the Majority

By 2050, the U.S. population is expected to increase from 282.1 million to 439 million. By as early as 2045, white people will be a minority in the United States. According to new projections from the Census Bureau, "ethnic and racial minorities will comprise a majority of the population of the United States in a little more than a generation." Minorities including Hispanics, Blacks, Asians, American Indians, and Native Hawaiians and Pacific Islanders "will together outnumber non-Hispanic whites." African Americans, Asian Pacific Islanders, and Hispanics made up more than one-third of the U.S. population in 2010, and the numbers have only continued to rise. By 2045, whites will represent 49.7 percent of America.[55] The Hispanic community is one of the greatest untapped markets we have ever seen. Already the largest minority in the United States, their numbers continue to grow faster than any other group. Between 2000 and 2010, the Hispanic population grew by 43 percent, or four times the nation's 9.7 percent growth rate. In real numbers, this was an increase of 15.2 million people of Hispanic descent and accounted for more than half of the total U.S. population increase of 27.3 million.

The total population of Hispanics in the United States today is 50.5 million people strong. Hispanics are also one of the most optimistic groups: most believe the struggling economy has hit them the hardest, yet conversely, they have the highest hopes for the future. According to a Pew Hispanic Research survey conducted in June 2016, Hispanics expected to improve their financial status.[56]

Factors affecting this trend are birth rates and immigration.[57] Immigration undeniably benefits the United States; the economic advantages are significant. Many immigrants are natural entrepreneurs, establishing companies, creating jobs, and driving innovation. Well-educated and highly trained foreign workers are inventive and productive. Expanded workforces increase business flexibility, allowing companies to quickly respond to changing demands. Larger labor forces also encourage specialization. Labor productivity rises as companies adjust to larger workforces and invest in employees.[58]

It is projected that minorities "will constitute a majority of American children under 18 by 2023 and of working-age Americans by 2039."[59] In almost one-third of U.S. states, nonwhite children outnumber all white children under 18 in 14 states—including Nevada, Hawaii, Georgia, and Maryland—plus the District of Columbia. Today the population of white children is 49.8 percent, and it is believed that the percentage will drop to 36.4 percent in 2060.[60] This forecast indicates that by 2050, "the number of Hispanic people will nearly triple, to 133 million from 47 million, to account for 30 percent of Americans." The Asian population is expected to increase to 41 million, or more than 9 percent of the U.S. population; and the black population will increase to 66 million, or 15 percent of the population over the same period. "Several states, including California and Texas, have already reached the point where members of minorities are the majority." As of 2015, the United States has 122 congressional majority-minority districts, which is approximately 28 percent of the nation's House district. Some of the states included in this list include Alabama, Arizona, Florida, Georgia, and California, which has the most majority-minority districts.[61]

For the first time in more than a century, the number of deaths now exceeds births among white Americans.[62] The aging white population has a significant impact on the trend toward diversity. The 2020 census will also highlight the sharp growth divide between the old and the young in America, as suggested by estimates from the Census Bureau's National Demographic Analysis. They show that between 2010 and 2020, the number of people over age 55 grew by 27 percent, which is 20 times larger than the growth rate of the collective population under 55 (1.3 percent). The largest driver of this divide is the baby boomer generation, who passed the age of 65 during the past decade, increasing the size of the 65- to 74-year-old age group by a half. By 2050, about 89 million Americans will be in that group.[63] The impact of these demographic changes on markets, customers, workforce composition, values, and ethics will be significant.

Educational Weaknesses and Gaps

A global study by the United Nations Educational, Scientific, and Cultural Organization (UNESCO) on educational levels revealed several trends that will have a significant impact on the workforce, not only in the United States, but on a global scale. "Globally, the number of children enrolled at the secondary level has tripled since 1970." In addition, "95 percent of primary school graduates continue their education at the lower secondary level in most countries in Central and Eastern Europe, Central Asia, and North America and Western Europe." The education of those entering the workforce is now being shaped heavily by globalization, which is characterized by the dominance of English "as the dominant language of scientific communication," the availability of "universal means of instantaneous contact and simplified scientific communication," and the "concentrated ownership of publishers, databases, and other key resources." This has created an "inequality among national higher education systems as well as within countries." Countries in Africa, for example, are not positioned with the same resources and educational standing. China and India, on the other hand, are "currently the world's largest and third largest academic systems."[64]

These educational trends and gaps affect the pool of applicants and current employees. For example, it is projected that the majority of the student population in the most developed countries will be comprised of women. It is also expected that "the mix of the student population will become more varied, with greater numbers of international students, older students, part-time students, and other types."[65] This diversity has already begun to be reflected in the U.S. workforce.

A 2012 McKinsey & Co. report titled *Education to Employment* demonstrated the challenging mismatch between our educational system and the job skills employers need:[66] 45 percent of U.S. employers reported that lack of skills is the "main reason" for entry-level vacancies and only 42 percent of worldwide employers believe new graduates are adequately prepared for work.[67]

Interestingly, the United States shows no gap in education attainment, with very high levels of literacy and women's enrollment in primary, secondary, and tertiary education.[68]

POINT/COUNTERPOINT

Student Education Debt and Loans: Whose Problem and Who Should Pay?

As of 2021, student loans exceed **$1.56** trillion, where approximately 54 percent of college attendees take on debt to pay for their education. The average amount of student loan debt per borrower is **$39,351** $35,359.[69] The average debt was $26,500. In 2018, a student who graduated left with $29,200 in loan debt.[70]

The U.S. Congress has approved new rates for federal loans, allowing undergraduates to borrow at a 3.9 percent interest rate for subsidized and unsubsidized loans. Graduate students will be able to borrow at 5.4 percent, and parents can borrow at 6.4 percent, at least for 2013.

Unlike federal student loans, private loans cost more because they offer less repayment flexibility and typically cannot be discharged in bankruptcy. Most student debt is difficult, almost impossible, to refinance—burdening borrowers with high rates in a low-rate environment and slowing the economy.

Nearly half of all complaints were related to struggling borrowers who were seeking a loan modification or other option to reduce their monthly payment.

The average American will also likely see interest rates increase as the Treasury increases rates to attract investors. Interest rates will also increase for mortgages, car loans, student loans, and credit cards. The cost of higher education is also creating a sense of more burden than benefit for some students. A Wells Fargo study found that one-third of millennials said they would have been better off working instead of going to college because of having to pay tuition.

Rising costs in education increases student loan debt. An art degree costs as much as a computer science degree. Which is more likely to result in a job? Lenders, in this case the government, should make a fact-based determination of a student's likelihood to graduate and get a job and their expected income. Prospective students applying for loans could be evaluated for a "creditworthiness" score. A student loan score would be based on a formula including their grade point average, major, and academic institution. Each of these variables is directly related to a student's ability to get a job upon graduation and repay their loans. For example, a STEM (science, technology, engineering, and mathematics) major at MIT would yield a higher score and loan compared to a religious studies major at a lesser-ranked school.

Instructions: Each student individually will adopt *either* the Point or CounterPoint argument and justify their reasons (with arguments using this case and other evidence/opinions). Then, either in teams or designated arrangements, students share their reasons. Afterward, the class is debriefed and there is further discussion.

POINT: Students should pay their debts—they borrowed, they pay. If the government accepts to pay part of the remainder, what precedent does this set in a capitalist, market economy? It's time to stop treating all degrees alike. Some degrees result in jobs, others don't. Create a scoring system and even backdate it. Those degrees that have high job potential should have different payback terms than those that don't. If the loans are not paid, the economy continues to suffer and we all pay. Next, people will want the government to pay for their mortgages, car loans, and then what?

COUNTERPOINT: The government should forgive and absorb all of the student loan debts. The loans and terms made were and are unstable and are nearly impossible to collect from every student. Students are assets to the future of this country. Why treat them like their loans—as liabilities? Education is the foundation of democracy. Should students be encouraged to become hourly wage workers at low-tech jobs? Learning how to think creates good citizens, a middle class, and entrepreneurs—and their degrees don't have to be only in computer science.

SOURCES

Bastrikin, A. (2020, April 12). Student loan debt statistics. Educationdata.org. https://educationdata.org/student-loan-debt-statistics/.

World Economic Forum. (2012). The global gender report 2012. Geneva: WEF. http://www3.weforum.org/docs/WEF_GenderGap_Report_2012.pdf.

Mainstreaming Disabled Workers

Hiring and mainstreaming qualified disabled workers is increasing in importance because of the combined effects of the shrinking and aging of the workforce. The International Labour Organization estimated that approximately 15 percent of the world's population (1 billion people) have a disability, and that "unemployment among persons with disabilities is as high as 80 percent in some developing countries."[71] Disabilities affect a large percentage of the workforce. In 2019, only 19.3 percent of people with a disability in the United States were employed.[72] "One-third of the employers surveyed said that persons with disabilities cannot effectively perform the required job tasks. The second most common reason given for not hiring persons with disabilities was the fear of costly special facilities." Disabilities are categorized as permanent (e.g., physical disabilities), temporary (e.g., those resulting from injury or stress), and progressive (e.g., AIDS, alcohol and drug addiction, cancer). An assessment from the National Organization on Disability/Harris Survey of Americans with Disabilities concluded that disabled Americans are three times as likely to live in poverty as the general public, twice as likely to drop out of high school, and twice as likely to be constrained by transportation options; also, three times as many individuals with disabilities have less health care than the general public. Understanding that these numbers are concerning, there are plenty of resources to help disabled workers get into the workforce. Job accommodations, job searching, and job training resources, to name a few, can create a fair playing field for disabled workers to have the same opportunity to work a job compared to someone who is not disabled.[73] It is interesting to note that "everybody is just one car wreck away, a diagnosis away, a progressive condition away from joining the ranks of the disabled."[74] Employers who hire persons with disabilities report they are more likely to be loyal, appreciative to their employers, and able to think outside the box.

Balancing Work and Life in Families

As more dual-career and child-rearing couples enter the workforce, conflicts and problems evolve over roles and responsibilities as families cope with workplace demands. Working family models illustrating these tensions have evolved over decades. Four such models, which are summarized in Figure 7.2, include:

1. An early model depicting complete separation of work and family life and issues, in which in this study of cisgender men worked and women maintained the family.

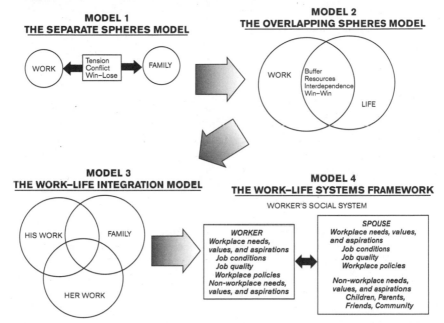

Figure 7.2

Evolution of Work and Family Life Systems Models

Source: Adapted with permission from Barnett, R. (1999, March). A new work–life model for the twenty-first century. *Annals of the American Academy of Political and Social Science,* *562,* 143–158.

2. An overlapping model of "work" and "family life" spheres, in which the boundaries were still fuzzy but roles were recognized as being interrelated.
3. A model that defined multiple roles and responsibilities, including "his work," "her work," and "family" obligations. Like the previous two models, this model was based on scarcity and zero-sum assumptions · (i.e., a fixed number of resources that resulted in win–lose situations) regarding the allocation and use of resources and responsibilities at home and at work.
4. The most recent work–life systems model, which assumes a systems perspective in which roles and responsibilities are not seen as competitive, isolated, or overlapping in undefined ways between family members and the organization and community are built into individual and family responsibilities, which are shared to optimize the well-being of the entire system (company, employees, and families). In this fourth model, the emphasis also shifts from individual and family to include workplace needs, values, and aspirations; job conditions; and quality of life. Company policies are recognized as part of the work–life equation and include flextime and part-time arrangements.

Having a strong work–life balance has positive impacts on the lives of individuals and couples. Reasons to move toward maintaining a strong work–life balance include:[75]

- Less stress and fatigue
- More control of your time
- Being better able to make decisions and meet commitments
- Being healthier

With personal benefits, others are also positively affected as well. "To develop and learn, children need warm, loving attention and quality time with you. Quality time is when you're physically and emotionally present with your child." In a relationship, spending quality time is very important as it is considered a solid building block to a relationship. A strong work–life balance allows for the time and energy to develop relationships with your significant other and child.

With the attack of the Covid-19 virus (coronavirus) in 2020, the struggle to maintain balance between work and life moved to a new setting: home. Even though many people were forced to work at home, many still struggled to finish work efficiently as well as spend quality time with the family. While this advice applied to this pandemic, it also applies post-coronavirus as well. During the week, create a routine to minimize distractions (which includes at least 30 minutes of physical movement), stay connected with peers and colleagues, and dress for work (this mainly applies to working at home), meaning put on proper attire. During the weekends, reduce the amount of time checking your e-mail, spend time engaging in relaxing activities, maintain some form of physical activity (e.g., taking a walk outside), and stay connected with friends and family.

A 2021 Deloitte Global Human Capital Trends survey of executives stated that their organization's move since Covid-19 to remote work had a positive impact on well-being. However, the sustainability of remote ways of working depends on the duration of the virus and responses to it. Moreover, because of Covid-19, Deloitte realized that organizations suddenly found themselves called upon to prioritize workers' physical and mental well-being as a matter of survival, as protecting their health and alleviating their stress became critical to operations. Work and life, health, safety, and well-being became inseparable. Recognizing the inextricable link among our well-being, our work, and our lives has led more organizations to think deeply about ways they can design well-being into work itself so that both workers and the organization can thrive moving forward.[76]

Several companies have consistently been ranked among the top 10 of the Best Companies to Work For. These companies include Abbott, A.T. Kearney, AbbVie, Adobe, ADP, American Express, Astellas Pharma, Blue Cross Blue Shield of Massachusetts, and Bank of America.[77]

In the following sections, we turn to topics regarding how employers have dealt with, and are dealing with, the legal and ethical issues of changing workforces.

7.2 The Changing Social Contract between Corporations and Employees

Covid-19 has shaken the concept of social contracts between organizations (corporations) and employees:

"The pandemic exposed the fragility of social contracts. To thrive in the future, businesses must play a role in rebuilding these contracts."[78] For many organizations and businesses—especially those that did not survive the virus—there will be no contract. For those that did, many will thrive, as many are now. While the nature of the so-called social contract between employer and employee cannot be predicted at this time, this section summarizes a brief history of the elements of this contract. You might ask as you read this section, Will the nature of this contract return to pre-Covid-19 standards and practices? Will there be some changes and other newer or different elements added? How radically might elements of this contract change? We have already mentioned that many reputable corporations and institutions (e.g., 'Best Companies to Work For') suggest that employee health, and emotional and physical stability, must be considered during the virus. Also consider that most of the sections and content in this chapter contribute to the changing nature of this social contract: generational differences, needs, educational level, aspirations; changing age and skills of employees (and employers); family needs, demands, rights, responsibilities; environmental changes that include post-Covid-19, climate change, industry shifts, and so on. Let's start with how the social contract has evolved.

The social contract that has historically defined the employee–employer relationship is known as the "employment-at-will (EAW) doctrine." Basically, the EAW doctrine holds that the employer can dismiss an employee at any time for any reason, as long as federal and state laws and union contracts are not violated; likewise, employees are also free to terminate their employment with a company whenever they choose and for whatever reason. While this doctrine has been the dominant view of the employment relationship in the United States, parts of the doctrine have eroded since its inception and may continue to do so with Covid-19.[79] The EAW doctrine has been in effect since 1884, when the *Payne v. Western & Atlantic R.R. Co.* judgment ruled that "all may dismiss their employees at will, be they many or few, for good cause, for no cause, or even for cause morally wrong without being thereby guilty of legal wrong." Essentially, the EAW doctrine can be defined as "the right of an employer to fire an employee without giving a reason and the right of an employee to quit when he or she chooses."[80] If employees are unprotected by unions or other written contracts, they can be fired, according to this doctrine. As the insert "Read Carefully before Signing," shown in Figure 7.3, illustrates, employees can be and are asked to acknowledge how tenuous their "contract" with a company can be.

The EAW doctrine evolved as part of the laissez-faire philosophy of the industrial revolution. Between the 1930s and 1960s, however, exceptions to the doctrine appeared. Federal legislation since the 1960s has been enacted to protect employees against racial discrimination and to provide rights to a minimum wage, to equal hiring and employment opportunities, and to participation in labor unions. Over time, the following exceptions to the EAW

Figure 7.3

Employee Contract under the EAW Doctrine

Read Carefully before Signing

I understand that refusal to submit to the testing noted [elsewhere] or a positive drug screen result will eliminate any consideration for employment.

I also certify that the statements and information furnished by me in this application are true and correct. I understand that falsification of such statements and information is grounds for dismissal at any time the company becomes aware of the falsified notification. In consideration of my employment, I agree to conform to the rules and regulations of the company and acknowledge that my employment and compensation can be terminated, with or without cause, and with or without notice, at any time, at the option of either the company or myself. I further understand that no policy, benefit or procedure contained in any employee handbook creates an employment contract for any period of time and no terms or conditions of employment contrary to the foregoing should be relied upon, except for those made in writing by a designated officer of the Company.

I agree and hereby authorize XYZ, Inc. to conduct a background inquiry to verify the information on this application, other documentation that I have provided and other areas that may include prior employment, consumer credit, criminal convictions, motor vehicle and other reports. These reports may include information as to my character, work habits, performance, education and experience along with reasons for termination of employment from previous employers. Further, I understand that you may be requesting information from various federal, state and other agencies which maintain records concerning my past activities relating to my driving, credit, criminal, civil, and other experiences, as well as claims involving me in the files of insurance companies. I authorize all previous employers or other persons who have knowledge of me, or my records, to release such information to XYZ, Inc. I hereby release any party or agency and XYZ, Inc. from all claims or liabilities, whatever that may arise by such disclosures or such investigation.

_____   _____
Date of Application   Signature of Applicant

---

doctrine have evolved: (1) the good faith principle; (2) the public policy principle; and (3) implied contracts.

Good Faith Principle Exception

Some states have other obligations that must be addressed by employers, like "good faith" or "fair dealing" practices.[81] A good faith principle is based on the premise that employers should practice fairness and reasonableness in their actions with employees. For example, an employer should demonstrate that opportunities were offered for a terminated employee to improve performance before the employee was fired. Companies that demonstrate fairness in their dealings and policies with employees show good faith.[82]

Public Policy Principle Exception

Since the 1970s, state court decisions have limited the EAW doctrine. Specifically, state courts have upheld employees' rights to use legal action against their employers if an employee termination violated "public policy" principles; examples include (1) if employees were pressured to commit perjury or fix prices; (2) if employees were not permitted to perform jury duty or file for workers' compensation; (3) if employees were terminated because they refused to support a merger; and (4) if employees reported alleged employer violations of statutory policy (whistle-blowing).[83]

Implied Contract Exception

An important 1981 California Appeals Court decision, *Pugh v. See's Candies, Inc.*, ruled that, in a noncontractual employment arrangement, an implied promise from the employer existed. The employer could not act arbitrarily with its employees regarding termination decisions when considering the following factors: (1) duration of employment, (2) recommendations and promotions received, (3) lack of direct criticism of work, (4) assurances given, and (5) the employer's acknowledged policies.[84] Other implied contract exceptions include statements in employee and personnel handbooks, manuals, guidelines, letters offering employment, and verbal statements made to employees regarding job security and promises of continuing employment.[85]

Although the EAW doctrine has undergone change, it remains the cornerstone of U.S. labor law, as is illustrated in Figure 7.3. States vary on the application of the EAW doctrine, but the U.S. Eighth Circuit Court of Appeals favored employers. The federal court has stated that it will not act as a "superpersonnel board" of a company. Figure 7.3 is a copy of a contract an employee must sign before beginning work at this reputable company in Massachusetts. It is an example of a strongly worded EAW-oriented contract.

At issue in the EAW doctrine is the continuing debate over the nature of property and property rights. Each organization defines property rights and responsibilities offered to managers and employees, such as severance payments, pensions, stock options, access to resources, and golden parachutes. Employers also view employees' labor, time, and effort as part of their property. At issue in the EAW doctrine is whether an employee's education, skills, and other intangible assets are seen as the employee's "property," and if so, whether employees have certain rights regarding these assets. Due process is one such right that accompanies the EAW doctrine.[86]

The debate will continue over whose "property" and rights take precedence and whose are violated and on what grounds, between employer and employee, especially in disputed firings that do not involve clear legal violations of employee rights, such as blatant discrimination. One scholar has noted that "the present-day debate revolves mainly around utilitarian issues. To what extent is the welfare of society advanced by preserving or limiting the traditional prerogatives of employers? Employers typically favor employment-at-will not because they want to fire without cause but because they would rather avoid the need to account for their personnel decisions in court and face the possibility of stiff punitive awards. Even advocates of greater employee protection recognize the dangers of the courts becoming too deeply involved in business decision making."[87]

The next section presents employee rights and employer responsibilities and offers recommendations to managers for avoiding arbitrary termination decisions.

7.3 Employee and Employer Rights and Responsibilities

Employers and employees have rights and responsibilities that each should honor with respect to the other. This section discusses these mutual responsibilities, some of which stem from rights by law and legislation, while others are based on ethical principles. A values-based, stakeholder management approach views the employer–employee relationship as one grounded on mutual trust and reciprocal responsibility. Although laws and legislation serve the purpose of protection for both parties, without trust that is demonstrated in fair and equitable treatment of basic rights and responsibilities, one or both parties stand to lose. Nevertheless, not all employers or employees have a personal, professional, or organizational ethic that respects the other's rights in all situations. Historical attitudes, negative prejudices, and stereotypes sometimes surface in institutionally unjust practices toward individuals and groups. On the other hand, employers must protect their property and assets against illegal and unethical practices of certain employees. When voluntary trust and mutual respect fail and harm is done to employers or employees, the legal system can be evoked.

The EAW doctrine was a transition from a feudal European governance context to a modern pluralistic U.S. context. Employers still control private property and proprietary rights over their intellectual property. Employees claim their constitutional rights to individual freedom, liberty, and control over their private lives. Employers try to maximize productivity and profits, to sustain financial growth and stability, to minimize costs, to improve quality, to increase market share, and to stabilize wages. Employees seek to increase their wages and benefits, to improve working conditions, to enhance mobility, and to ensure job security while demonstrating mutual respect for the value of their labor. No perfect boundary exists between employer and employee rights in a capitalist market economy.

Before discussing specific rights and responsibilities between employers and employees, this section begins by defining "rights" and two premises based on this definition. Then, two organizing concepts that underlie employee rights are suggested: balance and governmental rights. The concept of balance is based on utilitarian ethical reasoning, and that of moral entitlement is based on Kantian nonconsequentialist reasoning. Although these concepts are not mutually exclusive, it is helpful to understand the logic behind them in order to argue their merits and shortcomings as they apply to specific workplace controversies.

Moral Foundation of Employee Rights

The ideal relationship between employer and employees is one based on mutual respect and trust. Trust generally leads to open communication, which in turn provides an environment of collaboration and productivity. In many companies, this is unfortunately not the case. Power and authority relationships between employers and employees are, by definition, asymmetrical. Employees are generally, as stated by J. Rowan, in a "comparatively inferior bargaining position with respect to their employers. This inequity opens up possibilities for various sorts of exploitation, such as inadequate compensation, discrimination, and privacy invasions, all of which have been known to occur." Rowan also notes that "employee rights are complex, in that managers, as a prerequisite for making ethically sound decisions, must assess which alleged employee rights are legitimate . . . and must weigh them against the rights of those in other stakeholder groups."[88]

A right can be understood as a "moral claim." A right is moral when it is not necessarily part of any conventional system, as are legal rights. A right is a claim because it corresponds with a duty on the part of the person against whom the right is held. For example, I claim that I have a right to be safe in my workplace. I hold this claim against my employer because the employer has the duty to provide me with this safety. Under particular circumstances, my moral claim can be argued and disputed. It may not be an absolute claim.

The moral foundation for employee rights is based on the fact that employees are persons. One generic right that all persons have is a right to freedom, including the concept of negative freedom (i.e., the right not to be coerced or inhibited by external forces). Regarding employees, this right to freedom is a claim "that when managers choose to hire employees, they must bear in mind that they are dealing with persons, and the (positive and negative) freedom of their employees is therefore to be respected."[89] The second generic right of employees is the right to well-being. This right follows from individuals' having interests, which are preconditions for pursuing goals. Interests and the pursuit of goals are morally important because they are not satisfied when a person does not have well-being. When employees cannot satisfy their job-related goals, interests, and requirements because of work-related conditions, an employee's right to well-being may have been violated. With regard to these arguments on the moral foundation of employee rights, Sanford Jacoby has noted, "Employees should at all times be treated in a way that respects them as persons."[90] We might add that the same observation holds true for employers; they also should be treated with respect as individuals.

The Principle of Balance in the Employee and Employer Social Contract and the Reality of Competitive Change

As common law and custom have evolved from the EAW doctrine to implied employee rights, employers have the opportunity to consider more than stockholder and financial interests when dealing with employee stakeholders. A values-based stakeholder management perspective views the employee–employer relationship from a win–win foundation. Both employers and employees act from a base of values. Employer–employee working relationships are enhanced when the values of the organization reflect and align stakeholder with stockholder interests. Productivity, innovation, and personal and professional growth are more likely to result from this type of alignment.

In a highly competitive, globalizing environment in which intellectual skills, flexibility, and speed of work are emphasized, traditional views of company ownership and employee loyalty change. Employees' and workers' needs can also be diminished in polarizing political climates where governmental bodies and coalitions funded by interest groups seek to implement special demands. The evolving social contract between employers and employees still recognizes employers' power over their physical and material property, but the contractual relationship between employer and employee aims in principle at balance, mutual respect, integrity, and fairness. The employer's business interest can and should be balanced against the employee's welfare, interests, and willing contribution to add value. In the early twenty-first century, small and mid-size employers are also pressured to balance global economic demands and tighter profit margins with employee interests. Larger firms continue to reduce their workforce and cut costs through outsourcing and offshoring. Although employers generally have more power than employees in the contractual relationship, employees in the United States, for example, are still citizens under the protection of the Constitution. Employees must also balance their self-interests and motivations with the need of the organization to succeed, which is necessary for the organization to provide employment.

It is interesting to note that the principle of balance in the employer–employee relationship has been historically prevalent in some of the developed Asian countries, such as Japan, South Korea, Singapore, and Taiwan. In Japan, in particular, the Confucian tradition of harmony has underscored the cooperative relationship between unions and companies.[91] European countries, including Germany and France, have also enacted laws that protect employee benefits and welfare. Some of these countries have traditions that include socialism and strong populist social policies. Some of these traditions and practices are also beginning to change under the competitive pressures of economic downturns, the use of information technology, and global competition. For example, lifelong employment in many Japanese companies is no longer guaranteed. Offshoring and outsourcing are now practiced at Sony, Matsushita, and Toshiba, to mention just a few firms.[92]

Rights from Government Legislation

Employee rights are based on principles determined by law. Certain government rights (federal, state, and local) of the employee are not negotiable in written or implied contracts—for example, rights related to the minimum wage; sexual harassment; discrimination based on race, creed, age, national origin, gender, or disability; and the right to assemble. Although employee rights based on certain legislation are not always negotiated according to employer–employee self-interests, these rights can be disputed, depending on circumstances. Reverse discrimination, to be discussed later, is one such example. Although private corporations are the property of the owners, certain employee legal rights are still within a corporation's boundaries.

Employer Responsibilities to Employees

Employers are obliged to pay employees fair wages for work performed and to provide safe working conditions. Review and answer the questions in the box titled, "Who Has Rights in this Situation?" After you have answered and discussed the questions, what, if anything, did you learn about your and other classmates' values and beliefs regarding employee–employer responsibilities, obligations, and rights?

Fair Wages

Fair wages are determined by factors such as what the public and society support and expect, conditions of the labor market, competitive industry wages in the specific location, the firm's profitability, the nature of the job and work, laws governing minimum wages, comparable salaries, and the fairness of the salary or wage negotiations.[93] As we will see later in this chapter, fair wages for comparable jobs held by men and women are not always paid.

Full-time working women had median weekly earnings of $857, or 80.4 percent of the $1,006 median for men. Full-time working Black women earned a median weekly wage of $742 compared with those for white women of $873. Median earnings of full-time employed Hispanics was $763—lower than those of Blacks ($823), whites ($1,096), and Asians ($1,360).[94]

Based on the Institute for Women's Policy Research wage gap fact sheet, "If the pace of change in the annual earnings ratio continues at the same rate as it has since 1960, it will take another 45 years, until 2058, for men and women to reach parity."[95]

Who Has Rights in This Situation?

Aparna Jairam (a high-tech employee in India) isn't trying to steal your job (you're a high-tech U.S. employee). That's what she tells me, and I believe her. But if Jairam does end up taking it—and let's face facts, she could do your $70,000-a-year (U.S.) job for the wages of a Taco Bell counter-jockey—she won't lose any sleep over your plight. When I ask what her advice is for a beleaguered American programmer afraid of being pulled under by the global tide that she represents, Jairam takes the high road, neither dismissing the concern nor offering soothing happy talk. Instead, she recites a portion of the 2,000-year-old epic poem and Hindu holy book, the Bhagavad Gita: "Do what you're supposed to do. And don't worry about the fruits. They'll come on their own."

QUESTIONS

1. Do you agree with Aparna? Why or why not? Please explain.
2. On what, if any, ethical grounds could you either justify or reject her assessment? Explain.

SOURCE

Pink, D. (2004, February). The new face of the silicon age. *Wired Magazine*, *12(2)*. http://www.wired.com/wired/archive/12.02/india.html.

Safe Working Environment

Employers also are obliged to provide workers with a safe working environment and safe working conditions. The Occupational Safety and Health Administration (OSHA) and federal laws and regulations provide safety standards and enforce employer institution of the company's own safety standards. The problems of employers providing—and of employees accepting—safe working environments stem from (1) lack of knowledge and of available, reliable information about levels of health risks; (2) lack of appropriate compensation proportional to the level of occupational risk; and (3) employees accepting known risks when the employer does not offer any safer alternatives. When the option is employment versus no employment, workers, especially in low-income, noncompetitive employment regions, often choose jobs with hazardous risks to their health or life. Employees have a right to know about unsafe working conditions, as we also discuss later in the chapter.

Employers should pay competitive wages commensurate with the occupational risks associated with a profession, job, or work setting. For example, race car drivers would not be expected to receive the same pay as college professors. Employers also are expected to provide full information on the risks and health hazards related to the work, products, and working environments to all employees exposed to those risks. Finally, employers also should offer health insurance programs and benefits to employees exposed to workplace hazards. Not all employers, especially with recent economic conditions, meet these obligations. Employers who cannot provide health and protection of employees in high risk, potentially unsafe environments should not be in that business.

Many companies are proactive in developing standards and monitoring for safe working conditions. Apple, for example, announced in February 2012 that it would audit the working conditions at its overseas factories and make the findings public through the Fair Labor Association. The company has made a public commitment to hold its supply chain accountable for appropriate, safe working conditions. "Apple has said that if the companies manufacturing its products do not measure up to its labor and human rights standards, it will stop working with them." Apple, like many manufacturers, has not been immune to incidents with unsafe working conditions. Company reports indicate previous instances of "excessive overtime, underage workers, improperly disposed hazardous waste and falsified records." In 2010, "137 workers at an Apple supplier in eastern China were injured after they were ordered to use a poisonous chemical to clean iPhone screens." In 2011, "two explosions at iPad factories killed four people and injured 77." It is expected that there will be repercussions across the electronics industry, as Apple is an industry leader, and many of the suppliers are used by multiple companies within the industry. Apple was the "first technology company to join the Fair Labor Association," joining in January 2012. More recently, Apple has had privacy issues with consumers and the government.[96] Apple factories in China's Henan region have also been at the center of reports about employee suicide, exceptionally low wages, excessive overtime, among others.[97]

Working Conditions That Empower Employees

Although employers are not required by law to offer employees working conditions that provide meaningful tasks and job satisfaction, doing so can lead to increased performance, job satisfaction, and productivity. Employees work most productively when they can participate in the control of their tasks, when they are given responsibility for and autonomy over their assignments, and when they are treated with respect.[98] Quality of work life (QWL) programs that have provided employees with more autonomy, participation, satisfaction, and control in their work tasks have demonstrated positive results.[99] Many companies that have organized self-designing work teams, quality circles, and learning communities to tap into employee creativity and abilities have also provided opportunities for innovation. There is an increase in companies offering opportunities for employees to practice their own religious and spiritual rituals during the workday. Employers and employees both gain when personal and organizational needs are met. Working environments that can provide conditions for this alignment are increasing in order to attract and retain talent.

Employee Rights and Responsibilities to Employers

Employees are responsible for fulfilling their contracted obligations to the corporation; for following the goals, procedural rules, and work plans of the organization; for offering competence commensurate with the work and job assignments; and for performing productively according to the required tasks. Other responsibilities include timeliness, avoiding absenteeism, acting legally and morally in the workplace and while on job assignments, and respecting the intellectual and private-property rights of the employer.

Employee Rights in the Workplace

Labor, along with money and materials, is considered capital in a free-market system. However, labor is not the same as materials and money. Labor also means human beings who have general constitutional rights that should not be relinquished between working hours.[100] Yet, clashes of interests and of stakes between employee rights and management demands frequently occur. The boundary between an employer's private property and an employee's individual rights is often blurred in everyday experience. Understanding employee rights is part legal and part ethical because these rights must be viewed and interpreted within corporate policy, procedures, and particular circumstances. In some instances, there are clear violations of an employee's rights; other times there are "gray" or uncertain, areas. When employees and employers cannot agree on whose rights are seriously violated, third-party negotiation, arbitration, and even settlement may be required. This section presents major types of employee rights in the workplace:

- The right not to be terminated without just cause
- The right to due process
- The right to privacy

- The right to know
- The right to workplace health and safety
- The right to organize and strike
- Rights regarding plant closings

When the coronavirus caused the worldwide pandemic, the United States implemented the Families First Coronavirus Response Act (FFCRA). This act "requires employers to provide employees with paid sick leave or expanded family and medical leave for specified reasons related to Covid-19" and implemented and enforced by the Department of Labor's Wage and Hour Division (WHD). The Act stays in effect until December 31, 2020. All employees of covered employers are eligible for:[101]

- Two weeks (up to 80 hours) of paid sick leave at the employee's regular rate of pay where the employee is unable to work because the employee is quarantined and/or experiencing Covid-19 symptoms and seeking a medical diagnosis.
- Two weeks (up to 80 hours) of paid sick leave at two-thirds the employee's regular rate of pay because the employee is unable because of a bona fide need to care for an individual subject to quarantine, or to care for a child (under 18 years old) whose school or child care provider is closed or unavailable for reasons related to Covid-19, and/or the employee is experiencing a sustainably similar condition as specified by the Secretary of Health and Human Services.
- Up to an additional 10 weeks of paid expanded family and medical leave at two-thirds the employee's regular rate of pay where an employee, who has been employed for at least 30 calendar days, is unable to work due to a bona fide need for leave to care for a child whose school or child care provider is closed or unavailable for reasons related to Covid-19.

These rights become even more important in a society that rapidly transforms technological and scientific inventions into part of the human workplace environment.

Just Cause Termination

A basic principle in disciplinary termination cases is that the employer must have "just cause" for imposing the action. A test for determining whether there is "just cause" was developed by Arbitrator Daugherty in the celebrated Enterprise Wire case (46 LA 359, 1966 and 50 LA 83). An absolute "no" answer to any one or more questions in this guideline indicates that the employer's action was "arbitrary, capricious and/or discriminatory in one or more respects, thereby signifying an abuse of managerial discretion and allowing the arbitrator to substitute his judgment for that of the employer."

1. Was the employee adequately warned of the consequences of his conduct?
2. Was the employer's rule or order reasonably related to efficient and safe operations?

3. Did management investigate before administering the discipline?
4. Was the investigation fair and objective?
5. Did the investigation produce substantial evidence or proof of guilt?
6. Were the rules, orders, and penalties applied evenhandedly and without discrimination to all employees?
7. Was the penalty reasonably related to the seriousness of the offense and the past record?[102]

As a principle, it also has been argued that workers should have three rights regarding work to maintain self-respect:

- The right to employment
- The right to equal opportunity
- The right to participate in job-related decisions[103]

These rights are less entitlements than goals and depend on market conditions. Just cause termination is problematic when other forms of employer discrimination are determined, such as discrimination because of age, gender, disability, race, national origin, and other Title VII areas. For example, an Ohio jury awarded a 68-year-old woman $30.6 million in an age discrimination lawsuit after a jury ruled that the company violated her rights by refusing to give her another job within the company when it terminated her from a management position.[104]

Due Process

Due process is one of the most important underlying rights employees have in the workplace because it affects most of their other rights. Due process refers to the right to have an impartial and fair hearing regarding employers' decisions, procedures, and rules that affect employees. As applied in the workplace, due process essentially refers to grievance procedures.

At a more general level, due process rights protect employees from arbitrary and illegitimate uses of power. These rights are based on the Fifth and Fourteenth Amendments of the Constitution, which state that no person shall be deprived of "life, liberty, or property, without the due process of law."

Patricia Werhane states that the following corporate procedural mechanisms are needed to ensure employees' right to due process:[105]

- Right to a public hearing
- Right to have peer evaluations
- Right to obtain external arbitration
- Right to an open, mutually approved grievance procedure

The right to due process applies to other employee rights, such as those involving privacy; safety and health; safe working environments; holding meetings and gatherings; and hiring, firing, and other human resources decisions.

Right to Privacy

Employees' right to privacy remains one of the most debated and controversial rights. It raises these questions: Where does the employer's control over employee behavior, space, time, and property begin and end? What freedoms and liberties do employees have with employer property rights? What rights do employers have to protect their private property, earnings, and costs from employees? The U.S. Constitution does not actually refer to a person's right to privacy; the working definition of employees' right to privacy has come to mean "to be left alone." Privacy in the workplace also can refer to employees' right to autonomy and to determine "when, how, and to what extent information about them is communicated to others."[106] The extent of an employee's privacy in the workplace remains an unsettled area of controversy. The definition of what constitutes an employee's privacy is still somewhat problematic, including the notion of psychological privacy (involving an employee's inner life) and the notion of physical privacy (involving an employee's space and time).[107] In the 1965 *Griswold v. Connecticut* case, the Supreme Court ruled that the Constitution guarantees individuals a "zone of privacy" around them into which the government cannot intrude. Proponents of this definition argue that this zone includes personnel records and files and protection against polygraph and psychological testing and surveillance in the workplace. The ruling also is intended to protect employees in their after-work activities; their need for peace and quiet in the workplace; their dress, manners, and grooming; and their personal property in the workplace. Identifying this "zone of privacy" has proved complicated, especially in cyberspace and the use of technological surveillance.

Technology and Employee Privacy

Although employee privacy rights remain largely undefined regarding uses and abuses of emerging technologies in the workplace, the following main types of court-upheld privacy violations and permissible employee privacy inquiries can serve as guidelines. Court-upheld privacy violations include:

1. Intrusion (locker room and bathroom surveillance)
2. Publication of private matters
3. Disclosure of medical records
4. Appropriation of an employee's name for commercial uses
5. Eavesdropping on employee conversations and retrieving or accessing employee e-mail (if unauthorized)

Permissible employee privacy inquiries include:

1. Criminal history inquiries
2. Credit history inquiries
3. Access to medical records[108]

Conflicts of Interest

Employee responsibilities to employers become complicated when conflicts of interest appear; that is, when an employee's private interests compete or are not aligned with the company's interests. More obvious conflicts of interest arise in a number of situations, such as taking or offering commercial or personal bribes, kickbacks, gifts, and insider information for personal gain.

The so-called gray areas are more problematic for determining whose interests are violated at the expense of others. For example, an employee quits a firm, joins a competitor, and then is accused by the former employer of stealing proprietary property (i.e., passing on intellectual property, sharing trade secrets, or offering a competitive advantage by divulging confidential information). Whose interests are violated?[109] Some courts have used a "balancing model" based on utilitarian logic to resolve trade-secret-protection cases; that is, an employee's interest in mobility and opportunity is weighed against the employer's right to decide the extent of protection given to confidential information. For example, the following three criteria have been used to decide whether trade secrets have been divulged by employees:

1. True trade secrecy and established ownership must be shown.
2. A trade secret must have been disclosed by an employee, thus breaching a duty of confidentiality.
3. The employer's interest in keeping the secret must outweigh the employee's interest in using the secret to earn a living and the public's interest in having the secret transmitted.

Courts also use other considerations in these types of rulings—for example, contract obligations, promises made, truthfulness, confidentiality, and loyalty. The point here is that as technology and expertise become more sophisticated and as employee mobility—and downsizing—increase, workplace and courtroom criteria regarding the proof of conflict of interest also grow more complicated. Although a utilitarian model is used to help determine conflict-of-interest court cases, such as trade secrecy, other essential considerations are ethical principles such as rights, duty, and justice for determining right and wrong; violations of loyalty, confidentiality, or truthfulness; and harm done to either employers or employees.

Other Employee Rights and Obligations to Employers

Workplace theft has been estimated by the U.S. Department of Commerce to cost in excess of $40 billion a year in the United States.[110] Employers and many managers would like to use testing and other related techniques to prevent and detect crime in the workplace. They are, however, particularly concerned about employee privacy rights regarding testing and what may constitute a violation of employee rights.

Polygraph and Psychological Testing

Here are some of the issues surrounding the use of polygraphs and psychological testing:

1. These tests are not reliable or valid; they are only indicators.
2. The tests, to some extent, can be manipulated and influenced by the operators.

3. The tests may include irrelevant questions (such as those pertaining to gender, lifestyle, religion, and after-work activities) that invade a person's privacy.
4. Employees do not have control over the test results or how the information is used.

Researchers in the field of honesty testing have concluded that only 1.7 percent (at worst) to 13.6 percent (at best) of such tests are accurate.[111]

Workplace Surveillance

There is no comprehensive federal law in the United States regulating the extent to which employers can monitor employees in the workplace. And recent trends toward flexible working arrangements and work-from-home policies have made this issue even more murky for individual companies. Most privacy and workplace monitoring policies are governed by a wide range of state laws that often contradict each other, are too ambiguous, or are simply not advanced enough to keep up with technology.[112] Prosecutors federally rely on the Fourth Amendment that protects American citizens against "unreasonable search and seizure" of their person or belongings without a warrant issued by a judge stating probable cause. However, this language has a vague context in the workplace, where technology and online presence plays such an integral role in people's work lives. Because the federal government has left this so open-ended, it has been up to the states to make individual privacy laws to govern the issue of workplace monitoring.[113] "Surveillance of employees at work (that is, employers using technology to spy on and invade workers' privacy) is also a subject of concern. Software programs are used to monitor workers who use computer terminals. Although there are pros and cons of surveillance videos in the workplace (as Ethical Insight 7.2 shows), there are no clear-cut answers as to whether or not to use such equipment to monitor employee performance. Employers can detect the speed of employees' work, number and length of phone calls made and received, breaks taken, when machines are in use, and so on. Although some form of work-related monitoring is certainly legal and even necessary, the ethical issues that the American Civil Liberties Union (ACLU) raise are the possible invasion of employee privacy and fair treatment. What type of information does an employer have a right to, and what effects do stress and anxiety from monitoring have on employee welfare? The Electronic Communications Privacy Act renders electronic eavesdropping through computer-to-computer transmissions, private videoconferences, and cellular phones illegal.

A study released by the Society for Human Resource Management, a trade association in Alexandria, Virginia, showed that 80 percent of the organizations in the study used e-mail. Only 36 percent of those groups had policies concerning e-mail use, and only 32 percent had written privacy policies. The issue of individual employee privacy remains somewhat undefined in the workplace.[114]

Ethical Insight 7.2

Pros and Cons of Employers Using Video Surveillance

Pros	Cons
Increased safety: Improves the security of employers and employees.	*Potential invasion of privacy:* Camera installation in improper locations and video footage monitored and stored inappropriately presents liability for invasion of privacy claims and costly legal actions.
Theft deterrent: Saves companies by preventing stolen products.	
Prompts good behavior: Monitoring can encourage productive behavior.	
Provides evidence of a crime: Proof of stolen goods can be provided with electronic monitoring.	*Can provide false sense of security.*
	Lowers morale: Can promote a lack of trust, negatively affecting an employee's work performance.

Questions

1. How would electronic video surveillance affect you and your performance in the workplace?
2. With the evolving hybrid workplace/home model, would surveillance work any differently in your opinion? Explain.
3. Can you identify with an employer's need and justification for this equipment? Explain.
4. What other means of monitoring employee performance would you recommend and why?

Source: Miller, B. (2019, September 25). Pros and Cons of Employee Monitoring. *HR Daily Advisor.* https://hrdailyadvisor.blr.com/2019/09/25/pros-and-cons-of-employee-monitoring/.

Internet Use in the Workplace

This is another undefined area regarding employee use of technology that requires the employer's development of "appropriate use policies" (AUPs). Covid-19 has in part blurred some of the traditional boundaries of what is expected and demanded of employees' use of technology in the workplace, since many employees still have to use technology at home to perform their tasks. Still, as people return to the workplace, such issues will again be raised. The use of the Internet in workplaces for personal reasons can both decrease and increase employee productivity depending on whether or not the organization has an Internet use policy, individual employee responsibility, effective communication of those policies, and other factors related to employee dissatisfaction. Social media is a particularly tricky culprit—many companies have turned to social media for advertising and communication among employees; however, the temptation and access to the Internet for personal reasons can be excessive. Based on Statista .com data, in 2017 it was calculated that 90 percent of U.S businesses were using social media for marketing purposes.[115] However, cyberloafing and cyberslacking—i.e., employee uses of the Internet that are not job related—occur. This includes using workplace internet for personal use, playing computer games, and browsing social networking sites.[116]

Mitigating more serious risks are also necessary. Consider the following example: "Let's say a manager at a Fortune 500 company posted a disparaging Facebook comment about one of his clients. His boss saw the comment and asked him to remove it, but it was too late. Someone forwarded the comment to the client, and the company lost a huge piece of business and took a serious blow to its reputation. The person who posted the comment also lost his job."[117]

Companies must find the appropriate balance of Internet use for personal and professional reasons, as the Internet (particularly social media) is such an integrated part of the lives of employees and can have many benefits to the company. AUPs are a good start.

Labor and employment practices state that "if a worker is using a computer in a company office, on company time, privacy is what the employer says it is."[118] Without AUPs, Internet use in the workplace remains a guessing game between employer and employee. An employee Internet use policy depends on the company, its corporate culture, and the nature of its business. The policy must have the involvement and endorsement of top-level leadership. Monitoring capability, with employee awareness, must also accompany the policy. "A clear AUP policy effectively removes employee expectations of privacy on the Internet, eliminating potential lawsuits."[119] All use policies should also be spelled out clearly with no ambiguities and with simple, easy, enforceable rules. Part of such a policy involves the security of data for the entire company because the reputation of the system and violations of it involve not only employees but also all stakeholders. A policy on Internet use can help companies by (1) saving employee work time; (2) preserving phone lines and computer disk space for uses that are vital to company business; (3) preventing exposure of sensitive company data stored on computers to outside attack; and (4) preventing the creation of conditions that enable employee harassment.

Guidelines for employers regarding employee privacy include:

- Inform employees not to assume privacy in the workplace.
- Require employees to acknowledge the company's privacy policy in writing.
- Use private information only for legitimate purposes.
- Limit access to private information about employees to only those with a need to know.
- Secure employee medical records separately from other personnel files.
- Obtain signed permission releases and waivers before using an employee's name or photograph in any commercial advertisement, promotional material, or training film.[120]

With the coronavirus causing everyone to practice social distancing, the most popular way people are connecting with each other is through video chat. Since the first U.S. Covid-19-related death was recorded on February 29, 2020, applications and services like Zoom, Google Classroom, and Microsoft

Teams have seen significant spikes in usage. Offices and schools have moved into our basements and living rooms. Meetings are being conducted using online applications wherever and whenever.[121]

Dating in the Workplace

As employees, pre- and perhaps post-Covid-19, spend more time in the workplace, it is not uncommon for attraction and dating to occur. Companies believe that when in a work environment, everyone stays professional, meaning they maintain clear boundaries between employee personal and business interactions. Establishing these boundaries is important to maintain the success of the business. Extra caution is especially necessary when the work relationship involves someone in a supervisor or managerial position or anyone in an authority role. The reasons for this include their status as role models, access to sensitive information, and their ability to affect the employment of individuals in subordinate positions.[122] An annual survey of workplace romance noted that, in 2010, 60 percent of workers claimed to be involved in a workplace romance. This is an issue that affects all employees, not just those engaging in the relationships. For example, the survey also revealed that "53.2 percent of those surveyed say they've known a married co-worker who had an office affair, and 40.4 percent say they're acquainted with a married or committed co-worker who's had a romantic liaison while on a company business trip."[123] A 2013 poll taken by work–life and benefits consultants Workplace Options reported that 84 percent of 18- to 29-year-olds said they'd date a co-worker, versus 36 percent of Gen X-ers (ages 30–45) and only 29 percent of boomers (ages 45–65). Three-quarters of millennials (71%) "see a workplace romance as having positive effects such as improved performance and morale. Also, 40 percent of millennials would engage in a relationship with a boss, versus just 12 percent of older employees."[124] Issues leading to liability and ethical dilemmas can arise whenever problems in the dating relationships occur, especially when one party is more powerful and demands favors from the other. Gossip, accusations, and even sexual harassment complaints can and do occur. The guidelines offered in Figure 7.4 can help protect both employers and employees.

Figure 7.4

Quick Tips for Office Romance

- Find out if the company has a policy on dating; if not, check in with human resources or the legal/professional department.
- Be professional and maintain your dignity.
- Stay away from those in higher and lower positions; power differences add complexity to an already possibly gray area.
- Date someone outside your work/office area if possible.
- Discuss and confront personal issues after working hours and off-site.
- Plan for the worst.
- If relationship-related issues get too complicated, think about leaving.

Source: Adapted from Doyle, A. (2019, December 12). How to handle an office romance: Tips for handling office relationships. *About.com.* http://jobsearch.about.com/od /careerdevelopment/a/office-romance.htm.

Drug Testing and Privacy Rights

During the coronavirus crisis, drug testing has been difficult to administer in many workplaces since there's a labor shortage and the tests are difficult to administer.[125] Privacy is also an issue in drug testing. Advocates for employee drug testing argue that company health costs and the costs associated with sick and lost (nonproductive) days are affected when employees contract serious diseases, such as AIDS, or suffer from drug and alcohol addiction. Also, in certain industries (e.g., airlines or nuclear plant operations) where drug abuse can cost the lives of innocent people, screening drug abusers is viewed as in the public interest. Those who oppose forced employee drug testing argue that the practice violates employees' rights to due process and privacy.

The following guidelines can be used by companies for policy development in drug-testing programs:[126]

1. Tests should be administered only for jobs that have a clear and present potential to cause harm to others.
2. Procedural testing limitations should include previous notice to those being tested.
3. Employees tested should be notified of the results.
4. Employees tested should be informed that they are entitled to appeal the results.
5. The employer should demonstrate how the information will be kept confidential (or destroyed).

Four steps managers can take to develop corporate policy guidelines to prepare for privacy regulation in general are:[127]

1. *Prepare a "privacy impact statement."* An analysis of potential privacy implications should be part of all proposals for new and expanded systems.
2. *Construct a comprehensive privacy plan.* The privacy impact statement provides the input for planning; the plan specifies all that has to be achieved.
3. *Train employees who handle personal information.* Make employees aware of protecting privacy and of the particular policies and procedures that should be followed.
4. *Make privacy part of social responsibility programs.* Keep organizational members informed about company plans regarding privacy issues, with or without regulatory pressures.[128]

Genetic Discrimination

Should employers perform DNA testing on employees when several areas of discrimination could surface? As examples, (1) employment based on a person's predisposition to a disease could negatively and unfairly affect hiring, firing, and benefits; and (2) insurance companies could obtain an employee's genetic information and would also be able to deny a person certain benefits.

Since over 157 million people in the United States receive health care insurance through their employer health plans, genetic testing could help employee health and lower health risks; "an individual's genome is also a catalog of the genetic variants that may raise or lower risk for various diseases." Still, an ethical dilemma remains—namely, if an employee is able to receive a genetic test paid for by the employer and conducted by a third-party genomic testing company that would provide the (*preventive* health care) results as a benefit to employees, would that be acceptable? The question is whether or not those (possibly negative) results could affect the employee's employment with that company should the results be known.[129]

The Right to Know, and Workplace Health and Safety

Every employee is entitled to a safe, healthy workplace environment, because 1 in 10 employees in private industry suffers from an industrial accident or disease while working. Information about unsafe, hazardous workplace conditions and some form of protection from these hazards are needed.[130] Employees have a right to know the nature and extent of hazardous risks to which they are exposed, and to be informed and trained about and protected from those risks. Right-to-know laws have been passed in 20 states since the mid-1980s.[131] "OSHA covers most private-sector employers and employees in all 50 states, the District of Columbia, and other U.S. jurisdiction either directly through federal OSHA or through an OSHA-approved state plan."[132]

OSHA is the federal agency responsible for researching, identifying, and determining workplace health hazards; setting safety and health standards; and enforcing the standards. These remain major tasks. Critics of OSHA claim they are too overwhelming for one agency to monitor and execute effectively. The missions and budgets of government regulatory agencies—including OSHA—are also a function of the politics of the governing administration and Congress.

Covid-19 presented serious challenges to workplace safety and health—life and death for employees across industries. OSHA in collaboration with the CDC offered guidance to inform employers and workers in most workplace settings "outside of healthcare to help them identify risks of being exposed to and/or contracting COVID-19 at work and to help them determine appropriate control measures to implement."[133] Recommended guidelines and mandatory safety and health standards are offered to help employees and employers work safely and in health.

The Right to Organize and Form Unions

Workers have a right to organize, just as owners and managers do. Individuals, as workers and citizens, have the right of free association to seek common ends. This also means employees have a right to form unions. Although unions have a right to exist, they have no special rights beyond those due organizations with legal status.[134]

Plant Closings and Employee Rights

Companies have the right to relocate and transfer operations to any place they choose. If firms can find cheaper labor and raw materials, lower taxes, no unions, and other business advantages for making a profit elsewhere, they often close plants and move. Companies also close plants because of loss of competitiveness, financial losses, and other legitimate economic reasons. The ethical questions posed to corporate managers regarding plant closings are: What rights do the employees who are affected by the closing have? What responsibilities does the company have toward the affected communities, and even toward the national economy?

Since August 1988, companies with more than 100 employees must by law give 60 days' notice to workers before closing. Employees also have moral rights—to be treated fairly, equally, and with justice—when companies decide to relocate or close. Employees have the right to be compensated for the costs of retraining, transferring, and relocating; they have rights to severance pay and to outplacement and support programs that assist them in finding alternative employment; and they have the right to have their pension, health, and retirement plans honored.[135]

Employees also should be given the right to find a new owner for the plant and to explore the possibility of employee ownership of the plant before it is closed.[136] These rights extend beyond workers and include the welfare of the communities where the plant operates. Plant closings affect jobs, careers, families, and the local tax base, and can even negatively affect the regional and national economies when sizable operations are shut down or moved abroad.

Whatever the motivations for corporate closings or transfer of facilities, the rights of employees and local community groups stand, even though these rights are often negotiated against the utilitarian interests of corporations in specific economic contexts. As mentioned earlier, with globalization and increased pressures on corporate profits, plant closings have become almost commonplace. Responsible employers keep employees informed of planned facility closings.[137]

The Family and Medical Leave Act

The Family and Medical Leave Act (FMLA) was enacted into law in 1993, eight years after it was introduced in Congress by Christopher Dodd, William Clay, and Patricia Schroeder. The final rules were established in 1995. The FMLA entitles eligible employees to a maximum of 12 weeks of unpaid leave per year for the birth or adoption of a child, to care for a spouse or immediate family member with a serious health condition, or when an employee is unable to work because of personal illness. The 12 weeks need not be used consecutively because intermittent leave or reduced work schedules are allowed under the act. To be considered eligible, an employee must have been employed for a continuous 12-month period and for at least 1,250 hours during the year preceding the leave.

Companies that employ at least 50 people within a 75-mile radius are mandated to offer such leave. The employer is required to maintain any preexisting health coverage during the leave. Once the leave is concluded, the employee must be reinstated to the same position or an equivalent job. An equivalent position must have the same pay, benefits, working conditions, authority, and responsibilities.

Employers have the right to request a 30-day advance notice for foreseeable absences and may require employees to present evidence to support medically necessary leave. Employers may request employees to obtain a second medical opinion at the employer's expense. Employers may deny reinstatement of employment to "key employees." Such employees must be among the 10 percent of highest-paid company employees, and their absence must have a serious economic impact on their organization. It is the duty of employers to inform employees of their status as "key employees" when they request a leave.

Major problems with the FMLA, from employees' experience, have been serious illnesses (e.g., *Price v. City of Fort Wayne*); from employers' perspective, rising health care and company costs; and from government's viewpoint, administrative requirements (e.g., *Viereck v. City of Gloucester City*). Employers often unintentionally violate the sometimes confusing and contradictory FMLA.[138] The courts have also tended to rule in favor of employees who have less serious and even minor illnesses. Finally, based on a seven-year study of more than 7,500 adults, it was found that the burden of not having a national or state-by-state family paid leave policy falls heaviest on the middle class and the working poor. About 24 percent of Americans workers, which is 33.6 million people, do not have paid sick leave; 92 percent of those who are in the top quarter of earnings (with an hourly wage greater than $32.21) have some form of paid sick leave; 51 percent of the lowest quarter (paid $13.80 or less an hour) and 31 percent earning $10.80 or less an hour have paid sick leave. During the Covid-19 pandemic, some employers are trying to help their workers by offering temporary sick leave or requiring them to work remotely.[139] The Department of Labor's survey titled *Family and Medical Leave Act in 2012: Final Report* shows that FMLA "continues to make a positive impact on the lives of workers without imposing an undue burden upon employers, and employers and employees alike find it relatively easy to comply with the law."[140]

The COVID-19 crisis caused the Department of Labor to signal employees, and to those "caring for ill family members, check with the Department of Labor (DOL) for information on whether such leave is covered under the Family and Medical Leave Act (FMLA). Under the FMLA, covered employers must provide employees job-protected, unpaid leave for specified family and medical reasons. Employees on FMLA leave are entitled to the continuation of group health insurance coverage under the same terms as existed before they took FMLA leave."[141]

■ 7.4 Discrimination, Equal Employment Opportunity, and Affirmative Action

It is difficult to imagine that throughout most of the nineteenth century, women in America could not vote, serve on juries, issue lawsuits in their own name, or initiate legal contracts if they lost their property to their husbands.

In an 1873 Supreme Court decision, *Bradwell v. Illinois,* a woman had "no legal existence, separate from her husband, who was regarded as her head and representative in the social state."[142]

It is also difficult to imagine the legal status of Black people in the United States in 1857. In the Dred Scott case, one of the opinions of the Supreme Court considered Blacks as "beings of an inferior order . . . and so far inferior that they had no rights that the white man was bound to respect."[143]

As stated earlier, the following momentous events and movements in the United States have awakened again discrimination and racist practices in American institutions and businesses: the crisis of George Floyd's murder, the Black Lives and MeToo movements, the attack on the U.S. Capitol, and voter suppression legislation. Black individuals are more likely to be stopped and arrested by police than whites. Income disparities between whites and minorities continue to rise. Median wage differences among Black, white, and Hispanic men, women, and families persist. It is against this background that the doctrines, laws, and policies of discrimination, equal opportunity, and affirmative action must be considered. Corporations are, as noted earlier in the text, again reviewing existing policies and procedures to address discrimination, equity, and inclusion issues and opportunities to create a more socially just workplace.

Discrimination

Discriminatory practices in employer–employee relationships include unequal or disparate treatment of individuals and groups.[144] Unequal or preferential treatment is based on irrelevant criteria, such as gender, race, color, religion, national origin, or disability. Systematic and systemic discrimination is based on historical and institutionally ingrained unequal and disparate treatment against minorities, the disadvantaged, and women.

Examples of contemporary and systemic discrimination in employer–employee relationships are found in practices such as recruitment, screening, promotion, termination, conditions of employment, and discharge.[145] These practices are attributed to closed employment systems and practices resulting from seniority systems, "old boy networks," and arbitrary job classifications. Recruiting procedures that are biased toward certain groups and that do not openly advertise to minority groups are discriminatory. Screening practices that exclude certain groups and that use biased tests or qualifications are discriminatory. Promotion procedures that have "glass ceilings" (i.e., invisible discriminatory barriers to advancement) for women and minority groups are discriminatory.[146] Seniority tracks that favor white males or other groups over minorities or women are discriminatory. Terminating employees on the basis of sex, age, race, or national origin is discriminatory.

Equal Employment Opportunity and the Civil Rights Act

Title VII of the Civil Rights Act of 1964 makes discrimination on the basis of gender, race, color, religion, or national origin in any term, condition, or privilege of employment illegal. The law prohibits discrimination in hiring, classifying, referring, assigning, promoting, training, retraining, conducting apprenticeships, firing, and dispensing wages and fringe benefits. The Civil Rights Act also created the Equal Employment Opportunity Commission as the administrative and implementation agency to investigate complaints that individuals submit. The EEOC negotiates and works with the Department of Justice regarding complaints; however, the EEOC cannot enforce the law except through grievances. The 2021 updates on EEOC laws are found at https://www.eeoc.gov/.

The Civil Rights Act of 1991 extended, for the first time, punitive damages to victims of employment discrimination. This law states that job bias on the basis of gender, disability, religion, or national origin will be punished as severely as job discrimination based on race. It also makes it easier for job-bias plaintiffs to win lawsuits. This legislation shifts the legal burden of proof to the employer, who must defend any intentional or unintentional employment bias, especially if the practice in question has a "disparate impact" on minorities or women. Under this law, the employer must demonstrate that the alleged discriminatory act is "job-related for the position in question and consistent with business necessity."[147] "Job-related" and "business necessity" are undefined and are determined by the courts. The act specifies that employers with more than 500 employees could be liable for up to $300,000 in compensatory and punitive damages. Smaller companies are liable for less, depending on the number of workers they employ.

The Equal Employment Opportunity Act of 1972 amended the 1964 act to empower the EEOC to enforce the law by filing grievances from individuals, job applicants, and employees in the courts. All private employers with 15 or more employees fall under the jurisdiction of the revised act, with the exception of bona fide tax-exempt private clubs. All private and public educational institutions and employment agencies are covered by the law. Labor unions (local, national, and international) with 15 or more members are included. Joint labor-management committees that administer apprenticeship, training, and retraining programs are also under this law's jurisdiction.

There were 72,675,charges filed through Title VII in 2019, which resulted in recovery of over $244 million in monetary benefits to workers who had been discriminated against.[148]

Age and Discrimination in the Workplace

The Age Discrimination in Employment Act (ADEA) of 1967, revised in 1978, prohibits employers from discriminating against individuals based on their age (between ages 40 and 70) in hiring, promotions, terminations, and other employment practices. In 1987, ADEA again was amended when Congress banned any fixed retirement age. The EEOC also issued a final rule in 2001 that aimed at prohibiting contracts requiring terminated employees to give back severance benefits if they challenged their terminations under the ADEA. "The new regulation takes effect at a time when several large corporations have announced significant layoffs. In recent years, companies have increasingly tried to tie severance deals during mass terminations to waivers of ADEA rights, as many employees who lose their jobs in such actions are over age 40 and covered by the statute."[149]

A 2019 ageism study conducted by Hiscox found that 21 percent of U.S. workers aged 40 or older said they had experienced age discrimination—age 51 being the most common; only 40 percent of those discriminated against, reported it. Age discrimination also applies to younger individuals. Hanigan Consulting Group of New York surveyed 170 recent graduates, some scheduled to receive master's and doctoral degrees. The firm found that some applicants were asked questions that clearly violated anti-discrimination laws, such as: Do you intend to get married and have children? What will your boyfriend think of you working long hours? How old are you? Are you married? The basic guideline, according to a Boston attorney with Seyfarth Shaw, is "if the question is not business–related and there is no legitimate business reason for asking it, then do not ask it."[150]

Comparable Worth and Equal Pay

The Equal Pay Act of 1963, amended in 1972, prohibits discriminatory payment of wages and overtime pay based on gender. The law, in large part, is based on the doctrine of "comparable worth." This doctrine and the Equal Pay Act hold that women should be paid wages comparable to men who hold jobs that require equal skill, effort, and responsibility and that have the same working conditions. This law addresses this inequity and also applies to executive, professional, sales, and administrative positions. Although women have made substantial professional progress over the past 30 years, those gains now seem to have lost momentum and even stalled. Women in the United States in 2021 earn 82 cents to the dollar paid to men for comparable work.[151] Key indicators such as pay, board seats, and corporate-officer posts all reflect a leveling off or drop in recent years. Although the gap between men's and women's pay narrowed significantly through the 1980s, gains since then have been partly erased by a drop every few years.

Covid-19 further exacerbated discriminatory practices against women's careers and pay. In the workforce. "Thirty-four million women work in jobs officially classified as essential; and women represent the majority of workers in several occupations, including health care, education, personal care and sales and office occupations."[152] And even though women have served essentials roles in the U.S. economy during the COVID-19 pandemic, they continue to be discriminated against in pay, promotions, and other benefits men receive.

Affirmative Action

Affirmative action programs are a proactive attempt to recruit applicants from minority groups to create opportunities for those who otherwise, because of past and present discriminatory employment practices, would be excluded from the job market. Affirmative action programs attempt to make employment practices blind to color, gender, national origin, disability, and age. Although the doctrine of equal opportunity states that everyone should have an equal chance at obtaining a job and a promotion, affirmative action goes further. For example, Richard DeGeorge stated, "Affirmative action implies a set of specific result-oriented procedures designed to achieve equal employment opportunity at a pace beyond that which would occur normally."[153]

Affirmative action programs were designed to set goals, quotas, and time-frames for companies to hire and promote women and minorities in proportion to their numbers in the labor force and in the same or similar occupational categories within the company. Courts have both supported and eroded affirmative action approaches in the Civil Rights Act. Because of the changing social, political, and demographic landscape in the United States, different membership on the Supreme Court, and evidence of reverse discrimination (discussed below), changes in affirmative action law are occurring. Affirmative action remains a controversial topic and policy. Individuals' rights are violated when affirmative action programs seek to protect particular groups. Also, in a market economy where individual achievement based on merit is encouraged and rewarded, it seems unfair that arbitrary quotas should supersede those who do excel. On the other side of the controversy are advocates of affirmative action who claim that the playing field still is not level in U.S. corporate, educational, and other institutions whose officers select, hire, reward, and promote based on race, gender, national origin, ability, and other biases.

Four arguments have been offered to explain and summarize affirmative action as it applies to hiring, promotions, and terminations:

1. Affirmative action does not justify hiring unqualified minority group members over qualified white males. All individuals must be qualified for the positions in question.
2. Qualified women and minority members can be given preference morally, on the basis of gender or race, over equally qualified white males to achieve affirmative action goals.
3. Qualified women and minority members can be given preference morally over better-qualified white males, also to achieve affirmative action goals.
4. Companies must make adequate progress toward achieving affirmative action goals, even though preferential hiring is not mandatory.[154]
   Updates on affirmative action laws and mandates can be found at https://www.dol.gov/agencies/ofccp/faqs/AAFAQs.

Ethics and Affirmative Action

The ethical principles behind affirmative action are often debated. Affirmative action as a doctrine is derived from several ethical principles that serve as the basis for laws.

First, the *principle of justice* can be used to argue for affirmative action, by claiming that because white males have historically dominated and continue to unfairly dominate the highest-paying, most prestigious employment positions in society, members of groups who have been excluded from comparable employment opportunities because of past and present discriminatory practices deserve to be compensated through affirmative action programs embodied in equal opportunity laws. Opponents of affirmative action argue that it is unfair and unjust that the distribution of benefits be based only on a few categories (race, sex, ethnicity) rather than on achievement or other criteria.

Second, a *utilitarian principle* can be used to support affirmative action by claiming that such programs help the majority of people in a society. Opponents argue that affirmative action cannot be shown or proven to work and suggest that its benefits do not exceed its costs.

Finally, using a *rights principle*, proponents of affirmative action can argue that protected groups have a right to different treatment because these groups have not had equal or fair access to benefits as other groups have. In fact, the rights of minorities, women, and other underprivileged groups have been denied and violated regarding access to education, jobs, and other institutional opportunities. Opponents using the rights principle argue that the rights of all individuals are equal under the law. The controversy continues as the economic, social, political, and demographic environments change.

Reverse Discrimination: Arguments against Affirmative Action

Arguments against affirmative action are directed toward the doctrine itself and against its implementation of quotas. The doctrine has been criticized on the grounds that nondiscrimination requires discrimination (that is, reverse discrimination). Reverse discrimination is alleged to occur when an equally qualified woman or member of a minority group is given preference over a white male for a job or when less-qualified members of an ethnic minority are given hiring preference over white males through a quota system. Affirmative action, opponents argue, discriminates against gender and race—that is, white males. Some even say affirmative action discriminates against age: namely, white, middle-aged males.

Another major argument against affirmative action says that individuals are held responsible for injustices for which they were not and are not responsible. Why should all contemporary and future white males, as a group, have to compensate for discriminatory practices others in this demographic category once committed or now commit?

Although these claims have some validity, proponents of affirmative action argue that injustices from discrimination have been institutionalized against minority groups. It happens that white males continue to benefit from the competitive disadvantages that past and present discriminatory practices have created for others. To compensate and correct for these systemic disadvantages based on race, gender, and other irrelevant (i.e., not related to employment) characteristics, social affirmative action goals and programs must be implemented. Still, the law is not a perfect means to correct past or present injustices. People of all races will continue to be hurt by discrimination and reverse discrimination practices. In the meantime, the court system will continue to use civil rights laws, affirmative action guidelines, and moral reasoning to decide, on a case-by-case basis, the justice and fairness of employment practices.

In June 2002, the Supreme Court upheld the equal protection clause of the Fourteenth Amendment, which guarantees equal treatment under the law, by condoning the University of Michigan Law School's practice of using race to help integrate the institution's student body. The second Supreme Court opinion ruled that the admissions program in the university's undergraduate school violated the equal protection clause of the Constitution by giving minorities a bonus of 20 points in a 150-point system for race. "Two white students have sued the university claiming they were denied admission in favor of less-qualified minorities before the Supreme Court ruled. They want a federal judge to award damages to 30,000 white and Asian students who may have been illegally denied admission to make way for other minority students." A related 2021 U.S. Justice Department ruling found that Yale University's admissions policies had not violated Asian-American rights. "A multiyear investigation, the Justice Department said, found that white and Asian-American applicants were one-eighth to one-fourth as likely to be admitted as African American applicants with the same academic credentials." This finding is likely to be challenged going forward.[155]

Ethical Insight 7.3

The Pros and Cons of Affirmative Action

Affirmative action encompasses policies and procedures designed to make education and employment opportunities available to minority men and women of all races. It was created to address inequalities of present and past historical and institutional discrimination that prevent persons of different races from accessing education and employment in schools, universities, police and fire departments, and other public offices, as well as jobs in the private sector.

Affirmative Action

Opponents	Advocates
1. Perpetuates reverse discrimination.	1. Helps "level the playing field" by providing access to education and jobs that minorities and less advantaged groups would not otherwise be able to obtain.
2. Promotes the less qualified over the more qualified, instead of opening doors to the historically underrepresented.	
3. Perpetuates repressed groups continuing to be underprivileged for their benefit.	2. Integrates otherwise closed institutions and corporations with individuals from diverse groups more reflective of the general population.
4. Disadvantages mainstream groups for injustices they did not cause and with which they do not agree.	3. Is the "right thing to do." Three centuries of discrimination requires compensatory justice.

Questions

1. Which side of the arguments do you accept as most reasonable and realistic? Explain.
2. Why does the "Opponents" reasoning have validity?
3. Why does the "Advocates" reasoning have validity?
4. Does a level playing field exist in the society in which you live? Explain.

UCLA law professor Richard H. Sander has argued that racial preferences end up producing fewer black lawyers each year than would be produced by a race-blind system. Sander's opponents disagree with his methods and analysis. The debate over just and unfair affirmative action policies and procedures, especially in university admittance policies, continues to evolve. The Supreme Court on June 14, 2021, postponed a decision that challenged Harvard's use of racial affirmative action, "likely putting off for several months a case that could end nationwide practices that have boosted the admission of Black and Latino students for decades."[156]

7.5 Sexual Harassment in the Workplace

The MeToo Movement has reawakened the ongoing abuses of workplace sexual harassment. Sexual harassment was not a specific violation of federal law before 1981. It now may be difficult to imagine flagrant acts of sexual violation against women, but as recently as 20 years ago, when women worked in mines, they, like their male counterparts, were stripped and soaked in axle grease in a primitive hazing ritual, and then, unlike the male employees, the women were tied to wooden supports in spread-eagle positions.[157] The list of sexual harassment cases in all sectors of the public and private sectors of government and business has a long history, past and present. Sexual harassment remains among the most prominent civil rights issues in the workplace.

Some of the largest and most publicly visible cases include Supreme Justice Clarence Thomas's accusation by Anita Hill, his former colleague and a law professor, of using inappropriate language and sexually harassing her and female colleagues in their workplace. Hill's claims were not a lawsuit, and Thomas denied all allegations. Thomas's U.S. Senate nomination to the Court in 1991, when the allegations were made, was barely approved by a vote of 52–48. No legal suit was filed, and the allegations were neither proved or disproved. Another case was made by Paula Jones who was a state employee when former president Bill Clinton was governor of Arkansas. Jones alleged that Clinton exposed himself and asked her for oral sex in a hotel room. Clinton denied the allegations. Jones's 1998 lawsuit was dismissed since she didn't state a legal claim. A settlement was reached when Jones dropped her suit against him in exchange for $850,000. No admission of guilt or an apology was made. (Clinton had four other sexual harassment lawsuits brought against him.) A 1998 suit against Mitsubishi Motors by female plant workers at the company's Normal, Illinois, plant resulted in a $34 million settlement. The company then adopted a "zero tolerance" policy for sexual harassment. More recently, in 2020, discrimination and harassment allegations were brought against major companies like Amazon, McDonald's, and Pinterest.[158]

A meta-analysis on sexual harassment showed an organization's climate was a factor in sexual harassment incidences. Also, victims experienced post-traumatic stress disorder, loss of work, decreased organizational commitment, poor job satisfaction, and problems with physical and mental health. "Since 2000, 99 percent of Fortune 500 companies have paid settlements in at least one discrimination or sexual harassment lawsuit . . . that's not including the cases without a public record or incidents victims didn't report. . . . In 2019, the Equal Employment Opportunity Commission received more than 7,500 sexual harassment complaints, and 72,000 complaints about racial, sex, age, religious and other types of discrimination."[159]

What Is Sexual Harassment?

The Supreme Court ruled in 1986 that sexual harassment is illegal under Title VII of the 1964 Civil Rights Act and that when a "hostile environment" is created through sexual harassment in the workplace, thereby interfering with an employee's performance, the law is violated, regardless of whether economic harm is done or whether demands for sexual favors in exchange for raises, promotions, bonuses, and other employment-related opportunities are granted.[160]

Under Title VII, the EEOC guidelines (1980) define sexual harassment as follows:

> Unwelcome sexual advances, requests for sexual favors, and other verbal or physical conduct of a sexual nature constitute sexual harassment when (1) submission to such conduct is made either explicitly or implicitly a term or condition of an individual's employment, (2) submission to or rejection of such conduct by an individual is used as the basis for employment decisions affecting such an individual, or (3) such conduct has the purpose or effect of unreasonably interfering with an individual's work performance or creating an intimidating, hostile, or offensive working environment.

The courts have defined sexual harassment as conduct ranging from blatant grabbing and touching to more subtle hints and suggestions about sex. Forms of sexual harassment include the following:[161]

- Unwelcome sexual advances.
- Coercion.
- Favoritism.
- Indirect harassment.
- Physical conduct.
- Visual harassment. For example, courts have ruled that sexual harassment was committed when graffiti was written on men's bathroom walls about a female employee and when pornographic pictures were displayed in the workplace.

Sexual harassment continues to be reported across industries, including outstanding companies such as Walmart. Moreover, in 2018, men's sexual harassment charges in the workplace were reported at 13 percent across the United States.[162] Diversity training programs are now offered in many larger reputable U.S. firms.

More women are speaking out under the protection of Title VII of the amended Civil Rights Act and because of the support of a successful movement called "MeToo." Initially, the group was founded in 2006 to help survivors of sexual violence find pathways to healing; then it gained much national attention because of the viral #metoo hashtag that sparked sexual harassment conversations and elevated them to a new level. Along with helping victims heal from past experiences, women use their voices to "disrupt the systems that allow for the global proliferation of sexual violence."[163] They emphasize perpetrators being held accountable for their wrongdoings and want authorities to implement strategies to prevent any of these wrongdoings happening again in the future.

The MeToo movement has been a force for change in the United States and has greatly impacted the international world as well.[164] The 2019 International Labour Organization (ILO) Convention on Violence and Harassment at Work agreed to make major changes to resolve harassment issues in the workplace. "These include the adoption of national laws prohibiting workplace violence and taking preventive measures, as well as requiring employers to have workplace policies on violence. The treaty also obligates governments to provide access to remedies through complaint mechanisms, victim services, and to provide measures to protect victims and whistle-blowers from retaliation." When the ILO initially passed these changes in 2019, 10 countries were on board with implementing these changes: Argentina, Belgium, France, Iceland, Ireland, Namibia, Philippines, South Africa, Uganda, and Uruguay.[165] With support from many citizens and public pressure, more countries are expected to follow suit. It is also predicted that countries will partake in national reform even in countries that do not ratify the treaty.

POINT/COUNTERPOINT

Instructions: Each student individually will adopt *either* the Point or Counter-Point argument and justify their reasons (with arguments using this case and other evidence/opinions). Then, either in teams or designated arrangements, students share their reasons. Afterward, the class is debriefed and there is further discussion.

POINT: The MeToo movement was/is successful in the United States and other countries. Courts, police, and other public and private agencies and institutions have acted on sexual discrimination cases and lawsuits and delivered justice to victims.

COUNTERPOINT: While the MeToo movement has achieved part of its purpose, it also has backlashes that have harmed/destroyed (many innocent men's) reputations, careers, and lives; it has also weakened and strained many women's ability to obtain and keep gainful employment, and develop potential workplace relationships. Unfortunately, it also introduces the risk to women of retaliatory actions from suitors.

Who Is Liable?

The EEOC guidelines place absolute liability on employers for actions and violations of the law by their managers and supervisors, whether or not the conduct was known, authorized, or forbidden by the employer. Employers also are liable for coworkers' conduct if the employer knew, or should have known, of the actions in question, unless the employer shows, after learning of the problem, that the company took immediate and appropriate action to correct the situation. Employers may be liable for harassment of nonemployees under the same conditions as those stated for coworkers.[166]

Moreover, under EEOC guidelines, employers are responsible for establishing programs (and standards) that develop, train, and inform employees about sanctions and procedures for dealing with sexual harassment complaints (see Figure 7.5). It is in the employer's economic and moral interest to institute such programs because courts mitigate damages against companies that have harassment prevention and training programs. Some of the leaders in

Figure 7.5

Sample Corporate Sexual Harassment Policy

1. Sexual harassment is a violation of the corporation's EEO policy. Abuse of anyone through sexist slurs or other objectionable conduct is offensive behavior.
2. Management must ensure that a credible program exists for handling sexual harassment problems. If complaints are filed, they should receive prompt consideration without fear of negative consequences.
3. When a supervisor is made aware of an allegation of sexual harassment, the following guidelines should be considered:
   a. Obtain information about the allegation through discussion with the complainant. Ask for and document facts about what was said, what was done, when and where it occurred, and what the complainant believes was the inappropriate behavior. In addition, find out if any other individuals observed the incident, or similar incidents, to the complainant's knowledge. This is an initial step. In no case does the supervisor handle the complaint process alone.
   b. If the complaint is from an hourly employee, a request for union representation at any point must be handled as described in the labor agreement.
   c. The immediate supervisor or the department head and the personnel department must be notified immediately. When a complaint is raised by, or concerns, an hourly employee, the local labor relations representative is to be advised. When a complaint is raised by or concerns a salaried employee, the personnel director is to be advised.
4. The personnel department must conduct a complete investigation of the complaint for hourly and salaried employees. The investigation is to be handled in a professional and confidential manner.

Source: Based on the General Motors corporate policy on sexual harassment.

establishing sexual harassment policies and programs are NYNEX, AT&T, DuPont, Corning, and Honeywell, to mention only a few.

Tangible Employment Action and Vicarious Liability

A currently prominent feature of harassment cases is the concept of "tangible employment action," which Supreme Court Justice Anthony Kennedy described as "hiring, firing, failing to promote, reassignment with significantly different responsibilities or a decision causing a significant change in benefits."[167] An employer's defense against claims of harassment has been created in cases in which a hostile environment was evident but no tangible employment action occurred. As explained in the Supreme Court decision (in the case *Burlington Industries v. Ellerth*), Kimberly Ellerth's harasser threatened to take steps against her if she didn't comply with his wishes. Since he never carried out the threat, Ellerth's employment status was not negatively affected. However, her harassment was severe and pervasive, and Burlington was held liable for that instead.[168]

Severe and pervasive harassment that has no tangible employment action characterized another case, *Faragher v. City of Boca Raton*. In this case, it was determined that lifeguard Beth Faragher had been repeatedly harassed by two male supervisors for several years. She complained to other beach supervisors, but to no avail. Attorneys for the city argued that she had not complained to authorities at a high-enough level. This defense laid the foundation for another key concept the Court stressed: "vicarious liability."[169]

Employers, under this concept, could be liable for harassment if it is committed by *anyone* present in the workplace and if it is brought to the attention of *any* manager or supervisor. Employers are liable for harassment by anyone who is present in the workplace (coworkers, customers, vendors), if the employers know or should have known about the harassment. Moreover, employers are liable for harassment by all supervisors, whether the employer knew about the harassment or not. This represents a significant change in sexual harassment liability.

Employer Guidelines with Extended Liability Rulings

Employers should:

- Exercise reasonable care to prevent and correct for any harassment. There should be an anti-harassment policy and a complaint procedure present, made known to every employee, readily available, and used in training. The EEOC enforcement guidelines provide an excellent source of training materials.
- Quickly and effectively address all harassment complaints.[170]

Individual Guidelines

Although sexual harassment often occurs as part of a power issue (i.e., people in more powerful positions exert pressure over people in less powerful posts), a frequent observation is that men and women tend to see sexual harassment differently. This certainly does not justify legally or morally unwelcome sexual advances. It does suggest, however, that employers need to provide adequate education, training, and role-playing between the sexes so that gender differences in perceptions and feelings on what constitutes sexual harassment can be understood. Some practical guidelines that employees (men, in this instance) can use to check their motives and behavior regarding sexual harassment include the following:[171]

- If you are unsure whether you have offended a woman, ask her. If you did offend her, apologize and don't do it again.
- Talk over your behavior with noninvolved women and with men you can trust not to make a mockery of your concerns.
- Ask yourself how you would feel if a man behaved toward your daughter the way you feel you may be behaving toward women.
- Also, ask yourself if you would act this way if the shoe were on the other foot, if the woman were your boss or if she were physically stronger or more powerful than you.
- Most of all, don't interpret a woman's silence as consent. Silence is, at least, a "red light." Through silence, a woman may be trying to send you a signal of discomfort. Be very certain that your comments or behaviors are welcome, and if they are not, stop them.

Sexual Harassment and Foreign Firms in the United States

Two foreign companies operating in the United States have reacted differently to sexual harassment charges; this is a perilous area where the law and societal norms are rapidly changing. These companies' reactions have exposed them to increased liability. One of the firms, Astra, a Swedish pharmaceutical firm, fired its CEO of the U.S. subsidiary and two other top managers. The other company, Mitsubishi, denied all charges, maintained that the EEOC is wrong, and mounted a full-scale public relations campaign to discredit complainers. Both companies lacked one of the most basic requirements consultants recommend: a clear and strongly written policy on sexual harassment.[172]

Companies have the obligation of training and supporting their employees who work and conduct business internationally on harassment and discrimination laws. "When in Rome, do as the Romans do" does not mean do nothing, act immorally, or act from your own intuition as an employee representing your company. As Figure 7.6 illustrates, many countries have specific laws on employment discrimination and sexual harassment. Some are not the same as those in the United States. For example, Venezuela, as of January 1, 1999, has a new employment discrimination statute that prohibits sexual harassment and punishes this crime by a prison term from 3 to 12 months. The offender must also pay the victim twice the amount of economic damage in regard to lack of access to positions, promotions, or job performance that resulted from the sexual harassment.[173]

7.6 Whistle-Blowing versus Organizational Loyalty

The decision to become a whistle-blower frequently requires breaking with the very group that we have viewed as critical to our financial success, if not

Figure 7.6

Survey of Harassment and Its Crimination Law

Jurisdiction	Prohibitions on Employment Discrimination	Prohibitions on Sexual Harassment	Legal Basis
Argentina	Yes	Yes, by judicial ruling	Section 16, Argentine Constitution
Australia	Yes	Yes	Race, Sex, and Disability Acts
Belgium	Yes	Yes	Article 10, Belgian Constitution; Royal Decree of September 19, 1997
Brazil	Yes	No	Article 5, Brazilian Constitution; Section 461, Brazilian Labor Code
Canada	Yes	Yes	Human rights laws of each province
Chile	Yes	Yes	Article 19, Constitution; Article 2, Labor Code
Colombia	Yes	No	Article 53, Constitution; Article 10, Labor Code
Czech Republic	Yes, by judicial decision	No	Decision No. 13/94, Constitutional Court
Egypt	Yes	No, except by extension of Civil Code	Article 40, Constitution
France	No	Yes	Article L 122-46, French Labor Code; Article 27, Law of December 31, 1992
Germany	No	Yes	Section 2, Article 31, Constitution; Disability Act; Employee Protection Act
Hong Kong	Yes	Yes	Sex Discrimination Ordinance; Disability Discrimination Ordinance
Hungary	Yes	No	Article 5, Hungarian Labor Code
Ireland	Yes	Yes	Employment Equality Act
Italy	Yes	Yes, by judicial decision	Law No. 125 of April 10, 1991
Japan	Yes	Yes	Equal Employment Opportunity Act

Figure 7.6 *—continued*

Jurisdiction	Prohibitions on Employment Discrimination	Prohibitions on Sexual Harassment	Legal Basis
Mexico	No	Yes	Section 153, Mexican Penal Code
Netherlands	Yes	Yes	Article 3, Dutch Labor Conditions Act; Article 7, Dutch Civil Code
People's Republic of China	Yes	No	Article 12, Labor Law of the PRC (1995)
Philippines	No	Yes	Republic Act 7877 (1995)
Poland	Yes	No	Articles 32 and 33, Constitution; Labor Code
Republic of South Africa	Yes	No	Act No. 66, South African Labor Reform Act of 1995
Russia	Yes	No	Russian Labor Law of 1995
Singapore	Yes, by age only	No	Retirement Act
Spain	Yes	Yes	Articles 9, 14, and 35, Spanish Constitution; Section 34.3.95 of Spanish Employment Act
Sweden	Yes	Yes	The Act on Equal Opportunities at Work
Switzerland	No	Yes	Article 3, Law on Equal Treatment of Women and Men
Taiwan	No	Yes	Article 83, ROC Social Order Maintenance Act
Thailand	Yes	Yes	Constitution; Labor
Ukraine	Yes	No	Article 42, Labor Code of the Ukraine
United Kingdom	Yes	Yes	Sex, Race, and Disability Discrimination Laws
Venezuela	No	Yes	Law on Violence Against Women and Family

Source: Adapted with permission from Maatman, G., Jr. (2000, September 11). Harassment, discrimination laws go global. *National Underwriter, 104(37),* 3. For a 2020 update of 63 countries' discrimination laws and policies, see DLA Piper. (2021). Employment discrimination. https://www.dlapiperintelligence.com/goingglobal/employment/index.html?t=09-discrimination.

our very survival. The decision entails destabilizing one's life and placing all the essential underpinnings of our financial security—and the security of those who depend on us—at total risk. It is easy to understand that such a decision is accompanied by a good deal of anxiety and stress. "Since the beginning of October [2020], the [Securities and Exchange] Commission has awarded 28 individuals over $176 million in whistle-blower awards, which already surpasses the total dollar amount awarded in the entirety of any prior fiscal year."[174]

Among all the rights discussed in this chapter, one of the most valued by a U.S. citizen is freedom of speech. But how far does this right extend into the corporation, especially if an employee observes an employer committing an illegal or immoral activity that could harm others? What are the obligations and limits of employee loyalty to the employer? Under what, if any, circumstances should employees blow the whistle on their supervisors, managers, or firms?

Whistle-blowing is "the attempt of an employee or former employee of an organization to disclose what he or she believes to be wrongdoing in or by the organization."[175] Whistle-blowing can be internal (reported to an executive in the organization); external (reported to external public interest groups, the media, or enforcement agencies); personal (harm reportedly done only to the whistle-blower); and impersonal (harm observed as done to another).[176] Whistle-blowing goes against strong U.S. cultural norms of showing loyalty toward an employer and colleagues and avoiding the "snitch" label. However, strong cultural norms regarding fairness, justice, a sense of duty, and obedience to the law and to one's conscience also exist. A moral dilemma can occur when a loyal employee observes their employer committing or assisting in an illegal or immoral act and must decide what to do.

Whistle-blowers may not only lose their job but may experience negative and damaging repercussions in their profession, marriage, and family life. Dr. Jeffrey Wigand, head of research at Brown and Williamson Tobacco Company from 1989 to 1993, testified that the company knew and controlled the nicotine levels in its products. His testimony, along with that of others, helped the government initially win a substantial lawsuit against the tobacco industry. As the film *The Insider* accurately documented, Wigand paid an enormous personal price as a witness.[177]

Not all whistle-blowers undergo such traumatic fates as the example offered here. Michael Haley, a federal bank examiner, won $755,533 in back pay, future loss of income, and compensatory damages under the federal whistle-blower statute and another amended federal statute. He had worked as a bank examiner for the Office of Thrift Supervision (OTS), starting in 1977. He inspected OTS-regulated banks, evaluating the soundness of their operations. He was terminated after he reported violations in federal banking laws and regulations regarding a forced merger.[178]

Under what conditions is whistle-blowing morally justified? Richard De-George discusses five conditions:[179]

1. When the firm, through a product or policy, will commit serious and considerable harm to the public (as consumers or bystanders), the employee should report the firm.

2. When the employee identifies a serious threat of harm, they should report it and state their moral concern.
3. When the employee's immediate supervisor does not act, the employee should exhaust the internal procedures and chain of command to the board of directors.
4. The employee must have documented evidence that is convincing to a reasonable, impartial observer that the employee's view of the situation is accurate; and evidence that the firm's practice, product, or policy seriously threatens and puts in danger the public or product user.
5. The employee must have valid reasons to believe that revealing the wrongdoing to the public will result in the changes necessary to remedy the situation. The chance of succeeding must be equal to the risk and danger the employee takes to blow the whistle.

The risks to whistle-blowers can range from outright termination to more subtle pressures, such as strong and hidden criticisms, undesirable and burdensome work assignments, lost perks, and exclusion from communication loops and social invitations.[180] Twenty-one states have laws protecting corporate and governmental whistle-blowers from reprisal, so that after resigning or being fired, whistle-blowers can be reinstated with back pay and compensation for physical suffering. However, experience shows that the government's actual protection to whistle-blowers is weak because of the many subtle forms of retaliation, such as those just listed.

The Whistleblower Program proposed under the Dodd-Frank Wall Street Reform and Consumer Protection Act took effect on August 12, 2011. This program offers monetary awards to eligible whistle-blowers for information provided to the SEC. To be eligible, the tip provided to the SEC must be of high-quality information and must lead to a "Commission enforcement action in which over $1,000,000 in sanctions is ordered. The range for awards is between 10 percent and 30 percent of the money collected." Although this provides incentive for the disclosure of potential fraud to the SEC, it may also have negative repercussions for companies and whistle-blowers. Companies now have greater motivation to prevent whistle-blowing to the SEC, as SEC action may lead to monetary sanctions, loss of reputation, and other damage.[181]

When Whistle-Blowers Should Not Be Protected

The most obvious condition under which whistle-blowers should not be protected is when their accusations are false and their motivation is not justifiable or accurate. The following instances are when whistle-blowers should not have freedom of speech against their employers:

- When divulging information about legal and ethical plans, practices, operations, inventions, and other matters that should remain confidential and that are necessary for the organization to perform its work efficiently.
- When an employee's personal accusations or slurs are irrelevant to questions about policies and practices that appear illegal or irresponsible.

- When an employee's accusations do not show a conviction that wrongdoing is being committed, and when such accusations disrupt or damage the organization's morale.
- When employees complain against a manager's competence to make daily work decisions that are irrelevant to the legality, morality, or responsibility of management actions.
- When employees object to their discharge, transfer, or demotion if management can show that unsatisfactory performance or violation of a code of conduct was the reason for the decision.[182]

Factors to Consider before Blowing the Whistle

Whistle-blowing is a serious action with real consequences. It often involves a decision to be made among conflicting moral, legal, economic, personal, family, and career demands and choices. No single answer may appear. A stakeholder analysis can help the potential whistle-blower identify the groups and individuals, stakes, priorities, and trade-offs when selecting among different strategies and courses of action.

Listed here are 12 factors that a person should consider when deciding whether to blow the whistle on an employer (based on multiple sources):

1. Make sure the situation warrants whistle-blowing. If serious trade secrets or confidential company property will be exposed, know the harm and calculated risks.
2. Examine your motives.
3. Verify and document your information. Can your information stand up in a hearing and in court?
4. Determine the type of wrongdoing and to whom it should be reported. Knowing this will assist in gathering the type of evidence to obtain.
5. State your allegations specifically and appropriately. Obtain and state the type of data that will substantiate your claim.
6. Stay with the facts. This minimizes retaliation and avoids irrelevant mudslinging, name-calling, and stereotyping.
7. Decide whether to report to internal contacts or external contacts. Select the internal channel first if that route has proved effective and less damaging to whistle-blowers. Otherwise, select the appropriate external contacts.
8. Decide whether to be open or anonymous. Should you choose to remain anonymous, document the wrongdoing and anticipate what you will do if your identity is revealed.
9. Decide whether current or alumni whistle-blowing is the best alternative. Should you blow the whistle while you are an employee or resign first? Resigning should not be an automatic option. If the wrongdoing affects others, your decision is not only a personal one, but you are also fulfilling moral obligations beyond your own welfare.
10. Follow proper guidelines in reporting the wrongdoing. Check forms, meeting deadlines, and other technicalities.

11. Consult a lawyer at every step of the way.
12. Anticipate and document retaliation. This assists your effectiveness with courts and regulatory agencies.

Managerial Steps to Prevent External Whistle-Blowing

Managers have a responsibility to listen to and respond to their employees, especially regarding the observations of and reporting of illegal and immoral acts. Chapter 6 discussed mechanisms such as "ethics offices," ombuds programs, and peer-review programs. These are part of a corporation's responsibility to provide due process for employees to report personal grievances, to obtain effective and just resolution of them, and to report the wrongdoings of others, including employers. There are four straightforward and simple steps that management can take to prevent external whistle-blowing:

1. Develop effective internal grievance procedures and processes that employees can use to report wrongdoings.
2. Reward people for using these channels.
3. Appoint senior executives and others whose primary responsibilities are to investigate and report wrongdoing.
4. Assess large fines for illegal actions. Include executives and professionals who file false or illegal reports, who knowingly market dangerous products, or who offer bribes or take kickbacks.

Preventing, reporting, and effectively and fairly correcting illegal and immoral actions, policies, and procedures are the responsibilities of employers and employees. Management cannot expect employees to be loyal to a company that promotes or allows wrongdoing to its stakeholders. Whistle blowing should be a last resort. A more active goal is to hire, train, and promote morally and legally sensitive and responsive managers who communicate with and work for the welfare of all stakeholders.

Chapter Summary

The demographics of the workforce since the beginning of the twenty-first century continue to change. Two decades into the century, Covid-19 is challenging for employers and employees who have managed to survive. Changes include the survival of those who are able to keep a job and their positions in struggling companies and organizations; the health issues, if not death, of employees and employers; the aging of employees; the "shrinking" of the workforce; an increasing number of women and minority entrants; the demand for work–life balance from singles and dual-career families; the gap in educational levels; and a greater demand for the skills of disabled workers. The changes in the composition of the workforce signal changes in work-related values and motivations. The Black Lives Matters and the MeToo movements have been awakenings with regard to racial and gender relations.

Corporations and managers can expect moral tensions to rise regarding other issues as well: age discrimination, health care needs, conflicting communication, generational differences, and requests for more balanced and flexible work schedules. "One size fits all" management techniques do not work.

The social and psychological contract between corporations and employees is also changing. The original employment-at-will doctrine serves as the basis for employment between employer and employee; however, over the years, this doctrine has been complemented by the doctrine of implied employee rights. Most firms, large and small, use a mix of the two doctrines. Two underlying concepts of employee rights are balance and governmental rights. Whether or not and the extent to which the post-Covid-19 workplace will change the social contract between employer and employee will be seen. The evolving hybrid workplace, increase in communication technologies of work, and changing nature of work itself will affect this relationship.

The nature of legal and moral relationships between employers and employees is also changing. Employers rely on federal and state laws to guide their employee policies and procedures. However, many employers implement benefits and policies aimed at motivating and supporting employees' well-being. Work–life resources and insurance coverage for employees' same-sex partners are such examples.

Court decisions have supported and maintained racial affirmative action practices at the university admittance level, with a few exceptions only recently. Although EEOC policies and affirmative action practices remain a part of federal law, some states are showing less acceptance of these laws and procedures. Current and future issues related to sexual harassment and reverse discrimination will continue to shape legal and moral guidelines for corporations. Conflicts regarding due process, privacy, safety, drug testing, sexual harassment, technology monitoring, and other workplace topics will continue to be resolved through court cases and legislation; their resolution will influence corporate policies in the future.

Sexual harassment laws and guidelines for employers and employees and the moral dilemma of organizational loyalty versus personal ethics will always be important issues. The justification for whistle-blowing and guidelines for potential whistle-blowers must be considered by employees, before blowing the whistle, and by corporations, to prevent external whistle-blowing.

Questions

1. Identify two major trends in the changing demographics of the workforce. Include a trend that you as a student or employee could be or are now affected by.
2. Identify moral tensions and/or conflicts that could lead to illegal and/or unethical behavior associated with the changes you gave in question 1.
3. What are three major factors an employer should consider to avoid arbitrarily terminating an employee, especially post-Covid-19? What steps would you take if you were terminated by an employer who arbitrarily fired you now?

4. What problems do you see occurring when employees date in a company? What additions or changes would you make to the tips and suggestions offered on dating in the chapter?

5. Do you believe dating should be permitted among employees in the workplace without formal policies setting boundaries and rules? Why or why not?

6. Do you believe managers and company officers should date lower-level employees with less power and status? Why could this situation present ethical dilemmas?

7. What does the term "legal and moral entitlement" mean to you as an employee or future employee? Give an example. Do you agree that employees have legal and moral entitlements in the workplace? Explain.

8. Do you believe there is now an "equal playing field" regarding access to educational institutions, jobs, and other employment opportunities for all individuals and groups in the United States? Explain. Do you believe women should still be a protected group under Title VII of the Civil Rights Act? Explain. Do you believe minorities of different races in the United States, other than Caucasian, should still be protected? If so, which group(s)? If not, explain why not.

9. What are some arguments for and against "reverse discrimination"? Is the "playing field" in U.S. corporations more level now?

10. Describe criteria used to determine whether verbal or physical actions constitute sexual harassment. What are some specific types of sexual harassment? Have you been sexually harassed in a work setting? Can you describe what happened and the outcome?

11. What should employees expect from their employers and their companies now in terms of rights and obligations, after Covid-19? Explain. Is loyalty to an employer a "dead" or "dying" concept now? Why or why not?

12. Do you believe whistle-blowing is justifiable in corporations? Would, or could, you blow the whistle? Under what circumstances would you be compelled to blow the whistle as an employee in an organization? Offer an example.

13. Should corporate managers prevent whistle-blowing? Why or why not? Explain.

14. How can employers prevent whistle-blowing?

Exercises

1. Argue the pros and cons of eliminating standards such as test scores, grade point averages, and other objective criteria for admitting minorities and members of protected groups to universities and colleges. Do you believe such objective criteria should be eliminated by university and college admissions committees? Explain.

2. Select an employee right in the workplace from the chapter. Give an example, based on your own outside reading or experience, of a situation involving this right. Was it violated? How? What was the outcome? What should the outcome have been? Why?

3. Identify an example from your own experience, or that of someone you know, of discrimination or sexual harassment. Did this experience influence your view of affirmative action or employee protection programs? If so, how?

4. Write a paragraph describing a situation from your experience in which you felt justified that you had cause to blow the whistle. Did you? Why or why not? Under what circumstances do you feel whistle-blowing is justified?

5. Think of three people you know from the different generations discussed in the chapter. Of these people, who is and is not satisfied with their work and jobs? Explain why they are or are not satisfied. Refer back to the generational differences and values in the chapter. To what extent did "generational differences" contribute to your analysis of the individuals' work satisfaction? To what extent did "ethical reasons" affect their work satisfaction? Explain.

6. Create a "for" and "against" set of arguments regarding the "employment-at-will" doctrine in the present economic and demographic environment. After you make a complete set of arguments, which position do you support? Did your views change after this exercise? Why or why not?

What's Going on Here?

Bill Smith and Lana Kane seemed to have had some "bad chemistry" the day they met. Bill, a 23-year-old recent graduate and now working on his MBA, has been with the Marketing Group for a year. He is eager to excel, thrives on instant (especially positive) feedback, and is accustomed to participative, entrepreneurial work relationships. Upper-level management has been impressed with his work and has given him "free rein" on most assignments, since the Marketing Group had been without a director for the past year. Lana, who is 51, has been with the company for nine years and has just been assigned to head up the Marketing Group. Lana is accustomed to a more structured, orderly approach and also takes her seniority seriously. Bill was preparing a presentation on a new, promising product launch for the company's CEO and officers when he found an e-mail from Lana asking to review and approve his presentation before he submits it to Ralph, the CEO.

Lana's e-mail was critical of several of Bill's ideas, and she asked to meet with him. At their one-on-one meeting the following afternoon in Lana's office, they immediately started clashing. Lana politely but straightforwardly read her responses to Bill's e-mail, and Bill couldn't remain silent. He challenged her on every point, refusing to accept her logic. Lana grew tense and finally lashed out at Bill saying, "Can't you be more open to different perspectives? My role is to offer criticism to improve our efforts, not only to always give praise." Bill was frustrated and hurt that Lana couldn't see the same talent in him that upper management saw. "Why is she so stubborn and controlling?" he thought as he folded up the paper with her comments about his presentation. Nervously pondering the situation before leaving her office, he thought, "Maybe I should talk to Ralph about her. If I have to work with this style, I should pack my bags today." At the same time, when Lana looked at Bill's expressions, she thought, "I'm not sure this guy 'gets it.' He's bright but too spoiled, and not tough-skinned enough to take helpful criticism. I wonder if I should talk to human resources about him?"

Questions

1. What are the problems in this situation?
2. What potential "ethical" dilemma or issue could arise from this situation?
3. What perspective(s) in this chapter could help diagnose this evolving issue?
4. What should be done to prevent an issue from erupting into a conflict and between whom?

Case 19

Women on Wall Street: Fighting for Equality in a Male-Dominated Industry

"WASHINGTON—President Biden set off a heated identity politics debate less than 24 hours into his presidency when he signed a gender discrimination order that has drawn heat from critics who accuse him of erasing women's rights. Language in the order would allow transgender women to participate in women's sport leagues. The policy seeks to enforce a Supreme Court ruling from last year that prohibits discrimination on the basis of someone's gender identity and sexual orientation" (Bowden, 2021).

On Wall Street and the financial services industry in particular, it's tough being a women, since the business cultures are known to be male-dominated. "All of the top banks are run by men. A Catalyst study reports that women account for less than 17 percent of senior leaders in investment banking. In private equity, women comprise only 9 percent of senior executives and only 18 percent of total employees, according to a 2017 report by Preqin. At hedge funds and private debt firms, the numbers are similarly low—women hold just 11 percent of leadership roles" (Boorstein, 2018).

The following case documents major issues women have had, and continue to have, getting promoted and earning the same or comparable wages and bonuses as their male counterparts in the financial services industries and Wall Street in particular. It seems that only some class-action lawsuits that succeed and are brought on by the courage, rights, and expert legal help have brought awareness to these issues. Here are some of those lawsuits and the stories underlying them.

Allison Schieffelin and Morgan Stanley

On June 12, 2004, Morgan Stanley agreed to pay $54 million to settle dozens of claims from women who alleged that the securities firm denied them pay increases and promotions because of their gender. The case, filed by the Equal Employment Opportunity Commission (EEOC) on September 10, 2001, resulted from repeated complaints by Allison Schieffelin, a 43-year-old former convertible-bond sales clerk who worked in the firm's institutional-stock division for 14 years. Schieffelin earned more than $1 million a year, making her one of the highest-paid and highest-ranking women on Wall Street to publicly challenge the industry's pay and promotion practices. Schieffelin claims that she was trapped under a glass ceiling and continuously denied promotion to managing director despite being the top performer in her department. The EEOC claims that in addition to being repeatedly denied promotions and pay raises, women employees in Schieffelin's division "endured coarse behavior and lewd comments from their male colleagues and supervisors." Moreover, firm-organized sales outings with clients to golf resorts and strip clubs excluded women.

Of the $54 million settlement, $12 million was paid directly to Schieffelin. About $40 million will be used to settle complaints from an estimated 100 current and former female employees of the institutional-stock division. The remaining $2 million was used to enhance anti-discrimination training at the firm. In addition to the monetary settlement, Morgan Stanley must also fund a program to have an appointed outsider monitor hiring, pay, and promotion practices for a three-year period. Although the settlement seems large, it is merely "pocket change" to a firm like Morgan Stanley; the $54 million represents approximately 2 percent of the $2.45 billion in profits the firm earned in the first half of fiscal year 2004.

Background on *Schieffelin et al. v. Morgan Stanley*

Allison Schieffelin first complained of Morgan Stanley's working environment in a 1995 written review of her boss, stating, "He makes the convertible department and the firm by extension an uncomfortable place for women." During that same year, she also submitted an internal complaint about "unwelcome advances" from one of her male managing directors. At the time, she thought that management would be pleased with the tactful manner in which she handled the issues; however, today she feels management placed her on a "watch list" instead.

In December 1998, after three years of withstanding the men's locker-room-type atmosphere, in which the male employees openly "swapped off-color jokes and tales of sexual exploits and treated their female colleagues as inferior," Schieffelin took her harassment and discrimination complaints beyond the firm's executives to the EEOC. She hoped that the firm would see that she had been a dedicated employee throughout her entire career and that the issues with the firm's pay and promotion practices needed to be amended. Instead, she claims the firm "embarked on a campaign to get me to quit." She was fired in October 2001 for what the firm claims to be misconduct after a heated confrontation with her supervisor; however, both Schieffelin and the EEOC viewed her firing as illegal retaliation for her discrimination complaints. One year after Schieffelin complained, Morgan Stanley's New York convertibles department, the department in which Schieffelin worked, promoted Gay Ebers-Franckowiak to managing director—the first female managing director in that department; many people believe that this was no coincidence.

Morgan Stanley denied all discrimination charges and claimed that their female employees were and are treated equally. The EEOC planned to reveal evidence at the trial proving otherwise. The anticipated evidence indicated that some male employees of the firm ordered breast-shaped birthday cakes and hired strippers to entertain at office parties. The evidence supposedly provided statistics regarding the disparities between female and male promotion and pay within the firm. The trial was scheduled to begin July 12, 2004; however, a settlement was wrapped up mere minutes before opening arguments began. As part of the settlement, payroll statistics that showed whether or not there was a pattern of discrimination were sealed.

An Isolated Occurrence or an Industry-Wide Problem?

The allegations made against Morgan Stanley are not new to the securities industry. Several previous cases, in addition to statistics produced by the Securities Industry Association (SIA), indicate that sex discrimination is a persistent problem on Wall Street.

In April 2004, Merrill Lynch agreed to pay $2.2 million to Hydie Sumner as part of a class-action lawsuit brought by more than 900 women claiming the financial giant had a long history of gender discrimination. Sumner wanted her old job back; she also said that she wanted to be a Merrill Lynch manager in order to make changes at the firm. "I thought, one day, I'll be a manager and I'll have a choice, and I won't manage like him [Stephen McAnally, former manager of the Merrill Lynch San Antonio office]," said Sumner. As of early 2005, Merrill Lynch paid Sumner $1.9 million but was fighting the other $300,000, indicating that this payment would "not be considered until the issues relating to Ms. Sumner's reinstatement at the firm are resolved."

In a more recent lawsuit, Stephanie Villalba, former head of Merrill Lynch's private client business in Europe, sued for $13 million on gender-bias charges. She claimed that her male boss had difficulty accepting her in a senior position and, as a result, she was "bullied, belittled, and undermined." In early 2005, an employment tribunal in the United Kingdom ruled in favor of "Villalba's claim of victimization on certain issues, that included bullying e-mails in connection with a contract, but found no evidence of a 'laddish culture' at the bank." Villalba intends to appeal the ruling.

In February 2004, Susanne Pesterfield, a former broker for Smith Barney, settled her case with the investment firm on the eve of an arbitration hearing. She alleged that during her seven years at the firm she endured a "pattern of sexual harassment and a male-dominated culture that included trips to strip clubs." She described a working environment that was "hostile to women and in which women weren't given the same opportunities to succeed as men were given." She claimed that her male colleagues were better paid and received better leads for potential clients.

Pesterfield's accusations were not new to Smith Barney. A class-action lawsuit brought by female employees in 1996 led to a 1998 settlement in which the firm's parent company, Citigroup, Inc., paid out close to $100 million. The infamous case has been referred to as the "Boom-Boom Room," in reference to the basement "party room" in the Garden City branch of what was then Shearson Lehman Brothers, wherein discrimination and sexual harassment occurred. Among other things, the conversations that took place among the male employees went beyond their accomplishments on the trading floor to include their latest accomplishments in the bedroom. Shearson's manager took a "boys will be boys" approach that encouraged obscene comments and lewd behavior.

In her book, *Tales from the Boom-Boom Room,* Susan Antilla provides a detailed account of the workplace culture at Shearson. According to Antilla, "It was a time when men in branch offices of brokerage firms were encountering significant numbers of female colleagues for the first time. For some of them, it was unsettling." In the late 1990s, many well-educated women entered the financial services industry in hopes of finding great opportunities. Instead, they found an industry that continued to be dominated by white males and an environment that belittled and repressed women.

The acts of alleged sex discrimination abound; nearly 3,000 women filed claims in 1996 and 1997 against Smith Barney and Merrill Lynch. Although most of the women settled, some did not, including Nancy Thomas, Sonia Ingram, Laura Zubulake, Deborah Paulhus, and Neill Sites. Perhaps most notable is the case of Nancy Thomas, a broker at Merrill Lynch for 18 years. Among the numerous allegations of sex discrimination made by Thomas, one is particularly salacious. Thomas alleges that in 1991 "someone left her a package in the mailroom with a dildo, lubricating cream, and an obscene poem." An arbitration hearing was held in New York on September 13, 2004; arbitrators scheduled an additional 18 hearing sessions through July 2005. Merrill Lynch maintained that none of the testimony given as of late November 2004 "support[ed] even one of Thomas's allegations."

Wall Street's Glass Ceiling—the Numbers Tell the Story

The *2003 Report on Diversity Strategy, Development, and Demographics* produced by the SIA presents data suggesting there has been little improvement in the advancement of women in the securities industry in recent years, and that biased pay and promotion practices are not just outdated. Even though Wall Street firms seem to be making attempts to improve the workplace environment for women, statistics prove that a strong glass ceiling still exists. There was a gradual decrease in the percentage of women in the industry between the years 1999 and 2003 (43 percent and 37 percent, respectively), and management positions in 2001 and 2003 continued to be dominated by white males. In 2003, white males held 85 percent of (branch) office manager positions, 76 percent of the managing director positions, and 79 percent of the executive management positions. This compares to 85 percent, 81 percent, and 75 percent for the three position categories in 2001. The same is true for line positions such as brokers (80 percent in 2001 versus 78 percent in 2003), investment bankers (77 percent versus 71 percent), and traders (71 percent versus 74 percent). On the other hand, "white women and men and women of color continue to comprise the majority (89 percent) of the staff and junior level positions."

These numbers become even more disturbing when one considers that women are not new to the profession. In 1974, women held 33.8 percent of all securities industry jobs, with 6.5 percent being management positions. Muriel F. Siebert, chair of Muriel Siebert & Co. and the first woman with her own seat on the New York Stock Exchange, has worked on Wall Street since the 1950s. She claims that highly educated and successful women are consistently "dropping out" of the industry and changing careers because they feel they have no chance of reaching top management positions.

Catalyst, a nonprofit research organization working to advance women in business, conducted a study of female professionals in the securities industry. Published in 2001 as *Women in Financial Services: The Word on the Street,* the results indicated the top-three barriers to women's advancement were lack of mentoring opportunities, commitment to personal and family responsibilities, and exclusion from informal networks of communication. The survey also highlighted the differences in the viewpoints of male and female professionals with respect to the advancement of women. While 65 percent of women believed they had to work harder than men to get the same rewards, only 13 percent of men believed this to be true; 51 percent of women felt they were paid less than men for doing the same work, while only 8 percent of men agreed with this statement. In addition, 50 percent of men believed that women's opportunities to advance to senior leadership in their firms had increased greatly over the preceding five years, but only 18 percent of women agreed. Many of the women who file complaints, as well as their lawyers, maintain that the perceptual divide between genders is a serious issue. They argue that the men in charge at Wall Street firms do not recognize the existence of a problem, and therefore they fail to look at the statistics and to see the "big picture."

Mandatory Arbitration and Coercion Prevent Statistics from Appearing in Court

In 1986, the Supreme Court ruled that sexual harassment is illegal under Title VII of the 1964 Civil Rights Act. However, recent statistics and settlements in gender discrimination suits suggest that the glass ceiling, at least within the securities and investment banking businesses, still exists. What makes Wall Street such a laggard when it comes to the treatment and advancement of women? One factor could be that before 1999, any employee of a Wall Street firm was required to resolve all disputes in a "closed-door negotiation process" rather than in a public hearing. As the rest of corporate America was hit with discrimination lawsuits in the 1980s and 1990s, the problems occurring on Wall Street remained, for the most part, behind closed doors. After the Boom-Boom Room case and the Merrill Lynch suit in the late 1990s, the Securities and Exchange Commission removed the mandatory arbitration requirement for Wall Street employees who had civil rights claims. As a result, "the National Association of Securities Dealers and the New York Stock Exchange changed their arbitration rules in a way that permitted employees to sue under federal discrimination statutes in federal court."

Why Should the Securities Industry Make Changes?

Sex discrimination lawsuits have been costly, in terms of money and negative publicity, for securities firms. Avoiding such costs in the future is a strong motivation for change, but not the only one. Another powerful reason is the increasingly influential role of women in business. In 1998, women owned close to 8 million U.S. businesses, which was one-third of the total, and "more than 40 percent of households with assets of $600,000 or more [were] headed by women." In 2004,

10.6 million firms were at least 50 percent female-owned; 48 percent of all privately held firms were at least 50 percent female-owned.

Moreover, as more working women approach retirement age and younger women rise in the ranks, securities firms desire to increase their female clientele. As a result, there is an increasing demand for female brokers to serve the needs of this "new" client base. Women investors tend to prefer doing business with a friendly, trustworthy adviser rather than just a person with financial expertise, and thus they aim to establish a personal relationship with their brokers/advisers. To serve an increasingly diverse client base, investment firms must recognize that they will need a diverse group of employees who recognize and react appropriately to the needs of their clients.

In 2013, one of the United States' largest privately held life insurers, New York Life, announced plans to hire up to 3,700 new agents with at least half being women or individuals representing (in the company's own words) "cultural markets," under which it includes individuals "serving the African American, Chinese, Hispanic, Korean, South Asian, and Vietnamese markets." This will be in addition to the 62 percent of new hires last year in those categories. Like publicly traded insurer Allstate, whose staff is made up predominantly by women (58.9 percent), New York Life understands that having a staff that is gender and racially diverse is going to give it a better chance to grow its business.

Who Wins, Who Loses?

Richard Berman, the judge in *Schieffelin et al. v. Morgan Stanley*, described the $54 million settlement as a "watershed event in protecting the rights of women on Wall Street." Many others, including Elizabeth Grossman, an EEOC lawyer on the case, hope that the settlement will act as a revelation for not only Morgan Stanley but other Wall Street firms as well. The settlement may cause other firms within the securities and investment banking industry to reevaluate their pay and promotion practices. Additional complaints may also surface because of the settlement.

Although some people view the settlement in a positive light, others see a negative side. As part of the settlement, claimants agreed not to disclose any of the statistics and facts that would have been presented in the case. Although the women who will share the $54 million settlement scored a big win, some people believe that Morgan Stanley and other securities firms "scored an even bigger win" by preventing embarrassing statistics from being revealed in the courtroom and to the public.

The securities and investment banking firms seem to have a "what the public doesn't know, won't hurt them" attitude. Unless the compensation and promotion statistics of those firms are exposed to the public, Wall Street businesses will continue operating within its current culture. In "Money Talks, Women Don't," an article about the Morgan Stanley settlement, Susan Antilla stated, "Ingrained cultural misconduct changes only when customers, colleagues, and the public get wind of the nasty facts and companies are embarrassed. Those who can afford to keep their problems quiet may never have to change."

Today on Wall Street

While some aspects of work on Wall Street have improved for women, changing the culture of an entire industry cannot happen overnight, especially if firms are reluctant to admit that a problem exists. Antilla suggests that there has been reluctance to address the discrimination and harassment issues even after they were revealed in the Boom-Boom Room and Merrill Lynch lawsuits of the late 1990s: "When it came to acknowledging that there was still a problem to work on—violators to stop and biases to correct—Wall Street had become a little like the dysfunctional family hiding the crazy uncle in the attic. Everyone knew sexual harassment was there and indeed had put much energy into urgently and quietly negotiating the crises that resulted from it. But hardly anyone spoke openly about the problem—called the doctor, if you will—and started the real work of making things better."

A 2021 *Wall Street Journal* article regarding Pimco, a major investment firm, illustrates a continuing pattern shown in this case: "Letter to Pimco Execs Alleges Discrimination toward Women Employees." It often seems that the more things change, the more they stay the same:

> Current and former employees of Pacific Investment Management Co. wrote to the investment firm's senior executives alleging a pattern of abusive and discriminatory behavior toward women and urging them to take steps to fix gaps in pay and promotions.

> The letter, which was signed by 21 women, was sent Thursday to Pimco's top leaders, including its chief executive, Emmanuel Roman, and the firm's investment chief, Dan Ivascyn. Three of the women who cosigned the document have filed lawsuits against Pimco in the past two years, alleging gender or racial discrimination. Pimco is fighting the lawsuits.

Today, firms are more likely to have diversity programs and sexual harassment training. Many companies have altered their recruiting processes, and several have established partnerships with support organizations that promote equal opportunities in professions for women and minorities. Some companies are working at changing the "tone at the top" by promoting women to top positions and challenging old attitudes within the companies. For example, in late 2002, Smith Barney hired its first woman chief executive, Sallie Krawcheck. Since then, the company has fired some of its most successful brokers for mistreating female coworkers, thereby sending a message that such behavior will not be tolerated—even in the most valued employees. Despite these efforts, the industry statistics and continual lawsuits suggest that women in the financial services industry are not playing on a level playing field quite yet.

Indeed, as one Wall Street observer, Dan Ackman, a columnist for *Forbes* magazine, noted: "Beyond the numbers, nearly every woman on Wall Street will tell you there are, to this day, subtle and not-so-subtle double standards and a still pervasive atmosphere of harassment." And as the business writer John Churchill reports, "Many complainants claim the firms have just become subtler in their discrimination, rigging teams, for instance, so that when men retire or change firms, the most lucrative accounts they leave behind get assigned to other members of the old-boy network, not to the most senior broker in the office." Consequently, the most important question with respect to sexual discrimination in the securities and investment banking industry may be: What must happen in order for a true and pervasive cultural change to take place on Wall Street?

Questions for Discussion

1. Is business ethics relevant to the topic and examples in this case, or is this just business as usual? Explain.
2. What are the ethical implications of the onetime arbitration requirement that prevented Wall Street employees from seeking redress through the court system?
3. Why is the securities and investment banking business male-oriented and dominated?
4. Why does sex discrimination seem to persist on Wall Street in spite of the negative publicity of lawsuits and monetary costs of settlements?
5. What can or should be done to transform the persistent culture of sex discrimination on Wall Street?
6. Would you like working on Wall Street as a woman? Explain.
7. As a man or woman, what lessons would you take from this case if you accepted a professional job in a Wall Street firm?

Sources

This case was developed from material contained in the following sources:

Ackman, D. (2004, July 14). How Schieffelin beat the street. *Forbes.com.*

Allen, E. (2004, April 24). San Antonio woman wins Merrill Lynch suit, becomes voice for discrimination. *Knight Ridder Tribune Business News*, 1.

Antilla, S. (2003). *Tales from the Boom-Boom Room.* New York: HarperCollins Publishers.

Antilla, S. (2004, July 21). Money talks, women don't. *New York Times,* A19.

Antilla, S. (2004, August 9). In the companies of men: A rash of gender-discrimination suits suggests the Morgan Stanley payout may be only the beginning. *NewYork-Metro.com.*

Antilla, S. (2004, November 29). Merrill's woman problem: What men didn't know. *Bloomberg.com.*

Appleson, G. (2004, July 12). Morgan Stanley settles sex bias case. *ABCNews.Go.com.*

Baer, J. (2021, January 29). Letter to Pimco execs alleges discrimination toward women employees: Former, current female employees request better pay and promotions for women. *Wall Street Journal.* https://www.wsj.com/articles/letter-to-pimco-execs-alleges-discrimination-toward-women-employees-11611951608.

Boorstein, J. (2018, June 26). It's still tough to be a woman on Wall Street—but men don't always notice. *Makelt.com.* https://www.cnbc.com/2018/06/25/surveyon-wall-street-workplace-biases-persist---but-men-dont-see-t.html)

Bowden, E. (2021, January 21). Biden sparks TERF war with gender discrimination order. *New York Post.* https://nypost.com/2021/01/21/joe-biden-sparks-terf-war-with-gender-discrimination-order/.

Calian, S. (2004, June 9). Merrill faces gender-bias suit. *Wall Street Journal,* C15.

Churchill, J. (2004, August 1). Where the women at? *RegisteredRep.com.*

Discrimination claim—Merrill bites back. (2004, September 2). *Here Is the City News.*

Kelly, K., and DeBaise, C. (2004, July 13). Morgan Stanley settles bias suit for $54 million: Last-minute deal avoids sex-discrimination trial; $12 million for Ms. Schieffelin. *Wall Street Journal,* A1.

Langton, J. (2002, December 5). The *Boom-Boom Room* details travails of women on Wall Street. *Knight Ridder Tribune Business News,* 1.

Marsh, A. (1998, September 21). Women are from Venus, men are from Wall Street. *Forbes, 162(6),* 94.

McGeehan, P. (2002, February 10). Wall Street highflier to outcast: A woman's story. *New York Times,* 3-1.

McGeehan, P. (2004, July 14). Discrimination on Wall St.? The numbers tell the story. *New York Times,* 1.

Millar, M. (2005, February 3). Merrill Lynch faces appeal over sexual discrimination ruling. *PersonnelToday.com.*

Mollenkamp, C. (2004, February 23). Deals and deal makers: Former broker at Smith Barney settles sexual harassment case. *Wall Street Journal,* C5.

Securities Industry Association. (2003). Key findings. *Report on diversity strategy, development, and demographics,* 16–17.

Stephanie Villalba loses sex discrimination case. (n.d.). *Femalefirst.co.uk.* Accessed March 19, 2021, http://www.femalefirst.co.uk/business/182004.htm.

Top facts about women-owned businesses. (2004). Center for Women's Business Research.

Williams, S. (2013, July 18). Wall Street's secret weapon: Women. *Motley Fool.* http://www.fool.com/investing/general/2013/07/18/wall-streets-secret-weapon-women.aspx.

Notes

1. Safer, M. (2007, November 17). The "Millennials" are coming: Morley Safer on the new generation of American workers. *CBSNews.com*. https://www.cbsnews.com /news/the-millennials-are-coming/. See also Statista Research Department. (2021, January 20). U.S. population by generation 2019. https://www.statista.com/statistics /797321/us-population-by-generation/; Fry, R. (2020, April 28). Millennials overtake baby boomers as America's largest generation. *PewResearch.org*. https://www.pewresearch .org/fact-tank/2020/04/28/millennials-overtake-baby-boomers-as-americas-largest -generation/.

2. Indeed Career Guide. (2020, November 27). Characteristics of Generation X professionals. https://www.indeed.com/career-advice/career-development/generation-x -professional-characteristics.

3. GenerationZ.AU.com. (2021). Characteristics. https://generationz.com.au/articles /characteristics/#:~:text=Gen%20Z%20is%20part%20of,with%20influence%20be yond%20their%20years.

4. Bank, D. (n.d.). Civic Ventures, MetLife Foundation, Encore Colleges. http:// calbooming.sdsu.edu/documents/Encore_Colleges.pdf

5. U.S. Department of Labor. (2004). *DOL annual report, fiscal year 2004—performance and accountability report*. Strategic goal 1: A prepared workforce. https://www.dol.gov/sites /dolgov/files/general/reports/2004annualreport.pdf.

6. National Journal Group. (2011, July 6). Media advisory: Policy summit—"The Workforce Mosaic." *PRNewswire*. http://www.prnewswire.com/news-releases/media -advisory-policy-summit---the-workforce-mosaic-125070149.html; Conlin, M. (2001, April 2). Job security, no. Tall latte, yes. *BusinessWeek*, 62–64. Many of these trends are also found in the 2008 online editions of Data Dome research (http://datadome.com), and the McKinsey and Rand reports. See also O'Toole, J., and Lawler III, E. (2006). *The new American workplace*. New York: Palgrave Macmillan.

7. Bridge. (2016). 7 Trends for workforce 2020: How to make today's ever-changing workplace work for you. *GetBridge.com*. https://sewi-astd.org/resources/Pictures/7%20 TRENDS%20FOR%20WORKFORCE%202020.pdf.

8. Bank (n.d.), op. cit. Also based on the discussion of Tapscott, D. (1996). *The digital economy*, 296–303. New York: McGraw-Hill; Washburn, E. (2000, January–February). Are you ready for generation X? *Physician Executive, 26(1)*, 51–56.

9. This section is based on the following sources: Dishman, L. (2021). Is now a good time to change careers? More workers are feeling good about it. https://www.fastcompany .com/90607167/is-now-a-good-time-to-change-careers-more-workers-are-feeling -good-about-it; Tapscott (1996), op. cit., 301; Howe, N. (2000). *Millennials rising*. New York: Vintage Books.

10. Remote Work: The Pros and Cons for Employers. (2020, June 22). *LawDepot.com (blog)*. https://www.lawdepot.com/blog/remote-work-pros-and-cons/.

11. Bureau of Labor Statistics. (2012, February 1). Employment projections: 2010–2020 summary. https://www.bls.gov/news.release/archives/ecopro_02012012.pdf; Hedge, J. W., Borman, W. C., and Lammlein, S. E. (2006). *The aging workforce: Realities, myths, and implications for organizations*. Washington, DC: American Psychological Association.

12. Safer (2007), op. cit.

13. Bureau of Labor Statistics. (2019). Employment projections: 2018–2028. https:// www.bls.gov/news.release/archives/ecopro_09042019.pdf.

14. U.S. Department of Labor (2004). *DOL annual report, fiscal year 2004—performance and accountability report*. Strategic Goal 1: A Prepared Workforce. https://www.dol.gov/sites/dolgov/files/general/reports/2004annualreport.pdf, accessed June 7, 2020.

15. Beard, J. R., Biggs, S., Bloom, D. E., Fried, L. P., Hogan, P., Kalache, A., and Olshansky, S. (eds.). (2011). *Global population ageing: Peril or promise*. Geneva: World Economic Forum.

16. Ibid. See also Davidson, G., Lepeak, S., and Newman, E. (February 2007). The impact of the aging workforce on public sector organizations and mission. *IPMA-HR*.

17. Volini, E., Schwartz, J., Denny, B., Mallon, D., Van Durme, Y., Hauptmann, M., Yan, R., and Poynton, S. (2020, May 15). The postgenerational workforce. *Deloitte Insight*. https://www2.deloitte.com/us/en/insights/focus/human-capital-trends/2020/leading-a-multi-generational-workforce.html.

18. Washburn (2000), op. cit.; Howe (2000), op. cit.; Mui, N. (2001, February 4). Here come the kids: Gen Y invades the workplace. *New York Times*, sec. 9, p. 1, col. 3.

19. National Association of State Treasurers (NAST) Foundation. (n.d.). Silent generation (born between 1926–1945). *Tomorrow's Money*.

20. Rabinowitz, D. (2012, December). When men were men and women wore girdles. *WSJ.com*. http://online.wsj.com/news/articles/SB10001424127887324461604578191492784955084.

21. Kaye, B. (2012, January 1). Four generations: Develop and engage them at work. *Leadership Excellence*, 20.

22. Ibid. Boomers statistics. (2012). *Boomers Web*.

23. Gallup. (2013). *The 2013 state of the American workplace, employee engagement insights for U.S. business leaders*, 36.

24. Ibid., 42.

25. Stahl, A. (2019, September 10), How Generation-Z will revolutionize the workplace. *Forbes.com*. https://www.forbes.com/sites/ashleystahl/2019/09/10/how-generation-z-will-revolutionize-the-workplace/#708ebc874f53.

26. PricewaterhouseCoopers. (2013). *PwC's NextGen: A global generational study 2013*. Summary and compendium of findings. https://www.pwc.com/gx/en/hr-management-services/pdf/pwc-nextgen-study-2013.pdf; Ethics Resource Center. (2013). *Generational differences in workforce ethics*. Arlington, VA: ERC, 2.

27. Curtis, J. (n.d.). How to work with and manage millennials (Generation Y). *Money Crashers*. https://www.moneycrashers.com/work-with-manage-millennials-generation-y/.

28. Gallup (2013), op. cit., 36.

29. Weiss, J. (2000). *Organization behavior and change*, 2nd ed., 18–23. South-Western College Publishing; Brack, J. (2012). Maximizing millennials in the workplace. UNC Kenan-Flager Business School.

30. Addison Group. (n.d.). Age is just a number: The truth behind generational stereotypes at work. https://addisongroup.com/insights/insight/age-is-just-a-number-the-truth-behind-generational-stereotypes-at-work/, accessed March 19, 2021.

31. Rudolph, C. W., and Zacher, H. (2020, May 8). COVID-19 and careers: On the futility of generational experiences. *Elsevier Public Health Emergency Collection*. https://www.ncbi.nlm.nih.gov/pmc/articles/PMC7205708/.

32. Ibid.

33. Shaw, H. (2013). *Sticking points: How to get generations working together in the 12 places they come apart*. Carol Stream, IL: Tyndale House Publishers.

34. This section is based on, but not limited to, Marston, C. (2007). *Motivating the "What's in it for me?" workforce*, ch. 9. Hoboken, NJ: John Wiley.

35. Marston (2007), op. cit., 146. Balance requires negotiation, and negotiation is facilitated by knowing the expectations, attitudes, and needs of the employee as well as the requirements and resources of the organization.

36. Gallup (2013), op. cit., 42.

37. Beheshti, N. (2019, January 23). Improve workplace culture with a strong mentorship program. *Forbes.com*. https://www.forbes.com/sites/nazbeheshti/2019/01/23/improve-workplace-culture-with-a-strong-mentoring-program/#23a9386f76b5.

38. Kahn, S. (2020, March 6). Women with access to higher education changed America—but now they're bearing the brunt of the student debt crisis. *Time.com*. https://time.com/5797922/women-higher-education-history/#:~:text=Today%2C%20for%20myriad%20reasons%2C%20American,of%20students%20on%20college%20campuses.

39. Kelly, J. (2020, January 13). Women now hold more jobs than men in the U.S. workforce. *Forbes.com*. https://www.forbes.com/sites/jackkelly/2020/01/13/women-now-hold-more-jobs-than-men/#5548320f8f8a.

40. The Impact of Feminism in the Workforce. (2017, November 6). *Trisparkmedia.com*. https://trisparkmedia.com/2017/11/06/impact-feminism-business/.

41. Warner, J., Ellmann, N., and Boesch, D. (2018, November 20). The women's leadership gap. *AmericanProgress.org*. https://www.americanprogress.org/issues/women/reports/2018/11/20/461273/womens-leadership-gap-2/.

42. Wellington, S., Brumit Kropf, M., and Gerkovich, P. (2003, June). What's holding women back? *Harvard Business Review*. http://hbr.org/2003/06/whats-holding-women-back/ar/2.

43. Ibid.

44. American Civil Liberties Union. (2014, April 25). Windsor v. United States. *ACLU.org*. https://www.Aclu.org/lgbt-rights/windsor-v-united-states-thea-edie-doma.

45. Ibid.

46. Smith, Gambrell & Russell, LLP. (2014, Winter). The sweeping effect of the Windsor decision. *SGR Insights, 35*. https://www.sgrlaw.com/ttl-articles/the-sweeping-effect-of-the-windsor-decision/#:~:text=The%20U.S.%20Supreme%20Court's%20recent,persons%20in%20same%2Dsex%20marriages.&text=In%20Windsor%2C%20the%20Supreme%20Court,constitutional%20principles%20of%20equal%20protection.

47. Ibid.

48. Ahuja, M., Barnes, R., and Chow, E. (2013, June). How the Supreme Court ruled on same-sex marriage. *WashingtonPost.com*. https://www.washingtonpost.com/wp-srv/special/politics/how-supreme-court-could-rule-on-gay-marriage/.

49. U.S. Supreme Court rules gay marriage is legal nationwide. (2015, June 27). *BBC News*. https://www.bbc.com/news/world-us-canada-33290341; see also American Civil Liberties Union. (2021). Know your rights: LGBTQ rights. *ACLU.org*. https://www.aclu.org/know-your-rights/lgbtq-rights/; and Biskupic, J. (2020, June 16). Two conservative justices joined decision expanding LGBTQ rights. *CNN.com*. https://www.cnn.com/2020/06/15/politics/supreme-court-expanding-gay-rights/index.html.

50. Belge, K. (2012, January 26). Where can gays legally marry? *LesbianLife.About.com*.

51. Ibid.

52. Human Rights Campaign. (n.d.). Marriage Equality around the World. https://www.hrc.org/resources/marriage-equality-around-the-world, accessed March 19, 2021.

53. FindLaw Staff. (2020, May 19). What is domestic partnership? *FindLaw*. https://family.findlaw.com/domestic-partnerships/what-is-a-domestic-partnership.html.

54. National Conference of State Legislatures. (2020, March 10). Civil unions and domestic partnership statutes. https://www.ncsl.org/research/human-services/civil-unions-and-domestic-partnership-statutes.aspx.

55. Frey, W. H. (2020, March 14). The US will become "minority white" in 2045, Census projects. Youthful minorities are the engine of the future growth. *Brookings.edu.* https://www.brookings.edu/blog/the-avenue/2018/03/14/the-us-will-become-minority-white-in-2045-census-projects/.

56. Lopez, M. H., Morin, R., and Krogstad, J. M. (2015, June 8). Latinos increasingly confident in personal finances, see better economic times ahead. *Pew Research Center.* https://www.pewresearch.org/hispanic/2016/06/08/2-latinos-are-optimistic-about-their-finances-in-the-next-year-and-upward-economic-mobility-for-their-children/.

57. Ibid.

58. Bandow, D. (2013, September 16). Immigration benefits the U.S., so let's legalize all work. *Forbes.com.* http://www.forbes.com/sites/dougbandow/2013/09/16/immigration-benefits-the-u-s-so-lets-legalize-all-work/.

59. Ibid.

60. Saenz, R., and Poston D. L., Jr. (2020, January 9). Children of color projected to be majority of U.S. youth this year. *PBS.org,* https://www.pbs.org/newshour/nation/children-of-color-projected-to-be-majority-of-u-s-youth-this-year.

61. Majority-minority districts. (n.d.). *Ballotpedia.* https://ballotpedia.org/Majority-minority_districts, accessed March 19, 2021.

62. Yen, H. (2013, June 13). Census: White majority in U.S. gone by 2043. *NBCNews.com.* https://www.nbcnews.com/news/us-news/census-white-majority-u-s-gone-2043-flna6C10303232.

63. Ibid.

64. UNESCO Institute of Statistics. (2011). Global trends in secondary education. *Global Education Digest.*

65. Ibid. See also Altbach, P., Resiberg, L., and Rumbley, L. (2009). *Trends in global higher education: tracking an academic revolution.* Paris: UNESCO.

66. Bersin, J. (2012, December 10). Growing gap between what business needs and what education provides. *Forbes.com.* http://www.forbes.com/sites/joshbersin/2012/12/10/growing-gap-between-what-business-needs-and-what-education-provides/.

67. Barton, D., Farrell, D., and Mourshed, M. (2012). *Education to employment: Designing a system that works.* McKinsey & Company. https://www.mckinsey.com/industries/public-and-social-sector/our-insights/education-to-employment-designing-a-system-that-works#.

68. World Economic Forum. (2012). *The global gender report 2012.* Geneva: WEF. http://www3.weforum.org/docs/WEF_GenderGap_Report_2012.pdf.

69. Nitro College. (2021). Average student loan debt in the U.S., 2021 statistics. https://www.nitrocollege.com/research/average-student-loan-debt; see also Bustamante, J. (2021, April 4). *EducationalData.org.* https://educationdata.org/student-loan-debt-statistics.

70. Bastrikin, A. (2020, April 12), Student loan debt statistics. *EducationData.org.* https://educationdata.org/student-loan-debt-statistics/.

71. United Nations. (n.d.) Factsheet on persons with disabilities. https://www.un.org/development/desa/disabilities/resources/factsheet-on-persons-with-disabilities.html.

72. U.S. Department of Labor. (2021, February 23). Persons with a disability: Labor force characteristics—2019 (Press release). Bureau of Labor Statistics. https://www.bls.gov/news.release/pdf/disabl.pdf.

73. Campaign for Disability Employment. (n.d.). What can you do? Resources for job seekers and employees. https://www.whatcanyoudocampaign.org/where-to-learn-more/resources-for-job-seekers-and-employees/#Top.

74. Ibid. See also Eckberg, J. (2004, September 26). Disabled workers can solve short-fall. *Cincinnati Enquirer.*

75. Work–life balance: tips for you family. (n.d.). *RaisingChildren.net.au.* https://raisingchildren.net.au/grown-ups/work-child-care/worklife-balance/work-life-balance'.

76. Business Talent Group. (n.d.). Maintaining work–life balance during COVID-19. https://resources.businesstalentgroup.com/btg-blog/maintaining-work-life-balance-covid-19, accessed March 19, 2021. See also Fisher, J. (2021). Designing work for well-being: The end of work/life balance. Deloitte. https://www2.deloitte.com/us/en/insights/focus/human-capital-trends/2021/workforce-trends-2020.html.

77. See Best Companies for Multicultural Women. (n.d.). *Working Mother.* https://www.workingmother.com/best-companies-for-multicultural-women-2020, accessed March 19, 2021. Survey results were compiled and summarized for the years 2007–2011.

78. Ernst & Young (EY). (n.d.) *Megatrends 2020 and beyond*, EYQ 3rd ed. https://assets.ey.com/content/dam/ey-sites/ey-com/en_gl/topics/megatrends/ey-megatrends-2020.pdf.

79. Radin, T., and Werhane, P. (2003, April). Employment-at-will, employee rights, and future directions for employment. *Business Ethics Quarterly*, 113–130.

80. Fulmer, W., and Casey, A. (1990). Employment at will: Options for managers. *Academy of Management Review, 4*, 102.

81. Flynn, G. (2000). How do you treat the at-will employment relationship? *Workforce, 79*, 178–179.

82. Williamson, J., and Kleiner, B. (2003). New developments concerning the covenant of good faith and fair dealing. *Management Research News*, 35–41.

83. See Autor, D., Lii, J. D., and Schway, S. (2004, May). The employment consequences of wrongful-discharge laws: Large, small, or none at all? *American Economic Review*, 440–446.

84. Fulmer and Casey (1990), op. cit., 102. See also Williamson and Kleiner (2003), op. cit., 35–41.

85. Lousig-Nont, G. (2003, April). Seven deadly hiring mistakes. *Supervision*, 85–88.

86. For a discussion of these issues, see Awney, R. (1920). *The acquisitive society*, 53–55. New York: Harcourt, Brace & World; Reich, C. (1964). The new property. *Yale Law Review, 73*, 733; also the Supreme Court case Perry v. Sindermann.

87. Boatright, J. (2000). *Ethics and the conduct of business*, 3rd ed. Upper Saddle River, NJ: Prentice Hall, 265.

88. Rowan, J. (April 2000). The moral foundation of employee rights. *Journal of Business Ethics, 24*, 355–361.

89. Ibid., 358.

90. Jacoby, S. (1995). Social dimensions of global economic integration. In Jacoby, S. (ed.), *The workers of nations: Industrial relations in a global economy*, 21–22. New York: Oxford University Press. See DeVito, L. (2013). Kennedy Consulting, Research & Advisory. HR Transformation Consulting Market. *Seoul Journal of Business.*

91. Choi, J. T. (June 2004). Transformation of Korean HRM based on Confucian Values. *Seoul Journal of Business, 10(1)*, 1–26. http://s-space.snu.ac.kr/bitstream/10371/1785/1/SJBv10n1_001.pdf?origin=publication_detail.

92. Hiroshi, O. (2010). Lifetime employment in Japan: Concepts and measurements. *Journal of the Japanese and International Economies, Elsevier, 24(1)*, 1–27.

93. Velasquez, M. (1998). *Business ethics*, 4th ed., 439–440. Upper Saddle River, NJ: Prentice Hall.

94. U.S. Department of Labor. (2020, April 15). Usual weekly earnings of wage and salary workers first quarter 2020 (Press release). Bureau of Labor Statistics. https://www .bls.gov/news.release/pdf/wkyeng.pdf.

95. National Committee on Pay Equity. (2014, February 18). Wage gap is stuck. http:// www.pay-equity.org/.

96. McAlister, Z. (2012, January 27). Apple CEO responds to reports of inhumane working conditions for factory workers. *Financial Post*. https://financialpost.com/technology /apple-ceo-responds-to-reports-of-inhumane-working-conditions-for-factory-workers; see also Vesteinsson, K. (2020, January 16). U.S. government challenges Apple on encryption (again). https://www.hrw.org/news/2020/01/16/us-government-challenges-apple-en cryption-again.

97. Jacobs, H. (2018, May 7). Inside 'iPhone City,' the massive Chinese factory town where half of the world's iPhones are produced. *Business Insider*. https://www.businessinsider .com/apple-iphone-factory-foxconn-china-photos-tour-2018-5.

98. Hackman, J. R., Oldham, G., Janson, R., and Purdy, K. (1975, Summer). A new strategy for job enrichment. *California Management Review, 17*, 56–58.

99. Bjork, L. (1975, March). An experiment in work satisfaction. *Scientific American, 232(3)*, 17–23; see also Simmons, J., and Mares, W. (1983). *Working together*. New York: Knopf.

100. DeGeorge, R. (1990). *Business ethics*, 3rd ed. New York: Macmillan; Ewing, D. (1977). *Freedom inside the organization: Bringing civil liberties to the workplace*. New York: McGraw-Hill.

101. U.S. Department of Labor. (n.d.). Families First Coronavirus Response Act: Employee paid leave rights. Wage and Hour Division. https://www.dol.gov/agencies/whd /pandemic/ffcra-employee-paid-leave, accessed March 19, 2021.

102. Hawaii State AFL-CIO. (n.d.). "Just cause" guideline. http://www.hawaflcio.org /J-coz.html; Just cause: Using the seven tests. (n.d.). *UEUnion.com*. https://www.ueunion .org/stwd_jstcause.html.

103. Meyers, D. (1988). Work and self–respect. In Beauchamp, T., and Bowie, N., (eds.), *Ethical theory and business*, 3rd ed., 275–279. Upper Saddle River, NJ: Prentice Hall.

104. For an updated source on this topic by the National Employment Law Project, see Anderson, T. (2001, May 2001). Elsewhere in the courts. . . . *Security Management, 45*, 105.

105. Werhane, P. (1985). *Persons, rights, and corporations*, 118. Upper Saddle River, NJ: Prentice Hall.

106. DesJardins, J., and McCall, J. (1990). A defense of employee rights. *Journal of Business Ethics, 4*, 367–376.

107. Ibid.

108. Zall, M. (2001, May–June). Employee privacy. *Journal of Property Management, 66*, 16–18.

109. Beauchamp, T., and Bowie, N., (eds.). (1988). *Ethical theory and business*, 3rd ed. Upper Saddle River, NJ: Prentice Hall, 264. See also ch. 5 in *Ethical theory and business*, 6th ed. (2001), also published by Prentice Hall.

110. Post, J., Lawrence, A., and Weber, J. (1999). *Business and society*, 9th ed. Boston: McGraw-Hill, 378.

111. Dalton, D., and Metzger, M. (1993, February). Integrity testing for personnel selection: An unsparing perspective. *Journal of Business Ethics, 12(2)*, 147–156.

112. Mehl, B. (2020, November 26). The state of employee privacy and surveillance in 2021. *KisiBlog.* https://www.getkisi.com/blog/state-employee-privacy-surveillance; Carroll, A. (1993). *Business and society: ethics and stakeholder management,* 3rd ed., 371–372. Cincinnati: South-Western.

113. Mehl (2020, November 26), op. cit.

114. Samuels, P. (1996, May 12). Who's reading your e-mail? Maybe the boss. *New York Times,* 11; also Guernsey, L. (1999, December 16). On the job, the boss can watch your every online move, and you have a few defenses. *New York Times,* G1, 3. For a list of specific information regarding telephone, computer, e-mail, and social media monitoring, see also Privacy Rights Clearinghouse. (2019, March 25). Workplace privacy and employee monitoring. https://privacyrights.org/consumer-guides/workplace-privacy-and-employee-monitoring.

115. Guttmann A. (2019, May 13). Social media marketing penetration in the U.S. 2013–2019. Statista.com.

116. Salary.com. (2013, July 29) Wasting Time at Work Survey 2013. https://www .salary.com/chronicles/2013-wasting-time-at-work-survey/#:~:text=This%20year%20 that%20number%20is,day%20while%20on%20the%20clock.

117. Laviano, C. (2011, November 16). Internet ethics: Managing social media at work. *Talent Management.*

118. Martin, J. (1999, March). Internet policy: Employee rights and wrongs. *Human Resources Focus,* 13, 76.

119. Ibid.

120. Zall (2001), op. cit., 18. See also an excellent source on employee and company policy uses of the Internet: CurrentWare. (2021). How to manage personal use of the Internet in the workplace. https://www.currentware.com/personal-use-of-the-internet/#should-they.

121. Koeze, E., and Popper, N. (2020, April 7). The virus changed the way we internet. *New York Times.* https://www.nytimes.com/interactive/2020/04/07/technology/coronavirus-internet-use.html.

122. Society for Human Resource Management. (n.d.). Employee dating policy. https://www.shrm.org/resourcesandtools/tools-and-samples/policies/pages/cms _006713.aspx, accessed March 19, 2021.

123. Adams, S. (2010, February 5). The state of the office romance, 2010. *Forbes.com.* http://www.forbes.com/2010/02/05/workplace-love-sex-leadership-careers-affairs.html.

124. Fisher, A. (2013, June 7). Why your office romance is your employer's business. *Fortune.* https://fortune.com/2013/06/07/why-your-office-romance-is-your-employers -business/.

125. Nagele-Piazza, L. (2020, October 17). COVID-19 complicates companies' concerns about workplace drug testing. Society for Human Resource Management. https:// www.shrm.org/hr-today/news/all-things-work/pages/covid-19-complicates-concerns -about-workplace-drug-testing.aspx.

126. DesJardins and McCall (1990), op. cit., 367–376.

127. Goldstein, R., and Nolan, R. (1975, March–April). Personal privacy versus the corporate computer. *Harvard Business Review, 53(2),* 62–70. In addition to these guidelines, another source that provides drug testing guidelines is Bernardo, M. (1994). *Workplace drug testing: An employer's development and implementation guide.* Washington, DC: Institute for a Drug-Free Workplace.

128. For an updated list of mandatory guidelines for federal workplace drug testing programs, see the Substance Abuse and Mental Health Services Administration (SAMHSA).

(2021, March 15). *Drug-free workplace guidelines and resources*, U.S. Department of Health and Human Services. https://www.samhsa.gov/workplace/resources.

129. See Wagner (2013), op. cit., 107n. See also Bickel, N. (2020, November 5). Genetic testing: Employee perk or privacy hazard? University of Michigan News. https://news.umich.edu/genetic-testing-employee-perk-or-privacy-hazard/.

130. DesJardins and McCall (1990), op. cit., 367–376.

131. OMB Watch (http://www.ombwatch.org) and Enviro.BLR.com are websites to view updated employee, consumer, and employer right-to-know legislation and information across industries and products.

132. Occupational Safety and Health Administration. (2017). Workers' rights. https://www.osha.gov/Publications/osha3021.pdf.

133. OSHA. (2021). Protecting workers: Guidance on mitigating and preventing the spread of COVID-19 in the workplace. https://www.osha.gov/coronavirus/safe work.

134. DeGeorge (1990), op. cit., 322–324. Also see https://www.dol.gov/general/topic /termination/plantclosings.

135. Velasquez, M. G. (1988). *Business ethics: Concepts and cases*, 2nd ed. Upper Saddle River, NJ: Prentice Hall, 388; Velasquez (1998), 463–467.

136. Carroll (1993), op. cit., 371–372.

137. U.S. Department of Labor. (2018, February). Employment law guide: Other workplace standards: notices for plant closings and mass layoffs. https://webapps.dol.gov/elaws /elg/layoffs.htm.

138. Fletcher, M. (2001, May 21). Employee leave and law. *Business Insurance, 35,* 3.

139. Desilver Drew. (2020, March 12). As coronavirus spreads, which U.S. workers have paid sick leave—and which don't? Pew Research Center. https://www.pewresearch .org/fact-tank/2020/03/12/as-coronavirus-spreads-which-u-s-workers-have-paid-sick -leave-and-which-dont/.

140. More information on the Family and Medical Leave Act is available through the Wage and Hour Division of the U.S. Department of Labor at https://www.dol.gov /agencies/whd/fmla.

141. U.S.Department of Labor. (n.d.). COVID-19 and the Family and Medical Leave Act questions and answers. https://www.dol.gov/agencies/whd/fmla/pandemic, accessed May 26, 2021.

142. Kanowitz, L. (1969). *Women and the law,* 36. Albuquerque, NM: University of New Mexico Press; also quoted in Velasquez (1988), op. cit., 324, and Velasquez. (1998), op. cit., 387–392.

143. Fehrenbacher, D. (1978). *The Dred Scott case*. New York: Oxford University Press.

144. DesJardins and McCall (1990), op. cit.

145. Feagin, J., and Feagin, C. (1986). *Discrimination American style*, 2nd ed., 23–33. Malabar, FL: Robert Krieger; Velasquez (1998), op. cit., 391.

146. Krasner, J. (2001, May 20). Hitting the glass ceiling. *Boston Globe*, G1.

147. Noah, T., and Karr, A. (1991, November 4). What new civil rights law will mean: Charges of sex, disability bias will multiply. *Wall Street Journal,* 31.

148. U.S. Equal Employment Opportunity Commission. (2021). Title VII of the Civil Rights Act of 1964 charges: FY 1997–FY 2020. https://www.eeoc.gov/statistics/title-vii -civil-rights-act-1964-charges-charges-filed-eeoc-includes-concurrent-charges.

149. Excerpts from: Supreme Court opinions on limits of Disabilities Act. (2001, February 22). *New York Times,* A20.

150. Discrimination interviewer questions sometimes illegal. (2001, May 20). *Boston Globe*, H2. Also quoted in this section is Lowe, J. (2021, April 7). Ageism in the workplace in 2021. https://www.laborsoft.com/blog/ageism-in-the-workplace-in-2021

151. Payscale. (2021). The state of the gender pay gap in 2021. https://www.payscale.com /data/gender-pay-gap#:~:text=In%202021%2C%20women%20earn%2082,every%20dollar%20earned%20by%20men.&text=As%20PayScale's%20crowdsourced%20data%20 weights,lower%20paid%20and%20hourly%20workers.

152. Laughlin, L., and Wisniewsk, M. (2021, March 23). *Women represent majority of workers in several essential occupations.* US Census Bureau. https://www.census.gov/library/stories /2021/03/unequally-essential-women-and-gender-pay-gap-during-covid-19.html.

153. DeGeorge (1990), op. cit., 322–324.

154. Updates on affirmative action, EEOC, and discrimination legislation can be found at the Department of Labor website at http://www.dol.gov/dol/topic/hiring/affirmativeact .htm.

155. Hartocollis, A. (2021, February 3). Justice Department drops suit claiming Yale discriminated in admissions. *New York Times.* https://www.nytimes.com/2021/02/03/us /yale-admissions-affirmative-action.html. For a 2019 update on the status of affirmative action, see also Back, C. J., and Hsin, S. (2019, January 31) "Affirmative action" and equal protection in higher education. Congressional Research Service Report R45481. https:// fas.org/sgp/crs/misc/R45481.pdf.

156. Biskupic, J. (2021, June 14). Supreme Court effectively delays challenge to Harvard affirmative action policies for several months. *CNN.com.* https://www.cnn.com/2021 /06/14/politics/supreme-court-harvard-admissions-lawsuit/index.html.

157. Strom, S. (1991, October 20). Harassment rules often not posted. *New York Times,* 1, 22.

158. Kaminsky, M. (2020, September 16). Five biggest sexual harassment cases. https:// www.legalzoom.com/articles/five-biggest-sexual-harassment-cases. Baker, P. (1998, November 14). Clinton settles Paula Jones lawsuit for $850,000. *Washington Post.* https:// www.washingtonpost.com/wp-srv/politics/special/clinton/stories/jones111498.htm. CNNMoney. (1998, June 11). Mitsubishi settles for $34M: Automaker and EEOC agree on terms in largest sexual harassment case in history. http://money.cnn.com/1998/06/11 /companies/mitsubishi/. Sonnemaker, T. (2020, December 31). 2020 brought a wave of discrimination and harassment allegations against major companies like Amazon, McDonald's, and Pinterest. These are some of the year's high-profile legal battles. https://www.businessinsider.com/every-company-that-was-sued-discrimination-and-harassment-lawsuits-2020 -2021-1.

159. Willness, C., Stell, P., and Lee, K. (2007, Spring). A meta-analysis of the antecedents and consequences of workplace sexual harassment. *Personnel Psychology,* 127–162. See also Sonnemaker, T. (2020, December 31). 2020 brought a wave of discrimination and harassment allegations against major companies like Amazon, McDonald's, and Pinterest. These are some of the year's high-profile legal battles. *BusinessInsider.com.* https:// www.businessinsider.com/every-company-that-was-sued-discrimination-and-harassment-lawsuits-2020-2021-1.

160. Machlowitz, M., and Machlowitz, D. (1986, September 25). Hug by the boss could lead to a slap from the judge. *Wall Street Journal,* 20; Wermiel, S., and Trost, C. (1986, June 20). Justices say hostile job environment due to sex harassment violates rights. *Wall Street Journal,* 2.

161. Hayes, A. (1991, October 11). How the courts define harassment. *Wall Street Journal,* B1; Lublin, J. (1991, October 11). Companies try a variety of approaches to halt sexual harassment on the job. *Wall Street Journal,* B1.

162. Catalyst. (2019, December 5). Sex discrimination and sexual harassment: Quick take. https://www.catalyst.org/research/sex-discrimination-and-sexual-harassment/.

163. Me Too. (n.d.). History and inception. https://metoomvmt.org/get-to-know-us /history-inception/. The #MeToo movement can be defined "as a social movement against sexual violence and sexual assault that advocates for females who survived sexual violence to speak out about their experience"; see Ming, Y. (n.d.). The philanthropic meaning of the #MeToo movement. Learning to Give. https://www.learningtogive.org /resources/philanthropic-meaning-metoo-movement#:~:text=.%2C%202018, accessed March 19, 2021.

164. For positive and negative impacts, see Bower, T. (2019, September–October). The #MeToo backlash. *Harvard Business Review*. https://hbr.org/2019/09/the-metoo-backlash; Torres, N. (2020, January–February). #MeToo's legacy. *Harvard Business Review*. https:// hbr.org/2020/01/metoos-legacy.

165. Roth, K. (2020). Two years after #MeToo erupts, a new treaty anchors workplace shifts. *Human Rights Watch*. https://www.hrw.org/world-report/2020/country-chapters /global-1#.

166. Mastalli, G. (1991). Appendix: The legal context. In Matthews, J., Goodpaster, K., and Nash, L. (eds.), *Policies and reasons: A casebook in business ethics,* 2nd ed., 157–158. New York: McGraw–Hill.

167. Long, S., and Leonard, C. (1999, October). The changing face of sexual harassment. *Human Resources Focus*, S1–S3.

168. Ibid.

169. Ibid. For an update on "vicarious" liability, see Aparna, S. (2020, June 8). A case for vicarious liability for sexual harassment at workplaces. *Law School Policy Review & Kautilya Society*. https://lawschoolpolicyreview.com/2020/06/08/a-case-for-vicarious-liability-for -sexual-harassment-at-workplaces/.

170. The Business and Legal Resources website (www.blr.com) is an excellent source of training for HR employees and employers. Material in this section is also based on Long and Leonard (1999), op. cit.

171. Foreman, J., and Lehman, B. (1991, October 21). What to do if you think you may be guilty of sex harassment. *Boston Globe*.

172. Johannes, L., and Lublin, S. (1996, May 9). Sexual-harassment cases trip up foreign companies. *Wall Street Journal*, B4.

173. Maatman, G., Jr. (2000, July). A global view of sexual harassment. *HR Magazine, 45*, 158.

174. Steeley, B. (2000, September). Evaluating your client as a possible qui tam relator. *Practical Litigator, 11(5)*, 15. See also Securities and Exchange Commission. (2021, January 14). SEC awards nearly $600,000 to whistleblower (Press release). https://www.sec .gov/news/press-release/2021-7.

175. Hoffman, H., and Moore, J. (1990). Whistle blowing: Its moral justification. In James, G. (ed.), *Business ethics: Readings and cases in corporate morality*, 2nd ed., 332. New York: McGraw–Hill.

176. Ibid., 333.

177. Dwyer, J. (1995, November 21). Whistleblowing a warning tune. *New York Daily News*.

178. Haley v. Retsinas, 1998 U.S. App. LEXIS 4654 (8th Cir. Ct., March 16, 1998), No. 97–1946; see also http://caselaw.findlaw.com/us-8th-circuit/1199989.html.

179. DeGeorge (1990), op. cit., 208–214.

180. Near, J., Miceli, M., and Jensen, R. (1983, March). Variables associated with the whistle-blowing process (Working paper series 83–111), Ohio State University, College of Administrative Science, Columbus, 5. Cited in Carroll (1993), op. cit., 354–355.

181. Carroll (1993), op. cit., 356; Securities and Exchange Commission. (2012). Whistleblower program. http://www.sec.gov/spotlight/dodd-frank/whistleblower.shtml. The SEC's Office of the Whistleblower website at www.sec.gov/whistleblower has additional information.

182. Maatman (2000, July), op. cit., 158.

8

BUSINESS ETHICS AND STAKEHOLDER MANAGEMENT IN THE GLOBAL ENVIRONMENT

OPENING CASE

The global economy has been constrained during the Covid-19's pandemonium. Although comprised of separate economies with a multitude of stakeholders and stockholders by country and region, it remains a complex grid of interconnected networks of resources. Pre-Covid, advances in technology made it possible for "goods, services, and people to cross borders in large volumes and at unprecedented speed. Still, since 1990, trade flows grew 1.5 times faster than global GDP [gross domestic product], and cross-border capital flows expanded at three times the rate of GDP growth." In January 2020, pre-Covid-19, trade flows were expected to reach 2.7 percent compared to GDP growth of 2.5 percent.[1] Currently, as the pandemic endures, international trade in goods is continuously falling. "Data published on June, 11, 2020, showed that merchandise trade fell by 5 percent in the first quarter of the year and pointed to a 27 percent drop for the second quarter, and a 20 percent annual decline for 2020."[2] An economic recovery is still uncertain for the coming months ahead. However, a 2021 PwC 24th Annual Global CEO Survey of 5,050 CEOs worldwide indicated that CEOs were optimistic regarding their plans to respond to new threats, transform their operating model, and create a more sustainable future. In the midst of extraordinary challenges and uncertainty, and countless personal tragedies, leaders are under pressure to make decisions on managing the immediate impact of the pandemic and its consequences, decisions that will shape the state of the world for years to come. What might be the silver linings in the crisis and how might leaders use this moment to build a more prosperous, equitable and sustainable world?"[3]

■ 8.1 The Connected Global Economy and Globalization

The global economy and environment consists of a dynamic set of relationships among financial markets, cultures, politics, laws, technologies, government policies, and numerous stakeholders and stakeholder interests, as noted earlier. Covid-19 has constrained all aspects of human life and competition from different regional players across the globe. Institutions, companies, organizations, individual citizens, families, and communities that are served by multinational enterprises (MNEs) have suffered from the effects of the virus. Yet globalization, while tattered, is still intact. This chapter presents different dimensions of globalization, before and during the pandemic, that affect new and experienced managers and professionals and people in every nation. A major difference presently is that Covid-19 is recurring with variants of the virus. While vaccines are being distributed, there is agreement that this crisis will pass, as have previous natural disasters, but the consequences have been severe. Ethical Insight 8.1 defines and describes globalization in this broader and changing context.

Ethical Insight 8.1

What Do We Mean by Globalization?

Globalization is about an increasingly interconnected and interdependent world; it is about international trade, investment, and finance that have been growing far faster than national incomes. It is about technologies that have already transformed our abilities to communicate in ways that would have been unimaginable a few years ago. It is about our global environment, communicable diseases, crime, violence, and terrorism. It is about new opportunities for workers in all countries to develop their potential and to support their families through jobs created by greater economic integration. With

Covid-19, it is also about sharing scientific and medical expertise and discoveries to help quell the disease.

Globalization is also about international financial wealth, crises, and workers in developed countries who fear losing their jobs to lower-cost countries with limited labor rights. And it is about workers in developing countries who worry about decisions affecting their lives that are made in faraway head offices of international corporations. Globalization is therefore about risks as well as opportunities. We must deal with these risks at the national level by managing adjustment processes and by strengthening social, structural, and financial systems. And at the global level, we must establish a stronger international financial architecture and work to fight deadly diseases like Covid-19, to turn back environmental degradation, and to use communications to give voice to the voiceless.

The world's current population is 7.7 billion and has been expected to rise to 9.7 billion in 2050. "The population of sub-Saharan Africa is projected to double by 2050," while Europe and Latin America expect declining populations by 2100. "The Latin America and Caribbean region is expected to surpass Europe in population by 2037 before peaking at 768 million in 2058."[4] Despite the dramatic changes that 2020 brought, there are varying predictions of the world economy. One far-reaching scenario is that the world economy will have rapid growth and that by 2050, the global market is projected to double its current size, even as the UN forecasts the world's population will only grow by a modest 26 percent." This prediction suggests that four emerging economies will become the world's largest economies, such China, India, United States, Indonesia, and Brazil. Another near-term scenario from a report sponsored by the UN Department of Economic and Social Affairs states that the global economy will lose "nearly $8.5 trillion in output over the next two years [from 2020] due to the Covid-19 pandemic, wiping out nearly all gains of the previous four years. The sharp economic contraction, which marks the sharpest contraction since the Great Depression in the 1930s, comes on top of anaemic economic forecasts of only 2.1 percent at the start of the year."[5] From an ethics perspective, the UN report noted that Covid-19 pushed over 34 million people globally into extreme poverty in 2020.

We cannot turn back globalization. Our challenge is to make globalization an instrument of opportunity and inclusion—not of fear and insecurity. Globalization must work for all. There are more challenges ahead, and bigger ones. As we go forward, the voices of the poor must be our guide.

Time is short. We must be the first generation to think both as nationals of our countries and as global citizens in an ever-shrinking and more connected planet. Unless we hit hard at poverty, institutional racism, bigotry, disinformation and misinformation that promulgates autocratic nationalism, and the ruinous effects of Covid-19, we will not have a stable and peaceful world, shaped by the decisions we make and the courage and responsible leadership that is reemerging today.

Sources: Wolfensohn, J. D. (2001, April 2). The challenges of globalization: The role of the World Bank. WorldBank.org. https://documents.worldbank.org/en/publication/documents-reports/documentdetail/391781468762627948/the-challenges-of-globalization-the-role-of-the-world-bank; U.S. Census Bureau. (2020, June 25). U.S. and world population clock.

https://www.census.gov/popclock/; UN Department of Economic and Social Affairs. (2019, June 17). Growing at a slower pace, world population is expected to reach 9.7 billion in 2050 and could peak at nearly 11 billion around 2100. https://www.un.org/development/desa/en /news/population/world-population-prospects-2019.html; Cilluffo, A., and Ruiz, N. G. (2019, June 17). *PewResearch.org.* https://www.pewresearch.org/fact-tank/2019/06/17/worlds-popu lation-is-projected-to-nearly-stop-growing-by-the-end-of-the-century/; Galloway, L. (2020, March 23). Five superpowers ruling the world in 2050. *BBC.com.* http://www.bbc.com/travel /story/20200322-five-superpowers-ruling-the-world-in-2050; Wolfensohn, J. D. (2004, February 16). Financing the Monterrey Consensus—Remarks at the conference: Making globaliza-tion work for all. *WorldBank.org*; World Bank. (2007). *Global economic prospects: Overview and global outlook.* http://documents1.worldbank.org/curated/en/943761468762323157/pdf/381380REPL ACEM1nomic1Prospects12007.pdf.

We begin by identifying the forces underlying the globalization process in general, and then present ethical issues that companies in the global environment face. Business and ethical competencies that managers and professionals need to compete when doing business internationally are presented. We discuss the societal "dark side" of ethical issues and globalization, followed by a presentation of MNEs as stakeholders and their host-country relationships. We conclude by identifying negotiation methods for making ethical decisions, taking cross-cultural contexts into consideration.

Globalization and the Forces of Change

Because globalization involves the integration of technology, markets, politics, cultures, labor, production, and commerce, it encompasses the processes and results of this integration and disintegration. The economic benefits of globalization are both large and measurable. Globalization "expands trade flows and allows consumers to enjoy a range of goods and services vastly larger than that produced by their domestic economy. International financial flows enhance the efficiency with which capital and know-how are allocated."[6] The pre-Covid-19 global economy has been estimated at $86 trillion. GDP is expected to rebound for the largest economies; the 2021 partial-year estimate is $59.9 trillion.[7] Although globalization has facilitated economic growth over several decades, this process is also vulnerable to forces in the environment, as discussed in this chapter. Pre-Covid-19 threats to economic stability and growth were the national bankruptcies and debt crises across the globe, subprime-lending crisis, out-of-control investment practices, dysfunctional governmental regulation, rising oil and energy prices, environmental catastrophes (like the 2011 earthquake in Japan), and global terrorism, all of which continue to generate costs to businesses and the public. The most recent threats to economic stability and growth include the economic confrontation/friction between major powers, national autocratic and corrupt regimes, domestic political polarization, destruction of natural ecosystems, cyber-ransom attacks, and uncontrolled fires.

Of particular ethical and human concern is the increase in global poverty and income disparity. "More than a third of the world lived in extreme poverty 30 years ago. Today, less than 10 percent of people live on $1.90 a day or less." About 736 million people, or 85 percent of people who are extremely poor, are located in just five countries since 2015.[8] The poorest 40 percent of the world's population accounts for 5 percent of global income. The richest 20 percent accounts for three-quarters of world income."[9] However, the global poverty rate was cut in half between 1990 and 2010.[10]

The Covid-19 pandemic is predicted to erase almost of the progress from the last five years, and it is predicted that 40 to 60 million people will fall into extreme poverty ($1.90/day). "The global extreme poverty rate could rise by 0.3 to 0.7 percentage points to around 9 percent in 2020. Additionally, the percentage of people living on less than $3.20 a day could rise by 0.3 to 1.7 percentage points to 23 percent or higher, an increase of some 40 million to 150 million people."[11] These conditions create and add to the instability of governments, the rule of law, and political regimes, and to the influence of global and domestic terrorism.

Growth has been shown to decrease poverty. Growth has frequently been much more effective at reducing poverty in countries with low-income inequality than in countries with high-income inequality. Promoting equality, particularly among different religious, ethnic, or racial groups, also helps reduce social conflict.[12]

But as countries recover from Covid-19, stabilize, and continue to grow, possibilities for positive change can occur. However, unless growth trends dramatically upward, "it is not possible to maintain the trend rate of poverty reduction with so many fewer individuals ready to cross the line." The geography of poverty will be transformed. China passed the point years ago with more citizens above the poverty line than below it. In 2020, there were hardly any Chinese left consuming less than $1.25 a day; everyone will have escaped poverty. But there is still a long way to go. According to UNICEF, "22,000 children die each day due to poverty. . . . Nearly a billion people entered the 21st century unable to read a book or sign their names." There are 2.2 billion children in the world; one billion live in poverty.[13]

Entering a post-Covid-19 era, responsible and accountable leadership at all levels of government, business, and other organizations is required to ensure effective governance and performance. Before turning again to the macro-level stakeholder global environment, we turn to the topic of leadership, managerial and professional skills, and ethical capacities needed in a changing global environment.

POINT/COUNTERPOINT

Is Globalization Retreating or Moving toward a Rebound?

Globalization is the web of relationships between economies worldwide by way of international trade and investments. Protectionism is "an economic policy that attempts to protect domestic businesses from foreign competition and labor markets, usually by imposing trade barriers like tariffs" (Masterclass definition).

Instructions: Each student in this exercise must select *either* the Point or CounterPoint argument, defend that choice, and state why you believe either one or the other. Be ready to argue your choice as the instructor directs. Afterward, the class is debriefed and there is further discussion as a class.

POINT: Globalization is retreating ("slow-balization"). High tariffs and trade wars during the Donald Trump administration (which could rebound in 2024) have slowed and diminished globalization. In addition, globalization is on the decline because it creates unequal economic growth between rich and poor countries; exploits cheaper labor markets; and causes job displacement. Other costs of globalization (e.g., military protection for poorer countries and protection for all against cyberattacks) also exert unfair and unreasonable costs on industrialized nations. It isn't fair for countries struggling because of post-Covid-19 impacts to continue supporting those countries that can't support themselves even under "normal" conditions. (The Covid-19 crisis is responsible for shrinking global trade by 9.2 percent in 2020–2021.) The United Kingdom's exit from Brexit happened for similar reasons.

COUNTERPOINT: Globalization will expand. Globalization is inevitable in a complex, ever-changing world. The globalization process increases economic growth by increasing the international exchange of goods. It brings technological advances and information sharing; facilitates production, making it more affordable by creating a global market that allows businesses more access to production opportunities and consumers; and increases trade and investments in larger, otherwise nonexistent global financial markets. New goods and services are also produced from interdependence and technology sharing. Note that pre-Covid-19, the global economy expanded in 2019. Assisting poorer countries is the right thing to do, and economically speaking, "a rising tide lifts all ships." Also, China is moving to exert its economic influence and prowess over economically poorer but mineral rich countries (e.g., Africa). Globalization can create a fairer economic "playing field."

SOURCE

Irwin, D. (2020, December 17). Globalization in retreat. *Wall Street Journal*, R13; MasterClass. (n.d.). 3 examples of globalization. Accessed March 1, 2021, https://www.masterclass.com/articles/how-globalization-works-pros-and -cons-of-globalization#3-examples-of-globalization.

■ 8.2 Managing and Working in a Different Global World: Professional and Ethical Competencies

Young Global Leaders (YGL) in government and business shared their views at the 2020 Annual Summit regarding responsible leadership during a global crisis. "Since the onset of the COVID-19 pandemic, leadership has been put to the test. To emerge from the crisis stronger and more resilient requires re-thinking what it means to lead by prioritizing purpose, trust, empathy and inclusivity."[14] Their four takeaways mirror those of the major global consulting firms: (1) a strong sense of purpose enables adaptability, (2) involving more stakeholders boosts trust, (3) there's power in empathy and compassion, and (4) leadership means no one is left behind.

At a Servant Leadership Research Roundtable years before Covid-19, several scholars noted that global leaders need several key attributes:

1. Openness to other cultures and flexible
2. Awareness of verbal and nonverbal differences in communication with a person from another culture
3. Awareness that management practices developed in one culture may not be easily transferred to another
4. Awareness of the cultural influences on behavior
5. Adaptiveness
6. Loyalty, honesty, and ethical behavior
7. Multidisciplinary perspectives, which are needed for problem solving[15]

Although there are no definitive empirical or longitudinal studies that confirm skills of an ideal global manager or professional, research offers expertise areas for succeeding in international and global careers.[16] Figure 8.1 illustrates one such example. Figure 8.2 extends the managerial competencies with ethical dimensions of those skills. For example, having a managerial "multidimensional perspective" (i.e., "extensive multifunctional, multicountry, and multi-environment experience") would be complemented by having a "multidimensional ethical perspective," which would in turn require experience in managing cross-cultural country values and ethical orientations.

Figure 8.1

Global Leadership Skills

How can the profit of an International manager be described?
Illustration of a Global Manager (fictional) Profile

• **Multidimensional perspective**
Extensive multifunctional, multicountry, and multienvironment experience

• **Line management proficiency**
Successful track record in overseas projects and assignments

• **Good decision making**
Successful in making tactical and strategic decisions

• **Resourcefulness**
Skilled in getting known and accepted by host country's stakeholders

• **Culturally sensitive**
Can effectively deal with people from a variety of cultures

• **Culturally adaptive**
Quick and easy to adapt to foreign culture; cross-cultural experiences

• **Team-building skills**
Able to create culturally diverse working groups

• **Mental maturity**
Endurance for the rigors of foreign posts (culture shock)

• **Negotiating skills**
Track record of conducting successful (international) business negotiations

• **Change-agent skills**
Track record of successfully initiating and implementing organizational changes

• **Visionary ability**
Quick to spot and respond to political and economical threats and opportunities

Source: Based on Rainer Busch. (April 24, 2008). Global leadership skills. *RainerBusch.de.* http://www.rainerbusch.de /GLS-24-04-2008-Busch.pdf, accessed March 2, 2012.

Figure 8.2

Complementary, Managerial Ethical, and Social Responsibility Competencies

• **Multidimensional perspective** Extensive multifunctional, multicountry, and multienvironment experience	• **Multidimensional/ethical perspective** Multifunctional and multicountry business experience in leading with ethical values
• **Line-management proficiency** Successful track record in overseas projects and assignments	• **Line-management social responsibility** Socially responsible capacity in cross-cultural projects and assignments
• **Good decision making** Successful in making tactical and strategic decisions	• **Ethical decision making** Ability to negotiate ethically cross-culturally
• **Resourcefulness** Skilled in getting known and accepted by host country's stakeholders	• **Ethical resourcefulness** Skilled in getting known and accepted by host country's stakeholders for ethical reputation
• **Culturally sensitive** Can effectively deal with people from a variety of cultures	• **Cross-cultural ethics awareness** Can effectively communicate with others' cross-cultural values
• **Culturally adaptive** Quick and easy to adapt to foreign culture; cross-cultural experiences	• **Cross-cultural values adaptation** Quick and easy to adapt to different values while maintaining core ethical principles
• **Team-building skills** Able to create culturally diverse working groups	• **Team-building and social responsibility skills** Able to adapt to ethical differences of diverse working groups and relationships
• **Mental maturity** Endurance for the rigors of foreign posts (culture shock)	• **Moral maturity** Ability to work with rigors of different professionals' moral maturity
• **Negotiating skills** Track record of conducting successful (international) business negotiation	• **Negotiating skills across country cultures** Track record in successfully negotiating conflicting country norms and outcomes
• **Change-agent skills** Track record of successfully initiating and implementing organizational changes	• **Change-agent ethical skills** Track record of acting ethically in leading organizational change
• **Visionary ability** Quick to spot and respond to political and economic threats and opportunities	• **Stakeholder management skills** Quick to spot and respond to ethical issues in political and economic situations

Source: Based on Rainer Busch. (April 24, 2008). Global leadership skills. *RainerBusch.de.* http://www.rainerbusch.de/GLS-24-04-2008-Busch.pdf, accessed March 2, 2012. Adapted by Joseph W. Weiss, 2014. All rights reserved.

Many large companies outsource the assessment process for selecting managers and professionals to work abroad. Other firms have in-house assessment centers to evaluate, select, and train professionals for international and global work.

Shared Leadership in Teams' Competency

Global leadership also depends on teams. Research on workplace attitudes and values across 53 nations and regional groupings by professors at the Graduate School of Management in Claremont found that "teams that perform poorly tend to be dominated by the team leader, while high-performing teams have a shared-leadership structure. But beware: There are some risks executives run by sharing the reins. And [the] research suggests also that success may depend on the particular country where a business is operating."[18]

The researchers noted that it is more difficult to share leadership if members share values from a society that is based on unequal distribution of power. Those who occupy leadership positions are less likely to share their authority, since they likely believe it is something they have earned. Likewise, followers may be reluctant to share leadership because they view control as the sole prerogative of the appointed leader. Followers may also judge a leader to be weak if the leader attempts to hand over the reins. Countries that are more egalitarian and where power is more decentralized include Argentina, Australia, Austria, Britain, Canada, Denmark, Finland, Germany, India, Ireland, Israel, Italy, Jamaica, Japan, the Netherlands, New Zealand, Norway, South Africa, Sweden, Switzerland, and the United States. Of course, not every professional from a country in either of these two groupings shares that country's value system; this research is only an indicator. Use Ethical Insight 8.2 to discover how you identify your preferences for team leadership, based on your country of origin as well as your beliefs about effective teams and leadership.

Ethical Insight 8.2

Country Culture Counts: Potential for Shared Leadership

Countries that accept unequal power distribution in organizations and institutions; centralized decision making; **inegalitarian:** Arab countries, Belgium, Brazil, Chile, Colombia, Costa Rica, East Africa, Ecuador, El Salvador, France, Greece, Guatemala, Hong Kong, Indonesia, Iran, Korea, Malaysia, Mexico, Pakistan, the Philippines, Panama, Peru, Portugal, Singapore, Spain, Taiwan, Thailand, Turkey, Uruguay, Venezuela, West Africa, and Yugoslavia

Countries that do not accept unequal power distribution; decentralized decision making; **egalitarian:** Argentina, Australia, Austria, Britain, Canada, Denmark, Finland, Germany, India, Ireland, Israel, Italy, Jamaica, Japan, the Netherlands, New Zealand, Norway, South Africa, Sweden, Switzerland, and the United States

Questions

1. What is your country of origin? In which country have you lived, studied, or worked the longest?
2. Which decision-making style do you prefer in a team: centralized or decentralized? Explain.
3. Which leadership decision-making style do you believe would allow for more ethical decisions: (a) centralized/single leader or (b) decentralized/shared leadership? Explain.
4. What has been your experience in observing how more ethically oriented teams have performed? Were those teams centralized, authoritarian or decentralized, egalitarian in their leadership decisionmaking? Explain.

Source: Pearce, C. (2008, July 7). Follow the leaders. *Wall Street Journal.*

Under the heading "Passing the Mantle," the Claremont researchers provide the following leadership insights:

- *The Mistake:* When companies put together teams of employees, they usually hamstring the group right from the start by appointing one team member to lead the crew.
- *The Alternative:* Leadership should be shared among team members, according to whoever has the most expertise for the job at hand. Our research shows that when teams share leadership, their companies usually see big benefits.
- *The Caveat:* Shared leadership doesn't work in all situations—for instance, if the teammates haven't had time to learn each other's strengths and gauge who should be in charge at any given time. Shared leadership also faces big hurdles in some cultures, such as those that generally favor strong central authority.[19]

To summarize, people's cultural backgrounds, based on country differences, can affect their effectiveness as a global team leader and member. Of course, this type of difference is not the only factor determining team effectiveness. Yet, being aware of the effects of cultural background (on oneself and others) is important—not only for team membership but also for ethical decision-making differences, as we discussed earlier and will address again later in the chapter.

During the Covid-19 crisis, major studies have shown that leaders and team members would benefit from being and showing an increased emphasis on empathy; being purposeful, calm, clear, and confident; being both action-oriented and reflective, inspiring, resilient, aware of mindsets, and courageous.[20]

Global Ethical Values and Principles

The world's top-10 most influential values-based surveys in 152 languages, in this order are: Family, Relationships, Financial Security, Belonging, Community, Personal Growth, Loyalty, Religion/Spirituality, Employment Security, and Personal Responsibility.[21] A lack ethical values generally results in unethical practices across geographic boundaries that affect nation-states as well as corporations doing business in different countries. There is a need for both legal regulation and ethical motivation, as has recently been demonstrated in the United States and internationally by overly aggressive actions against Black and minority individuals taken by law enforcement, the rise of domestic and destructive terrorism, and autocratic, corrupt leaders. A classic example, which has repercussions in 2021, was the blatant illegal and unethical practice that has affected global business is South Africa's previous apartheid system that was supported by several local laws from 1948 to 1986. These laws condoned and even enforced racial segregation that protected white supremacy and domination. "Firms with subsidiaries operating in SA were bound by the apartheid legislation even though each of the laws could be ethically faulted."[22] Within that system, MNEs had to decide whether to continue supporting a system of racial discrimination and slavery by doing business in South Africa during that time or leave. Other forms of questionable ethical behavior by different countries will be discussed later in this chapter, including child labor, intolerable working conditions for employees, foreign firms paying below living wages for cheap labor, exporting proven hazardous products to different countries, and MNEs' usurping poorer countries' environmental and natural resources to gain profit. For these reasons, global values and principles were developed by international agencies and institutions to inform and constrain all corporations doing business across national borders from illegal and unethical acts such as apartheid.

Examples of Global Principles and Values

There are different universal sets of values and ethical standards that are shared by MNEs. The Global Sullivan Principles are one such source. "These principles were developed by Leon Sullivan (the first African-American to be appointed to the board of a major corporation—General Motors) in 1977. General Motors was the largest American employer of black South Africans at the time."[23] Over 30 prestigious firms have agreed to these principles, which are shown in Table 8.1. Other such global codes, principles, and statements of universal rights include the Caux Round Table Principles for Business, the Amnesty International Human Rights Principles for Business, the Asian Pacific Economic Cooperation Forum Business Code of Conduct, the Ceres Principles, the Clarkson Principles of Stakeholder Management, the International Labour Organization (ILO) Declaration of Fundamental Principles and Rights at Work, the Organisation for Economic Cooperation and Development (OECD) Guidelines for Corporate Governance, the OECD Guidelines for Multinational Enterprises, and the United Nations (UN) Declaration of Human Rights.

Table 8.1
Global Sullivan Principles of Social Responsibility

The Principles

As a company which endorses the Global Sullivan Principles we will respect the law, and as a responsible member of society we will apply these Principles with integrity consistent with the legitimate role of business. We will develop and implement company policies, procedures, training and internal reporting structures to ensure commitment to these Principles throughout our organization. We believe the application of these Principles will achieve greater tolerance and better understanding among peoples, and advance the culture of peace. Accordingly, we will:

- Express our support for universal human rights and, particularly, those of our employees, the communities within which we operate, and parties with whom we do business.
- Promote equal opportunity for our employees at all levels of the company with respect to issues such as color, race, gender, age, ethnicity, or religious beliefs, and operate without unacceptable worker treatment such as the exploitation of children, physical punishment, female abuse, involuntary servitude, or other forms of abuse.
- Respect our employees' voluntary freedom of association.
- Compensate our employees to enable them to meet at least their basic needs and provide the opportunity to improve their skill and capability in order to raise their social and economic opportunities.
- Provide a safe and healthy workplace; protect human health and the environment; and promote sustainable development.
- Promote fair competition including respect for intellectual and other property rights, and not offer, pay, or accept bribes.
- Work with governments and communities in which we do business to improve the quality of life in those communities—their educational, cultural, economic, and social well-being—and seek to provide training and opportunities for workers from disadvantaged backgrounds.
- Promote the application of these Principles by those with whom we do business.

Source: Sullivan, The Rev. Leon H. (n.d.). The global Sullivan principles. *Mallenbaker.net.* Accessed May 12, 2012, https://csridentity.com/globalsullivanprinciples/

Mary Guy's (1991) 10 core values also serve as a practical set of universal principles:[24]

1. Caring
2. Honesty
3. Accountability
4. Promise keeping
5. Pursuit of excellence
6. Loyalty
7. Fairness
8. Integrity
9. Respect for others
10. Responsible citizenship

Does One Set of Values "Fit" All?

Can one set of values apply to different cultures? According to some, universal "principles and common values are often—and wrongly—dismissed because actual behavior does not appear to coincide. The apparent incoherence between expressed values and observed behavior does not make values irrelevant to cross-cultural comparisons."[25] Researchers have cited empirical data from a study that included France, Germany, the United States, Japan, Mexico, South Africa, Argentina, Chile, Russia, Nigeria, and India to argue that although culture is a carrier of values, "values are not solely derived from one's culture."[26] In other words, there are universal principles and values that are not, nor should they be, culturally derived; rather, these principles should transcend cultures for the greater good of all. As we discuss in the last section of this chapter, issues emerge not only from the problem of identifying or agreeing on a set of universal ethical principles, but also when there is a clash between individuals, groups, and/or organizational interests that are constrained or denied by one or more of these principles. Doing the right thing may violate cultural norms in several cultures; some universal principles may take precedence over some cultural values for the common good, as well as for the rights of certain individuals and groups.

Know Your Own Cultural and Core Values, Your Organization's, and Those with Whom You Are Working

Corporate leaders and professionals working in different countries and globally need to know (1) their own cultural and ethical values and principles; (2) those of their organization or company; and (3) those of the individuals, team, and organization in whose culture they are working. Without this knowledge, two particular "ethical traps" may face individual professionals, teams, and companies:

1. *Acting ethnocentrically* is demonstrating "the belief in the inherent superiority of one's own ethnic group or culture; a tendency to view alien groups or cultures from the perspective of one's own."[27] Acting from one's own cultural preferences without awareness of or concern for others' cultural values also has ethical consequences that can result in negative reactions from others and your failure to achieve business goals. Critics have accused the U.S. government of acting ethnocentrically in some of its policies and preemptive approaches to imposing democracy on some Middle Eastern countries. Some North American and European corporations in previous decades and empires have also acted ethnocentrically in their use and destruction of poorer countries' resources for competitive gain.

2. *Moral (and cultural) relativism* is based on "the view that no culture is superior to any other culture when comparing systems of morality, law, and politics. It's the philosophical notion that all cultural beliefs are equally valid and that truth itself is relative, depending on the cultural environment."[28] At a cultural level, acting from this theory equates to "when in Rome, do as the Romans do," or do what your company believes is right at the time and in the immediate circumstance. If you had been working with an American company in South Africa in the 1970s, you may very well have been acting from this principle. You would have been, as noted earlier, accepting the practice of state-condoned racial discrimination. Some of the larger petroleum

companies working in conjunction with other cohorts have been described as acting from a relativistic ethic to satisfy their own profits at the expense of the environment and poorer working peoples who are barely surviving with increased energy and fuel prices.

A method you can use to understand your own cultural values and ethical principles—and those of your team and even organization—in an international setting comes from Joseph Badaracco at Harvard University. His method is presented in Chapter 2 and uses three key questions to consider before acting or taking a position in a "defining moment." The following is an extension of that method.[29] We have added a cross-cultural dimension to the probes.

For individuals, the key question is "Who am I?" First, ask and discern, "What cultural values, attitudes, and habits might influence my decision?" Second, what are my *ethical principles-in-action* (i.e., principles practiced). Do I generally rely on a utilitarian ethic? Do I rely on justice, fairness, and duty principles? Am I an altruist, pragmatist? Do I respect the rights of others? Or do I make decisions based on relativism; that is, act from my own self-interest and cultural values only? Do I demonstrate virtues in my character and toward others? Also, am I flexible in my ethical thinking when dealing with others, or am I rigid and demanding? Third, with whom am I making this decision? Do I understand their basic cultural values? Do I know some of their ethical principles-in-action? With this understanding, you may then:

1. Identify your feelings and intuitions that are emphasized in the situation.
2. Identify your deepest values that are in conflict in the situation.
3. Consider the feeling and intuitions of the other(s) in the situation.
4. Identify what their values and ethics are and how these might affect the conflict in the situation.
5. Identify the best course of action to understand the right thing to do for you and the others.

In work groups, managers can ask, "Who are we?" (Again, consider each team member's cultural values as well as your own and ask how the team reflects any particular set of values. Identify the ethical principles-in-action of the team.) You can then address these three questions as a team in this situation:

1. What strong views and understanding of the situation do team members have—cross-culturally and within your own team?
2. Which position or view would most likely win over others in a way that would be least harmful culturally and organizationally to all affected?
3. Can we respond in this situation in a way that reveals the values we care about in this organization?

Company executives can ask, "Who is the company?" (What are its core values and ethical principles-in-action in this international context and global setting?) Three questions you can consider are:

1. Have I strengthened my position and the organization to the best of my ability, relying on my values and ethics?
2. Have I considered my organization's values and role vis-à-vis society's cultural values and interests (both in my society and that of another, if working abroad) in a bold and creative way?
3. How can I transform my vision based on these reflections into action that combines creativity, ethical responsibility, courage, and shrewdness?

As discussed in Chapter 2, these ways of reflecting on the contextual values and facts in a situation when a difficult decision must be made is not always easy, especially in a cross-national setting. Deciding between two or more positions that are culturally and even morally "right" for parties in conflict also requires moral courage, common sense, and shrewdness. Section 8.7 offers specific methods of negotiating conflicting values cross-culturally. Next, we discuss some ethical issues in business that professionals may encounter when working across national boundaries.

Cross-Cultural Business Ethical Issues Professionals May Experience

Some of the more predominant ethical issues that managers and professionals in international settings have experienced include (1) bribery and gifts, (2) sexual and racial discrimination, and (3) piracy and intellectual property protection. These are a sample of such issues. The cases in this book present additional issues.

Bribery: A Form of Corruption

A former senior manager at Siemens admitted building up an elaborate system of slush funds and shell firms at the request of his superiors to help Europe's biggest technology group win overseas contracts through bribes. Reinhard Siekaczek told a Munich court [on May 26, 2008] that he had informed his entire divisional board about the system and assumed that the whole group executive board knew about it from at least 2004. On the opening day of Germany's biggest post-war corporate corruption trial, Siekaczek described how managers signed off "commissions" on yellow Post-it notes which could be easily removed in case of raids or investigations. His damning testimony included allegations that his efforts to stop the widespread bribery at Siemens' fixed-line telecommunications equipment division (Com), where he was a sales manager, had fallen foul of his superiors who "didn't want to hear." Siekaczek, aged 57, is the first of up to 300 accused among Siemens' current and former staff to stand trial in a corruption scandal that the group itself admits involves at least €1.3bn (£1bn) in siphoned-off money. Six of its divisions are involved in a bribery system spanning the globe that has so far cost it €1.8bn to clear up, including a €201m fine from another Munich court. It could result in a multibillion-dollar penalty from the U.S. Securities and Exchange Commission as well as the loss of lucrative contracts.[30]

Bribery can be a serious matter. Bribery payments are estimated at $1 trillion worldwide.[31] Leaders' and professionals' careers can be lost, settlements and court costs can be substantial to companies, and reputations tarnished. Bribery is part of the definition of corruption ("Corruption: moral perversion, depravity, perversion of integrity, bribery, corrupt or dishonest proceedings, any corrupting influence or agency. Bribery: money or other valuable consideration given or promised with a view to corrupting the behavior of a person, a public official crime in some countries and not others").[32] Bribery is a global problem: "Bribery in developing countries often stems from multinationals based in the richest countries. Global financial centers play a role in allowing officials to move, hide and invest illicitly gained wealth. Principles and ethics vary between countries. Interestingly, the U.S. accepts domestic political or legislative influencing practices such as lobbying and campaign funding, while considering the same underlying activities corrupt in other countries. The responsibility to combat corruption is global and no country can hold itself above the solution."[33]

The organization Transparency International publishes a Buyers Payers Bribery Index, where a high average score indicates low bribery. The report shows a ranked list of the top-30 countries (out of 197 countries/territories around the world, that the UN recognizes) on bribery. (Note: China and India ranked last and are not shown on this short list.) The top 16 in this index are shown in Table 8.2.

International organizations that have addressed and ratified bribery in different countries' legislation include the OECD, the Organization of American States (OAS), and the Council of Europe (CoE).

In the United States, the Foreign Corrupt Practices Act (FCPA) was enacted in 1977 and substantially revised in 1988. The provisions of the FCPA prohibit the bribery of foreign government officials by U.S. persons and prescribe accounting and record-keeping practices that prohibit American companies from offering payments to foreign government officials for the purpose of obtaining or retaining business. "When the Act was passed in 1977, it

Table 8.2
Index 2020: Rank/Country/Average Score (0–10)

Rank	Score	Rank	Score
1 Denmark	88	9 Germany	80
1 New Zealand	88	11 Canada	77
3 Finland	85	11 U.K.	77
3 Singapore	85	11 Australia	77
3 Sweden	85	11 Hong Kong	77
3 Switzerland	85	15 Austria	76
7 Norway	84	15 Belgium	76
8 Netherlands	82	16 U.S.	25

Source: Transparency International. (2020). *Corruption Perception Index https://www.transparency.org/en/cpi/2020/index/nzl#*

received substantial backing from American business because they could not compete fairly in overseas markets where bribery was accepted. The FCPA's anti-bribery regime—along with the adoption of treaties like the . . . [OECD's], which required signatory countries to outlaw all financial crime—has helped to level the playing field abroad for U.S. business."[34] "The fact that the FCPA deals only with bribes made to foreign government officials acts to exclude from the FCPA . . . payments to foreign persons who are not governmental officials. Additionally, the fact that the FCPA deals only with bribes that are intended for the purpose of obtaining or retaining business acts excludes grease or facilitating payments from the scope of the FCPA. A grease or facilitating payment is a payment made to expedite or secure the performance of a routine government action. Routine government actions include obtaining permits or licenses, processing official papers, clearing goods through Customs, loading and unloading cargo, and providing police protection."[35] U.S. individuals who cannot defend their actions with regards to the FCPA's anti-bribery provisions can face harsh penalties. "U.S. companies can be fined up to $2 million while U.S. individuals (including officers and directors of companies that have willfully violated the FCPA) can be fined up to $100,000 and imprisoned for up to five years, or both. In addition, civil penalties may be imposed."[36]

The U.S. Department of Justice (DOJ) and the Securities and Exchange Commission (SEC) have been more aggressive in enforcing and prosecuting the bribery section of the FCPA. Note the following example:

In December 2007, Lucent agreed to settle parallel DOJ and SEC FCPA enforcement actions by paying $2.5 million in combined fines and penalties for improperly recording travel expenses and other things of value to employees of Chinese companies that were owned or controlled by the state (SOEs). Such individuals are deemed to be "foreign officials" under the FCPA's anti-bribery provisions.

Pursuant to a DOJ non-prosecution agreement, Lucent acknowledged that from at least 2000 to 2003, it spent over $10 million on approximately 315 trips involving over 1,000 employees of Chinese SOEs that had a disproportionate amount of sightseeing, entertainment, and leisure. According to the government, while the trips Lucent paid for were "ostensibly designed to allow the Chinese foreign officials to inspect Lucent's factories and to train the officials in using Lucent's equipment . . . the officials spent little or no time in the United States visiting Lucent's facilities [but instead] visited tourist destinations throughout the United States, such as Hawaii, Las Vegas, the Grand Canyon, Niagara Falls, Disney World, Universal Studios, and New York."[37]

Also, the FCPA's penalties and levied fines have significantly grown in size. In December 2008, "the U.S. Department of Justice announced that the German conglomerate Siemens AG, along with its subsidiaries in Argentina, Bangladesh, and Venezuela, agreed to plead guilty to conspiring to commit violations of the U.S. Foreign Corrupt Practices Act. The criminal fines imposed, totaling more than $450 million, are by far the largest in the history of the FCPA, and are supplemented by more than $350 million in ill-gotten profits."[38]

Table 8.3
Foreign Corrupt Practices Act: 10 Biggest FCPA Cases and Penalties

Company	Country	Penalty	Year
Airbus SE	Netherlands/France	$2.09 billion	2020
Petroleo Brasileiro S.A.-Petrobras	Brazil	$1.78 billion	2018
Telefonaktiebolaget LM Ericsson	Sweden	$1.06 billion	2019
Telia Company AB	Sweden	$1.01 billion	2017
MTS	Russia	$850 million	2019
Siemens	Germany	$800 million	2008
VimpelCom	Netherlands	$795 million	2006
Alstom	France	$772 million	2014
Societe Generale S.A.	France	$585 million	2018
KBR/ Halliburton	United States	$579 million	2009

Source: Cassin, H. (2020, February 3). Airbus shatters the FCPA top ten. *FCPA Blog.* https://fcpablog.com/2020/02/03/airbus-shatters-the-fcpa-top-ten/.

On January 28, 2020, "Airbus SE (Airbus or the Company), a global provider of civilian and military aircraft based in France, has agreed to pay combined penalties of more than $3.9 billion to resolve foreign bribery charges with authorities in the United States, France and the United Kingdom arising out of the Company's scheme to use third-party business partners to bribe government officials, as well as nongovernmental airline executives. Airbus entered into a deferred prosecution agreement with the department in connection with a criminal information file on Jan. 28, 2020 in the District of Columbia charging the Company with conspiracy to violate the anti-bribery provision of the Foreign Corrupt Practices Act and conspiracy to violate the Arms Export Control Act (AECA) and its implementing regulations, the International Traffic in Arms Regulations (ITAR). Airbus engaged in a multiyear and massive scheme to corruptly enhance its business interests by paying bribes in China and other countries and concealing those bribes."[39]

When doing business in developing countries where corruption and particularly bribery is prevalent, it is worth taking the following precautions:

• Read and understand the legislation and its enforcement on corruption and bribery in that country.
• Read and understand the FCPA and the OECD guidelines on corruption.
• Know your business associates and partners where you do business.
• Take an active role in education, compliance, and due diligence.[40]

Gifts versus Bribery

The COVID-19 pandemic during 2020–2021 did not affect anti-corruption enforcement as might have been expected. The Department of Justice and Securities and Exchange Commission remained active, "bringing major cases that set new records and issuing new updates to long-standing FCPA guidance."[41]

A key question for new and even seasoned international business professionals is: When is a gift really a bribe? Peter Madsen, executive director of the Center for the Advancement of Applied Ethics and Political Philosophy at Carnegie Mellon University in Pittsburgh, stated that "hard and fast rules . . . tend to get blurry in international business settings. Even Fortune 500 companies with laudably firm policies have trouble in this area. . . . Relativism is rampant . . . and when you're talking business, cultural relativism becomes a really big problem."[42]

In most parts of the world, especially some less-developed nations, Asia, the Middle East, parts of Europe and the United States, business professionals are expected to "pay to play." Narayan Manandhar, former president of Transparency International in Nigeria, offered a distinction: "Personally, I like to see the bribe located at an intermediate position in a continuum where at one extreme you can put extortion and at the other, a gift. A bribe becomes extortion when it is demand-driven. If a medical doctor asks for a bribe inside an operation theater or an emergency room, it is clearly a matter of extortion. You have been blackmailed to pay the bribe. A bribe could turn into a gift if it is supply-driven. People have asked me whether tips paid to a waiter in a restaurant are a bribe or a gift. Normally, it is not a bribe. It is a gift as there is an element of voluntariness or the absence of a quid pro quo situation."[43]

The OECD uses the acronym GIFT, which expands as "(1) Genuine, (2) Independent, (3) Free, and (4) Transparent. First, the gift must be genuine, that is, offered in appreciation for something which you have done well, in accordance with your functions as a public official, without any encouragement. Second, the gift must be independent in a sense that it does not affect your functioning in the future. Third, it must be free from any obligations to the donor, or his/her family or affiliates. Fourth, it must be transparent. You must be able to declare the gift in a completely transparent way, to your organization and its clients, to your professional colleagues, and to the media and the public in general."[44]

Racial and Sexual Discrimination in the Global Context

Two other areas in which professionals working globally are likely to experience ethical issues are racial and sexual discrimination. The Black Lives Matter movement in the United States became a global phenomenon.[45] Although these issues and sexual harassment were discussed in Chapter 7, here we expand these topics to cross-cultural settings. "Discrimination is an assault on the very notion of human rights. Discrimination is the systematic denial of certain peoples' or groups' full human rights because of who they are or what they believe. International law guarantees human rights to all without distinction based on race, color, sex, language, religion, political or other opinion, national or social origin, property, birth, or other status. Governments are obliged to take essential measures to ensure the right of all to be free from discrimination," according to Amnesty International.[46] Globalization, the widening gap between income groups, the "global war on terror," and the post-9/11 environment have created opportunities and problems with regard to unintended consequences regarding racial discrimination. A brief sample of countries that have immigrant populations illustrates the potential for and experience with racial discrimination. The United States continues to deal with the need for labor while wrestling with "illegal immigration" from Mexico. England has one of the most diverse working populations in the world, with East Indian immigrants representing a large segment of that population (Black/ African/Caribbean/Black British are 3 percent, which is the largest ethnic group after white).[47] Germany must deal with integrating Turkish workers and immigrants. Dubai, the United Arab Emirates, and Saudi Arabia all import labor—of the 1.5 million residents of Dubai, one million are immigrants (Dubai population in 2020 is 3.8 million, of which 88.52 percent are immigrants).[48] "Argentina's population is European (mostly Spanish and Italian descent) and mestizo, which is mixed European and Amerindian ancestry (97.2 percent), Amerindian (2.4 percent), and African (0.4 percent).[49] One of the difficulties in assessing and addressing persistent forms of racial discrimination in Argentina is the lack of adequate information about the population, particularly the indigenous and immigrant communities."[50] Racial discrimination doesn't only occur between native residents and immigrants of host countries. As noted above, discrimination is practiced in different forms, including in MNEs as well as within an international labor force. Racial discrimination here refers to the workplace and generally involves acts relating to hiring, wage inequalities, treatment of employees, working conditions, and promotions.

A world survey on workplace discrimination shows the disparity in opinions about racial discrimination and also calls on governments to act to prevent such acts:[51]

- Majorities in 15 out of 16 nations [polled] agree that employers do not have the right to discriminate. Asked whether employers should be allowed to "refuse to hire a qualified person because of the person's race or ethnicity," on average three out of four (75 percent) say employers should not be able to base hiring decisions on race, while just 19 percent believe they should.

- Majorities against workplace discrimination are largest in France (94 percent), China (88 percent), the United States (86 percent), Indonesia (84 percent), Britain (83 percent), and Azerbaijan (82 percent).

- India stands apart from the other countries polled. Although a plurality opposed such discrimination, an unusually high 30 percent says that employers should be allowed to reject job seekers because of race or ethnicity. Relatively large minorities also agree that employers should be free to hire whom they choose in Nigeria (34 percent) and South Korea (41 percent), though in both cases, majorities are opposed (64 percent and 58 percent, respectively).

- Indonesians (80 percent) and the Chinese (77 percent) believe overwhelmingly that the government should try to prevent discriminatory hiring practices, followed by Azerbaijanis (72 percent), the French (69 percent),

Americans (69 percent), Britons (69 percent), Ukrainians (65 percent), Mexicans (64 percent), and Iranians (61 percent). More modest majorities agree in Russia (58 percent), Egypt (56 percent), Nigeria (56 percent), the Palestinian territories (53 percent), and South Korea (53 percent).

- Two countries differ: Turkey and India. Only 23 percent of Turks say that the government has the responsibility to take measures against workplace discrimination, and 43 percent say it does not. Among Indians, just 27 percent say that government has this responsibility, while 20 percent say it does not.

Companies hiring and integrating employees into their firms benefit from having corporate leaders and cultures that do not tolerate racial discrimination. Lack of respect and fairness from employers in their hiring, promotion, and reward practices leads to employee turnover, absenteeism, and lower performance. Employees usually turn first to their supervisors in the chain of command to report or discuss discrimination problems. If the company has no formal or written policy, the employee must decide whether or not to pursue the issue with others in the organization or go outside. Corporations can benefit from establishing such policies and procedures along with training to support their workforce.

The UN Human Rights Council moved to establish a new subsidiary body, the Expert Mechanism on the Rights of Indigenous Peoples, on December 13, 2007. Other UN agencies, nongovernmental organizations (NGOs), and different countries' human rights groups, such as the European Commission against Racism and Intolerance (ECRI), which was established by the first Summit of Heads of State and Government of the Council of Europe Member States, all continue to implement policies, help create laws, and monitor racial discrimination not only in workplaces but also in different societies. Companies moving to different countries and those already serving different countries need to familiarize their officers and professionals with the work of these UN bodies and NGOs. Many large, established MNEs have partnered and worked with such bodies for decades.

Sexual Discrimination

The MeToo movement also went viral internationally and has influenced new legislation in different countries.[52] Sexual discrimination is generally part of laws dealing with other types of discrimination and rights, such as race, age, national origin, gender, religion, and language. Not all countries have laws or even policies dealing with sexual harassment and/or discrimination specifically against women, or men. In a cross-national survey published in 2000, France, Germany, Mexico, the Philippines, Switzerland, Taiwan, and Venezuela had no "prohibitions on employment discrimination." Several countries also had no "prohibitions on sexual harassment" in the workplace—Ukraine, Singapore, Russia, Republic of South Africa, Poland, China, Hungary, Czech Republic, Colombia, and Brazil. Note that "in Europe, there is an increasing focus on behaviors described as 'moral harassment,' 'mobbing,' or 'workplace bullying,' all of which subordinate concern about the integration of women in the workforce to concern about the rights of all workers."[53]

Companies working globally that follow universal principles and values will adopt sexual-harassment and discrimination policies and be clear that women are included in such policies. Since leadership and professional talent in many regions of the world are at record shortages, companies cannot afford to exclude the protection of competent women leaders and professionals from these policies: "Laws that protect workers from sexual harassment conceive of sexual harassment in a number of different ways: as discrimination based on sex, as an offense against dignity, or as an issue of health and safety in the workplace. The discrimination conception of sexual-harassment law reflects an understanding that such law is designed to protect a vulnerable group—in this case mainly women—that is the target of inappropriate sexual behavior in the workplace. From this viewpoint, laws prohibiting sexual harassment must be implemented so as to remove an obstacle to the integration of women in the workforce. . . . Many countries have adopted the anti-discrimination model of sexual harassment law in an attempt to protect the rights of women in the workplace."[54]

Piracy and Intellectual Property Protection

Intellectual property (IP) is best defined in the context of a quote from a U.S. Trade Representative: "Innovation is the lifeblood of a dynamic economy here in the United States, and around the world. We must defend ideas, inventions and creativity from rip off artists and thieves."[55] When any materials or products are patented, trademarked, and copyrighted in the United States or other countries, these items are assumed to be protected under law. Brands are valuable commodities. When imitated, copied, and abused, the owners and originators of the brand are harmed.

IP theft is estimated at $250 billion annually, according to the U.S. Commerce Department. IP theft is estimated at $600 billion annually in cost to the U.S. economy.[56] The Internet Crime Complaint Center reported "467,361 complaints of suspected Internet crime, with reported losses in excess of $3.5 billion. The top three crime types reported by victims in 2019 were phishing/vishing/smishing/pharming, non-payment/non-delivery, and extortion."[57]

The illegal sharing of music files has been facilitated by the Internet and has become a practice of global piracy. That debate is ongoing. However, when countries protect or do not punish piracy of IP, the issue moves to a different level and can involve government-to-government and global issues. For example: "The threat to IP from backroom thieves who produce counterfeit and pirated products is absolutely the most pervasive threat to the global economy as a whole. The U.S. Chamber of Commerce estimates that counterfeiting and pirated products account for 5 to 7 percent of the global economy, costing the United States alone over 750,000 jobs, which socks U.S. industry for a loss of sales in the area of $250 billion. "Trade in counterfeit and pirated goods has risen steadily in the last few years—and now stands at 3.3 percent of global trade," about $509 billion.[58] The Chamber has directed its efforts, via trade missions and educational programs, toward China, Brazil, South Korea, and Russia with the goal of encouraging enhanced enforcement of IP protection laws within."[59]

Priority watch list countries are China, Indonesia, India, Algeria, Kuwait, Saudi Arabia, Russia, Ukraine, Argentina, Chile, and Venezuela.[60] The Bahamas, Bulgaria, Croatia, the EU, and Latvia have been removed from the watch list monitored by the United States. Intellectual piracy between countries is also viewed in the context of trading agreements and how countries adopt stricter laws to prevent, decrease, and stop observed violations.

Taking a more entrepreneurial view of IP piracy are researchers who state that even if over 80 percent of the software and music consumed in China and India is pirated, the estimated piracy rates in the United States are at about 30 percent. Also, the governments of China and India are becoming serious about laws enforcing IP; their motivation is to accelerate their country's science and technology base. "Instead of obsessing about these issues, companies should aim for a rapid rate of innovation that makes life difficult for imitators and pirates in developed and developing countries alike. Rapid innovation may not reduce piracy, but it will help ensure that pirates' products are viewed as consistently inferior, and thus less desirable."[61] Furthermore, "Companies can also reduce piracy by making their products or services more affordable. This is what Microsoft is now attempting with the introduction of Windows XP Starter Edition, a no-frills and low-priced version of its operating system for India, Brazil and many other emerging markets." U.S. and international firms could reduce IP leakage "by dispersing R&D and production across China, India and other locations."[62]

Companies operating in other countries where IP violations are prevalent need to have clearly stated policies and procedures that are communicated and supported with training for those employees who are responsible for handling these issues with the firm's stakeholders.

■ 8.3 Societal Issues and Globalization: The Dark Side

At a larger societal level, it is difficult to determine whether the process of globalization is the cause or effect of the forces driving this phenomenon. Certainly governments, MNEs, and transnational corporations (TNCs) affect this process, but they too are influenced by the forces driving the changes. In this section, we discuss some of the broader "dark side" issues of globalization before discussing the role of MNEs. The process of globalization may be producing "losers"; that is, countries that cannot share in the wealth- and health-generating processes, activities, and outcomes of globalization because they are either excluded from or ignored with respect to the positive side of globalization, including technology development and use, education, and economic development. However, many of the issues discussed here are being addressed by UN agencies, NGOs, and country governments. Corporations and strategic alliances are attacking problems with the natural environment, as discussed in previous chapters.

Critics generally argue that globalization has caused, or at least enhanced, the following problems: crime and corruption; drug consumption; pollution of the environment; massive layoffs that occur when companies move to regions that offer cheaper labor; decreases in wages; the erosion of individual nations' sovereignty; and the Westernization (led by Americanization) of culture, standards, and trends in entertainment, fashion, food, technology, ways of living, and values. These are not all of the issues related and attributed to globalization, but they are substantial ones that also affect the economies and populations that comprise the environments in which businesses operate.

International Crime and Corruption

"In Eastern Europe, traffickers ship girls through the Balkans and into sex slavery. Russians launder money through tiny Pacific islands that have hundreds of banks but scarcely any roads. Colombian drug barons accumulate such vast resources that they can acquire a Soviet submarine to ship cocaine to the United States. . . . It is clear that the globalization of crime is a logical outcome of the fall of Communism. Capitalism and Communism, ideologies that served as intellectual straitjackets for Americans and Soviets, allowed them to feel justified in unsavory proxies to fight their cold war."[63] The *Global Trends 2015* report estimates that corruption costs $500 billion annually, equivalent to 1 percent of the global economy. The report also states that in the illegitimate economy, narcotics trafficking has projected annual revenues of $100 billion to $300 billion. Identity theft in the United State is estimated to net $16.8 billion (2017), declining to $14.7 billion (2018) because of the shift to embedded chip cards.[64] Every third cigarette exported is sold on the black market.[65] The Corruption Perception Index (CPI)—based on the perceptions of ordinary citizens, business leaders, and experts and developed by the nonprofit group Transparency International—shows that the most corrupt countries in 2019 were Somalia, South Sudan, Syria, Yemen, Venezuela, Sudan, Equatorial Guinea, Afghanistan, North Korea, and Libya. The United States ranked as the 23rd least-corrupt country. Table 8.4 shows recent survey results of the global CPI. It is interesting to note that some of the leading industrialist nations did not rank at the top for noncorrupt activities.

Economic Poverty and Child Slave Labor

Child labor rates are slowing down. Since 2000, according to the International Labour Organization, the number of children working as child laborers has declined from 246 million to 168 million, 85 million of whom still work in hazardous conditions.[66] An exception is in Sub-Saharan Africa, "which has the largest proportion of child laborers (29 percent of children aged 5 to 17) and is increasing." Most child laborers continue to work in agriculture. Only one in five are paid. "In all regions, boys and girls are equally likely to be involved in child labor . . ."with girls far more likely to be involved in unpaid household services."[67] The overwhelming majority are unpaid family workers.[68] Child labor among girls has fallen by 40 percent since 2000, compared to 25 percent for boys. Child labor exists in both developing and industrialized countries, but mostly in South and Southeast Asia, South America, Africa, and increasingly in Eastern Europe, where there is

Table 8.4

Ranking of Countries' Public Sector Corruption, according to the 2013 Corruption Perceptions Index

Least "Corrupt"			Most "Corrupt"		
Rank	Country	Score	Rank	Country	Score
1	Denmark	87	153	Uzbekistan	25
1	New Zealand	87	158	Madagascar	24
3	Finlandia	86	158	Zimbabwe	24
4	Singapore	85	160	Eritrea	23
4	Sweden	85	161	Nicaragua	22
4	Switzerland	85	162	Cambodia	20
7	Norway	84	162	Chad	20
8	Netherlands	82	162	Iraq	20
9	Germany	80	165	Burundi	19
9	Luxembourg	80	165	Congo	19
11	Iceland	78	165	Turkmenistan	19
12	Australia	77	168	Democratic Republic of the Congo	18
12	Austria	77			
12	Canada	77	168	Guinea Bissau	18
12	United Kingdom	77	168	Haiti	18
16	Hong Kong	76	168	Libya	18
17	Belgium	75	172	Korea, North	17
18	Estonia	74	173	Afghanistan	16
18	Ireland	74	173	Equatorial Guinea	16
20	Japan	73	173	Sudan	16
21	United Arab Emirates	71	173	Venezuela	16
21	Uruguay	71	177	Yamen	15
23	France	69	178	Syria	13
23	United States of America	69	179	South Sudan	12
			180	Somalia	9

Source: Transparency International. (2019). Corruption Perceptions Index 2019: Overview of 180 countries. Switzerland Global Enterprise. https://www.s-ge.com/en/article/news/20201-c2-corruption-perceptions -index.

an economic transition from a command economy to a market economy.[69] The 20 years of progress combating child labor is at risk because of the Covid-19 crisis. "According to the brief, Covid-19 could result in a rise in poverty and therefore to an increase in child labor as households use every available means to survive."[70]

Globalization has bypassed Africa; in Sub-Saharan Africa illiteracy is high and modern infrastructure (telecommunications, reliable electrical power) do not exist. The gap in per capita GDP between the richest and poorest countries in the world is about 140:1. This gap will increase as the shift from industrial- to knowledge-based economies continues to occur. Third World countries must modernize around new technologies in order to gain the benefits of globalization.

Some regions of the Ivory Coast continue to attract child-labor traffickers (those who buy, enslave, and sell children to work on industrial projects and plantations used for cocoa and chocolate production).[71] It has been reported that young children, even six years old, work as many as 110 hours a week. On average the children earn less than $2 a day. Some less than $1 a day. It is believed that 10 percent of the world's children are subject to modern child labor, about 152 million children. Around 85 million work under hazardous condition. Moreover, children less than 14 years old in poverty in Bangladesh can work on average, 64 hours a week. Children make up 25 to 30 percent of the workers on farms producing cocoa, coffee, cotton, rubber, tea, tobacco, and other crops in countries such as Kenya, Brazil, and Mexico. Profit generated from child slavery is estimated to have reached $75.8 billion in 2020. One in four children is a victim of human trafficking and forced into labor. In African countries, children are being sold as slaves for about $37.[72]

The Third World includes not only all of Sub-Saharan Africa, but also large parts of the Middle East and much of South Asia and Central and South America. "Hunger is common; disease is rampant; infant mortality is high; life expectancy is short."[73] Notable economists from the Group of Eight (leading industrial countries) conclude that solutions to Third World poverty must include "systematic attempts to change incentives at every level in the global system—from the gangsterish Third World governments that exploit their citizens to the international institutions that prop them up through continued lending."[74]

The Global Digital Divide

Article 19 of the International Covenant on Civil and Political Rights (1966) states that "everyone shall have the right to freedom of expression; this right shall include freedom to seek, receive and impart information."[75] "The term *digital divide* refers to the gap between those individuals, households, businesses, and geographic areas, at different socioeconomic levels, who have access to information and communication technologies (ICTs) and use the Internet for a wide variety of activities, and those who do not." Currently, "70 percent of the world population is still excluded from the use of information technologies."[76] It is estimated that 59 percent of the world population is actively using the Internet, as of 2020, or almost 4.57 billion people. "The countries with the highest Internet penetration rates worldwide are the United Arab Emirates (UAE), Denmark, and South Korea. At the opposite end of the spectrum is North Korea, with virtually no online usage penetration among the general population, ranking last worldwide."[77]

It was noted, even in 2011, that "the digital divide is growing wider across the world as broadband access becomes out of reach for many in emerging markets."[78] Research by analysts Richard Hurst and those at Ovum showed that broadband costs are significantly greater for those in emerging countries. "According to a survey of 19 emerging markets, it was found that some countries are charging over triple what developed nations have to shell out for what is increasingly seen as a basic human right. In South Africa, for instance, entry level services went as high as $1,443 per year, with high end services reaching an enormous $6,000."[79] Consumers in Africa pay one of the highest rates. The average cost across the African continent is 7.12 percent of monthly income, and in some cases one gigabyte (1GB) of data costs more than a fifth of average earnings. "Citizens of Chad, [the Democratic Republic of] Congo, and the Central Africa Republic must all pay more than 20 percent of average earnings for 1GB of mobile broadband data. By contrast, the most affordable rates in the continent are in Egypt at 0.5 percent and Mauritius at 0.59 percent." Therefore, an estimated 49 percent of the world's population remains offline.[80]

One-third of the world's population is disconnected from, and has no access, to the Internet. This fact continues to broaden the divide between the haves and the have-nots and between First and Third World countries. Less than 1 percent of online users live in Africa. About 13.6 percent of Central Africans were Internet users on December 31, 2019.[81] Less than 5 percent of computers are connected to the Internet in developing countries. The developed world has almost 50 phone lines for every 100 people, compared to 1.4 phones per 100 people in low-income countries. Countries excluded from the global economy are those that cannot and do not build access to the Internet. Wireless technologies offer encouraging signs for Third World country access to First World technologies.[82] The EU has committed to concentrate its efforts on formulating information on society policies, focusing on EU coordination, Internet governance, and financing. The United States, technology MNEs, and other regional alliances are also working to fund and supply less-advantaged countries with Internet capabilities.[83] Alliance for Affordable Internet (A4AI) is an initiative that "brings together businesses, governments, and civil society actors from across the globe to deliver the policies needed to reduce the cost to connect and make universal, affordable Internet access a reality for all." The A4AI is hosted by the World Wide Web Foundation. Some sponsors of A4AI are Google, Sweden Sverige, Facebook, Huawei, Intel, Microsoft, and many others.[84]

Westernization (Americanization) of Cultures

Globalization has brought "Americanization" (some critics say American imperialism) to other cultures through fast-food commerce (McDonald's, the *Fast Food Nation,* and *Food, Inc.* phenomenon discussed in Chapter 5). "McDonaldization"[85] is "the process by which the principles of the fast-food restaurant are coming to dominate more and more sectors of American society as well as the rest of the world."[86] George Ritzer, the author of *The McDonaldization of Society*, argues that "McDonaldization affects not only the restaurant business but also education, work, the criminal justice system, health care, travel, leisure, dieting, politics, the family, religion, and virtually every other aspect of society."[87] (Ritzer states toward the end of his book that "McDonaldization will someday pass on when the nature of society has changed so dramatically that they can no longer adapt to it."[88])

In addition to fast food, the Internet has brought instant exposure to all forms of American culture: entertainment, film, news, music, and art. Values and ways of living underlie these influences and are not always welcome in many countries—France, China, Singapore, and countries in the Middle East, to name a few. Serious ethical questions are asked that are related to problems and threats of globalization through Westernization: "Does globalization result in cultural and economic homogenization through a heightened emphasis on consumerism? Do local and global values change as a result of international integration that promotes the conversion of national economies into environmentally and socially harmful export-oriented systems for competition in geographically and culturally transcendent 'world markets'?"[89]

American-based advertising to children, in particular, also has come under criticism in the United States. Juliet Schor's 2004 book, *Born to Buy*, examines American contemporary culture in which advertising significantly affects children age 18 months through 13 years. Schor's research shows that children shopped "50 percent more than the preceding generation, both with their parents and on their own. The supermarket was the predominant consumer arena. . . . Commodities have become increasingly influential especially in social dynamics within schools."[90]

Children's advertising also affects the foods children eat, the clothes they buy, the product brands they know and select when shopping, advice on relationships with parents and friends, and what they watch on TV and in the cinema. They are also influenced by social media. According to Schor, one remedy of this process would be the "decommercialization of food, media space, and the outdoors." She advocates for a "national comprehensive curriculum in gardening, menu planning, eco-literacy, and science and nutrition."[91] The point here is that American advertising—like entertainment, media, and film—is becoming another export that carries habits and a way of life that other cultures may find unacceptable.

Loss of Nation-State Sovereignty

Critics also protest that globalization erodes the ability of governments to protect the interests of their citizens against more powerful MNEs. At conflict are the benefits of economic globalization and the laws and institutions within these nations' own boundaries. Part of the debate centers on the argument that market forces are global and must be dealt with by global businesses.

There is also tension over sovereignty between nations and MNEs regarding power and influence. A classic example was the rejection of the proposed merger between General Electric (GE) and Honeywell by the European Commission's antitrust authorities. That merger, it was argued, would have left public interest behind, because these companies bring different legal and regulatory traditions across the Atlantic. Opinions differed among American and European antitrust officials as to GE's dominant market position. Other mergers blocked by the EU include Deutsche Telekom and Beta Research; Volvo and Scania; and MCI WorldCom and Sprint. On the other hand, Microsoft's fine by the EU on monopoly charges indicates that the global environment is a playing level where international law applies.[92]

Loss of nation-state arguments diminish when evidence is provided that MNEs cannot, and do not claim to, protect citizens during wars and regional conflicts; collect taxes; distribute benefits; build roads and infrastructure; care for the environment; or protect the rights of individuals, groups, and the elderly. In fact, governments subsidize and support companies when needed. In the immediate aftermath of the 2001 terrorist attack on the World Trade Center, the U.S. airlines suffered sizable financial losses. It is estimated that 2007–2008 losses in the industry were $5.2 billion.[93]

Other industries (e.g., railroad, automobile, agribusiness, aerospace) have also been subsidized by government funds. Still, it is argued that "globalization will continue to chip away at the power of the nation-state. As the Europeans know from their experience over the last 50 years, surrendering some degree of national autonomy is a natural and inevitable concomitant of growing economic interdependence."[94] The degree to which nation-states share and/or give up power, influence, and sovereignty to global companies—and the types of power, influence, and sovereignty they do give up or share—is and will be a continuing subject of debate.

8.4 Multinational Enterprises as Stakeholders

An MNE or TNC is generally regarded as "an enterprise comprising entities in more than one country which operate under a system of decision-making that permits coherent policies and a common strategy. The entities are so linked, by ownership or otherwise, that one or more of them may be able to exercise a significant influence over the others and, in particular, to share knowledge, resources and responsibilities with the others."[95] MNEs and TNCs are corporations that "own or control production or service facilities outside the country in which they are based."[96] Companies go global to enhance profit by creating value, building and increasing markets, and reducing costs. Costs are reduced by locating and using raw materials, skilled labor, land, and taxes at lower costs. Value can also be added by joint-venturing with other national and regional partners who have market reach, global skills, experience, and resources.

A 2012 *Harvard Business Review* article notes an interesting trend: the role of MNEs in the U.S. economy has been declining. Most U.S. MNEs have expanded faster overseas; however, MNEs still accounted for 75 percent of the labor productivity growth in the United States from 1977 to 2000. About half of the new job growth of MNEs came from Brazil, Russia, India, and China (or the "BRICs"). "Leaders of global corporations are voicing concerns about a deep set of U.S. challenges—complex taxation, inadequate worker skills, crumbling infrastructure—that inhibit hiring and investment in America. In contrast, corporate leaders see dynamic opportunities in countries like China and India."[97] In the following sections, we provide historical context for viewing MNEs with updates as well.

Power of MNEs

Although MNEs often reflect and extend their home nation's culture and resources, many are powerful enough to act as independent nations. This section focuses on MNEs as independent, powerful stakeholders, using their power across national boundaries to gain comparative advantages, with or without the support of their home country. The following facts indicate the power of MNEs:[98]

- Worldwide employment by U.S. MNEs decreased to 33.4 million workers in 2008. Employment in the United States by U.S. parent companies decreased to 22.9 million workers. The employment by U.S. parents accounted for almost one-fifth of total U.S. employment in private industries. Employment abroad by the majority-owned foreign affiliates of U.S. MNEs increased 1.7 percent, to 10.5 million workers.
- Worldwide capital expenditures by U.S. MNEs increased 4.1 percent in 2008, to $708.2 billion. Capital expenditures in the United States by U.S. parents increased 2.3 percent, to $519.7 billion. Capital expenditures abroad by majority-owned foreign affiliates increased 9.1 percent, to $188.5 billion.
- Sales by U.S. parent companies increased 3.2 percent in 2008, to $9.5 trillion. Sales by majority-owned foreign affiliates increased 10.9 percent, to $5.52 trillion.
- "Worldwide current-dollar value added of U.S. MNEs increased 2.0 percent to $5.3 trillion. Value added by U.S. parents, a measure of their direct contribution to U.S. gross domestic product, was nearly unchanged at $3.9 trillion, representing 22.9 percent of total U.S. private-industry value added. Value added by majority-owned foreign affiliates (MOFAs) increased to $1.4 trillion. Value added by MOFAs was largest in the United Kingdom, Canada, and Ireland.
- Worldwide expenditure for property, plant, and equipment of U.S. MNEs increased 2.0 percent to $853.2 billion. Expenditures by U.S. parents accounted for $653.6 billion and MOFA expenditures for $199.6 billion.
- Worldwide research and development expenditures of U.S. MNEs increased 3.3 percent to $354.9 billion. U.S. parents accounted for expenditures of $298.3 billion and MOFAs for $56.6 billion.[99]

The world's largest companies are shown in Table 8.5. They include Walmart, Sinopec Group, Royal Dutch Shell, China National Petroleum, State Grid, Saudi Aramco, BP, Exxon Mobil, Volkswagen, and Toyota Motor. Of the 500 global companies in 2019, 121 are U.S firms, 119 are Chinese, and 52 are Japanese.[100]

The dominant goal of MNEs is, as noted earlier, to make a profit and take comparative advantage of marketing, trade, costs, investment, labor, and other factors. At the same time, MNEs assist local economies in many ways, as is explained below. The ethical questions that critics of MNEs have raised are partly reflected in the following statement by the late Raymond Vernon, noted Harvard professor and international business expert: "Is the multinational enterprise undermining the capacity of nations to work for the welfare of their people? Is the multinational enterprise being used by a dominant power as a

Table 8.5
World's Largest Companies 2020

Search Rank	Company	Revenues ($b)	Profits ($b)
1	Walmart	$523,964	$14,881
2	Sinopec Group	407,009	6,793
3	State Grid	383,906	15,842
4	China National Petroleum	379,130	4,433
5	Royal Dutch Shell	352,106	88,210
6	Saudi Aramco	329,784	88,210
7	Volkswagen		15,542
8	BP	282,616	4,026
9	Amazon	282,760	11,588
10	Toyota Motor	275,288	19,096

Source: Fortune. (2020). Global 500. https://fortune.com/global500/2020/search/.

means of penetrating and controlling the economies of other countries?"[101] The next subsection addresses these questions in a discussion of the mutual responsibilities and expectations of MNEs and their host countries.

Misuses of MNE Power

Corporations cannot act as if they operate in a social vacuum. Society's values changed after September 11, 2001, and in order to maintain legitimacy, organizations are now expected to take into consideration a new social framework where society expects them to go beyond mere financial decisions and do "the right thing." This change is evident from the hundreds of shareholder resolutions, lodged in recent years, relating to social issues. It is also reflected in the new environment of corporate social responsibility and increased disclosure. The stream of corporate failures, the subprime-lending crisis, and the fragility of the U.S., European, and global financial systems have led to critics questioning more closely the motives and many practices of MNEs and large corporations' management in general.[102] From an ethical perspective, we ask: Why are some MNEs not paying their fair share of taxes in countries where they are located? Why are MNEs pushing their costs of doing business onto taxpayers and the public? Why are MNEs not treating the environment as a public good instead of as a "negative externality"—that is, as a "spillover" cost from businesses to third parties? Why are MNEs not treating and paying local labor better in developing—and even some developed—countries? Why are some markets treated less equally and equitably—for example, why do some pharmaceuticals not put the same warning labels on drugs in poorer, less regulated markets that they do in more developed, richer countries? Why are children and women in some developing countries discriminated against in labor practices by some MNEs? Of course, not all MNEs violate international law or take advantage of less-developed countries' markets and peoples; however, our interest here is discussing ways in which MNEs operate (and have operated) in host countries, in order to explore more socially responsible practices.

Crises since the birth of the MNE after World War II have raised international concern over the ethical conduct of MNEs in host and other countries. Not long ago, the Ford-Bridgestone/Firestone tire crisis was international in nature. These companies were not forthright early on with their consumers about defects known by the companies. Union Carbide's historic chemical spill disaster in Bhopal, India, resulted in thousands of deaths and injuries and alarmed other nations over the questionable safety standards and controls of MNE foreign operations. Nestlé's marketing of its powdered infant milk formula that resulted in the illness and death of a large number of infants in less-developed countries raised questions about the lack of proper product instructions issued to indigent, less-educated consumers. (Nestlé's practice resulted in a boycott of the company from 1976 to 1984.)

The presence of MNEs in apartheid-era South Africa raised criticisms over the role of large corporations in actively supporting apartheid or government-supported racism. Because MNEs had to pay taxes to the South African government and because apartheid was a government-supported policy, MNEs—it is argued—supported racism. Several U.S.-based MNEs that operated in South Africa witnessed boycotts and disinvestments by many shareholders. Many MNEs, including IBM and Polaroid, later withdrew. Post-apartheid South Africa has seen the reentry of companies from all countries. Another long-standing moral issue is the practice of MNEs not paying their fair share of taxes in countries where they do business and in their home countries. Through transfer pricing and other creative accounting techniques, many MNEs have shown paper losses, thereby enabling them to avoid paying any taxes.

Critics claim that many MNEs are not fulfilling their part of the implicit social contract discussed in Chapters 4 and 5. Some of these critics include Richard Barnet and John Cavanagh in their book *Global Dreams*, David Korten in *When Corporations Rule the World*, Tom Athanasiou in *Divided Planet: The Ecology of Rich and Poor*, Paul Hawken in *The Ecology of Commerce*, and William Greider in *One World, Ready or Not*.[103] MNE practices that are subject to criticism include committing corporate crimes, exerting undue political influence and control, determining and controlling plant closings and layoffs, and damaging the physical environment and human health. Evidence regarding these claims showed, for example, that 11 percent of 1,043 MNEs studied were involved in one or more major crimes over a 10-year period. The crimes that have been committed in the past included foreign bribery, kickbacks, and improper payments. A small sample of those firms included Enron, World-Com, Adelphia, American Cyanamid, Anheuser-Busch, Bethlehem Steel, Allied Chemical, Ashland Oil, and Beatrice Foods.[104]

Large corporations (along with trial lawyers and labor unions) also have immense influence through political action committees (PACs). The organization Common Cause noted that the majority of soft money contributions to both American parties in 1999 came from corporate business interests. With regard to plant closings and "downsizings," critics are concerned that some MNEs are more concerned with a particular profit margin than with their share of responsibility to community and society. After all, taxpayers support roads and other external conditions that allow corporations to operate in a country. Although corporations are not expected to be a welfare system for employees, critics note that large companies are expected to share in the social consequences of their actions, especially when, for example, plant-closing decisions are made to reap the benefits of cheaper labor in another country.

Finally, there is historical evidence that several large corporations have harmed the physical environment and the health of their employees and local communities. Classic crises cases discussed in Chapter 5 regarding asbestos manufacturing, oil spills, chemical plant explosions, toxic dumping, and industrial air pollution demonstrate corporate misuses of the environment in recent history. The external and human costs that communities, governments, the environment, and taxpayers have had to pay for these misuses of power have been documented.

In the following sections, two perspectives regarding global corporations' responsibilities—that of the MNE and that of the host country—are discussed.

MNE Perspective

"A rising tide lifts all ships." MNEs enter foreign countries primarily to make profit, but they also create opportunities host countries would not have access to without these companies. Although MNEs benefit from international currency fluctuations, available labor at cheaper costs, tax and trade incentives, the use of natural resources, and access to more foreign markets, these companies also benefit their host countries through foreign direct investment and in specific ways, such as:

- Hiring local labor
- Creating new jobs
- Co-venturing with local entrepreneurs and companies
- Attracting local capital to projects
- Providing for and enhancing technology transfer
- Developing particular industry sectors
- Providing business learning and skills
- Increasing industrial output and productivity
- Helping to decrease the country's debt and improve its balance of payments and standard of living

Moreover, MNEs open less-developed countries (LDCs) to international markets, thereby helping the local economy attract greatly desired hard currencies. Also, new technical and managerial skills are brought in, and local workers receive training and knowledge. Job and social-class mobility is provided to inhabitants.[105] Some MNEs also establish schools, colleges, and hospitals in their host countries. For example, although Nike has been criticized for its international child labor practices, it is also true that by contracting with factories abroad, it has helped employ more than half a million workers in 55 countries. Eighty-three percent of Nike's workforce in Indonesia consists of women who would not otherwise be employed.[106] Another company, Patagonia, Inc., has given 1 percent of its annual sales to environmental groups

MNE Global Stakeholder Management Issues and Ethical Concerns

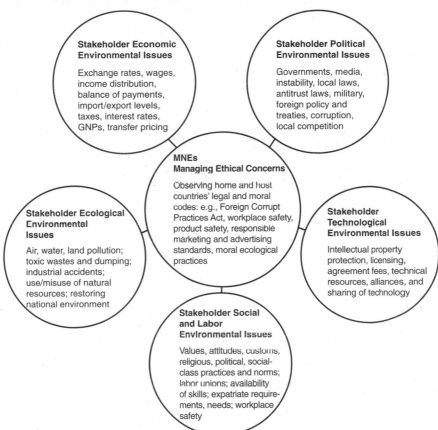

Source: © 2021 Joseph W. Weiss, Bentley University, Waltham, MA.

and gives employees up to two paid months off to work for nonprofit environmental groups. The company also routinely permits independent human rights organizations to audit any of its facilities and participates in the Apparel Industry Partnership (AIP) to set standards to expose and monitor inhumane business practices in their industry. Cadbury is another example of a company that has practiced highly ethical standards abroad. In India, the company hired local workers and instilled new work-related ethical values in its plant.[107]

The MNE must manage overlapping and often conflicting multiple constituencies in its home- and host-country operations. Figure 8.3 illustrates some of the major environmental and stakeholder issues the MNE must technically and ethically balance and manage in its foreign location. From the MNE's perspective, managing these stakeholder issues is difficult and challenging, especially as the global economy presents new problems.

MNE executives and other managers also complain about what they consider unethical practices and arbitrary control by host-country governments. For example, local governments can and sometimes do the following:

• Limit repatriation of MNE assets and earnings.
• Pressure and require MNEs to buy component parts and other materials from local suppliers.
• Require MNEs to use local nationals in upper-level management positions.
• Require MNEs to produce and sell selected products in order to enter the country.
• Limit imports and pressure exports.
• Require a certain amount or percentage of profit to remain in or be invested in the country.

Finally, MNEs can face the threat of expropriation or nationalization of their operations by the host government. More recently, MNEs must assume high-stakes risks, liabilities, and responsibilities in the area of safety, especially since September 11. The airline industry, in particular, has been hit very hard by this unpredictable crisis. The crisis itself, along with the "fallout" over laxness in safety standards and enforcement, has taken a heavy toll on all U.S. and most international carriers. The price of doing business safely has escalated.

Host-Country Perspective

Six criticisms of the presence and practices of MNEs in host and other foreign locations are discussed here.

1. MNEs can dominate and protect their core technology and research and development (R&D), thus keeping the host country a consumer, not a partner or producer. The Brazilian government, for example, has counteracted this by having entry barriers and laws that, since the 1970s, have protected against the complete control of its own electronics industries by foreign manufacturers. It is also argued (or feared) that Japan's MNEs could in the long term dominate certain critical industries (such as the electronics industry and perhaps the automobile industry) in the United States and use American labor more as assemblers than as technology R&D partners.
2. MNEs can destabilize national sovereignty by limiting a country's access to critical capital and resources, thereby creating a host-country dependency on the MNE's governments and politics.
3. MNEs can create a "brain drain" by attracting scientists, expertise, and talent from the host country.
4. MNEs can create an imbalance of capital outflows over inflows. They produce but emphasize exports over imports in the host country, thereby leaving local economies dependent on foreign control.

5. MNEs can disturb local government economic planning and business practices by exerting control over the development and capitalization of a country's infrastructure. Also, by providing higher wages and better working conditions, MNEs influence and change a country's traditions, values, and customs. "Cultural imperialism" is imported through business practices.
6. MNEs can destroy, pollute, and endanger host-country and LDC environments and the health of local populations. For example, the mining of and dangerous exposure to asbestos continues in some LDCs and in Canada.

Obviously, these criticisms do not apply to all MNEs. These criticisms represent the concerns of host-country and LDC governments that have suffered abuses from MNEs over the decades. Tensions in the relationships between MNEs and host countries and other foreign governments will continue, especially in the least-developed settings. Whenever the stakes for both parties are high, so will be the pressures to negotiate the most profitable and equitable benefits for each stakeholder. Often, it is the less-educated, indigent inhabitants of LDCs who suffer the most from the operations of MNEs.

More global companies are beginning to self-monitor and contribute to host-country education, consumer awareness, and community programs (e.g., Shell has written a primer on human rights with Amnesty International; Hewlett-Packard offers consumer education programs and computer training in host countries).

■ 8.5 Triple Bottom Line, Social Entrepreneurship, and Microfinancing

Positive trends in large and small businesses (globally and locally) include the "triple bottom line" philosophy and practices, social entrepreneurship, and microfinancing. These movements and practices are based on related premises and have in common a theme that serving society and the environment is also profitable. These are not new trends, but they are becoming more popular and acceptable ways of doing business, given the social, environmental, and moral problems businesses have and are experiencing at the expense of societies worldwide.

The Triple Bottom Line

The triple bottom line is "a kind of balanced scorecard that captures in numbers and words the degree to which any company is or is not creating value for its shareholders and for society."[108] This philosophy is based on "the sustainability imperative"—that is, the realization that in order for the environment to be preserved and society to benefit from business, corporations must respect the "interdependence of various elements in society on one another on the social fabric. Sustainability means operating a business in a way that acknowledges the needs and interests of other parties . . . and that does not fray but rather reinforces the network of relationships that ties them together."[109] The triple elements of this scorecard argue that business activity should be measured in economic, environmental, and social costs and benefits. The economic dimension includes sales, profits, return on investment (ROI), taxes paid, monetary flows, and jobs created; the environmental dimension includes air and water quality, energy usage, and waste produced; and the social dimension includes labor practices, community impacts, human rights, and product responsibility. "The sustainability sweet spot," which is where "increase profits and market share" and "address climate change and public health" intersect, indicates where a corporation's profits can be made. This has been demonstrated in several companies. Examples are healthy products from Tropicana and Quaker Oats, PepsiCo's environmental policy and procedures changes, Toyota's hybrid cars, and GE's clean technology ("ecomagination") products.

Social Entrepreneurs and Social Enterprises

A social enterprise is "an organization or venture that advances its social mission through entrepreneurial, earned income strategies."[110] "A social entrepreneur is a person who pursues novel applications that have the potential to solve community-based problems. These individuals are willing to take on the risk and effort to create positive changes in society through their initiatives. Social entrepreneurs may believe that this practice is a way to connect you to your life's purpose, help others find theirs, and make a difference in the world (all while eking out a living)".[111] Social entrepreneurship and enterprises date back to the 1960s and 1970s and include nonprofits, community groups, youth social entrepreneurial groups, as well as the private and governmental sectors.[112] Some NGOs are also related to social enterprises. In 2008, *Fast Company* magazine's Social Capitalist Awards honored 45 social entrepreneurs "who are changing the world."[113]

Microfinancing

This related movement is making a difference for the poor globally.[114] Microfinancing involves "very small loans, typically less than $100 . . . made to the rural poor in developing countries who normally do not qualify for traditional banking credit. This is often the only way they can establish a business and lift themselves out of poverty."[115] Microfinancing is the idea of Professor Yunus, who in 1976 founded the Grameen Bank after a famine in Bangladesh. In 2008, the bank had 6.6 million borrowers, of whom 97 percent were women. The Nobel Peace Prize was awarded to Yunus and his Grameen bank in 2006 for this practice. "Grameen, which means village, is an idea that has spread to more than 40 countries including Sri Lanka where women's banks were already a familiar concept."[116]

Covid-19 has added significantly to the financial stress on those in developing countries who depend on microfinance services. With the pandemic causing countries to move to lockdown, many microfinancing firms face challenges and threats to their own existence.[117]

Dvara Trust, a private firm in southern India, estimated that more than 90 percent of borrowers are unable to pay back. This compares to the 5 percent of default rates before Covid-19. Traditionally microfinance payments are made through an agent who visits borrowers' businesses to obtain cash. Since that country went into lockdown with social distancing regulations, payments could not be made. Still, investors and banks expect to be repaid. "Most of these microfinance Institutions (MFIs) have a cushion of a couple of months' cash. When that is exhausted, their future will be in jeopardy."[118]

8.6 MNEs: Stakeholder Values, Guidelines, and Codes for Managing Ethically

Guidelines for managing international ethical conduct have received detailed attention and effort over the past four decades in the areas of consumer protection, employment, environmental pollution, human rights, and political conduct.[119] Figure 8.3 illustrates issues and ethical concerns that MNEs must manage. The driving institutional forces behind the development of global ethical values, published guidelines, and universal rights include the UN, the ILO, the OECD, the Ceres Principles, the Conference Board, and the Caux Round Table Principles for Business.

The underlying normative sources of the guidelines that these global organizations have developed include beliefs in (1) national sovereignty, (2) social equity, (3) market integrity, and (4) human rights and fundamental freedoms.[120] Richard DeGeorge specifically offers the following guidelines that MNEs can use in dealing with LDCs:

1. Do no intentional harm.
2. Produce more good than harm for the host country.
3. Contribute to the host country's development.
4. Respect the human rights of their employees.
5. Respect the local culture; work with, not against, it.
6. Pay their fair share of taxes.
7. Cooperate with the local government to develop and enforce just background institutions.
8. Assume the ethical responsibility of attending to the actions and failures of the firm (which comes with majority control of the firm).
9. For multinationals that build hazardous plants, ensure that the plants are safe and operated safely.
10. Assume responsibility for redesigning the transfer of hazardous technologies so that such technologies can be safely administered in host countries.[121]

Other developments involving global companies and business ethics include the following: (1) global companies are, as discussed earlier, developing and using core principles relevant to their business practices; (2) codes of ethics with minimum social responsibility standards (e.g., gender discrimination and environmental responsibility) are being adopted and employees are being trained on them; and (3) a broad consensus for ethical requirements is being articulated. The Conference Board, a global network of businesses, academic institutions, governments, and NGOs in more than 60 countries, is working to define global business practice standards, core principles for doing business across cultures, and the requirements for the support of and cooperation between business and nonbusiness institutions.[122]

Covid-19 has impacted almost every country in the globe. It is clear MNEs must implement actions and new guidelines to provide a safe environment for workers. The UNI Europa has provided a set of recommendations to "help trade union alliances and European works council members to build workplace protection and ultimately save lives." The recommendations are:

1. Postpone annual/ordinary and negotiation meeting.
2. Request an online extraordinary meeting on Covid-19.
3. Request regular updates from management on Covid-19 in writing.
4. Share information about the situation in each country between yourselves.
5. Urge management to deal with the crisis on the basis of social dialogue.
6. Request an physical (in-person) extraordinary meeting to take place as soon as the Covid-19 crisis is over.
7. Contact your European trade union federation.

Multinational companies must also provide a safe environment for workers. Multinationals are crucial to contribute to flatten the curve.[123] The U.S. Centers for Disease Control and Prevention (CDC) has provided the following guideline for businesses and employers:[124]

- Actively encourage sick employees to stay home.
- Consider conducting daily in-person or virtual health checks.
- Identify where and how workers might be exposed to Covid-19 at work; encourage workers to wear a cloth face covering at work if the hazard assessment has determined that they do not require personal protective equipment (PPE).
- Separate sick employees; employees who appear to have symptoms upon arrival at work or who become sick during the day should immediately be separated from other employees, customers, and visitors, and sent home.
- Take action if an employee is suspected or confirmed to have Covid-19 infection; wait 24 hours before cleaning and disinfecting to minimize the potential for other employees being exposed to respiratory droplets.
- Educate employees about steps they can take to protect themselves at work and at home.
- For employees who commute to work using public transportation or ride sharing, consider offering the following support: if feasible, offer

employees incentives to use forms of transportation that minimize close contact with others.
• Implement flexible sick leave and supportive policies and practices.
• Establish policies and practices for social distancing.

Some pre-Covid classic guidelines that continue to influence policies and practices of global companies are presented next, with the expectation that a post-Covid environment may well return to many of these practices and policies. The following MNE guidelines are summarized under the categories of employment practices and policies, consumer protection, environmental protection, political payments and involvement, and basic human rights and fundamental freedoms.[125]

Employment Practices and Policies

• MNEs should not contravene the workforce policies of host nations.
• MNEs should respect the right of employees to join trade unions and to bargain collectively.
• MNEs should develop nondiscriminatory employment policies and promote equal job opportunities.
• MNEs should provide equal pay for equal work.
• MNEs should give advance notice of changes in operations, especially plant closings, and mitigate the adverse effects of these changes.
• MNEs should provide favorable work conditions, limited working hours, holidays with pay, and protection against unemployment.
• MNEs should promote job stability and job security, avoiding arbitrary dismissals and providing severance pay for those unemployed.
• MNEs should respect local host-country job standards and upgrade the local labor force through training.
• MNEs should adopt adequate health and safety standards for employees and grant them the right to know about job-related health hazards.
• MNEs should, minimally, pay basic living wages to employees.
• MNEs' operations should benefit the low-income groups of the host nation.
• MNEs should balance job opportunities, work conditions, job training, and living conditions among migrant workers and host-country nationals.

Consumer Protection

The following two items summarize best ethical and socially responsible practices for protecting consumers in a host country:

• MNEs should respect host-country laws and policies regarding the protection of consumers.
• MNEs should safeguard the health and safety of consumers by various disclosures, safe packaging, proper labeling, and accurate advertising.

Covid-19 has brought several changes that affect consumers' behavior. New protocols and guidelines are necessary for the safety of the consumer, such as social distancing and hygiene protocols. Because of the lockdowns that many countries implemented, online consumer demand has grown, pressuring e-commerce distribution network delays and disruptions. Online content providers have experienced increased traffic, leading them to reduce the quality of streaming. Also, "governments and businesses have taken actions to ensure affordable access to quality broadband services." As more individuals rely on the Internet, the government and communication operators in some countries have agreed to make this service more affordable, including accepting late fees for vulnerable consumers. As demand increases for online shopping, businesses must protect the personal information of consumers, such as name, address, and credit cards.[126]

Environmental Protection

The following items summarize best ethical and socially responsible practices for protecting a host country's environment:

- MNEs should respect host-country laws, goals, and priorities concerning protection of the environment.
- MNEs should preserve ecological balance, protect the environment, adopt preventive measures to avoid environmental harm, and rehabilitate environments damaged by operations.
- MNEs should disclose likely environmental harms and minimize the risks of accidents that could cause environmental damage.
- MNEs should promote the development of international environmental standards.
- MNEs should control specific operations that contribute to the pollution of air, water, and soils.
- MNEs should develop and use technology that can monitor, protect, and enhance the environment.

Political Payments and Involvement

There are two basic, foundational cautions that argue against MNEs taking, giving, or being involved in any way with bribes and illegal payments and related politics with host-country representatives:

- MNEs should not pay bribes or make improper payments to public officials.
- MNEs should avoid improper or illegal involvement or interference in the internal politics of host countries.

Basic Human Rights and Fundamental Freedoms

The following items broadly summarize the general principles underlying universal human rights and fundamental freedoms of all people that should be observed by MNEs:

- MNEs should respect the rights of all persons to life, liberty, security of person, and privacy.
- MNEs should respect the rights of all persons to equal protection of the law, to work, to choice of job, to just and favorable work conditions, and to protection against unemployment and discrimination.
- MNEs should respect each person's freedom of thought, conscience, religion, opinion and expression, communication, peaceful assembly and association, and movement and residence within each state.
- MNEs should promote a standard of living to support the health and well-being of workers and their families.
- MNEs should promote special care and assistance to motherhood and childhood.

William Frederick states that these guidelines should be viewed as a "collective phenomenon" because all do not appear in each of the five international pacts they originated from: the 1948 UN Universal Declaration of Human Rights, the 1975 Helsinki Final Act, the 1976 OECD Guidelines for Multinational Enterprises, the 1977 ILO Tripartite Declaration of Principles concerning Multinational Enterprises and Social Policy, and the 1972 UN Code of Conduct on Transnational Corporations.[127] The guidelines serve as broad bases that all international corporations use to design specific policies and procedures; these corporations can then apply their own policies and procedures to such areas as "child care, minimum wages, hours of work, employee training and education, adequate housing and health care, pollution control efforts, advertising and marketing activities, severance pay, privacy of employees and consumers, and information concerning on-the-job hazards."[128]

■ 8.7 Cross-Cultural Ethical Decision Making and Negotiation Methods

"You are a manager of Ben & Jerry's, [owned by Unilever], in Russia. One day you discover that the most senior officer of your company's Russian venture has been 'borrowing' equipment from the company and using it in his other business ventures. When you confront him, the Russian partner defends his actions. After all, as a part owner of both companies, isn't he entitled to share in the equipment?"[129] These and so many other international business situations confront managers and professionals with dilemmas and gray areas in their decision making. As one author noted, "Global business ethics has now become the ultimate dilemma for many U.S. businesses."[130]

"Transnationals operate in what may be called the margins of morality because the historical, cultural, and governmental mores of the world's nation-states are not uniform. There is a gray area of ethical judgment where standards of the transnational's home country differ substantially from those of the host country. . . . There is yet no fixed, institutionalized policing agency to regularly constrain morally questionable practices of transnational commerce. Moreover, there is no true global consensus on what is morally questionable."[131] Scholars and business leaders agree that solving ethical dilemmas that involve global, cross-cultural dimensions is not easy. Often there are no "quick fixes." Where other laws, business practices, and local norms conflict, the decision makers must decide, using their own business and value judgments. Ethics codes help, but decision makers must also take local and their own company's interests into consideration. In short, there is no one best method to solve international business ethical dilemmas. From a larger perspective, external human rights and corporate monitoring groups are also needed to inform and advise corporations before dilemmas occur about human rights and methods that can prevent abuses of local workers and private citizens.

External Corporate Monitoring Groups

Corporations and their leaders are ultimately responsible for articulating, modeling, and working with international stakeholders to enforce legal and ethical standards in their firms as they do business around the world. Many do. However, as noted earlier, gray areas and lack of universal laws and norms leave loopholes that companies and local groups might use as competitive but harmful cost-saving advantages (e.g., not providing even "living wages" to the poor women and children they employ, polluting the environment, and using undue political influence to beat out competition). Numerous international groups that work with and monitor MNEs regarding human rights include—but are not limited to—Amnesty International (promotes and advocates human rights), OECD (developed guidelines for MNEs), ILO (publishes and works in the area of human rights), NGOs (combat corruption, ensure adequate labor conditions, and establish standards for economic responsibility), Transparency International (monitors and publishes the international Corruption Perception Index), Apparel Industry Partnership (which develops codes of conduct regarding child labor practices and working conditions related to "sweatshops" and subcontractors), and the Caux Round Table (an executive group formed in Switzerland that published the noted Caux Principles and works with other international business professionals on developing and implementing universal ethics codes).[132] These groups work with, and some are composed of, MNE executives, governments, legislators, local citizenry, and other stakeholders worldwide to inform, monitor, and assist MNEs with ethical global business practices. Sandra Waddock states:

> Demands for greater corporate transparency and accountability as well as anticorruption measures are fostering significant new accountability, reporting, and transparency initiatives among coalitions of business, labor, human rights, investor, and governmental bodies. . . . A database created by the International Labour Organization and available over the Internet lists nearly 450 web sites of industry and business associations, corporate, NGO and activist groups, and consulting organizations that have developed and are promulgating a wide range of relevant policy initiatives. These initiatives include a mix of transparency and reporting initiatives, codes of conduct, principles, and fair trade agreements. Responses to these demands are varied. Many companies,

particularly those under NGO and social activist pressures to reform labor and human rights abuses in their supply chains, have formulated their own codes of conduct. Notable among these companies are Levi Strauss, Nike, and Reebok, all significant targets of activism.[133]

   In the following section, several guidelines are discussed to complement principles and "quick tests" presented in Chapter 2.

Individual Stakeholder Methods for Ethical Decision Making

In an international environment, the temptations can be strong, and the laws looser, or less obvious. Pressure from headquarters to make the bottom line can also weigh heavily. "Sometimes people confuse norms with ethics—exploitation of child labor, bribery and kickbacks may be the norm, but that doesn't mean they're right—and that's what companies need to deal with," says Joseph Reitz, who is codirector of the International Center for Ethics in Business at the University of Kansas. "There's lots of evidence that companies insisting on doing business in the right way may suffer in the short term, but in the long run they do well."[134]

   Or do they? When confronted with cross-cultural ethical dilemmas, conflicting norms, and potentially illegal acts in international situations, individual employee and professional stakeholders need guidelines. Professionals and executives preparing to work abroad should ask for country-specific training on regional and local laws, customs, and business practices. As noted earlier, these professionals need to know their own firm's acceptable and unacceptable policies and procedures regarding negotiations and business dealings. This section introduces some—but obviously not all—guidelines that are a beginning step to becoming aware of the cultural differences and potential ethical consequences of doing business in other regions and countries.

   DeGeorge offers the following general tactics that serve as a basic start for preventing, as well as solving, ethical dilemmas internationally:[135]

   1. Do not violate the very norms and values that you want to preserve and that you use to evaluate your adversary's actions as being unethical. Seek to pursue with integrity economic survival and self-defense tactics. Winning a tactical battle unethically or illegally is not the goal.

   2. Use your moral imagination, because there are no specific rules for responding to an ethical opponent. Stakeholder analysis can help. Explore different options. Use literature, stories, and lives of heroes and saints for creative responses instead of rules.

   3. Use restraint and rely on those to whom the use of force is legitimately allocated when your response to immorality involves justifiable force or retaliation. Use minimal force that is justified as the ultimate solution, realizing that force is a reaction to unethical acts and practices.

   4. Apply the principle of proportionality when measuring your response to an unethical opponent. The force you use should be commensurate with the offense, the harm suffered, and the good to be gained.

5. Use the technique of *ethical displacement* when responding to unethical forces. This principle consists of searching for clarification and a solution to a dilemma on different, higher levels than the personal (e.g., as discussed in Chapter 1, look at the problems from these levels: international, industry, organizational, structural, and national or legislative policy).

6. Use publicity to respond to an unethical practice, adversary, or system. Corruption (i.e., unethical and illegal practices and actions) operates best in the dark. Using publicity judiciously can mobilize pressures against the perpetrators.

7. Work jointly with others to create new social, legal, or popular structures and institutions to respond to immoral opponents.

8. Act with moral courage and from your values, personally and corporately.

9. Be prepared to pay a price, even a high one. Innocent people sometimes must pay costs that others impose on them by their unethical and illegal activities.

10. Use the principle of accountability when responding to an unethical activity. Those who harm others must be held accountable for their acts.

Getting to Yes

Solving a moral dilemma in an international context is not easy. Roger Fisher, Bruce Patton, and William Ury's *Getting to Yes: Negotiating Agreement without Giving In*, remains a classic primer for negotiating. Their four-step approach includes:

1. Separate the people from the problem.
2. Focus on interests, not on positions.
3. Insist on objective criteria; never yield to pressure.
4. Invent options for mutual gain.

The authors note that it is always necessary to determine your best alternative to a negotiated solution before starting a negotiation.[136]

Building on Fisher, Patton, and Ury's method, Nancy Adler states that formal negotiations, especially in an international or cross-cultural context, proceed through four stages:

1. Build interpersonal relationships (learn about the people)—separate people from the problem.
2. Exchange task-related information—focus on interests, not positions.
3. Persuade—invent options for mutual gain, instead of relying on preconceived positions, high pressure, or "dirty tricks."
4. Make concessions and agreements—use objective decision criteria.[137]

Understand the Local Culture First

Is local culture important, or are people across cultures becoming more alike, especially with globalization and for those working in MNEs? Studies show that although organizations are becoming more alike in their structures and technologies, individuals maintain and even emphasize their cultural behaviors even more. National culture explains more about employees' attitudes and behaviors than does age, gender, role, or race.[138] When communicating and negotiating in different cultural contexts, gaining an understanding of the local culture in preparing for the negotiation is recommended before using any specific negotiation technique. Cultural miscues and disconnects are grounds for creating and exacerbating ethical problems and dilemmas. Consider, then, these cultural differences before problem solving or negotiating with counterparts:

- What are the dominant, underlying values of the culture? (Are groups, families, and collectives and their decisions valued over individuals and individual decisions, or vice versa?)
- How formally or informally are relationships viewed? (Is it necessary to get to know someone before negotiating, or is jumping to the facts first acceptable?)
- How do people understand and value rules versus spontaneity and bending rules? (Do friendships come before rules, or are rules seen as unbreakable and applicable to all?)
- How are authority and power viewed? (Is position and status valued more than experience? Is the boss more often seen as being right regardless of "the facts"?)
- Is age respected as indicating wisdom and authority?
- To what extent does the culture avoid or embrace uncertainty and risk? (Are people threatened by ambiguity and therefore avoiding unpredictability?)

Sources that address these and other comparative cultural differences are readily available.[139]

Table 8.6 shows different negotiating strategies among North Americans, Japanese, Chinese, and Latin Americans, based on cultural values and characteristics. Can you see how ethical problems and dilemmas could arise from communication miscues among professionals from these countries negotiating a complex transaction?

It is helpful to understand how other cultures perceive, understand, and perhaps even stereotype American cultural characteristics. (Obviously, not everyone from every culture reflects all of their culture's characteristics.) For example, characteristics most commonly associated with Americans from the different nationals reveal interesting patterns (e.g., although Americans were largely seen as industrious, inventive, intelligent, decisive, and friendly by an interview sample of French, Japanese, Western Germans, British, Brazilians, and Mexicans, Americans were also seen as nationalistic, rude, and self-indulgent by Japanese; sophisticated by western Germans; nationalistic by Brazilians; and greedy by Mexicans).[140] Becoming self-aware of one's cultural characteristics (attitudes, values, behaviors, and others' perceptions of us) is an important step toward business transactions in order to prevent and negotiate ethical dilemmas.

Table 8.6

Four Typical Styles of International Ethical Decision Making/Negotiating Strategies with American, Japanese, Chinese, and Brazilian Cultures

American Negotiators	Japanese Negotiators	Chinese (Taiwanese) Negotiators	Brazilian Negotiators
Preparation and planning skill	Dedication to job	Persistence and determination	Preparation and planning skill
Thinking under pressure	Perceive and exploit power	Win respect and confidence	Thinking under pressure
Judgment and intelligence	Win respect and confidence	Preparation and planning skill	Judgment and intelligence
Verbal expressiveness	Integrity	Product knowledge	Verbal expressiveness
Product knowledge	Demonstrate listening skill	Interesting	Product knowledge
Perceive and exploit power	Broad perspective	Judgment and intelligence	Perceive and exploit power
Integrity	Verbal expressiveness		Competitiveness

Source: LeBaron, M. (2003, July). Culture-based negotiation styles. *BeyondIntractability.org.* https://www.beyondintractability.org/essay/culture_negotiation.

Four Typical Styles of International Ethical Decision Making

At a more macro-level, George Enderle identified four distinctive international ethical decision-making styles that companies often use when making decisions abroad:

1. Foreign Country style is when a company applies the values and norms of its local host—"when in Rome, do as the Romans do."
2. Empire style is when a company applies its own domestic values and rules; this can be an imperialistic practice.
3. Interconnection style is when a company applies shared norms with other companies and groups; national identities and interests are transcended and blurred, as when states make commercial decisions and rely on formal trade agreements, such as the United States-Mexico-Canada Agreement (USMCA) or EU membership, to offer agreed-on processes and solutions.
4. Global style is when a company abstracts all local and regional differences and norms, coming up with a more cosmopolitan set of standards and solutions for its actions in the host country.[141]

The Foreign Country and Empire styles have obvious drawbacks in reaching ethical decisions. The Foreign Country style may result in gross injustices and inequities that are inherent in the norms adopted. Some local-country norms and business practices, for example, do not prohibit child labor. The

Empire style is a form of imperialism that disregards local norms and practices. The Global style, seemingly the "right answer," also presents problems. This style imposes its own interpretation of a "global morality and truth" on a host culture and norms. The Global style can also suffer from shortcomings shared by the Foreign Country and Empire styles. The Interconnection style "acknowledges both universal moral limits and the ability of communities to set moral standards of their own. It balances better than the other types a need to retain local identity with the acknowledgment of values that transcend individual communities. The drawbacks of this style are practical rather than moral." Companies and individual employees usually do not have quick or direct access to a commonly shared local, national, and international source to advise on a particular issue. Of the four styles, the Interconnection style appears to be less arbitrary and absolutist.[142] Another option is creative ethical navigation, which Thomas Donaldson and Thomas Dunfee term "integrative social contracts theory" (ISCT). This is not really a "style" of decision making; rather, it is the process of a decision maker navigating among "hypernorms," company interests, and local norms, as explained in the following section.

Hypernorms, Local Norms, and Creative Ethical Navigation

It would be helpful to have a set of norms that everyone agreed on. Hypernorms represent such an ideal. "Hypernorms are principles so fundamental that, by definition, they serve to evaluate lower-order norms, reaching to the root of what is ethical for humanity. They represent norms by which all others are to be judged."[143] Hypernorms relate to universal rights: for example, the right not to be enslaved, the right to have physical security, the right not to be tortured, and the right not to be discriminated against. However, the problem even with hypernorms is that when "rights," local traditions, country economic systems, or business practices conflict, decisions have to be made; in such cases, it is necessary for managers or professionals to use their hypernorms as a starting principle but then to be creative in considering the local context and competing norms. Reaching a win–win situation without violating anyone's norms is an ideal goal. An example of such a troublesome gray area, along with a suitable solution, is offered by Donaldson and Dunfee:

> Consider another situation confronted by Levi-Strauss, this time involving hypernorms connected with child labor. The company discovered in the early 1990s that two of its suppliers in Bangladesh were employing children under the age of fourteen—a practice that violated the company's principles but was tolerated in Bangladesh. Forcing the suppliers to fire the children would not have insured that the children received an education, and it would have caused serious hardship for the families depending on the children's wages. In a creative arrangement, the suppliers agreed to pay the children's regular wages while they attended school and to offer each child a job at age fifteen. Levi-Strauss, in turn, agreed to pay the children's tuition and provide books and

uniforms. This approach allowed Levi-Strauss to uphold its principles and provide long-term benefits to the host country.[144]

Donaldson and Dunfee's "Global Values Map" illustrates conflicting local-country versus foreign-company norms and values that can clash when negotiating business contracts across cultures. The challenge for business professionals is to creatively navigate among value and norm differences to reach agreement on acceptable business practices. Donaldson and Dunfee introduce "hypernorms," which as previously noted are universal values acceptable to all cultures and organizations. "Consistent norms" are culture-specific values but are still consistent with both hypernorms and other legitimate norms. Ethical codes of companies, such as Johnson & Johnson's Credo (see Chapter 6), are examples of consistent norms. When the norms of a "foreign-company" representative clash with the local norms of a host-country business professional, each must seek "moral free space" to negotiate value and norm differences. Both parties can encounter inconsistent norms when each holds to their own values and preferences, which may conflict with hypernorms and/or local business practices. Either party can experience illegitimate norms—values or practices that transgress hypernorms (e.g., exposing workers to asbestos or other carcinogens)—when negotiating individual business interests. In the "moral free space," a company and host-country professional can explore how to reach a negotiated deal that satisfies both their values and norms, while each gives up certain practices to do so. The previous example illustrates such a negotiating process: Levi Strauss had to decide among a "hypernorm" (child labor is wrong) while embracing its own company norms ("consistent norms"—children cannot be hired or used by company suppliers). At the same time, the Bangladesh suppliers endorsed child-labor practices ("illegitimate norms" from the perspective of Levi Strauss & Co.). An agreement had to be reached that would benefit the children and their families and the Bangladesh suppliers. The company and the Bangladesh suppliers, each desiring and needing the benefits of a negotiated contract, entered the "moral free space" and worked out what seems to have been a win–win situation for all parties involved—and an arrangement that brought no harm to any party.

Finding such creative solutions to international moral dilemmas involves balancing and combining business pressures, legal enforcement, and political will. A company attempting to make tough decisions with local groups could also seek to do so with the cooperation of other companies, local government officials, or even an external human rights group, as the Interconnection style of decision making would suggest. The ultimate decision may very well entail no compromise after reflecting on the situation, the hypernorm, and a company norm. Still, the methods discussed here can allow a decision maker—individual or global or company team—to look for options without getting trapped into blind absolutes, amoral gray zones, or relativism. Entering "moral free space" requires flexibility and negotiating. A more recent study extending Donaldson's decision-making method is found is found in F. Ast, "The Deliberative Test: A New Procedural Method for Ethical Decision Making in Integrative Social Contracts Theory" (*Journal of Business Ethics*, 155 [2019]: 207–221).

Chapter Summary

The global environment has and is being affected by the Covid-19 pandemic, the effects of which are still unpredictable depending on resources, vaccines, and help from advanced economic states. This environment also consists of MNEs managing a dynamic set of relationships among country governments, international organizations, and each other. Elements of those relationships consist of financial markets, cultures, political ideologies, government policies, technologies, and laws. There are estimates of between 40,000 to 100,000 MNEs doing business across national boundaries, 60,000 MNCs worldwide, controlling over 500,000 subsidiaries, and contributing to the global economy. It is likely these numbers will increase. Also, emerging markets in countries referred to as the BRICs (Brazil, Russia, India, and China) have and are facing challenges from Covid-19 as well from climate change, poverty, and return-to-growth possibilities, if these factors can be controlled. New and competitive opportunities created by information technologies and the "flattening" of boundaries through the emergence of global supply chains, outsourcing, and China's "cost innovation" business model abound through mass production.

Globalization is the integration of technology, markets, politics, cultures, labor, production, and commerce. Globalization is both the process and the result of this integration. The global economy is expected to expand at a 3.6 percent annual rate over the long term, resulting in world GDP swelling to $90 trillion in 2020.[145] "The economic fallout could include recessions in the U.S., Euro-area and Japan, the slowest growth on record in China, and a total of $2.7 trillion in lost output-equivalent to the entire GDP of the U.K." Because of the global pandemic, GDP growth for the first quarter of 2020 slowed to 1.2 percent that year.[146] As the complexity and volatility of the global environment increases, the probability of ethical dilemmas and conflicts is also enhanced. The post-9/11 world has also created different constraints and costs on business and nations: the economic, legal, moral, and social pressures businesses face have several industries continuing to struggle for survival and profitability.

Forces that have accelerated globalization include the end of communism and the opening of closed economies; information technologies and the Internet, which accelerate communication and productivity within and across companies globally; entrepreneurship and entrepreneurs who are more mobile, skilled, intelligent, and thriving worldwide; free trade and trading agreements among nations; the flow of money through the World Bank and the International Monetary Fund (IMF), which offers a conduit to bring needed capital to countries participating in building the global economy; the growth and the spread of transnational firms, which open new markets and create local employment; and a shift to service economies and educating workers using technologies, which has also propelled innovation and productivity worldwide. A question commonly asked is: Will globalization and accelerated business integration across national borders be slowed or rejuvenated through new and changing business, governmental, and entrepreneurial alliances, including ongoing corruption and "bubbles" bursting in different national economies felt around the world?

The "dark side" of globalization includes corporate crime and corruption, child slave labor, Westernization (Americanization) of values, the global digital divide, and loss of nation-state sovereignty. Also, critics argue that the "McDonaldization of society" delivers cultural values as well as fast food. This is a debatable issue and was discussed in the chapter.

The power of MNEs, or global companies, lies in their size, economic prowess, and ability to locate and operate across national borders. MNEs offer benefits to their host countries by employing local populations, investing capital, co-venturing with local entrepreneurs and companies, providing enhanced technology, developing particular industry sectors, providing business learning and skills, and increasing industrial output and productivity.

MNEs also abuse their power by committing corporate crimes, exerting undue political influence and control, determining, and controlling plant closings and layoffs, and damaging the physical environment and human health. Guidelines drawn from more than four decades of international agreements and charters were summarized to illustrate a consensus of host-country rights that have been used to help MNEs to design equity into their policies and procedures.

Finally, principles from *Getting to Yes: Negotiating Agreement without Giving In* were extended to include understanding cross-cultural characteristics of decision makers to prevent ethical dilemmas and negotiate complex business transactions. A creative model was summarized that allow companies to reach agreements among conflicting hypernorms (universal rights), consistent norms (company ethics and values codes), and illegitimate norms. Being able to balance local cultural norms, a company's norms, and competing business practices involves creative and responsible navigation and decision-making skills based on personal, professional, company, and universal values.

Questions

1. Briefly characterize the emerging competitive global business environment, and identify some of the forces that define it. Also, do you believe the Black Lives Matter and the MeToo movements in United States have influenced global business and international cultural environments? Explain.
2. What is "globalization"? What are some of the forces driving this process?
3. What competencies do you (a) have and (b) need if you were to join—or are already working for—a global company in which you would spend time in different countries?
4. What differences, if any, in your ethical principles and morals do you believe you would have to adjust to in negotiating with other cultures (see Table 8.6)?
5. What adjustments to your values and ethical decision-making style have you had to make in teams in your own culture, and with others from different cultures in your studies and/or work? Explain.
6. What is the difference between a gift and a bribe? How would you, as a representative of your company, respond to the offer of a questionable bribe from an international government or business professional? Explain.

7. Does globalization result in cultural and economic homogenization (alikeness) through a heightened emphasis on consumerism, or is this an exaggeration? Explain and defend your position.

8. Do local and global values change as a result of international integration? Why or why not? If so, in what ways? Offer a few examples.

9. Do you believe that globalization "promotes the conversion of national economies into environmentally and socially harmful export-oriented systems for business competition" that is not in the best interests of consumers? Why or why not? Defend your position.

10. Explain what the "dark side" of globalization means to you. Offer some examples. Offer an additional issue that could be considered a dark side of globalization. After doing so, offer a realistic solution that could either eliminate, change, or transform the dark side of your issue.

11. Do you believe Facebook, TikTok, Twitter, and other such social networking sites are, will, or can promote more commonly shared values of people across cultures—knowing that some countries have their own such websites in their language? Explain.

12. Are you or have you thought about becoming a "social entrepreneur"? Do you believe this practice and movement can help make a difference in the world? Explain.

13. Explain the differences in perception and experience with regard to moral issues for (a) a host country viewing an MNE and (b) an MNE viewing a host country. Which perspective are you more inclined to support or sympathize with? Why?

14. In a paragraph or list, describe dominant cultural characteristics of yourself as could be seen from another country or regional perspective. Include some of your core values. Then proceed to the next question.

    Using your description, what difficulties or misunderstandings, based only on your answer, would you predict that you might encounter when negotiating an ethical dilemma with someone who had opposite cultural characteristics? Explain.

Exercises

1. Argue and defend your positions on the following statements:
   (a) The United States is already and will continue to lose its status as a central, pivotal global superpower, including its cultural and values influence, in the world in the next 10 to 20 years, if not sooner.
   (b) Censorship restrictions in other countries on such information technology as Google and other websites are justifiable; the United States and other Western nations should not try to impose their values and norms on censoring practices.
   (c) A "global set of ethics" is impossible. Each culture and region of the world should have its own ethics as well as values and cultural differences.

(d) To succeed, globalization must involve justice and fairness practices from First World countries toward Third World nations and peoples.

(e) Although it is preferable that transnational and multinational companies act ethically, it is really not practical in every region of the world, including the United States.

(f) MNEs cannot financially afford to follow the guidelines in Section 8.5; it would be too costly for them.

(g) When two MNEs are both right on a controversial issue—for example, violation of patent or intellectual property rights—ethics should be avoided and other, more concrete issues should be used to resolve the dispute.

(h) Without transnational companies and MNEs doing business in poorer countries, peoples of those countries who are striving to survive would suffer even more.

2. Offer an example of and explain why one of your own values or an ethical standard you deeply believe in and follow might conflict with a different cultural or regional ethic in—for example, China, Russia, the Middle East, or the United States (if you are from a different culture). How flexible would you be, or not be, in negotiating one of your core beliefs in another culture? What would be your constraints on being flexible and changing your value-based position? Explain.

3. Evaluate and argue different sides of this statement: "McDonaldization is not a 'bad' thing. Everyone has a choice of what and how much to buy and consume. People are lucky to have a low-cost food option like McDonald's."

Real-Time Ethical Dilemma

You (Jane) are a 29-year-old single woman who has an MBA and has been working in your current marketing position for a year. Your firm recently opened a new pilot branch in a somewhat remote Russian location. The CEO of your company believes there are real growth opportunities for your firm's products in that region and also wants visibility. The company has decided to launch a small office there for visibility as well as to introduce the product. You are one of the most outgoing and talented marketing professionals in your firm. It is believed that you'll make a positive impression and represent the company well. There is a small community of American business professionals there who will assist you.

Country values there are very different from what you are accustomed to. You overhear a discussion between two of your male colleagues who were recently in that country completing arrangements for the office. One says, "Jane's going to have some interesting challenges with the men she has to do business with. . . . It's like the Wild West." The other answered, "Yeah, she's got some real surprises coming." Your research suggests that country laws and norms on issues you take for granted (like women's rights and sexual harassment) are not well defined.

You have a conflict over wanting to advance with your company but not wanting to take this assignment. You are aware that the CEO has his mind set. In fact, you've already had a discussion expressing your concerns and fears. He brushed your issues aside when he told you earlier, "Jane, try it. You need the international exposure and experience." The second time you approached him with your concerns, he blurted out, "Look, Jane. I understand your concerns, but this is important to me and our company. There are some people there who can help you. I know it's going to be a challenge. But after a couple of years, you'll thank me." You still don't feel right.

Questions

1. What do you do, and why?
2. If you do decide to go, what specific preparations should you make?
3. If you decide not to go, draft out the dialogue you would have with your CEO.

Real-Time Ethical Dilemma

You are attending a sexual-harassment training seminar for local managers in your company's branch office in a Middle Eastern, predominantly Muslim, country. You were flown over with the trainers to observe their techniques and become familiar with the training materials because you, as a new human resources staff member, would be expected to give this course. The course has been a success for managers in the United States. The same materials have been perfected and are being used in the United States. The instructors call on local Muslim managers (men and women) to role-play and openly share stories about sexual harassment that involved them or that they had heard about. Near the end of the half-day session, several of the host-country employees uncharacteristically walk out. The trainers are dazed and become upset.

Questions

1. What do you think went wrong?
2. What would you do in this case if you were one of the trainers?
3. Read the epilogue that follows, then return and answer this question: Who should do what, if anything, with the Muslim managers after this cultural mishap? Why?

Epilogue

Assume the trainers have been briefed on research that noted that "in 1993, a large U.S. computer-products company insisted on using exactly the same sexual-harassment exercises and lessons with Muslim managers halfway around the globe that they used with American employees in California. It did so in the name of 'ethical consistency.' The result was ludicrous. The managers were baffled by the instructors' presentation, and the instructors were oblivious of the intricate connections between Muslim religion and sexual manners.

"The U.S. trainers needed to know that Muslim ethics are especially strict about male/female social interaction. By explaining sexual harassment in the same way to Muslims as to Westerners, the trainers offended the Muslim managers. To the Muslim managers, their remarks seemed odd and disrespectful. In turn, the underlying ethical message about avoiding coercion and sexual discrimination was lost. Clearly sexual discrimination does occur in Muslim countries. But helping to eliminate it there means respecting—and understanding Muslim differences."[147]

Cases

Case 20

Plastic in the Ocean: An International Climate Change Problem

One of humanity's largest looming existential threats is climate change. Bill Gates, founder of Microsoft, predictor of an all-encompassing virus that turned out to be Covid-19, now predicts what he says—based on the "overwhelming majority of scientists"—is a "looming climate disaster on a scale the world has never seen," if not changed in the next 30 years, starting now (Cooper, 2021). Gates claims that diminishing, containing, and limiting—if not eliminating—warming greenhouse gases and carbon dioxide into the atmosphere, will require "innovations in every aspect of modern life—manufacturing, agriculture, transportation. . . ." In fact, it will require "changing everything in the economy" as we know it. Again, if this is not accomplished, the devastation to human life will make what has and is happening from Covid-19 appear small in scale. Anderson Cooper, the CBS commentator who interviewed Gates for *60 Minutes*, asked Gates about one consequence of how climate change would affect migrations of people: "You're talking about hundreds of thousands of people trying to move from North Africa to Europe every year?" Gates responded, "Exactly. The Syrian War was a 20th of what climate migration will look like. So, the deaths per year are way—10 times greater than—than what we've experienced in the pandemic" (Cooper, 2021).

Gates currently has already invested $2 billion of his own fortune, with many more investments promised, in different industries to change the way products and services are conceived, manufactured, and distributed. He is also receiving contributions to his strategy implementation from several known billionaires.

Plastics Dumping in Oceans, Part of the Larger Problem

What does plastic dumping in the oceans have to do with climate change? "In our oceans, which provide the largest natural carbon sink for greenhouse gases, plastic leaves a deadly legacy. . . . As our climate changes, the planet gets hotter, the plastic breaks down into more methane and ethylene, increasing the rate of climate change, and so perpetuating the cycle" (Duong, 2021).

The use of plastic ballooned with the globalized economy following WWII. Plastics provided the world's economy with a cheap and durable alternative that could be mass-produced and utilized across almost all aspects of production, packaging, and consumption. *Earthday.org* provides the following statistics on plastic consumption: 480 billion plastic bottles were sold worldwide in 2016, one trillion single-use plastics are used annually, half a billion plastic straws are used every day, and the world uses 500 billion plastic cups every year (Earth Day Network, 2019). Unfortunately, our global addiction to plastic has created a worldwide crisis.

Moreover, "the world's production of plastic pollution since the 1950s is about 8.3 million tons, with projections expected to reach 640 million tons by 2035. With a huge reliance on plastic for our daily lives, the worldwide production per year is 300 million tons. 50 percent of the plastic output is expressly for single-use. The management of this colossal amount of plastic is not sufficient. Every year, approximately 8 million tons of plastic finds its way into our oceans, and 90 percent of the ocean's trash is from plastic" (Gaytravel.com, 2020).

Plastic biodegradation "estimates range from 450 years to never" in dark and cold oceans (Parker, 2018). Our heavy reliance on plastics, along with an extremely long breakdown period, have resulted in large swaths of plastic accumulating in the ocean in garbage patches that have become increasingly publicized of late. A lack of understanding, control, legislation, and social responsibility have impacted all five levels of business ethics: individual, organizational, association, societal, and international.

Why and How Did This Become a Global Environmental Problem?

Plastics came to prominence in WWII and beyond. "World War II necessitated a great expansion of the plastics industry in the United States, as industrial proved as important to victory as military success. The need to preserve scarce natural resources made the production of synthetic alternatives a priority" (Science History Institute, 2016). The benefits and scale of plastic were put on full display in WWII and producers took notice, utilizing the new polymer to drive down costs and innovate new products. Plastics are highly flexible, extremely durable, easy to manufacture, could be totally synthetic, and are cheap to mass-produce. "In product after product, market after market, plastics challenged traditional materials and won, taking the place of steal in cars, paper and glass in packaging, and wood in furniture" (Science and History Institute, 2016). The ramp-up of plastic use in the United States accelerated "by lower manufacturing costs and elimination of Food and Drug Administration restrictions on the use of plastics in food packaging" (Conner and O'Dell, 1988, 17). The introduction of plastics in food packaging has also led to the single-use plastic issue we are experiencing today.

From the 1950s to now, "plastic became an increasingly common component of textiles, electronics, appliances, automobiles, tires, aeronautics, agricultural equipment, electrical wiring, building materials, consumer products, and packaging" (Dauvergne, 2018, 24). The scale and increasing plastic production and utilization have been exponential. The entire global economy has been propelled by plastic production and consumption, resulting in a disastrous pollution problem.

Plastics have long been polluting the oceans, outpacing public awareness, but that is now changing. "Part of the explanation for this delayed realization relates to the distance and relative invisibility of marine plastic sinks in the center of ocean basins and on the sea floor" (Mendenhall, 2018, 291). "Poor management of waste on land was a significant source of plastic debris," with the worst contributors of plastic by volume coming from coastal Asia, Africa, and the United States (Mendenhall, 2018, 292). One source identifies Vietnam, Bangladesh,

Pakistan, Burma, and North Korea as having the highest rates of mismanaged waste in the world (Tibbets, 2015, 92). Another source, the 2020 U.S. Environmental Protection Agency (EPA) plan that addressed marine litter, named five Asian nations—China, Indonesia, the Philippines, Thailand, and Vietnam—"as responsible for more than half of the plastic waste flowing into the oceans every year (Parker, 2020). U.S. and U.K. residents, however, "produce more plastic waste per person than any other nation, with Americans generating an average of 105kg (231lbs) of plastic per year. The British are close behind, throwing away almost 99kg (218lbs) annually" (Parker, 2020). Plastic pollution is becoming so pervasive that "by 2050 the ocean will contain more plastic by weight than fish" (Laville and Taylor, 2017).

Plastic in the ocean is a problem that has several direct and indirect consequences. "Between 60–90 percent of marine litter is plastic, with over 9 million metric tons of plastic flowing into the oceans in 2015. The main source of this plastic pollution is litter from consumer packaging and products, a category that includes beverage bottles, shopping bags, bottle caps, food containers, straws, cigarettes butts, and cling wrap" (Dauvergne, 2018, 23). The first and most apparent is the destruction of marine life and habitats. Marine life can suffer from entanglement or ingestion of plastics. "Entanglement or ingestion can reduce the quality of life, survival chances, and reproductive viability of marine animals, or kill them through strangulation, suffocation, or starvation" (Mendenhall, 2018, 293). Additionally, plastics are destroying marine habitats by smothering them. Ocean plastic is accumulating in large garbage patches because of "Ekman transport, a current effect created by the complex interaction of the Earth's rotation and wind patterns. Five such accumulation zones have been identified: two in the Atlantic, two in the Pacific, and one in the Indian Ocean" (Mendenhall, 2018, 292). Plastics will continue to accumulate in these garbage patches for the foreseeable future. Plastics are presenting an enormous issue, in the short and long term, for marine wildlife and habitats around the world.

Plastic in the ocean is also having an impact on humans. In addition to becoming part of the global climate change impending disaster in 30 or fewer years, as stated earlier, a visible impact is coastal pollution that is becoming more apparent, affecting residents as well as country economies and livelihoods that depend on tourism. Additionally, humans are indirectly affected by the consumption of marine wildlife that is living in an increasing polluted world. The impact of plastic trickles up to humans by way of "trophic transfer, moving up the food chain through predator-prey relationships" (Mendenhall, 2018, 293). Trophic transfer is not a new phenomenon and historically has been used to explain the risk of mercury content and the risk associated with the consumption of fish. The application of trophic transfer to plastics is a relatively concept. "Scientists at Ghent University in Belgium recently calculated people who eat seafood ingest up to 11,000 tiny pieces of plastic every year" (Laville and Taylor, 2017). Unfortunately, little is known about the short- and long-term impacts of this type of plastic consumption. "We lack a full understanding of the total pollutant loads associated with chemical additives in plastics. In terms of animals who eat plastics, little is known about the degree and rate of absorption, and the effects of long-term exposure to these toxins" (Mendenhall, 2018, 293). The impact that plastic is having on humans presents a consumer protection rights issue as well. All consumers have "the right to a healthy environment: to live and work in an environment which is nonthreatening to the well-being or present and future generations" (Consumers International, 2011). And, again, the issue looming much larger is Gates's and other notable scientists' predictions that we have 30 years or less to contain and hopefully eliminate all forms of pollutants that add to the changing global climate crisis that will threaten all life as we know it on this planet.

Stakeholders and Solution Paths

Leaders include stakeholders and stockholders, government and nongovernment officials, public and private companies, profit and nonprofit agencies, associations, and community groups and citizens: all who use, consume, and have a stake in the complete supply chain of plastics are involved in stopping plastic pollution—not only in the oceans, but in use everywhere. More specifically, "in 2019, 187 nations within the United Nations [UN Environment Program] amended the 1989 Basel Convention, which governs trade in hazardous materials, to include plastic waste. The historic treaty created a legally binding framework to make global trade in plastic waste more transparent and better regulated" (Duong, 2021). This amendment "will result in a cleaner ocean within five years and allow developing nations like Vietnam and Malaysia to refuse low-quality and difficult-to-recycle waste before it ever gets shipped" (Duong, 2021). Also, the Natural Resources Defense Council (NRDC)—an international nonprofit environmental organization "with more than 3 million members and online activists," consisting of "lawyers, scientists, and other environmental specialists" who work "to protect the world's natural resources, public health, and the environment" (www.nrdc.org)—is particularly focused on stopping pollution in the oceans.

The National Geographic website lists global actions being taken to stop ocean pollution (Howard et al., 2019). Finally, a large part of this responsibility rests with individual citizens, including you and me. What is our "plastic footprint" now with regard to the use and disposal of plastics that could end up being dumped into an ocean?

Questions for Discussion

1. What, if anything, did you learn from reading this case and the "Notes" section below that you didn't know before?
2. What is/are the main issue(s) in the case, and who are the stakeholders?
3. How would you describe your "footprint" with regard to your habits in using any form of plastic?
4. How would you describe the relevance of "ethics" to the main points and takeaways from this case? (Refer to your learning from this book as well as your own thinking.)
5. Argue a position that using plastics is not as big a problem as the media and scientists claim, that it is probably no bigger a problem than the pollution that

cruise ships, for example, create (https://foe.org/projects/cruise-ships/; https://daily.jstor.org/the-high-environmental-costs-of-cruise-ships/; http://www.beachapedia.org/Cruise_Ship_Pollution).

Resources

For important and impressive graphics, charts, and graphs showing international and cross-national statistics and trends over time for plastic production, visit the following websites:

https://ourworldindata.org/grapher/displaced-plastic-chinese-import-ban?country=~CHN

https://www.grandviewresearch.com/industry-analysis/global-plastics-market

https://www.plasticsoupfoundation.org/en/plastic-problem/plastic-environment/plastic-production-decomposition/?gclid=CjwKCAjwhMmEBhBwEiwAXwFoEaFiHa1hyUT3INcOhciWVso_7MX82b6_FFgkbAcA41AciFhyCLvXvhoCZz4QAvD_BwE

Sources

This case was developed from material contained in the following sources:

Bilefsky, D. (2019, June 10). Canada plans to ban single-use plastics, joining growing global movement. *New York Times.* www.nytimes.com/2019/06/10/world/canada/single-use-plastic-ban.html.

Conner, D. K, and Odell, R. (1988, January). The tightening net of marine plastics pollution. *Environment: Science and Policy for Sustainable Development, 30(1)*, 16–36. doi:10.1080/00139157.1988.9930865.

Consumers International. (2011). What are consumer rights? http://www.consumersinternational.org/who-we-are/consumer-rights.

Cooper, A. (2021, February 15). Bill Gates: How the world can avoid a climate disaster. *60 Minutes* interview with Bill Gates. CBS News. https://www.cbsnews.com/news/bill-gates-climate-change-disaster-60-minutes-2021-02-14/.

Dauvergne, P. (2018, July). Why is the global governance of plastic failing the oceans? *Global Environmental Change, 51*, 22–31. doi:10.1016/j.gloenvcha.2018.05.002.

Deutsche Welle. (2019, March 15) World agrees on first global commitment to curb single-use plastics. www.dw.com/en/world-agrees-on-first-global-commitment-to-curb-single-use-plastics/a-47938697-0.

Duong, T. (2021, January 22). UN hopes to reduce ocean plastic waste within five years. *EcoWatch.* https://www.ecowatch.com/plastic-waste-ban-un-oceans-2650065625.html?rebelltitem=2#rebelltitem2.

Earth Day Network. (2019, January 8). Fact sheet: How much disposable plastic we use. www.earthday.org/2018/04/18/fact-sheet-how-much-disposable-plastic-we-use/.

Gaytravel.com. (2020, November 4). 60+ facts about plastic pollution in the world and our oceans (2021). https://www.gaytravel.com/gay-blog/plastic-pollution-in-the-ocean-statistics.

Gross, A. (2019, May 21). UK presses ahead with ban on single-use plastics. *Financial Times.* https://www.ft.com/content/f00869c2-7bdd-11e9-81d2-f785092ab560.

Howard, B. C., Gibbens, S., Zachos, E., and Parker, L. (2019, June 10). A running list of action on plastic pollution. *National Geographic.* https://www.nationalgeographic.com/environment/2018/07/ocean-plastic-pollution-solutions.

Laville, S., and Taylor, M. (2017, June 28). A million bottles a minute: World's plastic binge "as dangerous as climate change." *The Guardian*. www.theguardian.com /environment/2017/jun/28/a-million-a-minute-worlds-plastic-bottle-binge-as -dangerous-as-climate-change.

Mendenhall, E. (2018, October). Oceans of plastic: A research agenda to propel policy development. *Marine Policy, 96*, 291–298. doi:10.1016/j.marpol.2018.05.005.

Parker, L. (2018, May 16). We depend on plastic. Now, we're drowning in it. *National Geographic*. www.nationalgeographic.com/magazine/2018/06/plastic-planet -waste-pollution-trash-crisis/#close. Also see, same article, excerpts in https:// www.energytoday.net/environmental-health-impact/we-made-plastic-we-depend -on-it-now-were-drowning-in-it/.

Parker, L. (2020, October 30). U.S. generates more plastic trash than any other nation, report finds. *National Geographic*. https://www.nationalgeographic.com /environment/2020/10/us-plastic-pollution/.

Science History Institute. (2016, December 20). The history and future of plastics. www.sciencehistory.org/the-history-and-future-of-plastics.

Tibbets, J. H. (2015, April). Managing marine plastic pollution: Policy initiatives to address wayward waste. Spheres of Influence, *123(4)*, 91–93. https://doi.org/10 .1289/ehp.123-A90.

Case 21

Sweatshops: Not Only a Global Issue

The Idea

Imagine that every day you go to work you are exposed to toxic chemicals without having any protective clothing or safety training, and that the workplace has poor ventilation and poor fire safety. Suppose that you are subject to physical and verbal abuse at the hands of your employer and that there is a lack of drinking water in the workplace. Suppose further that you are paid only a couple of dollars per day and forced to work excessive overtime hours. Would these be satisfactory working conditions—for anyone, anywhere in the world? Conditions such as these are found in businesses commonly known as sweatshops. "Migrants are constantly in a state of danger . . . they are in a constant state of stress. But they are needed and are beneficial to those that keep on exploiting them," said Svetlana Gannushkina of the human rights group Assistance for Citizens (Kovalyova, 2013). And with Covid-19, the sweatshop system in America was no different. One Los Angeles reporter recently noted that the garment industry generally has had workers performing tasks in unsanitary conditions even before Covid-19 for wages as low as $ 4.60 an hour (Dean, 2021). Such conditions resemble sweatshops.

The Move

Sweatshops exist throughout the world and in a variety of manufacturing industries, including apparel, shoes, toys, and electronics, among others. To the surprise of some, sweatshops also exist in major metropolitan areas such as New York City and Los Angeles. Moreover, human trafficking exists in these settings that hire cheap labor and pay slave wages. They have become most notoriously famous within the footwear and apparel (or garment) industries. In these two industries, easy portability of work and technology from one region to another, or one country to another, has facilitated the ongoing presence of and reliance on sweatshop factories. For instance, from a historical perspective, apparel manufacturing has been a very mobile industry. It has migrated from Britain to New England in the United States, to the Southeastern United States, to Mexico and Asia, with companies constantly pursuing less-expensive workers, a practice often referred to as "the race to the bottom." In this race, clothing wholesalers and retailers have developed a manufacturing supply chain of a large number of contractors and an even larger number of subcontractors, all with the aim of securing the absolutely lowest cost anywhere in the world. Each move in the race to the bottom has been more fleeting than the preceding one, with an excruciating toll being exacted from the workers at the lowest rungs of the "economic food chain" for the predatory benefit of others higher up and at the top.

Of course, this race to the bottom has not been confined to the footwear and apparel businesses. It is occurring in the production of computers, printers, laptops, and other electronics equipment. It can be found in any type of business that supplies products to large retailers—like Walmart and Target—that operate on the basis of a low-price strategy.

The Problem

A Georgetown study showed that people were more likely, for example, to endorse the use of questionable labor practices involved in a Caribbean vacation for themselves but tend to oppose that use if the vacation in question is for their friends.

"This phenomenon, known as moral hypocrisy, is used by consumers in situations to benefit themselves but not others," study author Neeru Paharia explains. "They also made economic development justifications, such as convincing themselves that sweatshops are the only realistic source of income for workers in poorer countries, without which they wouldn't develop, that the labor offers products not otherwise affordable to low-income people and it's OK because 'companies must remain competitive.'

"A great sale or exclusive offer can increase the desirability and value of a product, which can further justify the labor practices used to create the product," Paharia says. "The strength of a brand and consumer loyalty may also influence reasoning—causing consumers to view companies such as Nike and Apple as subsidiaries that are not directly involved with the labor conditions" (Paharia 2013).

The Fight

Unfortunately, most companies that are "benefiting from sweatshop labor around the world are doing nothing about it." According to the Investor Responsibility Research Center, just 12 percent of Standard & Poor's 500 companies have formal requirements that their suppliers address labor issues, and only 4 percent have requirements that address all the issues—including the freedom to organize bans on child labor, forced labor, and discrimination—considered to be important by the International Labour Organization.

In April 2013, a Bangladeshi factory building collapsed killing more than 1,100 employees. Following this horrific sweatshop-related disaster, opinions from every side of the aisle have been pouring in over how to stop these practices. Yet it is hard to get away from the fact that without the sweatshop, the employees would have no job whatsoever.

Given that sweatshop conditions exist around the world, what can be done to counter these assaults on human dignity and human rights that affect the most vulnerable people in the "economic food chain"? Not surprisingly, in the context of prevailing macroeconomic conditions and pent-up demand for low-cost production, the prospect of black-market sweatshops becomes all too real. The problem could be addressed at the other end of the supply chain. Western retailers should be required to display details of their full supply chain to consumers and invest in monitoring conditions at all stages. The "fair trade" concept could then be applied to all types of industries, allowing consumers the choice of paying a small premium on products produced in acceptable working conditions.

During the past several years a number of avenues of activism against sweatshops have emerged. For example, in the United States, student-led anti-sweatshop demonstrations and protests pressured some 200 colleges and universities into adopting "no-sweat" purchasing policies—especially for clothing emblazoned with the schools' logos. Ten universities in Canada also have "no-sweat" buying policies, as do several U.S. and Canadian cities. The Worker Rights Consortium (WRC) campaigns against sweatshops and helps to police factory compliance with "no-sweat" codes of business conduct. The WRC "does complaint-based and spot monitoring of plants that supply goods to its over 100 member universities."

In 2003, the Fair Labor Association (FLA), whose members include companies such as Adidas-Salomon, Eddie Bauer, Inc., Levi Strauss & Co., Liz Claiborne Inc., Nike Inc., the Phillips-Van Heusen Corporation, and Reebok International Ltd., as well as about 175 colleges and universities, began publicizing audits of factories regarding possible sweatshop conditions, including labor and human rights violations. These publicized audits put "pressure on Walmart, Disney, Gap, and every other company that does labor monitoring, to release their audits, too." In May 2004, Gap, Inc. issued its first social responsibility report in which it acknowledged that "many of the overseas workers making the retailer's clothes are mistreated and [the company] vowed to improve shoddy factory conditions by cracking down on unrepentant manufacturers." Gap uncovered "thousands of violations at 3,009 factories scattered across roughly 50 countries," including unacceptably low pay, psychological coercion and/or verbal abuse, lack of compliance with local laws, workweeks in excess of 60 hours, poor ventilation, and machinery lacking operational safety devices. Then Gap CEO Paul Pressler said, "We feel strongly that commerce and social responsibility don't have to be at odds."

These are some of the more notable efforts that have been undertaken to combat sweatshop conditions around the world. They have met with varying degrees of success. Ultimately, however, true success only will be found in putting the brakes on the "race to the bottom" and in establishing an acceptable minimum level of conditions and compensation for workers on the lowest rungs of the "economic food chain"—acceptable minimums that will ensure them a living wage, protect their rights, and respect their dignity as human beings.

Currently, three major groups oversee factory inspections to monitor sweatshop conditions. These are Social Accountability International (SAI), with members including Toys "R" Us and Otto Versand, the German direct-mail giant; the FLA, which was established by footwear and apparel makers such as Nike, Reebok International, and Liz Claiborne; and the Ethical Trading Initiative (ETI), a London-based organization composed of European unions, companies, and nonprofits. All three groups have codes of conduct that specify standards and also oversee factory monitoring targeted toward enforcing their codes and remedying violations of the standards.

Because there is considerable variation in the methodologies used by SAI, FLA, and ETI, many companies have engaged in some form of self-monitoring.

For instance, "Wal-Mart says it inspects thousands of supplier factories each year in dozens of countries. But since no outside body such as SAI or the FLA is involved and Wal-Mart won't release its audits or even its factories' names, the public is left to take the company's word for it." However, the perceived confusion among the methodologies of SAI, FLA, and ETI appears to be on the verge of changing as a consequence of an ambitious 30-month experiment called the Initiative on Corporate Accountability and Workers' Rights, which is being sponsored by six anti-sweatshop activist groups and eight global apparel makers. This initiative seeks "to devise a single set of labor standards with a common factory-inspection system that will 'replace today's overlapping hodgepodge of approaches with something that's easier and cheaper to use—and that might gain traction with more companies.' If it works, the 30-month experiment would create the first commonly accepted global labor standards—and a way to live up to them.

"This 30-month experiment is a great first step in bringing order to the piecemeal manner in which even the biggest companies set and monitor workplace conditions across the developing world. But a much broader solution is required to make real progress against sweatshop conditions. There are currently only about 100 large, mostly Western companies actively involved in the anti-sweatshop movement. Their efforts over the past decade are laudable but ultimately insufficient because thousands of other manufacturers don't participate. Building consensus around basic universal standards for particular industries, say apparel or consumer electronics, is crucial. Otherwise, why should one manufacturer incur the cost of upgrading and continually monitoring its workplace standards if it has to compete with factories without the same obligations?"

Questions for Discussion

1. Why are sweatshops so common around the world?
2. Why are sweatshops viewed with disgust and abhorrence? Does a sweatshop accomplish anything positive?
3. What is a reasonable objective (or set of objectives) for addressing sweatshop conditions throughout the world? Explain your answer.
4. What is your assessment of the potential of the Initiative on Corporate Accountability and Workers' Rights for making significant progress in alleviating sweatshops around the globe?
5. Do you think "moral hypocrisy" has any effect in the fight to improve working conditions in sweatshops? Explain your reasoning.

Sources

This case was developed from material contained in the following sources:

Bernstein, A. (2003, June 23). Sweatshops: Finally, airing the dirty linen. *Business Week, 3838,* 100–101.

Bernstein, A. (2005, May 23). A major swipe at sweatshops. *Business Week, 3934,* 98.

Brown, G. (2004, April 8). Vulnerable workers in the global economy. *Occupational Hazards, 66(4),* 29–30.

Brown, G. (2006, June). Why sweatshops won't go away: Nike's actions are the exception to the rule. *Industrial Safety & Hygiene News,* 71.

Burrows, P. (2006, June 19). Stalking high-tech sweatshops. *Business Week, 3989,* 62.

Dean, S. (2020). The sweatshops are still open. Now they make masks. https://www.sandiegouniontribune.com/business/story/2020-04-21/making-masks-and-making-less-than-minimum-wage.

Hammond, K. (1997, November 7). Leaked audit: Nike factory violated worker laws. *MotherJones.com.* http://www.motherjones.com/news/feature/1997/11/nike.html.

Herskovitz, J. (2013, May 16). The cost of no sweatshops: South Africa struggles not to be Bangladesh. *Voice of America.* https://www.voanews.com/africa/cost-no-sweatshops-s-africa-struggles-not-be-bangladesh.

June, A. W. (2003, July 4). In its first major report, anti-sweatshop group cites violations. *Chronicle of Higher Education, 49(43),* A23.

Kovalyova, A. (2013, June 5). Vast underground migrant sweatshop found beneath Moscow street. *NBCNews.com.* https://www.nbcnews.com/news/world/vast-underground-migrant-sweatshop-found-beneath-moscow-street-flna6C10207577.

Liedtke, M. (2004, May 13). Gap acknowledges labor violations. *WashingtonPost.com.* http://www.washingtonpost.com/wp-dyn/articles/A22681-2004May12.html.

Malone, S. (2005, February 8). Tempest in a t-shirt: Book offers new look at globalization. *WWD: Women's Wear Daily, 189(28),* 15.

Meyer, A. (2020, April 29). Inside the fight to end labor exploitation in L.A. garment factories. https://fashionista.com/2020/10/la-garment-workers-ethical-fashion-manufacturing-sweatshops.

Mitchell, J. (2013, May 19). Benjamin Powell: In defense of sweatshops. *DallasNews.com.* https://www.dallasnews.com/opinion/commentary/2013/05/17/benjamin-powell-in-defense-of-sweatshops/.

Paharia, N. (2013, June 28). Consumers think sweatshops OK if "shoes are cute," research reveals. *Georgetown.edu.* http://www.georgetown.edu/news/paharia-sweathshop-products-study.html.

Stamping out sweatshops. (2005, May 23). *Business Week, 3934,* 136.

Wells, D. (2003, September–October). Global sweatshops and ethical buying codes. *Canadian Dimension, 37(5),* 9–11.

Case 22

The U.S. Industrial Food System

"The way we eat has changed more in the last 50 years than in the previous 10,000. But the image that's used to sell the food, it is still the imagery of agrarian America." In the grocery store we see labels picturing pastures and names of farms on the labels; in reality, however, it is a handful of corporations bringing our food to market, not farmers. Corporations use farm-fresh images to create a specific brand image. The biggest names in the industry are ADM, Cargill, ConAgra, IBP, Monsanto, Swift, and Tyson. These multinational corporations control our food from seed to supermarket and have different methods of communicating information about that food to consumers. In the 1970s, the top-five beef packers controlled 25 percent of the market. Today, the top-four companies control more than 80 percent of the market. Meat-packers, slaughterhouses, seed manufacturers, and food processors operate like monopolies in their control of the U.S. food industry.

The corporations running the food supply chain in the United States are constantly enhancing production to create larger quantities of food at lower costs. More efficient production processes allow for the distribution of food products to more parts of the world. Yet, the process is not without concern. Food industry jobs are often endangering to employees. Animals are raised and treated in controversial conditions; and many employees find themselves responsible for treating meat with chemicals like ammonia, which creates health issues like diabetes, obesity, and cancer. This, in turn, increases demand for medical professionals and the need for prescription drugs. The effect on stakeholders may even go as far as increasing American reliance on fossil fuels, aggravating the deportation of illegal farm workers whose labor is essential to this food industry, and further increasing children's addiction to sugar and sweetening substitutes. Where's the efficiency in that?

A Brief History of Food since 1800

In the early 1800s, the independent farmer was considered the bedrock of American democracy. It wasn't until the 1950s that the McDonald brothers introduced a factory assembly line to a commercial kitchen for the first time. The assembly-line process taught workers a single task, significantly increased efficiency, and, in essence, created the fast-food industry. Today, "McDonald's is the nation's largest purchaser of beef, pork, and potatoes—and the second largest purchaser of chicken." This strong purchasing power gives fast-food franchise giants, like McDonald's and Burger King, influence over food supply. This has resulted in diminished need for independent farmers; in fact, prison inmates in the United States now outnumber farmers. Without a network of independent farmers, once the backbone of this country, our food supply must now be controlled by major corporations. Throughout history we have never seen food companies this large and with this much power.

The processing/refining of our foods has also changed significantly in the last century. Americans generally no longer eat "whole" foods like vegetables, fruits, and whole grains; instead, they rely primarily on processed foods. Processing makes more money for corporations, but at what cost to the consumer? "It is a fact that the chronic diseases that now kill most Americans can be traced directly to the industrialization of food: the use of chemicals to raise plants and animals in huge monocultures; the superabundance of cheap calories of sugar and fat produced by modern agriculture; and the narrowing of the biological diversity of the human diet to a tiny handful of staple crops, notably wheat, corn, and soy. These changes have given us the Western diet that we take for granted: lots of processed foods and meat, lots of added fat and sugar, lots of everything—except vegetables, fruits, and whole grains."

The Industrial Food Supply Chain

Unethical activity takes place at all steps of the industrial food supply chain: the animals; the growers of our food, the workers in their factories, the influence extended on our legal system, the planet Earth, the health care system, and ultimately the consumer.

The Treatment of Animals

Cows, natural-born grazers of grasses, are now raised on feedlots called Concentrated Animal Feedlot Operations (CAFO), created after World War II to make the production of meat more efficient. On CAFOs, cattle's diet consists mainly of corn, which fattens them quickly, but also animal by-products including cow's blood (a substitute to mother's milk when cows are taken from mothers at less than 24 hours old), out-of-date domestic pet food, antibiotics, and even poultry litter. Until 1997, cows were even fed broken-down cow parts, until the Food and Drug Administration (FDA) banned it after discovering it led to mad cow disease. Cows are housed in small pens, never allowed to graze in pastures, and stand in pools of their own excrement. What was formerly a well-functioning system—cattle grazing on the waste of crops fertilizing the soil, making it rich to grow more crops—is now a system resulting in two new inefficiencies: (1) a fertility problem on the farm, requiring chemical fertilizers to remedy; and (2) a pollution problem in the feedlot, which is often not remedied at all.

A fatal consequence of cattle's new diet is the creation of *E. coli* 015:H7 in the cow's stomach, which, in turn, lives in the meat purchased and consumed by consumers. The acid in our stomachs cannot destroy *E. coli* 015:H7. The virus can and has killed humans, including two-year-old Kevin Kowalcyk of Colorado, an otherwise healthy boy. Without the human intervention of feeding corn to cattle, this virus would never even exist. Studies have shown that if cattle were removed from feedlots and allowed to graze on grass for just a few days before slaughter, 80 percent of *E. coli* would be eliminated. Yet the cattle industry and the United States Department of Agriculture (USDA) consider that an impractical solution to the problem.

The 2008 documentary *Food, Inc.* also reveals the disturbing treatment of chickens in the food industry. Like cattle, chickens are fed corn and antibiotics

582 ■ Business Ethics

to fatten them more quickly and efficiently. The time to maturity has been reduced by more than 30 percent since the 1950s. Chickens are fattened so quickly that their bones, muscles, and internal organs are not strong enough to support them. The disturbing footage in *Food, Inc.* shows several birds who can take only a few steps before collapsing beneath the weight of their supersized corn-fed breasts. White meat is of the highest demand in the fast-food industry. The chickens live in tight quarters, stepping over each other and in each other's waste. The animals never see any sunlight, living in a large tunnel-like chicken house required by large corporations like Purdue and Tyson.

The Treatment of Growers and Factory Workers

Chicken growers typically begin the process by building one or more poultry houses and signing a contract with one of the major chicken retailers in the country (i.e., Tyson or Purdue). The building of two poultry houses can land the grower with a mortgage of about $500,000, whereas the average yearly salary of a grower was only $18,000 in 2009. This grower then must conform to all regulations set by the corporation, including costly equipment purchases and upgrades to the poultry houses. Failure to do so results in a loss of contract. One grower interviewed in *Food, Inc.* discussed the stench and illness inside the poultry house. She developed an allergy to all antibiotics as a result of growing chickens. Chickens spend their entire lives as corporate property. Why don't corporations grow their own chickens? They have found that outsourcing to chicken growers produces the same results at a much lower cost. Once the animals are fully grown, catchers are sent in to collect them. The chicken catchers hired by corporations were formerly poor Americans but are now primarily undocumented Latino workers.

Slaughterhouse workers are said to have one of the most dangerous jobs in the country. Both *Food, Inc.* and Eric Schlosser's book *Fast Food Nation* discuss the horrific conditions, life-threatening injuries and illnesses, lack of unions, low number of inspections, minimum-wage salaries, and nonexistent benefits faced by employees working in meat-processing plants. These conditions are true of employees who either clean the facilities or handle the meat. Most often, it is illegal immigrants performing the most treacherous and lowest-paying jobs.

Poor conditions are also found in the growing process of other foods of popular demand. The profession of potato farmers, for example, has drastically changed. Potatoes, which once thrived on farms in Maine, are now mass-produced in Idaho. It is estimated that about 2 cents out of every $1.50 order of fast-food fries makes it back to the farmer. Like the chicken grower, the average potato farmer is more than $500,000 in debt before even earning a penny.

The fast-food service industry itself is also a source of worker exploitation. Fast-food chains rely heavily on unskilled, low-paid workers. "The roughly 3.5 million fast food workers are by far the largest group of minimum-wage earners in the United States."

Growers, farmers, and factory or service workers put themselves at risk both financially and physically.

The Legal System

Government subsidies make corn a natural choice for animal feed. Corn is now the cheapest food source available and fattens the animals most quickly. This is a result of farm bills passed with pressure from congressional lobbyists representing the big companies like Cargill, Smithfield, Tyson, and others. NAFTA resulted in cheap American corn in Mexico, putting approximately 1.5 million Mexican corn farmers out of business. Large meat processors like IBP (Iowa Beef Packers) actively recruited in Mexico for cheap labor in their slaughterhouses. *Food, Inc.* shows footage of the government taking illegal immigrant workers into custody at their homes but never at the slaughterhouses. The film suggests that the Smithfield meat processor has an arrangement with the government to provide the whereabouts of 15 illegal aliens each day at their homes in exchange for the government's avoidance of the corporation's factories.

In 1977, Senator George McGovern chaired the Senate Select Committee on Nutrition and Human Needs to probe the link between diet and the increase in chronic diseases like heart disease, cancer, obesity, and diabetes. The committee found that during wartime, when U.S. consumption of meat and dairy was down, rates of heart disease similarly dropped. They also noted that in countries where diets are based mostly on plants, rates of chronic diseases were "strikingly low." The committee went on to publish dietary guidelines suggesting that Americans cut back on red meat and dairy products. The threatened red meat and dairy industries forced the committee to change its recommendation from "reduce consumption of meat" to "choose meats, poultry and fish that will reduce saturated fat intake." In the next election, three-term Senator McGovern was ousted, demonstrating the potential repercussions for politicians who take on the food industry.

In the 1980s, a U.S. law was passed allowing companies to put a patent on life. As a result, the corporation Monsanto owns a genetically modified organism (GMO), a type of soybean, grown in the United States. These specific soybeans were created to withstand the spraying of pesticide on crops (another Monsanto product). The GMO soybean withstands pesticides and herbicides better than any other. Farmers must now purchase fresh seed from Monsanto every year or take the serious and expensive risk of being sued by Monsanto and put out of business. These seeds are proven to grow more efficiently, but no one yet knows the health consequences humans face from eating GMOs. Interestingly, *Forbes* magazine named Monsanto the "Company of the Year" in 2010. The article explained Monsanto's plan to reach other nations, such as China, which will need GMO grains to raise enough steak to feed the masses and bring the Western diet to Asia.

"Every day in the United States, roughly 200,000 people are sickened by food borne disease, 900 are hospitalized and fourteen die." After the two-year-old mentioned above tragically died as a result of eating beef containing *E. coli* O15:H7, his mother became an advocate, fighting for higher safety standards in our food industry. For several years she has been working to have a bill passed into law:

the Meat and Poultry Pathogen Reduction and Enforcement Act of 2003, also known as "Kevin's Law." This law would give the USDA the power to close down plants that produce contaminated meat. This bill is still not a law.

Food, Inc. shows viewers that many politicians and regulatory committee members have ties to large food industry corporations. For several years, the chief of staff to the USDA was a former chief lobbyist to the beef industry, and the head of the FDA was the former executive vice president of the National Food Processors Association. In January 2010, the Supreme Court ruled to "overturn a 20-year-old Supreme Court ruling that barred corporations from spending freely to support or oppose candidates." Corporations are now able to pour as much money as they want into advertisements for or against a particular candidate. The food industry giants are among the wealthiest corporations in the world.

The Planet

The use of fertilizers on crops inhibits the crops' ability to obtain nutrients from the soil, resulting in a less nutritious fruit or vegetable. Additionally, growing only one crop repeatedly, as opposed to varying crops, further depletes the soil of nutrients. We are left with a downward spiral in the nutritional content of our fruits and vegetables. When the vitamin levels found in an apple from 1940 were compared to one grown today, only about one-third of the nutrients were present in today's apple. In addition to the depletion of nutrients in produce, the relatively new year-round need for out-of-season plants, particularly citrus, around the world requires the use of additional fertilizers, irrigation systems, and fossil fuels to plant, harvest, and transport.

The Fallout of the American Diet

Corn, wheat, and soybeans are very highly subsidized commodities in the United States that can be found in nearly every product in the supermarket. High fructose corn syrup, for example, is very common. This translates to a large increase in the sugar and empty calories found in American diets. Government subsidies make bad calories cheaper for consumption. Obesity, cancer, and diabetes are on the rise in every country that adopts the Western, or American, diet of processed and fast food.

As Senator McGovern's committee discovered in the 1970s, evidence points to the correlation of chronic diseases and industrialization of food in America. Farms today can "produce more calories per acre, but each of those calories may supply less nutrition than it formerly did. Nutritionists have known for years that a diet high in whole grains reduces one's risk for diabetes, heart disease and cancer," yet the industry makes more money off refined grains that can be stored and manufactured into a wider variety of packaged foods for purchase. This creates a greater demand on the U.S. health care system and drug industry.

Big Organics

As an alternative to conventional food products, organic meat and produce offer several improvements. Companies like Stonyfield Farms are growing over

20 percent annually. Organics is the fastest-growing segment in the food industry. They are not as sustainable as independent farmers, but big organic corporations are improving the industry by using fewer pesticides and working to educate consumers.

Food Industry Corporations

The giant conglomerates make outlandish profits, billions of dollars more than their nearest competitors. They run their factories in hiding. None of the top corporations would agree to be interviewed for either of Michael Pollan's books (*In Defense of Food* and *The Omnivore's Dilemma*) or the documentary *Food, Inc.*

Ethical Implications

The stakeholder victims of the U.S. food industry are many: consumers, growers, farmers, factory workers, and service industry workers. Additional stakeholders include the shareholders of the food companies and professionals in the medical industry, health insurance industry, oil industry, transportation, government, and even foreign nations that are adopting the Western diet.

Over the last century the marketplace set a demand for larger quantities of cheaper food. Individuals were suffering from malnutrition, and during the Great Depression people could not afford to eat. The issue was how to make farming more efficient and increase the availability of products. However, in the attempt to make things more efficient, new, and larger problems have resulted, changing the issue to one of a food and health crisis.

Stakeholders include the owners, customers, employees, suppliers, competitors, government, unions, customer advocate groups, and illegal immigrants. At first glance, it seems that these stakeholders are working in the best interests of many of the consumers. These stakeholders provide customers with accessible food products, they employee thousands in the United States, and they form relationships with countless suppliers. On closer inspection, however, the products created by the food industry that are readily available to customers are, in fact, leading to the increase in chronic diseases and rising health care costs. Employees are working in unsafe and often illegal situations with few or no benefits. Suppliers and farmers are being exploited. Many of these groups do not understand that they are victims. The government appears to be in a collaborative relationship with the industry. Politicians receive money from industry giants. Times are finally beginning to change with the new organic movement, however. Consumers are more educated about what the food system is doing to the health of their families. Stores like Whole Foods are catering to the highly educated consumer. Even Walmart has begun selling organic foods, as it recognizes the shift in consumer demands.

Still, the U.S. food industry is in a crisis. Every time a child dies or an adult becomes sick due to *E. coli* in their food, the consumers, executives, and government should be outraged. Why hasn't Kevin's Law passed? Each year when health care costs rise, rates of cancer and heart disease skyrocket, and nutrients in foods are diminished, alarm bells should be sounding.

Conclusion

Consumers are becoming more educated, and the food industry is slowly shifting to provide more options. Farmers markets are seeing a resurgence as consumers demand healthier, greener options. As *Food, Inc.* pointed out, we don't buy the cheapest car, so why buy the cheapest food? Quality does matter. As consumers educate themselves and make demands for less processed foods, the industry will have to respond to changing demands.

Questions for Discussion

1. What are the most significant issues in this case, and are these really that important to you?
2. Who are a few of the major stakeholders and their stakes in this case?
3. Are the issues in this case national or global in nature? Explain.
4. Who is responsible, and why, for problems presented and argued in this case?
5. Are there any positive steps being taken to rectify the problems this case presents? If so, please identify them.

Sources

This case was developed from material contained in the following sources:

Kenner, R., and Pearlstein, E. (Producers), and Kenner, R. (Director). (2008). *Food, Inc.* [Motion Picture]. USA: Magnolia Pictures.

Langreth, R., and Herper, M. (2010, January). The Planet versus Monsanto. *Forbes, 185(1),* 64–69.

Pollan, M. (2006). *The omnivore's dilemma.* New York: Penguin Group.

Pollan, M. (2008). *In defense of food.* New York: Penguin Group.

Schlosser, E. (2002). *Fast food nation.* New York: Houghton Mifflin Company.

Tedford, D. (2010, January 21). Supreme Court rips up campaign finance laws. *NPR .org.* http://www.npr.org/templates/story/story.php?storyId=122805666.

Weise, E. (2003, June 10). Consumers may have a beef with cattle feed. *USAToday .com.* http://www.usatoday.com/news/health/2003-06-09-beef-cover_x.htm.

Notes

1. Brodzicki, T. (2020, January 2). Outlook for global trade in 2020. ihsmarkit.com, https://ihsmarkit.com/research-analysis/outlook-for-global-trade-in-2020.html.

2. United Nations Conference on Trade and Development. (2020, June 11). Global trade continues nosedive, UNCTAD forecasts 20% drop in 2020. *UNCTAD.org*. https://unctad.org/en/pages/newsdetails.aspx?OriginalVersionID=2392. Also see PwC 24th Annual Global CEO Survey. (2017–2021). A leadership agenda to take on tomorrow. https://www.pwc.com/gx/en/ceo-agenda/ceosurvey/2021.html?WT.mc_id=CT3-PL300 -DM1-TR2-LS4-ND30-TTA9-CN_CEO-Survey2021-GlobalCEOSurvey-Google &gclid=Cj0KCQjw-LOEBhDCARIsABrC0Tm50YKFgpVKCLXjPhN2wz-IDJXD j2DOc4jSFY6m-MC8qYVJybCYyYQaAqFrEALw_wcB&gclsrc=aw.ds.

3. World Economic Forum. (2020, May). Challenges and opportunities in the post-COVID-19 world, 6. http://www3.weforum.org/docs/WEF_Challenges_and_Opportunities_Post_COVID_19.pdf.

4. Cilluffo, A., and Ruiz, N. G. (2019, June 17). World's population is projected to nearly stop growing by the end of the century. *PewResearch.org*. https://www.pewresearch .org/fact-tank/2019/06/17/worlds-population-is-projected-to-nearly-stop-growing-by -the-end-of-the-century/.

5. UN Department of Economic and Social Affairs. (n.d.). COVID-19 to slash global economic output by $8.5 trillion over next two years. United Nations. https://www.un .org/en/desa/covid-19-slash-global-economic-output-85-trillion-over-next-two-years, accessed March 7, 2021.

6. Ernst & Young. (2010). Tracking global trends: How six key developments are shaping the business world. *EY.com*. https://www.eycom.ch/en/Publications/20130129 -Tracking-global trends/download.

7. Desgardins, J. (2019, September 10). The $86 trillion world economy—in one chart. *World Economic Forum*. https://www.weforum.org/agenda/2019/09/fifteen-countries-re present-three-quarters-total-gdp; PwC Global (2021, January). Global economy watch: Pre-dictions for 2021. https://www.pwc.com/gx/en/research-insights/economy/global-economy -watch/predictions-2021.html.

8. Barne, D., and Wadhwa, D. (2019, December 20). Year in review: 2019 in 14 charts. *WorldBank.org*. https://www.worldbank.org/en/news/feature/2019/12/20/year-in-review -2019-in-charts.

9. *The Economist*. (2013, June 12). Poverty: Not always with us. http://www .economist.com/news/briefing/21578643-world-has-astonishing-chance-take-billion -people-out-extreme-poverty-2030-not; Barne and Wadhwa (2019), op. cit.

10. World Bank Group. (2020). Poverty and shared prosperity 2020. https://www .worldbank.org/en/publication/poverty-and-shared-prosperity.

11. Ibid.

12. Human Development Report. (2013). *The rise of the south: Human progress in a di-verse world*. New York: United Nations Development Programme. http://www.undp.org /content/dam/philippines/docs/HDR/HDR2013%20Report%20English.pdf.

13. Ibid.

14. Jabari, M. (2020, October 15). 4 lessons for a radical rethink of leadership in the post-COVID-19 era. World Economic Forum.

15. This list is based on works by Professor Kathleen Patterson, whose academic pro-file and references are found at https://www.regent.edu/faculty/ph-d-kathleen-a-patterson/,

and in Russell, R. F. (2002, May). A review of servant leadership attributes: Developing a practical model. *Leadership & Organization Development Journal 23(3)*, 145–157.

16. World Economic Forum. (2020, October). The Future of Jobs Report. http://www3.weforum.org/docs/WEF_Future_of_Jobs_2020.pdf.

17. These lists are based on the research of Armstrong, M. (2006). *Handbook of HR management practice*. London: Kogan Page; and of Henley, as shown in Hurn, B. (2006). The selection of international business managers: Part 1. *Industrial and Commercial Training, 38(6)*, 279–286.

18. Pearce, C. (2008, July 7). Follow the leaders. *Wall Street Journal*. http://online.wsj.com/article/SB121441363110903891.html? mod=djem_jiewr_HR.

19. Ibid.

20. Korn Ferry. (2020). The COVID-19 Korn-Ferry leadership guide: Strategies for managing through the crisis. https://www.kornferry.com/content/dam/kornferry/special-project-images/coronavirus/docs/KF_Leadership_Playbook_Global_FINAL.pdf.

21. Neufeld, D. (2020, November 5). The world's most influential values, in one graphic. *Visual Capitalist*. https://www.visualcapitalist.com/most-influential-values/.

22. Fisher, J., and Bonn, I. (2007). International strategies and ethics: Exploring the tensions between head office and subsidiaries. *Management Decision, 45(10)*, 1563.

23. Ibid.

24. Guy, M. E. (1991). Using high reliability management to promote ethical decision making. In Bowman, J. S. (ed.). *Ethical frontiers in public management,* 193. San Francisco: Jossey-Bass.

25. Garofalo, C. (2003). Toward a global ethic: Perspectives on values, training, and moral agency. *International Journal of Public Sector Management, 16(7)*, 496–497.

26. Gilman, S. C., and Lewis, C. W. (1996). Public service ethics: a global dialogue. *Public Administration Review, 56*, 520.

27. "Ethnocentric." (2012). *Dictionary.com*. http://dictionary.reference.com/browse/ethnocentric.

28. Cultural relativism—illogical standard. (2012). *All about Philosophy*. http://www.cultural-relativism.com/.

29. Badaracco, J. Jr. (1998). A guide to defining moments, the discipline of building character. *Harvard Business Review, 76(2)*, 114.

30. Gow, D. (2008, May 26). Siemens boss admits setting up slush funds. *Guardian.co.uk*. http://www.guardian.co.uk/business/2008/may/27/technology.europe.

31. The global bribery crackdown. (2009, February 18). *GrowthBusiness.co.uk*. http://www.growthbusiness.co.uk/growing-a-business/business-regulations/996112/the-global-bribery-crackdown.thtml.

32. Keston, J. (2007, December 16). Doing business overseas? Then let's talk about corruption. *LocalTechwire.com*.

33. Ibid.

34. Kenton, W., (2020, June 10). Foreign Corrupt Practices Act (FCPA). *Investopedia.com*. https://www.investopedia.com/terms/f/foreign-corrupt-practices-act.asp.

35. Foreign Corrupt Practices Act. (2017). *FindLaw.com*. http://library.findlaw.com/1997/Jan/1/126234.html.

36. Ibid.

37. Koehler, M., Brown, S., Bruch, G., Chilton, B., King, I., and Simon, D. (2008, February 14). The FCPA perils of hosting foreign customer visits. *Mondaq.com*. http://www.mondaq.com/article.asp?articleid=56878.

38. Shearman & Sterling, LLP. (December 2008). Siemens agrees to largest settlement in history of FCPA. *Shearman.com*.

39. Department of Justice. (2020, January 31). Airbus agrees to pay over $3.9 billion in global penalties to resolve foreign bribery and ITAR case (Press release). https://www.justice.gov/opa/pr/airbus-agrees-pay-over-39-billion-global-penalties-resolve-foreign-bribery-and-itar-case.

40. Based on Keston (2007), op. cit.

41. WilmerHale. (2021, February 1). Global anti-bribery year-in-review: 2020 developments and predictions for 2021. JD Supra LLC. https://www.jdsupra.com/legalnews/global-anti-bribery-year-in-review-2020-4631196/.

42. MacDonald, J. (2006, January 25). When does a gift become a bribe? *Christian Science Monitor*. http://www.csmonitor.com/2006/0125/p13s01-lire.html.

43. Manandhar, N. (2007, December 23). Bribe versus gifts. Canada Foundation for Nepal. http://cffn.ca/2007/12/bribe-versus-gifts/.

44. Ibid. Also see WilmerHale (2021), op. cit.

45. Maqbool, A. (2000, July). Black Lives Matter: From social media post to global movement. *BBC News*. https://www.bbc.com/news/world-us-canada-53273381.

46. Amnesty International. (2012). Discrimination. *Amnesty.org*. http://www.amnesty.org/en/discrimination.

47. CIA World Factbook. (2019, December 7). United Kingdom demographics profile 2019. https://www.indexmundi.com/united_kingdom/demographics_profile.html#:~:text=white%2087.2%25%2C%20black%2FAfrican,3.7%25%20(2011%20est.

48. GMI Blogger. (2020, April 28), United Arab Emirates population statistics (2020). https://www.GlobalMediaInsight.com/blog/uae-population-statistics/.

49. CIA World Factbook. (2021, February 25). South America: Argentina. https://www.cia.gov/the-world-factbook/countries/argentina/.

50. Amnesty International. (2008). Publics around the world say governments should act to prevent racial discrimination. *WorldPublicOpinion.org*. https://drum.lib.umd.edu/bitstream/handle/1903/10652/WPO_Race_Mar08_art.pdf;jsessionid=F0FF946261A1D2860554664FA158F169?sequence=3.

51. Ibid.

52. Human Rights Watch. (2020). Two years after #MeToo erupts, a new treaty anchors workplace shifts. *HRW world report 2020*. https://www.hrw.org/world-report/2020/country-chapters/global-1.

53. Stop Violence Against Women. (2007, July 13). Approaches to and remedies under sexual harassment law. http://www.stopvaw.org/Approaches_to_and_Remedies_under_Sexual_Harassment_Law.html.

54. Ibid.

55. Congressional Research Service. (2020, May 12). Intellectual property rights and international trade. https://fas.org/sgp/crs/row/RL34292.pdf.

56. Rosenbaum, E. (2019, March 1). 1 in 5 corporations say China has stolen their IP within the last year: CNBC CFO survey. *CNBC.com*. https://www.cnbc.com/2019/02/28/1-in-5-companies-say-china-stole-their-ip-within-the-last-year-cnbc.html.

57. Federal Bureau of Investigation. (2020, February 11). FBI releases the Internet Crime Complaint Center 2019 Internet Crime Report (Press release). https://www.fbi.gov/news/pressrel/press-releases/fbi-releases-the-internet-crime-complaint-center-2019-internet-crime-report.

58. OECD. (2019, March 28). Trade in fake goods in now 3.3% of world trade and rising (Press release). https://www.oecd.org/newsroom/trade-in-fake-goods-is-now-33-of-world-trade-and-rising.htm.

59. Burgess, C., and Power, R. (2008). *Secrets stolen, fortunes lost: Preventing intellectual property theft and economic espionage in the 21st century,* ch. 4. Burlington, MA: Syngress Publishing.

60. Office of the United States Trade Representative. (2019, April). Special 301 Report. https://ustr.gov/sites/default/files/2019_Special_301_Report.pdf.

61. Gupta, A. K., and Wang, H. (2007, April 28). How to get China and India right: Western companies need to become smarter—and they need to do it quickly. *Wall Street Journal* (Eastern edition), R4.

62. Ibid.

63. Smale, A. (2001, August 16). The dark side of the global economy. *New York Times,* 3. https://www.nytimes.com/2001/08/26/weekinreview/the-world-the-dark-side-of-the-global-economy.html.

64. Insurance Information Institute. (n.d.). Facts + Statistics: Identity theft and cybercrime. https://www.iii.org/fact-statistic/facts-statistics-identity-theft-and-cybercrime, accessed July 1, 2020.

65. Smale (2001), op. cit.

66. International Labour Organization. (2017, September). International programme on the elimination of child labour (IPEC). http://www.ilo.org/ipec/lang--en/index.htm#a1.

67. UNICEF Global Database. (2019, October). Child labor data. https://data.unicef.org/topic/child-protection/child-labour/, accessed July 1, 2020.

68. International Labour Office. (2010). *Accelerating action against child labour: Global report under the follow-up to the ILO Declaration on Fundamental Principles and Rights at Work.* Geneva: ILO. http://www.ilo.org/ipecinfo/product/viewProduct.do?productId=13853, accessed February 6, 2021.

69. Ibid.

70. International Labour Organization. (2020, June 12). COVID-19 may push millions more children into child labour—ILO and UNICEF (Press release). https://www.ilo.org/global/about-the-ilo/newsroom/news/WCMS_747583/lang--en/index.htm.

71. UNODC, United Nations Office on Drugs and Crime. (2020). Global Report on Trafficking in Persons. https://www.unodc.org/documents/data-and-analysis/tip/2021/GLOTiP_2020_15jan_web.pdf.

72. The World Counts. (2020). Number of children sold as slaves. https://www.theworldcounts.com/challenges/people-and-poverty/child-labor/child-slavery-facts/story.

73. Warsh, D. (2001, July 29). The next 50 years. *Boston Globe,* E2.

74. Ibid.

75. Global Freedom of Expression, Columbia University. (2021). United Nations Human Rights System. https://globalfreedomofexpression.columbia.edu/law-standards/united-nations-human-rights-system/. Article 19 states: "(1) Everyone shall have the right to hold opinions without interference. (2) Everyone shall have the right to freedom of expression; this right shall include freedom to seek, receive, and impart information and ideas of all kinds, regardless of frontiers, either orally, in writing or in print, in the form of art, or through any other media of his choice. (3) The exercise of the rights provided for in paragraph 2 of this article carries with it special duties and responsibilities. It may therefore be subject to certain restrictions, but these shall only be such as are provided by

law and are necessary: (a) for respect of the rights or reputation of others; (b) for the protection of national security or of public order . . . , or of public health, or morals."

76. Peacock, A. (2020). *Human rights and the digital divide.* New York: Routledge, Taylor & Francis.

77. Clement, J. (2020, June 4). Worldwide digital population as of April 2020. *Statista.com.* https://www.statista.com/statistics/617136/digital-population-worldwide/.

78. Finnegan, M. (2011, August 15). Global broadband digital divide widens. *TechEYE.net.* http://harlechnnorfolk.blogspot.com/2012/02/global-broadband-digital-divide-widens.html.

79. Ibid.

80. Monks, K. (2019, October 22). Africans face most expensive internet charges in the world, new report says. *CNN.com.* https://www.cnn.com/2019/10/22/africa/internet-affordability-africa/index.html.

81. Internet World Stats. (2020, March). Internet users statistics for Africa. *InternetWorldStats.com.* https://www.internetworldstats.com/stats1.htm.

82. GSMA. (2020). The State of Mobile Internet Connectivity 2020. https://www.gsma.com/r/wp-content/uploads/2020/09/GSMA-State-of-Mobile-Internet-Connectivity-Report-2020.pdf.

83. Ibid. Change to European Commission. (2021). Communication from the Commission to the European Parliament, The CounciL, The European Economic and Social Committee and the Committee of the Regions, 2030 Digital Compass: The European way for the Digital Decade. https://ec.europa.eu/info/sites/default/files/communication-digital-compass-2030_en.pdf

84. Alliance for Affordable Internet (A4AI), Who We Are, a4ai.org. https://a4ai.org/who-we-are/members/, accessed June 2, 2020.

85. Ritzer, G. (2004). *The McDonaldization of society.* 4th ed. Thousand Oaks, CA: Pine Forge Press. Also see Ritzer, G. (2006). *McDonaldization: The reader.* 2nd ed. Thousand Oaks, CA: Pine Forge Press.

86. Ritzer (2004), op. cit., 1.

87. Ibid., 2.

88. Ibid., 212.

89. Ibid.

90. Schor, J. (2004). *Born to buy: The commercialized child and the new consumer culture.* New York: Scribner, 125.

91. Ibid.

92. Beattie, A. (2020, March 30). Why did Microsoft face antitrust charges in 1998? *Investopedia.com.* https://www.investopedia.com/ask/answers/08/microsoft-antitrust.asp.

93. MacInnis, L. (2008). Airlines set to lose $5.2 bln in 2008—IATA. *Reuters.* https://www.reuters.com/article/sppage023-l3518534-oisbi/airlines-set-to-lose-5-2-bln-in-2008-iata-idINL351853420080904.

94. Trautwein, H. M. (2013). Economic thinking about transnational governance: Blind spots and historical perspectives (Working paper no. 13). Universitat Bremen, Center for Transnational Studies. https://ideas.repec.org/p/zen/wpaper/13.html.

95. Draft United Nations Code of Conduct on Transnational Corporations. (1983). United Nations Conference on Trade and Development, Division on Investment and Enterprise. https://investmentpolicy.unctad.org/international-investment-agreements/treaty-files/2891/download#:~:text=%5BThe%20term%20%22transnational%20corporation%22,of%20decision%2Dmaking%2C%20permitting%20coherent.

96. Rahman, M. (1973). *World economic issues at the United Nations: Half a century of debate.* Norwell, MA: Kluwer Academic.

97. Slaughter, M., and Tyson, L. (2012, March). A warning sign from global companies. *Harvard Business Review,* 74–75.

98. Bureau of Economic Analysis. (2018, August 24). Activities of U.S. multinational enterprises: 2016 (Press release). https://www.bea.gov/news/2018/activities-us-multinational -enterprises-2016.

99. Bureau of Economic Analysis. (2019, August 23). Activities of U.S. multinational enterprises: 2017 (Press release). https://www.bea.gov/news/2019/activities-us-multina tional-enterprises-2017.

100. Fortune. (2020). Global 500. https://fortune.com/global500/.

101. Vernon, R. (1971). *Sovereignty at bay.* New York: Basic Books.

102. Bureau of Economic Analysis (2018), op. cit.

103. A helpful analysis with recommendations can be found in Human Rights Watch. (2020). Holding companies to account: Momentum builds for corporate human rights duties. *HRW world report 2020.* https://www.hrw.org/world-report/2020/country-chapters/global-2.

104. Corporate Finance Institute. (2015). Top Accounting scandals. https://corpo ratefinanceinstitute.com/resources/knowledge/other/top-accounting-scandals/. Citations for the following section are also taken from Meyer, B. S., Estrin, S., and Meyer, K. (2007, March). Determinants of employment growth at MNEs: Evidence from Egypt, India, South Africa, and Vietnam. *Comparative Economic Studies, 49(1),* 61–80. For a recent source on "just cause" job protection by the National Employment Law Project, see also I. Tung, P. Sonn, and J. Odessky (2021). "Just cause" job protections: Building racial equity and shifting the power balance between workers and employers. https://s27147 .pcdn.co/wp-content/uploads/Just-Cause-Job-Protections-2021.pdf.

105. See Beyer, J. (1999, September). Ethics and cultures in international business. *Journal of Management Inquiry, 8(3),* 287–297.

106. Akst, D. (2001, March 4). Nike in Indonesia, through a different lens. *New York Times,* 3; Dutton, G. (2008, March 26). How Nike is changing the world, one factory at a time. *Ethisphere.*

107. Cadbury is also a leader in cutting emissions in the environment. See Cadbury announces aggressive emissions reduction plan. (2007, July 7). *Ethisphere.*

108. Savitz, A., and Weber, K. (2006). *The triple bottom line.* San Francisco: Jossey-Bass, xiii.

109. Ibid.

110. Social Enterprise Alliance. (n.d.). What is social enterprise? *Social Enterprise Alliance.* https://socialenterprise.us/about/social-enterprise/, accessed March 12, 2020.

111. The 45 entrepreneurs who are changing the world. (n.d.). *Fast Company.* http://www .fastcompany.com/social/2008/index.html. James, A., and M. James. (2021, April 24). Social Entrepreneur. https://www.investopedia.com/terms/s/social-entrepreneur.asp#:~:text =A%20social%20entrepreneur%20is%20a,in%20society%20through%20their%20initiatives.

112. Banks, J. (1972). *The sociology of social movements.* London: Macmillan; Hsu, C. (2005, October 31). Entrepreneur for social change. *U.S. News & World Report.*

113. The 45 entrepreneurs who are changing the world (n.d.), op. cit.

114. Christen, R. P., Rosenberg, R., and Jayadeva, V. (2004, July). Financial institutions with a double-bottom line: Implications for the future of microfinance (Occasional paper). Consultative Group to Assist the Poorest, 2–3.

115. Q&A: So what is microfinancing? (2006, October 13). *BBC.co.uk.* http://news .bbc.co.uk/1/hi/business/6047364.stm.

116. Ibid.

117. CGAP. (2020, June). Microfinance and COVID-19: A framework for regulatory response. *CGAP.org.* https://www.cgap.org/research/publication/microfinance-and-covid-19-framework-regulatory-response.

118. *The Economist.* (2020, May 5). For microfinance lenders, Covid-19 is an existential threat. *Economist.com,* https://www.economist.com/finance-and-economics/2020/05/05/for-microfinance-lenders-covid-19-is-an-existential-threat.

119. For a helpful introduction to this topic, see Frederick, W. (1991). The moral authority of transnational corporate codes. *Journal of Business Ethics, 10,* 165–177.

120. Ibid., 168–169.

121. DeGeorge, R. (1993). Ethics in personal business—a contradiction in terms? *Business Credit, 102(8),* 45–46. DeGeorge, R. (2006). *Business Ethics.* 6th ed. N.p.: Pearson, 514.

122. Berenbeim, R. (October 2000). Globalization drives ethics. *New Zealand Management, 47(9),* 26–29.

123. UNI Europa Global Union. (2020, April 17). Stepping up multinational corporations' responses to Covid-19. *Uni-europa.org.* https://www.uni-europa.org/2020/04/stepping-up-multinational-corporations-responses-to-covid-19/.

124. CDC. (2020, May 6). Guidance for businesses and employers: Plan, prepare, and respond to Coronavirus Disease 2019. https://www.cdc.gov/coronavirus/2019-ncov/community/guidance-business-response.html#more-changes.

125. Frederick (1991), op. cit., 167.

126. OECD. (2020, April 28). Protecting online consumers during the COVID-19 crisis. https://www.oecd.org/coronavirus/policy-responses/protecting-online-consumers-during-the-covid-19-crisis-2ce7353c/.

127. Frederick (1991), op. cit., 167.

128. Ibid.

129. Puffere, S., and McCarthy, D. J. (1995, Winter). Finding the common ground in Russian and American business ethics. *California Management Review, 37(2),* 20–46; Donaldson, T., and Dunfee, T. (1999, Summer). When ethics travel: The promise and peril of global business ethics. *California Management Review, 41(4),* 45.

130. Davis, M. (1999, January–February). Global standards, local problems. *Journal of Business Ethics, 20(1),* 38.

131. Maynard, M. (2001, March). Policing transnational commerce: Global awareness in the margins of morality. *Journal of Business Ethics, 30,* 17, 27.

132. Cattaui, M. (2000, Summer). Responsible business conduct in a global economy. *OECD Observer, 221/222,* 18–20; Berenbeim, R. (1999, September 1). The divergence of a global economy: One company, one market, one code, one world. *Vital Speeches of the Day, 65(22),* 696–698; Morrison, A. (2001, May). Integrity and global leadership. *Journal of Business Ethics, 31(31),* 65–76; Palmer, E. (2001, June). Multinational corporations and the social contract. *Journal of Business Ethics, 31(3),* 245–258.

133. Waddock, S. (2004, April). Creating corporate accountability: Foundational principles to make corporate citizenship real. *Journal of Business Ethics, 50(4),* 313.

134. *The Economist.* (2003, February 10). Integrity, on a global scale. *Economist.com.*

135. DeGeorge, R. (1993). *Competing with integrity,* 114–121. New York: Oxford University Press.

136. Fisher, R., Patton, B. M., and Ury, W. L. (1992). *Getting to yes: Negotiating agreement without giving in,* 2nd ed. Boston: Houghton-Mifflin.

137. Adler, N. J. (2001). *International dimensions of organizational behavior,* 4th ed. Mason, OH: South-Western/Thomson Learning. The 5th edition (2007) is published by South-Western College Publishers.

138. Lubatkin, M., Calori, R., Very, P., and Veiga, J. (1998). Managing mergers across borders: A two-nation exploration of a nationally bound administrative heritage. *Organization Science, 9(6),* 670–684; Laurent, A. (1983). The cultural diversity of Western conceptions of management. *International Studies of Management and Organization, 13(1–2),* 75–96.

139. See Hofstede, G. (1980, Summer). Motivation, leadership, and organization: Do American theories apply abroad? *Organizational Dynamics,* 42–63. See also Hofstede, G. (1991). *Cultures and organizations: Software of the mind: Intercultural cooperation and its importance for survival.* London: McGraw-Hill; Hampden-Turner, C., and Trompenaars, F. (1997). *Riding the waves of culture: Understanding diversity in global business,* 2nd ed. New York: McGraw Hill; Hall, E. T. (1976). *Beyond culture.* Garden City, NY: Anchor Press; Adler (2001), op. cit.

140. Adler (2001), op. cit.

141. Énderle, G. (2015). Exploring and conceptualizing international business ethics. *Journal of Business Ethics,* 127(4), 723–735.

142. Ibid.

143. Donaldson, T., and Dunfee, T. W. (1994, April). Toward a unified conception of business ethics: Integrative social contracts theory. *Academy of Management Review, 19(2),* 265.

144. Ibid.

145. Bain & Company (2011). The Great Eight: Trillion-dollar growth trends to 2020. https://www.sec.gov/Archives/edgar/data/1534155/000153415516000067/ex1015bain breif8macrotrendsr.pdf.

146. Orlik, T., Rush, J., Cousin, M., and Hong, J. (2020, March 6). Coronavirus could cost the global economy $2.7 trillion. Here's how. *Bloomberg.com.* https://www.bloomberg .com/graphics/2020-coronavirus-pandemic-global-economic-risk/.

147. This real-time ethical dilemma example comes from Donaldson, T., and Dunfee, T. (1999, Summer). When ethics travel: The promise and peril of global business ethics. *California Management Review, 41(4),* 60.

■ Index

Page numbers followed by *f* denote figures. Those followed by *t* denote tables.

A

Electronic Frontier Foundation, 3
electroencephalography (EEG), 333
Eli Lilly, 121
Ellerth, Kimberly, 482
empathetic marketing, 358f
empathy, 358f
Empire style, 560
Employee Retirement Income Security Act of 1974 (ERISA), 185
employee rights: due process as, 461; employer's responsibilities and, 456–459; employment-at-will doctrine and, 451; moral foundations of, 454; plant closings and, 470; polygraph and psychological testing and, 463–464; privacy as, 462–463; in workplace, 459–463; workplace surveillance and, 464
employees: business ethics attracting, 16; conflicts of interest and, 459, 462–463; drug testing of, 468; employer's responsibilities to, 456–459; empowerment of, 459; ethical behavior of, 384; food supply working conditions of, 582; key, 471; rights and responsibilities of, 454; social contracts between corporations and, 451–453; union organization, rights of, 469. See also workforce
employee stock option programs (ESOPs), 85
employers: contract under EAW doctrine, 452f; employee rights and responsibilities of, 456–459; fair wages obligation of, 456–457; genetic discrimination by, 468–469; good faith principle of, 452; implied contracts by, 453; polygraph and psychological testing by, 463–464; safe working environment, obligation of, 458; sexual harassment and liability of, 481–482. See also workplace
employment-at-will (EAW) doctrine, 451, 452f, 453, 490; employee contract under, 452f

empowerment, 249; of employees, 459; of teams, 251
EmSense, 334
Endangered Species Act, 230
Enderle, George, 560
Energy Independence and Security Act, 230
Energy Policy Act (EPACT), 230, 329
Enron, 4, 224; ethics code of, 23; loans to, 130; scandal of, 224; weak culture of, 382
environment: causes of pollution in, 309; changing, 3–12; conscious capitalism creating better, 252; crisis concerning, 170; demographic, 10; economic, 9; employment influenced by, 9f, 10; ethics of ecology, 310–311; fracking influencing, 327–328; government, 10; green marketing, 311–312; laws protecting, 229–230, 309–310; legal, 10; regulations for, 312; rights and treatment of, 312–313; safe working, 458; social, 10; technological, 9; toxic air pollution in, 306–307, 307f; water pollution and scarcity in, 307–309
environmental justice, 311–312
Environmental Protection Agency (EPA), 302, 571
Equal Credit Opportunity Act (ECOA), 228
Equal Employment Opportunity Commission (EEOC), 150, 473, 494
Equal Pay Act of 1963, 474
equal protection clause, 477
Equifax, 198
equity, 223; -based compensation, 218; brand, 359, 386; issues (raising of), 73; MNE policy design incorporating, 564; moral authority and, 67f; private (Wall Street), 494; professional stakeholders and, 389; return on (overemphasis on), 246; return on (premium), 253; social, 551; traders, 148
Erbitux, 119, 121, 226

Joseph W. Weiss is professor of·management at Bentley University, where he teaches leadership, business ethics, and careers. He received an Innovation Teaching Award and is on the honor roll of the Organizational Behavior Teaching Society. He has been a Fulbright Program Specialist and serves as an evaluator for Russian professors and professionals applying for awards in the United States. He is past chair of the Academy of Management's Management Consulting Division and Minitrack Chair of the Hawaii International Conference on System Sciences' IT/Project Management track. He consults and advises companies and organizations as a 360-degree leadership assessment consultant.

Dear reader,

Thank you for picking up this book and welcome to the worldwide BK community! You're joining a special group of people who have come together to create positive change in their lives, organizations, and communities.

What's BK all about?

Our mission is to connect people and ideas to create a world that works for all.

Why? Our communities, organizations, and lives get bogged down by old paradigms of self-interest, exclusion, hierarchy, and privilege. But we believe that can change. That's why we seek the leading experts on these challenges—and share their actionable ideas with you.

A welcome gift

To help you get started, we'd like to offer you a **free copy** of one of our bestselling ebooks:

www.bkconnection.com/welcome

When you claim your **free ebook**, you'll also be subscribed to our blog.

Our freshest insights

Access the best new tools and ideas for leaders at all levels on our blog at ideas.bkconnection.com.

Sincerely,

Your friends at Berrett-Koehler

Berrett–Koehler
Publishers

Berrett-Koehler is an independent publisher dedicated to an ambitious mission: *Connecting people and ideas to create a world that works for all.*

Our publications span many formats, including print, digital, audio, and video. We also offer online resources, training, and gatherings. And we will continue expanding our products and services to advance our mission.

We believe that the solutions to the world's problems will come from all of us, working at all levels: in our society, in our organizations, and in our own lives. Our publications and resources offer pathways to creating a more just, equitable, and sustainable society. They help people make their organizations more humane, democratic, diverse, and effective (and we don't think there's any contradiction there). And they guide people in creating positive change in their own lives and aligning their personal practices with their aspirations for a better world.

And we strive to practice what we preach through what we call "The BK Way." At the core of this approach is *stewardship,* a deep sense of responsibility to administer the company for the benefit of all of our stakeholder groups, including authors, customers, employees, investors, service providers, sales partners, and the communities and environment around us. Everything we do is built around stewardship and our other core values of *quality, partnership, inclusion,* and *sustainability.*

This is why Berrett-Koehler is the first book publishing company to be both a B Corporation (a rigorous certification) and a benefit corporation (a for-profit legal status), which together require us to adhere to the highest standards for corporate, social, and environmental performance. And it is why we have instituted many pioneering practices (which you can learn about at www.bkconnection.com), including the Berrett-Koehler Constitution, the Bill of Rights and Responsibilities for BK Authors, and our unique Author Days.

We are grateful to our readers, authors, and other friends who are supporting our mission. We ask you to share with us examples of how BK publications and resources are making a difference in your lives, organizations, and communities at www.bkconnection.com/impact.